D1075452

# MARIA EDGEWORTH

A Literary Biography

THE EDGEWORTH FAMILY, 1787, by Adam Buck

EMMELINE LOVELL ANNA HONORA
MARIA R. L. EDGEWORTH MRS. E. EDGEWORTH
HENRY CHARLOTTE SNEYD BESSY WILLIAM

# MARIA EDGEWORTH

A LITERARY BIOGRAPHY

BY

MARILYN BUTLER



OXFORD
AT THE CLARENDON PRESS
1972

*Oxford University Press, Ely House, London W. 1*

GLASGOW NEW YORK TORONTO MELBOURNE WELLINGTON
CAPE TOWN IBADAN NAIROBI DAR ES SALAAM LUSAKA ADDIS ABABA
DELHI BOMBAY CALCUTTA MADRAS KARACHI LAHORE DACCA
KUALA LUMPUR SINGAPORE HONG KONG TOKYO



PRINTED IN GREAT BRITAIN
AT THE UNIVERSITY PRESS, OXFORD
BY VIVIAN RIDLER
PRINTER TO THE UNIVERSITY

# ACKNOWLEDGEMENTS

IN the writing of this book I was much aided by the general advice and guidance of Dr. Roger Lonsdale and Miss Rachel Trickett, and by specific suggestions from Miss Mary Lascelles, Professor H. W. Donner, Mr. David Fieldhouse, Mr. Angus MacIntyre, and Mr. J. S. G. Simmons. The National Library of Ireland, custodians of many of the Edgeworth papers, have generously allowed me to study them in the Bodleian Library, Oxford; my thanks are due to the staff of both libraries, and to those of University College London, and the Bibliothèque Publique et Universitaire, Geneva, for the speed and courtesy with which they have met my requests. I am further indebted to the Librarians of the National Library of Ireland, University College London, and the Bibliothèque Publique et Universitaire, and to the trustees of the National Library of Scotland, for permission to quote from manuscripts in their possession.

For family papers and family lore my debt to Mrs. M. L. Butler and to Miss R. F. Butler and her sisters is very great. All have in addition given me leave to reproduce the portraits and sketches in their possession. But above all I owe an incalculable debt to Mrs. Christina Colvin, who has allowed me to draw on her unrivalled familiarity with the Edgeworths and their correspondence. Far more, with her wide knowledge of the period she has supplied me time and again with illustrative material extending well beyond the Edgeworths and their immediate circle. Indeed, the patience and generosity with which she has criticized, corrected, and encouraged has been a major source of pleasure throughout the writing of this book.

I should also acknowledge the contribution of the Principal and Fellows of St. Hilda's College; of Mrs. Jean Hemingway and Mrs. Anne Calvin; and, last but not least, of my small sons who tolerated and my husband who unfailingly encouraged the whole enterprise.

M. S. B.

*St. Hilda's College, Oxford*
*November 1971*

# CONTENTS

# LIST OF PLATES

# ABBREVIATIONS

## MEMBERS OF THE EDGEWORTH FAMILY AND OTHER FREQUENT CORRESPONDENTS

CSE — Charles Sneyd Edgeworth (1786–1864), ME's stepbrother.

DAB — Daniel Augustus Beaufort (1739–1821), geographer, father of RLE's fourth wife Mrs. FE.

ED — Étienne Dumont (1759–1829), utilitarian, penologist, and man of letters.

Mrs. EE — Mrs. Elizabeth Edgeworth (1753–97), *née* Sneyd, RLE's third wife and ME's stepmother.

Mrs. FE — Mrs. Frances Anne Edgeworth (1769–1865), *née* Beaufort, RLE's fourth wife.

ME — Maria Edgeworth (1768–1849), novelist.

Mrs. R — Mrs. Margaret Ruxton (1746–1830), *née* Edgeworth, younger sister of RLE.

RLE — Richard Lovell Edgeworth (1744–1817), scientist, educationalist, and father of ME.

SR — Sophy Ruxton (1776–1837), elder daughter of Mrs. R and cousin of ME.

## FREQUENTLY CITED BOOKS AND PERIODICALS

*Black Book* — H. J. and H. E. Butler, *The Black Book of Edgeworthstown and Other Edgeworth Memories*, 1927.

*Ed. Rev.* — *Edinburgh Review.*

*Letters from England* — Mrs. Christina Colvin, *Maria Edgeworth: Letters from England, 1813–44*, 1971.

*Mem.* — Mrs. Edgeworth, [Harriet Butler, and Lucy Robinson], *Memoir of Maria Edgeworth*, with a selection from her letters, 3 vols., privately printed, 1867.

*Memoirs of RLE* — *Memoirs of Richard Lovell Edgeworth*, begun by himself, and concluded by his daughter, 2 vols., 1820.

*QR* — *Quarterly Review.*

*REL* — *Review of English Literature.*

Slade — Mrs. B. C. Slade, *Maria Edgeworth: A Bibliographical Tribute*, 1937.

References to ME's novels are to the first Collected Edition of 1825.

All manuscripts referred to (unless otherwise stated) are in the Edgeworth–Butler and Beaufort–Edgeworth collections of letters in the National Library of Ireland and in the possession of the (Edgeworth) Butler family: see Bibliography. In cases where a letter has been published the additional reference is given after a semicolon, but the text followed is, wherever possible, that of the manuscript.

# INTRODUCTION

FROM 1800, when she published *Castle Rackrent*, to 1814, when Scott published *Waverley*, Maria Edgeworth was easily the most celebrated and successful of practising English novelists. Her eminence was comparable to Fanny Burney's two decades earlier. For both women success in novel-writing led to social success and a place in London Society. At the time, the art of both was taken seriously, and by good judges—for they were by a large margin the best novelists available, although this was not perhaps saying much. Maria Edgeworth headed a field in which the other runners were, for example, Mrs. Hamilton, Mrs. Opie, and Hannah More. The competent Mrs. Inchbald had retired from writing by 1800, and William Godwin and Madame d'Arblay herself performed far below their best during Maria Edgeworth's heyday. Yet there is no hint of *faute de mieux* in Maria Edgeworth's first reviews. The enthusiasm of her reviewers is reassuringly positive. The notoriously aggressive John Wilson Croker did not think Maria Edgeworth's productions perfect, but he did compare them with *Don Quixote* and *Gil Blas*, and in some respects he thought Miss Edgeworth did better than Fielding. Francis Jeffrey of the *Edinburgh Review* was much less qualified. He thought Maria Edgeworth's tales 'actually as *perfect* as it was possible to make them'.

Maria Edgeworth's success with her contemporaries was not just a *succès d'estime*. The public bought her novels in large numbers, ensuring that almost all went into at least three editions within a few years of first appearing. Her publishers paid her up to £2,000 for a single work, a remarkable sum before Scott did even better; Murray offered Jane Austen a conditional £450 for *Emma*. Most interesting of all is the impression Maria Edgeworth made on her fellow writers. Jane Austen admired her sufficiently to send her a copy of *Emma*, and to tease her publicly in a well-known passage of *Northanger Abbey*. Byron thought the impression of intelligence and prudence left by her novels very profound. Stendhal, not generally an easy critic to please, described her tale *Vivian* as 'excellente comédie de caractère et roman, excellent dessin à la Michel-Ange'. Scott claimed that he owed his own successful career as a novelist about Scotland to her Irish example. Turgenev is reported to have said that his sketches of the Russian peasantry were inspired by hers. Ruskin declared that he had read her tales, and her long novel *Patronage*, 'oftener than any other books in the world, except the Bible . . . they are it seems to me the most re-readable books in existence'.[1]

Almost everyone who has written about Maria Edgeworth in the last hundred years has had to rely heavily on the compliments paid her by others. Arguably, what Scott in particular wrote about her is better known than anything she wrote herself, even *Castle Rackrent*. After forty years as a well-known writer and apparently a key figure in the evolution of the novel, even before her death she began to dwindle in importance. Today the fact that she influenced Scott (even if it is believed) is not enough to convince the world at large that she contributed anything significant to literary history, since Scott has also been a victim of fluctuating fashions. Nowadays the public is not much more likely to read Maria Edgeworth as a living author than to read Mrs. Opie or Hannah More.

But although the lavish praise once given to her tales has been discounted since the middle of the nineteenth century, the compliments she received as a woman are a different matter. She had a personality that has always had a strong appeal for the kind of biographer, almost invariably a woman, that likes to like her subject. She was humorous, affectionate, and modest. Moreover, she was a celebrated talker and often very quotable. Meeting her in London in her later years was an experience that often found its way into the copious diaries, letters, and reminiscences of the period. With a small handful of exceptions, the accounts her celebrated acquaintances gave were enthusiastic. In 1820 she went to Paris and Geneva, in 1823 she was in Scotland, and she visited London half a dozen times from 1813 onwards. She made friends everywhere in the intellectual reaches of high Society. Scott's son-in-law, John Gibson Lockhart, who was not given to raptures, always felt obliged to introduce some statutory reservations, and yet he

[1] Letter to Henry Acland, n.d. [? 1855]; Bodleian Library, MS. Acland d. 72.

did like her very much. 'Miss Edgeworth is at Abbotsford, and has been for some time; a little, dark, bearded, sharp, withered, active, laughing, talking, impudent, fearless, outspoken, honest, whiggish, unchristian, good-tempered, kindly ultra-Irish body. I like her one day, and damn her to perdition the next.'[1]

Better still from the popular biographer's viewpoint, she wrote highly entertaining letters herself. Particularly when she was away from home, she got up early in the morning to write to her family and friends, and dashed off her descriptions of people and conversations with amazing speed and fluency. Letters were a good medium for her, since she had a sharp eye for character and an ear for dialogue. Read in quantity, her letters are *too* good-tempered; most people whose letters have been their literary fortune have had more than a dash of vinegar, and this she lacks. Still there is something very pleasing about her good humour, and about her style, a distinctive blend of eighteenth-century poise with unpretentious homeliness. Even though there is not enough acid to put her in quite the first rank of letter-writers, nearly all her biographers, and more than one twentieth-century critic, have claimed that the letters are better reading than the novels.

Yet, like other judgements about her, this too remains open to question. When Maria Edgeworth's life is seen as a whole, the self-portrait she gives in her letters appears less complete than her biographers, or indeed the friends of her later life, ever realized. There was more contrast in her life, and also more anxiety and unhappiness, than she wanted to reveal. Furthermore, the novels that she produced in middle life, although too impersonal ('she has no more heart than a post', Byron said, quite wrongly, after reading them) have certain advantages over the letters. Intellectually they are much more ambitious, which was why Scott and (perhaps) Turgenev found them so peculiarly interesting. The tradition of domestic biography, for which Maria's personality as revealed in the letters has had such an appeal in the last hundred years, has tended to censor or misrepresent the very qualities which established her reputation, and which ought to make her of real literary interest still.

[1] Letter to 'Christopher North', Aug. 1823, quoted by Mrs. Gordon, *'Christopher North', a Memoir of John Wilson*, 1862, ii. 58–9.

The common picture of a kind and entertaining old woman has outlasted any other impression of Maria Edgeworth because it comes from much more accessible sources. To begin with biographers have been able to draw on the anecdotes and casual references of a score of celebrated acquaintances. Far more important, they have had Maria Edgeworth's own letters—or rather the relatively small proportion of her letters that have so far been published. The fullest and most influential selection by far is in the *Memoir of Maria Edgeworth*, edited by her stepmother and stepsisters, and published in 1867.

This book has shaped posterity's view of Maria Edgeworth more decisively than anyone has recognized. The *Memoir* was privately printed, and has always been very difficult to obtain. Many critics and biographers who have written about Maria Edgeworth have probably never seen it. But Augustus Hare largely derived *his* selection in 1894 from the *Memoir*, and Hare's two volumes have always been regarded as the standard version of the Life and Letters. For better or worse, all subsequent critics and biographers have tended to rely on Hare. Even when a new study has been able to claim that it contains unpublished material, this has always been taken from letters picked out for the author by members of Maria Edgeworth's family. No version of the Life has hitherto gone back beyond the *Memoir* to the unselected evidence about Maria Edgeworth presented by the 2,000-odd letters written by her that survive, and the almost equally large body of letters from members of her immediate family.

It would be quite wrong to suggest that Maria Edgeworth's family have been suppressing information about her all these years. On the contrary, the *Memoir of Maria Edgeworth* is a careful selection from the correspondence, which gives a very fair picture of her as the authors saw her. It is true that they took some liberties with the texts of the original letters, for the rules of scholarship were less stringent then than now. Important cuts and some bewildering elisions were also made, often in order to spare the feelings of living people. But there was no serious tampering with the truth, as the editors saw it. They were not trying to hide guilty secrets—not, at any rate, secrets about Maria herself.

On the other hand, this was a family *Memoir*. It was written by three women who had lived for many years in the same household as Maria Edgeworth. They meant it as a memorial, which means obviously that it is not the same book that a dispassionate observer would have written. For one thing its emphasis lies where it was natural for the authors to place it, on Maria Edgeworth as a social being—not as a woman in society, which would be quite another matter, but as a friend. This is not necessarily the most helpful viewpoint from which to study an author. Furthermore the *Memoir*'s picture is 'true', even within these limits, for only part of Maria Edgeworth's life. The nominal author, Mrs. Frances Edgeworth, first met her in 1797, when Maria was twenty-nine years old.[1] Mrs. Edgeworth's principal assistant, Harriet Edgeworth, later Harriet Butler, who has been an influential witness about the detail of her stepsister's life, was not born until 1801. Her first hand testimony can scarcely begin before Maria Edgeworth's most productive period as a novelist was over. Mrs. Edgeworth's other co-author, her youngest daughter Lucy Robinson, was born in 1805. Mrs. Edgeworth, Mrs. Butler, and Mrs. Robinson were sometimes inaccurate in the facts they gave about the early years, for which they had had to rely partly on letters, partly on family tradition, partly on the memories of others. In any case the one volume of the *Memoir* which deals with Maria's first forty-nine years is obviously much less exhaustive (and reliable) than the two volumes which go from 1817 to Maria's death in 1849. Since every novel but one was written by 1817, it is the years covered by the first volume that most concern the student of literature.

The *Memoir*'s bias in favour of Maria Edgeworth the good friend, and Maria Edgeworth in old age, has been reflected unconsciously in virtually everything written about her. The corpus of biography and criticism is not great, and it divides into two groups, the late nineteenth-century and the modern. Since the vogue for Maria Edgeworth the novelist was over, the interest shown in her in the late Victorian period was almost entirely personal. Between the early 1880s and the

[1] The *Memoir* was not published until 1867, two years after Mrs. Edgeworth's death at the age of ninety-six. It is probably safe to assume that most of the narrative was written by her daughters.

first World War (busy years also for Janeites and for admirers of the Brontës and Mrs. Gaskell), more than half the books ever written about Maria Edgeworth appeared. The first and best-researched of these was by an American, Mrs. Grace Oliver's *Study of Maria Edgeworth, with Notices of her Father and Friends*, published in Boston in 1882. Next year two English books were devoted partly or wholly to Maria's life and career, Anne Thackeray Ritchie's *Book of Sybils* and Helen Zimmern's *Maria Edgeworth*. Two decades later there were more biographical studies, Emily Lawless's *Maria Edgeworth* (1904) and Constance Hill's *Maria Edgeworth and her Circle in the Days of Buonaparte and Bourbon* (1910), followed by Alice Paterson's more specialized *The Edgeworths: A Study of Later Eighteenth Century Education* in 1914.

The only interest of most of these books nowadays is as an illustration of how influential myths can gain ground. All the biographers were women, and they all seemed bent on making Maria Edgeworth attractively feminine. In this effort the *Memoir* understandably lent them a great deal of support. The Maria Edgeworth both of the *Memoir* and of nineteenth-century biography was 'a regular jolly old bird' (as one young woman who married into the family described her in 1846). The trouble was that a lot of the fiction did not seem to match the woman. How could the jolly old bird have taken it into her head to write the immensely serious novel *Patronage*? There were also the educational books to explain away. *Castle Rackrent*, with its comic central figure, fits the image of its author reasonably well—but what about the other Irish tales, which deal with the land question, sectarian quarrels, and political jobbery? None of these fitted at all; but the late Victorian imagination had a favourite resource in cases, or apparent cases, of split personality—the sinister *alter ego*. Dr. Hyde and Svengali are products of this period, and so in his way is Richard Lovell Edgeworth.

Maria Edgeworth certainly did have a father who played a central part in her life. The facts that were known about him could be presented in an extremely unfavourable light. He was the inventor of innumerable half-understood gadgets (i.e. an eccentric), an educator (i.e. a would-be controller of other people's minds), and, in spite of his manifest respectability, a kind of Bluebeard—the husband of four wives and father of twenty-two children. Edgeworth had come in for some hostile criticism in his lifetime, but this was nothing compared to the inferences that were drawn between 1880 and 1900. Evidence was marshalled, and in some cases invented, to show that the novels had been tampered with. If Maria was to be presented as an entirely amiable and feminine woman, she must have an unamiable father, because women like that do not write, from choice at least, about education, class, and economic relationships. 'For our part, after reading her letters, with which her father certainly did not meddle, we are inclined to lay most of her faults [as a novelist] to the charge of that monitor and guide, whose assistance she so much over-rated.'[1]

Without going back to first-hand evidence, it has proved almost impossible for twentieth-century critics and literary historians to shake off this peculiarly insidious legend. Virginia Woolf lent it her wit and authority in *The Common Reader*, and recently Professors Donald Davie and W. L. Renwick have referred to Edgeworth's interference as an undisputed fact. Among the small and undistinguished band of twentieth-century biographers of Maria Edgeworth, only P. H. Newby in his perceptive monograph has even hinted that there could be other ways of interpreting Maria's relationship with her father:

> Richard Lovell Edgeworth's influence over his daughter was not, as has sometimes been imagined, the superficial one of censor, nor is it true that he inserted sermons on utility into his daughter's lively novels. . . . The trouble lay deeper. Edgeworth's crime was not so much that he was a rather pompous and opinionated utilitarian but that he so conducted himself as to cause his daughter to love him uncritically and therefore adopt his opinions on literature and life unquestioningly.[2]

Yet even this relatively mild account of 'Edgeworth's crime' puts the onus on him for the faults of the novels: how justly will emerge in the book that follows. In the circumstances, the most useful twentieth-century studies of Maria Edgeworth have been specialist books with fresh facts to offer. Selections from family manuscripts were for example published in *The*

[1] Helen Zimmern, *Maria Edgeworth*, 1883, p. 80.
[2] *Maria Edgeworth*, 1950, p. 18.

*Black Book of Edgeworthstown and other Edgeworth Memories, 1585–1817*, 1926, by H. J. and H. E. Butler (granddaughter and great-grandson of Richard Lovell Edgeworth). Mrs. B. C. Slade's *Maria Edgeworth, 1767–1849: a Bibliographical Tribute*, 1937, produced many new details about the writing and publishing of individual tales and novels, although it also put into general currency a considerable number of fresh mistakes of its own. Meanwhile fresh batches of the letters have appeared to fill out still further the picture of Maria the older woman and friend. There have been several selections of her letters to Scott in the 1820s, as well as her letters to Sir Samuel and Lady Romilly from 1813 to 1818, and to the Irish family of Moore from about twenty years later. The best of all her individual letters, her description of a visit to the west of Ireland in 1833, has been published as *A Tour of Connemara.*[1] Mrs. Christina Colvin's *Maria Edgeworth: Letters from England, 1813–1844*, 1971, contains much the biggest group of Maria Edgeworth's letters to appear since Augustus Hare's *Life and Letters* in 1894. But these letters again have the disadvantage for the student of literature that they were written in Maria Edgeworth's later life, in 1813 and after. By this time she had passed the peak of her literary influence, and had only three stories for adults left to write.

It would be a perverse biographer who sat down to compose a portrait from which her charm and humour in old age are deliberately omitted. On the other hand a different picture of Maria Edgeworth emerges from a perspective that is not personal but literary. Just what did Scott (or for that matter Turgenev) read into her novels that was so well worth copying? Scott himself now seems to be receiving his long-overdue reassessment; but even during the twilight of his reputation earlier this century, no one denied that in his day Scott had as wide an influence on European literature as any English writer has ever had. A formative influence on him, if Maria really was that, ought to arouse some interest; especially when she also attracted the notice of Stendhal and Turgenev, the pioneers of the two greatest European traditions in the novel. The fact is that Maria's most important stories, together with

[1] Full details of all these publications are given in the bibliography below, pp. 506–9.

the personal and intellectual influence that went into them, reveal a great deal about the roots of early-nineteenth-century realism. To understand why she succeeded is to have a clearer insight into the conditions that brought the major Victorian novels into existence.

Two years before Maria Edgeworth died, the publishers Simpkin and Marshall wrote to inform her of their intention to bring out a new edition of her tales and novels, similar to the collected edition of Scott's Waverley novels which appeared in 1829. They wanted Maria to supply a preface and notes along the lines of Scott's; she was to give supplementary information about the background to the tales, and provide a sketch of the circumstances in which each one was written. Maria declined the opportunity.

> In truth I have nothing to say of them but what my dear father has said for me in his prefaces to each of them as they came out. These sufficiently explain the moral design; they require no national explanations, and I have nothing personal to add. As a woman, my life, wholly domestic, cannot afford anything interesting to the public: I am like the 'needy knifegrinder'—I have no story to tell.[1]

The latter part of this characteristically self-effacing declaration has a great deal of truth in it; so much, that in trying to supply the information sought by Simpkin and Marshall I have had to avoid altogether the kind of format they proposed. Indeed, despite the title, the reader will find that in the first part of this book Richard Lovell Edgeworth looms larger than his daughter, and rightly so: no account of the origins of the novels can exclude parts of Edgeworth's experience, or the continuous interaction from Maria's earliest years between her mind and her father's. The nature of the Edgeworths' ideas on education and their experience of Irish politics are both more relevant to the novels than any simple event, of the kind which provides the staple of the narrative in more active lives. What is needed is not so much a study of what Maria Edgeworth did, but of how her novels originated, in so far as this is a process which can be tackled within the compass of a biography. And if, therefore, as in *Tristram Shandy*, it takes

[1] *Mem.*, iii. 259. The knifegrinder is the representative of the needy apostrophized in George Canning's *Sapphics*, a parody of Southey's *The Widow* (*Anti-Jacobin*, 27 Nov. 1797).

the heroine some time to be born, and even longer before arriving at the age of five, this is no mere matter of chance: the gestation period of the novels was long, and it involved both a family and a wider intellectual circle. If Maria Edgeworth was a key figure in the development of the English novel, it was not because she had a creative talent equal to that of Jane Austen, but because her training and background made her seem more serious and more relevant to her times than any novelist immediately available for comparison.

# Part I

# APPRENTICESHIP:
# TO 1799

# I

# INHERITANCE

MARIA EDGEWORTH was born into a family whose history was typical of the Anglo-Irish gentry. In about 1585 two brothers, Edward and Francis Edgeworth, came to Ireland in the hope of advancing themselves in their respective professions, and both succeeded. Edward, who in England had been a chaplain to the Earl of Leicester, died Bishop of Down and Connor in 1595. The lawyer Francis was appointed in 1606 to the Irish office of Clerk of the Crown and Hanaper, and in 1619 nearly 600 acres of land were granted him around Mastrim, Co. Longford, which later in the seventeenth century became known as Edgeworthstown. This grant was in accordance with James I's policy of settling Protestants of English descent on lands confiscated from Irish Catholics.

Family fortunes in the seventeenth century ebbed and (rather more rarely) flowed with the unstable conditions of English government in Ireland. Like other members of their newly established breed, the Edgeworths had few natural ties with the peasantry who now became (to use the English concept) their tenants. Differing in religion and in traditions of land tenure from the common people, the Anglo-Irish did not belong to their localities with the same naturalness as the English squirearchy in the sister country. Typically, the seventeenth-century Edgeworths showed very little interest in their estate, except as a source of revenue. They were gentlemen first, soldiers and courtiers afterwards, landowners last of all. They put their hopes of further advancement on the English court, and were in London or Dublin as often as they were in County Longford.

John Edgeworth, who succeeded to the estate in 1627, was very much a Cavalier in politics and in his style of life. His extravagance often forced him to retire to his home, the castle of Crannelagh, near Edgeworthstown, but even when there he failed to retrench. 'A constant table was kept for the better sort, and a long table in the Hall for all comers of the inferior sort; which table was constantly supplied with meat, ales, pipes and tobacco, to the great joy of the common Irish and to the great detriment of his fortune.'[1] In spite of his free spending Edgeworth was not generally popular with his tenants, for during the Great Rebellion of 1641 his house was sacked by a Catholic mob, and his wife and three-year-old son barely escaped with their lives.

In the 1650s John Edgeworth made a bid to restore the family finances by an adroit second marriage with an English widow named Bridgman. Finding that it was not she but her daughter who was heir to the fortune he had in view, he then induced his son, another John, to elope with his stepdaughter on the eve of her fourteenth birthday. The two Edgeworths, father and son, were thus real-life prototypes of the dashing Irish adventurers who were to make such frequent appearances in eighteenth-century stage comedy. Nor did the resemblance to popular conception stop there, for the young couple were as giddy and feckless as John Edgeworth the elder, and after inheriting the estate in 1668 they managed it in much the same style as he had done. Thanks to two extravagant trips to London, and to the younger John's lifelong addiction to gambling, they were already in severe straits before the war of 1689 brought ruin. King James landed at Kinsale on 12 March of that year, and in June the head of the Edgeworth family and his eldest sons—in company with the majority of Protestant landowners—found themselves temporarily dispossessed, outlawed, and attainted. Catholics once again surged into the property, and two of the three Edgeworth houses, the castle at Crannelagh and a summer residence at Kilshrewly, Co. Longford, were burnt to the ground.

Sir John (who had been knighted by Charles II, because, it was believed, that monarch had an eye for his pretty wife) spent his last years in London hanging about the Court, very much a Mr. Dorrit now that he was in his decline; he kept up a remarkable appearance of dignity, but his real occupation

[1] Like much of the detail in this section, from the family annals written by ME's grandfather, Richard Edgeworth (1701–70), in his record of the estate known as the 'Black Book' (for which see below, p. 502); this passage quoted *Black Book*, p. 11.

consisted of begging for himself and his family. When he died in January 1700/1 his only certain legacies to his eldest son Frank were personal debts, for the estate was in inextricable confusion. Even when Sir John had got back his land with the victory of King William, he had stayed at Court rather than go home to put things to rights, and during his absence two of his six sons, Robert and Ambrose, had successfully purloined parts of the estate.[1] Moreover, Robert had prejudiced their mother's mind against Frank, who accordingly became further embroiled in disputes about the payment of her dower.

Frank was honourable, brave, and well-intentioned, but he was not the man to get out of financial trouble. Like his father and grandfather before him he was 'unbusinesslike, casual and extravagant, with a fondness for good wine, which he often carried to excess'. After the death of his first wife, Dorothea, he tried to follow his father's example by marrying an heiress, but on his way to conclude a match with the daughter of the Earl of Donegal he stayed overnight with a family called Cullum, at Lisnamcan, Co. Cavan. Inopportunely he got drunk that night, and when he woke in the morning he discovered that he had been married to the unlovely Miss Dorothy Cullum—whose dowry, a rather too modest £1,500, was never paid. When this wife died, Frank's third marriage to Mary Bradston was for love. His money troubles got worse, but he went on living in a fine style; he had an elegant house in Dublin, and in 1706, when he must have been near to bankruptcy, he apparently built himself another at Edgeworthstown. Two years later his financial situation was quite desperate. In May 1709 he and his wife were in Dublin, and in some danger of starvation; the only money they had to live on for a month was £10 borrowed from a friend. Early in June Frank caught a fever with pneumonia, and died on 7 June 1709. His wife, who had nursed him, caught the

[1] Robert's name especially became a by-word in the elder branch of the family for dishonesty, treachery, and absence of family feeling, and ME was influenced by its associations in naming characters in her novels. The rascally litigious cousin in *Patronage* who temporarily disinherits the senior branch of the family is called Sir Robert Percy, and striking incidents which occur in the lawsuits in that novel are taken from early-eighteenth-century Edgeworth family history (see below, p. 498). In one of ME's best-known children's stories, *Little Dog Trusty*, the good brother is Frank and the bad brother Robert.

infection and died a week later, though not before an attempt had been made to arrest her for debt.

The careers of these three Edgeworths, John, Sir John, and Frank, could be paralleled in dozens of anecdotes about the Anglo-Irish squirearchy of the seventeenth and eighteenth centuries; Maria based her most celebrated book, *Castle Rackrent*, on the story of just such a dynasty. The Rackrents are sportsmen, litigants, drunkards, gamblers, duellists, adventurers in marriage; Maria did not give them a characteristic that she could not have found among her own predecessors. The Edgeworths of earlier times are beyond question the real models for the four generations of the Rackrent family. Some incidents in the tale are borrowed from local gossip, but the well-documented Edgeworths are always the richest source.[1] In her grandfather's narrative in the 'Black Book' Maria had an outline which strongly resembled the plot of *Castle Rackrent*—a family saga compounded of debts and prosperous marriages; successive landlords who were selfishly oblivious of their tenants, and yet were strikingly endowed with personal charm, humour, and finally pathos.

Maria owed the greater part of her material to the grandfather she never met, Richard Edgeworth, whose imagination was thoroughly possessed by the generations of the family. Richard was Frank's only surviving son, so that in 1709 he succeeded at the age of eight to what was left of the estates in Co. Longford. His sudden orphaning seems to have made a deep impression on him; at any rate, he grew up determined to avoid the mistakes of his father and of the spendthrifts who preceded him. Richard was cautious, hard-working, sensible about money, and—again unlike his forefathers—more than a little dull. He was brought up by a sensible guardian, Edward Pakenham, who helped him to realize his ambition to train as a lawyer. All his life Richard retained a belief in the

[1] Tracing the history of the direct line gives an inadequate idea of the extent of ME's borrowings from her grandfather's narrative: e.g. Richard observes of one of his cousins, a clergyman, that he seemed to think 'a readiness for single combat to be one of the cardinal virtues'; ME's Sir Kit Rackrent was of the same breed. A descendant of Robert's who was milked by his wife's relations seems to have provided hints both for Sir Condy Rackrent and for the blacksmith-Earl in another Irish tale, *Ennui* (*Memoirs of RLE*, i. 37–41).

wisdom of training a future landowner to the law (and his son and granddaughter Maria inherited the same conviction).[1] If the worst should happen, it was prudent to have a gentlemanly profession in reserve; and even at best the Irish landowner's path was likely to be strewn with litigation. The Edgeworth line henceforth became careful, prudent, economic, and decidedly different from the commoner traditions of the Anglo-Irish landed gentry.

After reading for the Bar at the Middle Temple in London in the early 1720s, Richard went to law with his uncles to regain possession of his estate. By 1726 he was sufficiently in command of his resources to begin building or rebuilding the house at Edgeworthstown which henceforward became the family home.[2] The following year the tiresome business of his grandfather's will was at last settled in his favour, and in a few more years he found himself in easy circumstances. In 1732 he married, left the Bar, and retired to his estate at Edgeworthstown. He wanted nothing better than to administer the lands he had won back, and he was to spend the rest of his life perfecting his rent-rolls and the other records of the estate to hand on to his descendants as, next to the estate itself, 'the most useful legacy I could leave'.[3]

Richard's wife was a very different woman from the beauties or wealthy widows earlier Edgeworths had chosen. Jane Lovell was the daughter of a Welsh judge, Samuel Lovell, and granddaughter of Sir Salathiel Lovell, Recorder of London at the time of the Revolution in 1688. Jane brought a new element into the family: she was the first member in whom any interest in books or education is recorded. She and Richard had eight children, of whom four survived infancy—Thomas, Mary, Richard Lovell, and Margaret. Since Thomas was destined to be the heir, Richard decided to make his other son a

[1] A legal education is recommended in *Professional Education* (1809), and favourably depicted in the two novels *Ennui* (1809) and *Patronage* (1814). Training future landowners in the law was of course a common practice in the seventeenth and eighteenth centuries, but not everyone made such a moral virtue of it as the Edgeworths.

[2] See below, pp. 81–3.

[3] The next two generations did find the records invaluable, for example to prove contested boundaries in the lawsuits that were so common a feature of the Irish landlord's life. ME wrote a manuscript continuation to her grandfather's volumes, cited below, p. 422.

merchant, and by the time the boy was five he was being taught arithmetic with special care, to prepare him for book-keeping in later life. But the following year, 1750, Thomas died, leaving Richard Lovell heir to the property, so that henceforward his father always hoped he would be a lawyer.

In middle and later life Richard Lovell showed important traits that he probably learnt from his father. He became a prudent and efficient manager, without the slightest inclination (in the words of Richard's admonitory preface to his family records) to 'lavish away his estate in idleness, debauchery or extravagance'. But his steadiness was not obvious to others until well after his father was dead, and in the old man's lifetime the differences in his son's tastes and temperament were much more striking than the resemblances. The two of them felt this for themselves; there was no outright quarrel, but they did not get on well together.

Nothing illustrates the contrast between them more clearly than the way they handle the same family anecdotes. Richard is far more accurate in his 'Black Book' than Richard Lovell in the briefer account of his ancestors with which he begins his published *Memoirs*.[1] Although not uninterested in his predecessors as individuals, the father cares most about them as landlords, and the point of most of the episodes he relates is the getting, or more frequently the squandering, of money. Richard Lovell concentrates exclusively on producing a gallery of remarkable people. He is fascinated by the combination of traits that go to make up an individual as complex as his great-grandmother, Lady Edgeworth; although of course he never met her, she takes her place among the long succession of eccentrics and waifs who are glimpsed, impressionistically, in his disconnected but strangely haunting volume of autobiography.[2] His gift was for seeing, not for writing, but thus far Richard Lovell Edgeworth was a novelist *manqué*.

[1] e.g. on at least three occasions RLE attributes an anecdote to the wrong person. Cf. *Memoirs of RLE*, i. 11, 16, and 19, with *Black Book*, pp. 11, 19, and 33–4: the latter version, from the father's narrative, is the more authoritative.

[2] Virginia Woolf, who disliked RLE and was perhaps unduly influenced by the clumsiness of his style, praises his people, places, and episodes, which 'live with a peculiar beauty, fantastic, solemn, mysterious, in contrast with Edgeworth, who is none of these things' ('Lives of the Obscure', *The Common Reader*, 1st ser., 1925, p. 118). The imagination that retained these impressions—and passed many more to Maria—was nevertheless his.

Afterwards he thought that his father had lacked insight into human nature—at least into his own[1]—and, although this may have been unfair, the elder Edgeworth's watchfulness for signs of imprudence made him unsympathetic to the boy, and thus greatly reduced his influence over him.

Jane Edgeworth was a more successful parent. Her favourite author, Locke, had inspired her with the belief that a child's mind and character were formed by his environment rather than by heredity, and she devoted herself to her children's education from their infancy. Like her husband, she had a clear view of the kind of man she wanted Richard Lovell to be. She admired strength and independence of character, and would urge her son never to fall in with the views of his school-fellows, or with the common run of people, merely in order to be popular. She would read literature with Richard Lovell primarily in order to teach him the difference between right and wrong. Later he recalled studying Shakespeare with her, particularly the Roman plays, which were full of examples of fine, disinterested conduct. Jane Edgeworth thought *Julius Caesar* an instructive play, and *Coriolanus* even better; rather oddly, she considered Coriolanus himself a happy model for her son.

> The contempt which Coriolanus expresses for the opinion and applause of the vulgar, for 'the voices of the greasy-headed multitude', suited well with that disdain for low company, with which I had been first inspired by the fable of the lion and the cub. It is probable that I understood the speeches of Coriolanus but imperfectly; yet I know, that I sympathised with my mother's admiration, my young spirit was touched by his noble character, by his generosity and, above all, by his filial piety, and his gratitude to his mother.[2]

If there were dangers in seizing on this particular example, Jane avoided them, for Richard Lovell grew up no more emotionally dependent on her than he was on the good opinion of the world in general. She succeeded in giving him that contentment with himself which made it easy for him to do without the approval of others.[3]

[1] *Memoirs of RLE*, i. 231–2.

[2] Ibid., 35–6.

[3] Jane's success in forming RLE's character along the lines she intended is the nominal theme of his volume of autobiography, although in fact outweighed in literary interest by what was probably meant to be secondary, the richness of his incidental experiences.

While the boy was an adolescent it was by no means clear that either father or mother would have a permanent influence with him. He went to a series of schools in England and Ireland noted for their teaching of Latin and Greek, but in general he lacked the stimulus of clever companions, and at home in the holidays he took up the usual rural amusements of hunting and shooting.

As he was preparing to go up to Trinity College, Dublin, in 1759, his elder sister Mary celebrated her marriage to a neighbouring gentleman, Francis Fox, of Fox Hall, Co. Longford. There was hunting, feasting, and dancing at Edgeworthstown, and for three nights Richard Lovell never went to bed at all. On the dance floor he was tireless, and during the intervals, when others were snatching rest or sleep, he was still working off his energies by feats of agility. One night, when the dancing was over, the young people went off and had what was known as 'a raking pot of tea'.[1] This was a drink taken in the early hours of the morning to give a new lease of life to a weary party. As a joke one of the young men put a white cloak round his shoulders to resemble a surplice, and announced his intention of marrying Richard Lovell to his favourite partner, the daughter of a curate who had once taught him Latin. Someone produced the key of the door as the ring, and the 'priest' gabbled through part of the wedding ceremony, to the great amusement of the company.

Next morning Richard Edgeworth was far from amused. He felt he knew all about hasty marriages that ended in one side's robbing the other of a fortune. In litigious Ireland some very improbable suits came before the courts, and Richard was afraid the girl's family might claim that a marriage really had been solemnized. He instigated a suit of *jactitation of marriage* in the ecclesiastical courts; that is, he sued to have the marriage annulled, to do which he had first to prove that it *had* taken place. Richard Lovell regarded his father's behaviour over this prank as one more instance of his pedantic fussing. Meanwhile the elder Richard was confirmed in his opinion that his son was growing up in the worst traditions of the family.

On 26 April 1760, a month before his sixteenth birthday, Edgeworth entered Trinity College, Dublin. The slackness of Trinity authorities and the riotousness of the students is well

[1] Cf. *Castle Rackrent*, i. 52, and note in glossary.

attested by Oliver Goldsmith's experiences there in the 1740s. Edgeworth himself later commented drily that 'it was not the fashion in those days to plague fellow-commoners with lectures'.[1] Once again he was unlucky in his contemporaries, and he was drawn into a favourite student occupation, hard drinking. Drunkenness insensibly began to lose its appeal, however, as hunting and shooting had already done. The pessimistic Richard Edgeworth was unaware of it, but before he was seventeen Richard Lovell had lost any taste for becoming the traditional type of Anglo-Irishman.

Imagining that the boy would never settle down to work in Dublin, Edgeworth decided to send him to Oxford, to the care of an old friend whom he thought of as a sober hard-working lawyer, the very model of everything a man should be. He had known Paul Elers in the 1720s as a law student destined by his industry for success, even though he was only the son of a German immigrant, a potter who in spite of original techniques had not had much commercial success. Since returning to Ireland at the end of his student days at the Temple, Edgeworth had corresponded with Elers, but never met him, and he knew no more than that Elers had long since married an heiress of the Hungerford family. A girl destined to inherit an estate in Oxfordshire 'of eight hundred pounds a year, highly improvable, well wooded and within a ring fence'[2] seemed an excellent match for a potter's son (though on his father's side Elers came of an old German landed family); Anthony Hungerford was considered broadminded when he accepted Elers as a son-in-law. But it seemed essential to him that the young man should give up practising at the Bar in London, to settle instead on his wife's estate at Black Bourton; and Elers was temperamentally unsuited for the life of a country gentleman. While he dabbled a little at the law and at his books, he left the management of the estate to his wife, who in turn left it to the servants. In 1754 he became involved unsuccessfully in the famous and expensive Oxfordshire election campaign.[3] After this the family was always in difficulties for money.

[1] *Memoirs of RLE*, i. 74. [2] Ibid., 82.

[3] Although Elers rates only passing mention (as a Whig J.P. supporting the New

Edgeworth's decision to trust his son to Elers, of all people, was highly ironic, since the latter had turned into the very kind of improvident landlord Edgeworth detested. There was a solemn exchange of letters between the two men, in which Edgeworth described his son's character, obviously in very despondent terms, and Elers honourably warned him in reply that he had several pretty daughters of marriageable age. Was it wise to throw the young people together? Edgeworth was impressed at the delicate sense of honour shown by his friend, and not at all deterred at the thought of the daughters. In October 1761, Richard Lovell entered Corpus Christi College as a gentleman commoner, and, probably before October, was admitted into the 'excellent but antiquated house' at Black Bourton.[1]

With his usual indolence Elers did little or nothing to hinder the intimacy that as he had foreseen rapidly developed between Edgeworth and his daughters. Richard Lovell enjoyed his first weeks at Bourton Place. 'I laughed, and talked, and sang with the ladies, and read Cicero and Longinus with their father, who, notwithstanding my youth, and my propensity to female society, filled many of my hours with agreeable conversation.'[2] The girls were not especially beautiful or interesting, but they had the charm of naturalness and high spirits, and the eldest, Anna Maria, particularly caught his fancy.

It is conceivable that Richard Lovell seduced the girl, although he never admitted as much afterwards. Whatever happened occurred before his visit to Bath, an exposure to polished society which completely opened his eyes to Anna Maria's ignorance and want of style. He went back and laid the whole matter before Elers, telling him that he did not love Anna Maria, but that since he had encouraged her to fall in

Interest) in R. J. Robson's *Oxfordshire Election of 1754*, 1949, family sources indicate that he engaged himself deeply in the hope of being rewarded by the political patronage of local magnates like the Duke of Marlborough. In practice what happened was that he ruined his chances of making money from law, because most of his natural clients around Black Bourton were Tories.

[1] Bourton Place was pulled down at the end of the eighteenth century. Among the celebrated Hungerfords of more prosperous times were Sir Thomas, d. 1377, the first man formally entitled Speaker of the House of Commons; his son Sir Walter, also Speaker, who fought at Agincourt; and Sir Edward (1632–1711), who gave his name to Hungerford Market at Charing Cross in London.

[2] *Memoirs of RLE*, i. 90–1.

love with him he felt bound to offer her marriage. Perhaps understandably, Elers's sense of honour was this time less in evidence, and he had no hesitation in accepting the proposal on Anna Maria's behalf.

Richard Lovell did not ask his father for permission because he knew that it would not be granted. In Scotland he could legally marry Anna Maria before he was twenty-one, and so, in 1763, to Scotland they went.[1] They returned as husband and wife to Black Bourton, and in May 1764, before Richard Lovell was twenty, he was the father of his first son (also called Richard). The imminence of the baby's birth forced Richard Edgeworth to bow to the inevitable: cautious as ever as to the legal status of a potential heir to Edgeworthstown, he gave the consent which was necessary to have the couple legally re-married on 21 February 1764 at Black Bourton. Later the same year they set out for Edgeworthstown, taking the baby with them.

It was a sad homecoming for more reasons than one. On arrival Richard Lovell found his mother very ill, and she died a few days afterwards. Jane had no opportunity to form an opinion of Anna Maria, and Richard Lovell was relieved that it was so, for Anna Maria's limitations became more and more apparent. Since 1761 Richard Lovell had been reading with Paul Elers, who generously continued to pour out on his son-in-law the stores of knowledge he had withheld from his own children. The three years at Corpus Christi College had been more fruitful than his earlier formal education, and Edgeworth could now claim to be well-read among classical and to some extent among modern writers. But the more he read the more bitterly he was aware of the aridity of his marriage, since Anna Maria read little or nothing.

The year he spent with his wife at Edgeworthstown was the dreariest of his adult life. 'I never passed twelve months with less pleasure or improvement.' In desperation he returned to a boyhood hobby, mechanics. He was thrown back on his own inventiveness, for there were no books to guide him and even the tools available were indifferent. As a boy he had been

[1] RLE's account, which there is no surviving documentary evidence to corroborate.

impressed by an orrery, a model which represented the movements of the sun, earth, and moon, and now he first designed, then made one for himself out of wood. 'I calculated the wheel-work accurately, and invented a movement, to represent the obliquity of the moon's orbit, and its change, which I afterwards found to be the same as what is usually employed in this sort of machinery.' He implied afterwards that Anna Maria's pronounced lack of interest in his achievement made their relationship even cooler than before.[1] At last Richard Edgeworth decided that it would be best for the couple to take themselves back to England, in order for Richard Lovell to qualify as a barrister at the Temple. In 1765, probably to everyone's relief, Richard Lovell and Anna Maria went off to set up home for themselves.

On their journey through England they stopped at Chester to visit an aunt of Anna Maria's, and thus by chance Edgeworth was able to see a travelling exhibition known as the Microcosm. Among other things this machinery 'represented various motions of the heavenly bodies with neatness and precision'. Its appeal for Edgeworth was obvious: he came back so often, and asked so many questions, that the good-natured showman told him how the model worked. In the course of their conversation the man mentioned the names of other ingenious gentlemen he had met in the various towns where he had exhibited. Among them was Dr. Darwin of Lichfield, Erasmus Darwin, who, the showman said, had designed a carriage that could turn about in its own length without loss of stability. Here was another problem in mechanics to fascinate Edgeworth, and he immediately made up his mind to tackle it. As he observes in his *Memoirs*, at this point in his life he might equally well have gone to the House of Commons, heard a great debate, and been fired with political ambition. Bored at home, he needed an outlet for his prodigious energy, and the years 1764–5 determined that the outlet was to be practical science.

The home that Richard Lovell and Anna Maria rented was an unpretentious house in the Berkshire village of Hare Hatch, in the Thames valley between Reading and Maidenhead.

[1] *Memoirs of RLE*, i. 109–10.

There was a modest garden, which Anna Maria managed with the help of a manservant who also had responsibility for a phaeton and two ponies. The couple had one other manservant and two maidservants—a much smaller household than either was accustomed to. Their house bordered on a common, around which some quite wealthy people lived, and the Edgeworths were soon recruited into local Society. On two or three evenings a week couples went to one another's houses for tea, cards, and conversation, walking back to their own homes by about ten o'clock at night. Anna Maria found the domesticated, admirably inexpensive life at Hare Hatch very congenial. Unlike her parents she was a good manager, in her element when growing her own vegetables and administering the servants, and she did not aspire to an evening occupation that was intellectually more ambitious than cards. Her husband, on the other hand, rapidly became bored; later in life he marvelled that he could ever have taken part in Hare Hatch amusements.[1]

The obvious alternative was London, and before long Richard Lovell had effectively made his escape. His first openings came through Anna Maria's distinguished connections on her mother's side. Three elderly ladies, the Misses Blake, lived in Great Russell Street, Bloomsbury, and by visiting them Edgeworth once again came into contact with people of rank. The company at Great Russell Street was not exactly fashionable, nor very young, but it was polite. Moreover, some of the visitors who came to the house were in touch with a wider world. One evening Edgeworth was entertaining the gathering by imitating the feats of one 'Comus', a stage magician who was enjoying a vogue in London that season, and he did it so successfully that he was brought to the notice of another amateur magician, the fashionable Sir Francis Delaval. For the time being Edgeworth's way in high Society was made.

Edgeworth's account of Delaval makes him out as no doubt he actually appeared to a rather inexperienced twenty-two-year-old: a handsome rake, now approaching middle age, who mixed in London with the lively set surrounding the Duke of York, could recall some amusing episodes during his two campaigns for Parliament at Andover, and was still energetically employed, on his own behalf and that of his sister

[1] Ibid., 119.

Lady Stanhope, in the pursuit of some wealthy partner to relieve them of their financial difficulties.[1] Delaval might almost have had a family affinity with Edgeworth's own rakish forebears, and Edgeworth seems to have viewed his exploits in much the same light. He describes them in a tone of moral neutrality, as evidence merely of human oddity, and incidentally also illustrations of 'the manners of the times'.

In fact Delaval's career was a great deal more sordid than Edgeworth appreciated. The eldest son of a *nouveau riche* family whose house, Seaton Delaval in Northumberland, was built by Vanbrugh, he had always been kept short of money and had come to London to seek his fortune by any means that offered. His Parliamentary career was undertaken as the most convenient insurance against imprisonment for debt. Edgeworth gives an engaging account of the practical joke planned and carried out by Delaval and his friend the actor Samuel Foote, which ended in Delaval's winning for himself the hand of the wealthy widow Lady Nassau Paulet. According to Edgeworth, Delaval himself dressed up as a fortune-teller who advanced the love intrigues of half the town by his cunning predictions.[2] The reality seems to be that Delaval hired the 'fortune-teller', another actor, Jemmy Worsley, to persuade the fat, half-deranged fifty-year-old widow that her destiny lay in a match with the penniless twenty-three-year-old libertine, and, when she showed signs of wanting to escape, he fell back on an even more unsavoury fraud. Delaval had promised Foote a percentage of the widow's fortune if he would seduce her, so that in case of difficulty Delaval could blackmail her by threatening to expose her relations with Foote. It was not for nothing that two years afterwards Walpole laconically

[1] Francis Blake Delaval, b. 16 Mar. 1727; M.P. for Hindon, 1751, Andover, 1754 and 1761; m. Isabella, widow of Lord Nassau Paulet and daughter of the Earl of Thanet, 8 Mar. 1750. When in 1755 his debts were calculated at £45,000 he was disinherited by his brothers and sisters. After his exploits at the taking of Cherbourg, 1758, he was made a K.B. in 1760. In 1759 his sister Anne became the third wife of Sir William Stanhope, who was reputedly impotent; the couple separated two years later. For taking the singer Ann Catley out of her father's house and allegedly living off her earnings, Delaval had to defend an action heard in Westminster Hall, 1764. Following the many disappointments of his last four years, he died on 8 Aug. 1771: the entertainment value of his life was such that his obituaries were much longer than Gray's, who had died ten days earlier. (Cf. Horace Walpole to Wm. Mason, 9 Sept. 1771; *Walpole's Correspondence*, ed. W. S. Lewis, 1955, xxviii. 20.)

[2] *Memoirs of RLE*, i. 138.

described Delaval as a man 'married by one Foote, a player to Lady Nassau Paulet, who had kept the latter'.[1]

Edgeworth had his version from Delaval's own lips, and no doubt the latter, having heard the story of Edgeworth's own unworldly marriage, tailored his life history so that it would not shock too deeply. The picture Sir Francis gave of himself coincided not so much with the phrase of Lady Stanhope's brother-in-law, Lord Chesterfield—'that most consummate puppy and impudent jackanapes'—as with Horace Walpole's observation, none the less revealing for being ironic, that he was one of the three most fashionable men in England. It was flattering for Edgeworth to be singled out by such a man, and delightful to be drawn into lively company which shared his own taste for mechanical contrivances; even if Delaval's motives in devising 'illusions' often seemed some way removed from the pure spirit of scientific inquiry. The most interesting deception Sir Francis and Edgeworth worked on originated in a substantial bet. For £500 they guaranteed that they would be the first people in London to know the result of a celebrated horse-race being run at Newmarket. Their opponents, led by Lord March, future Duke of Queensberry, thought that by posting fast horses along the ninety miles of road they could have the result of an afternoon race in town by nine at night. Edgeworth claimed he could have it by five: not of course by faster horses, but by a telegraph, a series of machines with giant pointers which could relay messages translated into a prearranged code from one vantage-point to another. After a few trials between houses in London, unfortunately, Edgeworth felt so sure of winning the bet that his sense of honour obliged him to hint as much to the other side; Delaval's view of his young friend's conscience is not recorded in so many words. The other party withdrew, Delaval lost a certain £500, and a Newmarket–London telegraph was not set up in 1766. Had it been, it would have pre-dated by three decades the system of Chappe in France which first brought the telegraph into regular use.

When Edgeworth first met Delaval the latter still had a chance to recoup his fortunes. He was M.P. for Andover;

[1] Horace Walpole to Horace Mann, 13 Mar. 1751; *Correspondence*, xx. 231. A more accurate version of Delaval's marriage than was available to RLE is given by Francis Askham in his *Gay Delavals* 1956, to which the above account is indebted

he had his Star of the Order of the Bath (of which, Foote said, he was so proud that he wore it on his cork jacket when swimming in the Thames); best of all he was a widower, and therefore free to have a second try at the easiest of all methods of acquiring money. As soon as Edgeworth met him in 1766 he became a party to one of Sir Francis's marital ploys, for he was put to work as stage manager to an amateur performance of Rowe's *The Fair Penitent*, in which Delaval had designedly cast the Duke of York and Lady Stanhope as the young lovers. In order to work on this production, for which Sir Francis used a private theatre in Petty France, Edgeworth went to stay for six weeks in Delaval's house in nearby Downing Street, where in addition to the actors Foote and Macklin, and the often disreputable hangers-on of the Duke of York, he met his first sprinkling of scientists. The experience was dazzling, for in that short time, as the *Memoirs* observe, he 'saw more of what is called *the world*' than he was likely to 'have seen elsewhere in as many years'.[1] It was in fact most of what he did see of high-life London until in his old age his daughter Maria became famous; so that in less than two years Delaval determined Edgeworth's future picture of fashion and, for half her life, Maria's too.

The experience lasted no longer, for within two years Delaval's affairs had taken on a very different aspect. The Duke of York died suddenly in Rome in 1767, and in the General Election of the following year Delaval lost his parliamentary seat at Andover. His creditors closed in on him, and he was obliged to give up the house in Downing Street, with all its ingenious contrivances.

From 1768 Edgeworth was away from London a great deal, and so he cannot have seen so much of Sir Francis in his decline—for Delaval at forty was fat and ageing—as he had seen in relative success only two years earlier. When they did meet Sir Francis told him of a pain in his chest, and forecast that he had not long to live; in the course of one such conversation, which took place in a London steam-bath in, presumably, August 1771,[2] Delaval suddenly added an unexpected

[1] *Memoirs of RLE*, i. 121–2.

[2] Ibid., 155–7. There was evidently some confusion in RLE's mind about dates, since he represents the death of Delaval as occurring shortly after the Duke of

confession. Although he had maintained his outward appearance of gaiety, he was sick of the futility of the life he had led. Two days later he was found dead in his bed, a circumstance so generally unexpected that an autopsy was performed to establish that his death was from natural causes. Many years later Maria was to draw on many features of Delaval's life and death—the political escapades, the fashionable notoriety, the outward appearance of gaiety, the private confession to a young friend, the pain in the chest which the gay world knew nothing of—for one of her best-remembered characters, Lady Delacour in *Belinda*.[1]

Although Edgeworth was fascinated by Delaval's liveliness, and by his circle of friends, he had little personal respect for him. It was a different matter with another friend he made in the same year, the eighteen-year-old Corpus Christi undergraduate Thomas Day, who exercised a strong and lasting moral appeal. During the vacations Day lived with his mother and stepfather near Hare Hatch, but he disliked his stepfather and found the society of their neighbours tedious. One day in 1766, therefore, he walked across the common to introduce himself to Edgeworth.

Thomas Day (1748–89) had inherited £1,000 a year from his father, a Collector of Taxes, who died when his only son was a year old. While at Oxford Thomas read widely in the classics, particularly singling out Lycurgus, Plato, Xenophon, and Socrates, from whom he imbibed an earnest passion for the pursuit of virtue and integrity.[2] He admired the Stoic personal ideals, and looked back with veneration (as did so many eighteenth-century moralists) to the simplicity and integrity of the early days of the Roman republic. At about this time, perhaps as a result of Edgeworth's influence, he discovered the modern primitivist Rousseau, and found his austerities so appealing that he became a disciple for the rest of his life.

Day's person was large, awkward, and unkempt. In private, when alone with friends like Edgeworth and, later, James Keir, he was eloquent and witty, and his letters could be humorous;

York's. He may have been deliberately trying to telescope the period of his friendship with Delaval because of the latter's notoriety.

[1] See below, pp. 309 ff.

[2] J. Keir, *An Account of the Life and Writings of Thomas Day, Esq.*, 1791, pp. 7–8.

but in general company he was either tongue-tied or severe, and both his clothes and his table manners gave real offence. The lively Edgeworth was so amused by his new friend's social peculiarities that he remembered a score of incidents, and indeed gave them so much weight in writing about Day in his *Memoirs* that it is as a great eccentric that Day has come down to us. Even Edgeworth commented in retrospect how odd it seemed that the bear-like Day should at once have had so strong an attraction for a young man who was superficially his exact opposite, graceful and witty, a dancer, a lover of parties and feminine company.[1] In reality these differences were less significant than the fact that Day appealed at a profound level to the values by which Edgeworth had been brought up: he conformed to Jane Edgeworth's ideal of the independent man who rejected popularity and lived by his principles. In trying to characterize his friend long after his death, Edgeworth recalled 'that highmindedness which distinguished him from other men'. 'During three and twenty years, that we lived in the most perfect intimacy, I never knew him swerve from the strictest morality in words or actions.'[2] Edgeworth clearly associated the streak of misanthropy in his friend with the underlying virtue; and in doing so he responded to one of the most fundamental eighteenth-century ethical traditions. Not merely for Edgeworth, but for the distinguished and practical circle of industrialists to whom Edgeworth introduced him, Day became something of a secular saint. He was the philanthropist, the private man, who in his public character railed against an over-soft civilization with tongue and pen.

In his youth, when Edgeworth knew him best, Day's target was a decadent and trivial society, in the social sense; later on, when he took up politics, demanding a 'return' to pure representation and civic virtue, he refused to contaminate himself by standing for Parliament.

> How is it possible that I should descend to the common meanness of the bought and buying tribe, or stoop to solicit the suffrages of the multitude, more than I have hitherto done the patronage of the great. . . . It was not in the forum, amidst the tribe of begging, cringing, shuffling, intriguing candidates, but in their farms, and amidst

[1] *Memoirs of RLE*, i. 180–1. [2] Ibid., 182.

their rural labours, that the Romans were obliged to seek for men, who were really animated with an holy zeal for their country's glory, and capable of preferring her interest to their own. I would neither pretend to the magnanimity, nor to the abilities of those illustrious men, whom we are more inclined to admire than imitate, but I pretend to all their indifference to public fame, and to all their disinterestedness.[1]

Edgeworth must have been reminded of Coriolanus, although Day's own favourite Roman model was Cincinnatus, who refused to leave his farm until prevailed upon to do so for the sake of the republic. In preferring a life of retirement, in which he did good to the poor, Day joined the long line of much-admired eighteenth-century Honest Men, including John Kyrle (Pope's Man of Ross), Ralph Allen of Somerset (commemorated by Fielding as Squire Allworthy), Fanny Burney's Mr. Albany, and many another active philanthropists of real life and fiction. To lose sight, in the midst of Day's eccentricities, of the continuing appeal of the tradition for which he stood, is to underrate the good sense of the more practical men to whom he personified one kind of moral ideal.

Profound as it was, Day's intellectual influence was at once qualified by that of the other new friends Edgeworth made between 1766 and 1770. When, after settling in at Hare Hatch, he began to make a carriage after Darwin's design, all he had to work on was the general description of the showman at Chester. 'It was so constructed, as to turn in a small compass, without danger of over-setting, and without the incumbrance of a crane-necked perch.'[2] Edgeworth's version was so successful that Delaval commissioned a second, and Edgeworth submitted a model to the Royal Society of Arts.[3] His sense of honour being what it was, he was anxious not to claim sole credit for the invention, and he informed both the Society and Darwin himself where his idea had originated. In reply the Doctor invited Edgeworth to call on him, and Edgeworth

[1] Letter to Dr. John Jebb [1780], quoted Keir, op. cit., pp. 121–3.

[2] *Memoirs of RLE*, i. 111.

[3] The RSA, a kind of lesser Royal Society, was an institution which specialized in encouraging designs which were industrially and commercially useful. RLE's name figures in their records several times between 1766 and 1771, as well as in their journal, *Museum Rusticum et Commerciale*.

did so the following summer, 1766. Darwin, who had been labouring under the impression that his visitor was a coach-maker, was delighted by the polished and amusing young gentleman who appeared—so much so that he wrote off at once to his friends in Birmingham, the industrialists Matthew Boulton and Dr. William Small, urging them to come to Lichfield to meet 'the greatest conjuror I ever saw'.[1]

In reality his introduction via Darwin to Midlands industrialists marked the end of Edgeworth's days as a private gentleman-amateur and a dabbler in conjuring tricks. His *Memoirs* are so personal and anecdotal that they do not give a proper sense of the intellectual importance to him of his new friends. Darwin himself, the first, remained one of the most intimate. Like Edgeworth he was of the gentry, and had been at Cambridge before going on to Edinburgh to complete his training as a doctor. Again like Edgeworth, he was humorous, and loved company, although in physical bulk and odd personal mannerisms Darwin was built on a more Johnsonian scale. He was a good doctor by the standards of his profession in the period. Many of his remedies were, needless to say, incorrect; but he believed in making notes, in comparing his observations with those of other doctors, and in ceaseless experiment.

Whether in England or Ireland Edgeworth always continued to consult Darwin as a doctor, although occasionally the advice that came back gave more amusement than enlightenment. Darwin had an obsessive belief that liquor was the cause of a great range of diseases, and he was well aware of the reputation of the Irishmen as drinkers. When Edgeworth consulted him about a stomach disorder in 1786, therefore, the doctor eloquently warned him of the consequences of his supposed addiction to the bottle, ending his letter, Maria says, 'God keep you from whiskey—if he can'.[2] The recollection of Darwin as a lovable and entertaining companion remained for many years in the Edgeworth family.

> Maria had been a good deal in his company with her father at different times, and thought him not only a first-rate genius, but one of the most benevolent, as well as wittiest of men. He stuttered, but far from this lessening the charm of his conversation, Maria

[1] Quoted by Robert E. Schofield, *The Lunar Society of Birmingham*, 1963, p. 45.

[2] *Memoirs of RLE*, ii. 83.

used to say that the slowness with which his words came forth, added to the effect of his humour and shrewd good sense.[1]

The Lunar group into which Darwin introduced Edgeworth was in time to have a nucleus of fourteen, but in 1766 the practice of holding regular meetings was only recently established, and the circle consisted probably of less than half a dozen members.[2] In addition to Darwin they included Small, Boulton, and the potter Josiah Wedgwood, who lived at some distance from the rest at Etruria in Staffordshire. Within a short time the engineer James Watt and the industrial chemist James Keir, both Scotsmen, had been introduced to the circle and had come to settle in Birmingham. Although the geographical area from which Lunar membership was drawn was limited to the Midlands, there was nothing parochial about the group—they had close ties with the leading intellectual figures of Glasgow and Edinburgh, they kept abreast of experimental work on the Continent, and they were in continuous contact by letter with Benjamin Franklin in Philadelphia.

From 1765 they had made it a practice to meet as regularly as they could at Matthew Boulton's house near Birmingham, in order to exchange information and test new ideas. Because moonlight made the journey easier for those travelling from a distance, they chose the Monday nearest the full moon, and it was this that gave the society its picturesque name. Edgeworth attended meetings when he could between 1766 and 1771, with long gaps for the periods when he was in London or Ireland. But although this era of his life shows Lunar influence at its greatest, he never moved out of its orbit. The effectiveness of the group as a centre for ideas did not depend on the meetings alone, but also upon frequent and detailed letters, and Edgeworth continued to write to Darwin, Wedgwood, Keir, and Watt all their lives. Even when he had settled permanently in Ireland the group retained its hold on

[1] *Mem.*, i. 99. This is, however, an example of the *Memoir*'s relative inaccuracy in dealing with ME's early years (see Introduction, above, p. 5). The impression of Darwin reported here is based on ME's meeting with him in July 1799. She had probably not seen him since about 1780, when she was twelve, and she was never 'a good deal in his company with her father'.

[2] For details of the membership and intellectual pursuits of the circle at different times see Schofield, *The Lunar Society of Birmingham*. This study contains the fullest account of RLE as a practical scientist.

him, for when he was intellectually isolated in a remote countryside it provided him with a stimulus and an audience.

Although only about half the members were practising industrialists, the factor binding the group together was their interest in bringing scientific investigation to bear on industrial problems. They were in their informal way a pioneer industrial research establishment, and the businessmen among them owed at least part of their success to the existence of the group as a whole. This, at least, is likely to be the verdict of the historian of science; it is less familiar to the literary public, who have always been far readier to take Watt and Wedgwood seriously than Edgeworth and Erasmus Darwin.

Darwin has long been no more than a celebrated crank of literary mythology, although the remarkable intellectual achievement of the conception of heredity set out in *The Botanic Garden* entitles him to a better fate.[1] Edgeworth has achieved the same kind of notoriety as 'the man who almost invented the telegraph, and did, in fact, invent machines for cutting turnips, climbing walls, contracting on narrow bridges and lifting their wheels over obstacles'.[2] The air of superiority with which his inventions are listed is not a twentieth-century phenomenon; literary London has never been technologically minded, and in their day Samuel Rogers, John Wilson Croker, and Thomas Moore found it equally impossible to take the mechanical Mr. Edgeworth seriously.[3] Professor Donald Davie summarized a long tradition when he remarked that 'it is hard to be fair to a man like Edgeworth. A crank, one might argue, is only a genius who doesn't come off.'[4] A man who invents machines may, however, be neither a genius nor a crank; and if the feasibility of his projects, and their relevance to the needs of the time, are fair enough tests, Edgeworth can be shown to have brought a rational mind to bear on that major preoccupa-

[1] Ernst Krause, author of what is still in many respects the authoritative book on Darwin, describes him as the first man 'who proposed and consistently carried out, a well-rounded theory with regard to the development of the living world'. *Erasmus Darwin. With a Preliminary Notice by Charles Darwin*, 1879, p. 211. Desmond King-Hele also gives an account of his importance in his popularly written but generally authenticated *Erasmus Darwin*, 1963, *passim*.

[2] Virginia Woolf, 'Lives of the Obscure', *The Common Reader*, 1st ser., 1925, pp. 151–2.

[3] See below, pp. 230–1.

[4] *The Heyday of Sir Walter Scott*, 1961, p. 67.

tion of eighteenth-century industrialists—vehicles, roads, canals, and alternative means of transportation.

The machine which could climb walls, for example, a subject of urbane amusement ever since he described it in his *Memoirs*, was a continuous-track vehicle on the same principle as the modern caterpillar tractor. Of all his designs, this was the one which Edgeworth considered had most practical potential, and he persevered with it, building over a hundred working models in the course of the next thirty years. More regular carriages also absorbed him intermittently to the end of his life, and on minor points of design, such as springing, he was successful. Like all the group he was fascinated by the potentialities of railways and exercised about the best means of powering the engine. In 1768 he made a model of 'a waggon drawn by fire, and a walking table which will carry 40 men',[1] and demonstrated it to a committee of the Society of Arts early in 1769. Samuel Smiles says that he tried to persuade Watt to design a steam locomotive,[2] and in their correspondence the two continued to debate the subject for many years; on 7 August 1813, for example, Edgeworth was still maintaining that 'an iron rail-road would be a cheaper thing than a road on the common construction'. This was the year of his *Essay on the Construction of Roads and Carriages*, which, as has often been pointed out, describes a method of road-making closer to modern practice than his contemporary McAdam's. Robert E. Schofield's observation about the *Essay* could be applied to most of Edgeworth's achievements in mechanics. 'The work contains little in the way of theory or calculation; it was as a book of sensible, pragmatic recommendations for planning, building and repairing roads, of workable ideas in carriage and wagon design that it became popular.'[3]

Meanwhile Anna Maria gave birth in May 1766 to a second son, 'Lovel', an ailing baby whose burial is recorded at Black Bourton on 26 May 1766. The following year she was pregnant again, and once more she retreated to her parents' home to

[1] Erasmus Darwin to Josiah Wedgwood, 14 June 1768, quoted by Eliza Meteyard, *Life of Josiah Wedgwood*, 1865, ii. 43. Cf. Minutes of Society of Arts for 1768–9.

[2] *Lives of Boulton and Watt*, 1865, p. 336.

[3] *Lunar Society of Birmingham*, p. 410.

have the child. It was at Black Bourton, in the fast disintegrating former home of the Hungerfords, that Maria Edgeworth came into the world on 1 January 1768.[1]

The mechanical experiments in which her father was happily absorbed at the period when Maria Edgeworth was born were ultimately to enrich her life and help to extend her education far beyond what was common for a woman, although she never regarded herself as an accomplished scientist. The circle into which her father had won an entry had even more influence on her adult attitudes and tastes. But the immediate effect of Edgeworth's intellectual occupations in her infancy was a negative one, for it widened the sense of estrangement between her parents and often took her father away from home. Afterwards Edgeworth was anxious to establish that he really had not neglected Anna Maria. It may well be true, as he insisted, that he 'lived more at home than is usual with most men of my age. . . . Except paying one visit to Sir Francis Delaval, three or four short visits to Birmingham and Lichfield, a visit to my father in Ireland, and the days necessary for keeping terms at the Temple, I never dined or slept from home ten times during five or six years.'[2] This way of putting it obscures the fact that the visit to Ireland lasted from the spring to the autumn of 1768; moreover Edgeworth went away accompanied by Thomas Day, for whom Anna Maria had conceived an intense dislike. The following year, when he was keeping the necessary terms at the Temple, he did so by sharing lodgings in London with Day and Day's friend John Bicknell. At other times Edgeworth invited Day to the house at Hare Hatch so continually that he was almost an inmate, and when the two were not arguing for hours about metaphysics or education, Edgeworth was likely to be absorbed in mechanics or chemistry[3]—with the result that Anna Maria felt neglected, and said so. Edgeworth found his wife's capacity for complaint one of the most tiresome things about her. 'She lamented about

[1] ME's date of birth is usually given as 1 Jan. 1767, but she seems to have considered 1768 correct, and the Black Bourton records on the whole support her. For a re-examination of the evidence see Christina Colvin and Marilyn Butler, 'A Revised Date of Birth for Maria Edgeworth', *N. & Q.*, September 1971.

[2] *Memoirs of RLE*, i. 184.

[3] RLE also invited the chemist James Keir to stay for several months at his house in 1769, thus inaugurating a friendship between the two families which survived into a second generation. See below, p. 442.

trifles; and the lamenting of a female, with whom we live, does not render home delightful.'[1]

It was in this domestic atmosphere that Maria Edgeworth spent her first years. Afterwards she could recall little of her mother—a soft red dress, beautiful blue eyes, a white skin—'but she did recollect that she was always crying'.[2] The two of them paid long visits to Black Bourton; Anna Maria perhaps preferred the home of her easy brothers and sisters to a Hare Hatch frequented by Thomas Day. Maria later remembered the indulgent way in which she was treated by the family at Black Bourton. 'Here the vivacity of her early wit was encouraged, and the sallies of her temper were unrepressed by her soft-hearted mother and tender aunts.'[3] The favourite companion of her childhood seems to have been her brother Richard, who was four years older, although after another interval of two years a sister, Emmeline, was born.

Edgeworth was not likely to forget the Elers's bad record in educating young children, and Maria's first lessons were obviously not neglected as her aunts' and uncles' had been. She seems for example to have known how to read by the time she was five. But Edgeworth himself had no hand in teaching her, which means that her early experience was very different from that of her younger brothers and sisters, and from the ideal environment for bringing up children which she and her father afterwards described in their books. A decade later Edgeworth began to formulate his ideas about the importance of the family, with the father at home supervising the education of his children. Nothing of this sort was in his mind when Maria herself was passing through the important first five years of life; although her brother Richard saw more of their father than she did.

From 1767, when his son was three, Richard Lovell conducted the experiment of bringing him up according to the ideas put forth by Rousseau in *Émile*. During the next five years the boy was not wearied with the dreary learning by rote which other children were subjected to, but instead was encouraged to observe, ask questions, and learn about the

[1] *Memoirs of RLE*, i. 184.

[2] From cancelled manuscript draft of *Memoir* in Lucy Edgeworth's hand.

[3] *Mem.*, i. 1.

things around him. So far the experiment seems to have been essentially successful, for, in addition to picking up a precocious knowledge of mechanics, young Richard seemed admirably quick-witted, and very self-reliant. In fact he was too self-reliant; there was nothing in the art of child-management in the period that could show his teachers, or, in the end, his father, how to cope with such wilfulness as Richard showed. The outcome of the experiment with Richard belongs to the future; but during its earlier more successful phase Maria was incidentally affected, since in order to maintain the system Richard Lovell had to take the boy with him whenever he went away for any length of time. It cannot have mattered to the baby that she was alone with her mother for six months in 1768 while her brother was in Ireland, but she also had to do without him for over a year in 1772–3, when she must have missed him more.

It was while the Midlands and London were taking more of his attention than Hare Hatch that, in 1770, Edgeworth's circumstances totally changed. At the end of 1769 he had been summoned back to Ireland because his father was ill. At first there seemed to be no danger—a slight cut in one of the old man's toes had merely become infected. But the surgeons treating him in Dublin proved helpless to prevent the infection from spreading, and after lingering painfully for many months Richard Edgeworth died on 6 August 1770, at the age of sixty-nine.

Inheriting the estate made such a difference to Richard Lovell's income that he could now choose the way of life that best suited him. Although he had just (in 1769) completed the necessary terms to qualify as a barrister, it was part of Richard Lovell's general disagreement with his father that he had never liked the thought of the law as a profession. He at once decided not to be called to the Bar. He could have settled at Edgeworthstown, as his father would certainly have wanted, but his first experience as a landlord was not encouraging. At twenty-six Richard Lovell was easy-tempered; he also wanted to make a good first impression on his tenants. He soon discovered that he really could not grant every favour that was asked of him, and, more woundingly, that some of the hard-luck stories he had listened to were pure fabrication. He made sterner resolutions for the future, but for the time being at least could not feel that it was his vocation to be a landlord.[1] A much-loved younger sister, twenty-two-year-old Margaret Edgeworth, who had been courted by Day on his visit to Edgeworthstown two years earlier, might have been a factor to keep him in Ireland; but shortly after the death of her father she unexpectedly married a very different man from Day, an Anglo-Irish army officer of conservative views—John Ruxton, of Black Castle, Co. Meath. For the time being, therefore, Edgeworth left his estate to the mercy of an agent, while he rejoined Anna Maria and the children at Hare Hatch.

Not, however, in order to stay with them. For several months now Edgeworth had seen nothing of his friend, who had been abroad in France pursuing a remarkable educational project of his own,[2] but Day returned before Christmas and took a house at Stow Hill, near Lichfield. Edgeworth at once went off to visit him—and thereby virtually ended, it seems, his normal home life at Hare Hatch with Anna Maria.

Through Darwin Edgeworth had long since been accepted in Lichfield literary society, which was no longer graced by Samuel Johnson or David Garrick, but nevertheless maintained a high opinion of itself. The centre of polite intellectual life in the town was the Bishop's Palace, occupied by Thomas Seward, prebendary of Lichfield and editor of Beaumont and Fletcher; the Canon's daughter Anna, who had already achieved some celebrity as a poet, was the acknowledged feminine leader of the circle. Later in life Anna became an absurd figure, both as a woman and as a writer. She was precious, sentimental, histrionic, self-important, and, as both the Edgeworth and Darwin families discovered, malicious.[3]

[1] *Memoirs of RLE*, i. 234–5. RLE's experience in taking over his estate, both now and later, is used extensively in ME's tale *Ennui*; see below, pp. 88–9.

[2] This plan was the one most often associated with Day's name, the scheme to train a foundling girl in perfect seclusion after the example of Rousseau's Sophie, in the hope that she would make an ideal wife. Day took two girls to France, but returned to Lichfield only with the one he preferred, Sabrina Sidney. As his behaviour at Lichfield indicates, he was never single-minded about marrying Sabrina; she finally offended him over a trivial matter in 1773 and was sent away to eight years of genteel retirement. In 1781 she married Day's friend John Bicknell, who died, leaving her unprovided for, in 1784. During her long widowhood she was housekeeper to Dr. Charles Burney the younger at Greenwich.

[3] Anna Seward (1747–1809) published, or attempted to publish, attacks on both families—by implication on the Edgeworths in her *Monody on the Death of*

But in these early days of Edgeworth's acquaintance with her, youth and good looks were still on her side. Indeed, on one of his earlier visits to Lichfield onlookers had noticed her inclination to flirt with a not unwilling Edgeworth.[1]

The favourable impression that Edgeworth made in society as a young man is reflected in the welcome he received at Lichfield. He was well-read, ingenious, amusing, good-humoured; or, as Anna Seward characteristically put it, he was 'the lively, the sentimental, the accomplish'd, the scientific, the gallant, the learned, the celebrated Mr. Edgeworth'.[2] Even afterwards, when she disliked him, she was obliged to recall that 'his address was gracefully spirited, and his conversation eloquent. He danced, he fenced, and winged his arrows with more than philosophic skill.'[3] Presumably the last phrase is a reference to rather more than the taste for archery which Edgeworth was to introduce to Lichfield. He enjoyed the company of women, for whom, as his *Memoirs* show, he had a strong streak of intuitive sympathy; he was not a philanderer, but his record of success with the opposite sex is as notable as Thomas Day's record of failure.[4] Because his written style is heavy it is difficult to remember how entirely different he was physically from the somewhat leaden impression he has left of himself on the page. Again and again the impression which struck people who met him was his phenomenal energy. At fifteen he had danced all night for three nights and performed acrobatics in the intervals. At

*Major André*, 1780 (for which see below, p. 48 n.), and on Darwin in her *Life of Darwin* (1804); the latter was however heavily cut before publication after strong representations from Darwin's family and friends, including RLE. Anna's uncensored views of RLE particularly can be found in those of her letters which are published in H. Wickham, *Journal and Correspondence of T. Sedgwick Whalley*, 2 vols., 1863. Her motives for turning on her former friends are too complex for analysis here; in 1769 she was emotionally much involved in the proposed engagement between Honora Sneyd and the Swiss-born John André; and perhaps she hoped to marry Darwin in the period 1777–80, when he was a widower, before his second marriage to Mrs. Pole. Her resentments were intense, particularly when she was activated by jealousy.

1 An account of their first meeting is given in *Memoirs of RLE*, i. 166–7.

2 Quoted by Schofield, *The Lunar Society of Birmingham*, p. 57.

3 Anna Seward, *Life of Darwin*, 1804, pp. 16–17.

4 With his ever-growing families of children RLE was not from a materialistic point of view a brilliant match, but all four of the women to whom he proposed accepted him; the wealthy bachelor Day suffered as many refusals.

eighteen he danced so well that a professional who saw him remembered him afterwards as 'the best dancer in England'.[1] It seemed appropriate that among his inventions were vehicles designed to move him at superhuman speed—a one-wheeled phaeton in which he whirled rapidly across foot-bridges, a sailing-carriage in which he was swept along by the wind, a gigantic wheel which a single man could propel much faster than any man could run. Edgeworth retained this remarkable physical vitality into old age. When people remembered him they usually depicted him doing something. Often what they recalled was his ceaseless flow of talk (which his enemies were to characterize as 'rattling'), but sometimes it was movement of a more startling order:

> My father's activity began to be discussed & Capt. B[eaufort] said he saw him & he must have been 55 at least—as they [were] standing before the Dining room fire my father made 2 steps forward & holding himself perfectly erect sprang right across the large oval table clear over all the bottles & glasses & lighted aplomb as light as a feather on the other side!—he once cutting a caper & clapping the soles of his feet together cracked a walnut between them!—it having been stuck on to his shoe with wax.[2]

The charm of his vitality had already won the hearts of such diverse personalities as Day, Delaval, and the Lunar industrialists, and needless to say now that he had settled down for some time near Lichfield it ensured that he was welcome daily at the Bishop's Palace. It was there, in the early months of 1771, that Edgeworth became involved with Honora Sneyd, and she with him.

Honora was the nineteen-year-old daughter of Major Edward Sneyd, who came originally from Staffordshire, but now had an appointment at Court as a Gentleman Usher. Since the death of his wife in 1757, Sneyd's eight children had been looked after by different relatives or family friends. Honora, the second surviving daughter, was brought up in Canon Seward's house as a foster-sister to Anna. Honora had a reputation both for beauty and intelligence, and there was a quality about her that caused her to be almost venerated by enthusiasts—such, for example, as both Anna and Richard

[1] *Memoirs of RLE*, ii. 149–50.

[2] Harriet Butler to Michael Pakenham Edgeworth, 13 Sept. 1838.

Lovell. The latter now felt that the regard for excellence which his mother had given him could be applied for the first time to a woman. 'Her person was graceful, her features beautiful, and their expression such as to heighten the eloquence of everything she said. I was six and twenty; and now, for the first time in my life, I saw a woman that equalled the picture of perfection, which existed in my imagination.'[1]

But he was not free to marry; and, rashly, he conceived it his duty to stay in Lichfield during 1771, attempting to master his passion, while Thomas Day paid laborious court to Honora on his own behalf. Edgeworth attempted to persuade Anna Maria to set up house with him in the vicinity, but after a limited visit she declined to stay. To the surprise of both Edgeworth and Day, Honora replied decisively in the negative to the letter Day sent proposing marriage, countering, indeed, his rather untimely observations on the duties of woman with a few ideas of her own about their rights. Day was shocked rather than heart-broken, however, and within a few weeks he had fallen in love again—this time with a newcomer to Lichfield, Honora's sister Elizabeth.

Edgeworth's own preference for Honora was far too deep-seated to shake. He might concede that Elizabeth had a healthier appearance than her sister, more fashion, wit, vivacity, 'and certainly more humour. . . . She had, however, less personal grace; she walked heavily, danced indifferently, had much less energy of character, and was not endowed with, or had not then acquired, the same powers of reasoning, the same inquiring range of understanding, the same love of science, or, in one word, the same decisive judgment as her sister.'[2]

While he thought of Honora as Day's future wife, Edgeworth had been able to keep his feelings under control, but now that no rivalry to a friend was implied his passion for her returned in all its intensity. It was essential for him to get away; he let it be known that he was going to France, and that after his return he would settle not in England but in Ireland. This was probably a real decision, for he gave up the house at Hare Hatch and took Anna Maria and the younger children to

[1] *Memoirs of RLE*, i. 240–1. Cf. H. Wickham, *Journal and Correspondence of T. Sedgwick Whalley*, i. 343, for Anna Seward's extravagant praise of Honora.

[2] *Memoirs of RLE*, i. 252–3.

Black Bourton for the six months or year he proposed to be away. Shortly afterwards, one autumn day in 1771, Edgeworth, Day[1], and young Richard crossed the Channel to France.

Their destination was Lyons, where Edgeworth took lodgings for the winter with M. Charpentier, head of the city's Military Academy.[2] By December he was receiving letters from his wife in (to judge from his replies) her habitual tone of complaint:

> Since I began this Letter I have received your Last—And am sorry to find that you are displeased with me—You tell me I defer'd letting you know that I determined to stay at Lyons—I assure you upon my honour I wrote either to you or Charlotte the very day I determined to stay here, and I believe the very hour after I had taken Lodgings—so that I am certain I had not given you any real reason upon that account to be uneasy.

The letter as a whole is framed in the same soothing, conciliatory terms. 'You need not be afraid of his [young Richard's] forgetting you: He has too good a heart to forget you.'[3]

Before the end of the winter he had found an occupation that was particularly to his taste. Lyons was built on a confined site, which a group of businessmen had subscribed to enlarge by having the Rhone diverted into a new channel. Every day Edgeworth went to observe the methods used to build the new embankment, some of which seemed to him unnecessarily cumbrous. He suggested that they should use what he described as a moving platform—a kind of conveyor-belt—to tip a full load into the boat; another platform on the boat could then tip the sand and gravel into the gap.[4] Edgeworth was encouraged

[1] Day by now had a motive of his own for travelling; he had proposed to Elizabeth Sneyd, who had replied that she would not consider marrying him until he acquired more polish. His painful efforts to learn French deportment were not to be crowned with success, for when he returned Elizabeth 'confessed that Thomas Day, *blackguard*, as he used jestingly to style himself, *less* displeased her eye than Thomas Day, fine gentleman'. Anna Seward, *Life of Darwin*, 1804, p. 44.

[2] The father of Charlotte Charpentier or Carpenter, one day to be wife of Walter Scott: at the time of RLE's arrival in the house Charlotte was a baby of one year old. Before the *Memoirs* were written, as the Edgeworths were well aware, rumours circulated about the unhappiness of the Charpentiers' marriage and Charlotte's possible illegitimacy. RLE, no scandal-monger, went out of his way (*Memoirs*, i. 263) to suggest that at the very relevant time he knew the couple no such stories were current.

[3] RLE to Mrs. Anna Maria Edgeworth, à l'Académie, Lyons, 8 Dec. [1771].

[4] RLE's sketch is reproduced in Desmond Clarke's *The Ingenious Mr. Edgeworth*, 1965, facing p. 96.

to build his conveyor-belt, and afterwards pressed to do more. He was in his element. Richard's education was neglected—Edgeworth decided, abruptly, to hand over responsibility for it to a Catholic seminary in the town. There was no longer any immediate prospect of going home, or settling at Edgeworthstown. In the spring of 1772 he sent for Anna Maria, who came with one of her sisters to spend the summer with him at Lyons.

Maria and Emmeline stayed behind. Most of the time they were probably at Black Bourton, but for a while they were with Anna Maria's aunts in Great Russell Street. The Misses Blake were elderly, and they lived in some style, so that the two children must have passed a lot of their time with servants.[1] Maria afterwards said nothing of her feelings at this period, or of how she felt when at the age of four she was deprived not only of her father (whom she was accustomed to doing without) but also of the mother who had always looked after her. It seems from what followed, however, that the months without Anna Maria affected her a great deal. She now entered one of the few really unhappy periods of her life.

Anna Maria came back again to Bourton Place in the autumn of 1772. Her husband had been very preoccupied while she had been with him; so much so that after her return she supposed he was probably too busy to read her letters.[2] There had been few compensations in Lyons for her and she soon became 'weary of French society'.[3] To add to her misery, she found herself pregnant again soon after arriving in France, and she had a horror of staying in a foreign country to have the child. At the time she left, escorted by Mr. Day (who, after a year learning French gallantry, was coming home to propose to Elizabeth Sneyd), Anna Maria had some hope that Richard Lovell would follow her before the end of the year—for the engineering project at Lyons had to be suspended in the depths of winter. Instead, Edgeworth became engrossed in the design of the flour mills that were to be built on the reclaimed land. When he wrote, it was to postpone his return for some months.

[1] The Edgeworths later became very critical of the practice of leaving children with servants. See *Practical Education*, ch. iv, and the opening chapters of *Harrington*.

[2] RLE to Anna Maria Edgeworth, 12 Jan. [1773].

[3] *Memoirs of RLE*, i. 272.

He had also to break it to her that his affairs in Ireland were faring so badly that he would have to go there in the spring. He was aware Anna Maria felt that her own preferences were seldom considered and so he framed her a letter that was probably as positively kind as he could make it:

> Last summer I chose our place of Residence Chuse you this summer and let it be where you will I give you my honor to reside there without hesitation—Your last letter was written with too much *Duty*—I don't know where you learn'd the Idea of the word Duty I know you did not learn it from me—a mutual regard founded upon a Similarity of Sentiment a desire to please but above all a desire to *be* pleased is worth all the duty in the world—Will you agree to be unmarried again?—I mean as to the contract made between ourselves—and shall we make a new one?—If you will give it under your hand I will *seriously*—You become more agreable to me every day—and I hope the reason is that you become more deserving—Your character really and truly is mended and is I think a very desirable one—let the *past* be *past*—And I will return to England with a real desire to be *pleased* and to please.[1]

He was proposing that they should bury the memory of their marital misdemeanours—her fruitless complaints and inability to share in his interests, his mental infidelity, whether with mechanics, with Day, or with Honora. The letter was ironically timed, since it was probably the last Anna Maria received from him. In March 1773, ten days after she had given birth to her third daughter (Anna), Anna Maria died, probably of puerperal fever.

She had taken her two little daughters to the house at Great Russell Street for the baby's birth, and Maria afterwards had several recollections of episodes there about the time of her mother's death. She remembered being led to the bed for a last kiss; and, probably about the same time, being taken out by the three stately old ladies, dressed in black, to play in the gardens at the back of the British Museum.[2]

Afterwards Maria did not discuss her feelings about her mother, or reveal directly how she felt about her death, but she was a very disturbed child at this time. A whole number of incidents are recorded which were put down to 'naughtiness',

[1] RLE to Mrs. Anna Maria Edgeworth, 12 Jan. [1773].

[2] *Mem.*, i. 1–2.

and punished accordingly. Towards the end of that March, either at Great Russell Street or at the home in London of Anna Maria's brother, Captain Elers, Maria caused outrage by throwing tea in someone's face. She was

> accordingly imprisoned by her Aunts between two doors . . . . Suddenly she heard a voice which she says she has a distinct recollection of thinking quite different and superior to any she had heard before—and the doors being opened she saw a gentleman in black and her imagination was instantly struck with the idea of his being sublimely superior to all she ever saw before.[1]

It was Richard Lovell Edgeworth, who had come back from Lyons on learning of the death of his wife. Whatever comfort there may have been for Maria in this reunion, it was of short duration, for Edgeworth had someone else to think of besides the children. When he reached London he found a letter waiting for him from Day with news of Honora. The two friends immediately arranged to meet at Woodstock, where Day confirmed what Edgeworth most wanted to hear—she was well, and unattached. He hurried on to Lichfield in order to propose without more loss of time. Honora accepted him at once, and neither her father nor Canon Seward insisted on the conventional interval of six months or a year after Anna Maria's death. Within four months of being left a widower, on 17 July 1773, Richard Lovell remarried.

The financial troubles of the estate demanded his presence at home, and the high-minded Honora had no objection to beginning her married life in the depths of the Irish countryside. The journey to Edgeworthstown with Anna Maria's four children was not without incident, for in Dublin Maria committed another of her outrages. After landing from the packet they went to their hotel. The child was surrounded by strangers; four months earlier she had not known her father by sight, and she may never have met Honora until the time of the marriage. She was intensely miserable:

> Yesterday Maria was talking of her childhood and saying how unhappy she was[.] She remembered in Dublin getting out of a garret window on the window stool when she was about 6 yr old and some passenger running in and telling the maid of the child's

[1] Harriet Butler to Michael Pakenham Edgeworth, 3 Jan. 1838.

danger and when the maid said as she took her in 'Do you know you might have fallen down and broken your neck and been killed' and Maria answered 'I wish I had—I'm very unhappy'—so piteous the idea of so little a child being so very wretched.[1]

Yet another incident occurred after their arrival at Edgeworthstown. Maria wilfully trampled 'through a number of hotbed frames that had just been glazed, laid on the grass before the door at Edgeworthstown; she recollected her delight at the crashing of the glass, but immorally, did not remember either cutting her feet or how she was punished for this performance'.[2] She certainly would have been punished, for both Honora and Edgeworth put her behaviour down to the fact that she was spoilt. The amiable, lax Elers sisters had not been in the habit of administering reproof; and obviously there would have been no consistency in the discipline Maria received from the servants she had been left with at other times. Honora believed that speedy and consistent punishment was very important in bringing up a young child.

It is my opinion that almost everything that education can give, is to be given before the age of 5 or 6—therefore I think great attention & strictness should be shewn before that age; particularly, if there is anything refractory or rebellious in the disposition, that is the time to repress it, & to substitute good habits, obedience, attention, & respect towards superiors.[3]

The severity with which Maria was handled was sufficiently marked to attract the attention of outsiders. Edgeworth's eldest sister Mary, Mrs. Francis Fox, was one of those who took Maria's part:

She was punished one day for being naughty and my aunt Fox coming pitied her and my father said 'since you pity her so much take her to yourself' which she did and in the carriage said to her 'Now my dear I shall never chastise you unless you deserve it' and Maria mused all the way to Foxhall on what chastise could mean.[1]

Unfortunately it was not long before 'Aunt Fox' herself became a target for Maria's aggression. Her aunt had a checked sofa cover, and one day Maria amused herself by

[1] Harriet Butler to Michael Pakenham Edgeworth, 3 Jan. 1838.

[2] *Mem.*, i. 2.

[3] Mrs. Honora Edgeworth to Mrs. R, Edgeworthstown, n.d. [? 1776].

cutting out the squares. This was bad enough, but a display of bad manners in public was worse:

There was company one evening and tea and cakes of which Maria eat so much that being desired to buckle her shoe she could by no means stoop to reach her foot and looking for help she saw a Miss Nugent who having been playing on the fiddle her natural instinct taught her must be an underling—and called to her to do it for her—My aunt Fox was so enraged at this insolence that she never forgave it.[1]

From the Elers women she had not learnt the *savoir-faire* that even a five-year-old would have acquired among the Sneyds and Edgeworths. Her rudeness to Miss Nugent might not have been insolence so much as an ignorant child's mistake, but it gave profound offence to her well-bred relatives. As for her fully intentioned acts of mischief, these were regarded by the family (as they would have been by almost any parent at the time) simply as wrongdoing. No one apparently linked them with the distress she felt at the death of her mother and the coming of a strange stepmother. The idea that she wanted to attract attention because for some time she had been deprived of it could not have occurred in these terms even to intelligent bystanders.

On the other hand hostility between a child of a previous marriage and a new stepmother *was* a recognized phenomenon, with the stepmother traditionally playing the villain's part. Some of Honora's relatives had apparently tried to dissuade her from marrying Edgeworth, on the grounds that it was notoriously difficult to handle someone else's children.[2] And at first Edgeworth's family and friends did suspect that Honora was harsher to some of Edgeworth's children than she should have been. After Honora's death Edgeworth referred back to the difficult first years between 1773 and 1775:

Though her timely restraint of you, and that steadiness of behaviour, yielding fondness towards you only by the exact measure

[1] Harriet Butler to Michael Pakenham Edgeworth, 3 Jan. 1838.

[2] Draft obituary of Honora by RLE for the *Gentleman's Magazine*, in the form of a letter to 'Mr. Urban'. This notice was composed mainly to correct the facts given by Anna Seward in her *Monody on the Death of Major André*. (In 1780 Honora's former fiancé was captured by the Americans while dealing with Benedict Arnold, and hanged as a spy.) Anna's account of André's relations with Honora was typically mischievous, but RLE's denial seems never to have been published.

of your conduct, at first alarmed those who did not know her, yet now, my dearest daughter, every person who has the least connection with my family is anxious to give sincere testimony of their admiration of those very circumstances which they had too hastily, and from a common and well-grounded opinion, associated with the idea of a second wife.[1]

What Edgeworth claimed in this letter was apparently true. The sympathy that Maria got (from Aunt Fox, for example) quickly evaporated. Maria was indiscriminately exasperating, while once Honora's character was known it became inconceivable that she could be guilty of spitefulness to a child. Her severity was highly principled, as even Maria recognized:

She felt great awe of her at the time, but she was long afterwards sensible of her justice, and of the habits of exactness and order in which she trained her. The surpassing beauty of her presence struck Maria, young as she was, at her first acquaintance with her: she remembered standing by her dressing table and looking up at her with a sudden feeling of 'How beautiful!'[2]

Anyone familiar with Maria's scale of personal values recognizes the hidden reservations in this paragraph. When she grew up Maria placed great value on warmth, expressiveness, what she half-defensively came to describe as 'petting'; and, especially, she disapproved of a mother who exacted awe from her children.[3] As a child she could not generalize her reaction in this way, but she does seem to have felt frightened of her stepmother. In 1773 Honora had not yet had children of her own, and her ideas about handling Edgeworth's were, to put it mildly, theoretical. She set a high standard of conduct for herself, and she expected the children to try to live up to her example. If they succeeded in improving themselves (a term frequently on her lips) she meant to reward them with her friendship. Two of her letters to Maria contain obviously sincere offers of friendship—but both are conditional, because Honora did not conceive of a child as a friend, especially so ill-behaved a child as Maria. It was enough therefore to utter, in a postscript to one of Edgeworth's letters,

my most earnest wishes that you may become everything he

[1] RLE to ME, 2 May 1780; *Mem.*, i. 7.

[2] *Mem.*, i. 3.

[3] In Lady Davenant in *Helen*, for example, she depicts a mother who is over-severe. See below, p. 476.

approves, & then, I am sure your character will be such, as (were you a stranger to me) would make me wish you for the Friend of your affectionate Mother.[1]

The strictness which now characterized the Edgeworth household originated with Honora, but Edgeworth, chastened by his failure with Richard, was perfectly ready to support her. The trouble in both Maria's case and Richard's was that the right moment had already been lost. It is probably no accident that Honora declared a child had to be disciplined before the age of 'five or six'—Maria's age when she first met her. The disciplinary problems that Maria and Richard created between 1773 and 1775 seemed fully to justify the generalization. A fair idea of what went on is given in some manuscript notes which Edgeworth made in 1778 after reading one of Mrs. Barbauld's first books on education.[2] At one point he puts forward his belief that children from the age of three should be made to dress themselves and make their beds, an uncommon task for a young child in this period of servants and elaborate clothes. He says he knows two children of between four and five who do both successfully, and here he must be referring to his two youngest daughters Anna (Anna Maria's last child) and Honora, who was born just over a year later. He explains how successful what we know was his wife's system had been in this case. The children had been told they would get no breakfast if they failed, and neither had failed as many as five times.

Since Anna was one of the children who gave least trouble, it is worth noting what she thought of the methods used on her. When she revisited Edgeworthstown thirty-three years later, after an interval of seventeen years, she saw with surprise that her father had become much milder, 'so that he appears in a much more amiable light', and that his children now had as much liberty as anybody else's.[3] It may also have been Anna who in the early years of her married independence revealed that Edgeworth's older children were not brought up in the cheerful progressive atmosphere described in *Practical Education*.

[1] Mrs. H. Edgeworth, PS. to letter of RLE to ME, Great Berkhamstead, 1778. Cf. Mrs. H. Edgeworth to ME, 10 Oct. 1779.

[2] See below, p. 61.

[3] Mrs. Anna Beddoes to Leonard Horner, Edgeworthstown, 3 Aug. 1811 (Bodleian Library, Oxford, MS. Eng. lett. d. 222, f. 55).

Coleridge was pleased with the story when it reached him. 'J. Wedgwood [the younger] informed me that the Edgeworth's were most miserable when children; and yet the father in his book is ever vapourizing about their happiness.'[1]

If Anna was miserable, she had less cause than Richard and Maria between 1773 and 1775. Edgeworth was pleased to be able to point to little Anna's favourable response to discipline, in contrast with his older children's habit of resisting it:

> No motive, no force, no art can govern a child that has been threatened frequently and that has frequently escaped the evil with the apprehension of which it has been kept in suspense. Nothing but repeated instances of the fact could have convinced me of the amazing incredulity of children, who have been ill educated. I at first attributed many parts of their conduct to stupidity, and afterwards to Obstinacy, which, as I at length discovered, arose merely from want of belief in the threats that were denounced against them or the promises with which they were encouraged. . . . If for instance a child were repeatedly told that he should be whip'd for a particular fault and if the threat were never put in execution for three or four of his first years another person might threaten and execute his threats in vain for many months before he could convince a child that whipping was a certain consequence of his fault.[2]

Richard probably was whipped, for Lyons had seen the final breakdown of the attempt to educate him according to Rousseau's system. While Edgeworth was busy with his engineering schemes, his son was able to defy first an English tutor brought out to teach him, later the French priests at the seminary to which he was sent. The combined efforts of his father and Honora at Edgeworthstown fared no better. From 1776 to the end of 1778, Richard was sent off to school at Charterhouse, and in 1779 he went away to sea, never returning to his father's household during Honora's lifetime.

Maria was sent away even earlier. In 1775, after only two years, Edgeworth decided that she should go to Mrs. Latuffiere's school at Derby. And the decision was evidently one which was forced on Edgeworth, because the combined school fees of

1 S. T. Coleridge to his wife, 19 Sept. 1798; *Letters*, ed. E. H. Coleridge, 1895, i. 261.

2 Notebook in RLE's hand on Mrs. Barbauld's *Lessons for Children*, pp. 56–8, dated in pencil 1777, probably 1778.

Richard and Maria—£100 a year—added up to considerably more than he could afford at the time.

Mrs. Latuffiere's pupils were the daughters of north Midlands landed gentry and of industrialists like the Edgeworths' friends in later years, the Strutts of Derby. The school was pleasant, well run, and by what were to become the Edgeworths' standards, no more than conventional. The subjects taught were not as a whole academic, for example, although Edgeworth afterwards believed that girls should have the same syllabus as boys. From Mrs. Latuffiere Maria learnt the routine accomplishments of the better-taught upper-class women of the period, such as French, Italian, dancing, embroidery, and handwriting. The last was taught particularly well: when the seven-year-old Maria arrived at the school in the autumn of 1775 she could barely write, but by March she was able to compose her first letter home, in an elegant copperplate painstakingly formed between two pencilled lines:

> Dear Mamma, It is with the greatest pleasure I write to you, as I flatter myself it will make you happy to hear from me. I hope you & my Dear Papa are well: school now seems agreeable to me: I have begun French and Dancing: I intend to make great [*crossed out*] improvement in everything I learn: as I know it will give you great satisfaction to hear that I am a good Girl: my cousin Clay sends her Love to you; mine to my Brothers and Sisters, who I hope are well: Pray give my Duty to Papa, and accept the same from Dear Mamma
>
> Your dutiful Daughter
>
> Mary Edgeworth.[1]

She had not felt at home when she first arrived, it seems, but she had settled down during the winter. Mrs. Latuffiere took satisfaction in adding on the same sheet that the 'Dear Child' had been 'good and attentive lately', and promised that if, as she supposed, Mr. and Mrs. Edgeworth could not come to fetch Maria away for the summer holidays, a Miss Scott would be delighted to look after her until the autumn term began. In fact, Mrs. Latuffiere did not have much cause

[1] Letter dated 30 Mar. 1776, the only one signed by ME in this way; her name appears on a copy of the Black Bourton baptismal register for 31 Oct. 1768 in the same form. 'Cousin Clay', whom I have not been able to identify, is presumably a family connection of the Sneyds.

to complain of her reserved but clever pupil. In return, Maria remembered her and the other teachers afterwards 'with gratitude and affection'.[1] She had been as anxious to learn as they to teach, and they had got on excellently.

But her happiness at school depended quite as much on her relations with her fellow pupils, and here the evidence suggests that Maria felt less at her ease. A portrait of just such a schoolgirl as she must have been is given in her tale *The Bracelets*, which she wrote when she was twenty and afterwards published in *The Parent's Assistant*.[2] In this story a prize offered to the most assiduous pupil is easily won by a girl called Cecilia. Then the headmistress announces that she means to award a second prize, to the girl who is best liked by the rest of the class. The very qualities which enabled Cecilia to win the first time, egotism, competitiveness, and love of praise, now stand in her way. Cecilia, who cannot bear not to win, examines herself to see why the others do not like her. The self-analysis which occurs at this point in the story must be autobiographical:

> Her mother died when she was very young; and though her father had supplied her place in the best and kindest manner, he had insensibly infused into his daughter's mind a portion of that enterprising, independent spirit which he justly deemed essential to the character of her brother. This brother was some years older than Cecilia, but he had always been the favourite companion of her youth. What her father's precepts inculcated, his example enforced; and even Cecilia's virtues consequently became such as were more estimable in a man than desirable in a female. All small objects and small errors she had been taught to disregard as trifles; and her impatient disposition was perpetually leading her into more material faults; yet her candour in confessing these, she had been suffered to believe, was sufficient reparation and atonement.[3]

Cecilia, finding that competitive women are not liked, decides to reform herself, to become pleasing, meek, and feminine—like her admirable friend Leonora, who 'had been habituated to that restraint which, as a woman, she was to expect in life. . . . Yet, notwithstanding the gentleness of her temper, she was in reality more independent than Cecilia.

[1] *Mem.*, i. 2. [2] See below, p. 155.
[3] *The Bracelets, Parent's Assistant,* 1796, pt. 2, vol. i, 57–8.

She had more reliance in her own judgment, and more satisfaction in her own approbation.'[1]

With Leonora the Edgeworthian heroine is born, well-educated but gentle, modest, domestic; and, most typically, a wife and mother, the hub of a secure and happy family. Caroline in *Letters for Literary Ladies* (1795), Lady Anne Percival in *Belinda* (1801), Ellen Elmour in *Almeria* (1802), Emma Granby in *The Modern Griselda* (1804), another Leonora in the tale of that name (1806), Selina Sidney in *Vivian* (1812), Mrs. Percy and her daughter Caroline in *Patronage* (1814), Lady Annaly and her daughter Florence in *Ormond* (1817)—there are nearly as many of them as there are tales. Conceivably real-life women contributed something to this most persistent character: Margaret Ruxton, *née* Edgeworth, for example, was one wife and mother who came to be idolized by Maria; and the schoolgirl Leonora probably owed something to Maria's own school friend, Fanny Robinson. In general, however, the Leonora figure is too unspecific to suggest a real-life original. She is rather the woman Maria wanted to be, and felt she was not—secure, strong in herself, and (emotionally most essential of all) greatly valued by the tight-knit domestic circle round her. By the time Maria was a schoolgirl, perhaps by the time she first arrived as a five-year-old at Edgeworthstown, that dominant characteristic of hers, what her father was to call her 'inordinate desire to be beloved',[2] had already been born out of her sensation that she was not loved enough.

Like Cecilia, Maria did her utmost to excel at school, and she exulted in the praise which Mrs. Latuffiere regularly sent home.[3] This was not the road to popularity with the other girls, but luckily Maria discovered that she could command one device which gave her some sort of standing at both the schools she went to.

Maria was remembered by her companions both at Mrs. Lataffiere's [*sic*] and at Mrs. Davis's [*sic*] for her entertaining stories, and she learned with all the tact of an improvisatrice to know which tale was most successful by the unmistakable evidence of her auditors wakefulness, when she narrated at night for the amusement of those

[1] *The Bracelets, Parent's Assistant*, 1796, pt. 2, vol. i, 59.

[2] See below, p. 477 n.

[3] e.g. in a letter to Charlotte Sneyd, Mrs. Honora Edgeworth's youngest sister, Derby, 19 Oct. 1780.

who were in the bedroom with her. Many of these stories were, of course, taken from the books that she read; among those of her originals she recollected only one which was specially applauded: of an adventurer who had a mask made of the dried skin taken from a dead man's face, which he put on when he wished to be disguised, and kept buried at the foot of a tree.[1]

This was a form of success, at any rate. There were also times at Mrs. Latuffiere's when she acted like any ordinary unselfconscious ten- or twelve-year-old:

. . . pray ask her [*an old schoolfellow*] if I was a grave sedate young Lady at Mrs. Lataffiere's [*sic*]; Has she forgot our leaping off the top scaffold at the hazard of our necks, of our noses at least, and our having the foolscap on for walking on the Rails of the stairs going to the Drawing Room & Miss Ford's popping out upon us and crying *So Ladies*! and a thousand other pretty pranks she'll divert you with up in the corner by the fireplace where you and I have chattered many a livelong hour.[2]

The fact remained that she did not make any significant friendships at school. It was never the emotional centre of her life; her home was that, even when she was unable to go there.

After her arrival at Mrs. Latuffiere's she apparently did not go back to Edgeworthstown, where the family remained till 1777. Then, luckily for her, Edgeworth and Honora moved with the younger children to a house at Northchurch, near Berkhampstead, Hertfordshire, and Maria was able to go home regularly for the Christmas and summer holidays. She now began to impress her father and stepmother by her good behaviour and painstaking efforts to please. There was no longer a trace of the child who had thrown tea or jumped on greenhouse frames. 'Maria is at home and behaves extremely well.'[3]

While at school she had to rely on letters to maintain the all-important link with home. Edgeworth and Honora encouraged her intense interest in the family by sending bulletins

[1] *Mem.*, i. 10. The *Memoir*'s errors in spelling the names of both ME's schoolmistresses is a reminder that neither the nominal author, Mrs. F. Edgeworth, nor the daughters who assisted her, Harriet Butler and Lucy Robinson, knew ME until many years later. See Introduction above, p. 5.

[2] ME to Fanny Robinson, 6 Dec. 1783 (copy).

[3] RLE to Mrs. R, Beighterton, 4 Jan. 1780.

of minor colds and accidents, but the tone adopted by Honora, especially, was chilly:

I hope Mr. and Mrs. Latuffiere will authorize you to inform us, that your behavior has merited their esteem, & that you have endeavor'd to improve yourself in everything which you have had an opportunity of learning—your being taught to dance may enable you to alter your common method of holding yourself if you pay attention to it, & I must say you wanted improvement in this respect very much when you were here.[1]

Edgeworth also harped on the future woman rather than the child he was actually writing to:

With a benevolent heart, complying Temper, & obliging manners, I should make no doubt, that by your mother's assistance you might become a very excellent, & an highly improved woman—Your person, my dear Maria, will be exactly in the middle point, between beauty and plainness—handsome enough to be upon a level with the generality of your Sex, if accompanied with gentleness, Reserve, & real good sense—Plain enough to become contemptible, if unattended with good qualities of the head & heart.[2]

Neither of them responded (in their letters, at least) to Maria's insecurity and anxiety to establish an intimacy with them. Maria had asked Honora 'many times' if she might write to her, but Honora merely told her judiciously: 'I am always glad to hear from you, when you have inclination to write, but I wish you never to consider it as a task.'[3] Then Maria did write, after the summer holidays of 1779, but this was an occasion when Honora had promised to write first. A repressive answer made its way to Derby: 'I assure you, my dear Maria. . . that . . . I shall not be displeased with you for omitting anything which I had before told you, I did not expect.'[4] Long afterwards Maria was to compare Honora's letters with her sister Elizabeth's, and to observe that the latter's were 'in my opinion far more agreeable'.[5]

The fault was not however all on one side. Badly though Maria wanted to communicate with home, she too wrote

1 Mrs. H. Edgeworth to ME, 5 Feb. 1778.
2 RLE to ME, Great Berkhamstead (Northchurch), n.d. [1778].
3 Mrs. H. Edgeworth, PS. to RLE's letter from Gt. Berkhamstead of 1778.
4 Mrs. H. Edgeworth, Beighterton, 10 Oct. 1779.
5 ME to ?CSE, n.d. [1817].

inexpressive letters, judging by Edgeworth's exasperated response on one occasion: 'Your last letter appeared to me more en fille d'Ecole than your former letters—Indeed it is impossible to write without having something to say: at least it ought to be impossible.'[1] He begged Maria to take him into her confidence—'I wish to have letters from you familiarly'[2]—and to foster the relationship between them he began to set her writing tasks to do for him. The first, in 1779, was a well-known Arabian fable, which he began and asked her to finish. The second, set in the following spring, was to be an original composition, a fable of her own on the subject of Generosity.

Maria wanted nothing more than to get on a footing of intimacy with her father. Once they were in a coach together, and he exerted himself to amuse her by arousing her interest in the things they saw, and regaling her with his vast fund of anecdote. She never forgot this, nor another occasion when he came to see her at school:

> I had not for some years the happiness to be at home with him. . . . But even during the years that I was absent from him his influence was the predominating power in my early education. It is now above forty years ago, but I have a fresh and delightful recollection of his first coming to see me at school on his arrival from Ireland. I recollect the moment when . . . he stopped and said with a look & voice of affection which went to my heart,
>
> Tell me my dear little daughter if there is anything you wish for or want—and remember what I now say— *You will always through life find your father your best and most indulgent friend.*[3]

Edgeworth had no idea at the time how she valued this expression of his interest in her, nor how after this she would treasure his rather thoughtless correspondence:

> His power of exciting early affection & ambition to deserve his approbation was great—It is the first and best power a preceptor & parent can possess. I never can forget the delight & pride I felt in receiving letters from him when I was at school.—The direction—The handwriting within—even the breaks erasures & blots are present to me.[3]

[1] RLE to ME, Beighterton, 8 Nov. 1779. [2] Ibid., 6 Apr. 1780.

[3] Cancelled manuscript pages for RLE's *Memoirs*, in ME's hand, [?1818] (National Library of Ireland MS. 11132, 1st folder). Many of the more intense passages ME wrote for the *Memoirs* were cut down or cancelled in accordance with the advice of her friend Etienne Dumont. See below, p. 407.

Edgeworth afterwards came to admit that in the first three years of their marriage especially he and Honora had been too exclusively interested in one another.[1] In Ireland it had been the estate and the gardens which kept them happily occupied in one another's company. Honora, so austere in expressing herself to Maria, is an entirely different woman writing to her own friends about her daily life with her husband:

I believe I do not so frequently speak of the happiness of our union as he does—my disposition has more natural reserve in it, than his . . . Enfin mon amie, il me semble vraiment que nous somes fait [*sic*] l'une pour l'autre — et si j'allois vous dire tout le bien que je pense de lui vous auriez une assez longue lettre — Je vous ai ecrit en tres mauvais Francais but I fell into it, I know not how, when I was speaking on this subject — It seems as if one might write in French without being ashamed of Boasting for when I speak of Lovell—we seem so much one, that I fancy I am speaking of myself.[2]

Later, mechanics and literature were the interests which drew them together. In theory one of the objects of moving from Edgeworthstown back to England in 1777 was to enjoy more intellectual company than was available in Ireland; in practice their social life had to be very restricted, for, thanks to mismanagement of his estate while he was an absentee, Edgeworth's income had fallen from an estimated £1,650 (Irish) in 1770 to only about £1,000 a year in 1777. They had to live at Northchurch in a very modest way, and to restrict their entertaining to such old friends as Day and Wedgwood. But this scarcely affected the great intellectual richness of this period in their lives, for they read voraciously and made considerable progress in their joint pursuits—pursuits which, to be sure, effectively excluded the older children at the time from the most interesting part of their parents' lives, but which were also to bring incalculable benefits, especially to Maria, in time to come.

The Edgeworths' work in education, founded during the critical years 1777–80, is often misunderstood (like Edgeworth's mechanics) by those not fundamentally interested in it, because

[1] *Memoirs of RLE*, i. 344.

[2] Mrs. H. Edgeworth to Miss Mary Powys, 3 May 1775 (copy).

it is easily confused with his earlier dabbling with the ideas of Rousseau. In fact the breakdown of the experiment with Richard, and Edgeworth's growing preference for Lunar practicality, had turned his attention to an entirely different educational approach.

Thomas Day, on the other hand, remained an ardent disciple of the imaginative, theoretical Rousseauistic tradition, as his *Sandford and Merton* (1783–9) illustrates.[1] But it is interesting that Day's great Lunar friend Keir, a profound admirer of Day's values in general, by no means went with him on the subject of Rousseau.

According to the ideas of this celebrated writer [Rousseau], society is an unnatural state in which all the genuine worth of the human species is perverted; and he therefore recommends that children should be educated apart from the world, in order that their minds may be kept untainted with and ignorant of its vices, prejudices and artificial manners. Nothing surely can be more absurd than the principle of this plan of education, or more impracticable in execution; for society is not only natural to man, but also necessary, if not for his existence, yet certainly for the attainment and perfection of those qualities which give him the pre-eminence over all other animals, and which are the principal subjects of comparative excellence among men. An education therefore which has not society in view must be defective, not only in that instruction which ought to explain our duties and relations, but also in the acquisition of our most important habits, particularly that of controlling our selfish impulses for the sake of general order and happiness.[2]

Keir had been educated at Edinburgh; he was probably a typical Lunar member in that his moral and social philosophy originated not on the Continent, but in the Scottish circle of Adam Smith and Adam Ferguson;[3] and his belief in Social

[1] Although Day's celebrated book was stimulated by RLE's interest in writing for children, and hence often associated with the Edgeworths' work in the same field, its plot turns on the contrast between Tommy, the sophisticated effete little aristocrat, and Harry, the more natural, robust farmer's son. ME was often to pass strictures on some aspects of high life, but she never even remotely condemned the existing social framework. Nor did she or her father hold any brief for primitivism.

[2] *An Account of the Life and Writings of Thos. Day, Esq.*, 1791, pp. 25–6.

[3] For the influence of Scottish social theory on the Edgeworths, see below pp. 76–7.

and Civilized Man, as opposed to Natural Man, was eventually to convey itself to the Edgeworths, with interesting results. But at this period of his life at least Edgeworth would not have objected to Rousseau on ethical grounds; indeed there is very little evidence that he thought much in general concepts.[1] He gave up Rousseau because he was powerfully under the influence of Lunar pragmatism—which meant that he did not want to waste time on a system which seemed to have little practical relevance, if indeed it was workable at all.

By the time Edgeworth needed a new system of teaching small children to replace Rousseau's,[2] he was at Northchurch with Honora; and Joseph Priestley had come within the Lunar orbit. Priestley, although primarily distinguished as a chemist, was a man of remarkably varied interests, among them education. As a Dissenter he had been excluded from the established English institutions of education, the grammar and public schools and the two universities.[3] Where they could, the children of Dissenters attended instead their own academies, and the example and influence of these had a profound influence on the best English educational thinking in the eighteenth century.

Priestley was associated with two of the best of the Dissenting academies: he had been a pupil at Daventry and a master at Warrington, where he taught language, oratory, criticism, and the history, law, and constitution of England. Other subjects on Warrington's unusually up-to-date syllabus included literature, German, and natural history, which was a branch, at least, of science. Priestley's *Essay on a Course of Liberal Education*, 1768, is based on the courses he gave at Warrington. With its emphasis on reasoning capacity in preference to parroted

[1] RLE strikingly demonstrated his indifference to theory while in France in 1772–3. He actually met both Rousseau and some of the *philosophes*—certainly the Abbé Morellet, perhaps d'Alembert and Marmontel (see *Memoirs of RLE*, ii. 272–3, and below, p. 249); yet he got in touch with the latter group not out of interest in their ideas, but because he had designed his flour mill for Lyons, and he wanted d'Alembert to verify the mathematical calculations.

[2] For the dates of birth of the Edgeworth children, see below, p. 489.

[3] Small and the other doctor, William Withering, were also excluded as Dissenters; Wedgwood, Boulton, and Watt went straight from school into the workshop; only Edgeworth, Day, and Darwin among the Lunar group went to Oxford or Cambridge. For the educational background of the Lunar group and an interesting discussion of their ideas in this field see Brian Simon's chapter 'Forerunners of Educational Reform', in his *Studies in the History of Education, 1780–1870*, 1960.

learning, and its utilitarian assessment of the subjects that should be taught, the book is representative of the strong educational tradition which the English manufacturing classes inherited from Locke.

Edgeworth wholly agreed with Priestley about the case for modernizing the syllabus. It was indeed an old issue, for there had been demands for reform since Tudor times, and in the eighteenth century it could well be argued that schoolboys were not being trained to understand the universe according to Newton, let alone to pilot the industrial revolution. Although Edgeworth's own formal education had been traditionally classical, in his books he was to go even further than Priestley in recommending modern subjects, notably chemistry and mechanics. In *Émile* Rousseau had declared that we should educate for mankind, not for a profession; the English liberals, at once more pragmatic and less revolutionary, wanted to do the reverse.

So far Edgeworth belongs recognizably to the Lunar group, but his real contribution to thinking on education lies elsewhere. What he was at first looking for in 1778 was no more than a satisfactory means of teaching his children Anna and Honora to read. He examined 'upwards of forty Books, written for the use of children', which would have included primers, Aesop's and other fables, collections of 'beauties' from famous authors, Newbery's recent pioneering publications, even perhaps vulgar chap-books. Out of all this, Edgeworth declared: 'I could not select three pages that were suited to their capacities; and there is scarcely any folly or any vice, of which they might not learn the Rudiments, in this collection, if it were written in language which they could comprehend.'[1] Fortunately he then came upon a newly published experiment, Anna Laetitia Barbauld's *Lessons for Children from Two to Three Years Old*, in which the vocabulary was simple, the backgrounds homely, and the lessons kept short. The two girls learnt to read in six weeks, and Edgeworth, delighted, composed a seventy-page 'Letter to Mrs. Barbauld', in fact a general essay, in which he set down his observations, and the moral he drew from them.

[1] RLE to Mrs. Barbauld, n.d. [1778]. (Apparently a draft; although it seems likely that no copy was ever sent, as there is no reference to it later, or record of a reply. For the Edgeworths' first meeting with Mrs. Barbauld, see below, p. 141.)

Edgeworth was now fully aroused to the problems of actual teaching, as opposed to educational theory; and fresh depth and direction were shortly given to his interest by Lunar, or rather Anglo-Scottish, attempts to put the study of the mind on to a more scientific basis. In 1778 or 1779 Edgeworth came upon Priestley's abridgement of Hartley's *Observations on Man*, a highly influential book in which Priestley drew attention to the importance of Hartley's doctrine of the *association of ideas*—the most coherent account yet, he believed, of the mind's reception and ordering of external impressions.[1] By the mid-eighteenth century psychology was beginning to emerge as a separate study from general philosophical inquiry; and the relevance of psychology to education was potentially immense. What struck Edgeworth about *Hartley's Theory* was the prospect that psychology, and thence education too, might cease to be subjective and speculative, and, if Hartley's work were correctly applied, might be counted among the sciences.

The subject of teaching children to read, for example, could be approached more analytically through the child's responses. The first principle, Edgeworth decided, was that children's books must be pleasing. The child who found pleasure in reading would read on, whereas the child who found it drudgery would escape to play as soon as he was allowed to. Therefore, Edgeworth thought, the teacher should fall in with the child's natural preference, and tell him a story.

Secondly, the writer for children must try to make an absolutely clear mental impression. The child must know the meaning of every word, or he must be able to guess it, or to understand it when his mother explained it to him. The experiences of the children in the story must also fall within the area of his understanding. Edgeworth had already praised Mrs. Barbauld's simple language and familiar setting, but Priestley and Hartley supplied the reason why her clarity helped the child to learn. So long as the child responded to what he met in his reading, he would himself, by the associative process of the human mind, combine that experience with an infinitely proliferating number of fresh impressions. He would

[1] *Hartley's Theory of the Human Mind, or the Principle of the Association of Ideas, with essays relating to the subject of it, by Joseph Priestley*, 1775, p. xxiv. Hartley's book first came out in 1749.

relate the significantly chosen single instance to analogous cases: intellectually and imaginatively, what he read would become part of him.

Edgeworth's informed conviction that children's literature must be based on a knowledge of children was to be crucial in his daughter's career as a writer for this special audience. As the first English classic writer for children, she later derived much of her originality and merit from the attention she paid to establishing an intimacy with her young readers. The pilot work preceding many of hers was a story written by Edgeworth and Honora in 1779, about two children called Harry and Lucy, who get up in the morning, make their beds, and eat their breakfast. The purpose is frankly educational: the children ask a great many questions and their parents supply the answers, in well-judged phrases calculated to make brick-making, or many another process, intelligible to the very young.[1]

In spite of the book's slightness and apparent naïvety, Edgeworth had a high opinion of its importance. He sent a copy to Priestley early in 1780, asking if Honora might dedicate it to him, 'as she learnt from his writings of the Doctrine upon which it is founded'.

> Her chief design has been to associate with the objects, which are every day unnoticed by the generality of children ideas of analogy, causation and utility: she proposes to pursue this plan and hopes with the assistance of her friends to introduce into different parts of her work the first principles of many sciences or rather the facts upon which those principles are founded.[2]

The phrase 'with the assistance of her friends' is probably significant. What Edgeworth and Honora seem to have been thinking of was nothing less than reproducing the area of Lunar inquiry, with Lunar assistance, in elementary books

[1] The story was intended to form the second volume in a set of three; it was actually printed as *Practical Education*, vol. ii, in Feb. 1780, but never published, for domestic reasons given below. The first and third volumes were not written. A slightly emended version of the story was published under the names of R. L. and Maria Edgeworth as the first of the *Harry and Lucy* series, 1802.

[2] RLE to J. Priestley [copy], n.d. [early 1780]. Wedgwood was also shown the text. Priestley approved warmly of the design of applying associationism to education (letter to RLE of 20 Feb. 1780), but disappointed RLE by failing to make constructive proposals.

for children. They meant to make a practical start on a modest scale in filling the enormous gap in scientific and technical education. The preface of their story explained that it was an attempt to co-operate with the natural process by which the mind developed, as far as this was understood. The intention (of the complete work, at any rate) was to plant the seeds of science, morality, and other departments of thought in the small child's conscious or partly conscious mind.

> The following little book is part of a work, the object of which is to unfold in a simple and gradual manner such of the leading principles of human knowledge, as can be easily taught to children from four to ten years of age; to inculcate the plain precepts of morality, not by eloquent harangues, but by such pictures of real life, as may make a child wish to put himself in the place of the characters intended to excite his emulation, to give by the assistance of Glossaries clear and accurate ideas of every word, which is in the least difficult, and as much as possible to lead the understanding from known to unknown problems and propositions.

In fact this is the manifesto not of a single book, but of the whole series of *Early Lessons* completed between 1801 and 1825 by Maria Edgeworth.[1]

Volume iii of the original *Practical Education* promised to be equally interesting. In it Edgeworth apparently hoped to open the whole issue raised in his mind by Hartley, of the nature of the child's responses to learning. What could a child of four, six, eight, fourteen be expected to understand? What was he likely to remember? A whole new field of experiment should be opening in educational psychology, and Edgeworth and Honora began to collect the data for a study to meet the need.

Their idea was not to devise another 'system' of education, or to discuss the merits of existing systems, to adjudicate between the school of Locke and the school of Rousseau. As scientists they felt that the need was to establish facts, through trying out on real children, lesson by lesson, what could be learnt and what could not. Honora set to work compiling a register of children's reactions to new knowledge and experience;[2] not

[1] See below, pp. 165–8.

[2] Of the various notebooks of the register that survive, two are in Honora's hand, and date from 1778 to 1779. See Bibliography, below, p. 501.

only was she responsible for the data but for the original principle, Edgeworth claimed afterwards, 'that the art of education should be considered as an experimental science':[1]

> She had observed the advantage of Experiments in many branches of philosophy and was surprized to find that systems [of] Education were supported upon uncertain Theories and Speculation and were as contradictory and capricious as the diversity of Tastes and the wildness of imagination could invent—She thought if proper Experiments were made upon different Children from their earliest years, if these Experiments were registered, if the answers & questions of children at different ages, Capacities and Educations were preserved & compared . . . some knowledge of the effects of different instruction might be acquired, their apparent might be distinguished from their real proficiency, and the success or failure of different Experiments might lead to some certainty upon a Subject of such extensive importance.[2]

Honora's practice of testing an educational idea on a real child, and later, without his being aware of it, making a note of his response, was taken over afterwards by Mrs. Elizabeth Edgeworth and by Maria. For the latter keeping the educational register was to become an education in itself. It taught her to value precision and objectivity, and trained her to a habit of observation and note-taking that extended into other spheres, including, as we shall see, the sphere of story-writing. This strictly literary connection between the two activities is one reason why it is essential to understand the educational work in which Maria was so shortly to become a partner. But it is also important to understand why all her life Maria persisted in placing so high a value on the family's educational achievements (which she rated a great deal higher than her own fiction). In her volume of the *Memoirs* she remarks that she would prefer her father to be remembered for 'having made this first record of experiments in education' than for any other single thing he had done; and she quotes with pride the continental critic who in writing of *Practical Education* confirms that 'this is the first time, that the idea of making education an experimental science has ever been developed'.[3]

[1] Appendix to *Practical Education*, 1798, ii. 734.

[2] MS. draft of letter from RLE to the *Gentleman's Magazine*, n.d. [1780–1].

[3] *Memoirs of RLE*, ii. 187. For the influence and reputation of *Practical Education* then and subsequently, see below, pp. 171–2.

Edgeworth's period of residence at Northchurch with Honora thus saw his second major phase of intellectual growth. Like the first a decade earlier, the era of mechanics and the Lunar society, it was marked by only the faintest traces of concern for the well-being of his daughter Maria. The effect on Maria of everything that was happening to Edgeworth during these years was paradoxical. Her father's absence and his involvement in other interests was more than merely painful to her at the time; it must have been a principal cause of the timidity and dependence that marked her for most of her life. On the other hand, she was to find that his adventures away from home supplied her with material for her novels which a sheltered spinster found it difficult to obtain—*Belinda*, for example, borrows both its plots from episodes in her father's life between 1766 and 1771.[1] And unquestionably the lucid well-trained intellect which is one of her chief attractions as a writer owes everything to her father; most of all perhaps to the conscientious programme of 'improvement' which he and Honora settled down to at Northchurch while Maria laboured at Derby on handwriting, needlework, and French.

The best evidence as to what Edgeworth read, and what he was shortly to get Maria to read, is the long list of books of every subject which she cites as authorities in the 1798 *Practical Education*. New books of course afterwards continued to be received at Edgeworthstown, and in great numbers;[2] but when it comes to aesthetics, a field in which the family was not very actively interested, it is noticeable that Maria in 1798 is on the whole content with books her father might easily have discovered before 1780—Burke's *On the Sublime and Beautiful* (1756), Kames's *Elements of Criticism* (1762), and Reynolds's *Discourses* (from 1769). Many people carry the imprint all their lives of the atmosphere of the years in which they were undergraduates; Maria Edgeworth has the intellectual stamp of a generation, or half a generation, earlier than that of her own early adulthood.[3] It is true that Burke and Kames at times show a sensitivity to the responses of the individual

[1] See below, p. 309.

[2] See below, pp. 219–20.

[3] For the similarity between her manner and that of graphic artists of the 1770s, see below, pp. 143–5.

reader which anticipates the subjectivism of the early nineteenth century; but elsewhere, and as a whole, Maria's aesthetic authorities are neo-classical in spirit, and they help to explain why her writing was traditional in form, and impersonal in tone, not only while other writers were breaking free, but while she herself was attempting to deal with wholly new kinds of matter.

The programme of reading was interrupted suddenly in the spring of 1779. While Edgeworth was away in Ireland on business he received news that Honora had caught cold and become feverish. He was alarmed, for the Sneyd family was a very unhealthy one; her mother and five sisters had died of tuberculosis, and Honora herself had been threatened with the disease at fifteen. He came home as fast as adverse winds would allow, and first consulted Darwin, who confirmed that Honora had consumption, though he would not commit himself as to how far it had taken hold.

The Edgeworths went to stay with Day near London so that they could consult other doctors. These included the celebrated Dr. William Heberden (Johnson's doctor), who told them at once, as humanely as he could, that there was no hope. 'He advised me to attend more to the ease of my beloved wife, and to the palliation of symptoms, than to the pretensions of any medical help, that held out hopes of recovery.'[1] They followed his advice. Instead of going to Bristol to take the waters, or basing hope on other fashionable 'cures', they took a house for the winter at Beighterton, near Shifnal, in Shropshire, which gave them access to Darwin, the various members of the Sneyd family, and other old friends.

If Edgeworth and Honora had been absorbed in one another before, they were more so now. In the great majority of letters Edgeworth wrote this winter, Honora's health was the sole topic. After November she was generally too ill to write letters (she did not write again to Maria), and usually too ill to enjoy the company of friends, but she longed to see her sister-in-law Margaret Ruxton. All winter Edgeworth was writing to Margaret, begging her to leave her husband and young family in Ireland to give Honora what comfort she could. As late as

[1] *Memoirs of RLE*, i. 365.

January 1780 he did not think there was immediate danger, although 'my own opinion has long induced me to fear the worst; the worst evil that ever can befal me!'[1] Two months later the news was worse and the tone of Edgeworth's letters desperate. 'Alas my beloved sister you are coming to a Scene which from Justice if not from friendship I should spare you . . . Such is the nature of the human mind that I should feel the utmost joy in having her secured to me even for another summer.'[2] Soon afterwards Honora drew up her 'will', a characteristic document in that, like most of her writing for adults, it shows the strength of her mind and the extent to which her thoughts centred on Edgeworth—for her own two children do not figure in it:

> I am possessed of one thing of value—it is the picture of my dearest, & valued Husband—when I die I leave it in trust to him, beging [*sic*] him to present it, to that Woman whom he shall think worthy to call his, for her to wear, so long as they both shall LOVE—
>
> At the end of that time, which I hope may be their lives, I desire, my beloved Husband, to let it become the property of *that* Child of all his Children then living, who has given him the greatest happiness, & shewn, & *felt* the greatest love, attention, & respect towards him;—To become hers, at his Death, or his Wife's Death, or after Marriage, as he shall direct.[3]

In his *Memoirs*, where he gives a moving account of Honora's last days, Edgeworth refers to a Journal which he kept to try to occupy his mind. It survives, to give a most sympathetic picture of their marriage. During the last week in April Edgeworth stayed with Honora almost all the time, going to bed himself only from about half past three in the morning till six. The Journal breaks off before the end and the story is completed in the *Memoirs*. Honora was urging Edgeworth to remarry, and she thought he should choose her own younger sister Elizabeth —the same sister whom Day, to Edgeworth's astonishment, had come to prefer to Honora nine years earlier. Then, at six in the morning of Sunday, 30 April, not long after he had gone to rest, he was called back to her bedside. She was at the very point of death, and in a few minutes he had lost her.

1 RLE to Mrs. R, Beighterton, 4 Jan. 1780.
2 RLE to Mrs. R, Beighterton, 8 Mar. 1780.
3 Written in Mrs. Honora Edgeworth's hand, Apr. 1780.

Honora's year-long illness and death, which were shattering to Edgeworth, had implications for Maria too. She was with them at Lichfield in the summer, and at Beighterton at Christmas, so that she saw how her father was suffering. He had little time to write to her during Honora's illness, but he did go out of his way to compose a long formal letter two days after Honora's death. Part of this letter has already been quoted; previous biographers have used it to demonstrate how unfeeling Edgeworth was, and it is certainly an example of his remote early style in addressing Maria; yet as far as she was concerned, the last sentence must have been full of meaning: 'My writing to you in my present situation will, my dearest daughter, be remembered by you as the strongest proof of the love of / Your approving and affectionate Father.'[1]

Edgeworth at first reacted to Honora's death as his strenuous notions of right conduct dictated he should. Mrs. Ruxton finally arrived, the day after Honora died; Edgeworth could only tell her that later he should feel his loss more than he felt it now. He went to stay with Day, but once again said little. Then he arranged that August to take his children to Scarborough, where Elizabeth Sneyd planned to go with a family party. The purpose of this joint holiday was to decide if indeed they should get married.

Edgeworth had no personal inclination whatsoever to marry Elizabeth. On the other hand Honora's advice had a virtually binding force, and he had become wretched about the motherless condition of the younger children, Anna (seven), Honora (six), and Lovell (five). He therefore proposed to Elizabeth at the end of the summer, and she accepted him. Later he explained to Mrs. Ruxton why it seemed best that they should get married as quickly as possible:

> If we defer it for any time, which we would do if we thought it for the best, perhaps I shall send all my little Children to you for I cannot bear their present orphan State—left for weeks without a father's or a mother's care—Alas! Sister Je ne suis pas si gai que je n'etois — Honora (I told you it would be so) becomes every day a greater loss to me.[2]

[1] RLE to ME, 2 May 1780; *Mem.*, i. 7. See above, pp. 48–9. For a very unfavourable reaction to the tone of this letter, see Emily Lawless, *Maria Edgeworth*, 1904, pp. 34–5.

[2] RLE to Mrs. R, Beighterton, 28 Nov. 1780.

The marriage could be achieved only in the face of great hostility from both families. Major Sneyd and Canon Seward objected on the grounds that marriage with a deceased wife's sister was unlawful (though not at this time in civil law). The Bishop of Lichfield denounced it from the pulpit, so that they were unable to marry in his diocese, and when they tried to marry in Weston parish church, where Honora was buried, a letter from Major Sneyd to the clergyman again frustrated them. Edgeworth's family joined the attack; Margaret Ruxton, who strongly disapproved of the marriage, had heard even in Ireland that the couple were living together, and believed it. Edgeworth sent detailed letters proving that Elizabeth had never passed a night unchaperoned. To his sister, if to no one else, he was also ready to lay bare his feelings on the eve of his wedding:

I am surprized that you could think for a moment that I should hazard the Character of a woman that is to be my wife, or that, were she not my wife, is the Sister of the beloved, the unrivalled object of my affections . . . I am just returned from Brereton hall where I have passed three weeks very agreeably or rather *as* agreeably as possible in my present situation of mind—For alas my mind turns in spite of every effort to *Honora & to a wish of joining her*.[1]

The best prospect of evading the Sneyds and their sympathizers was London, and eventually in December Edgeworth had the banns called three times at the parish church of St. Andrew's in unfashionable Holborn—'among 100 city names—nobody heeding'.[2] The marriage went off without a hitch on Christmas Day, in the presence of no one but the witnesses, one of whom was Day; afterwards Edgeworth took Elizabeth back to the old house at Northchurch.

Maria did not join them there until the end of January or early February because no way presented itself of escorting her from Derby to Hertfordshire. Edgeworth wrote to tell her how sorry he was: 'It has given your mother and me very great

[1] RLE to Mrs. R, Beighterton, 28 Nov. 1780. Elizabeth was staying with her family friend Lady Holte at Brereton Hall, Cheshire. RLE's movements at this time are given in detail in his letter to Mrs. R of 26 Jan. 1781.

[2] Harriet Butler to Honora Beaufort (both ME's stepsisters), Jan. 1849. Honora, a daughter of Mrs. Elizabeth Edgeworth, had written from London to get a record of the details of her mother's marriage from the 81-year-old Maria, the last survivor in the family of that time.

concern that it has been out of our Power to have you with us this Christmas: but we hope that circumstances will give us an opportunity of making you more than amends', and Elizabeth added a postscript declaring that she wanted 'to supply the place of the kind mother you have lost'.[1] On 22 January Edgeworth wrote to Josiah Wedgwood, who shortly intended coming to London, to ask him to escort Maria from Lichfield. This was her last departure from Mrs. Latuffiere's school, since Edgeworth had now chosen for her a more fashionable institution in Mrs. Devis's, at Upper Wimpole Street in London.

The most important factor in Maria Edgeworth's life, her relationship with her father and the rest of her family, was on a different footing after Edgeworth's remarriage. Whereas Honora and Edgeworth had written almost obsessively in their letters about one another, Elizabeth and Edgeworth seemed to accept that it was the former's function to be 'an attentive and successful [mother to] my children who improve under her care'.[2] In 1781 Dick, the incorrigible scapegrace, went away again to sea, leaving Maria and Emmeline at school, and the younger children settling down in the atmosphere created by their new stepmother—and 'it is impossible that female gentleness and the strongest desire to please can be more apparent in any woman than Mrs. E.'[3] The children became in effect the beneficiaries of Honora's death. Such a thought did not occur to Edgeworth, who never allowed another woman quite to fill the place of Honora in his life. He taught all his children, Elizabeth's included, that Honora's superiority was beyond question. But in private they seem to have doubted it, both because of the frigidity of her outward manner, and because of the way she took Edgeworth's attention from everyone else. Maria preferred Elizabeth, and so, understandably, did Elizabeth's own children from the evidence that came their way. Many years later one of them, another Honora (born in 1791), was reading some old family letters:

> These all confirm the high opinion I was early taught to form of the nobleness of her [Honora's] character [,] its perfect truth—&

[1] RLE to ME, Northchurch, 31 Dec. 1780.

[2] RLE to Mrs. R, London, 25 Apr. 1781.

[3] RLE to Mrs. R, 9 Mar. 1781.

fearlessness of *selfish* consequence—while they give me a much stronger idea than I ever had of the tenderness and gentleness of her feelings & of the warmth & gratitude of her affections—When I read the glowing expressions of joy & gratitude at the accomplishment of a union which seemed for the first years to have produced perfect happiness one can't help regretting its cruel termination & yet how much of happiness was enjoyed by one of those two—for many years afterwards—& of how much value was his life—after this life—& how many more human creatures he made good & happy than he would have done—had that one engrossing attachment been permitted to continue![1]

As though to illustrate her point, the letter Edgeworth wrote to Maria the autumn after Honora's death expressed a wholly new relationship between them, one in which even a twelve-year-old might have much to give. 'My dearest daughter—I received your letter with more pleasure, than I have felt for some time; continue to cultivate your heart [for] it is from the heart the fruit of happiness must spring.'[2]

This encouragement came when Maria needed it, since she was never to settle down at Mrs. Devis's. Why Edgeworth sent her there is something of a mystery; perhaps he thought the London school would give her manners a polish they would not receive in Derby—and it may have done so, although much of the effort Mrs. Devis's staff put into making her fashionable was so much wasted time:

Maria went through all the usual tortures of backboards, iron collars, and dumb-bells, with the unusual one of being swung by the neck to draw out the muscles and increase the growth, a signal failure in her case. She had so little taste for music, that the music-master very honourably advised her to give up learning to play on the pianoforte.[3]

If Maria had been pretty and confident, she would have had no reason to fear Mrs. Devis's, for as old-established landed gentry—middling gentry, as Edgeworth called it[4]—the Edgeworths and Sneyds were acceptable in Society. But at thirteen

[1] Honora Edgeworth to Fanny Wilson, *née* Edgeworth, 17 June 1829. Cf. ME's letter to ?CSE of 1817, quoted above, p. 56.

[2] RLE to ME, 4 Nov. 1780. 'For' crossed out in MS.

[3] *Mem.*, i. 9. A fashionable family's view of the school is given by Mrs. Warenne Blake in *An Irish Beauty of the Regency*, 1911, *passim*.

[4] *Letters from England*, p. xxxii.

she had grown into a painfully shy girl, and there was nothing about her appearance to lend her confidence. Even allowing for the shorter average height then than now, she was very small—four feet seven inches when she was twenty-one years old—and most of her features were not pretty. Maria herself always exaggerated when on the topic of how ugly she was, although in later life she could do it without pain. On meeting the Duchesse de Dino, Talleyrand's niece, for example, in December 1830, she commented 'little, and ugly—plain, I should say—nobody is ugly now but myself'.[1] Ugliness was not a joke at Mrs. Devis's, where fashionable girls were being educated to make good marriages. This was one race where the competitive Maria could not make the running.

She did make a friend at Mrs. Devis's in Fanny Robinson, daughter of Sir George Robinson, Bt., of Cranford Hall, near Kettering. It is from Maria's letters to Fanny, written shortly after she left school in 1782, that we know what her life at Mrs. Devis's was like. Fanny had teased her at school with being 'a grave sedate young lady',[2] and Maria seemed to be doing her best to live up to the description in what was at first a remarkably priggish correspondence. She lectured Fanny on the economic condition of Ireland, on prudence in writing letters, and, most severely of all, on novel-reading:

> You desire me to read *Julia de Roubigni* if I should meet with it. I won't promise you that I will for though I am as fond of Novels as you can be I am afraid they act on the constitution of the mind as Drams do on that of the body—But your recommendation will induce me to read any other species of books.[3]

Thomas Day had asked her to write a 'dialogue on happiness' for him, and after leaving Mrs. Devis's she was still busy on this, or on some other work with a similar theme. She asked for Fanny's help, but defensively, since at school she had been laughed at for her bookishness:

> You know I used to be laughed at for my definitions & told that I should set up by a lamp like the philosophers of old; but however I am not to be ridiculed out of a good thing—a girl of fifteen & a

[1] ME to SR, London, n.d. [Dec. 1830]; *Mem.*, iii. 42.
[2] ME to Fanny Robinson, 6 Dec. 1783 (mid-nineteenth-century copy).
[3] ME to Fanny Robinson, 15 Sept. 1783 (copy).

philosopher where joined sound ridiculous to be sure; but if we attend to the thing and not to the name the ridicule vanishes immediately, for surely there is nothing ridiculous in a girl of fifteen's attending to the feelings of her own mind & endeavouring to find out what makes her more or less happy—& what does a philosopher do more than this or what else is meant by a philosopher?[1]

She was conscious that the kind of occasion which made Fanny happy made her miserable. She therefore begged Fanny to analyse herself carefully and send her the result. Could it really be possible that Fanny was happier at a Ball than anywhere else? If so, where did the appeal lie? Was it in the preparations? the music? the dress? the praise? the bustle? Apparently it was essential for Maria's thesis that the preparations should prove more pleasurable than anything else. As for herself, she did not like any of it:

Our tastes do not in these respects, *I believe*, agree—but I see the obvious cause for their disagreeing—you have a very agreeable person, agreeable manners, & many external accomplishments which I want, you are active nimble & dance well, I am awkward & dance very ill, it is not therefore in the least surprizing that you should be happy in a ballroom . . . or that I on the contrary with every *personal* disadvantage & others which arise from awkwardness & mauvaise honte should feel myself much less at my ease in company than among friends who set little *comparitive* [*sic*] value on such qualifications—*comparitive* value I said for because I want them myself I would not depreciate them in others; I know their value, for I know the want of them; and the pain arising from that want is certainly the most exact measure of their worth.[1]

The episode is interesting in showing how Day influenced Maria at this early period of her life. She went to stay with him twice during 1781, once in July and once in September. Day was now living in retirement in an austere and isolated house at Anningsley in Surrey. He had married at last in 1778—not the orphan he christened Sabrina Sidney, whom he had been bringing up to resemble Rousseau's Sophie, nor indeed any other daughter of nature, but the combative, philosophical Miss Esther Milnes, a Yorkshire heiress, who had enthusiastically embraced her husband's ideas about a simple, useful life lived apart from society. Day was impractical, and existence with

[1] ME to Fanny Robinson, n.d. [1782].

him can never have been comfortable: most of Mrs. Devis's other pupils would surely have found him grotesque, but not Maria. His contempt for fashion and other social frivolity, his positive preference for a virtuous and intellectual life led at home, no doubt gave her the incentive she needed to stick to the role of 'philosopher' that she was given at school. 'The lofty nature of his mind, his romantic character, his metaphysical enquiries, and eloquent discussions, took her into another world.'[1]

Even with Day's example to fortify her, she felt the pain of being odd. Her schoolfellows were suspicious of her intellectuality; Maria characteristically longed for their good opinion, and, even after she had left, tried to use Fanny as her intermediary: 'Pray tell me if I am ever spoken of and how.'[2] She was passionately grateful to Fanny 'because she has uniformly shewn me more love, attention and kindness than any friend of my own age ever showed me before'.[3] Although she seemed to have spent her childhood looking for friends, her emotional need of them was perhaps never greater than in 1781 and 1782. She was suffering from a disorder of the eyes which developed alarmingly at Mrs. Devis's in the summer of 1781; as an ailment it was painful, and, since her face swelled up, humiliating too. One doctor told her brutally to her face that she would go blind; and, as though all this were not enough, she had in her summer holidays to endure the well-meant intervention of Thomas Day, who considered Bishop Berkeley's remedy of a daily dose of tar-water as efficacious for eye trouble as for everything else.

Much of this was agonizing, but it was a real consolation to Maria that the threat of blindness at last brought her to the full attention of her father. During the last year Edgeworth had begun to notice qualities in Maria which touched him, especially her assiduity and her desperate desire to please. At thirteen she compared very favourably with Richard, and the tractable but uninteresting eleven-year-old Emmeline. Before the trouble was known to be serious, he added an anxious postscript to one of his wife's letters: 'We beg you not to think of writing or

[1] *Mem.*, i. 12.
[2] ME to Fanny Robinson, Oct. 1782 [copy].
[3] ME to Fanny Robinson, 18 Dec. 1784 [copy].

drawing or anything mental or ocular—except perhaps Arithmetic which requires no attention of the eyes.'[1] When in the autumn she became worse he seemed to be struck first by pity for himself:

> I have felt my dear daughter a great deal of [anxi]ety on your Account—[ ] long been in a course of Misfortune: The great loss which I sustained last year disappointment from your Brother and several other Circumstances were almost too much for me; they have injured my health & now when your present Mothers unremitting kindness gentleness attention & good sense begin to restore my mind to tranquility if you from whom I have lately expected much comfort & Satisfaction should lose your health it will be the cause of a very severe relapse into my former uneasiness . . . You have become every year more agreeable to me and promised to be a very amiable young woman & though it is vain for you or me to lament we cannot help perceiving that we have cause . . . [I de]sire you not to write [on m]y account. Until I hear that your Character & conduct is much changed for the worse I shall not suspect you of voluntary neglect to your affectionate father.[2]

Whatever may be thought of the element of egocentricity in these letters, they must have been intensely gratifying to Maria. 'You from whom I have lately expected much comfort and satisfaction'; in the past year she had evidently given him much, and there was a place for her in the vacuum left by Honora.

Maria did not go blind in 1782. In fact she went from misery to unexpected happiness. Ever since 1779, Edgeworth had been hesitating about where to set up home with his family. His inclination in 1781 seems to have leant towards Bath or Birmingham, around which so many of his Lunar friends were grouped; but his estate was suffering from his absence, and before Honora's death he had recognized, reluctantly, that duty called him to Ireland. It may have been from books, such as Adam Ferguson's *Essay on Civil Society* (1766), or more probably Adam Smith's *Wealth of Nations* (1776), that he acquired a much more positive and idealistic attitude towards his homeland between 1780 and 1782.[3] Perhaps the example of his friends the Lunar industrialists, most of whom were active

[1] Mrs. EE and RLE to ME, Brereton Green, Cheshire, 15 Aug. 1781.

[2] RLE to ME, Brereton Green, Cheshire, 23 Sept. 1781 and 26 Oct. 1781.

[3] There is no evidence as to the date when the Edgeworths first met the works of Smith and Young; both became formative influences, and were frequently cited as authorities in both letters and novels (see, e.g., below, p. 368 and p. 376).

philanthropists with a strong sense of civic responsibility, was finally enough to remind him that he too had an economic role, which he could play only at home on his estate. 1780 saw the publication of Arthur Young's *Tour in Ireland*, a survey of trade and agriculture, richly supported with statistics; 1781 brought Ireland tariff concessions, from a Westminster hard-pressed on account of the American war. A man like Edgeworth, who for fifteen years had known the English Midlands in the bright morning of the industrial revolution, could hardly fail to feel full of hope that Ireland was at last about to experience the blessings of economic progress.

In January 1782 he told Wedgwood of his decision to go home, adding that 'if the inhabitants are excited to industry by the present opportunity of becoming manufacturers', Ireland could develop into the best remaining British possession.[1] The belief that he could play a part in his country's advancement gave him the sense of purpose he needed in an existence without Honora; it had the virtue that it was a fresh start, and, like care of the children, it took him outside himself. 'In the year 1782, I returned to Ireland, with a firm determination to dedicate the remainder of my life to the improvement of my estate, and to the education of my children; and farther, with the sincere hope of contributing to the melioration of the inhabitants of the country, from which I drew my subsistence.'[2]

When the journey began that June, it was nine years, all but a month, since Maria Edgeworth had last left England in the company of her father and a new stepmother, to set up home in Ireland.

[1] RLE to Jos. Wedgwood, Brereton Green, Cheshire, Jan. 1782.

[2] Memo. left by RLE at the end of the MS. of his part of his *Memoirs*; quoted by ME, *Memoirs of RLE*, ii. 1.

## II

## EDGEWORTHSTOWN HOUSE
## 1782–1799

NOT many pupils at Mrs. Devis's school would have rejoiced to be told that they were going to live at Edgeworthstown. It meant going into a society which was far more restricted than the social world in the English Midlands and South, where the family had lived for most of Maria's life. Intellectually she would have to surrender a great deal. Thomas Day had already given her food for thought, and he was only one of her father's circle of interesting friends with whom she would have come into contact if they had stayed in England. It was all very well for Edgeworth, who by now had got the intellectual nourishment he needed from direct contact with other people. His children would not have access to ideas at Edgeworthstown, except through books and through him. The girls of marriageable age were likely to be the ones that suffered most. It was soon evident that few husbands were to be had at Edgeworthstown—no Edgeworth daughter married an Irishman until the 1820s—and Maria's next sister, Emmeline, was to take every opportunity of staying with relatives and friends in England. But not Maria. She was happy to give up card-parties and balls, and delighted to be going to share a home with her father.

When she had arrived in Ireland in 1773, she had not cared if she fell from an attic window. This time, in very different circumstances, and with a different stepmother, her morale was high. The *Memoir* says that her return to Edgeworthstown made a vivid impression on her, and in two of her novels she draws extensively on her memories of that journey and arrival in 1782. Both *Ennui* and *The Absentee* have as a hero a young man of Irish origin, but brought up in England, who comes back to his Irish estate as a virtual stranger. Each time Maria deals with the situation, she gives it the charge of excitement she felt herself. Colambre, for example, 'exulted' in Dublin's beautiful bay, only to feel his heart swell with very different sensations when his first mob of Irish unemployed swarmed around him:

. . . instantly he found himself surrounded and attacked by a swarm of beggars and harpies, with strange figures and stranger tones; some craving his charity, some snatching away his luggage, and at the same time bidding him 'never trouble himself', and 'never fear'. A scramble in the boat and on shore for bags and parcels began, and an amphibious fight betwixt men, who had one foot on sea and one on land, was seen; and long and loud the battle of trunks and portmanteaus raged! The vanquished departed, clinching their empty hands at their opponents, and swearing inextinguishable hatred; while the smiling victors stood at ease, each grasping his booty; bag, basket, parcel, or portmanteau—'And your honour, where *will* these go?—Where *will* we carry 'em all to for your honour?' was now the question. Without waiting for an answer, most of the goods were carried at the discretion of the porter to the custom-house, where, to his lordship's astonishment, after this scene of confusion, he found that he had lost nothing but his patience; all his goods were safe, and a few *tinpennies* made his officious porters happy men and boys; blessings were showered upon his honour, and he was left in peace at an excellent hotel.[1]

Ireland constantly presented these violent contrasts between the beauty of natural settings and fine buildings, and the ugliness of the poverty of the common people. The journey from the Pigeon House on Dublin Bay (where Maria would have disembarked, as Colambre did) into the centre of the city took the visitor through Ringsend, which an early-nineteenth-century traveller described as 'one of the most squalid sinks of filth I ever beheld. Every house swarmed with ragged squalid tenantry, and dung and garbage lay in heaps in the passages.'[2] After Ringsend, the centre of Dublin could not fail to impress. The Edgeworths had chosen a good moment to tour the capital, since 1782, the year of Independence, also marked a climax in half a century of building and improvement. The Irish capital was already one of the most beautiful in Europe. The Wide Street Commission, established in 1757, had done much of its

[1] *The Absentee*, ch. 6; x. 107–8. Similar disreputable scenes among the porters who met the packet-boats are described by several real-life travellers to Dublin in this period.

[2] John Carr, *Stranger in Ireland*, 1806, p. 31.

work, and the Georgian heart of the city was laid out much as it is now. Most of the eighteenth-century public buildings were already there when Edgeworth took his family round the city, the fine Parliament House, built from 1728, the Royal Exchange, and the library and façade of Trinity College. So were the best of the private houses of the aristocracy: Leinster House, Charlemont House, Powerscourt House, the Provost's House at Trinity College had all gone up within the previous two or three decades. Of all Dublin's great eighteenth-century landmarks, only Gandon's imposing Customs House was still to come.

Having committed themselves for the time being to Ireland, the Edgeworths were gratified to feel that their capital was nothing to be ashamed of, and that Dublin possessed public and private buildings which rivalled the Georgian West End of London. Edgeworth must have been puzzled as to how so much progress had been made since his days as a student at Trinity College. The answer was that some Irish classes had done particularly well between the middle of the century and the outbreak of the American war—the landed gentry, for example, and the linen manufacturers and provision merchants of Dublin. These people had money to spend; so, in a very literal sense, had the public authorities:

> The Irish Parliament had plenty of money at its command, and was determined that its dominating neighbour should not have the use of it. Having failed to establish its authority over the surplus in 1753, it had taken care that henceforth no surplus should exist, and money was spent lavishly on local improvement—roads and canals, manufactures, and building.[1]

The result was that other English arrivals besides the Edgeworths were struck by the curious anomaly of Dublin life, the contrast between ostentatious spending and equally glaring poverty:

> You who were here so lately would scarcely know this city, so much is it improved, so rapidly is it continuing to improve. After the talk of the misery of the people in our Parliament, and in the Parliament here, I cannot but feel daily astonishment at the nobleness of the new buildings and the spacious improvements hourly

[1] Constantia Maxwell, *Dublin under the Georges*, 1936, p. 74.

making in the streets. I am sometimes tempted to suspect appearances, and to think I am at a table with a man who gives me Burgundy, but whose attendant is a bailiff disguised in livery. In a word, there never was so splendid a metropolis for so poor a country.[1]

Edgeworth, with his technical bent, noticed the discrepancy between the magnificent pretensions of the greater private houses and their faulty workmanship. Often a sudden want of capital had left them visibly incomplete.[2] As for Maria, she still looked at Ireland with an eye habituated to England. 'An Henglishwoman, born in Hoxfordshire',[3] and educated in Wimpole Street, was more likely to be struck by the old poverty than the new wealth.

Once they were out of Dublin and in the countryside the signs of poverty were all around them. The arrival at Edgeworthstown could not help being an exciting experience:

The tones and looks, the melancholy and gaiety of the people, were so new and extraordinary to her, that the delineations she long afterwards made of Irish character probably owe their life and truth to the impression made on her arrival at this time as a stranger. Though it was June when they arrived there was snow on the roses she ran out to gather, and she felt altogether in a new and extraordinary country.[4]

In spite of snow on the roses, Edgeworthstown as a whole was hardly a pleasing spectacle. Her father was shocked at the condition of the house and gardens: 'Wherever he turned his eyes, in or out of his house, damp, dilapidation, waste! appeared. Painting, glazing, roofing, fencing, finishing—all were wanting.'[5]

At best, Edgeworthstown House was not an impressive gentleman's home by English standards. Its gate was at the very end of the village street, and the house stood awkwardly at an angle just inside it. 'It had been built in my grandfather's time, in a bad situation, for the sake of preserving one chimney, that had remained of the former edifice.' The same crampedness characterized the interior. In the first half of the eighteenth century, when Edgeworth's father built the new house, it was

[1] Letter from an anonymous Englishman in Dublin to Wm. Eden, later Lord Auckland, 1785, quoted ibid., pp. 73–4.

[2] Cf. *Ennui*, ch. 6; vii. 49.

[3] Lady Clonbrony's favourite boast (in *The Absentee*) is a sly reference by the author to her own history.

[4] *Mem.*, i. 13.

[5] *Memoirs of RLE*, ii. 2.

fashionable to be able to see 'through a number of doors a *suite* of apartments. To gratify this fancy it was made a slice of a house, all front, with rooms opening into each other, through its whole length, without any intervention of passage. All the rooms small and gloomy, with dark wainscots, heavy cornices, little windows, corner chimneys, and a staircase taking up half the house, to the destruction of the upper story. In short, a more hopeless case for an architect, and for a master of a large family, could scarcely occur.'[1]

Edgeworth resisted the temptation to embark recklessly on 'improvements' which he could not afford, but over the years he employed ingenious mechanical contrivances and small structural alterations to make the interior more efficient and comfortable for his large family. A later inhabitant long afterwards remembered the house as it was in 1864, when her grandfather's personality was still distinctively stamped upon it:

. . . with its big rooms lined with books, its workshop, its clocks, its large maps on the walls, its innumerable ingenious mechanical devices, [the house] bore unmistakably the character of its master through several generations. From the central hall hung with family pictures, adorned with stuffed birds and foreign 'curiosities', opened on one side the dining-room and library. Drawing-room there never was in that house; the family room was the library, where all the family read and drew and worked together round the long centre table, with Maria's little desk-table in a corner. On the other side of the hall lay the workshop, where Richard Lovell worked in his day, and after him nearly all his family performed feats of carpentry after their own fashion with varying degrees of skill. Up the curving staircase crowned by a glass dome was a labyrinth of bedrooms of all sizes, the smallest being Maria's with its little bow-window added by her father, of which she was so proud, though even with this addition the room can hardly have measured ten feet square, and it was generally shared with a sister! And higher still was a series of small attics peopled by a host of children and servants. And down in the depths below a miscellaneous army of retainers worked in semi-darkness in a huge kitchen and offices, low-roofed and mud-floored, where as late as 1864 the cocks and hens roamed at their will.[2]

He found that by patching he could also do something to improve the external appearance of the house. When his

[1] *Memoirs of RLE*, ii. 5–6. [2] *Black Book*, pp. 251–2.

PLATE I

RICHARD LOVELL EDGEWORTH
Copy of the portrait by Hugh Douglas Hamilton

PLATE II

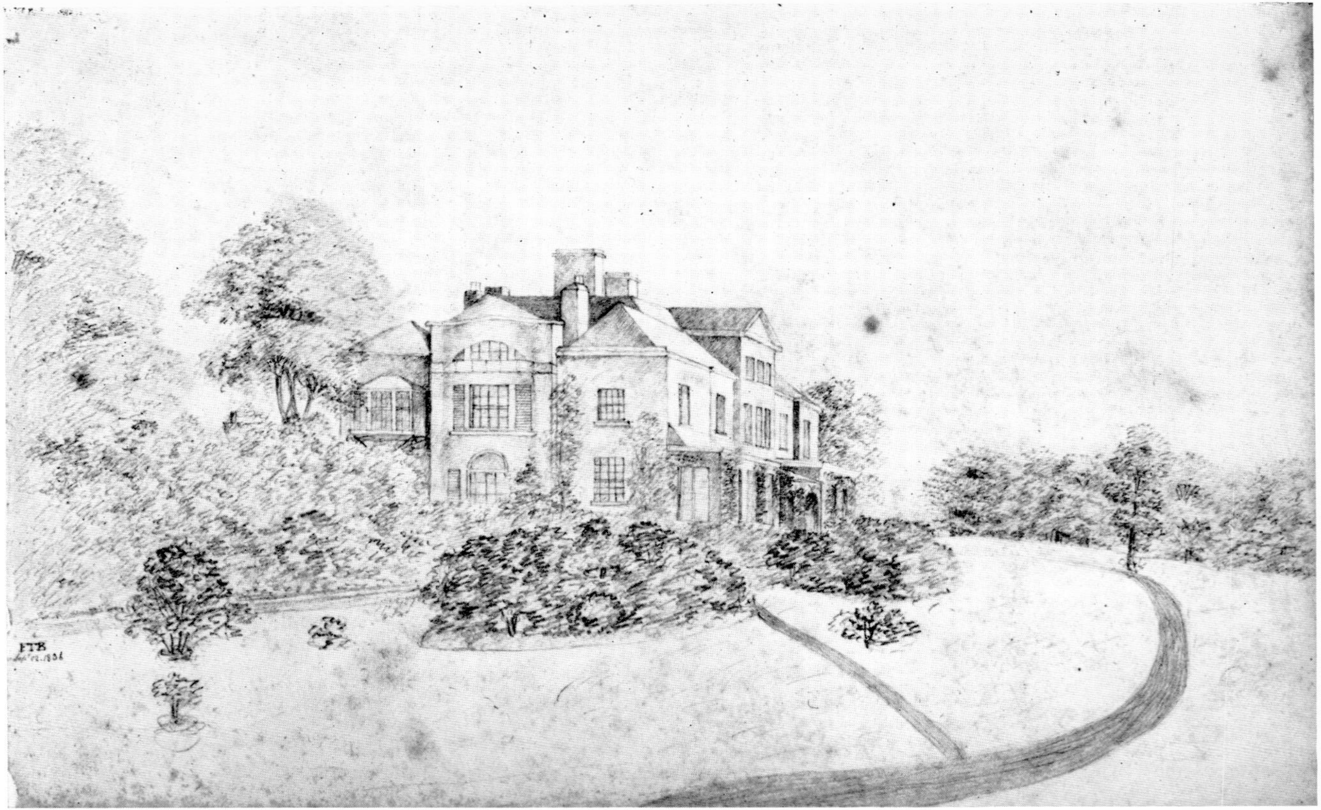

EDGEWORTHSTOWN HOUSE

Drawing by Francis Thomas Beaufort, 12 Sept. 1836, showing the window of Maria Edgeworth's room, extreme left

financial situation permitted he moved the entrance and made a recessed porch dignified by two columns. Meanwhile he had done his best with the grounds, although, in this generally flat part of Ireland, landscaping was an unpromising task:

> They appeared to have been originally laid out in humble imitation, on a small scale, of the frontispiece to Millar's Gardener's Dictionary, in the original Dutch taste. But the very day after his arrival, he set to work, and continued perseveringly, fencing, draining, levelling, planting, though he knew that all he was doing could not *show* for years. He contented himself with the reflection, that time and industry together might render the whole neat and cheerful.[1]

The result, as he hoped, was an unassuming setting well adapted for generations of energetic children to grow up in:

> The lawn, as it was called, contained many fine trees and had a path all round it, said to measure a mile, where endless family walks were taken. There were rich grazing fields, a wood haunted by herons and known as the 'cranery', a quarry and a great walled fruit-garden, all combining to make a demesne, in no wise remarkable, but a very pleasant spot, which old and young loved and enjoyed,—a homely oasis in the quiet and not very interesting country that surrounds it.[2]

But it was in relation to his estate that Edgeworth made his really significant changes. When it comes to appreciating Edgeworth's role as an Irish landlord, the past has to be borne in mind. Before his father's day, the estate had been milked for its revenue, and otherwise neglected; no landlord had lived on it for preference, or for any sustained length of time. Richard Edgeworth, on the other hand, had been a model landlord according to his own lights; he lived on the estate, secured it, and kept its papers scrupulously. But there is no evidence either that he was interested in new methods in agriculture, or that he tried to encourage or reward good tenants. He was a typical Anglo-Irish landlord in everything except his excellent book-keeping. When it suited his convenience, he granted very long leases to individual tenants. He had been unable or unwilling to prevent the peasants from dividing and subdividing the land

[1] *Memoirs of RLE*, ii. 8.

[2] *Black Book*, p. 252. RLE's efforts were to win the approval of one visitor: Wordsworth came to Edgeworthstown in 1829, and afterwards recalled that it was one of the few places where he had seen 'groves' in Ireland. Fanny Wilson to ME, 28 Dec. 1830; *Letters from England*, p. 456 n.

among their innumerable children to satisfy the hunger of each one for a few feet of soil. This was bad farming practice, because the units that resulted were hopelessly uneconomic, and the overworked land rapidly became exhausted. The careful leases which Edgeworth senior had drawn up contained many of the old semi-feudal clauses which were still common in eighteenth-century Ireland. Tenants had to do so many days' 'duty work' for the landlord each year, and pay him so many 'duty fowl'. On more carelessly run estates, the tenants got something back in kind from the landlord's open kitchen, and they had their cut from his timber and his peat. Not at Edgeworthstown, however. Edgeworth senior was not a harsh man, but he was more alive to the landlord's interests than to customs that favoured the tenants, and he gave little away.

Since his death, the Edgeworthstown estate had been run for nine years out of twelve by an agent. The period 1770–3, not generally bad for Irish farming, had seen a marked decline in the Edgeworthstown rent-roll, and now, after a five-year absence, Edgeworth had to meet a large bill for damage. Her father's bitter experience of agents is fully reflected in Maria's novels, especially *The Absentee*, in which the hero returns to his father's estate to see signs of physical dilapidation all round him. The peasants' hovels want paint, windows are broken, and roofs have fallen in. Behind the scenes whiskey-distillers and sellers flourish, and most of the tenants are in league with them. Nominally the agent in *The Absentee* is on the side of law and order, but in reality he is a criminal on a grander scale, who profits from tricking tenants out of their land, and from 'jobbing' in county politics. *The Absentee* no doubt painted a lurid picture, but the essence of its case against agents was sound. The landlord's interest was served by the long-term profitability of the estate, the agent's merely by raising the expected rent-roll twice a year—plus, if he was dishonest, a further profit for himself. Thus in the all-important drawing-up of leases, the agent was always tempted to put cash first. If a tenant had been so short-sighted as to improve land he held on a short-term lease, he was likely to have his rent put up when the lease fell in, and, if he could not pay, another tenant would be put in in his stead. A very long lease, for as many as three lives, naturally fetched a much bigger lump sum than a short lease, although the real annual rent brought in might be ludicrously low. The agents who had acted for Edgeworth since 1770 had committed some or all of these misdemeanours, and had reduced the value of the estate his father had left by more than a third.[1]

In her father's *Memoirs* Maria gives a full account of what Edgeworth set out to do in 1782.[2] First, and most important, he eliminated the agent, or middleman. He ran the estate himself, which meant getting to know each individual tenant and the quality of his holding. It also meant doing all the legal business himself, and here Edgeworth's more formal education at last stood him in good stead. He had to receive the rents twice a year (on 25 March and 29 September), and determine on what basis they should be renewed. He decided to make various changes from the usual Irish customs. Much of what he did was designed to ensure that he kept control over the land, a prerequisite if he was to modernize the estate. He would grant only short leases, and he introduced a system of fines which effectively stopped subletting by large tenants to small. Nor would he confirm subdivisions of land among members of the same family which the tenants themselves had made. Other innovations were designed to relieve the tenants of unreasonable burdens. He abolished *duty work* and *duty fowl*, although the old leases still entitled him to these. Instead he offered about the standard rate for work done for him, plus (the real incentive) unusually good labourers' cottages at a low rent. Since Edgeworth liked to be able to choose his tenants, he kept all rents moderate. Furthermore, he recognized that the insecurity of land tenure in Ireland was one of the peasants' greatest hardships. He granted *de facto tenant right* to those who had improved their land or were visibly industrious. The general absence of this right outside Ulster was to prove one of many bitter grievances relating to the land in nineteenth-century Ireland.

In this way Edgeworthstown was established as a model Irish estate. Edgeworth's aim was to educate his tenants to farm progressively, which meant instilling a far more co-operative spirit than was common in Ireland. Inevitably in this period,

[1] See above, p. 58.

[2] *Memoirs of RLE*, ii. 14 ff. ME obviously took great care with this chapter, which is presented, as she says, not as 'merely my hearsay opinion and belief, but as my evidence'. Although too detailed to quote from here, it is admirable material for the social historian.

he was a paternalist, and there was nothing egalitarian about any of his reforms. On the other hand, he meant the tenants to profit from improvements to the estate. His role in many ways resembled that of his friends the Midlands entrepreneurs. It was his capital that was at stake, and his initiative that determined what was done, but (if Adam Smith was right) the benefits would be shared by the whole community. In England such an attitude might not have meant a fundamental change in the relationship between many landlords and tenants, since on well-run estates the tenants' interests were already cared for, and everywhere the social scale was more gradual. In deeply divided Ireland a model estate like Edgeworthstown set a political as well as an economic precedent.

At first the attitude of the Edgeworthstown peasant was one of suspicion. As Edgeworth had found in 1770, the tenants were highly practised at making up for some of the inequalities of the Irish land system. They could put up with all kinds of folly and extravagance on the part of the landlord, provided they could sponge on his kitchen, steal his timber, extract a generous tip occasionally when he was in a good mood, and rely on his protection from the law if they fell foul of it. Most substantial landowners were magistrates, with very considerable powers over their tenants' liberties. The peasants expected their masters to distinguish between friends and enemies when they administered justice—between the good tenant and bad (or someone else's tenant), and, in many cases, between Protestant and Catholic. Edgeworth, with his half-English background and strong family tradition in the law, made no such distinction. His tenants can scarcely have welcomed his ideal of impartiality which meant that, unlike most of their neighbours in Co. Longford, they could not expect automatic 'protection'. After a while they came to accept his disinterestedness as a personal quirk which after all frequently served the underdog's turn: by the 1790s, at least, Edgeworth had the reputation of being 'the poor man's friend'.

In all dealings between landlord and tenant, Edgeworth insisted on a punctiliousness that belied his temperament, and he made Maria follow his example. He would not allow delay in the payment of rent, beyond what was strictly customary. After his over-indulgent start in 1770 he had completely given up random charity, though he believed in bonuses as a reward for industry, and an incentive to hard work in the future. In these matters he was of course acting in accordance with the new principles of political economy. His success in teaching discipline to the weaker and more impressionable Maria was very remarkable. Many years later, on his death-bed, he foretold that her warm heart would never be able to resist a hard case among the tenants, but he was wrong. She had learnt her lesson perfectly. At the time of the Famine, for example, we find her approving a regulation that barley for sowing should be doled out only to those who could produce a receipt for the last half year's rent.[1]

Such a condition may sound harsh in exceptional circumstances, but it was in line with the system that first Richard Lovell Edgeworth, later Maria herself, worked successfully on the estate for sixty years. Edgeworth believed that the first duty of both landlord and tenant was to fulfil their mutual contract, after which there would be plenty of opportunity to bestow favours. The Edgeworths showed a kindly paternalistic interest in their tenants; they lent them money, found jobs for their children, and kept in touch with them as far as America after they went away. In return the tenants soon accustomed themselves to their landlord's idiosyncratic way of doing things. Edgeworth was not a cold-blooded theorist, but a very responsive man, susceptible to genuine misery, and easily moved to laughter. 'His Honour, anyway is *good pay*.'[2] The Edgeworthstown tenants remained attached to their landlord's family throughout the next half century of class and sectarian strife, until the political ferment of the 1830s imposed strains that proved too strong for individual or family ties.

The first task for Edgeworth on his return to the neglected estate was to make a thorough survey of every holding. To do this he rode out daily in the second half of the summer of 1782. He had to have an assistant to go with him on these expeditions, taking notes of what was said by him, and by the tenants; at home he also needed a secretary to keep his records and accounts. His wife was expecting her second baby in September, and

[1] *Mem.*, iii. 251. See also M. Hurst, *Maria Edgeworth and the Public Scene*, 1969, *passim.*

[2] *Memoirs of RLE*, ii. 4.

his eldest son had left home. He therefore turned to the fourteen-year-old Maria, and it was she who went with him to meet the peasants (although she was frightened of horses) and sat by his side with the rent book in March and September. The result was that from the first she saw the Irish peasantry at their most impassioned and persuasive. From the day of the family's return the tenants flocked on to the lawn in front of the house, thanking Edgeworth for continuing their leases with profuse declarations of loyalty, or pleading and arguing with him if his decision had gone against them.[1] 'Alternately as landlord and magistrate, the proprietor of an estate had to listen to perpetual complaints, petty wranglings and equivocations, in which no human sagacity could discover truth, or award justice.'[2] The most vivid impression of the animated scenes they met this summer occurs in *Ennui*, where the hero describes his first days in residence on his Irish estate:

By this time my castle-yard was filled with a crowd of 'great-coated suitors', who were all *come to see—could they see my lordship? or waiting just to say two words to my honour*. In various lounging attitudes, leaning against the walls, or pacing backwards and forwards before the window, to catch my eye, they, with a patience passing the patience of courtiers, waited, hour after hour, the live-long day, for their turn, or their chance, of an audience. . . . How these subjects of mine had contrived to go on for so many years in my absence, I was at a loss to conceive; for, the moment I was present, it seemed evident that they could not exist without me.

One had a wife and six *childer*, and not a spot in the wide world to live in, if my honour did not let him live under me, in any bit of a skirt of the estate that would feed a cow.

Another had a brother in jail, who could not be *got out* without me.

Another had three lives dropped in a *lase* for ever; another wanted a renewal; another a farm; another a house; and one *expected* my lard would make his son an exciseman; and another that I would make him a policeman; and another was *racked*, if I did not settle the *mearing* between him and Corny Corkran; and half a hundred had given in *proposials* to the agent for lands that would be out next May; and half a hundred more came with legends of traditionary *promises from the old lord, my lordship's father that was*: and for hours I was forced to listen to long stories *out of the face*, in which there was such a perplexing and provoking mixture of truth and fiction,

[1] *Memoirs of RLE*, ii. 16–42. [2] Ibid., ii. 2–3.

involved in language so figurative, and tones so new to my English ears, that, with my utmost patience and strained attention, I could comprehend but a very small portion of what was said to me.

The days spent dealing with his tenants' affairs were drudgery to Lord Glenthorn, a character who had not been used to consulting anything but his own pleasure. The Edgeworths were fired by a new sense of duty, but even so there must have been times when they became exasperated. There was no escape anywhere out of doors from the clamorous peasantry:

On the fourth morning, when I felt sure of having despatched all my tormentors, I was in astonishment and despair on seeing my levee crowded with a fresh succession of petitioners. I gave orders to my people to say that I was going out, and absolutely could see nobody. I supposed that they did not understand what my English servants said, for they never stirred from their posts. On receiving a second message, they acknowledged that they understood the first; but replied, that they could wait there till my honour came back from my ride. With difficulty I mounted my horse, and escaped from the closing ranks of my persecutors. At night I gave directions to have the gates kept shut, and ordered the porter not to admit any body at his peril. When I got up, I was delighted to see the coast clear: but the moment I went out, lo! at the outside of the gate, the host of besiegers were posted, and in my lawn, and along the road, and through the fields; they pursued me; and when I forbade them to speak to me when I was on horseback, the next day I found parties in ambuscade, who laid wait for me in silence, with their hats off, bowing and bowing, till I could not refrain from saying, 'Well, my good friend, what do you stand bowing there for?' Then I was fairly prisoner, and held by the bridle for an hour.[1]

To have a part in scenes like these was a remarkable experience for an upper-class Englishwoman. As Mrs. Edgeworth rightly observed, Maria's tasks were doubly relevant in her evolution as a writer:

Her father employed her as an agent and accountant; an employment in which she showed marvellous acuteness and patience; it not only gave her habits of business and accuracy, but let her into a familiarity with the modes of thought and terms of expression among the people which she could in no other way have acquired. The exactness of arithmetical calculations far from disgusting her

[1] *Ennui*, ch. 7; vii. 65–7. Cf. *Memoirs of RLE*, ii. 2–3.

by its dryness, was agreeable to the honesty of her mind, and the apparently monotonous business of adding up columns of accounts was a pleasure to her, so much did she like to make her totals agree and complete her admirably kept account books.[1]

Her first reactions to the peasantry were probably as uninstructed and as fresh as Lord Glenthorn's in *Ennui*, but she was not suffered to revel long in the mere picturesqueness of her surroundings. Her father encouraged her to read about the Irish economy and constitution, and to write 'an enquiry into the causes of poverty in Ireland'. She was quickly 'immersed in Politics, among old newspapers, older pamphlets, Blackstone's *Commentaries*, Burgh's *Political Disquisitions*, De Lolme on *The Constitution of England*, &c, &c, &c.' Within two months she was listing her reading to Fanny Robinson, and giving an account of Ireland, which owed much more to her study of the law and political economy than to the fresh response her stepmother mentioned:

> The Irish are perhaps the laziest civilized nation on the face of the Earth; to avoid a moment's present trouble they will bring on themselves real misfortunes . . . for this indolence peculiar to the Irish Peasantry several reasons may be assigned, amongst others the most powerful is the low wages of labor 6d a day in winter and 8d in summer; the demand for labor must be very little indeed, in a country when the day labourers in it can find it answer to go over to a foreign nation, in search of employment . . .
>
> They live in a hut whose mudbuilt walls can scarcely support their weather-beaten roofs: you may see the children playing before the cabins sans shoes sans stockings sans every thing—The father of the family, on a fine summer's day standing in the sunshine at his door while his house is ready to fall upon his head and is supported only by two or three props of wood; perhaps out of charity you go up to him and tell him he had much better set about repairing his house.—he would answer you 'Oh (pronounced Ho) faith Honey when it falls it will be time enough to think of picking it up' . . .
>
> To conclude their character, the Irish are remarkably hospitable to strangers; friendly & charitable to each other; apropos, about charity, I must observe to you that the charity of the higher class of people in Ireland is one of the greatest checks to industry it encourages Idleness amongst the Poor & increases the numbers, or rather, the swarms of Beggars, which infest the streets of Dublin.

[1] *Mem.*, i. 14–15.

Let the rich raise the wages of labor, the rewards of industry, that would be true charity.—The lower class of Irish are extremely eloquent, they have a volubility, a fluency, & a facility of delivery which is really surprising . . . The Irish language is now almost gone into disuse, the class of people all speak English except in their quarrels with each other, then unable to give vent to their rage in any but their *own* they have recourse to that and they *throw* it out with a rapidity and vehemence which I can give you no idea of . . .[1]

The formality of the writing is as unlike Maria's lively later descriptions of Irish life as it could be (although the encounter between the earnest fourteen-year-old English girl and the peasant is full of comic possibilities). None the less, the reading Maria did at this time was a crucial part of her education, and it was what singled her out from her predecessors among writers of fiction. She would one day satirize the unread traveller who fell into the common errors of his kind—'the deducing general conclusions from a few particular cases, or arguing from exceptions, as if they were rules'.[2] With her constitutional authorities, and, better still, with Spenser and Sir John Davies, Arthur Young and Adam Smith behind her, she had a broad basis for forming accurate judgements about Ireland; and to the Edgeworths, getting the picture right as a whole was to seem an even more important virtue than achieving vividness in sketching a part.

Her father set her yet another task during the first weeks of their new life at Edgeworthstown. He gave her a newly published French book on education to translate, Madame de Genlis's *Adèle et Théodore: ou lettres sur l'éducation.* Although Maria's version was never published,[3] it had the advantage of bringing her into literary collaboration with her father for the first time, and of demonstrating to him that she was prepared to work at a piece of writing which, if printed, would have filled three volumes. With translation, as with most of the other tasks he set her, a careful attention to the given facts was much more valuable than invention or fancy. The bias of the training Edgeworth gave Maria's mind—a schooling in accuracy and lucidity, accompanied by a fund of real information—was

[1] ME to Fanny Robinson (copy), n.d. [Aug. 1782].

[2] *The Absentee*, ch. 6; x. 109. See below, pp. 371–3 and p. 376.

[3] See below, p. 148.

thus strongly apparent in the first weeks of his assuming responsibility for her education.

Edgeworth had never been so conscious of Maria as in the two years following their return to Edgeworthstown. Probably he never spent proportionately so much of his time with her and on her again. He said afterwards that he had neglected other business to train her in the affairs of the estate.[1] When he went to Dublin in December 1782 he sat up late at night to correct her translation. He was delighted with the way she performed the tasks he set her:

> My dear—I was going to say my Dearest Daughter [—] I received your letter with more pleasure than pride, and that is the humblest thing I ever said in my life—for indeed Maria I am not a little elated by the Success of our joint endeavours to turn the vivacity of genius to the sober certainty of useful improvement—What sincere satisfaction I shall feel in seeing you united to a man worthy of your merit—my whole mind has been turn'd to forming your Character for the enjoyment and the power of conferring permanent happiness—Indeed, were you to be disappointed in the reasonable and honourable hope of selecting from the mob of modern gentry one rational creature, who will esteem you as I do, yet the care that you have taken to form your Character will not be thrown away,—it will secure Serenity to the evening of your life;—and whilst I live will rivet the affections of a fond parent and a steady friend—I am interrupted [*sic*]—Enter a Baloon [*sic*]—Exit Daughter—
>
> manet
>
> Richard Lovell Edgeworth.[2]

Educating Maria supplied him with an intellectual interest; besides, she promised to be the intellectual partner he had missed since Honora died. His wife Elizabeth was certainly not unintelligent, and she and Edgeworth always treated one another with great affection and respect. But her health was not strong, and her record of childbearing might have taxed any constitution: she gave birth to four children in the first four years of her marriage, and later to five more, although only two of these survived early childhood. It soon became accepted

[1] See below, p. 102.

[2] RLE to ME, Dublin, 12 Feb. 1784. News of balloon experiments in France by the Montgolfier brothers and de Rozier created 'balloon mania' in England and Ireland in 1783–4; there were trial ascents in Dublin, as elsewhere.

that Maria had a special position in relation to her father's work which would have been unthinkable in Honora's day.

By early 1784, a year and a half after his arrival at Edgeworthstown, Edgeworth's letters were expressing conscious contentment again. Maria played her part in ministering to him: 'I acknowledge with pleasure that your company and affection have contributed much to my felicity since you lived with me.'[1] Educating a succession of children and maintaining a model estate kept him active, and made him feel useful. 'The perception of great improvement in everything about me will be one of the most delightful pleasures that I can enjoy.'[2] What had formerly been his private hobby, mechanics, took its place in a more disinterested pattern of life. 'I agree with you in thinking the cultivation of the Earth the most engaging & most lasting & certainly the most innocent amusement a man can follow. It has particular charms for me in this country as it gives great scope to my taste for mechanics.'[3]

Edgeworth had got over the black interval following Honora's death, and he was once again what his mother had managed to make him, admirably self-sufficient. The life he created for himself at Edgeworthstown suited him perfectly in that it kept him his own master, and, except when he chose to go in for politics, virtually independent of the outside world. His greatest pleasure was probably in watching his children develop, which is why he paid Maria a special kind of attention in 1782–4 that she did not get as a mature adult. He was quite satisfied with the conviction that his children had improved, and did not ask either for their gratitude, or for public recognition. There was nothing intense or possessive about his feelings for individual members of the family, and once they grew up he was inclined to devote his fresh energies to someone else—a younger child, a niece, or any young friend who seemed in need of encouragement.

It would be an exaggeration to say that Edgeworth did not continue to show an interest in Maria's progress, but she was one interest among many others, and the third child among

[1] RLE to ME, Dublin, 24 Feb. 1784.
[2] RLE to ME, Dublin, 3 Feb. 1785.
[3] RLE to Thomas Day, 5 Feb. 1787.

twenty-two. Edgeworthstown House was not his whole world, as it was Maria's. In 1785, for example, he was to become a founder-member of the Royal Irish Academy, and in 1786–7 to busy himself with experiments for reclaiming bogland, and for portable wooden railways.[1] Even earlier, from the month of his arrival in Dublin until 1785, he was busy with Irish politics.

June 1782 marked the very height of one of the most exhilarating periods in Ireland's history. In May the Dublin parliament's constitutional status had changed, with the abolition of the powers over it of the English Privy Council and House of Lords. In actual practice there was a great deal of illusion about this 'independence'. Real authority remained all along in the hands of ministers in London, who could not function in Ireland unless they had a majority in the Dublin parliament; as before, their majority was bought for them by political managers, the great borough-mongers, and paid for with pensions and places. To twentieth-century observers it has seemed that the corruption in the Irish House of Commons was an inevitable feature of an anomalous constitution;[2] but in 1782–3 it was fashionable among the Anglo-Irish to think otherwise. The American revolt a few years earlier had been both their inspiration and their opportunity. They did not see why they any more than the Americans should put up with the mere shadow of representation in their own government; and, since Ireland was now garrisoned almost entirely by Anglo-Irish Volunteers, many of them felt in the summer of 1782 that they should not delay exacting those reforms of the representation that would turn apparent independence into a reality.

In throwing himself from the first into this popular cause, Edgeworth had before him the example of Day, who had been passionately advocating constitutional reform in England from 1780. While still in Dublin on his journey from England, Edgeworth composed an Address to the Electors of Longford on electoral reform;[3] once home he was advocating a country-wide

[1] *Memoirs of RLE*, ii. 73–4.

[2] For recent accounts of the way in which the 'independent' Irish Parliament functioned, see Edith M. Johnston, *Great Britain and Ireland, 1760–1800*, 1962, and G. C. Bolton, *The Passing of the Irish Act of Union*, 1966.

[3] Given in *Memoirs of RLE*, ii. 49–50. Parts of RLE's address seem indebted to Day's Address to the Freeholders of Cambridge of 25 Mar. 1780; but RLE puts more

conference of Volunteers to pursue the same end; and when the conference was called, in Dublin in November 1783, he attended as one of the delegates from County Longford. Maria was aglow with excitement and pride about her father's role (which she greatly over-estimated). 'His address and exertions had as compleat success as he could have hoped—the heads of the Corps co-operated in his views, & there seems no doubt that a Reformation will take place in a *very* short time.'[1]

Maria was far too optimistic all round. By the time the Convention met, many gentlemen who had at first supported reform had had time for second thoughts; men in the Whig tradition like Henry Grattan, the Convention's Chairman Lord Charlemont, and indeed Edgeworth himself, feared the constitutional implications of imposing reform on a legally elected parliament by the threat of force. Others, including the eccentric Frederick Hervey, Bishop of Derry, with whom Edgeworth was on friendly terms, planned to make the maximum use of the Volunteers' arms and uniforms in order to frighten parliament into agreeing to their proposals. The most significant thing Edgeworth ever did on the Irish national scene was the modest part he played backstage in thwarting the Bishop's manœuvres;[2] Lord Charlemont was afterwards able to disperse the delegates to their respective counties—whereupon most of them discovered, not merely that the moment was lost, but that reform of a government designed to help the English rule Ireland was not on the whole in the interests of the Anglo-Irish Protestant gentry.

Both at the time and in retrospect, Maria was extremely proud of her father's political activities in 1782 and 1783. In campaigning for reform at the beginning, and in acting constitutionally at the climax, Edgeworth was with the respectable majority of the gentry, a company in which his daughter

emphasis than Day on the importance of improving agriculture and trade, and he altogether avoids radical touches such as 'subjects may alter their rulers, and [that] kings must expect allegiance no longer than they deserve it'.

[1] ME to Fanny Robinson, 15 Sept. 1783 (copy).

[2] See *Memoirs of RLE*, ii. 63–4. Part of RLE's account of a dinner-party at the Bishop's house was confirmed before publication of the *Memoirs* by Henry Grattan (Grattan to ME, 19 Aug. 1819); more significantly, the Bishop wrote RLE a letter of reproach shortly afterwards: 'I am not yet reconciled to your desertion of me on the *penultimam Diem* . . . which I fear has done the cause irreparable mischief' (Bishop of Derry to RLE, 12 Feb. 1784).

instinctively liked to see him. She gives full weight in the *Memoirs* to the Convention, and the events leading up to it; what she fails to do is to tell the complete story. Unlike most of his fellow landlords, Edgeworth did not cease active campaigning. In the following year he canvassed for one of the County Longford seats in Parliament,[1] and that winter, 1784–5, he was one of the few representatives of the gentry to attend a further Congress on reform in Dublin.[2] His fellow delegates included Napper Tandy, Todd Jones, Hamilton Rowan, William Drennan—all Dublin and Belfast radicals who in the 1790s were to belong to the revolutionary movement, the United Irishmen. The cause of reform had passed by now to a less respectable, landless class—merchants, lawyers, doctors—who provided the revolutionaries of the coming age, not just in Ireland but throughout Europe. It is not surprising that Maria, writing in a more conservative era after the Congress of Vienna, and anxious as ever to do her father credit, should omit from his biography the controversial side of his political life.[3] The fact that she does so, however, obscures the true picture of the Edgeworths' situation in polite Irish society during her formative years, and makes it difficult to understand the implicit political attitudes in her Irish tales; Edgeworth had detached himself from the run-of-the-mill Anglo-Irish gentry in 1784, and Maria in her fiction was to reflect that detachment to the full.

In spite of the size of the family at Edgeworthstown House, Maria was comparatively lonely between 1782 and the early 1790s. Emmeline remained away at school until about 1785, after which she often stayed with friends of the Sneyds in England. Anna, the oldest child at home after Maria, was still only nine in 1782. Their aunt, Margaret Ruxton, was taking a kindly interest in Maria 'from the time I was a child with inflamed eyes and swelled features for whom nobody else

[1] ME to Fanny Robinson, n.d. (copy; pencilled note on copy gives postmark of original as 27 Dec. 1784).

[2] For the fullest account of this occasion, and of the Irish radical movement in the period, see R. B. McDowell, *Irish Public Opinion, 1750–1800*, 1944, pp. 105 ff.

[3] ME's discreet omissions did not deceive John Wilson Croker, whose vindictive review of the *Memoirs* (*QR*, xxii, 1820) was probably politically inspired. See below, pp. 410–12.

cared'.[1] But the Ruxtons lived forty miles away, near Navan in County Meath; Maria seems neither to have seen them really often nor corresponded with them independently until the 1790s; and almost no companions offered themselves outside the family, or nearer home.

The Irish gentry were fewer in number and more scattered than in most parts of England, and they were inferior to their English counterparts in manners and education. The Edgeworths later claimed that the Rackrent type of squire belonged to the era before 1782, but some of the breed must have survived that year in County Longford. 'In general, formal large dinners and *long sittings* were the order of the day and night. The fashion for literature had not commenced, and people rather shunned than courted the acquaintance of those, who were suspected to have literary tastes or talents.'[2] For a while they saw something of a clergyman called Brooke, whose passionate admiration for Homer endeared him to Edgeworth. But their circle was in the main limited to two families, the Pakenhams and the Forbes. The Edgeworths and Pakenhams were interrelated, and Edgeworth's affection for Edward, Lord Longford, had survived from boyhood. At Pakenham Hall there was a large and cheerful family, 'a delightful domestic society', which Edgeworth and presumably even Maria loved to visit when they could. 'But Pakenham Hall was twelve miles distant from us, in the adjoining county of Westmeath. There was a vast Serbonian bog between us; with a bad road, an awkward ferry, and a country so frightful, and so overrun with yellow weeds, that it was aptly called by Mrs. Greville "the yellow dwarf's country".'[3] The result was that the two families exchanged visits not more than once or twice a year. Castle Forbes, the home of the Earl of Granard, was more accessible, since it was only eight or nine miles away along a better road. But it was not so attractive to the Edgeworths, except when Lady Granard's mother, Lady Moira, was staying there. This cultivated woman, daughter of the celebrated Methodistical Countess of Huntingdon, had sophisticated English literary

[1] ME to Mrs. R, Liverpool, 6 Apr. 1813; *Letters from England*, p. 15.

[2] *Memoirs of RLE*, ii. 13.

[3] Ibid., ii. 11. Mrs. Greville, a frequent visitor to Pakenham Hall, was Meliora, daughter of the Hon. and Revd. R. Southwell, wife of W. F. Greville, R.N., and sister-in-law of buff and blue Mrs. Crewe. Her family owned land in Co. Longford.

tastes which made her a leader of Dublin intellectual life. She was a tremendous asset at a social gathering in County Longford; and the Edgeworths were all the more grateful to her because she took kindly notice of Maria.

When Maria first came home to live there had been obvious defects in her temper: like many insecure people, she took offence when criticized. At home, under her father's enthusiastic encouragement, she gradually lost this tendency;[1] but in company she still experienced mortification because her talents went unrecognized. Lady Moira's interest in her was not enough, and she remained awkward and tongue-tied in front of strangers:

> She was at this time very reserved in manner, and little inclined to converse. To those who knew her in after years with all her brilliant wit, in the company of the first-rate talkers of French and English society, and her never-failing cheerfulness, and flow of conversation at home, this unwillingness to speak appears incredible. She was however, then in weak health, and felt great powers which were unvalued by the young and gay of ordinary society. She knew that her father appreciated these powers, and she was contented with his approbation.[2]

Edgeworth's approbation, and also his company, preferably tête-à-tête, thus continued to matter far more to Maria than hers ever could to him. 'My father's to come home tomorrow. Oh joy and jubilee!'[3]

Although estate business and her own reading took much of Maria's time, she was also involved in what became the main preoccupation of the Edgeworth women, the education of the younger children. From Emmeline's return in the mid eighties to Edgeworth's death in 1817, no child went away to school; thirteen of them received all of what would now be called primary and secondary education at home, without the intervention of any tutor or governess. Organization was necessary if the children were to learn to read and write and acquire something of all the different subjects. One device was to allocate a young child to an older sister or adult. From about 1787, or earlier, Mrs. Edgeworth became responsible for Elizabeth (Bessy), born 1781, Maria for Henry, born 1782,[4] and Emme-

[1] RLE to ME, Dublin, 3 Feb. 1785.

[2] *Mem.*, i. 13.

[3] ME to Fanny Robinson (copy), 6 Dec. 1783.

[4] Maria took this charge seriously and worried about Henry's progress. In the

line for Charlotte, born 1783. At certain times of day—after breakfast, for example, and in the evening—the family gathered around the library table. The children were offered books to read (adult books, necessarily) on any desired subject—history, biography, travels, literature, or science. Short passages which were considered to be within a particular child's comprehension had already been marked for him. When the child had read the passage, the adult teaching him would go carefully over the sense of it, word by word and idea by idea. Often the child was encouraged to read aloud, and then he was never suffered to read on (whatever the literary demands of rhythm and structure) unless his teacher was satisfied that he had mastered the meaning. The atmosphere at these sessions was pleasant, and the child was encouraged to ask questions.[1]

Since it was necessary for their professional future, Edgeworth taught his sons Latin during the family lesson time. A more characteristic occupation was arranging scientific experiments. At other times he did his estate business, or read, or wrote, in the midst of the children. Maria did the same. Intellectual work from breakfast time until the family went to bed was executed in the communal situation, and accompanied by the hubbub of questions and answers, or the steady flow of reading aloud.

Edgeworth's family was, he believed, unusually happy. He was able to boast that not 'one tear per month is shed in the house, nor the voice of reproof heard, nor the hand of restraint felt'.[2] For the adults of the family, too, there were seven years of tranquillity, although they were not wholly without their sorrows. Richard's misdemeanours continued to be a trial to his father. In 1783 he deserted his ship, and afterwards asked to come home, but Edgeworth would not have him there 'in a state of dereliction'.[3] With only an occasional trace of regret

later 1780s he was an unusually poor talker for his age; she feared that he was too timid, and wondered if her own cowardice had communicated itself to him (ME to Charlotte Sneyd, 3 Oct. 1787).

[1] Although the fullest formal account of the Edgeworths' education methods is provided by *Practical Education* (1798), there is a more vivid description of the reading-aloud technique in *The Good French Governess*, part of *Moral Tales*, 1801.

[2] RLE to Dr. Erasmus Darwin, 7 Sept. 1794; *Memoirs of RLE*, ii. 156. But cf. Josiah Wedgwood's remarks to Coleridge, quoted above, p. 51.

[3] RLE to Thomas Day, 8 July 1784. See also Edgar E. Macdonald, *The American Edgeworths*, privately printed, 1970, p. 15.

Edgeworth had washed his hands of his eldest son, and learnt to look upon his eldest daughter as a substitute. 'Had I a son as much my friend, or as worthy of my friendship nothing would be wanting to my domestic felicity.'[1]

At the beginning of October 1789 Edgeworth received a letter informing him that his good friend Day, with whom he had never ceased to correspond several times a year, had been killed in an accident. Day met his death in a manner most appropriate to his life, when a horse which he had tried to train by benevolence threw and killed him. This blow fell at a time when Edgeworth was already steeling himself against another catastrophe. Of all his children, the most obviously talented was perhaps Honora's daughter, born in 1774 and also called Honora. She was intelligent, sweet-tempered, and she had inherited her mother's good looks. Unfortunately this was not the only Sneyd inheritance. On 27 November 1788, her stepmother Elizabeth reported that Honora's health had grown weaker, and there could not be any doubt as to the disease since the symptoms were the same as her mother's. During 1789 Mrs. Ruxton took her away to Dublin in search of treatment, and there was talk of the seaside; but since everything was obviously useless, Edgeworth decided in the end to keep her at home in familiar surroundings. As winter came on the strain was felt by the whole family: 'Indeed my dear Aunt if you were to come in one of the coaches you would cheer my poor Father's heart & my Mother's and all our Hearts—It is the most melancholy thing imaginable to see my Father preparing to bear the loss of his second Honora.'[2]

Honora died early in February 1790, and Maria, watching her father anxiously, reported in detail to her Aunt Ruxton all the suppressed but evident symptoms of her father's 'anguish of mind'.[3] She says nothing in this letter of her own or anyone else's grief; it is a very characteristic feature of her letters, throughout life, that (except when her father himself died) she seldom seemed to think of herself as having any right to grieve

[1] RLE to ME, Dublin, 3 Feb. 1785. [2] ME to Mrs. R, 16 Dec. 1789.

[3] ME to Mrs. R, 11 Feb. 1790. Another talented daughter, Charlotte, died of tuberculosis in 1807, and again ME reacted in the same way; she saw her role as cheering her father, and she would not write about Charlotte's symptoms to Mrs. Ruxton, in case her father saw traces of tears on her face. (ME to Mrs. R, n.d. [Oct. 1806].)

openly at the loss of one of the family. Her role was always to comfort those who had prior claim, especially her father.

The following year, 1791, brought a break in Maria's life after nine years securely under Edgeworth's wing. Lovell, Honora's remaining child, who was now fifteen, also showed the familiar early symptoms of tuberculosis. He, Edgeworth, and Elizabeth set off for England to consult doctors: after leaving home in the early summer of 1791, they went first to Eastbourne, later to Clifton, and the first indications were that they would stay away for some time. Mary Powys, Honora's old friend, had arranged to come to Edgeworthstown during their absence to help look after the younger children, but Maria's knowledge of estate business meant that she became her father's real deputy. So much responsibility made her uneasy:

> For though the unbounded kindness and confidence my father and dear mother expressed towards me when we parted was enough to reassure a disposition more timid than mine naturally is, yet I cannot help feeling unusual timidity, when I look round me and think I am trusted with so valuable a charge . . . You, my dear aunt, who know the excessive kindness with which they treat me, more as a friend and equal, than as a daughter, can imagine how I miss the pleasures I have been SPOILED with.[1]

Her temperament made her cast about for a substitute for her father, and the answer was naturally the person who, as she later said, most resembled him, Mrs. Ruxton. Although they had been good friends for nine years, Maria's real emotional dependence on Margaret Ruxton appears to date from these months when Edgeworth was away. 'Now that my father & mother are gone, you cannot imagine with what pleasure I reflect that we have so good and kind a friend as you my dear Aunt Ruxton so near us; and much do I wish we could have the pleasure of your conversation & society, and much more I wish your superior tending Eye was over us. . . .'[2]

Mrs. Ruxton's children were Fitzherbert, who was to die in 1799, Richard, born 1775, Letty, born about 1773, Sophy, born 1776, and Margaret, born about 1779. Of these, Sophy was a particular favourite with Richard Lovell Edgeworth, who took an interest in her education, encouraged her taste for science by

[1] ME to Mrs. R, n.d. [summer 1791]; *Memoirs of RLE*, i. 20–1.
[2] ME to Mrs. R, n.d. [summer 1791].

proposing books for her to read, and often included special affectionate messages to her in his letters to her parents. Sophy came over to stay with Maria at Edgeworthstown in September 1791, and Maria reported to her aunt that she liked her cousin better and better. 'I don't wonder she is so great a favourite of my Dr. Father's.'[1]

In time Sophy became Maria's first confidante of her own generation since her schooldays; even so, it was Mrs. Ruxton who was the real magnet in that household. Earlier in the summer Mrs. Ruxton had asked Maria to write to her 'about *all that I think* [and all that] I feel'[2] an inducement to a frank correspondence that proved important in Maria's literary development.

Maria never seemed to write a letter at this time to her father or aunt without emphasizing her dependence on the older person; she liked for example to refer to herself as 'little i'. Her father had no wish to encourage this childish streak in her. On going away he made her a present of £500, for which she evidently wrote to thank him in her most emotional manner. His reply explaining his views for her was phrased kindly, but with much more detachment:

*I never meant payment!*

As to the sentimental part of your letter—a Father may oblige or be obliged by a grown up daughter . . .

You were obliged to me whilst I hazarded my affairs & gave up time in teaching you Business.

I have been obliged by your attention to my affairs for so many years after you had learn'd the Business—The Quantum of Obligation on either side I shall never enquire—not from the fear of finding myself in the lighter scale of the balance but from knowing & feeling that all obligation ceases the moment it is computed by the Giver—

I gave you £500 to make you independent for Subsistence—I think every grown up person should by degrees be rendered independent as to the necessaries of life—I shall always keep you dependent upon me for a degree of Esteem, affection entertainment & Sympathy that you will find it difficult to obtain from any but a husband & to a good husband I will make over all my rich possessions in your heart—I am therefore under no apprehension

[1] ME to Mrs. R, n.d. [Sept. 1791].
[2] ME to Mrs. R, n.d. [summer 1791].

of losing you & you may *sew* my name again to my Bond without offending your *Heart or Understanding*—that is your antithesis you know.[1]

The mention of a husband was no mere passing reference. Edgeworth's three eldest children at home, all girls, had arrived at marriageable age. Maria was twenty-three, Emmeline twenty-one, and Anna eighteen. Edgeworth decided to stay for the winter in the south of England, which meant that he and Elizabeth could make a family home for the younger children; but he felt that Maria at least, and preferably all three grown-up girls, should if possible have a season in London. His first thought was Esther Day, the widow of his old friend, and he wrote enthusiastic letters to her recommending Maria and Emmeline for their good sense and good behaviour. Meanwhile he addressed Maria again, with a more explicit intention even than before of fixing her mind on some object other than himself:

> Between Mrs. P[owys] Miss Smith Anna & you (Mrs. E is not amongst the accused) you have so pamper'd me with sweetmeats & delicacies of all sorts that I fear my appetite will be quite spoil'd—and by the by I shall offer a reward like the Roman Emperor's for some new praise—Your letter of the 17th I received yesterday with very great pleasure—I do sincerely believe that you think all the kind things you say—and I do as sincerely wish to see your fondness & enthusiasm turned happily upon a proper object—I never see a Gentleman of tolerable promise, that I do not immediately think of you; and instantly consider whether we should like him— . . . as soon as I know myself I will write to you to determine about your London visit—if that do's not take place I will endeavour to arrange some other method of passing the winter that shall be agreeable to you.[2]

Far from finding the prospect agreeable, Maria was horrified. The idea of a visit to Mrs. Day had been floated before, earlier in the year, and at that time Maria had made her feelings plain:

> I dare say that if I go I shall be amused for a time and happy in Mrs. Day's society. But I *do not* think of the Journey with pleasure—for I shall find neither Father or [*sic*] Mother ni Amant assurement . . . in the wide town of London—But however I shall have

[1] RLE to ME, Eastbourne, 17 Aug. 1791.
[2] RLE to ME, Princes Buildings, Clifton, 25 Sept. 1791.

learnt from *Experience* how happy compared with other situations my Home is—and that is all the good I expect.[1]

The worst part of going would be the still longer separation from her father. 'Most heavily shall I feel his absence if I am to spend the winter away from him—But I have had the seven years of plenty.'[2] Luckily—as Maria certainly thought—Mrs. Day pleaded ill-health, and Edgeworth fell back on a plan which Maria much preferred. On 14 October he sent her her 'marching orders' to bring six of the seven children to live for a season or so in lodgings at Clifton. Only the youngest, the two-year-old Thomas Day Edgeworth, was to stay behind with the Ruxtons, under Sophy's special care: it was a sign of Edgeworth's interest in Sophy that he wanted to make her, like his own daughters, a 'preceptrix'.[3]

By the time she left home Maria had developed other anxieties, which she confided to the Ruxtons. She suspected that her father, who (as she supposed) must have resumed his old place in sophisticated society, would probably now despise the humble occupations they had shared at Edgeworthstown. But her first letter after she rejoined him shows that once the family was together they quickly returned to domestic normality:

We live just the same kind of life that we used to do at Edgeworthstown and though we move amongst numbers, are not moved by them, but feel independent of them for our daily amusement. All the Phantasmas I had conjured up to frighten myself vanished after I had been here a week for I found that they were but phantoms of my imagination—As you very truly told me, my Father was not a Man for Card Parties &c and he is just as kind and fond of me as he used to be at Home, as you prophecied.[4]

In expecting anything else, Maria had failed to allow for the effect on her father of spending nine years at Edgeworthstown; and, perhaps even more important, the powerful posthumous influence of Thomas Day. Edgeworth had been working on his biography of his late friend in 1790,[5] and now, confronted again

[1] ME to Mrs. R, PS. in letter from RLE to Mrs. R, n.d. [early 1791].

[2] ME to Mrs. R, n.d. [Sept. 1791].

[3] RLE (and Mrs. EE) to Mrs. R, Clifton, 9 Oct. 1791. Thomas Day Edgeworth died in June of the following summer, 1792.

[4] ME to John Ruxton, Clifton, 29 Dec. 1791; *Mem.*, i. 27.

[5] RLE had nearly finished a biography of Day in 1790 when he learnt of the existence of Keir's (published 1791). The two men differed about the function of

in England with the conventional sociability he had been able to avoid in Ireland, he felt all the force of Day's strictures against society. Edgeworth found

'he could not endure, in favor of any pretensions of birth, fortune or fashion, the stupidity of a formal circle, or the inanity of common-place conversation . . . Sometimes, perhaps, he went too far, and at this period of his life was too fastidious in his choice of society; or when he did go into mixed company, if he happened to be suddenly struck with any extravagance or meanness of fashion, he would inveigh against these with such vehemence, as gave a false idea of his disposition . . . An inconvenience arose from this, which is of more consequence than the mere loss of popularity, that he was not always known or understood by those, who were really worthy of his acquaintance and regard.[1]

Many years later, when her own circle was larger, Maria called her father's retired habits at Clifton 'an error of system and practice'; but at the time she was delighted to find that 'the mode of life at a water-drinking place was not suited to him', and that, whatever the purpose of an English season had been, he still proposed to live as much as possible within the circle of his family and existing friends.

The Edgeworths' domestic habits at Clifton emerge both from the correspondence and from Maria's stories for children: five in *The Parents' Assistant* and two in *Moral Tales* have Bristol or its neighbourhood as a setting. During the next two years they lived in 'a nice house' in Princes Buildings, although the children found it narrow after their upbringing in the Irish countryside.[2] A regular occupation was a walk up the hill to the Downs, where the children ran about 'hunting fossils and clambering', and picking the fine variety of local flowers. Living in an English city was also good for some of their more literate amusements. Below in the town was an excellent library, for which Edgeworth acquired a ticket, and the children enjoyed occasional visits to the theatre or to exhibitions of scientific curiosities.

biography, RLE thinking it should be a detailed record of the chances, incidents, and influences that built up an individual, Keir preferring the more sedate format of the public memoir. RLE offered his material to Keir, but the latter, hardly seeing how to use it, urged him to publish separately. In effect RLE eventually did so by incorporating the material in his own *Memoirs*.

[1] *Memoirs of RLE*, ii. 142–5.

[2] ME to SR, Clifton, 9 Mar. 1792; *Mem.*, i. 31.

But because on the whole it was social people rather than scientists who presented themselves, the list of new friends is not long. They met and liked an Irishwoman 'of uncommon abilities', Mrs. Kierney, and her uncle, Mr. Lloyd, who 'has seen a great deal of the world, has read and thought a great deal, and speaks and *listens* extremely well'.[1] By mistake they also got to know two younger ladies, 'whom my father went to call upon under the impression that they were his cousins. They are prodigiously fine ladies, like the Miss Branghtons in *Evelina*. Mrs. Kierney says they have a joint more in their arms than anybody else.'[2] Their favourite acquaintance was a Miss Place, whom Maria liked the better for resembling Mrs. Ruxton. For three weeks in 1792, Mrs. Edgeworth's brother, William Sneyd, visited them, and Edgeworth at least met Sneyd's new wife, the former Mrs. Emma Cecil, *née* Vernon, with whom he had run away in 1789.[3] There are signs in Maria Edgeworth's fiction that she was very interested in this woman, or at least in her story, and it was one of the irritating curbs that society placed upon upper-class women writers that she could not with propriety get to know a divorcee.

Another visit which gave some variety to their life at Clifton was from Richard, the errant eldest son, who in the summer of 1792 returned from America to stay for a few weeks in his father's household. Richard carried off a gift from Edgeworth of £1,000 Irish so that he could establish himself as a farmer; but on a later visit, to Edgeworthstown in 1795, he was considering the idea of taking up law as a profession. He was very much in need of support from home, since he had settled down in South Carolina with a young wife, Elizabeth Knight. The Edgeworths were displeased with this marriage; not so much, to do them justice, because Elizabeth's father was a hatter, but because she was a Methodist, a creed for which they felt the intellectual contempt common in educated circles in the late eighteenth century.[4] Maria praised Richard in her letters from

[1] ME to John Ruxton, Clifton, 29 Dec. 1791; *Mem.*, i. 27. Hardress Lloyd, of Co. Tipperary, was uncle to the Ruxtons' friend Mr. Saunderson of Co. Cavan. ME took care to add that, although a bachelor, he was 'about sixty'.

[2] Ibid. The ladies' name is spelt 'Broughton' in the *Memoir*, but is correct in the MS.

[3] See Elisabeth Inglis-Jones, *The Lord of Burleigh*, 1964.

[4] Cf. *Belinda*, ch. 22; iii. 90.

Clifton with her usual indiscriminate enthusiasm for members of the family, and was still praising him in 1795; but when Richard died in America in September 1796, Edgeworth at least was dispassionate: 'All that he received from me in two years about £2,000 was spent and his way of life had become such as promised no happiness to himself or his family—it is therefore better for both that he has retired from the scene.'[1]

As a means of widening the family's social experience the stay in England was a failure. Maria might be pleased that Clifton was just like home, but her father was not. In the autumn of 1792 he toyed with moving to Plymouth or Bath for the season. Then the opportunity arose for Maria, at least, to try a new setting. Her old school friend Fanny Robinson, who was now married to the wealthy banker Charles Hoare, had recently returned to the country from Lisbon and had written urging Maria to come to stay with her. Maria did not want to accept, but Edgeworth insisted, and so to Mrs. Hoare, in October 1792, Maria went.

The visit to Fanny Hoare at Roehampton is of particular importance because it was Maria Edgeworth's only first-hand experience of London Society before her best-known novels were written. Many of her critics have had mistaken ideas about her familiarity with fashionable life: 'Nothing could be farther from the truth than to suppose Miss Edgeworth in Edgeworthstown as secluded, as far out of the swim, and confined to as narrow a round, as Miss Austen in Steventon and Chawton.'[2] Much later in her life Maria did move freely in London Society; but when she wrote *Belinda*, *Leonora*, *The Tales of Fashionable Life*, and *Patronage*, the great majority of her tales and novels set in England, she had no real experience of English metropolitan life apart from her visit to Mrs. Hoare.

At the time she avoided criticism of her hostess, but she did not conceal either from her family or from the Ruxtons that she was homesick:

> The more I see of others, the more I like the character, manners & way of life of my own family. She was exceedingly kind to me, and I spent most of my time with her as I liked; I say most, because

[1] RLE to Mrs. Powys, n.d. [1796.]

[2] D. Davie, *The Heyday of Sir Walter Scott*, 1961, p. 69. Cf. also W. L. Renwick *Oxford History of English Literature, 1789–1815*, 1963, p. 71.

> a good deal of it was spent in company where I heard of nothing but Chariots and Horses[,] Curricles and Tandems. Oh, to what contempt ⟨I expo⟩sed myself in a luckless hour by asking what a Tandem was! I know my dear Aunt you will say—this will do Maria a great deal of good—And so I believe it will—I believe it must enlarge the mind & improve the manners, though at the moment it may be disagreeable to hear opinions diametrically opposite to all one has been used to & to see a variety of characters entirely different from those we have been used to love & admire. Since I have been away from home I have missed the society and fondness of my Father, Mother and Sisters more than I can express to you and more than I beforehand should have thought possible, though I did expect to miss them very much—I long to see them all again;—even when I am amused I feel a void in my mind—and now I understand what an aching void is, perfectly well.[1]

By 1810, when Mrs. Hoare asked Maria Edgeworth to visit her again, Maria was much more outspoken about the failure of her stay in 1792. She told her aunt that she would not trust herself again 'in the fine lady's den'. 'There is no occasion for my quitting my happy home a second time to go to see one who could not find out that I was a good friend till the public told her I was an authoress.'[2] To Mrs. Inchbald, another authoress with a taste for retirement, she gave a vivid picture of the tedium and loneliness of the London visit: 'I remember once, when I had gone on a WILD-goose chase to a *friend's* house . . . I was just in the solitary, melancholy state you describe; and I used to feel relieved and glad when the tea-urn came into the silent room, to give me a sensation by the sound of its boiling.'[3] It was obviously an unhappy experience, and her strong attachment to her family was at the root of the trouble. 'I have missed the society and fondness of my Father, Mother and Sisters more than I can express to you.' She returned to Clifton resolved not to leave the family again if she could help it, and certainly not to go to strangers without them, a resolve that determined the social pattern of her life ever afterwards.

Although Maria had all along felt unenthusiastic about her

[1] ME to Mrs. R, Clifton, 6 Nov. 1792; partially published *Mem.*, i. 41–2.

[2] ME to Mrs. R [Aug. 1810].

[3] ME to Mrs. Inchbald, n.d. [Mar. 1810]; B.M., Egerton MS. 2158; J. Boaden, *Memoirs of Mrs. Inchbald*, 1833, ii. 177.

father's plans to find her a husband, her sisters were happy to co-operate. Anna indeed appears to have been determined to take the first good chance she was offered. In May 1793 a friend of Keir's, Thomas Beddoes, came to Clifton to open a new medical research unit. Although originally of yeoman stock in the county of Shropshire, Beddoes had studied medicine at Oxford, and had incidentally shown such promise in chemistry that in 1788 he was invited back to give lectures in that subject. He had just given up his Oxford lectureship when he came to Bristol.

Beddoes's interest at the moment was to try to find out through experiment whether the inhalation of oxygen, hydrogen, and other gases might be relevant in the treatment of pulmonary diseases such as tuberculosis. He had chosen Bristol for his location because the hot wells attracted patients who were suffering from the right diseases and wealthy enough to pay for expensive experimental treatment. But he found the householders of that respectable resort doubly reluctant to let their houses to him. He was a notoriously outspoken radical, who was said (though wrongly, in fact) to have been driven from Oxford because he had circulated an anti-clerical handbill.[1] Now he was proposing to fill the elegant houses and salubrious air of Clifton with evil-smelling, conceivably poisonous gases. Beddoes was in difficulties until his Lunar acquaintance Edgeworth interceded with an intended landlord on his behalf.

Beddoes, who was otherwise friendless in Bristol, spent much of the summer of 1793 in the Edgeworths' company, while a house in Hope Square was negotiated and his medical and chemical apparatus installed there. Before long he was in love with Anna. She was twenty, while Beddoes was thirty-three, short, fat, and on first acquaintance unprepossessing, with the ungainly manners that could not escape notice among well-born people of the period.[2]

In spite of his social deficiencies Beddoes succeeded with the Edgeworth children, who liked the experiments he showed them. Beddoes wrote to a friend that they 'jump about me, intreat me

[1] His resignation seems to have been voluntary and to have preceded the affair of the handbill. He objected to the poor academic standing of Chemistry in the University.

[2] A distinguished Viennese doctor who visited him ten years later had been warned—justifiably, as it turned out—that he would 'find in Dr. Beddoes a man whose *premier abord* was rather repulsive' (J. E. Stock, *Life of Beddoes*, 1811, p. 300).

to go to Ireland, and consider my occasional absence from dinner a serious calamity'.[1] Whether Anna went quite so far is in doubt, but she did prefer Beddoes's company at Clifton to the prospect of life at Edgeworthstown again with her family. The Edgeworths were due to go back to Ireland in the autumn. Before they left, Dr. Beddoes proposed, and Anna accepted him. He came to Edgeworthstown in March 1794, stayed for a few weeks before the marriage, and afterwards took Anna back to live at Clifton.

Although intellectually Edgeworth had much in common with Beddoes, he described him rather guardedly to the Ruxtons. It may be that he was unsure of Anna's motives in marrying, or doubtful about pneumatics as a source of income:

> Dr. Beddoes the Object of Anna's Vows is a little fat Democrat of considerable abilities, of great name in the Scientific world as a naturalist and Chemist—good humored good natured—a man of honor & Virtue, enthusiastic & sanguine & very fond of Anna. His manners are not polite—but he is sincere & candid . . . The Doctor will settle at Clifton and if he will put off his political projects till he has accomplish'd his medical establishment he will succeed and make a fortune—But if he bloweth the trumpet of Sedition the aristocracy will rather go to hell with Satan rather than with any democratic Devil.[2]

They remained an oddly assorted couple. This was the first observation to occur to the young Cornish chemist, Humphry Davy, when he came to the Pneumatic Institution as Beddoes's assistant in 1798:

> First, Dr. Beddoes, who, between you and me, is one of the most original men I ever saw—uncommonly short and fat, with little elegance of manners, and nothing characteristic *externally* of genius or science; extremely silent, and, in a few words, a very bad companion. His behaviour to me has been, however, particularly handsome . . . Mrs. Beddoes is the reverse of Dr. Beddoes—extremely cheerful, gay and witty; she is one of the most pleasing women I have ever met with. With a pleasing understanding and an excellent heart, she combines an uncommon simplicity of manners. . . .[3]

During their married life Beddoes remained deeply absorbed

[1] J. E. Stock, *Life of Beddoes*, 1811, p. 93.
[2] Postscript by RLE to letter from ME to Mrs. R, Clifton, 21 July 1793.
[3] H. Davy to his mother, 11 Oct. 1798; T. E. Thorpe, *Humphry Davy*, 1896, p. 27.

in his medical experiments and in a great variety of other subjects, political, social, and educational, to which he turned his pen with remarkable industry and rapidity. Anna, who was childless for several years, expended some of her vivacity and intelligence on their growing circle of intellectual friends. She became a hostess to the brilliant group of writers and scientists that gathered in Bristol in the 1790s. It is clear that she hungered for some further emotional or sexual satisfaction that her husband could not give her, that she tentatively sought it from Beddoes's friend Davies Giddy, and that after Davies Giddy married and her husband died—in the same year, 1808, but in the wrong order—she suffered from prolonged regrets about her relationships with both men. Anna herself lived on as a widow until 1824, to be a strong influence on the son who temperamentally appears to have resembled her, Thomas Lovell Beddoes.[1] It is ironic that of all Maria Edgeworth's apparently talented younger relatives, Anna's son was the only one to achieve a literary fame equal to her own. His morbid temperament and Romantic manner were as remote from his aunt and her domestic world at Edgeworthstown as they could have been.[2] Which is not surprising, since the mother to whom he seems to have owed his artistic tastes began her married life in reaction against the training, home, and father that Maria Edgeworth clung to with such tenacity.

The events of the 1790s in France divided families as well as nations, and the wider Edgeworth circle was no exception. Edgeworth held decided views in favour of the Revolution, an attitude shared of course by many of the Lunar group. There was never any reason to feel inhibited about expressing a radical opinion among the Lunar circle, as Edgeworth demonstrated well after England was at war with revolutionary France: 'America is a dreary unsociable puritannical abode—When peace permits if it ever will permit everybody who can speak French & who loves Freedom will go there.'[3] In Ireland, among

[1] Cf. A. C. Todd, 'Anna Maria, the mother of T. L. Beddoes', *Studia Neophilologica*, xxix, 1957.

[2] For ME's view of T. L. Beddoes, see below, p. 444.

[3] RLE to Erasmus Darwin, 2 Mar. 1795 [misdated 1794]. ME omits this letter from the sequence of correspondence she gives in *Memoirs of RLE*, ii; it should have appeared on p. 158.

a landed gentry outnumbered ten to one by land-hungry peasants who were traditionally pro-foreign because they were Catholic, views like this increasingly laid a man open to being misunderstood. From the first, characteristically, Edgeworth declined to moderate his tone. To the conservative Ruxtons he explained that the real threat to liberty in Britain came not from those tempted to follow the French example, but from the reactionaries—the King, Pitt, the Irish political Establishment. 'The monied & landed Interest are Whipped in with the old Cry of Church & State, and ten to one but in the bustle a leg or arm of the Liberty of the Press may be pulled off as if by accident.'[1]

Even more unpopular among his Anglo-Irish neighbours than his tolerance of the French revolution was his steady support of what was then known as Catholic Relief. He had come to feel that the aims of parliamentary reformers at the Convention were inadequate, because they had not included the principle of giving Catholics the vote on equal terms with Protestants. 'The number, and wealth, and knowledge of Protestant voters in Ireland, could not decently be considered as sufficient, to elect a fair and adequate representation of the people.'[2] His brother-in-law, John Ruxton, was like many ex-soldiers a conservative in politics, and Edgeworth seems to have given him some offence by the careless way he dashed off his views:

> As I do not know the or⟨ ⟩ tenure of Mr. R's estate I cannot be supposed to m⟨ean⟩ anything ⟨re⟩lative to him, when I say that the ⟨preser⟩vation of ⟨my⟩ Estate shall never be my Criterion ⟨of the⟩ part I s⟨ho⟩uld take in Politics—My firm pers⟨uasion⟩ that the Catholics *should* be represented num⟨erically⟩ & without relation to property is certainly ad⟨verse⟩ to my own interest possessed as I am now of⟨ ⟩ landed property by the right of Conquest—⟨That⟩ right has hitherto been sufficient for the com⟨mon⟩ purposes & common sense of mankind—Upon ⟨what⟩ foundation is another question . . .—It is my Dr Sister my firm belief that the Catholics must from the present state of European Politics necessarily obtain an entire participation of all the functions of Citizens.[3]

[1] RLE to Mrs. R, Clifton, 13 Dec. 1792.
[2] Memo. of 1817, *Memoirs of RLE*, ii. 63.
[3] RLE to Mrs. R, Clifton, 13 Dec. 1792.

Maria did not enter into the substance of the disagreement, for what chiefly concerned her was the fear that it might cause a rift between her father and the Ruxtons:

I hope . . . that all the black clouds in the political horizon will be dispersed and that Freemen will eat their pudding & hold their tongues . . . My father says that *I* may vent to you as much as I think proper my 'wailings & weak fears' that any circumstances should come to pass in which my Uncle & you & my father should be of different sides of the Question.[1]

In her letters to the Ruxtons from Clifton, Maria began for the first time to develop her characteristic adult manner as a correspondent. She was almost as anxious about her intimacy with them as she had been about the tie with her father during his absence, and her letters usually contained an obligatory passage which conveyed her affection—'I am tired of recollecting how kind and agreeable you were—Are you still the same Aunt Ruxton?'[2] Another staple ingredient was a humorous anecdote, or description of some amusing character she had met. And now she could also discuss her writing—for, while there was no estate business Maria could do with her father, she had thrown herself wholeheartedly into working with him on no less than three separate projects for publication.[3] Just as she emphasized the personal and literary topics, she avoided the political, and continued to do so in her letters for many years to come. The omission was so conscious that some years later, when Mrs. Ruxton herself asked Maria for her opinion on an issue, she flatly refused to give it. 'I am very proud of the honor you have done me in asking me to criticize upon a subject which I feel to be far above my capacity and information; were the subject any other but Politics you should find me pert and ready.'[4] When, rather later, she went out of her way to praise the speeches of a politician, William Windham, which she had been reading, she took care to limit her own area of competence:

[1] ME, earlier part of same letter.

[2] ME to Mrs. R, Clifton, 21 July 1793.

[3] i.e., *Letters for Literary Ladies* (1795), *Parent's Assistant* (1796), and *Practical Education* (1798). The two latter evolved directly from the work RLE had begun with Honora in 1778–80. For an account of the writing and publication, see below, Ch. III.

[4] ME to Mrs. R, Oct. 1796.

'I like Mr. Wyndhams speeches: he plays with his subject & is never upon stilts & consequently never stumbles in an awkward or ridiculous manner—As to his politics I know nothing[.] I only mean he *speaks* well whether on the wrong or right side of the question, like a true woman I trouble myself not to enquire.'[1] Mrs. Ruxton would have approved, for she was feminine in this sense herself, and preferred personalities and manners to abstract issues. But in any case there was the all-important question of the relationship between the two households, which mattered so much to Maria from the early 1790s onwards. As the years went on, management of the correspondence from the Edgeworth end increasingly devolved on her, and she avoided all abrasive subjects. 'I sometimes flatter myself I have been the means of drawing them [John Ruxton and her father] nearer together & this is a delightful feeling.'[2]

Maria even managed to find material to amuse the Ruxtons in County Longford on their return, although at times this cannot have been easy; for by the autumn of 1793, when the family arrived home, the Irish countryside was in a more disturbed state than they had ever known it. Since her letters habitually see the comic side of the disturbances,[3] it is easy to conclude that events outside her home impinged very little on Maria, but in reality this was not so. The pleasant world of Edgeworthstown House was as delightful to her, after Clifton and London, as it had ever been; but the appearance of the surrounding countryside had grown threatening, and it was to become uglier still in the years ahead.

The troubles had begun in Ulster in the late 1780s, with bitter sectarian feuding between bands of Protestants (the Peep o' Day Boys) and their Catholic opposite numbers, the Defenders, who, as their name implies, came into existence in order to protect themselves against attack. Defender outrages

[1] ME to SR, 18 Dec. 1803. Later in life ME became scathing on the subject of political naïvety in women. See the passage of *Helen* quoted below, p. 451.

[2] ME to Miss Mary Sneyd, Black Castle, 17 Nov. 1805.

[3] e.g., in writing of the Defenders' practice of blackening their faces with charcoal, ME declared that she was going to subject callers to the house to a careful scrutiny. 'A *very* clean face will in my mind be a strong symptom of guilt—clean hands proof positive, and clean nails ought to hang a man' (ME to Mrs. R, Jan. 1796; *Mem.*, i. 69).

were reported as far south as Dublin by 1790, they had forced down rents in Cavan and Meath by 1792, and, stimulated by the war with France and the granting of limited Catholic enfranchisement, they became a problem even in relatively peaceful counties like Longford between 1793 and 1795. But in the midland counties Defenderism had a different character from its original form in Ulster. There was no significant Protestant peasantry for disaffected Catholics to feud with. When they burnt down houses, mutilated cattle, and assaulted individuals, the targets of their violence were usually the landlords or the landlords' agents.

A clear picture of events in the county can be pieced together from the Edgeworth correspondence in this period.[1] Edgeworth, perceiving that agrarian grievances lay at the root of the trouble, took care to see that all his tenants were kept regularly employed, well housed, and effectively secure of their land.[2] In 1797 he was able to boast that no tenant of his had ever been a Defender.[3] It happened that in this period almost all the large landowners in the county were absentees; most of them lived in Ireland, perhaps in a neighbouring county, but they were not Longford residents. 'Is there any other county in Ireland', Edgeworth demanded of Lord Charlemont, 'where there is not one gentleman of two or three thousand pounds per annum resident during the whole year?'[4]

Instead the large estates were run by agents, with all the opportunity for abuse which that implied. There were also a number of smaller estates, owned by former agents, 'middlemen', or tradesmen, many of whom owed their recent rise to fortune to profits made a decade earlier in the American war; the same

[1] The Edgeworth evidence does not tally in every respect with the interpretation most commonly found in printed sources. Both Lecky and H. Senior, *Orangeism in Ireland and Britain*, 1966, write of ultra-Protestantism as a general problem in the midland counties only from about 1797. (Orangeism proper originated with the founding of the first Orange Lodge in Ulster in 1795.) RLE was of course very liberal, and he may have misinterpreted some of the facts. His letters of 1795 certainly claim that the poor Catholics were already being provoked by domineering ultra-Protestant landlords and magistrates—i.e. that agrarian grievances were strengthened by open religious hostility—earlier than has sometimes been supposed.

[2] See above, p. 85.

[3] *Letter to the Earl of Charlemont on the Tellograph and on the Defence of Ireland*, 1797, p. 1.

[4] Letter of 30 Apr. 1795 [misdated in printed text]; *H.M.C., 13th Rep., App. viii*, p. 272.

class did well, as indeed did the gentry, during the war with France. The new 'half-and-half gentlemen' were predominantly Protestant, and their strongholds were in the two towns of Longford and Ballymahon, to the south of the county. Elsewhere, in the countryside, Protestants were outnumbered by perhaps ten to one.

In the vacuum left by a strong resident gentry, the judicial, economic, and political running of Co. Longford fell into the hands of this newly risen class of men. As magistrates they fitted the description of their type given in a pamphlet of 1796: they were men of 'contracted minds and illiberal prejudices, corrupted by habits of dissipation and the insolent despotism they exercised over a prostrate defenceless peasantry'.[1] Edgeworth had several reasons to despise them and they in return to dislike him. Socially and educationally he was far above them. His manner of running his estate was a standing criticism of many of their practices. Lastly, he objected to the partisan spirit with which they administered justice—to the way, for example, in which a Protestant witness or plaintiff or defendant was openly termed 'an honest man'.[2]

By April 1795 such a state of lawlessness prevailed in County Longford that extraordinary action was necessary. Edgeworth gave a summary of the situation in his own locality to the nearest large landowner, Lord Granard.

> Eleven robberies upon the poorer sort of persons whose names I enclose have been committed within a few days immediately near this place—The inhabitants of the smallest farms crowd into this town and abandon their homes . . . Unless some effective means are devised industry will be neglected . . . The produce of the ground . . . will be the next object of depredation—Rents will be unpaid . . .[3]

He was anxious to keep the task of policing the county in the hands of substantial and moderate men, like Granard and himself, rather than see it fall into the hands of the extremist Protestants. He was prepared to raise a force at his own expense to maintain order for sixteen miles around Edgeworthstown, if he could get government authority and if others like Granard would do the same. Granard replied that Edgeworth's offer was

[1] Quoted by R. B. McDowell, *Public Opinion in Ireland, 1750–1800*, 1944, p. 216.
[2] *Memoirs of RLE*, ii. 205–9.
[3] RLE to Lord Granard, 10 Apr. 1795 [copy].

generous, but too private and local to meet the case, and he proposed to call a meeting of all the gentry of the county to transmit their united views to the government.[1]

Meanwhile the ultra-Protestant party was not inactive. A group of five or six magistrates from Ballymahon called a meeting of their own at Longford on 17 April, to which they omitted to invite either Granard or Edgeworth; Edgeworth, however, heard about it on the 16th and was in time to attend. The resolutions put to the meeting by the Ballymahon group (not one of whom, Edgeworth wrote, had 'fortune, knowledge, birth or education'),[2] urged the government to proclaim a state of insurrection in the county. Edgeworth, who saw this as nothing more than a manœuvre by the Protestant group to gain extra powers for themselves, opposed everything they suggested, and was voted down in a minority of one. Maria characteristically interpreted the meeting as a moral victory for her father:

> The meeting was composed of five or six Journeymen-Gentlemen who in their collective capacity call themselves the Granard Rangers & bully pickpockets most magnanimously, and in their individual capacity weigh out almonds and raisins, administer medicine & Law not gratis, and beat their wives (gratis)—The six above-described Gentlemen have thought proper to draw up re⟨quis⟩itions for the whole County in which they thank Lord Granard for his virtious conduct—literally spelled as my mother observed two thirds *vitious*—& moreover they all joined in one scrambling attack upon my Father—hoping to mortify him but on the contrary being at length mortified themselves to find that he received all their abuse with laughing contempt—'Go on my Lads! Go on![']  said he & on they went.[3]

Proclaiming a state of insurrection was a popular solution among many rural magistrates in the 1790s, but it tended to be resisted in Dublin, for the Administration felt unenthusiastic at the prospect of seeing the gentry once more as fully armed and as powerful as they had been during the heyday of the Volunteers. The official view was that pacification of the countryside should not be left to one local sectarian body, however 'loyal', but should be entrusted to units of the army based on regional centres. Therefore on this occasion Edgeworth had some reason

1 Lord Granard to RLE, 11 Apr. 1795 [copy].
2 RLE to Lord Charlemont, 30 Apr. [1795]; *H.M.C., 13th Rep., App. viii*, p. 272.
3 ME to Mrs. R, 20 Apr. 1795.

to laugh. On 22 April he set off for Dublin, where he already had an appointment to see the Lord Lieutenant and the Chief Secretary, and on 11 May he was back with troops. Not merely for Edgeworthstown either—'there are troops sufficient, he has just heard, have been sent from Athlone to Ballymahon'.[1] The government continued responsive to Edgeworth's appeals for help, and later in the year, when the band of Defenders active at Edgeworthstown had swelled from ten men to thirty, Pelham, the Chief Secretary, sent sixty men of the Limerick Militia.[2]

Although he got his own way this time, Edgeworth had made enemies in the county. Indeed he had few friends of any weight. This point was well demonstrated when in the February of 1796 there was a by-election for one of the two County Longford seats, and Edgeworth decided to contest it.

As with most Irish county seats, the issue in County Longford was decided by a handful of important landlords. The major influences on elections were the three great estate-owners, Lord Oxmantown,[3] Lord Granard, and Sir William Newcomen; Edgeworth and Lord Longford[4] were minor influences. A few years later Edgeworth told the author of a survey of Ireland that 'all political questions in the county were decided by four families', of which his own was one.[5] Elsewhere in the book the author summed up the situation in terms less flattering to Edgeworth's importance. He concluded that 'the Oxmantown estate returns one member; the election of the other is liable to be contested between Sir W. G. Newcomen and the Earl of Granard'.[6] Now the latter seat was already held by Newcomen;

[1] ME to Mrs. R, 11 May 1795.

[2] ME to Mrs. R, n.d. [1795]. Cf. the remarks on Protestant demands for excessive powers by the Lord Lieutenant, Lord Camden, quoted Thomas Pakenham, *The Year of Liberty*, 1969, p. 34.

[3] The well-known former M.P. Lawrence Parsons, 1749–1807, created Baron Oxmantown in 1792 and Earl of Rosse in 1806. He lived at Birr Castle, Co. Offaly, forty miles south of Longford, but he had inherited land in the county through his mother, a Harman.

[4] Although the Earls of Longford had some land in the county, Pakenham Hall itself is over the border in Co. Westmeath. Politically Lord Longford had 'but an indifferent interest in this county' (Edith M. Johnston, *Great Britain and Ireland*, 1962, p. 134).

[5] E. Wakefield, *An Account of Ireland, Statistical and Political*, 1812, ii. 615.

[6] Ibid., ii. 307. Other information on the state of the county seats is to be found in Edith M. Johnston, 'The Irish House of Commons in 1791', *Proceedings of the Royal Irish Academy*, 1957 (c), and *Return of Members of Parliament*, H.C. 69 (1878), vol. lxii, pt. 2.

it was Oxmantown's seat that had just fallen vacant, on account of the death of the previous member, his lordship's relative C. B. Harman. It seems clear that the three most powerful landowners had a gentleman's agreement not to contest one another's seat; so that by offering himself as a candidate Edgeworth was causing a great deal of normally unnecessary trouble and expense to Lord Oxmantown. Moreover, he could not hope to win unless the other two substantial landlords also chose to oppose Oxmantown, thus putting their own seat at risk when the next General Election came.

Some at least of the local gentry were prepared to swallow their personal dislike of Edgeworth: 'Mr. Edgeworth, "Dear Honora's" husband, has sett up for the County, and though a man *far* from being liked in Society, yet from his great Parts and independent principles, 'tis thought there cou'd not be found among us an abler or better representative.'[1] But private support like this could hardly affect the issue. Everything depended on how the great landlords instructed their freeholders. Edgeworth must have been hoping to profit by the enfranchisement of Catholic freeholders in 1793 and by the act of 1795 which was supposed to enforce residential qualifications. On his canvass he discovered that he really seemed to be very popular among the Catholics, apparently because his reputation as an impartial magistrate had spread around the countryside. 'Could the whole county be polled', wrote Maria, unusually wistful for democracy, 'my F[ather] would have ten voices to one.'[2] But he had miscalculated if he had expected votes from the Catholics. Early in 1796 there had not been much time for registration changes, and in fact these did not have much influence on county election results as yet. The issue was determined in the usual way. Lord Oxmantown campaigned vigorously (and, Edgeworth claimed, most corruptly) on behalf of his candidate and dependent, the impecunious Sir Thomas Fetherstone. After temporizing with Edgeworth at first, Granard and Newcomen also gave their support to Fetherstone. Edgeworth probably ended up with the votes only of his own

[1] Mrs. O'Connell to Sarah Ponsonby, 12 Jan. 1796; Mrs. G. H. Bell, *The Hamwood Papers*, 1930, p. 284.

[2] ME to Mrs. R, n.d. [Dec. 1795 or Jan. 1796]. Continuation of letter begun by Mrs. EE.

freeholders, and Lord Longford's (for this is the likely meaning of Edgeworth's observation to Mrs. Ruxton, 'Lord Longford has behaved most handsomely').[1]

Edgeworth was philosophical about his defeat in the election. 'I repeat to you that the warm attachment & approbation which I have met with on my canvass has more than repaid me for my trouble.'[1] He gave a lively if cynical summing-up of the proceedings in some commemorative verses, which in their unedited state were strictly for private circulation:

Granard sneaks forth with promises and lies
Points to the Church, the Army and—Excise.
In vain for me the crowded Chapels pray
In vain 'God speed you' cheers me on my way.
Can Poverty from Gold withdraw his hand?
A Guager's rod what Voter can withstand?[2]

Maria showed her usual capacity to feel her father's setbacks quite as acutely and probably longer than he felt them himself. 'My dearest Aunt I am not Philosopher enough not to feel, nor Hypocrite enough to pretend not to feel disappointment—however it is tempered by the Reflection—that my father has done all he could without *crawling*.'[3] There was also the great consolation that the family could now 'enjoy again his company and conversation', and hear him act out 'his lively pictures of all the figures he had seen on his travels', some of which were later to make a second appearance in Maria's books.[4]

Although he disliked the war with France, Edgeworth tried to make a modest contribution of his own to Ireland's defences. In the 1790s there was much discussion of the new French military device, the telegraph. He resurrected the old model he had practised on with Sir Francis Delaval, and suggested to the government that he should set it up between Dublin and various points along the coast. He even offered to defray about

[1] RLE to Mrs. R, 16 Feb. 1796.

[2] Copied in Mrs. EE to Mrs. R, Dec. 1795 or Jan. 1796. An extended but censored version of these lines is given in *Memoirs of RLE*, ii. 176. The poem recalls Day's poetic farewell to politics, quoted Keir, op. cit., p. 60. For jobbing in Irish politics, especially the road-making schemes implied by the 'guager's rod', cf. *The Absentee*.

[3] ME to Mrs. R, PS. to RLE's letter of 16 Feb. 1796.

[4] ME to SR, 27 Feb. 1796. For the literary use made of RLE's canvass, see below, Ch. VIII.

half the cost, which as he estimated it then was a gift to the government of about £500.[1] The telegraph business meant that from February 1795, when he first raised the subject, until late in 1796, Edgeworth (and of course his secretary Maria) were enmeshed in the formidable incompetence and corruption of Dublin politics. Getting even a cut-price military device accepted proved more difficult than an innocent outsider could have supposed. No one had any technical objection to Edgeworth's telegraph—the soldiers especially always seemed to like it—but no one stood to gain anything from seeing it set up. No doubt Edgeworth and his invention became a great nuisance at Dublin Castle, while from Edgeworthstown the administrators' indifference seemed equally infuriating.

The first obstacle to be surmounted was a slippery Secretary, Thomas Lewis O'Beirne, Bishop of Ossory, later Bishop of Meath, who seemed to bless the idea of a telegraph with no more than '*faint applause*'.[2] After a few months in which little progress was made, the 'Courtier-Bishop-Secretary' departed from office with his master, the controversial Viceroy Lord Fitzwilliam, and Edgeworth had to begin again with Fitzwilliam's successor, Lord Camden. In July 1795 Camden decided that the telegraph was unnecessary, which appeared to put an end to the idea for good.

But the following year, September 1796, when there were universal rumours that the French were on the point of invasion,[3] Edgeworth again applied to the government. A personal acquaintance of his, Lord Carhampton, was now the Irish Commander-in-Chief. This time the response was encouraging. Both Carhampton and civilian officials in Dublin seemed impressed by the cheapness and efficiency of Edgeworth's system, and in the autumn of 1796 he was certain that it was to be adopted. Then, in November 1796, there was a mysterious change of heart. With a few courteous phrases but no explanation, Edgeworth was suddenly told that his telegraph was not wanted after all; it seemed (or this was the interpretation he

[1] The telegraph he finally set up, from Dublin to Galway, in Dec. 1803, cost £2,000, of which half was paid by the government, half by RLE.

[2] ME to Mrs. R, n.d. [early 1795]. See below, p. 256.

[3] See W. E. H. Lecky, *History of Ireland in the Eighteenth Century*, 1892, iii. 457. The French fleet at last appeared off Bantry Bay in Dec. 1796, but no troops landed on this occasion.

put on it) that he had failed to employ the customary bribes and promises of jobs.[1] He retaliated by publishing a pamphlet, actually written by Maria, which connected the affair with the general dishonesty of public life, and the perpetual interference of Westminster; meanwhile he told his family and friends that he would probably leave Ireland, for he did not see how it could be defended.[2]

Later on, in her novels, Maria was to prove that she had absorbed her father's loyalty to the wider community and to its institutions (however corrupt in practice they might be). At the time she showed less regard for the whole than indignation at the behaviour of those raucously hostile parts who were most in evidence from Edgeworthstown. Her father came home after successive rebuffs, convinced each time that he had done his duty, and even that defeat was for the best as far as his own happiness was concerned. After the county election, for example, he remarked: 'At present I might be as advantageously employed in sweeping any other dirty place, as in assisting to cleanse the Augean stable.'[3] Even when his telegraph was rejected, he took consolation from the fact that he was a man 'who is genuinely happy in his private life, and who is disappointed more in what concerns others than in what touches himself'.[4]

Maria cared much more than her father about the world's good opinion. 'I fear, for I am not like my father, invulnerable to the dread of slander—I fear that much would be said & believed to my father's disadvantage were he at this crisis & circumstanced as he has been to quit the country.'[5] She was unlucky in identifying herself emotionally with someone who could not only endure unpopularity, but in a sense actually welcomed it. She was made of much more vulnerable material than her father. One way out was for her to pretend that what appeared to be defeats were really victories. Just as she had imagined the 'journeymen-gentlemen' recognizing her father's moral superiority, so she conceived of him—without any

[1] R. L. Edgeworth, *A Letter . . . on the Tellograph and on the Defence of Ireland*, pp. 28–9.

[2] *H.M.C., 13th Rep., App. viii*, p. 287.

[3] RLE to Mrs. R, 16 Feb. 1796.

[4] *A Letter . . . on the Tellograph*, p. 31.

[5] ME to SR, 3 Oct. 1798.

foundation in fact—glorying over Dublin courtiers in the affair of the telegraph. 'I fear he will never make "a successful *boow*", his part is to make others *boow* to him—and perhaps Courtiers are most ready always to boow to them who will not bend their own upright backs.'[1] But in general she had to recognize that the outside world did not value him according to her idea of his merits. Thus, while his unpopularity in the 1790s left him relatively indifferent, it affected her in a number of ways.

The general personal consequence must have been to strengthen her protective feelings for her father. While he was under attack from so many quarters she also had an additional motive to wax emotional about the Ruxtons: Edgeworthstown and Black Castle were islands of rational family harmony in a sea of self-interest and hatred. By the time events in Co. Longford reached their climax (1795–8), Maria was already an apprentice novelist, and, inevitably, her real-life relations with the outside world are an important factor in determining the presentation of society in her fiction. In her first group of high-life novels, which are all set in England, she depicts people of her own class in very unflattering terms: those characters in *Letters from Literary Ladies*, *Belinda*, *Almeria* and *The Dun* who choose to live in London, or who like parties, are most unlikely to lead happy lives. In each of the first three works, a retired family is introduced specifically for purpose of comparison with the fashionables. Caroline's family in *Letters for Literary Ladies*, the Percivals in *Belinda*, and the Elmours in *Almeria* are all affectionate, domesticated, and interested in serious subjects like education; they are of course a recognizable if idealized portrait of the Edgeworths themselves. After a gap, this idealized model family reappears in Maria's later tales, and individual members of the family as well as the general atmosphere of Edgeworthstown are portrayed in some detail in *Patronage*.[2]

Maria's general impression of the outside world as gossipy and vindictive must owe something originally to Thomas Day's diatribes against society, but Day's theories had been given fresh meaning by the family's unpopularity during her formative years between about 1785 and 1799. Her ideas about

[1] ME to Mrs. R, n.d. [early 1795].
[2] See below, p. 248.

metropolitan life and more narrowly politics were not of course based on first-hand knowledge, but on glimpses of her father's career in Dublin, and these in turn were considerably modified by her partisan feelings. The result is that her sketches of political life are even more biased than her portraits of life in high Society. The features of politics as she presents them are corruption and some very melodramatic forms of treachery; not one of her politicians appears to serve, or indeed to have heard of, a political cause.[1]

Not, of course, that she deliberately intended criticism of the English or Irish governments. When, after her long period of silence about politics, she began to utter views of her own, they were more conservative than her father's: she came to identify herself in a way Edgeworth never had with the landowning classes.[2] The difference between them is exemplified by their attitude to a political radical they both knew. In the 1790s Edgeworth chose as their publisher Joseph Johnson, who also published Godwin and Blake. Maria 'thought him a generous, able, kindhearted man', and accompanied her father to the Kings Bench Prison to see him when he was there for sedition in 1799. But left to herself she would not have chosen a man of his political views for a publisher, as her stepmother makes clear. 'He became too much connected with Godwin and Holcroft, and it was afterwards a disadvantage to Maria that her works were published by the printer of what were considered seditious and sectarian books.'[3]

The a-political, or perhaps quietist, views she expresses in her letters would lead one to expect her Irish tales to show a more middle-of-the-road political standpoint than Edgeworth's. This is not the case. They draw deeply on Edgeworth's political experience, and reflect all the main features of his ideas. *Ennui*, *The Absentee*, and *Ormond* have as heroes young landlords who are taught to lay aside personal pleasures and gratifications, and to think instead about the welfare of those who are dependent on them. Co-operation between landlord

[1] The political skulduggery in *Patronage* was condemned as implausible by contemporary politicians: e.g., see below, p. 346. Apart from Lord Oldborough in that novel—ME's one relatively sympathetic politician—all her figures in public life are drawn wholly or in part from Irish politics.

[2] See below, Ch. X.

[3] *Mem.*, i. 99.

and peasant on the Edgeworthstown model is steadily shown as the ideal to aim at; and while *Ennui* specifically condemns rebellion against the established order, all three tales put the positive emphasis on the need to educate the upper classes in their social responsibility, and the principal blame for all that has gone wrong on the failure of the Anglo-Irish to live up to their responsibilities in the past.

To some extent the whole class bias of Maria's Irish writing, its appearance of being directed against the landlords and their agents, is an accident. It must not be forgotten that *Ennui* and *The Absentee* are part of a series called *Tales of Fashionable Life*, which was explicitly designed to point out the vices of the upper classes, and that *Ormond* was a continuation of the series. Theoretically *Rosanna* (one of the *Popular Tales*), the two Irish plays in *Comic Dramas*, even the unpublished and very immature *Double Disguise* (1786),[1] all of which are aimed at a popular (or, in the last case, juvenile) audience, ought to redress the political balance. But they don't. It is true that in her comic drama Maria for once produces peasants who are lazy and quarrelsome and considerably less virtuous than their landlord. But none of these popular works deals with Irish life in the same detail, or as broadly, as the longer and intellectually more ambitious tales for Maria's own class; they carry no weight as political statements about Ireland.

Because she wrote novels, which gave her the ear of the public, and because she cared all too much about her father's reputation, she made much more effort to persuade the Anglo-Irish to follow Edgeworth's example as an enlightened landlord and magistrate than he bothered to do. On the face of it, it seems entirely improbable that someone of her character and opinions would have written political novels—it went quite against the grain for her to appear to set herself up as a critic of her own class. By inclination she was the least controversial of Anglo-Irishwomen, and it was only through complex personal circumstances that she became the author of three progressive, at times even radical, studies of the Anglo-Irish in Ireland.

[1] See below, pp. 152–3. The principal comic character in *The Double Disguise*, Justice Cocoa, a self-made man, a former grocer from Tipperary and enthusiastic Volunteer, is ME's only sympathetic portrait of an Irishman who has risen in the social scale—although in her *Popular Tales* especially she is fond of Englishmen who have made good.

Maria's personal defence at the time was to exclude the outside world as much as she could in favour of her happy domestic life among the Edgeworths and Ruxtons. Just as at Clifton writing had kept up her intimacy with her father, so now she made sure that the Ruxtons were involved in her career as an authoress. The fact that her aunt and her cousin Sophy were available to her as enthusiastic assistants was important, for both of them read a great deal, and Mrs. Ruxton especially was 'literary' rather than scientific in her tastes. Black Castle at this time had a different intellectual atmosphere from Edgeworthstown, because the children were all virtually grown up; conversation in the evening was between adults looking for interest and amusement, not, as at Edgeworthstown, between adults and school-children needing instruction. Maria spent her time at Black Castle in long entertaining talks with her aunt on the sofa (and the sofa is often mentioned affectionately in her letters afterwards). She prided herself on being the only person who could always make her serious cousin Letty laugh, but more frequently her function was to amuse her aunt and Sophy. Some time probably between 1793 and 1795, after Mrs. Ruxton had been ill, Maria regaled her with an imitation of the steward at Edgeworthstown, John Langan, whose accent, phrases, and gestures both Maria and her father could mimic perfectly.[1] Maria may have been thinking of this particularly successful visit when she complained wistfully after her brother Richard's last departure for America that there was no opportunity at home for quite that kind of laughter: 'Write to me Dear Sophy for since Richard's departure I have not been the merriest of mortals—not above nine laughs & a $\frac{1}{2}$ per day, and none, such as you & my good kind aunt used to hear when I attended her happy Levee.'[2]

The motive of producing material which would further entertain the Ruxtons spurred Maria on with her writing, and encouraged her to aim at an adult as well as at a child audience. Mrs. Ruxton insisted on being kept abreast of her 'authorship Self', and in return supplied her with books and recommendations of books of the lighter sort, particularly memoirs and novels. Works like Godwin's *Caleb Williams* as well as his

[1] The genesis of *Castle Rackrent*. For the likely date, see below, pp. 353–4.

[2] ME to SR, Oct. 1795.

*Political Justice*, Mrs. Radcliffe's *The Italian*, and various French tales and novels—such as Marivaux's *Vie de Marianne*—passed between Edgeworthstown and Black Castle, or were commented on in Maria's letters.

If it had not been for the Ruxtons, Maria would scarcely have needed to write letters in the 1790s; and (as so often in the period) the letters are among her most important productions, both because they helped her to develop an idiomatic prose style and because they have a literary merit of their own. Especially for the Ruxtons she evolved the formula which is so noticeable in the letters of the first half of her life—an affectionate opening paragraph, a lively anecdote or two (amusing but not damaging, so that the Ruxtons could regale friends with them afterwards), family news, and a full paragraph or page about reading and writing. Most of the letters are addressed to Sophy, whom Maria praises highly for steady good sense,[1] and to whose judgement she constantly appeals. But these appeals are probably a device to make Sophy and her mother feel involved. Addressing the letters to Sophy was even a device in its way; it enabled Maria to write with great freedom and intimacy to a young girl, but of course did not prevent the letters from being read out to her aunt, whose affection was what Maria really valued. Nothing that was said in the letters mattered so much as the overall impression they gave of modesty, lightness, and charm. To say that this impression was calculated seems to undermine it, which one would not wish to do. Good eighteenth-century familiar letters (and Maria Edgeworth knew some of the best models) are designed as artefacts, far more than most modern letters even of literate people; moreover they do not express the personality and opinions of the sender in a vacuum, but in the context of a specific friendship.[2] Letters, in short, cannot be taken at face value, as undesigned revelations of character. If they could, Maria Edgeworth in her late twenties would have been likeable and amusing, but timid, unwilling to hazard an opinion, and wholly happy to secure the approval of minds stronger than her own. Her novels were to reveal a more

[1] e.g. ME begins a letter of 22 Jan. 1794: 'It is more like the weakness of my mind, than the strength of yours . . . to imagine that you were neglected.'

[2] ME was particularly indebted to Gray's letters, which have much of this quality of reciprocated friendship in them. See below, p. 154.

rational and unselfconscious intellect than this; her actions later in life showed her reserves of strength; the earlier correspondence, Maria's first real literary achievement, merely projected that timid, clinging side of her personality which she wanted the Ruxtons to see, because she wanted to make that household a second Edgeworthstown.

As a letter-writer Maria owed little or nothing to her father. In fact Edgeworth's letters were notorious in the family, and he resignedly accepted the common opinion of them. Maria wrote her letters very quickly, but in youth at least she thought about them first, whereas Edgeworth tossed his off without prior thought in his big, bold semi-legible scrawl. ('What a pity so great a man should write with a skewer!')[1] He was willing to admit that he communicated better 'by living voice than by dead letter'.[2] He also accepted that by not choosing his words carefully he gave offence, or created confusion:

> I am sensible that I do not detail my thoughts sufficiently [in—*RLE wrote* and—] writing and that I am from that defect frequently misunderstood—this makes me less disposed to write to those whom I love the most than to persons about whom I am more indifferent—for surely the only proper motive for writing to our friends is to give them pleasure.[2]

On the other hand he did not quite coincide with Maria in her taste for compliment. 'I have written the Sublime—the Beautiful I leave to Maria.' He congratulated Mrs. Ruxton on 'the simple easy stile and the sentiments' of a letter he had received from Sophy: 'I meet with a great many young ladies who can write in a very fine stile, full of Sensibility & the jargon of the day; but such writing creates no feeling in my mind but disgust.'[3] Occasionally he paid compliments, but he preferred to end his letters with a brief affectionate sentence, and by the mid seventeen-nineties was refusing on principle to 'send his love' automatically at the foot of Maria's letters. A modern reader, looking over the notes he scribbled in the 1780s and 1790s, so full of news, views, and matter, so unconcerned with the personal effect he was creating, may feel that there was something to be said for his brusqueness when feminine convention,

[1] ME to Mrs. R, PS. to letter of RLE, 14 Oct. 1790. See also above, p. 40.
[2] RLE to Mrs. R, Clifton, n.d. [1792].
[3] RLE to Mrs. R, Clifton, 17 Apr. 1792.

particularly, inclined to be self-conscious and over-ceremonious. Edgeworth's idiosyncrasies might be the despair of his women-folk, but they were quite in keeping with the pithy and entertaining exchanges he had with Thomas Day or Erasmus Darwin.[1]

As though to underline this point, Edgeworth won a very valuable friend in this period on account of his odd manner of expressing himself by letter. Through the Ruxtons he had become acquainted in the 1780s with a scholarly clergyman, Daniel Augustus Beaufort. In 1786, when Edgeworth was at work draining bogs, Beaufort had written to him to say that he had heard that the bones of animals extinct in Ireland, such as moose, were to be found in the bogs. Could Edgeworth get such a skeleton on behalf of a friend of Beaufort's, Edmund Burke? As a liberal Whig Edgeworth was an enthusiastic admirer of Burke's. He had travelled with him through Wales when both were leaving Ireland, probably in 1765, 'and I think I have been the better, I need not say the wiser, ever since'.[2] Edgeworth had therefore been delighted to fulfil Beaufort's commission. Since then Dr. Beaufort had published his fine map of Ireland, with its accompanying *Memoir* (1792); but Edgeworth had seen little more of him, and he was living at the moment in London.

After the Edgeworths had returned from Clifton, in 1794–5, Edgeworth was busy altering the inside of his house, particularly the hall and passages, and refurnishing some of the rooms. He therefore wrote to Dr. Beaufort to ask him to buy some hangings that he needed, and opened the letter in his usual peremptory style. 'To have many friends & an excellent taste and an obliging disposition leads a man very often into a great deal of trouble & Inconvenience—for instance—I want. . . .'[3] Dr. Beaufort was highly amused. Unfortunately Edgeworth had not specified many of the details a man needs to know before he buys bedroom hangings, such as exact size and colour. So Beaufort wrote back, in his own more urbane manner: 'When a man of great wit & lively imagination employs a dull orderly fellow, in commissions of taste, he must expect to be *boddered* with questions. . . .'[4]

1 Many of these letters are published in *Memoirs of RLE*, ii. 68–179.
2 RLE to DAB, 27 Oct. 1786.
3 RLE to DAB, 26 June 1795 [misdated 1793].
4 DAB to RLE, Queen Anne's St., Cavendish Sq., London, n.d. [1795].

There followed a fearsome number, set out in Beaufort's beautifully neat scholarly hand. Edgeworth wrote back again good-humouredly: 'I make no doubt of your making such a choice as would please every eye at Edgeworthstown; but I am willing to become a dull plodding fellow such as we all know you to be & to answer all your questions *literatim* & *verbatim*.'[1] Although the correspondence was about nothing of any intellectual substance, it revealed their different qualities, and each of them liked what he learnt of the other. When Beaufort brought his family back to his parish of Collon, Co. Louth, in 1796, he and Edgeworth at once wrote and visited like old friends.

Beaufort and his wife had two sons, Francis, a sailor,[2] and William, a clergyman. There were also three daughters, Frances, Harriet, and Louisa. The eldest, Frances, who was born a year after Maria Edgeworth in 1769, was a particular friend of the Ruxtons, and early in 1797 Mrs. Ruxton and Sophy began to bring her into the literary circle made by Black Castle and Edgeworthstown. A lavish new edition of Maria's *Parent's Assistant* was planned, which unlike the edition of 1796 was to be illustrated, because Joseph Johnson, the publisher, thought that people would buy it in the more expensive form to give away as presents.[3] Like the rest of her family, Frances was interested in science, and she had also been taught to draw. The Ruxtons got Maria's permission to ask Frances to do some of the illustrations, while Maria asked Elizabeth Pakenham to do others.

Frances's drawings were ready by March 1797. While Edgeworth was paying a visit to her father he discussed them with her; he liked the modest, intelligent manner in which she listened to his criticisms and accepted them. Frances and her mother were invited to come to meet the family at Edgeworthstown that summer. Her father had stayed there in October 1787, but Frances had never been. Nor had she met Maria.

She went full of curiosity, because she had heard a lot about Edgeworthstown, not all of it from the Ruxtons. Edgeworth's

[1] RLE to DAB, 17 Aug. 1795.

[2] Francis, 1774–1857, later Rear-Admiral Sir Francis Beaufort, shared his father's interests and became hydrographer to the navy, 1829–55. From about 1801 he was one of RLE's closest friends, and in 1837 married Maria's half-sister Honora.

[3] The edition was published in 1800 with three illustrations signed FAB and one FE.

taste for mechanics, his method of running his estate, and his supposedly revolutionary politics had already contributed to a reputation for eccentricity. Frances, who came herself from a scientific and liberal household, was astonished at the difference between the rumours she had heard and the truth as she saw it:

The family are all you know chymists and mechanics, & lovers of literature & a more united more happy more accomodating more affectionate family never yet came under my observation. How enormous are the lies, how confounded the reports that have [been] told concerning them. How very malicious all the histories that I have heard from people who said they knew, but only envied the Edgeworths—If I could not praise as I do with sincerity & truth, I should have expatiated on the neatness and convenience of the house—the tables, the closets—the various inventions which ease both Master & Servant the unnumerable contrivances that answer perfectly well & the regularity & order that reign within & without.

Their very great & partial kindness to me, deserves gratitude, but truth alone has guided my pen . . . Our time was agreeably spent between reading & listening to Miss E reading some of her own compositions, & walking—added to the lively conversation of Mr. E who knows more anecdotes & tells them better than anyone I know. Mr. Lovell showed us some experiments in Chymistry & if it had not been for the intrusion of that foolish baronet Sir Thomas F[etherstone] would have performed that very curious one of separating the Atmosphere into the three kinds of air which compose it . . . on Saturday we took our leave . . . We went to dinner at Foxhall where we met the Ruxtons again . . . Lady Anne & Mr. Fox are good kind of people, very good, & he rather agreeable, but they appeared to us as flat after those we had just left, as boiled chicken would after venison.

Frances was an attentive observer, and noticed not merely the characteristics of different members of the family but also their relationships with one another. The nominal mistress of the household, Mrs. Elizabeth Edgeworth, had been slowly declining for many years. Reports of her health are poor after the autumn of 1791, when her daughter Honora was born, although she had a last baby, William, in 1794. Elizabeth had always been characterized by her sweet and accommodating manner—Maria once described her as 'the least *exigeante* person I have ever known'[1]—and even now Frances praised her natural

[1] PS. to letter of RLE to John Ruxton, n.d. [early 1791].

humour and cheerfulness. Her sisters, Charlotte and Mary Sneyd, had come to live permanently at Edgeworthstown in 1795, and Frances caught in a few words their sensible unassertive way of deporting themselves in their brother-in-law's household. Frances saw that the three Sneyd sisters were not a forceful element; Edgeworth was much the strongest personality, and it was by him that the children were guided. Emmeline was away in England, staying with Mrs. Powys, but Frances got a strong impression of the two grown-up children at home—Maria, still modest, but (now that she was an author) conveying a sense of having found a role within the family circle; and the twenty-two-year-old Lovell, much less easy and satisfied with himself:

> In the first place Mrs. E is still pretty though very ill & weak to the last degree: she is inclined to be cheerful & sometimes is comical—Her two sisters the Miss Sneyds are little tight looking Englishwomen civil & goodhumored to strangers, affectionate & attentive to the family & though very reserved, rather agreeable.
>
> —*Miss E—the Maria*—is little, being the same size as myself, her face is not pretty but very agreeable. She looks unhealthy–lively & has a sweet voice in speaking: her dress is neatness itself, & her manner pleasing to a degree that is equally distant from the affectation of concealing, or the vanity of displaying her talents.
>
> Next to her comes Lovell. He is a poet & a Chymist, seems much attached to his father & kind to the younger children, but he is not like his father & yet methinks he tries to be like him—a bad plan, comparisons cannot be to his advantage. . . .

Once again Edgeworth talked to Frances, advising her what books to read, and finding her a willing pupil. She found the conversation with him the best part of the visit, and was very sorry when they had to come to an end: 'Our time flew swiftly & we found ourselves arrived at the cruel hour which was to separate us, almost without being conscious of the succession of hours & days & without having seen or heard a third of what we wished.'[1]

By the end of that summer it became clear to the family at Edgeworthstown that Elizabeth was not likely to survive another winter. Maria began writing fortnightly bulletins in

[1] Frances Beaufort to her brother Wm. Beaufort, 2 July 1797 (copy in Harriet Butler's hand).

October to Mrs. Powys, which are full of the familiar symptoms. As in the case of earlier bereavements, Maria was preoccupied with her father's sufferings. He was very fond of Elizabeth, as his letters to Darwin, Beaufort, and other friends show, but this blow had been expected for many years and he was prepared for it. She died on 18 November 1797, and Edgeworth followed his usual practice of busying himself outside the home. In February 1798 he found himself a seat in parliament, for the pocket borough of St. John's Town. 'My mind had sunk to the resource of public life from the loss of private happiness.'[1]

At the same time he already had another source of comfort in mind. Within two months of Elizabeth's death he had privately spoken to Dr. Beaufort about the possibility of his marrying Frances. Beaufort was an unusually tolerant man, and he approved of Edgeworth as a friend, but a man of over fifty who had been three times widowed and had had sixteen children was not the most eligible son-in-law. Beaufort therefore responded cautiously by making inquiries about the circumstances of Edgeworth's last marriage, to Elizabeth. Edgeworth replied with his usual spirit, that husbands and wives should choose one another on rational grounds, rather than in obedience to one of the prevailing tyrannies—custom, fashion, or fathers.[2]

By this time the Ruxtons had guessed what might be afoot, because they had observed the interest Edgeworth had shown in Frances, and her liking for him. Maria too suspected something. One day when the Ruxtons were visiting Edgeworthstown, in January or early February, the three of them talked over the marriage that might be in the air, and differed sharply in their view of it. The Ruxtons not only liked Frances but thought her suited to Edgeworth, while Maria apparently suspected her of vanity and affectation, and was certain that she was not good enough for her father.[3] Unaware of anyone else's suspicions, Edgeworth asked Frances to marry him in February 1798, and was accepted.

When he broke the news to Maria formally, either at the end of February or beginning of March, she told him frankly that she was very unhappy about it. She believed the sole reason

[1] RLE to DAB, 2 Feb. 1798.
[2] RLE to DAB, 20 Jan. 1798.
[3] ME to Mrs. R and SR, Collon, 23 Apr. 1798.

was her doubt about Frances's worthiness, although of course she also had reason to feel jealous of a healthy, intelligent stepmother a year younger than herself. Edgeworth treated her objections with great tact and patience. He took the line that she must get to know Frances as intimately as he did; he showed her many of their letters, and took her with him in mid March to Collon in order to make further plans for their wedding.

By this time Frances was writing as though she had not one but two offended fiancés to placate. Edgeworth was annoyed because the Beauforts wanted to consult Mrs. Beaufort's family, the Wallers, and Maria because of some tactless joke Frances had made at Edgeworthstown in February.[1] Far from wishing to exclude Maria, it was her ambition, Frances wrote, to make one side with Edgeworth and Maria of an equilateral triangle. She hoped that the worst of their misunderstandings were over, and tried, still tentatively, to claim Maria as an ally: 'My heart has suffered so acutely these last four days that my head is perplexed, my mind confused & even my hand disobedient . . . Your uniform kindness is the reality which next to the return of your father's / confidence & affection / gives me most pleasure.'[2]

Maria's reply began rather stiffly, but became warmer as she arrived at the subject of her own well-established place in her father's affections:

> It is indeed the first, and warmest wish of my heart to please him, —for never father could deserve more, or exact less, from a daughter —I have implicit confidence, founded upon *happy experience*, in his judgement of character—all *his* friends, I hope are mine—the persons he most esteems & loves in the world are those for whom I have most affection & respect—and, if I may without presumption say so, my father's ideas, & mine, upon almost all subjects have so great a similarity, that I believe it to be morally impossible, that I should not become attached to one who fixes his heart.—That heart is so large, that, occupy as much of it as you will, dear Miss Beaufort, I need not fear, that there should not be ample room enough left for me . . .
>
> I do not wonder at your being a little surprised at my turning an innocent shadow into a formidable giant—but the giant & shadow have both completely vanished from my imagination.[3]

[1] Frances Beaufort to ME, n.d. [about 8 Mar. 1798].

[2] Ibid., another letter.

[3] ME to Frances Beaufort, 11 Mar. 1798.

Maria was probably not yet quite so happy as this paragraph implies, but during the next month she came round:

Since that time [*her conversation with her aunt and cousin in January or early February*] my feelings & opinions, have entirely changed—I am sure not from any mean, I hope not from any inadequate motives—Undoubtedly the wish to please my father is the first & warmest wish of my soul, but I am incapable of playing the hypocrite—I could not pretend, even to please him, that I liked anyone living, one degree better than I really did—It is therefore delightful to me my dear Sophy to be able to tell you from the bottom of my heart that I love your friend, that I see her now with your eyes, that I am sensible you judged impartially of her, that she is exactly suited to my father, will increase his happiness a hundred fold & will never diminish his affection for me—Indeed he never in his life shewed me so much affection, so much confidence as he has done since he became attached to her—and his goodness which would have touched a heart of stone has left an impression on mine (which is not I hope a heart of stone) that never can be effaced—However I did not mean to talk to you of his goodness just at present—I meant to have told you by what means & by what degrees I became attached as I now am to Miss Beaufort—

In the first place her appearence and manner when she came to Edgeworthstown last Feby. radically convinced me that Sophy had judged rightly of the perfect *simplicity* & innocence of her mind—When this prejudice was gone I was disposed to think well of her—The extreme surprise she shewed when my father first expressed attachment to her was the perfect proof to me that she had less vanity & more artless integrity than I could have supposed possible in the same circumstances—My father, in the next place, has been so *very* kind as to let me see a great part of the correspondence, which has passed between them & has told me a vast number of circumstances, which only he could tell me that have layed Miss B—'s character & Disposition most thoroughly open to me—I have had strong proofs both of the excellence of her temper & the superiority of her understanding—a superiority which I had never *suspected*—My dear Sophy I thank you for your steadiness in supporting your better judgment, when you saw that it was not pleasing to me.[1]

The marriage took place in Dublin on Edgeworth's fifty-fourth birthday, 31 May 1798. By this time Maria was able to promise Frances that she would always treat her with the respect due to her father's wife—she would be 'gratefully exact *en belle*

[1] ME to Mrs. R and SR, Collon, 23 Apr. 1798.

*fille*'.[1] The Edgeworthstown convention of rather formal good manners and conversation was probably what made this successful triumvirate possible. For the situation did work out as Frances had hoped. She came back to Edgeworthstown that June as mistress of the household, and was welcomed affectionately by all her husband's children, including Maria.

Although family harmony was secured at the start, Richard Lovell and Frances were not able to settle down for several months to a normal domestic routine. On their way home from Dublin they saw the body of a hanged man dangling between the upturned shafts of a cart—a demonstration of the violence that was becoming more open than ever in the Irish midlands, to trouble and even endanger their lives in the months ahead.

Since Edgeworth's setbacks in 1796 he had become active once more in national politics; his avowed aim in acquiring a seat in Parliament was to campaign for better provision for the education of the poor in Ireland.[2] At home his principal concern was to try to save Catholics from victimization by his Protestant fellow magistrates; indeed, it was his lack of militancy as a justice of the peace that had by now made him an object of intense suspicion to the partisan Protestants in County Longford.

In 1796–7 the government had at last acceded to demands that provincial gentry should be empowered to raise a force of Yeomanry to police the countryside. At first liberal Whigs like Grattan and Charlemont were in favour of the idea, because they imagined that like the old Volunteers the Yeomanry could be made up of both Protestants and Catholics, and thus bring the moderates of both sides together. That it should be recruited from both sects was certainly the government intention, but

[1] ME to Frances Beaufort, 16 Mar. 1798; *Mem.*, i. 81.

[2] The pocket borough of St. John's Town belonged to Lord Granard, who normally sold it outright, leaving the member free to vote as he chose. In a good year such a borough would fetch about £2,000 (Edith M. Johnston, 'The Irish House of Commons in 1791', *Proceedings of the Royal Irish Academy*, 1957 (c)); but at the General Election of 1797 money was tight and the price was generally forced down to about £1,200. In 1797 Granard's political ally Newcomen was returned twice, for the county as well as for St. John's Town, which was why the seat was available for disposal the following February. RLE may have got it cheap; he may even have got it for nothing, if Granard thought his nuisance value in future county elections sufficient.

historians have never doubted that many Protestant gentlemen evaded their obligation to recruit Catholics.[1] Edgeworth goes further than this. He claims that it was the general practice in County Longford to recruit only Protestants, and that the Yeomanry, galloping about the county in all their new-made bravado, aggravated the situation as much or more than the Defenders themselves. While the Yeomen were known by the peasantry as 'scourers of the country',[2] Edgeworth had no desire to have a corps at Edgeworthstown. By 1798, however, the unrest in the county was genuinely so serious that he was forced to change his mind and begin recruiting. Needless to say the Edgeworthstown Yeomanry was not like any other corps in the neighbourhood. Edgeworth recruited Catholics indiscriminately with Protestants, and one of his own sons marched in the ranks. The result was that his band became a source not merely of dislike but of active suspicion on the part of what were now known as the Orangemen of Co. Longford.

A gentleman of similar cultural background to Edgeworth, like Beaufort, for example, could perfectly well understand how a man could have at one and the same time a Whiggish veneration for the Constitution, a desire to protect his country against the French, a hatred of the war and a belief in Catholic emancipation; it was only in the unstable conditions of the Irish countryside that Edgeworth's progressive views took on the colour of a dangerous extremism. The point was that although Edgeworth did not believe in subversion, and was not a United Irishman, many of his neighbours thought he was. His most deeply reasoned opinions, on the importance of building up the Irish economy, would have been understood perfectly well in commercial centres like Dublin and Belfast: but at home in the depths of the Irish countryside, problems were not seen in economic but in political or rather religious terms. Even Edgeworth's management of his own estate, far from being taken as a good lesson in economics, was interpreted as a flagrant example of his 'soft' political line.

Edgeworth and his family were thus dangerously isolated when the Rebellion came. The peasant rising of 1798 was at first confined mainly to Wexford, and during the summer months

[1] e.g. H. Senior, *Orangeism in Ireland and Britain*, 1966, p. 59.
[2] *Memoirs of RLE*, ii. 205.

the Irish midland counties were not in revolt, although individual outrages were common. But at last the French took their opportunity. An army led by General Humbert landed at Killala in County Mayo on 22 August 1798, and after inflicting a notable defeat on a large Anglo-Irish army at Castlebar, it advanced eastwards on a course which would take it through Co. Longford. At this encouragement the Catholic peasantry of Longford did take up arms, though somewhat uncertainly. According to Edgeworth, whose account once again lacks confirmation, the frightened and ill-informed Catholic peasantry panicked in the crisis because they were told (by, unfortunately, a Catholic tenant of Edgeworth's) that the Orangemen were about to massacre them—indeed, that the killing had already begun with the murder of a priest. Meanwhile, at the end of the first week in September, Edgeworth found himself in a desperate situation. He had his small band of loyal yeomanry, but no arms for them to fight with. Because of a general shortage, or some mistake in the Ordnance Department at Dublin, or, as he believed at the time, by the deliberate malice of his opponents in the county like Sir Thomas Fetherstone, the weapons for his corps had never arrived.[1] After committing his family and tenants to the side of law and order, he found himself alone with them in a rebel-held countryside, with neither the army nor the Longford yeomanry likely to rescue them.

On 7 September Edgeworth felt obliged to abandon his home and move both household and corps to the Protestant stronghold of Longford. The citizens immediately tried to expel the corps, who, for fear of their lives, dared not disperse to their homes in the rebel-held countryside.

After an anxious few hours, during which the French came to within a few miles of the town, an Anglo-Irish army under Lord Carhampton won the decisive battle near Granard. The victory was received by a frenzied outburst of popular emotion in Longford. An excited mob waylaid Edgeworth near his inn and tried to lynch him. Later it emerged that the crowd had been harangued by a sergeant of one of the Protestant bands of militia, who claimed that Edgeworth was a French spy and had been signalling to his allies from the roof of the town gaol. There was no doubt about the strength of feeling against him

[1] RLE to DAB, 29 Sept. 1798.

in Longford, for eleven days later 'the popular phrenzy' in the town continued 'in full force',[1] and Edgeworth's political opponents, who evidently included men of substance, were applying to Dublin to have his corps impeached.

Edgeworth removed his family next morning to their home, which, as though to confirm Protestant suspicions, had indeed been deliberately spared by the Catholic rebels. After the nightmarish scenes of mob frenzy they had met with at Longford, their return to Edgeworthstown House made an impression which Maria remembered vividly more than twenty years later:

> Within the house everything was as we had left it—a map that we had been consulting was still open on the library table, with pencils and slips of paper containing the first lessons in arithmetic in which some of the young people had been engaged the morning we had been driven from home; a pansy, in a glass of water, which one of the children had been copying, was still on the chimney-piece. These trivial circumstances, marking repose and tranquility, struck us at this moment with an unreasonable sort of surprise, and all that had passed seemed like an incoherent dream. The joy of having my father in safety remained, and gratitude to Heaven for his preservation. These feelings spread inexpressible pleasure over what seemed to be a new sense of existence. Even the most common things appeared delightful; the green lawn, the still groves, the birds singing, the fresh air, all external nature, and all the goods and conveniences of life, seemed to have wonderfully increased in value, from the fear into which we had been put of losing them irrecoverably.[2]

The Edgeworths' correspondence in September and October shows how deeply the family was affected by the incident at Longford. Maria wrote: 'I can talk think write of nothing but this affair my mind is so full of it.'[1] Meanwhile her father was pressing the Lord-Lieutenant through the new Chief Secretary, Lord Castlereagh, for a Court of Enquiry into the episode; and excitedly telling his new father-in-law what he would do if he did not get it:

> I have a remedy in my own power which is far preferable to any which he can apply—I mean an appeal to the English public— . . . We, that is to say Maria (who is always meant by we, when writing

[1] ME to SR, 19 Sept. 1798. [2] *Memoirs of RLE*, ii, 232.

is in question) have notes taken during every part of the transaction —which are interesting & which she can make entertaining—Nobody but a bogtrotter can after such an appeal think that I could be more than an idiot if I staid in a country where neither innocence nor patriotic exertion could be protected by the Government against a sanguinary party—I declare to you most solemnly that I have lived in Ireland from no other motive than a sense of duty & a desire to improve the circle round me—I shall lose about 10,000 pound sunk in this country by removal but I shall live the remainder of my life amongst men, instead of warring against savages.[1]

Beaufort in reply showed his usual calm good sense. He cleverly argued that by fleeing the country Edgeworth would be playing into the hands of his detractors:

The envy of some persons, who feel the superiority of your talents, the prejudices of others, who know only some singularities of your history, and the dislike of such acquaintance as esteem a man only in proportion to his conviviality,—will induce too many to believe and propagate every evil report that may be raised upon your leaving Ireland.[2]

That December the sergeant who led the mob was court martialled. The verdict was rather inconclusive, and Lord Oxmantown, one of Edgeworth's old political opponents, could be seen openly prompting the accused; but, although this was scarcely satisfactory, Beaufort did at last persuade Edgeworth to drop the subject. He even persuaded him that to some extent he was to blame for being misunderstood, because he had kept his family so self-absorbed. Edgeworth was brought to agree 'that he ought to mix more with society, and make himself more generally known in Ireland'.[3] Beaufort, who, although a moderate, was personally popular with all parties, did a lot in 1799 to persuade the gentry of the midland counties that they had been mistaken about Edgeworth. 'From his aimiable, popular character in Ireland, and from his extensive acquaintance, possessing peculiarly the power of serving his friends in society, Dr. Beaufort knew how to contradict the misrepresentations of party, and to rectify the mistakes of ignorance, without ever exposing those he loved to envy, by indiscreet praise. Such a friend was peculiarly advantageous to my

[1] RLE to DAB, 29 Sept. 1798. [2] DAB to RLE, 5 Oct. 1798.
[3] *Memoirs of RLE*, ii. 237.

father.'[1] So much so that after his fourth marriage Edgeworth was no longer an isolated figure in the Irish midlands, and his family slowly adapted to a normal social life in a circle of gentry with whom they had interests in common.

The events of 1798 were so disturbing that it was not until the following spring that Richard Lovell and Frances were able to go to England on their wedding trip, taking Maria with them. This should have been a landmark in her education; for during three weeks in April spent travelling in the Midlands on the way to London, she visited Keir and Darwin's son Robert, walked around several factories in the Birmingham area, and saw the great ironworks at Ketley Bank.

Undoubtedly Maria was interested in the factories (her stepmother, who wrote long and lucid accounts of the trip, called some of the machinery at Ketley Bank 'beautiful as well as sublime');[2] and among the Keirs especially she made some lifelong friends. Yet this visit to England is most remarkable for the slightness of the contribution it made to Maria's experience, at least as reflected in what she afterwards wrote. Although she and her father had established themselves as educationalists in 1798 with the publication of *Practical Education*, they met no one of interest to them in London except Mrs. Barbauld.[3] After sightseeing and visiting galleries, museums, and a mechanical exhibition, they set off for Clifton, where on 5 June Mrs. Frances Edgeworth gave birth to her first child, a girl, also christened Frances but known in the family (like her mother) as Fanny.

Again, Bristol might have been expected to give Maria some new and perhaps more literary acquaintances, since their hosts

[1] Ibid., ii. 261–2. An enlightened Anglican clergyman who acts as a benevolent peacemaker among the hot-tempered partisans of the Irish political scene appears in ME's novel *Ormond*. (Dr. Cambrai). As even the French name indicates, he is intended for a portrait of Dr. Beaufort. See below, p. 383.

[2] Mrs. FE to DAB, Hill Top, nr. Birmingham, 23 Apr. 1799; Nat. Lib. of Ireland, MS. 13, 176 (4). In a letter to her sister Louisa Beaufort of 29 Apr. 1799 she spoke of the whip-making they had seen in Birmingham as 'a very beautiful manufacture'. Few of ME's letters from this visit have survived—none from the Midlands part of the tour—so that her stepmother's reactions have to stand in as a rough indication of her own.

[3] Anna Laetitia Barbauld (1743–1825), was introduced to the Edgeworths through the Keirs, and paid them two separate visits, one at their lodgings off the Strand and one at Clifton. She later corresponded with ME. See below, p. 220 n.

were Anna and Thomas Beddoes. In retrospect, however, Maria did not take Anna's circle at quite their own valuation: she later wrote in passing of 'self-opinionated provincialists of the Bristol school'.[1] As far as literature went Bristol's best days were over by 1799; Coleridge, Southey, and Thomas Wedgwood (who had stayed a year in 1797 with Dr. and Mrs. Beddoes as a friend and patient) had now all gone elsewhere.

The Edgeworths were probably more interested in the talented scientists with whom Beddoes had surrounded himself. The medical side of the Institution was superintended by the Swiss-born physician John King, who subsequently planned with Beddoes, but never executed, a major work on physiology. King wanted to marry Emmeline, although Edgeworth felt that it was socially and financially anything but a brilliant match. For nearly a year the chemical experiments which were the other side of the Institution's activities had been superintended by a twenty-one-year-old Cornishman, Humphry Davy; and Edgeworth, noticing his exceptional talent, characteristically gave him some fatherly advice. Davy's first biographer gives the decorous version of this conversation: 'When he was a very young man at Clifton, unknown to fame, Mr. E early distinguished and warmly admired his talents, and gave him much counsel, which sank deep into his mind.'[2] Dr. Paris had approached Maria for her recollections of this and other meetings, and presumably he was quoting what she told him. She was placed in an awkward situation, as she explained privately to her stepsister Fanny: 'I know no anecdotes of him fit for publication—I could not well furnish Dr. P with the only one I know that my father advised Sir H. early not to tell lies —and that he really did not *hate* him for it afterwards—I am not sure that he took his advice.'[3]

At the end of July Edgeworth, his wife, Maria, and the baby Fanny left Clifton for home, again taking a leisurely tour through the Midlands. At Birmingham with the Keirs once more, Mrs. Edgeworth was enthusiastic about their circle: 'I hope I shall see some more of the wonderful people of this neighbourhood as we do not go away till Monday. Watts [*sic*]

[1] ME to Mrs. FE, 23 Jan. 1822; *Letters from England*, p. 330.

[2] J. A. Paris, *Life of Sir Humphry Davy*, 1831, p. 59.

[3] ME to Fanny Wilson, 19 Feb. 1830.

and Bolton [*sic*] are as well worth seeing as the fire Engine that goes by their name.'[1]

Edgeworth and Maria went off by themselves to visit Erasmus Darwin and his family at Derby. Maria had not seen Darwin since she was a schoolgirl; it was their last meeting, for he died in 1802.

In expecting English literary life or the astonishing industrial landscapes of the Midlands to leave their mark on the mature Maria Edgeworth, one is demanding something of her that she never gave. Once or twice in her letters she attempts descriptions of industrial scenes; but the best known of them, an account of a visit to a Welsh copper factory in 1802, suspiciously resembles a painting composed by, perhaps, Wright of Derby. 'At first nothing but the sound of dripping water, then a robin began to sing among the rafters of the high and strange roof. The manufactory in which the men were at work was a strong contrast to this desolate place, a stunning noise, Cyclops with bared arms dragging sheets of red-hot copper, and thrusting it between the cylinders to flatten it. . . .'[2] Probably she was being consciously derivative when she wrote this, for Maria had little visual imagination, and knew it;[3] she disliked describing places, and when confronted with the technological miracles of her day she seems to have been genuinely puzzled as to what her response should be. Should she marvel at the achievements of science? or should she recoil, as well she might, at the dirt, the noise, and the inhuman scale of it all? Her best treatment by far of industrial England occurs in the late and little-read *Harry and Lucy Concluded*, in a scene in which she honestly presents her divided response—through the boy Harry, who resembles Edgeworth, a sense of admiration at the practical achievement; through the more literary girl, Lucy, a reaction akin to horror. Both children are impressed when they travel at night through a country in which flames seem to burst from

[1] Mrs. FE to Louisa Beaufort, Hill Top, nr. Birmingham, 27 July 1799.

[2] ME to SR, Loughborough, 25 Sept. 1802; *Mem.*, i. 111. In an undated letter to SR of 1801 she gave a vivid account of a trip down a coal-mine; but this was had at second hand from a visitor to Edgeworthstown.

[3] RLE told her she had 'no taste—and no Eyes'. In referring ruefully to this accusation, ME added: 'I am learning the use of my eyes main fast; and make no doubt please Heaven I live to be sixty I [shall] see as well as my neighbours' (ME to Mrs. R, 18 Nov. 1793). Her expectations were on the whole justified; see below, pp. 430–1.

the ground—'their deep red colour and pointed shape appeared against the dark night, far and wide as the eye could reach'. When they return next day they discover that it is the countryside surrounding a foundry, and an appalling place it is:

. . . they saw only a black dreary waste, with half burning, half smothering heaps of dross, coal and cinders. Clouds of smoke of all colours, white, yellow, and black, from the chimneys of founderies and forges darkening the air; the prospect they could not see, for there was none. It was a dead flat, the atmosphere laden with the smell of coal and smoke. The grass, the hedges, the trees, all blackened. The hands and faces of every man, woman, and child they met, begrimed with soot! The very sheep blackened! not a lamb even with a lock of white wool, or a clean face. Lucy said, that it was the most frightful country she had ever beheld.[1]

This, no doubt, is what the twentieth-century reader expects from a nineteenth-century spectator of an industrializing world. But it was written at a significantly late stage in Maria Edgeworth's career, and nothing like it appears in the novels she wrote earlier, in the first two decades of the century; nor do other novelists use this type of material until the 1840s. Compared with either Mrs. Gaskell or Dickens, therefore, Maria Edgeworth is not a novelist of the industrial revolution at all—or, rather, she is not one on their terms; she neither employs industrial settings, nor does the sense of revulsion characteristic of the second quarter of the century find any expression in her fiction.

On the other hand, the echo in her earlier description of Wright of Derby is not a matter of chance. Graphic artists were interested in industrial scenes from the mid eighteenth century, and in the 1760s and 1770s pictures were painted which better convey the Edgeworths' attitude to the external world than any literature of the period. This is the era of George Stubbs's *Anatomy of the Horse* (1766), a lucid, exact series of scientific studies of their subject; of Wright's *Philosopher giving that Lecture on the Orrery, in which a Lamp is put in place of the Sun* (1766) and *The Iron Forge* (1772), works which for all their classicism, and their touches of sentiment, enter direct into the real world of the Lunar industrialists; and the sunny, factual, harmonious drawings of the leading topographical artist, Paul Sandby

[1] *Harry and Lucy Concluded*, 1825, ii. 164–5.

(1721–98).[1] These first painters of the industrial revolution are detailed and objective; they paint the everyday working world, but at the same time present it against a landscape, and within an over-all composition, in which machines are perfectly in harmony: one is reminded of Mrs. Edgeworth's enthusiasm for steam-powered lifting gear which was 'beautiful as well as sublime'. Many an industrial design of the period perfectly conveys the Lunar ideology, by coupling scientific detail with the clarity and serenity typical of the still classical perspective of an age of Enlightenment. Maria inherited the same habits of thought: which explains why, although she saw much to interest her in England in 1799, she saw nothing to divert the direction in which her career as a novelist would develop. Her interest in the detail of how people of all classes spoke, dressed, acted; her almost sociological awareness that, however remarkable as individuals, people are studied most revealingly in terms of what they do to get their bread; all this, an interest in society rather than in place, was what made Maria Edgeworth typical of her time and was to make her significant in the development of the novel. And her attitude to people and society was not learned, it is clear, first-hand at Ketley Bank in 1799, but had already been absorbed during two decades of reading and listening, at home at Edgeworthstown.

[1] The Lunar group were in direct contact with many of these artists. Wedgwood, for example, who as a potter was an influential patron of art in the Midlands, commissioned paintings from both Stubbs and Wright, and numerous views of country houses and gardens from various topographical artists for the table service he made for the Empress Catherine of Russia.

# III

## A NOVELIST FOR THE NURSERY[1]

MARIA EDGEWORTH had begun to write stories by the time she was twelve, probably as literary exercises to improve her command of form and style. When her father asked her to write a tale for him, he suggested that the result should be 'about the length of a Spectator';[2] and the sententious Addisonian essay in the old-fashioned Addisonian style was probably the model they both had in mind. Clearly the entertaining tales of horror and adventure with which Maria regaled her schoolfellows at night had no connection with the literary pieces she composed by day.[3] Two or three fables for her father are the lightest of her recorded schoolgirl writings. The others consist of the 'dialogue on happiness' for Day, and, for Edgeworth again, the 'enquiry into the causes of poverty in Ireland'.[4]

Edgeworth's first request to Maria to write a story for him came in 1779: 'I send you part of an Arabian fable which I beg you to finish.'[5] The first story mentioned in the *Memoir* was written in April 1780, also at Edgeworth's suggestion. The subject he set was 'Generosity', and although the text did not survive Maria Edgeworth retained two useful impressions of it. One was that the contents did not match the title—and 'Where's the Generosity?' became a byword in family criticism. The second was that the style at times fell below eighteenth-century standards of exactness: there was, Maria remembered, 'a sentence of inextricable confusion between a man, a saddle, and a horse'.[6]

A single tale that she wrote in this early Addisonian manner did survive, to be published by an enterprising editor when she had made her name.[7] *The Mental Thermometer*, which is said to have been written when Maria Edgeworth was sixteen—

[1] E. V. Lucas, *Old Fashioned Tales*, 1905, p. ix.
[2] RLE to ME, 25 May 1780; *Mem.*, i. 8.
[3] See above, pp. 54–5.
[4] See above, p. 90.
[5] See above, p. 57.
[6] *Mem.*, i. 8.
[7] Juvenile Library, 1801, vol. ii.

that is, in 1784—is probably a fair guide to the style and quality of her juvenilia. The genre is that of the fashionable didactic tale, the main characters a young man and his elderly friend, a London merchant. The atmosphere of the fable is remote, the time unspecified, and the style, although admirably correct, very stiff by comparison with her later writing. The characters engage in long debates about who is happiest, and why. The older man gives the younger a present, a remarkable thermometer which, when held against the user, can tell him at what moment in his recent past he experienced his purest sensation of pleasure.[1] Once the use of the thermometer has been explained, the fable suddenly ends. Perhaps she once had it in mind to send her hero about the world, like Candide or Rasselas, in search of the secrets of felicity; if so she forgot her design, and was surprised long afterwards to be told that the story seemed unfinished.[2]

A more substantial literary attempt was the translation of Mme de Genlis's *Adèle et Théodore* which Edgeworth set Maria to work on within a month of their arrival at Edgeworthstown in 1782. Once again, the piece was undertaken primarily as an exercise; translation was another way of testing the precision and elegance of her English. The months that she spent toiling over Mme de Genlis's long text were undoubtedly a useful preparation for a writer. So was her father's insistence that she should get to the end of any task she took up, no matter how uncongenial it became.[3] She must have thrown herself with great energy into 'Adelaide and Theodore', since she completed the rough translation of one of the three proposed volumes in July and August, 1782. Polishing and revision, supervised by her father, took up the rest of the year. This was an aspect of authorship that Edgeworth was always to lay great stress on.[4] At times, as in this case, he found it a form of drudgery: 'it is not only a laborious but a very humble office to correct the writings of

[1] There is an obvious connection between the theme of this story and the 'dialogue on happiness' composed in 1782 for Day. ME's question to Fanny about the degree of pleasure she experienced in a ballroom is also presumably part of the same train of thought. See above, p. 74.

[2] i.e. to Dr. Aikin, brother of Mrs. Barbauld. CSE to RLE, 26 May 1807; Nat. Lib. of Ireland, MS. 13,176 (15).

[3] *Memoirs of RLE*, ii. 341.

[4] See below, p. 291.

another.'[1] Nevertheless he went over the first volume word by word, as he was to do with everything she wrote for publication in his lifetime.

While the first volume was at the printer's in London, the Edgeworths learnt of a rival version. Maria fulfilled her promise that she would go on to the end, although it now seemed likely that her translation would never appear before the public. 'I had just finished the third volume when a rival translation appeared in all its glory—one volume however is printed & my father thinks of compressing the two others into one & publishing them in Dublin.'[2] The new plan cannot have been carried out, for Edgeworth did not do the necessary work on the rough part of the translation. Many years later, in 1818, one of Maria's half-brothers, Charles Sneyd Edgeworth, proposed to publish Maria's complete translation of *Adèle et Théodore*. One of his other sisters warned him that although they did have a copy of the first volume, he would find the rest of the work in poor condition. 'You must remember that the first volume was the only one which had been corrected by my father—the two others were never looked over and therefore Maria fears will give you a great deal of trouble.'[3] This plan, like the earlier ones, came to nothing, and *Adelaide and Theodore* in Maria's version has apparently ceased to exist, either in print or in manuscript.

Although abortive in itself, her year of concentrated effort on the work of Mme de Genlis had the useful effect of bringing Maria into partnership with her father, as well as introducing her to a number of themes which were to recur regularly over the years in her own fiction.[4] *Adèle et Théodore* is, briefly, an

[1] RLE to ME, 3 Dec. 1782.

[2] ME to Fanny Robinson, 15 Aug. 1783. There is no known copy of the first volume which ME describes here as printed in London.

[3] Honora Edgeworth to CSE, 31 Oct. 1818. ME suggested that her brother should wait until Mme de Genlis's work was more in demand. Some time in the mid nineteenth century CSE found, on a Dublin bookstall, a copy of a translation of *Adèle et Théodore* bearing the imprint of the Dublin bookseller Luke White. Inside, strangely enough, were MS. corrections in RLE's hand. (M. Pakenham Edgeworth to Harriet Butler, n.d. [*c.* 1860].) But since three volumes of the translation published by Luke White are still in existence, it is difficult to see how this version can have been ME's, even though Pakenham Edgeworth believed it was.

[4] Stéphanie Félicité Brulart de Genlis, Marchioness de Sillery (1746–1830), was mistress to the Duc de Chartres, Philippe Egalité, and tutor to his children. Many of her educational ideas derived ultimately from Locke, but her work represented

exposition of educational theory and practice, purporting to be an exchange of letters between a lady who has retired to the country to devote herself to her children's education, and the lady's sophisticated friend in the capital. This format must have had a particular appeal to the Edgeworths in the first months of their retirement to the Irish countryside. So perfectly does it coincide with their own taste for experimental education in a domestic environment that echoes of *Adèle et Théodore* recur in novels written twenty or even thirty years later. Both *Letters of Julia and Caroline* (part of *Letters for Literary Ladies*, 1795) and *Leonora* (1805) resemble it in form as well as in content, and Madame de Genlis's virtuous domesticated matron may be a prototype for the most typical heroine of Maria's early novels.

Although *Adelaide and Theodore* thus eventually bore literary fruit, at the time it looked more like the end of Maria's career as an authoress. News that she was going into print reached Thomas Day, and greatly annoyed him. In spite of his progressive opinions on other issues, he passionately disapproved of female authorship, which did not coincide with his ideal of feminine simplicity: 'At one time, he was nearly of Sir Anthony Absolute's opinion, that the extent of a woman's erudition should consist in her knowing her simple letters, without their mischievous combinations.'[1]

When the publication of *Adelaide and Theodore* was cancelled, Day sent Edgeworth a sardonic letter of congratulation, which 'contained an eloquent philippic against female authorship'. Edgeworth wrote back and the correspondence, or Maria's memory of it, afterwards inspired the first part of *Letters for Literary Ladies*.[2] Edgeworth had never agreed with Day's views about the role of women, nor did he accept that women should not be authors, but he was too fond of Day to pursue a plan which aroused his violent disapproval. For the rest of Day's lifetime, therefore, he gave up his intention of turning Maria into an authoress.

At the same time he did not give up her education: he was urging Maria to read widely and experiment with writing. Exactly what she chose to imitate was left to her, but Edgeworth

at the same time so determined an effort to make Rousseau's system practicable that she shared the vogue still enjoyed by that writer in France and England.

[1] *Memoirs of RLE*, ii. 342.

[2] See below, p. 173.

intervened to ban one area of experiment. It was originally her father's view, and not Maria's own, that she should leave novels alone for the time being. In spite of her admiration for *Evelina*, he forbade her to read the newly published *Cecilia*.[1] Just at this time Fanny Robinson had the good fortune to meet Fanny Burney, now in the full blaze of her reputation as a novelist; and Maria, despite her father's attitude to *Cecilia*, inquired wistfully whether there was any hope that the authoress would enter into a correspondence with a young lady in Ireland. But Miss Burney was apparently not interested, and Maria had to content herself with self-improvement through the printed page.

Apart from the forbidden novels, her taste was catholic and her appetite tremendous. After the impressive programme of political economy and constitutional law which she undertook during her first summer in Ireland,[2] she was, by September 1783, deep in European history. After finishing the Abbé Raynal's *Anecdotes historiques, militaires et politiques de l'Europe*, she was reading Voltaire's *History of the Russian Empire under Peter the Great*, after which she proposed to go on to the same author's *History of Charles XII, King of Sweden*.[3] She had recently read Adam Smith's *Theory of Moral Sentiments* (and warmly recommended it to Fanny). At the same time she was immersed in French plays. By August she had read Mercier, by September Molière and some of Marivaux: '—You see I read several Books on different subjects at a time, not at once, did you ever try this method. I think you would find it succeed. Change of Employment refreshes without relaxing the mind.'[4]

It was in this area, of lighter literature, and plays in particular, that her own early attempts were concentrated. Although she was reading so much French theatre, she had reservations about some of its conventions:[4]

> . . . Moliere's [plays] entertained me much. The plots of all I have yet read of Marivaux I think too much alike & too uninteresting; indeed that is a fault I have met with in most French plays—the waiting women & valets are mere machinery to help the author through his plot and to bring their Masters and Mistresses in spite of fate together.[4]

[1] See above, p. 73, and ME to Fanny Robinson, 15 Aug. 1783.

[2] See above, p. 90.

[3] ME to Fanny Robinson, 15 Sept. 1783.

[4] Ibid. The punctuation of this copy is not necessarily ME's own.

It is interesting that her main criticism of French theatre was its absence of realism, or perhaps of humanity, in depicting the lower orders of society. The few English plays she read at this time, such as Addison's *The Drummer* and some of Sheridan, were not much better in this respect. Maria's objection to the practice of making mere dramatic conveniences of footmen and waiting-maids remained firm, and the plays she was to publish herself in later life departed from the more formal convention by characterizing members of the middle and lower classes:

The *popular plays* as we think of calling them have in them a mixture both of high & low life & endeavour to represent the follies of both & the connexion between both classes such as they really are in the world not as they are too often represented on the stage—where servants are only *machines* for carrying on the intrigues of the play or the intrigues of their masters & mistresses—From *fashionable* plays either of this day or even Congreve's or Farqhar's time the middle classes of society can surely learn nothing but a taste for profligacy—for laughing at *age* at fathers & husbands &c—Besides most of the characters are merely stage characters—like nothing that is or ought to be in real life—Yet as you say the middle & poorer classes have a taste for the drama & why shd not an attempt be made to afford them innocent amusement.[1]

Her first attempt at a natural middle-class comedy was written as early as 1786. But while she was still under the influence of established stage tradition the manner she adopted was portentous. Her first play was to have been called *Anticipation, or the Countess*. Maria sent a few sample scenes to Fanny, demanding to be told frankly what faults her friend saw in the performance. 'Are the gossips overdone? or would they *take* on the stage?'[2]

Fanny's negative was so devastating that Maria immediately destroyed every sheet of the play except one, which was required to do penitential duty as a paper pattern for a cap. She declared that Fanny had cured her 'of the Mania of Playwriting at least for the Winter season'.[3] But a year later she was describing her plans for more plays of her own—'and I am indeed just beginning a tragedy founded upon an anecdote in the life of Hyder Ali Mirza'. There followed two pages about the plot, a tangle of

[1] ME to Mrs. R, n.d. [1815 or 1816]; with reference to *Comic Dramas*, 1817.
[2] ME to Fanny Robinson, 15 Sept. 1783 [copy].
[3] Ibid., 6 Dec. 1783.

gallantry, villainy, and heroic deeds, which suggest that in action as in setting the proposed tragedy would have been a kind of pastiche of Dryden's *Aurengzebe*.[1]

Apparently the tragedy shared the fate of the comedy, for it is not referred to elsewhere. At this point there is a two-year gap in the evidence about what Maria was writing, and then, from 1786, a complete play survives. This is the unpublished *Double Disguise*, which was acted by the family at Edgeworthstown before Lord and Lady Longford at Christmas 1786.[2]

*The Double Disguise*, although in itself no more than unpretentious family entertainment, marks an important step in Maria Edgeworth's literary development. It is the first example of her consistent practice of turning her literary models into a more natural product, featuring ordinary people going about their common everyday business. She placed her characters in middle and low life, and set the action in a humdrum inn on the road between Liverpool and London. The plot is admittedly a mere vehicle, the conventional stage idea of a soldier returning from the wars in two successive disguises to test the fidelity of his lady.[3] Maria was further constrained by the duty to provide a suitable part for everyone in the household old enough to learn their lines. She cast herself as an English servant girl of the inn where the scene was set. The twelve-year-old Honora, the family's most accomplished actress, was the flighty heroine, Anna her gentle cousin, whose virtue wins the hero in the end. But it was in composing an appropriate part for her father that Maria interestingly stumbled on what was to become her particular vein. Edgeworth was a keen mimic, and liked entertaining his family with impressions of the Irish characters he met. The part Maria wrote for him was her first Irish sketch—

[1] ME to Fanny Robinson, 18 Dec. 1784.

[2] *Memoirs of RLE*, ii. 79–81. RLE describes the play in a letter to Darwin probably written early in 1787. The *Mem.* wrongly puts the performance in 1790, when Honora was dead. Mrs. Emmeline Gibbons, daughter of Maria's sister Emmeline, who inherited the MSS., understood that the performance was in '1778 or 9', which is impossibly early. The two MS. copies of the play, with cast-list of family actors, are in the Goschen deposit, Bodleian Library, Oxford (Dep. c. 134).

[3] ME liked this device of an arbiter for all the characters, who remains in disguise until the closing moments. She used it again in two later plays, *The Grinding Organ* (written 1808, published 1827) and *The Absentee* (written 1811 and published as a story 1812).

Justice Cocoa, a Tipperary grocer who has risen in the world and become an enthusiastic officer in the Volunteers.[1]

The change in manner between *The Mental Thermometer* and *The Double Disguise* is so great that it needs accounting for. There is no evidence that Maria Edgeworth ever engaged in conscious literary experiment; the two principal sources of pressure on her as a writer were, first, her wide-ranging, scientific, essentially factual education, and secondly an emotional dependence on her family that led her to produce work that was particularly likely to be well received by them.

This is not to say that she was exempt from literary fashion, or that any writer could be. In the very decade in which she was reacting against artifice in the drama and the tale, both Cowper (*The Task*, 1785) and Crabbe (*The Village*, 1783) were reacting against artifice in the pastoral poem:

I paint the Cot,
As truth will paint it, and as Bards will not.

The broad temper of the times was moving writers towards a more frank and detailed realism, and the Edgeworth family's tremendous appetite for fact was in itself merely a symptom of this. Nevertheless, it was the family climate of opinion that immediately influenced Maria; she was unaware at the time of truly contemporary English poetry, and, characteristically, she was never to put the case for realism in strictly literary terms.[2]

On her own account and as a teacher, she was consuming a very high proportion of non-fiction—science, travel, history, biography, and political economy. And, perhaps even more important, she was consciously trying to improve her manner as a letter-writer, a fact which helped both her style and her sense of intimacy with the reader. In spite of Edgeworth's complaints, Maria had come home from school with her 'missy' formulae intact, and for the first year her letters to Fanny Robinson are dreadfully correct. Luckily she soon fell under the

[1] See above, p. 125.

[2] For her attitude to 'truth' in literature, see below, Ch. V. Later in life, as ME gradually acquired rather more reading among the poets, both Cowper and Crabbe became favourites (see below, p. 219). It is also in keeping that one of the few poems she mentions repeatedly is Gay's *Trivia*—his 'town eclogue', which paints a scene so much at variance with the idealized countryside of literary convention.

influence of one of the most relaxed and agreeable letter-writers of the period, the best model she could have had:

> What easy sprightly letters Greys [*sic*] are . . . I daresay you have seen them.—They are not the stiff performances of an author written under the rod of Criticism and under the *Pressentiment* [*sic*] that they would be published as Authors letters usually are—All that I have ever seen of Pope's gave me that idea, the Style is too correct to be free & the Wit is too labored to be pleasing.[1]

At this date, however, Maria did expect her letters, if not to be published, at least to be passed around. She was even urging Fanny to show her correspondence to her critics at school, which meant that she had to take care to show herself to best advantage—prudent, serious-minded, and not 'satirical'.[2] After reading Gray's letters she abandoned some of the stiffness, replacing it at first with an equally self-conscious sprightliness:

> So many things come into my head when I think I have done with you that my postcripts are almost as long as my letters. Besides a post script is a most convenient receptacle for odd questions & odd thoughts—pell mell—
>
> So Miss Burlton's gone or going—You know she was always very fond of singing 'When I am a Widow, oh then! oh then!' Query) Was there aught prophetic in the song?
>
> Lord Lord how I have forgot my *prudence* within this twelvemonth![3]

It was several years, perhaps about a decade, before she developed her own mature manner as a letter-writer. A graceful easy style appears quite early, but what she also worked for, and took some time achieving, was the *persona* she wanted to present within the family, to her father and to the Ruxtons particularly.[4] She developed a real hatred of having her letters shown around because her ambition was to communicate freely with her aunt and Sophy, not with the world in general. Her subordination of everything like news and ideas to the central purpose of conveying a lively, likeable personality meant that she also had to

[1] ME to Fanny Robinson, 15 Aug. 1783 (copy). ME had just been reading Mason's *Life of Gray*, the first literary biography to make extensive use of letters.

[2] ME to Fanny Robinson, Aug. 1782 [copy].

[3] ME to Fanny Robinson, letter begun 15 Sept. 1783 (copy).

[4] See above, p. 113.

suppress the derivative literary element in her early letters, in order to be, or seem to be, simply 'natural'.[1]

The same impulse towards naturalness begins to show itself in the mid 1780s in her story-writing. *The Bracelets* (*c.* 1787) is the first story she set among children in day-to-day circumstances, and presented in her plain thoughtful narrative manner. In a way it is not a story for children at all, but a slice of fictionalized autobiography.[2] Even so, the homely style and setting connect it with better later work, and explain why it is the only story written in the 1780s which she thought it appropriate to publish in *The Parent's Assistant.*

But she had not yet found the formula of her successful stories of the 1790s, which, like the letters she wrote in that period, seem 'natural' because they are deliberately aimed at her own domestic circle. Her earliest stylistic ideals, precision, clarity, and elegance, came from the French authors she was reading and translating in 1782 to 1785—the playwrights, the writers for children, perhaps Voltaire, certainly Marmontel. This was an adult manner, appropriate if she was writing a story for herself, her father, and one or two other sympathetic grown-ups to read. (Daniel Augustus Beaufort, visiting Edgeworthstown in October 1787, recorded in his journal that 'Miss E. obliged me with a perusal of her Bracelets'.[3]) Her first attempt to write for the whole family was *The Double Disguise*, which she made suitably broad and popular. Within a few years the family demand for her stories was so great that she had changed her narrative style as well to suit it.

On many occasions, especially in the evening, or when an invalid had to be entertained, the most appropriate form of communal activity at Edgeworthstown was to listen to a book or story. In 1788 or 1789, when Mrs. Edgeworth was recovering from a confinement, Edgeworth amused the circle of adults and children with a saga of his own invention about a family of numerous children who went out into the world and experienced all kinds of exciting and romantic adventures. *The Freeman Family* was such a success that Maria wrote it down. As she

[1] See above, pp. 127–8. [2] See above, pp. 53–4.

[3] Journal in possession of Trinity College, Dublin, MS. K. 6. 57, p. 78. A MS. of *The Bracelets*, copied in four different unknown hands, is in the Bodleian Library, Oxford (MS. Eng. Misc. d. 647). See Mrs. C. E. Colvin, 'Maria Edgeworth's Literary Manuscripts in the Bodleian Library', *The Bodleian Library Record*, viii, 1970.

and her father rode together round the estate in the mornings, she would check the details to make sure that she remembered them correctly from the night before. Later, as the story became hers rather than his, she invented on her own account, until many years later Edgeworth's old tale served as a framework for her longest novel, *Patronage.*[1]

In the 1780s books for children suddenly became what they have been ever since, a substantial part of the booksellers' trade. It was not only Edgeworth who had noticed in the decade before the almost complete dearth of good reading-matter for children of the literate classes, and others had also been ready to follow the lead offered by Mrs. Barbauld's *Lessons.* A public that was increasingly mindful of the arts of domesticity, and moreover had been educated whether by Locke or Rousseau to recognize the importance of early education, was eager for simply written books that would be responsible as well as entertaining. If Edgeworth and Honora had published in 1780, they would have been among the pioneer writers of educational fiction for children. As it was, in the 1780s dozens of other authors took the field: the bookseller John Marshall, who in the early days almost cornered the market in instructional juvenile literature, listed no less than seventy books for children between 1780 and 1790.

Marshall's authors were headed by a group of redoubtable women, Mrs. Trimmer, the Kilner sisters, and Eleanor Fenn. The purpose of their writing was narrowly didactic, as Mrs. Trimmer made clear in the Preface to her *Fabulous Histories* of 1786 (better known to generations of children as *The History of the Robins*). Although these conversational birds, Dicksy, Flapsy, and Pecksy, became part of the folklore of innumerable families, the Edgeworths among them,[2] the author meant her fables 'to convey moral instruction applicable to themselves [*i.e. the children*], at the same time that they excite compassion and tenderness for those interesting and delightful creatures, on

[1] The first rough version of this story was finished as early as 1790. Maria then rewrote it between Nov. 1793 and May 1794, and she took it to England to work on again in 1799. All this time it appears to have been intended as a story for children. She used the same framework for one of her *Popular Tales—The Contrast—* published in 1804, and finally began work on the novel in 1809. Her father's version remained, she said, the most entertaining. *Memoirs of RLE*, ii. 344.

[2] See ME's allusion to it in her letter of May 1813, describing Étienne Dumont, which is quoted below, pp. 227–8.

which such wanton cruelties are frequently inflicted, and recommend *universal benevolence*'. This was all very well, but Mrs. Trimmer and her kind were too crude as moralists, and (as this quotation suggests) wrote too badly, to satisfy the standards at Edgeworthstown. Thomas Day's *Sandford and Merton*, 1783–9, with its considerable intellectual content and its sharp, secular spirit of social criticism, must have been far more to Edgeworth's taste. But even Day's book had a disadvantage compared with the ideal Edgeworth had tried to work out in the later 1770s: it was too Rousseauistic and theoretical.[1] The same objection could be raised against the two French authors who of all writers for children were probably most read at Edgeworthstown. Mme de Genlis gave only a thin narrative or dramatic cover to the ideas she had culled from Locke and Rousseau; and Berquin, though from a literary point of view more attractive, created children as precious and unworldly as figures from Watteau.[2] Since almost no books written in England except Day's aimed at this kind of intellectual standard, cultivated parents could only welcome the French pioneers. But the Edgeworths, who had been keeping their record designed to track the mental growth of real-life children, could not be unaware of the gap between the actual experience of Lovell, Bessy, Henry, and Charlotte, and even the best of the books they read.

*The Freeman Family* and presumably *The Bracelets* proved that Edgeworth and Maria could devise stories of their own which were more vivid and comprehensible to the audience of children. Maria now set out to invent a whole series of tales that met these requirements. Her attempts were written down on a slate, and only copied out on to paper if they had the approval of the family audience. Among the earliest to survive this test were *Dog Trusty* and *The Orange Man*, which according to the *Memoir* were written in 1790 or 1791.[3] The stories were not only for the Edgeworthstown children; in 1791 Margaret Ruxton, youngest of Maria's cousins, who was then about twelve, 'commissioned' Maria to write stories for her, and as usual Maria was glad to meet a request from Black Castle.

[1] See above, pp. 58–60.

[2] ME was reading groups of tales by each in 1784, Mme de Genlis's *Veillées du Chateau*, and Berquin's *Ami des Enfants*.

[3] *Mem.*, i. 21. These stories were first published in *The Parent's Assistant* in 1796, but from 1801 they appeared as part of the more juvenile *Early Lessons*.

When after Day's death Edgeworth no longer had scruples about letting Maria be an authoress, the field of children's literature was the obvious one. Other publishers were keen to break into Marshall's profitable near-monopoly, and they approached many writers, including Lamb, Ann and Jane Taylor, and Mrs. Sherwood, to turn their hands to books for children. Although seldom reviewed, juvenile books were listed in the magazines among new publications, so that even in Ireland, and without literary contacts in London, the Edgeworths cannot have been unaware of the tremendous growth in interest in this field where they had been privately assembling so much material.[1]

All Maria's early tales for children are quite unlike the 1780 *Practical Education*,[2] which comes into the category of an educational tool, not primarily a story. Even so, that pilot effort was not forgotten, and in 1791 Maria and her father apparently began to think of reviving the whole plan which Edgeworth and Honora had worked out: a series, that is, which would include a general essay on education for adults as well as reading books for children. As far as the stories at least went, it was Maria who set the pace: 'I am . . . very glad to hear that you are inclined to increase our three volumes—I beg you to encourage this propensity as it will add exceedingly to your happiness and to mine.'[3]

The thought that she was contributing to their joint happiness was just what was most likely to spur Maria on. It would have been too devious for her to calculate coldly that she had to find a new device if she was to maintain the large share of her father's attention which she had enjoyed in 1782–5. All the same, the younger children of the third marriage were now growing up to claim his time—Bessy, born 1781, Henry, born

[1] F. J. Harvey Darton produces interesting evidence of the high sales of Marshall's leading writers, and the best of their rivals, in the 1790s. 'Fifteen hundred to two thousand was usually the first printing, and the majority of the works mentioned here went into three or four reprints, or were amalgamated with others and perpetuated in a new form' (*Children's Books in England*, 1932, p. 169). Although there is little evidence about the size of edition of ME's first collections of stories, the rest of Darton's observations certainly apply to her. The best of her children's tales remained popular well into the nineteenth century, and indeed outlasted her work for adults. See Appendix B, p. 491.

[2] See above, pp. 63–4.

[3] RLE to ME, Clifton, 25 Sept. 1791.

1782, Charlotte, born 1783, and Sneyd, born 1786. Helping to teach them was a useful contribution Maria could make, but it did not bring her into proximity with her father. The peculiar advantage of writing stories for publication was that it restored her to the status of pupil, since he supervised and corrected everything she wrote. If they really produced another *Practical Education* together, it even made her a kind of amanuensis for her father, who had done the theoretical work on education a decade earlier. It is not clear how consciously Maria formulated in her mind at the start just how valuable writing was going to be in maintaining the all-important relationship (or relationships, since Mrs. Ruxton was to play her part too). Later on she certainly did know, for she frequently applied to her writing the phrase which emphasized Edgeworth's connection with it, attributing the books published under her own name to their 'literary partnership'.

Most of her first collection of children's stories were probably written at Clifton. *Lazy Lawrence*, *The False Key*, *Mlle Panache*, *The Mimic*, and *Old Poz* (a play), all of which probably first appeared in 1796,[1] are set in or around Bristol. Although one or two of the other stories have no specific location, all seem to be in England rather than in Ireland. Two are set in boys' schools, and employ themes and background material which were clearly supplied by Edgeworth.[2]

The group of children's stories which Maria Edgeworth published in 1796 include some minor masterpieces in the genre. *The Purple Jar* (which appeared in 1796 in *The Parent's Assistant* and then reappeared as part of *Rosamond* in 1801) is one of her most celebrated stories. Its heroine, Rosamond, needs a pair of shoes, but she would prefer to see the money spent on a purple jar which she has seen in a chemist's window. Her mother allows Rosamond to have her way, and the result is a disappointment

[1] No copy of a 1795 *Parent's Assistant* has ever been located, although an advertisement stating that it is published appears in *Letters for Literary Ladies* (1795). This lists the contents of the second volume as *The Purple Jar*, *The Bracelets*, and *Mlle Panache*, and these three stories make up pt. ii, vol. 1, of the edn. of 1796. On the other hand an undated letter of ME's, clearly from its contents written in mid 1796, refers to *The Parent's Assistant* as just coming out for the first time (*Mem.*, i. 73). The latter piece of evidence seems decisive.

[2] *Tarlton* and *The Barring Out*, which are both warnings to boys of the dangers of party spirit. See *Memoirs of RLE*, i. 47–52 and i. 258–9.

which is perfectly right in scale. Rosamond cannot go out for a proposed treat, because her father spots that she is 'slipshod', and the pretty glass is no consolation at all once the coloured water has run out of it. The impetuous, fallible Rosamond, based by family tradition on Maria herself, is one of the first real heroines of children's literature. Another attractive figure in the first collection is a sturdy, industrious boy called Jem, hero of *Lazy Lawrence*, who works at a number of ingenious and plausible odd jobs for two weeks to save his horse Lightfoot from having to be sold. By ingenuity, industry, and some luck, he scrapes together the necessary sum of money, only to have his hoard stolen from him the night before Lightfoot is due to be taken away. Jem's emotions at the moment when he discovers his loss are not dwelt on. The reader's sympathy is already with him, and words are hardly necessary.

Another picture of childish grief is given in *Simple Susan*, which Maria completed in 1798. Susan is a village girl whose father, an honest farmer, finds himself in difficulties over money. Susan works hard to raise the £9 he needs, and, when she finds that her efforts are not enough, she takes her remaining pet, a lamb, to the local butcher. The story is so pleasingly written that the moment of parting with the lamb is not mawkish but touching. Edgeworth read the story over and over again, and was always delighted with it:

> I have been reading *Simple Susan* this half hour and am really charmed with it—the perfect elegant simplicity & accuracy of description, the discrimination of character & the pathos which are to be met with in every page—will if it becomes known *at present* give it the preference of every story of the sort that has yet been written in any language.[1]

The happy ending seemed no less moving to Scott in his declining months: '"Ay, Miss Edgeworth: she's very clever, and best in the little touches too. I'm sure, in that children's story, where the little girl parts with her lamb, and the little boy brings it back to her again, there's nothing for it but just to put down the book, and cry."'[2]

After the first publication of *The Parent's Assistant*, Maria Edgeworth continued to work at more stories in the same

[1] RLE to ME, n.d. (? 1798 or 1800).

[2] J. G. Lockhart, *Memoirs of the Life of Sir Walter Scott*, 1837–8, vii. 338.

manner and for the same age-group of perhaps nine to twelve. As well as *Simple Susan*, a new edition of 1800 included for the first time *The Little Merchants* (which has an improbable Neapolitan setting), *Eton Montem* (based on a newspaper account of the Etonian custom), *The Basket Woman*, *Waste Not, Want Not*, and *Forgive and Forget* (the last two set once again in Bristol), and two rather slight Irish stories, *The White Pigeon* and *The Orphans*.

The age-group which Maria Edgeworth thought of at a particular time partly depended upon the age of her real-life audience. In 1792–5, the years in which she wrote the stories of the first *Parent's Assistant*, there were always at least two of Mrs. Elizabeth Edgeworth's children between the ages of ten and thirteen. After 1795 it was natural for Maria to extend her range to include a group of stories for older children, which duly appeared in 1801 under the title *Moral Tales*. Rather longer than her classic productions for *The Parent's Assistant*, the stories in *Moral Tales* are as a whole much less successful. They include *The Good French Governess*, which is incidentally interesting as a dramatized account of the Edgeworths' teaching methods, but has none of the narrative simplicity of *Simple Susan*. *Angelina*, a satire on novelettish sentimentality, is another story which holds the attention for incidental reasons. As a burlesque it is coarse and unamusing, but it interests as a commentary on the novel-writing school of Mary Wollstonecraft and Mary Hays, and as a parallel with the juvenilia of Jane Austen.

The loss of sureness of touch which Maria Edgeworth seemed to experience in writing for the older age-group is an interesting phenomenon, which is very relevant to her future career as a novelist for adults. Maria Edgeworth's stories for children of twelve and under are remarkably intimate. They have a strong and obvious appeal to the child reader, which, as Maria Edgeworth had learnt from her father, ought to be the first requirement of a story written for children.[1] The stories of *The Parent's Assistant* each have a sympathetic child as a focus for the reader's emotions. The young hero or heroine is being tested through taking on a task which is near the limit of his or her capacity. What is required of him is not a priggish conformity to adult norms of behaviour, but courage and determination to act on

[1] See above, p. 62.

his own, often in defiance of the adults and children around him. The virtues of the child heroes and heroines are energy, initiative, and persistence. The vices which appear in the 'bad' characters are not double-dyed villainy, but indolence, meanness, and thoughtlessness. The child reader is invited to identify with the protagonist as he experiences all kinds of difficulties and disappointments and finally emerges victorious.

Having found a first-class formula, Maria employs it again and again. Sometimes the child hero or heroine is tested deliberately by an adult, as in *The False Key* and *Waste Not, Want Not*. Sometimes it is the child—Jem, or Susan—who has determined to achieve a certain goal. Sometimes, as in *The Orphans* and *The Basket Woman*, the children are up against nothing but poverty. In every case, an adult is waiting on the fringes of the action, a wise and kindly parent, schoolmaster, guardian, or benefactor, who in the closing pages steps forward to distribute the appropriate rewards and punishments. It is the presence of this arbiter which gives the plot its clarity of outline and air of inevitability. A *deus ex machina* is seldom a convincing figure in stories about the adult world, but in a representation of the world of a child, whose destiny is shaped by adults, a just conclusion is not only allowable, but reasonably natural.

Another successful feature of the stories in *The Parent's Assistant* is the handling of setting. As the defects of her letters demonstrated, Maria was not by any means a descriptive writer, and until her career was almost over there was hardly an extended physical description in any of her stories.[1] Yet the tales of *The Parent's Assistant* do manage to give the impression of being 'placed' within a landscape, or inside a house. This is largely a matter of enlisting the reader's imaginative co-operation, for the information which Maria gives, although specific, is only fleetingly visual:

> In the pleasant valley of Ashton there lived an elderly woman of the name of Preston. She had a small neat cottage, and there was not a weed to be seen in her garden. It was upon her garden that she chiefly depended for support. . . .[2]

Instead of a general view of Susan's village, the reader hears

[1] *Helen*, 1834, is another matter. See below, pp. 430–1.

[2] From the opening paragraph, *Lazy Lawrence*.

about the triangle of common land where the children like to play. He also knows how Susan and Jem earn every penny of their treasures. Indeed, it would usually be possible to name the exact sum in the pocket of any of Maria Edgeworth's twelve-year-olds. Whatever is relevant to the immediate issue, and small sums of money always are relevant, is in large, clear focus. Sometimes, as in *The False Key*, we get a sense of the internal geography of a large town house. In *Waste Not, Want Not*, it is the external geography of Clifton and Bristol—the cathedral, the library, the shops and the Downs. In *The Mimic* it is a large house divided into rented apartments. None of these places is described, but the characters' movements are given with unselfconscious exactness. The first audience after all did know the exact landscape of many of these places. The stories convey a few everyday objects with the clarity which characterizes certain selective childhood memories. It is a technique which has no necessary place in adult fiction, but is peculiarly effective in stories for children.

Maria Edgeworth's formula for a plot and her knack with setting gave her her mastery over the tale, or *novelle*, for children. The achievement seemed the more remarkable at the time because there were no precursors. Before Maria Edgeworth, masterpieces like *Gulliver's Travels* and *Robinson Crusoe* were read by children, but there were no masters of writing for children. What writing was done deliberately for them was done largely by the uncultivated, often drawing on the popular oral tradition of nursery rhymes, ballads, and fairy tales; or it was done with a sharp eye on instruction. When cultivated men applied themselves to the subject of education, they did so at the theoretical level, and addressed themselves to the parents. Maria Edgeworth's strength was that she was both cultivated, and a woman. Her stories were beautifully written, with an elegance evident to the adult, yet, as her father had shown her, what mattered most was making them direct enough to please the child. Edgeworth had thought out the theory of writing for children, but on the whole it was women like his daughter who first mastered the technique. Success depended upon real familiarity with children. Edgeworth knew his much better than most men, but as an elder sister Maria lived with them more naturally still. Day by day she was in the middle of her audience, so that she knew (what so few educated men would have known) how much Jem's pennies mattered to him, or what a triumph it was when Susan baked the bread.[1]

All the same, Maria Edgeworth's mastery of the genre by the middle of the 1790s was too easily won. At least, her relative uncertainty when she came to write for the next age-group shows that she had not conquered the technique of the *novelle* in general. The three volumes entitled *Moral Tales* were intended for adolescents, an age-group for which it is notoriously difficult to write well. To begin with, the formula-plot would no longer serve. The central characters now had to seem like inexperienced, often inadequate adults, hovering awkwardly just within the grown-up world. Her most interesting teenage characters are Forester and Angelina, each of whom reacts—Maria thinks excessively—against adult social forms and conventions.[2] Making mistakes in the course of adjusting to adult life is a promising theme, but Maria was too bound to the idea of instructing the young to give her adolescent characters their heads. The benevolent guardian was still there, waiting to put the young people right in the final chapter. The *Moral Tales* are patronizing, and this the stories for younger children never were.

In another genre which she attempted mastery eluded her. Edgeworth was very fond of plays. He loved the energy and bustle of a performance in which all the children could participate, and since his friendship with Sir Francis Delaval he had been fond of contriving stage effects.[3] After *The Double Disguise* in 1786 Maria wrote only one more play, *Old Poz*, until, in 1798, Edgeworth suddenly decided that it would be a good idea to include a volume of plays in her series for adolescents. The first product of this idea was *Whim for Whim*, begun by Maria

[1] Harvey Darton attributes her literary pre-eminence among the first generation of children's writers to her humour, humanity, and to the fact that she created real children, not abstractions. 'They had to work out their own salvation as human beings, not in a groove' (*Children's Books in England*, p. 145).

[2] Forester was probably based on Thomas Day, although he was widely taken for Lord Ashburton (see below, p. 258). Angelina is supposed to have modelled herself on such romantic heroines as Mary Hays's Emma Courtney. As a burlesque heroine she was partially forestalled by Bridgetina in Mrs. Elizabeth Hamilton's *Memoirs of Modern Philosophers* (1800).

[3] See above, p. 28.

and her father in November 1798 and acted first at Christmas and then again early the following year.[1]

*Whim for Whim* deals with the stratagems and subsequently unmasking of Count Babelhausen, an Illuminatist. Other members of the cast include an elderly baronet who hates everything new, his nephew who hates everything old, a rich and whimsical widow, a disreputable French governess, and a rational heroine. After its Edgeworthstown performances the play was sent to Sheridan, who rejected it. Like *Angelina*, *Whim for Whim* belongs to contemporary literary warfare. The targets of the satire in both cases are philosophers of the supposedly self-indulgent German school, and, along with the philosophers, their English dupes. The play ends with the hero resolving that henceforth 'instead of pure reason, I will follow common sense'.

Early in 1799, before Sheridan rejected *Whim for Whim*, Maria began *Angelina* as a play, but rewrote it as a story before its appearance in *Moral Tales* in 1801. Sheridan's rejection of *Whim for Whim* put her off it, and she did not include it in the collection. *The Knapsack*, a short and thin drama set in Sweden, is in fact the only piece to survive in dramatic form. Although Maria never developed confidence in herself as a dramatist, she continued to write plays for performances on family occasions such as birthdays, and two sets were eventually published, *Comic Dramas* in 1817 and *Little Plays for Children* in 1827.

So far these pieces for children, successes and failures alike, were Maria's own. At the end of the 1790s she began to work directly on her father's old plan, not for stories but for textbooks: the latter henceforth accounted for most of her writing for children. The original 'Harry and Lucy' of 1780 had introduced the characters of a little boy and girl, who in the course of a number of natural conversations and encounters learnt about processes carried on in the world about them.[2] That appeared in a revised form as a volume of *Early Lessons*, 1801. Rosamond,

[1] The MS. of this unpublished play is in the Bodleian Library, Oxford (MS. Eng. misc. d. 648).

[2] See above, p. 63. In the intervening two decades other writers, notably Mrs. Trimmer and Dorothy Kilner, had been inspired by the success of Mrs. Barbauld's *Lessons* to compose instructive dialogues for children. However, the usual sphere of these philanthropic females is religion and morality; RLE's Lunar emphasis on science gives his work an appearance of originality even in 1801.

with her naïve follies, made the central character of another group of stories in the same collection, and Frank, who like Harry was a scientific little boy, was the focus for a third.

The only entirely new series of the three, *Frank*, was intended as a first introduction to science for Maria Edgeworth's half-brother William, born in 1794. Maria found *Frank* difficult to write, because it was a specialist business to produce a narrative which would be absolutely clear and interesting to the six-year-old, while at the same time establishing in his mind the different characteristics of the potato and the horse-chestnut, teaching him property rights, and going step by step through the process of making a kite. There are in *Frank*, as in *Harry and Lucy*, many inspired lessons, the material for which was probably supplied by Edgeworth: 'About eighteen pages of scientific matter was left to me by my father to make into a new volume of *Harry & Lucy* & this I have to do at this moment.'[1]

Maria, who usually enjoyed writing, sometimes seems to have found her part in piecing these lessons together and making the result palatable frankly uncongenial: 'I have done almost a little volume of *Frank*—shall do two vols of *Frank*—2 of *Rosamond*—2 of *Harry & Lucy* by degrees—However humble, & indeed often tiresome the task, I think it will do good & therefore I feel happy doing it, & determined to persevere.'[2]

After Edgeworth died she felt committed to more children's volumes, even though her own creative literary work was too painful to contemplate without him. Her father had left many unused notes, and it was always his intention to cover with this series of lessons the whole age range of childhood: that is to say, from the time the child learns to read through to the time, at about fourteen, when he graduates to adult books. Maria seems to have been left enough notes for a last series about Frank, and she could handle Rosamond for herself. But she had little scientific knowledge of her own, and she had to consult many friends before she could venture to offer fourteen-year-olds the four-volume *Harry and Lucy Concluded*, with all the relatively sophisticated scientific matter that it had to contain. She described her difficulties ruefully to Scott, and made it

[1] ME to SR, 16 Oct. 1813. The book referred to in this letter and the following quotation is *Continuation of Early Lessons*, 1813.

[2] ME to SR, 9 Aug. 1813.

plain that never before had she regarded herself as the principal author of books in the more strictly educational series:

I have been this year and a half, the same more or less spellbound in stupidity, writing four minnikin volumes of a child's book. I conceived that I could, would, and above all should and ought to finish a certain little *work* called *Harry and Lucy* which my father began for his own children some 40 years ago, and I know regretted he had not finished it. I had at various times helped him to continue it—my part being merely to spread amusement through it, while he furnished the solid knowledge and accurate principles of science. The toil, difficulty, mortification I have gone through in finishing these last volumes without him is not to be described . . . I have no science; and, as to accuracy, can compare myself only to the sailor who 'would never quarrel for a handful of degrees'. I trust my friends have saved me from public shame.[1]

She feared that this time she had found it impossible to supply 'as much of the amusement arising from incident and story, in this book as in some others'.[2] Her preface explained apologetically that she had done what she could to enliven the material by creating a domestic setting, breaking up her narrative into short scenes, and establishing a relationship between the two children in which the exchange of scientific information played a natural part. She really need not have been so much on the defensive. *Harry and Lucy Concluded* is not, of course, a work of literature in any ordinary sense, but the material in it has superabundant interest of its own. In the second volume, particularly, where the two middle-class children are taken on a tour of the industrial Midlands, most readers are likely to find their attention held by the family's journey on a canal, and Harry's trip down a mine. Some may agree with Lucy, that the great wonders of the industrial landscape tend to become progressively less intriguing as each machine is carefully explained. Others, like Harry, will find the passages of scientific explanation among the best in the book.[3]

The stories for children known as 'Maria Edgeworth's' should

[1] ME to Sir Walter Scott, 8 Apr. 1825; W. Partington (ed.), *Private Letterbooks of Sir Walter Scott*, 1930, pp. 269–70.

[2] Preface to *Harry and Lucy Concluded*, 1825, p. x.

[3] See above, pp. 143–4. Walter Scott was privately a Lucy, and he thought the whole approach of the *Harry and Lucy* series misconceived. See below, p. 397 n.

in fact be divided into two groups, much as she would have disliked seeing this done. Maria herself evolved out of her reading in French and English the 'tales' which constitute virtually an original literary form, and appear initially in *The Parent's Assistant* of 1796 and 1801, and in *Moral Tales* (1801). Richard Lovell and Honora Edgeworth initiated, Richard Lovell and Maria continued, a distinct genre of 'lessons', for the purpose of teaching facts about chemistry, physics, mechanics, and other sciences, as well as certain specific injunctions about behaviour—truth-telling, obedience to parents, and so on. *Early Lessons*, as the second group is generically known, offers to the parent who wishes to follow it a programme of education. He is meant to begin by introducing the child to the first part of *Frank*, for Frank is the simplest child, and his earliest adventures are suitable for the four- to six-year-old. When the child reader has mastered these he is ready to meet Harry and Lucy (in their first story, written in 1780), then Rosamond, and so on. Over the years the characters grow up. In 1821 we are seeing Rosamond between ten and thirteen. In the sequel to Frank, published in 1822, the hero grows from seven to eleven. Finally in 1825 Harry and Lucy complete the series by arriving (supposedly with their readers) at the age of fourteen.

Rosamond's place in the second group was originally of doubtful logic. Her first, most sparkling appearances, in *The Purple Jar* and *The Birthday Present*, were in *The Parent's Assistant*. In some respects she was an unusual figure in that context. She was higher in the social scale than most of the children in *The Parent's Assistant*, and she was more frequently to be found receiving instruction from a patient mother or father. By the time of the *Continuation of Early Lessons*, 1814, Rosamond's parents are ranging over subjects such as the spinning jenny, and this places her decisively in the second of the two broad general categories. For Maria's own stories *are* stories, not lessons. In her father's type the interest centres on the dialogue, since the purpose is to introduce as much solid information as possible in the very superficial guise of a fictional situation. Naturally the two groups do not compete as literature; nor, to do Edgeworth justice, do they compete as lessons. Educationally, his *Harry and Lucy* is brilliant, a model introduction to science which even today retains its freshness and excitement.

*Practical Education*, the major treatise on education which R. L. and Maria Edgeworth published jointly in 1798, had of course evolved together with the *Harry and Lucy* stories, as part of Edgeworth's earlier thinking on how learning could best be conveyed to the child's consciousness. Most parts of *Practical Education* do not resemble the treatises of Locke or Rousseau so much as a modern handbook for a student teacher, or for a parent needing inspiration over a wet weekend. There is a place in metaphysics for theorizing like Rousseau's, and the Edgeworths do not deny it;[1] but they argue that something else is meant by 'practical education'.[2]

*Practical Education* came out in two cumbrous quartos in 1798, and in three volumes, re-titled *Essays in Practical Education*, in 1801.[3] The first third, which deals largely with the training of pre-school children, is divided into chapters entitled On Toys, Tasks, Attention, Servants, Obedience, Truth, and so on. The central section of the book is made up of exact recommendations for teaching particular subjects—Grammar, Classical Literature, Geography, Chronology, Arithmetic, Geometry, Mechanics, Chemistry. There is a more general concluding section, on the relative importance of the faculties education aims to bring out in the child—Memory and Invention, Taste and Imagination, Wit and Judgement, Prudence and Economy.

Although Maria did more than half of the writing, the technical chapters were by Edgeworth himself. 'The work was resumed from a design formed and begun twenty years ago by Mr. Edgeworth; all that relates to teaching to read in the chapter on Tasks, the chapter on Grammar and Classical Literature, Geography, Chronology, Arithmetic, Geometry and Mechanics, were written by him.'[4]

[1] See above, p. 64.

[2] Cf. Preface to *Practical Education*. See also Schofield's description of Edgeworth's essay on road-making, which is quoted above, p. 35, and applies equally well to *Practical Education*.

[3] The change in title was made to meet widespread objections to the omission of religious education from *Practical Education*. The most eloquent criticism on this subject in print occurs in the *Bibliothèque Britannique*, xii, 1799, and in Abraham Rees's *Cyclopaedia* in the articles entitled 'Moral Education' and 'Intellectual Education'. Edgeworth also had to defend his book privately to his father-in-law, the Revd. D. A. Beaufort, and to the Bishop of Killala, who finally persuaded him to change the title.

[4] Preface to *Practical Education*, 1798, pp. ix–x.

From the educationalist's point of view these include most of the original and valuable parts of the book.[1] To take a single example of Edgeworth's ingenuity, in his remarks on teaching children to read he proposes a system of dots to distinguish the varying pronunciation of the vowels in English. When the child has mastered a sufficient number of words, his texts need no longer be prepared with dots by his teacher. This system is comparable with the technique of printing different sounding vowels in different colours, a method now in favour in some primary schools in England and America.

Two other specialist chapters were supplied at least in note form by others. Edgeworth's son Lovell, who was twenty-three at the time of publication, wrote 'the sketch of an Introduction to Chemistry'. It was the resourceful Thomas Beddoes who, while playing with the Edgeworth children at Clifton in the summer of 1793, worked out the genesis of the excellent chapters which begin the book—'Toys' and 'Tasks'. Children should be offered pencils, scissors, paste, tools, work-benches, and manageably sized implements for gardening. From the very earliest stages, babies' needs are sensibly catered for:

> A nursery, or a room in which young children are to live, should never have any furniture in it which they can spoil; as few things as possible should be left within their reach which they are not to touch, and at the same time they should be provided with the means of amusing themselves, not with painted or gilt toys, but with pieces of wood of various shapes and sizes, which they may build up and pull down, and put in a variety of different forms and positions; balls, pulleys, wheels, strings, and strong little carts, proportioned to their age, and to the things which they want to carry in them, should be their playthings.[2]

Few of the long list of toys they suggested were supplied by ordinary toy-manufacturers; some were not available at all. After Beddoes and the Edgeworths had thought out their ideas, in 1793–4, Beddoes considered backing a manufacturer in Bristol to make and sell the toys they recommended. A 'repository' of this kind is actually described in Maria's story *The Good French Governess* (*Moral Tales*, 1801). It is a warehouse stocked

[1] This opinion is shared by Alice Paterson in her monograph *The Edgeworths: A Study of Later Eighteenth Century Education*, 1914.

[2] *Practical Education*, 1798, i. 11.

with sturdy carts, small gardening tools, printing presses, looms, and furniture which takes to pieces and reassembles. In real life, unfortunately for the children of Bristol, it seems that Beddoes dropped his scheme before the factory came into existence.

From all that has been said of the contributions of others, and of the work initiated by Edgeworth much earlier, it will be evident that Maria's modest summary of her own part in making *Practical Education* is just enough:

> In the work of which I am now speaking, the principles of education were peculiarly his, such as I felt he had applied in the cultivation of my own mind, and such as I saw in the daily instruction of my younger brothers and sisters during a period of nearly seventeen years; all the general ideas originated with him, the illustrating and manufacturing them, if I may use the expression, was mine.[1]

*Practical Education* stood almost at the beginning of Maria's literary career, and her awareness that most of what was valuable in it emanated from Edgeworth became crucial in determining her literary outlook in the years ahead. 'So commenced that literary partnership, which[,] for so many years was the pride and joy of my life.'[1] With *Practical Education* and *Harry and Lucy*, Edgeworth had in reality said all that he and Honora had meant to say; Maria, to whom 'partnership' meant so much, was determined not to leave it there.

Was she—as literary readers probably suppose—generally mistaken about the merits of the educational ideas which she was to spend so much energy trying to popularize? Some twentieth-century educationalists have sided with her: one in particular called *Practical Education* 'the most important work on general pedagogy to appear in this country between the publication of Locke's *Thoughts* in 1693 and that of Herbert Spencer's *Essay on Education* in 1861'.[2] Yet its publication in 1798 did not after all do nearly as much for the name of Edgeworth as Maria afterwards achieved through popularizing its themes in her novels. The family were not sought after when they appeared in England in 1799. Even in educated circles in London a decade and a half later, Edgeworth was not so much an author

[1] *Memoirs of RLE*, ii. 190.

[2] A. Paterson, *The Edgeworths: A Study of Later Eighteenth Century Education*, pp. v–vi. Cf. Brian Simon, *Studies in the History of Education, 1780–1870*, 1960, p. 15.

established in his own right, as an obscure Irishman attempting to make capital out of his daughter's success.

*Practical Education* did have a considerable *succès d'estime* among progressives, particularly on the Continent, as the family were to have an opportunity of discovering in a few years' time. But in England it did not attract the prestige it deserved, partly no doubt on account of the date of publication. By 1798 many of the Lunar circle were dead, and Priestley, the other prominent educationalist among them, was in political exile in Pennsylvania; in England, where the political tide was strongly reactionary, it was not a year for welcoming progressive books.[1] Edgeworth had more honour in Bonapartist France than in his own country.

In any case he showed his usual indifference to reputation and success. Advanced though it was in scientific and teaching methods, the book did not represent in every sense 'practical education'. The omission of religious education brought down on his daughter's novels, as well as on his own works, the hostility of the growing forces of Evangelicalism.[2] Furthermore, the patient, flexible method of teaching Edgeworth proposed was difficult to work except in the ideal circumstances of his own home, where from 1795 four adults were continually available to instruct a family which never at one time exceeded seven children under twenty years of age. The *practical* need in nineteenth-century England was for a device which, like Lancaster's use of monitors, instructed the maximum number of children by means of the minimum number of teachers. Edgeworth's sensitive methods, directed at the individual child, were essentially experimental, and could never have been put to large-scale use.

For Maria, substantially cut off from the reaction of the wider world, there could be no doubt that in terms of absolute value the family's educational writing, and the large body of stories for children which supported it, was the real achievement of the decade 1791–1801. But by the beginning of the new century she had also made a diffident beginning as a writer of fiction for adults. In 1795 she published the immature *Letters*

[1] For a similar eclipse in the revolution of other members of the Lunar Society after the French Revolution on account of political reaction in England, see Schofield, op. cit., pp. 4–5.

[2] See below, pp. 341–2.

*for Literary Ladies*, a collection of three pieces of varying quality designed for adult readers. Since Thomas Day's views had for so long determined the question of whether or not she should publish, it was appropriate that she should begin with a discussion of female authorship. *Letter from a Gentleman to his Friend, upon the birth of a daughter*, which was probably written in 1793, is an attempt to reconstruct the ten-year-old correspondence between Day and Edgeworth which had put a temporary stop to Maria's public career.[1] *Letters of Julia and Caroline* is another fictionalized correspondence, between the domesticated 'philosopher', Caroline, and her flighty, romantic friend, Julia. The seven letters cover a span of several years, from the first theoretical debate between the two unmarried girls, one advocating sense, the other sensibility, to Caroline's final narration of how Julia, after leaving her husband for a lover, has died of shame. Not content with borrowing the format and some of the ideas of *Adèle et Théodore*, she seems to have taken some of the detail from real-life sources. The opening exchanges read as though they might recall some conversation between the retired and philosophic authoress and her fashionable friend Mrs. Charles Hoare, the former Fanny Robinson. Equally, Julia V—'s downfall has features in common with the career of Emma Vernon, who ran away with Mrs. Elizabeth Edgeworth's brother, William Sneyd, in 1789.[2] But in general, Julia, the silly sentimentalist who reads too many of the wrong books, and writes in too extravagant a style—'Kind Heaven, let not my soul die before my body!'—is a familiar enough butt of the women writers of the period, from Jane West and Elizabeth Hamilton to Jane Austen.

The third piece in *Letters for Literary Ladies, An Essay on the Noble Science of Self-Justification*, is much the best. An amusing essay on feminine methods of conducting an argument, it has all the characteristics of Maria Edgeworth's best mature style, elegance, humour, nice observation, and a day-to-day domestic setting. The material in this essay was too good to waste, and Maria Edgeworth later expanded it into a one-volume novel, *The Modern Griselda*.

The uneven quality and disparate nature of Maria Edgeworth's first work for adults suggests that she was not giving much thought to writing on her own for the ordinary public.

[1] See above, p. 149. [2] See above, p. 106.

Probably before *Letters for Literary Ladies* was published, between 1793 and 1795, she had produced a fourth short piece which was totally different again in style and content. Maria had acquired from her father the practice of collecting curious specimens of Irish speech, and she liked to entertain the family circle by mimicking the brogue and strange opinions of Edgeworth's steward, John Langan. It was Mrs. Ruxton who urged Maria to make a written version of her dramatic monologue, and she did so, inventing the saga of the Rackrent dynasty as a suitable story for such a character to tell. Two years after the narrative of the first three landlords was completed, Maria added the second section, Condy's story.[1] The piece was not mentioned in family correspondence until in 1798 D. A. Beaufort was asked if he had anything 'to add alter or correct in the Rack Rent families'.[2]

The accidental manner in which *Castle Rackrent* evolved over the years, and the family's hesitation over whether to publish it, are typical of the doubts and scruples Maria Edgeworth felt about novel-writing. In 1800, with a new version of *Parent's Assistant* coming out, and *Practical Education* acclaimed on the Continent, she could feel certain of her mission as an educational writer; no evidence available to her at home gave her any inkling that posterity, and indeed her own contemporaries too, would have more regard for *Castle Rackrent*.

The high degree of prestige which attached in Maria's mind to the educational work helps to explain a paradox about her career which has puzzled her admirers. Her most popular story for adults (*Castle Rackrent*) and her best tales for children (*The Purple Jar*, *Lazy Lawrence*, *Simple Susan*) were already written before 1800. But Maria, who had produced all these intuitively to amuse her domestic audience, had no idea of their literary value. She saw that the proper next step lay in writing fiction for the adult audience, but in 1800 as she laid her plans she was thinking in terms of two instructive series for the upper and middle classes; committing herself in effect to moralistic counterparts of *Early Lessons*, although she had already shown that it was in delineations of domestic life that her own talent naturally expressed itself.

[1] ME to Mrs. Stark, 6 Sept. 1834. See below, pp. 353–4.

[2] Mrs. FE to DAB, 28 Oct. 1798.

# Part II

# PARTNERSHIP: 1800–1817

# IV

## ABROAD AND AT HOME: 1800–1817

AFTER returning to Edgeworthstown from England in August 1799 Maria settled down contentedly to domestic life again. Now that the excitements of 1798 were over, it soon became clear that the family circle was entering a period of more than common stability. While Edgeworth was always the active force in the household, the personality of his successive wives was often enough to decide whether his individual children were happy or not. The gentle, humorous Elizabeth was much loved; but she had been fading for several years before her death in 1797, and during this time several of the older children were in want of active sympathy and encouragement.

Mrs. Frances Edgeworth had a kind of genius for supplying sympathy. Although her eldest stepdaughter, Maria, was actually a year older than she was, Frances's good sense and intelligence, her wry Beaufort humour, and her general responsiveness made her a natural confidante and adviser, so that she lived up to her nominal title of mother. Taking on a parental role was a family trait. Her father Daniel Augustus had always seemed not merely five years but a generation older than the naturally youthful Edgeworth.[1] Frances had a great deal of her father and her sensible, good-humoured mother in her. She was therefore an effective complement to her husband, and of all his wives uniformly the best with the children.

Edgeworth, although an enthusiastic parent, was a volatile man. He was less successful with some of his children than with others, and he certainly did not like them all equally.[2] Elizabeth,

[1] See for example above, p. 140.

[2] The children who attracted his censure at different times included Richard, Emmeline, Anna, Lovell, and (for a short period around 1808) William. Writing of Emmeline to Sneyd, he once observed 'I do not wish to retrace lines in my memory which are already sufficiently deep but I cannot from any customary sanction or irrational prejudice be induced to think that all those who are called my children have equal claims upon me' (28 Jan. 1808).

who, unlike Honora, but like her sisters Mary and Charlotte, had the Sneyd meekness and diffidence, could not make up to the children for their father's partialities. Frances, although she respected her husband, always retained her close contacts with her own family, so that an alternative ideal was present to her in the more equable Beaufort household. Her own six children tended not surprisingly to be happier and more stable as a group, as well as healthier, than the children of the previous marriages.[1] All the same, Frances's most remarkable achievement was to win the affection and increase the happiness of stepchildren who were already grown up when she met them.

She made an excellent friend to Maria, who readily admitted that at first she had entirely mistaken her stepmother's character. She addressed her as the 'friend who has taken so many thorns out of my imagination with a degree of patience skill & tenderness for which I shall be as grateful I hope as the lion was to Androcles'.[2] When at a time of great family sorrow Mrs. Edgeworth did as Maria entreated her, and went off to Dublin to be with her husband, Maria opened a letter to her in even more glowing terms: 'My dearest mother, for mother I will call you in spite of all physical impossibility—you are my mother in sense if not in age & a metaphysical possibility is a match any day for a physical impossibility. . . .' Typically, it was this adult characteristic of Frances, her steady good sense, that Maria singled out, in contrast to what she felt was her own immaturity. 'For once in my life you see . . . that even *I i* was right—neither too cowardly nor too rash—What a wonder!'[3] Maria's letters to Frances are not often among her best, partly because Maria had too much sense of what was proper to her own subordinate position, *en belle fille*, to make an informal companion of her stepmother.[4] Both in intimate matters and on the purely intellectual side there may have been surprisingly little contact between them. At the same time the strength of Maria's affection for Frances can be gauged from her comment to Étienne Dumont: 'You will understand that though she is

[1] Her children were Frances (Fanny), b. 1799, Harriet, b. 1801, Sophy, b. 1803, Lucy Jane, b. 1805, Francis, b. 1809, and Michael Pakenham, b. 1812. For their personalities in early adult life see Ch. XI below.

[2] ME to Mrs. FE, n.d. [summer 1803].

[3] ME to Mrs. FE, 19 Apr. 1807.

[4] See above, pp. 135–6.

my mother-in-law [*i.e. stepmother*] she is, next to my father, the friend I love best in the world.'[1]

Lovell, the heir, was (as Frances noticed when she first saw him) an unhappy individual.[2] She put his discontent down then to his desire to imitate and perhaps rival his father. He considered that Edgeworth was too strict with him, and other observers tended to confirm this; Charlotte Sneyd remembered afterwards that Lovell had been rebuked with 'greater warmth' than any of the other children.[3] On his way to the Continent early in the summer of 1802 in his usual aggrieved and rather self-pitying frame of mind, he yet had time for an emotional letter to Frances in which he thanked her for her friendship to him—'by all your family are you adored, and by me particularly'.[4] Charlotte, born 1783 and soon to be the eldest daughter left at home after Maria, was another stepchild whom Frances especially befriended. Their relationship was probably more intense and based on more shared interests than Frances's relationship with Maria. Charlotte expressed her gratitude in terms similar to Lovell's: 'You taught me how to draw and you taught me how to love.'[5]

This was a period when all Frances's warmth was needed to compensate for longstanding coolnesses between the older children. Emmeline was often away, but when at home she did not get on well with Maria. 'I have ever been of opinion that Emmeline had been prejudiced against me whether by persons or circumstances I know not.'[6] Maria felt that Charlotte did not like her either, although Charlotte's manner was apparently agreeable, even delightful, to virtually everyone else. Lovell was the most explicit about his dislike of his famous stepsister. 'Miss E the authoress bears the laurel so meekly and her temper seems so much improved that she is quite agreeable and she does not interfere with anybody the consequence is obvious nobody interferes with her, and we all go on as if there was no

[1] ME to ED, 9 July 1811.

[2] See above, p. 132.

[3] Letter to CSE of 19 Feb. 1808.

[4] Letter from England, May 1802. Lovell's tendency to carp is exemplified more than once, both in his letters from Geneva and afterwards, more understandably, when he wrote from Verdun.

[5] Charlotte Edgeworth to Mrs. FE, n.d.

[6] ME to SR, 22 July 1804.

such serpent in the house.'[1] Like Emmeline, Lovell was no longer at home from 1802, after which domestic life continued more smoothly.

It was clearly not easy for Maria to fit in with the siblings nearest her in age. In Emmeline and Lovell's case the trouble may have arisen because they were in conflict with their father, and Maria sided with him. Lovell especially seems to have resented her special position as her father's assistant, and to have felt jealous of her success as an author. Because she was a strong character, Frances provided a counterpoise to Edgeworth; it was no longer quite so important to be a favourite of his, or even on very good terms with him, when Frances was in a position of virtually equal authority. After 1803 less is heard of the friction between Maria and Charlotte, and in 1806 Maria even talks of 'the party quarré which of all others I like the best, papa, mamma, Charlotte and I'.[2]

Through her own family's connections Frances also did a great deal to transform the Edgeworths' social relationships in Co. Longford.[3] Once the wedding trip to England was over their calendar of engagements became much fuller than it had been before. At first their visiting circle was limited mainly to Co. Longford, Co. Cavan (immediately to the north), and to the three rich counties to the east of Co. Longford, which were well settled by the Anglo-Irish gentry—Westmeath, Meath, and the more remote Louth, where the Beauforts lived. But this apparently restricted area soon produced some cultivated and well-travelled new friends. For example, John Foster, former Speaker of the Irish House of Commons, had a nephew who shared Edgeworth's interests in trade and industry.[4] And Mrs. Tuite of Sonna, only ten miles away in Co. Westmeath, in October 1800 came to Edgeworthstown with her brother

[1] Lovell Edgeworth to Peter Mark Roget, 16 Aug. 1801; dossier Romilly, B.P.U., Geneva. Roget, a fellow student of Lovell's at Edinburgh, was the future author of the *Thesaurus*.

[2] ME to SR, 30 Jan. 1806.

[3] For her father's part in this process, see above, pp. 140–1.

[4] J. L. Foster, future Irish barrister, M.P., and judge, published an *Essay on the Principles of Commercial Exchanges, particularly between England and Ireland* in 1804. He gave ME material about visits to factories and coalmines in 1801, and a journey to Constantinople in 1805, both of which descriptions she entered in a notebook (perhaps for use in conversation). RLE had been at school with his father, William Foster, now Bishop of Clogher, and with his uncle the Speaker.

Richard Chenevix, who was 'acquainted with all the chemists and scientific men in France'.[1]

Edgeworth's troubles in the county in 1798 had arisen not on account of his estrangement from the gentry, but from the suspicion he generated among the ultra-Protestant middlemen, with whom neither Beaufort nor anyone else had much influence. In this direction too matters improved strikingly after 1800, largely because of Edgeworth's behaviour over the great political issue of 1800, Ireland's parliamentary Union with England. The people of real political influence in Co. Longford favoured the Union; so—in so far as their views were ascertainable—did the Catholics; but the Orangemen deeply resented a measure which they saw as reducing Ireland's prestige, undermining exclusively Protestant power in the country, and opening the door to granting further political rights to Catholics.[2]

Edgeworth was very much in favour of the Union. His belief that it would help Ireland's trade had been confirmed by his conversations with Midlands industrialists in 1799. 'The mercantile & commercial world with which we have mixed since we came to England speak of a Union as a thing that must be in a few months—& look upon it as madness in the Irish to oppose what they think so advantageous.'[3] The new House of Commons at Westminster, which was to be enlarged in order to admit 100 Irish M.P.s, would have a lower proportion of pocket boroughs than either of the old Parliaments at Westminster or Dublin; according to Edgeworth's calculations, nearly half the members would be County or City members (i.e. returned by a more or less genuine franchise) as opposed to only a third before.[4] Finally, he believed that Pitt would grant equal rights to Catholics once the Union was accomplished, and so he saw

[1] ME to SR, 20 Oct. 1800; *Mem.*, i. 103. Chenevix (1774–1830) became an F.R.S. in 1801 and returned to live in Paris in 1808.

[2] Among pro-Unionist gentry in the county Mrs. FE listed Oxmantown, 'his man' Fetherstone, Newcomen, and Longford (Letter to DAB, 31 Jan. 1800, Nat. Lib. of Ireland, MS. 13176 (5)). A government agent who visited a Col. Ahmuty at Brianstown, Co. Longford, in Oct. 1799, was assured that only the Catholics in the county favoured Union, 'and there was *scarcely* a Protestant in the county for it'. Cited W. E. H. Lecky, *A History of Ireland in the Eighteenth Century*, 1892, v. 304 n.

[3] Mrs. FE to DAB, Hill Top, nr. Birmingham, 23 Apr. 1799; Nat. Lib. of Ireland MS. 13176 (4). For the influence of these conversations on *Castle Rackrent*, see below, pp. 354–5.

[4] Draft of a letter to an unknown English peer [? Earl Spencer], 26 Jan. 1800.

it as the likeliest chance of removing the sectarian bitterness which was endemic in Irish life.[1]

What actually happened as the votes were taken in the Irish House of Commons in 1799 and 1800 has many touches of comedy, and demonstrates that politics was hardly the sphere in which Edgeworth appeared at his practical best. Yet there was also consistency of a kind in the way he acted. As he had shown in 1783, when once before he had sacrificed a cherished reform to the inviolability of Parliament, there were certain established forms and institutions which he would not challenge. Of all his beliefs, the most fundamental was perhaps in the *idea* that the representatives of the gentry were independent individuals, the very symbols of a free and manly people (the analogy with the early Roman republic was well to the forefront of his political thinking). He was convinced that the gentry of Ireland ought to carry the day; that the Bill ought not to be passed if 'the real voice of the country particularly of those who possess the property of the Kingdom is against it';[2] and that certainly it ought to be thrown out if the majority of members were in principle against it, but had been bought up by a corrupt oligarchy. Therefore he twice spoke in favour of the motion, in an attempt to carry gentry and members by reason; and twice voted against it, because he thought that money rather than conviction was winning the day.[3]

Needless to say, Edgeworth's refined dealings with his conscience cut little ice in County Longford. The fact that he was really for Union was not the point; he had voted against it,

[1] This was also a view put forward earlier by Adam Smith in *The Wealth of Nations* (v, ch. 3). The former United Irishman Hamilton Rowan, writing his autobiography in 1799, similarly welcomed the Union as heralding the end of a corrupt legislature and an aristocratic and sectarian form of government.

[2] RLE to Mrs. R, interlined message in letter from ME to Letty Ruxton, 29 Jan. 1800.

[3] Recent scholars have doubted whether corruption was really as extensive as the Bill's opponents claimed at the time. RLE thought it was, and could have cited the fact that two attempts were made to buy his vote (*Memoirs of RLE*, ii. 254–5), and that he was offered '3000 guineas for my seat during the few remaining weeks of the session' (RLE to Erasmus Darwin, 31 Mar. 1800; ibid., ii. 252). In *The Passing of the Irish Act of Union*, 1966, G. E. Bolton argues that the final vote reasonably represented Irish public opinion as a whole. RLE's apparently eccentric vote against his own conviction in favour of the view of many people he detested was cast precisely because he thought their voices were not being heard, as they had a constitutional right to be. Longford is of course only one county, and a small one.

thus enrolling himself at the eleventh hour in (as they would have put it) the 'patriot' party fighting to maintain the Protestant Nation. Other gentlemen who had formerly been popular with the local Protestants lost a great deal of prestige over the issue. Sir William Gleadowe Newcomen and Sir Thomas Fetherstone, the County members, and Luke Fox, member for Lord Granard's borough of Mullingar, had voted in favour, and, although one must clearly discount many of the scandalous inferences drawn at the time, there was certainly a widespread belief that two of the three were bought.[1] Lord Longford's uncle had publically declared himself the government's man during the first reading: 'Admiral Thomas Pakenham, a naturally friendly and goodhearted gentleman, that night acted like the captain of a press gang, and actually *hauled* in some members who were desirous of retiring. He had declared that he would act in *any* capacity, according to the exigencies of his party; and he did not shrink from his task.'[2]

There was a rapid transformation in the relative standing of the gentlemen of the county, and Daniel Augustus Beaufort was (perhaps somewhat cynically) delighted: 'I had great pleasure in hearing from the Speaker that it was, once more, Edgeworth for ever—Hurra! at *Longford*, and that Lords & admirals and Baronets, shrunk [*sic*] before him into a most diminutive Minority.'[3]

This sudden popularity was too unnatural to be sustained indefinitely, and some of Edgeworth's neighbours, notably an inveterately hostile farmer called William Bond, were soon to revert to type. But at least politics ceased henceforth to be a real bone of contention between Edgeworth and his neighbours. The Anglo-Irish had been castrated politically by the Union. It did not really matter any more that Edgeworth was more liberal than the gentry or half-and-half gentry of the county, since no one cared much about any of them at far-away Westminster. Edgeworth went on believing in Catholic Emancipation, but he no longer found much occasion to say so publicly.

[1] Newcomen was said to have had a debt to the Treasury cancelled, Fox to have been paid with a judgeship. Jonah Barrington, *The Rise and Fall of the Irish Nation*, 1833, pp. 467ff. and pp. 107ff.

[2] Ibid., p. 410. Admiral Pakenham contributed to ME's one direct portrait of a political 'jobber'. See below, pp. 249–50.

[3] DA to RLE, 14 Apr. 1800.

There was now a slow realignment in Irish politics which had the effect of bridging the gap between liberals like the Edgeworths and people who had once been far to their right. As Catholic agitation steadily increased during the next decades, 'Repeal' of the Union became a Catholic cry, while the Protestants came to see the measure as an instrument for their protection. Although the Edgeworths were tolerant in religious matters, and more benevolent than most landlords in their aims, they still thought that Ireland's economic future was tied up with England's. As the years passed, therefore, they became increasingly difficult to distinguish from the other moderates among the Protestant gentry.[1] The extreme strain between the family and their neighbours, their near-isolation among the thin ranks of Longford gentry, ended at the beginning of the nineteenth century.

During 1800 Maria saw less of her father than for some years before. In the 1790s they had produced *Practical Education*, and to a lesser extent the children's books, as part of a joint programme of work, and Maria had been involved in her father's affairs in Co. Longford and in the politics of the telegraph. For much of the first half of 1800, however, Edgeworth was kept away in Dublin by the prolonged series of debates about the Union. He wrote home disconsolately; while Maria in reply showed that her feelings for him lost none of their intensity when they were apart:

> I am sadly afraid that this Bill of Bills will keep you away longer than you expect—But now you have the cup at your lips I am sure you will like a good boy drink it to the dregs without making a wry face—and you shall have some home-made sweetmeats afterwards. . . Adieu Dearest father, friend and companion I am very happy—but I miss you & it is absolutely impossible that I should not—God prosper you in all your wishes—that would be a fatal prayer for anyone who did not know how to wish as wisely as you do.[2]

Maria was thus no more inclined than she had been earlier to assert her independence of her father; but the fact was that at this period she and he often found themselves differently occupied. When he could spare time from politics Edgeworth was thinking about mechanics. 'I persevere in my scheme for

[1] See below, pp. 452 ff.

[2] ME to RLE, n.d. [? Mar. 1800].

reviewing and improving agricultural machinery—& I hope when we meet that I shall have made some progress . . . Did you try my tin seed wheel?'[1] The following year he published a short piece, 'On Engraving Bank of England Notes', and his 'Essay on the Rail-Road'.[2] Meanwhile, between May 1800 and the spring of 1801, Maria was very busy with *Belinda*, a three-volume novel in the Fanny Burney tradition which Edgeworth had never much cared for.

There was thus the beginning of an apparent split between Richard Lovell's activities and Maria's; but although this divergence might seem to have become an objective fact, and to remain one for several years,[3] Maria refused to acknowledge it. She did so by not taking her own career as a writer of fiction seriously. Her few references to her growing fame in the outer world were flippant. When Sophy managed to convey that her brother Richard Ruxton was in awe of Maria's reputation, she was told she was 'a goose or a gosling whichever you like best . . . As you recommend Richard so humbly & patiently to my approbation, I shall certainly lay aside my gorgon terrors & as far as in me lies, endeavour not to strike him dead with the blaze of glories that surrounds the authoress of Pracl. Education, Early Lessons etc.'[4] Characteristically, even when she was joking the books she thought of were the ones she wrote with her father, not her two recent resounding successes, *Castle Rackrent* (1800) and *Belinda* (1801).

In her manner with strangers she was still almost as shy as she had been on coming to Ireland, a fact which astonished a Swiss tourist of 1801 who made a detour to Edgeworthstown in order to meet her:

Je me persuadois que l'auteur de l'ouvrage sur l'éducation, de tant d'autres productions utiles ou agréables, devoit se trahir par quelque chose de bien remarquable dans l'extérieur: je me trompois. Une petite taille; des yeux presque toujours baissés; l'air profondément modeste et réservé: peu d'expression dans les traits quand elle ne parle pas; tel fut le résultat de mon premier toisé. Mais quand elle parloit, ce qui arrivoit beaucoup trop rarement à mon gré, rien

[1] RLE to DAB, 26 Apr. 1800.

[2] In the *Monthly Magazine*, xii, 1801, and *Nicholson's Journal*, i. 1801.

[3] For RLE's relatively limited connection with ME's fiction in the first years of the century, see below, e.g., p. 203.

[4] ME to SR, 1 Aug. 1802.

de mieux pensé, et de mieux dit, mais toujours timidement exprimé, que ce qui sortoit de sa bouche.[1]

Marc-Auguste Pictet was an interesting visitor. At this time he was the Edgeworths most important publicist, although as yet they had very little appreciation of how much he had helped their reputation. With his brother Charles he was a founder-editor of the Genevese scientific and literary journal, the *Bibliothèque Britannique*, which has been described as 'certainly the most important cultural link existing between England and the Continent' during the Napoleonic Wars.[2] In 1798 and 1799 the Pictet brothers serialized Charles's translation of *Practical Education* in twelve substantial instalments, adding at the end a lengthy and generally sympathetic criticism. In the next three years they also published several children's stories, *Moral Tales*, selections from the glossary of *Castle Rackrent* ('Traits remarquables des mœurs des Irlandais') and from *Irish Bulls*, and two long extracts from *Belinda*.

The Edgeworths and Pictet became friends, although Maria's notions of decorum were upset when he published his impressions of them after his return home. During his two days with the family he was invited to give his opinion on the subject that was then under discussion, where they should go on their next journey overseas. Edgeworth had not forgotten Beaufort's strictures on the subject of taking his family into society, nor his obligation to try to find husbands for his two remaining grown-up daughters.[3] By now their prospects were very unequal. Charlotte, born in 1783, struck Pictet as 'jolie, fraiche comme la rose', while Maria, handicapped by her reserve and her unremarkable appearance, was already thirty-three. There are hints in Mrs. Beaufort's letters in 1800 and 1801 that she might marry an Irish baronet, Sir James Blackwood ('the sweeting . . . but that he is rather old and stiff')[4] but Maria's own view of the gentleman is not recorded. Presumably he never came

[1] *Voyage de Trois Mois en Angleterre, en Écosse et en Irlande*, Geneva, 1802, pp. 193–4. Success might have been expected to give ME confidence, but as late as 1812 RLE boasted that if anything it had made her more timid (Letter to ED, n.d. B.P.U.,Geneva). [2] H. W. Hausermann, *The Genevese Background*, 1952, p. 31.

[3] Elizabeth (Bessy), b. 1781, died of tuberculosis in 1800; Emmeline was planning to marry Dr. King of Clifton, although not as yet with RLE's encouragement.

[4] Mrs. Beaufort to Harriet Beaufort, 14 Aug. 1801; Nat. Lib. of Ireland, MS. 13176 (5).

to a proposal. Once about this time Maria confided to Lovell that she would have liked to have children of her own. But when Edgeworth suggested that a purpose of the trip they had in view was to find her a husband, her reaction was the same as it had been in 1791:

> The idea . . . of being shewn, & stared at & criticised as the author of Prac Ed &c would be highly disagreeable to me—I know my own defects of person too well to wish to be placed in '*horrid relief*'—The chance of my meeting, abroad, with any person who should have so much judgment & so little taste as to overlook these defects & in spite of them to become sincerely attached to me is I think scarcely worth calculating—There is 34 to one against me . . . I have no doubt that my happiness would be much increased by a union with a man suited to me in character, temper, & understanding, and *firmly attached to me*—but deduct any one of those circumstances and I think I should lose infinitely more than I should gain . . . Therefore I may well be content with that large portion of happiness which I actually enjoy—I am not afraid of being an old maid.[1]

Preparations for the trip went ahead in spite of Maria's qualms. Almost to the last moment no one had a fixed idea of where they were going. Edinburgh was proposed at one time, London at another. In the end Edgeworth decided to take Pictet's advice and go to Paris, a popular course with English travellers now that, following the Peace of Amiens of 27 March 1802, France and England had ceased to be at war for the first time in nine years.

Lovell, who was able to get away in May, went first to Paris, and then on to Geneva, making use in both cities of Pictet's wide circle of friends. He was spending what Edgeworth considered to be a phenomenal amount of money, and when his father's reproaches caught up with him at Geneva he merely replied that, after twenty years under restraint, it was time he took the bridle off.[2] The idea was that Lovell should join the rest of the family party, at a place yet to be decided, some time in 1803. Richard Lovell, Frances, Maria, Emmeline, and Charlotte set off from Edgeworthstown at the end of September 1802, after the half-yearly rent-day, leaving the younger children in the care of the Sneyd aunts. Emmeline's destination was Clifton, where

[1] ME to SR, n.d. [1802]. Cf. letter to Mrs. R quoted above, pp. 103–4.
[2] RLE's PS. to Mrs. FE to Mary and Charlotte Sneyd, Paris, 28 Oct. 1802.

she was to have her way and marry Mr. King—backed by Edgeworth's grudging consent, and a modest settlement of £75 a year. The others were not to attend her wedding, but were to pass more or less directly through England on their way to France.

In the Midlands they had time, as ever, for the survivors among Edgeworth's old friends. At Derby Richard Lovell renewed the acquaintance he had made in 1793 with William Strutt, and he drove out to call on Erasmus Darwin's widow at Breadsall Priory, the Darwins' new home four miles north of the town.[1] They made another brief stop for Josiah Wedgwood the younger at Etruria. Inquiring at a bookseller's in Leicester about the sales of the works for adults that Maria had produced in the last two years, they learnt that *Castle Rackrent* especially had done well; afterwards the bookseller introduced them to a local poet, Miss Watts, who (according to the amusing but rather snobbish account Maria sent home) was quite overwhelmed by the honour. 'Lady Delacour, O! Letters for Literary Ladies, O!'[2] In a Bond Street shop window they saw a print purporting to show characters from *Belinda*. 'Lady Delacour is a fat vulgar housekeeper & Belinda a stick worse a hundred times than sprawling Virginia.'[3] In spite of this evidence, the Edgeworths drew no conclusions about the English public's preference for Maria's two novels as against the educational writing. Once again they stayed in London without coming into contact with literary life. They dined with no one outside the family except one old friend and their publisher, Johnson, and after six days Maria's first impression was that she had 'walked about a great deal'.[4]

They crossed from Dover to Calais on 3 or 4 October. Instead of heading directly for Paris they made a short tour of Flanders first. From Gravelines and Dunkirk ('an ugly bustling town', at which Maria saw her first French play) they went on to Bruges, and thence to Ghent. They stayed at Ghent for two days, and gave four or five more to Brussels, on which

[1] Erasmus Darwin had died suddenly on 17 Apr. 1802, while in the middle of a letter to RLE (which is in the Edgeworth collection). See also *Memoirs of RLE*, ii. 263 ff.

[2] ME to Charlotte Sneyd, Nerot's Hotel, London, 27 Sept. 1802; *Mem.*, i. 115–17 (but the version in the *Memoir* tones down ME's ridicule of Miss Watts and her mother).

[3] ME to Mary Sneyd, Paris, 19 Oct. 1802.

[4] ME to CSE, Sittingbourne, Kent, n.d. [early Oct. 1802].

Maria bestowed her most favourable report to date—it was the town 'best calculated for the residence of English families'.[1] Her letters home while she was travelling were not in her freest, most amusing vein; she was over-anxious to reassure the family left at home that she cared more for them than for all the fine things she was looking at, and she did her utmost as always to avoid describing paintings, statues, buildings, or scenery. She was perhaps most influenced in favour of Flanders by several pleasant encounters she had there, including one with the Mayor of Bruges, who knew her name well through the *Bibliothèque Britannique*. It was becoming so apparent that Pictet had served them well that Maria already began to repent her hard opinion of him.

After brief stops at Valenciennes, Cambrai, and Chantilly, they arrived in Paris on 23 October. They went to the expensive Hotel de Courland, which looked out directly on to the Place de la Concorde; but the following day Edgeworth enlisted the help of one of Pictet's friends, the banker Benjamin Delessert, who helped him to find 'pretty little lodgings' at 527, Rue de Lille, which were a great deal cheaper; and this was a piece of good fortune because, they were told, the sudden influx of wealthy English into Paris had doubled the price of lodgings and many luxuries.[2]

The Delessert family was a key introduction; they were wealthy philanthropists with scientific tastes, who had befriended Rousseau and continued to entertain a progressive, rationalist circle in which the Edgeworths immediately felt at home. Within a few days of arriving in Paris they were invited to the home of Mme Delessert's daughter, Mme Gautier, where they met Edgeworth's old acquaintance, the 75-year-old Abbé Morellet.[3] Morellet invited them to his home, and Maria was charmed with it and with him. 'Everything in his house so convenient, so comfortable! so many inventions the same as my father's—so many of his ideas so like my Father's.'[4] Morellet conveyed gracefully that he returned her admiration. He told

[1] ME to SR, Brussels, 15 Oct. 1802.

[2] Mrs. FE to Mary Sneyd, Paris, 21 Nov. 1802.

[3] See above, p. 60 n. André Morellet, 1727–1819, the rationalist philosopher, political economist, and statistician, who before the Revolution had been the friend of Diderot, d'Alembert, Marmontel, Voltaire, Lord Shelburne, and Benjamin Franklin.

[4] ME to Mary Sneyd, 31 Oct. 1802.

her: 'A Paris on lit votre livre sur l'éducation — à Geneve on l'avale — à Paris on admire vos principes — à Geneve on les suit.'[1] Her name did indeed seem to be (in Mrs. Edgeworth's words) 'as well-known at Paris as at Edgeworthstown'.

The Edgeworths were soon much in demand by other hostesses—Mme Suard, wife of the journalist and critic Jean-Baptiste-Antoine Suard, the immensely wealthy *nouveau-riche* Mme Bidermann, Mme de Vindé,[2] Mme de Vergennes, and the celebrated Mme Récamier. The last-named obviously impressed them with her charm and beauty—sufficiently, indeed, for Maria to maintain a correspondence with her afterwards—but the world she moved in was never quite theirs. 'She is a charming woman surrounded by a groupe of admirers and flatterers', commented Mrs. Edgeworth, while Maria observed drily that she was 'ambitious of the *suffrage* des gens d'esprit'.[3]

Since she was writing to women, the Ruxtons and the Sneyd aunts, Maria took more space in her letters for the characters and manners of the women she met than for the men. Of all the Parisian ladies, the sixty-year-old Mme Delessert was the general favourite with the Edgeworth party. Characteristically Maria thought of comparing her with Mrs. Ruxton, which meant presumably that she had a dignified and gracious manner. Mme Gautier also met with their approval, though not so emphatically as her mother because she was more literary and more a woman of the world. At first Mme de Pastoret was not given one of the highest accolades—Maria could think of no higher comparison than Mrs. Saunderson, wife of the M.P. for Co. Cavan—but by 1 December she thought Mme de Pastoret resembled Edgeworth himself. As the creator of the woman of fashion Lady Delacour, Maria was inevitably fascinated by the individual nuances of style in the only circle of fine ladies she had ever met at first hand; the discriminations she learnt at Paris were to be reflected many times in the characters of the upper-class women she created after coming home.[4]

[1] Mrs. FE to Mary and Charlotte Sneyd, 28 Oct. 1802.

[2] ME's compliment to Mme de Vindé in *Émilie de Coulanges* is quoted below, p. 323.

[3] Mrs. FE to Mary Sneyd, 21 Nov. 1802, and ME to Mrs. R, 1 Dec. 1802.

[4] Mme de Pastoret was the original of Mme de Fleury in the tale of that name; Mme Delessert and Mme Gautier may have suggested Mrs. Hungerford and her daughter Mrs. Mortimer in *Patronage*. Mme Delessert certainly reminded ME

The days passed in a pleasant bustle; the Edgeworths went to museums, art galleries, scientific lectures, and exhibitions by day, and to a succession of social engagements by night. Edgeworth was in his element among men of science who accepted him as one of themselves. Their entry into French social life was less fraught with embarrassment than it might have been because under Bonaparte the subject of politics was either taboo, or touched on only guardedly.[1] On the whole it was a great relief to avoid controversy (although Edgeworth had determined not to seek an introduction to Bonaparte, a gesture by which he meant to make plain his opposition to tyranny). Meanwhile they could scarcely believe their good luck—that they were actually enjoying social success in a society that valued intellect as well as fashion.

> It is no easy matter to get into agreeable society at Paris; we hear that many English of rank and fortune far far superior to ours cannot force or win or buy their way into it—They put their trust in chariots and in horses—which are of little or no avail here except with *les nouveaux riches*, who are not worth seeing or hearing —The title of philosopher or rather of man of letters or science is the best possible title here[.] We see the French scavans mixing with most polite and elegant societies of both sexes . . . as essential to the formation of good company—At La Harpe's we met a few days ago—the celebrated French beauty Madame Récamier—the celebrated English wit Lady Elizabeth Foster—and a Russian Princess Dalgarouki . . . Would you have expected to meet such a lady in the study of a philosopher—Nothing but fashion could have brought her there and therefore I mention her as the strongest proof that literature and literary men are in high esteem here.[2]

Never having known London high life, Maria was unduly astonished at the heterogeneous quality of Parisian Society, and at its intellectual interests; she also under-rated the social advantage which interesting English visitors in fact enjoyed in 1802–3. Among her upper-class compatriots readily admitted

of the Duchess in *Leonora* (ME to M.-A. Pictet, 23 Sept. 1804; H. W. Haüsermann, *The Genevese Background*, p. 68). *Leonora* was influenced by Mme Gautier's advice (see below, p. 293). The dialogue of the French countess in *Émilie de Coulanges* and of the French characters in *Ormond* obviously owes much to experience gained in 1802–3 (see below, pp. 322–3 and p. 385).

[1] *Memoirs of RLE*, ii. 279ff.

[2] ME to Henry Edgeworth, 16 Jan. 1803.

to the salons was for example the Marquis of Lansdowne's son, Lord Henry Petty.[1] In later years in England he was to become one of Maria's warm friends; so too was his tutor and travelling companion, the Genevese Étienne Dumont. Maria found the latter the more interesting in 1802. After meeting him at Mme Gautier's she described him as 'very sensible and entertaining' and was 'sorry he is since gone from Paris'.[2]

One day in mid November four gentlemen called on Edgeworth to talk about science, and stayed several hours, to the lively enjoyment of both Richard Lovell and Frances. One of these visitors was a slight, reserved, highly intellectual Swede, Abraham Niclas Clewberg-Edelcrantz, a bachelor of forty-six who had been commissioned by his king to travel through Europe examining new inventions that might be adopted in Sweden. With such a brief, Edelcrantz was an interesting figure to Edgeworth; in fact the two men had a great deal in common. They were both gentlemen by birth, although of moderate means, and while both were interested in the arts,[3] they preferred mechanics. Edelcrantz had even invented a version of the telegraph which was used by the Swedish army a few years later. He called again in November, always apparently seeing the family as a group together. Then on 3 December, while Maria was in the middle of a letter to Mrs. Ruxton, Edelcrantz called and asked to see her privately:

> . . . Here, my dear aunt, I was interrupted in a manner that will surprise you almost as much as it surprised me, by the coming in of Monsieur Edelcrantz, a Swedish gentleman, whom we have mentioned to you, of superior understanding & mild manners: he came to offer me his hand and heart! !
>
> My heart, you may suppose, cannot return his attachment, for I have seen but very little of him, and have not had time to have formed any judgment, except that I think nothing could tempt me

[1] Lord Henry Petty, 1780–1863, himself became 3rd Marquis of Lansdowne in 1809. In politics he was a liberal Whig who held office intermittently from 1806 to 1863. At his country house, Bowood, he and his wife afterwards entertained a brilliant circle of politicians and intellectuals, among them ME.

[2] ME to Mary Sneyd, 31 Oct. 1802.

[3] Edelcrantz was the author of poems conveying fresh, accurate observations of nature, although they are not linguistically very interesting. His main task in the service of Gustav III had been the administration of the five royal theatres. An account of his life is given in a Swedish monograph, Karl Ragnar Gierow's *Abraham Niclas Clewberg-Edelcrantz*, Stockholm, 1964.

PLATE III

MRS. RUXTON
pastel

SOPHY RUXTON
aged 14
silhouette

PLATE IV

THE CHEVALIER EDELCRANTZ
Caricature by Johan Tobias Sergel

to leave my own dear friends and my own country to live in Sweden. . . .[1]

The bottom of the page is more than half torn away. It appears to have contained further objections to marriage with Edelcrantz, among them the existence of an elderly widowed mother whom he seems to have been supporting. Meanwhile Edgeworth, although sounding all the proper parental notes of tact and caution, quite apparently favoured Edelcrantz:

Before I left Edgeworthstown I stated as one of my reasons for wishing at this period to take Maria abroad that it was the only probable means of giving her excellent qualities an opportunity of engaging a partner for the remainder of her life—Yesterday a Swedish Chevalier [*knight of one of the Swedish orders*] a man of universal information polite manners & good character rich enough for a Swede 46 years old &c offered his hand, & I most sincerely believe his heart to Maria—She objects with reason & kindness to his distant settlement—as her heart is still her own she may without injury to her future happiness take time to consider—

It will give you & our dear Mary sincere satisfaction to be told that Maria's good sense never appeared so much mistress of her imagination—she sees that she is truly respected and much liked in this country and the first offer should not be instantly accepted—I like the gentleman—and no selfish consideration—need I say so to you!—no selfish consideration shall on my part obstruct her wishes—

I go this morning to make proper enquiries.[2]

On 8 December Maria wrote again to the Ruxtons. She had been under pressure for five days, and there are signs in her letter that she was upset, but her refusal to marry Edelcrantz remained as decided as before.

Now for love & wisdom—I have nothing new to tell you about our Swedish knight—I persist in refusing to think of 'leaving my country and my friends' to live at the Court of Stockholm &c &c, and he tells me (of course) that there is nothing he would not sacrifice except his duty—he has been all his life in the service of the king of Sweden, has places under him, and is actually employed in collecting information for a large political Establishment—thinks himself bound in honour to finish what he has begun—he

[1] ME to Mrs. R, Paris, 1 Dec. 1802; *Mem.*, i. 141.

[2] RLE to Miss C. Sneyd, Paris, begun 29 Nov., resumed 3 Dec. 1802.

says he should not fear the ridicule or blame that would be thrown on him by his countrymen for quitting his country at his age—but that he should despise himself if he abandoned his duty to gratify any passion—all this is very fine & I must add reasonable—but it is reasonable for him only; not for me—I have not ever felt anything for him but esteem & gratitude—& he says he could never be contented to be loved next to a father—I wish you were here! . . . write to me. . . .[1]

Whether Edelcrantz really would have made a suitable husband for Maria cannot be taken on trust. It was true that he had scientific interests in common with the Edgeworths, and that intellectually he was able; perhaps it was as a fellow intellectual that Maria appealed to him. Alternatively he may have thought that, either as her father's daughter, or as the author of celebrated books, she was a wealthy woman; Edelcrantz was a clever financier, as his administration of the royal theatres had shown. Never at any other point in his life did Edelcrantz reveal any interest in women or in marriage. He was a very reserved man, and might well have found it genuinely difficult to communicate his feelings either to the object of them, or to a third party; nevertheless it is reasonable to doubt whether he can really have felt much for Maria.[2] She needed above everything else to feel certain that she was loved, and, in spite of her suitor's admirable intellectual qualifications, she seems to have suspected that his emotion was not of the order needed to re-create the security she had found at Edgeworthstown in faraway Sweden. 'I agree with her [Charlotte Sneyd] in thinking that with such a father & such friends as I have much merit & strong affection must combine in a husband to make me happy in marriage.'[3]

Maria must have been able to sense that both Edelcrantz's personality and the circumstances of his life at the Swedish court would have involved her far from combatative spirit in a great deal of pain. He was an ambitious man who had risen

[1] ME to SR, 8 Dec. 1802; *Mem.*, i. 142. The *Memoir* omits the significant sentence about being loved next to a father.

[2] Dr. Gierow points to Edelcrantz's prolonged stay in England in the summer of 1803 as evidence of his inclination to re-open the question of marriage with ME (see Gierow, p. 257, and below, p. 201). This may be so, but it proves nothing about his motives or the nature of his attachment.

[3] ME to Mary Sneyd, 10 Jan. 1803. Cf. *Mem.*, i. 143.

from being a commoner to the ranks of the lesser nobility, so that his status was still inferior to that of the established hereditary nobility. His rise, coupled with his financial astuteness and a certain sharp, sarcastic turn to his tongue, had made him many enemies—who afterwards, in the last years of his life, succeeded in bringing him to trial on charges of embezzlement, although the charges could not be made to stick. However honest he may have been (and it is not certain he was honest), Edelcrantz never shrank from a fight, and his taste was assuredly not for a domesticated retirement. While Maria cannot have known much about her lover's circumstances, nor been able to see into his insecure future, a sound enough instinct prompted her to put safety first. Apparently against her father's advice,[1] she said goodbye to Edelcrantz at a breakfast on 26 January 1803, after which she never communicated with him again.

The decision to refuse what she suspected would be her only offer of marriage caused her so much pain that for once she was unable to maintain her cheerful manner with the family. 'While we were at Paris, I remember that in a shop where Charlotte and I were making some purchases, Maria sat apart absorbed in thought, and in so deep a reverie, that when her father came in and stood opposite to her she did not see him till he spoke to her, when she started and burst into tears.'[2] Even though she cast doubt on Edelcrantz's feelings, her own could not be disguised. She longed for marriage and children, and, in her impressionable way, was deeply moved by the man who offered them, and claimed to love her. The family considered Edelcrantz ugly, as most people did, but Maria was physically attracted to him. 'Her father rallied Maria about her preference of so ugly a man; but she liked the expression of his countenance, the spirit and strength of his character, and his very able conversation. The unexpected mention of his name, or even that of Sweden, in a book or newspaper, always moved her so much that the words and lines in the page became a mass of confusion before her eyes, and her voice lost all power.'[3] Her pleasure in the latter part of the visit to Paris was destroyed, and it was only by making a strong effort at self-command, 'at a time when few minds could have had motive sufficient to

[1] See below, pp. 217–18.
[2] *Mem.*, i. 142.
[3] Ibid., i. 144.

set them to work',[1] that she was able to exert herself for the rest of the party.

Her father still found Paris so congenial that he was talking in January and February of bringing the whole family to live there for one or two years; he had even begun negotiations for a house 'charmingly situated' near the Luxembourg Gardens.[2] But various events, lesser and greater, occurred to thwart this plan. On 21 January Edgeworth's favourable impression of France was shaken by his receiving a sudden order from the police to leave Paris within twenty-four hours. Protesting vehemently, Edgeworth retired that evening with Maria to a damp inn at Passy; friends offered their country houses, but he was afraid he would compromise them with Bonaparte's police if he accepted. Mrs. Edgeworth and Charlotte waited in their lodgings, while M. Pictet, M. le Breton, and others made representations on their behalf—so energetically that Edgeworth and Maria were back in Paris in forty-eight hours. At the time everyone believed that Bonaparte himself had expelled Edgeworth in the belief that he was brother to Louis XVI's chaplain, the Abbé Edgeworth.[3] Later they discovered that the order came from lower down. Even so, its arbitrariness showed the true colours of an authoritarian regime which was peculiarly disagreeable to a man with Edgeworth's ideas about the gentleman's right to dignity and freedom.

More decisively, the Edgeworths were influenced by growing evidence that France was preparing for war. Some of their French friends discounted these rumours, but M. le Breton, an officer of the Mint, knew better and firmly advised them to leave the country. By this time, late February, both Frances and

[1] Mrs. FE to Charlotte Sneyd, 10 Mar. 1803.

[2] *Memoirs of RLE*, ii. 291. ME's account of RLE's state of disillusionment with France at the time he left in March is far more strongly phrased than Mrs. FE's (*Mem.*, i. 158–60). Once again ME may have been influenced by her desire to present RLE as somewhat less liberal (i.e. in many connections pro-French) than he really was.

[3] The Abbé Edgeworth, 1745–1807, was born at Edgeworthstown Henry Essex Edgeworth. His father Robert, Rector of Edgeworthstown and first cousin to ME's grandfather, Richard Edgeworth, became a Catholic and went to France in 1749. The abbé, known in France as the Abbé Edgeworth de Firmont, became famous for his ministration to Louis XVI on the scaffold and his subsequent loyalty to the French royal family in exile.

Maria seemed ready to go home: Frances missed her little daughters, while Maria's unusually disturbed state of mind seems to be reflected in the mordant power with which she describes the most interesting experience of these last weeks, a meeting at last with an impoverished and embittered Mme de Genlis.[1] It was agreed, therefore, that they should go first to Edinburgh, where Henry was reported to be very unwell; then on to Edgeworthstown; and, if all went well, perhaps return to Paris later that summer. After several days of waiting at Calais for a fair wind, they crossed to Dover on 5 March 1803. But in London a letter was waiting for them from M. le Breton which altered everything, for it ended with a pre-arranged message in code—war was imminent. Edgeworth abandoned all hope of going back to France, and sent an urgent letter to Lovell in Geneva to follow them home at once.

When England declared war again early in May, Lovell, who had never received his father's summons, was only just beginning his journey home through France. He was arrested and interned for the next eleven years, six of them to be spent in dispiriting idleness at Verdun—'this abominable hole', as he called it, where 'the Genius of Ague had made ... his residence'.[2] It was a catastrophe that was felt acutely by an unfulfilled man of twenty-eight, and it effectively poisoned the rest of his life.

Long before this the Edgeworth party was in Edinburgh. They arrived at Dumbrick's Hotel on 19 March, after a leisurely journey up the Great North Road which was broken by visits to York and Durham. Henry had been very ill during the severe Scottish winter, but he had kept indoors, and his physician, the Professor of Medicine James Gregory, was now ready to pronounce that he had avoided tuberculosis for the time being.

With their minds set at rest the Edgeworths could enjoy themselves. Of all the places they had originally thought of visiting, Edinburgh was the most naturally congenial. They were able to mix with people like themselves, intellectual, rational, and progressive; they were in little danger of finding themselves out of place among mere socialites. Their principal host in Edinburgh was the Professor of Moral Philosophy,

[1] ME to Mary Sneyd, Edinburgh, n.d. [March 1803]; *Mem.*, i. 161–9.

[2] Lovell Edgeworth to M. N. Phillips, Verdun, 14 Aug. 1803.

Dugald Stewart, who had acted as teacher, host, and father-figure in turn to Lovell and Henry. As a survivor of the group of Scottish empiricists which had included Hume, Adam Smith, and Thomas Reid, Stewart was a figure out of Edgeworth's intellectual past.[1] His house attracted many clever men throughout this period; although not intellectually in the first rank of the school to which he belonged, Stewart was perhaps the most effective teacher and disseminator of ideas of his time, and his influence in progressive Whig circles was to remain profound for another twenty years. 'The evening parties at Lothian House appeared to us (though then fresh from Paris) the most happy mixture of men of letters, of men of science, and of people of the world, that we had ever seen.'[2]

Dugald Stewart's wife, the charming and able woman who in her own right kept the friendship of her husband's former pupils,[3] remained for many years a favourite correspondent of Maria's. Among other friends she made in Edinburgh were Dr. Gregory, the mathematician John Playfair, and the preacher and aesthetician Archibald Alison. But somehow she missed meeting the better-known literary men who also frequented Dugald Stewart's house in the Canongate. This after all was the year following the founding of the *Edinburgh Review*; but there is no evidence that she met Francis Jeffrey, for example, until some years after her father's death. Her friendship with Scott also began much later. The Edgeworths' failure to meet Scott in 1803 later struck Lady Scott as surprising, but her husband had a characteristic explanation. '"Why", said Sir Walter, with one of his queer looks, "you forget, my dear,—Miss Edgeworth was not a lion then, and my mane, you know, was not grown at all."'[4]

In spite of their high praise for Edinburgh as a literary centre, the only creative writer the Edgeworths met there was Elizabeth Hamilton (1758–1816), the author of works not dissimilar in

[1] See above, p. 59. ME had already sketched the idea of Stewart she had received from her brothers in the character of Dr. Campbell in *Forester* (*Moral Tales*, 1801).

[2] *Memoirs of RLE*, ii, 295. A general picture of Edinburgh society in this period which confirms the Edgeworths' impression of its brilliance is given in Lord Cockburn's *Memorials of his Time*, 1856.

[3] She was, for example, the 'Ivy' of John Ward, 1st Earl of Dudley's *Letters to Ivy*.

[4] *Life, Letters and Journals of George Ticknor*, 1876, i. 431.

style and range from Maria's own. Maria already admired her *Memoirs of Modern Philosophers* (1800), in which she used the character of Bridgetina to satirize philosophical novels of the school of Godwin and Mary Wollstonecraft. Later she was to produce minor works on education and—one of Maria's favourite novels—*The Cottagers of Glenburnie* (1808), a brisk, progressive study of the slovenly ways of the Scottish peasantry, which in its realism, its humour, and its impatience with traditional ways resembles Maria's own tales about Ireland. Maria and Elizabeth Hamilton liked one another: they corresponded at intervals and met again in 1813, when Mrs. Hamilton visited Ireland.

On their way home in early April the Edgeworths gave a day to Glasgow, but as usual little time to Dublin. Towards the end Maria especially seemed anxious to see her own friends and home again. She had insisted all along that travelling made no difference to her tastes, by which she meant that she still preferred her quiet domestic existence at Edgeworthstown. Like the tour of England in 1799, her journey had also made surprisingly little difference to her ideas. The visit to Edinburgh confirmed intellectual ties that had existed since her father fell under the influence of the Lunar circle and read Adam Smith. Paris was in itself of course a much more diverse society; but the Edgeworths had been received there primarily as the friends of Pictet and the authors of *Practical Education*. Although their Parisian friends sometimes assured them that they had enjoyed reading *Belinda* recently (in its French translation by M. Ségur), they seemed to have been virtually unaware of the extracts from *Castle Rackrent* and *Irish Bulls* which had also been carried by the *Bibliothèque Britannique*. And this was not only understandable, but, Maria thought, just. Both she and her father believed that the difficulty of translating her Irish stories was a symptom of their limitation. Long afterwards, on receiving a copy of *L'Absent*, Maria exclaimed: 'It is impossible that a Parisian can make any sense of it from beginning to end—beginning with Lady Clonbrony & Sir Terence O'Fay & ending with Larry!—but these are good lessons—to teach an author what is merely local & temporary.'[1]

[1] ME to Mrs. R, 1 Jan. 1814 [?1815]. Cf. also RLE's letter of 15 July 1815 to ME's French publishers, Galignani and Maradan, quoted below, p. 301.

In minor ways meeting so many people in Paris helped Maria's fiction. It gave her fresh material, and (for a while at least) it made her much less sweeping and doctrinaire about the fashionable life in which so many of her tales were set.[1] But both these were short-term advantages. In the most fundamental of her attitudes, that at best the fiction could never be more than a supplement to the educational work, Paris tended to confirm Maria's existing assumptions. Probably it also encouraged her to write about high life, which was much the same in England and France, rather than about the Irish peasantry. If anything, therefore, the effect of exposure to French society was to make Maria more conservative as a writer, and this is certainly significant, because for many years Paris was more important culturally in the Edgeworth household than London. Between 1803 and 1808 Maria seems to have read more imaginative books in French than in English, and after that the proportion of French books was still high. Out of 122 references between 1803 and 1813 to different books she was currently reading, thirty-eight of the titles, nearly a third, are French.[2]

Settling down again at home therefore brought few problems of readjustment for Maria, except the need to recover from her refusal of Edelcrantz. He continued to occupy her thoughts far more than one would suppose from reading her published correspondence. In the summer of 1803 she managed to do little work, and that autumn she was kept busy with tasks for her father; but in November she renewed her interest in fiction with a plan to write a story especially to please Edelcrantz. The great literary talking-point in Paris the previous winter had been Mme de Staël's *Delphine*, which, Maria said, was 'cried down universally' by the circles they moved in. Her own opinion, as she told her brother Henry at the time, was that it had fine passages in it; but it was 'tiresome & immoral or as a

[1] See above, p. 190 n., and below, p. 318. In retrospect ME undervalued the influence of her season abroad. 'I don't think I was much—if at all improved as a writer, by a winter in Paris or by a visit to Edinburgh or Dublin' (ME to ED, 9 July 1811; quoted at length below, pp. 224–5).

[2] She must have read more books than she writes about in her letters. But there is no reason to suppose that the proportion of French to English would be affected by the addition of more titles.

gentleman lately said *il manque d'etre abregé—eclairci et epuré'*.[1] Although the gentleman she quoted was not Edelcrantz, she knew that he too disapproved. Maria accordingly conceived in *Leonora* a story which was to be a strong, clear, pure reply to Mme de Staël, and so would appeal to the taste of all their Parisian friends, but to Edelcrantz in particular.

The painstaking work Maria did on *Leonora* over a period of two years must have helped to keep Edelcrantz alive in her mind. 'The idea of what he would think of it was I believe present to her in every page she wrote.'[2] In any circumstances it would have been difficult to exorcize the memory of him. For she soon discovered that Edelcrantz had come to England, and the knowledge that he lingered on there disturbed her peace with the possibility that they might meet again.

> To my surprise it [the last number of *Nicholson's Journal*] begins with 'Upon my late return from an Agricultural tour in Scotland &c[']' and it ends with A. N. E—z. so he is still in London! What to think of this or of any of his mysterious & inconsistent conduct I know not—and you will say it is not worth my while to consider—sooner said than done my dearest Sophy—Stay till you try—May you never try as I do. . . .[3]

In these circumstances her ability to confide in Sophy was a source of real comfort. Long before, Edgeworth had observed that steadiness was Sophy's great characteristic, and Maria could now confirm that she was both discreet and tough. Years later Maria summed up Sophy by comparing her with the Sneyd stepmothers' niece, Emma Sneyd:

> Her head & heart have almost risen to the level of Sophy Ruxton—steady & solid as Sophy—*safe* as her for a friend—safe in judgment & sincerity—almost not quite her equal in temper—inferior to her in natural ability—inferior in strength of mind I believe but am not sure—superior far-far in manners—& in all feminine unaffected feminine characteristics.[4]

For years Maria had been used to asking Sophy's advice. 'With all my wisdom, in print, I have not out of print, the clearest of all possible judgments—but then you have a good

[1] Letter of 16 Jan. 1803.

[2] *Mem.*, i. 143.

[3] ME to SR, 15 Feb. 1804. For a possible explanation of his conduct, see above, p. 194 n.

[4] ME to Mrs. FE, 4 Mar. 1819.

judgment—& my mother has, & my father, & what need I care if these are not actually lodged in my pericranium I have the use of them—What's yours is mine—you may thank your stars, at least on this occasion, that what's mine is my own.'[1] Where Edelcrantz was concerned Sophy seems to have stuck firmly to the same advice to Maria—not to think of him, and above all not to put herself in his way. The latter course was a temptation, since Maria received two invitations to visit England in 1804. One was from Mrs. Saunderson, who was now on visiting terms with them, and besides was a family connection of the Beauforts; this Sophy advised her decidedly to refuse. The second was from Emmeline. Maria was pleased that her sister, who had not always been friendly, should now ask her to go and stay at Clifton, but she was decided about what her answer should be:

> Independently of all other reason I could not possibly go to England at present without my father because —— is I believe still there—I have never mentioned *that* subject to E[mmeline] as I feared it might possibly implicate her . . . Now I can always with perfect truth say to my father—She knows nothing about the matter & therefore she *could* not influence me—You see my dear friend Sophy I use you worse—exactly because I have the most perfect dependence upon your strength of mind & cool judgment & warm friendship.[2]

In many respects Maria's friendship with the Ruxtons reached the height of its importance in her life between her return from Paris in 1803, and about 1807. Even after this Sophy continued for some years to be her only confidante on affairs of the heart (except perhaps Frances Edgeworth, whose private conversations with Maria at home are not recorded in any letters). The pleasure of talking intimately was one of the factors which took Maria to Black Castle at this time. Another was the Ruxtons' willingness to spend long hours hearing and discussing her stories, which contrasted with Richard Lovell's crowded day and competing interests.

Soon after their return Edgeworth had once again become busy with public affairs, but in Henry and Sneyd he now had two grown-up sons to help him. In August 1803 Dublin was shaken by Emmet's rising, and although this was not so serious

[1] ME to SR, n.d. [1802]. [2] ME to SR, 22 July 1804.

an affair as the general Rebellion of 1798, its reverberations were felt in the countryside. That month Edgeworth was 'almost harrassed to death' fortifying his house; although the county might be quiet, there was evidence of a spirit of disaffection on their very doorstep. 'A whole nest of *little* villains—10–11–12–13 years old have been discovered in Edgeworthstown who get together to drink unlawful toasts such as *Here's to the star which was lit in America, which shined in France & was quenched in Ireland*.'[1]

Ireland's situation was made more uneasy, as in the 1790s, by persistent rumours that the French were on the point of invasion. Once again Edgeworth pressed his invention of the telegraph on the government; and this time, perhaps because the family had become locally and nationally better known, Lord Hardwicke's Administration did not take long to accept. Everyone at Edgeworthstown who could write had to set to work that October making two full copies of the code. Just before Christmas Edgeworth set off with his wife's brother, Capt. Francis Beaufort of the Royal Navy, to build a chain of telegraph stations across the country from Dublin to Galway. 'God speed them—& keep Bonaparte away till the giant isosceles is ready on the coast to meet them.'[2] Edgeworth's absorption in defence and the telegraph explains why he had nothing to do with the early stages of *Leonora*, and did not know that *Modern Griselda* was being written until it was printed.[3]

Circumstances thus encouraged Maria to maintain her correspondence with the Ruxtons, and of all her letters to them, none are so entertaining or so well designed to give pleasure to a particular recipient as those of this period. In many respects these family letters, which are so different from the journal-letters she sent home from abroad, serve as informal notes for the novels; they contain for example some acute and memorable sketches of visitors to Edgeworthstown.[4] Her father did not approve of so much feminine gossip about personalities. She broke off once on the third side of a letter to her stepmother to exclaim in mock alarm: 'I have not yet done talking of *persons*—what will my father say to me?'[5] But Maria took as

[1] ME to SR, Aug. 1803. [2] ME to SR, 18 Dec. 1803.
[3] See below, p. 288. [4] See, for example, letters quoted on pp. 353–4 below.
[5] ME to Mrs. FE, Black Castle, n.d. [summer 1803].

much pleasure in 'scribbling' to Black Castle as in writing any tale, and she would get up early to finish her letters before breakfast, so that she had no need to account to her father for her time.

Compared with the strongly practical, utilitarian bent of everything on which Edgeworth spent his time, many of Maria's best letters have almost no content at all. In the absence of much news, she concocted entertainment out of mere wisps of material, such as an absurd accident to an acquaintance from which she could point the contrast between fashionable impracticality and plebeian Irish common sense:

. . . I hope when and wherever [Sophy] rides she will not buckle, strap, pin or otherwise entangle her limbs in her habit skirt, I have always thought this a most dangerous & detestable practise [*sic*] & yesterday heard a memorable instance in support of my opinion. Lady Anna Maria Cotton who was not long since shewing us how admirably she tied up her feet in her skirt & made a swathed mummy of herself on horseback was riding near Longford with a party of Knights & Squires & Lords & Lordlings & grooms of the stole & *grooms-companions* which are now more in request than Knights companions. The lady's horse took fright at a turf-kish & reared & backed & backed & reared till he fell backwards upon his fair mistress into the gripe of a dirty ditch 6 foot broad by I don't know how many deep; but deep enough to cover her Ladyship with water & mud up to her watchchain. . . .

The Lords & Knights and grooms-companions still in their saddles set roared out 'Oh my Lady Anna Maria!—Lady Anna Maria!' and lift[ed] up their hands & eyes to heaven as far as the care of their curb-bridles would permit. The servants dismounted but some only held their own horses heads, others only peeped into the ditch or listened to their masters & none ventured to the fair & noble lady's assistance. At last a farmer of the name of John Allen came riding up & the moment he saw the distressed damsel he like a true knight jumped off his horse & flew to her assistance. He set his foot upon the back of her Ladyship's steed which just appeared above water & pulled at the Lady's fair hand & arm with all his might & raised her from the back of the ditch but her foot & petticoats were fast in the stirrup, for this he was not prepared, with this unexpected resistance to his jerk, he lost his footing & he with his fair burthen in his arms fell into the ditch & floundered up to his middle.

Here is falling & floundering & dirt enough to delight even

Mr. Day's [*sic*] whom nothing diverted so much as people's falling down in the dirt, especially if they were ladies & gentlemen & well-dressed. Lady Anna Maria being daughter to a dutchess & accoutred in a regimental riding habit laced across the body with costly silver ribs like a man in armor and covered with bog-water & mud would inevitably have killed Mr. Day with laughter.[1]

John Allen grovelled and grappelled in the ditch repeating 'Upon my conscience Ma'am I can't find your foot!'—'By my soul Ma'am there's not a foot here to be had nowhere now.'—Her Ladyship at last directed him to her foot but when he had it in both his hands by no manner of means could he get the lump that he felt in the skirt & which he was instructed to call a foot, out of the stirrup. It was so tied & buckled there was no such thing under water or over as undoing it. Her knight errant with great presence of mind drew his knife from his pocket & cut the stirrup leather & brought up the lady stirrup and all & when he had set her upon dry land & was struggling out of the water himself what do you think her first words were—'Oh my poor horse! my poor horse! How shall I get him out?' John Allen provoked beyond all bounds retorted with an oath—'Your horse—let him get out as he can for me!'

How he got out or what the preux-chevaliers, who had never done more all this time than bow to their saddle-bows looking into the ditch, said for themselves when they got to the castle with their forlorn damsel in her piteous plight history does not say. Nor perhaps have you any curiosity to know.[2]

The majority of Maria's letters selected for publication are not like this: they date from later in her life and reflect both a wider circle of acquaintance and a wider range of interests.[3] But very little that was newsworthy was happening between 1803 and 1813, except that she was steadily writing her tales; and if the topics she takes up are gossipy and feminine, it is partly because, both at home and visiting, she was generally in the company of women.[4] Often it is the women among their

[1] This paragraph is enclosed in large brackets by ME, probably to warn her aunt to leave out the passage if she was reading the letter aloud.

[2] ME to Mrs. R, n.d. [? Mar. 1804].

[3] For the selections from her letters, see Introduction, above, p. 8, and bibliography.

[4] On a most exceptional occasion in Jan. 1810 there were seven adult males in the house to three females, and ME exclaimed in the accents of their servant Mrs. Billamore: 'I really . . . did not know the house, it looked so comicul' (ME to Mrs. R, 9 Jan. 1810).

neighbours rather than their husbands who attract notice in the letters:

Mrs. Tuite is a very clever woman with a great deal of conversation literary & anecdotal, but not philosophical or logical—So much the better aunt R will say—so much the worse Papa would say—Mrs. Smyth[e] I should prefer as a friend, Mrs. Tuite as a companion—Mrs. Smyth[e]'s manners are gentle conciliating & such as inspire affection & confidence—Mrs. Tuite's more brilliant & captivating.[1]

In conversation, in the content of her letters, and, at this time, in the scope of her tales, Maria was on her aunt's side of the question.[2]

In April 1805 Edgeworth was summoned to England as a witness into an inquiry into the judicial conduct of his friend Judge Fox, which was due to open in London on 17 May. His visit to London had some influence on Maria's life, although it was entirely negative. If Edgeworth had gone down well in London he would have made more positive efforts than he did over the next few years to take his family there. But his most distinguished social contact, Mrs. Edgeworth's family connection Lady Spencer,[3] showed a marked lack of interest in him. He met the rising Edinburgh Reviewer, Sydney Smith, and the politician Lord Melville, but did not like either as much as the octogenarian Dr. Charles Burney, who was described by Johnson twenty-six years earlier as 'a man for all the world to love';[4] quite apart from Burney's well-attested charm, it is probable that Edgeworth, who admitted to an Irish brogue, was not at his ease among the young, clever, and fashionable. He was seated next to Godwin (himself by now somewhat *passé*) at a dinner, but this meeting did not go entirely smoothly because of some perverse remarks made by Godwin. 'He says that the word moral tale is always associated in his mind with an indecent story—My father says this was such a nonsensical paradox that he did not attempt to argue against it—He found Godwin however less pedantic assuming and disagreeable than he had

[1] ME to SR, 8 Jan. 1804.

[2] See below, pp. 299–300.

[3] See below, pp. 293–4 and n.

[4] *Diary and Letters of Mme d'Arblay*, ed. A. Dobson, 6 vols., 1904–5, i. 203.

heard him represented.'[1] Edgeworth concluded that English Society as a whole was at fault for his mildly uncomfortable experiences. 'English assemblies have no charm for me—Society is not only a century behind French society, but it never can be so agreeable—there is certainly too much beef & pudding about Englishmen.' There is a note of sympathy in his reference to the homesickness of Judge Fox's wife: 'I never saw anybody so completely tired of any place as Mrs. Fox is of London.'[2]

A fortnight before leaving for London, on 12 April 1805, Edgeworth had had an alarming seizure of acute intestinal pain which terrified Maria. 'Where should I be without my father? I should sink into that nothing from which he has raised me.'[3] While he was away Maria in her turn became violently ill. The immediate cause of this was an accidental overdose of laudanum: she applied it to an aching tooth, and fainted clean away.[4] In May she assured Sophy that she was well again and going back to work, but this was not really so. The letters reaching Edgeworth in June gave him cause for disquiet, for he wrote solicitously begging her to 'eat often, take gentle exercise of various sorts, avoid the approach of fatigue, of heat, of cold'.[2] Maria suffered from a host of minor ailments all her life—violent headaches, erysipelas, and periodic bouts of sickness which were often brought on by allergy to certain kinds of food. This time it was more serious, and during the last seven months of 1805 she could write almost nothing. Towards the end of the year she went to stay with Mrs. Ruxton 'to refit', and after this, on 'the stock of health I brought back from Black Castle', she was able to resume her writing and her normal busy social life.

Although the latter flourished in the winter of 1805–6, all of Edgeworth's old enmities in Co. Longford were not forgotten. Their ultra-Protestant neighbour, William Bond, was a tireless litigant, and very good at predisposing judges in his favour. 'I need not torment you with a long history of the lawsuit,'

[1] ME to Mrs. R, 31 May 1805. Part of RLE's former prejudice against Godwin derived from the 'anti-matrimonial' views expressed by the latter in *Political Justice*.
[2] RLE to ME, London, 15 June 1805.
[3] ME to SR, May 1805.
[4] *Mem.*, i. 189.

wrote Maria resignedly, 'it is sufficient to tell you that as usual my father lost it.'[1]

In the spring and early summer of 1806 Maria was ill again. There were certain consolations for her this time in external events, especially the great occasion of the year within their social horizon, the marriage on 10 April of Kitty Pakenham to her old sweetheart Sir Arthur Wellesley.[2] In July that inveterate traveller Humphry Davy, paying his second visit to Ireland, came for the first time to Edgeworthstown. He thought poorly of the flat plain of County Longford, ringed by its amphitheatre of hills, but at Edgeworthstown House he enjoyed himself. 'Except the moral and intellectual paradise of the author of *Castle Rackrent*, nothing worthy of observation.'[3] Davy was an entertaining talker, and many of his anecdotes went into one of Maria's notebooks, for use in her tales and in conversation with her friends.[4] She was full of cheerful anticipation of the pleasure they would give to her circle at large, for a long convalescent holiday had been planned for Maria that summer, beginning with a week on her own with the Beauforts at Collon. The rest of the trip took her for once out of her usual surroundings, although not away from her friends: at the end of her visit Daniel Augustus Beaufort escorted her as far as Dundalk, in the north of Co. Louth, after which she went on alone in a hired chaise the ten miles to Newry. There she was met by Mrs. Ruxton and Sophy, who had taken a house along the coast on the other side of the sea-inlet, Lough Carlingford, and at the foot of the mountains of Mourne.

The trip to Rostrevor, beyond which lay Mrs. Ruxton's farmhouse, Fort Hamilton, took Maria into a kind of society which was quite new to her. She exclaimed in a letter at the 'mercantile taste' of the newly built villas around Rostrevor, and the modish 'gazabos' in the gardens; and to her upper-class ear the accents of some of the residents seemed even less

[1] ME to Mrs. R, 19 Mar. 1806.

[2] The Edgeworth circle viewed this event with much sentiment—more indeed than the bridegroom showed. When the future Duke of Wellington first saw Kitty again, after his absence of many years, he whispered: 'She is grown ugly, by Jove.' ME continued to meet the Duchess in London in later years.

[3] Davy's Journal, [July 1806], quoted by John Davy, *Memoirs of the Life of Sir Humphry Davy*, 1836, i. 278.

[4] For the use of a Davy anecdote in *Ennui*, see below, p. 247 and pp. 366–7.

acceptable. One Newry resident may have suggested features of both Lady Clonbrony and Mrs. Raffarty in the next Irish tale Maria was to write, *The Absentee*. 'Mrs T[hompson] is a vulgar, fine lady talking about the *pley* and the *pleyers*—Oh Ma'am you must dine with me and *stey* and go to the *pley*.'[1]

But the visit to Rostrevor was cut short by bad news from home: the twenty-three-year-old Charlotte was ill—dying, in fact, of tuberculosis—and Maria was needed at home to offer what comfort she could. Edgeworth confessed to her that in this crisis, with Frances as wretched as he was himself, he really needed her society.[2] When the blow fell, on 7 April 1807, both he and the surviving children of his Sneyd wives were deeply shaken. Honora's health was thought to have been endangered by excessive grieving; Sneyd, away in England, fell ill the following winter; and Henry, marked already as potentially tubercular, fell into a lingering illness in 1809 from which he never recovered.[3]

There is no sign that Maria was affected by Charlotte's death as deeply as the children of the same mother; but her letters in 1807 are less amusing than usual, which perhaps reflects the depression of spirits in the entire household. Eventually the outward routine at least returned to normal, and Maria embarked on a task she had been planning for some time, a second general work on education. Her father had been impatient for her to turn from the amusing anecdotal stories she was writing to something rather more solid, and Maria had reasons of her own for complying:

> I am now laying myself out for wisdom, for my father has excited my ambition to write a *useful* essay upon professional education: he has pointed out to me that to be a mere writer of pretty stories & novellettes would be unworthy of his partner, pupil & daughter & I have been so touched by his reason or his eloquence or his kindness or all together, that I have thrown aside all thoughts of pretty stories, & put myself into a course of solid reading. Now Sophy, dear Sophy! mixed with all this filial piety & obedience, &

[1] ME to Mrs. FE, n.d. [Aug. 1806]; Mrs. C. E. Colvin, 'Maria Edgeworth's Tours in Ireland', *Studia Neophilologica*, xlii, 1970, 322. For a comparable passage in *The Absentee*, see below, p. 377.

[2] ME to Mrs. R, n.d. [Oct. 1806].

[3] Henry, born 1782, was ME's particular protégé (see above, p. 99). From 1809 his letters became increasingly confused, although he had intervals of lucidity. He went to Madeira and never returned home, dying insane at Clifton in April 1813 at the age of 31.

goodness, &c, which I see you ready primed to praise, there is one little tiny grain of folly, which is visible to no eye but that of conscience & which I might keep snug concealed from you, if I pleased, but I do not please to cheat—I have the same lurking hope, which first prompted me to write *Leonora*—that it will be read & liked by —— vide page 63 of Monthly Magazine for Feb. 1805.[1]

As a study of vocational education for boys, *Professional Education* was outside Maria's natural sphere. It cost her two or more years' hard reading, and months of drudgery in the writing, and on top of everything she had the anxiety that only her father's name, not her own, was to appear on the title-page:

I am well repaid for all the labor it has cost me by seeing that my father is pleased with it & thinks it a *proof of affection* & gratitude —I cannot help however looking forward to its publication & fate with an anxiety & an apprehension that I never felt before in the same degree—for consider my father's credit is entirely at stake! and do you not tremble for me, even when you read the heads of the chapters & consider of how much importance the subjects are & how totally foreign to my habits of thinking or writing?[2]

She was kept busy on this often uncongenial task until she finished a complete draft in April 1808. Early that May she rested and recovered her interest in fiction by reading Mme de Staël's *Corinne*, a novel which both fascinated and disappointed her. 'In one word I am dazzled with the genius & provoked by the absurdities . . . As soon as I can recover the desire to *write* which has been somewhat satiated of late I shall look over the Tales which are lying by & shall perhaps write some new ones—I have not forgotten my promise to my dear Aunt—I am actually making notes for a story for *her*.'[3] Two weeks later she had written enough of her story for Mrs. Ruxton to read it aloud on her father's birthday, 31 May. It was called *Plain-sailing*, then *Mrs. Beaumont*, and finally *Manœuvring*; and it was very evidently written as a reaction to *Professional Education* rather than under its inspiration, for it is one of the most feminine of all Maria's tales.

1809 was an exceptionally sociable spring and summer. Among the visitors to Edgeworthstown were the Irish Primate

[1] ME to SR, 26 Feb. 1805. The reference in the last line is of course to Edelcrantz, although the *Monthly Magazine* gives details of another Swede, Brooeman, who had a similar commission from the Swedish king to travel.

[2] ME to SR, 23 Jan. 1808.

[3] ME to Mrs. R, 16 May 1808.

and various new English acquaintances, including the London hostess Lydia White, the young physician Henry Holland, and Mrs. Clifford of Perrystone Court, Herefordshire: all of whom became in time firm friends. But that September Edgeworth was taken ill with a severer disorder than he had ever previously had. He had a high temperature and an intense burning pain when he passed urine; kidney trouble was suspected. Maria reported him on the mend, although still weak and thin, in October; and in the new year he accepted a characteristic method of fully restoring himself. He accepted the role of adviser to the new government survey of the Irish bogs. 'It is bog, bog, bog, night and day', Maria wrote in exasperation, and later she recalled how he had gone 'often fifteen hours without food, traversing on foot, with great bodily exertion, wastes and deserts of bog, so wet and dangerous, as to be scarcely passable at that season, even by the common Irish best used to them'.[1]

All this while, since May 1809, Maria was theoretically busy on a new fashionable tale, *Patronage*. In 1809 she had published not only *Professional Education* but her greatest critical success to date, that group of stories begun in 1802 which were published together in three volumes as the first series of *Tales of Fashionable Life*. Their publisher was eager for a second three volumes to follow the first, but the elaborate, ambitious *Patronage* proved difficult to write, and Maria was evidently not sorry when a series of excuses enabled her to break off. In the summer of 1810 she fulfilled a commission for a friend—Mrs. O'Beirne, wife of the Bishop of Meath; for this couple had now become as decidedly a part of the Edgeworths' widening circle as they had formerly been associated with the hostile world of Dublin Castle.[2] The commission was to supply an introduction and notes for a book by a protégée of Mrs. O'Beirne, a Quaker lady called Mrs. Leadbeater. The book, *Cottage Dialogues Among the Irish Peasantry*, was a sober exercise in reporting real life, similar in spirit to *The Cottagers of Glenburnie*, which Maria's Scottish friend Elizabeth Hamilton had published two years earlier. Mrs. Ruxton had found the *Dialogues* difficult to get through, but Maria was prepared to disagree: 'Like a true commentator I have fallen

[1] *Memoirs of RLE*, ii. 316. RLE's MS. maps of Longford and Westmeath, made at this time (1810), are in the National Library of Ireland (16 D. 15).

[2] See above, p. 121.

in love with the *text* & begin to think there is no such author to be found as my author—I fear my notes are but rubbish—my father has not read them yet.'[1] The notes were a miscellany of anecdotes and facts, strongly reflecting the Edgeworths' intense interest in documenting the Irish social scene. This sociological bent had become noticeably stronger in Maria of recent years, since she had been forced to turn her mind to weightier general ideas than ever before both by her correspondence with Étienne Dumont and by her work on *Professional Education*. Even so, the personal motive always weighed as heavily with Maria as any other. For a brief period in 1810 she became quite an intimate of Mrs. O'Beirne's, and her work on *Cottage Dialogues* belongs in the context of their friendship. 'Besides the pleasure I have in doing anything for . . . Mrs Leadbeater I enjoy the satisfaction of its bringing me nearer to you, and affording me a pretence for troubling you thus frequently with letters.'[2]

That summer the family received a particularly welcome visitor in the Irish Solicitor-General, Charles Kendal Bushe. This witty and popular lawyer, who had been kind to Sneyd in the latter's first attempts as a barrister, was to be rewarded by a eulogy from Maria in *Patronage*.[3] Bushe liked Maria, but he had obviously heard stories which were not favourable to her father, and his first-hand impression confirmed them:

Society in that house is certainly on the best plan I have ever met with. Edgeworth is a very clever fellow of much talent and tho not deeply informed on any subject, is highly (which is consistent with being superficially) so in all. He talks a great deal and very pleasantly and loves to exhibit and perhaps obtrude what he wou'd be so justifiably vain of (his daughter and her works) if you did not trace that pride to his predominant Egotism, and see that he admires her because she is *his* child, and her works because they are *his* grandchildren. Mrs. Edgeworth is uncommonly agreeable and has been and not long ago very pretty. She is a perfect Scholar, and at the same time a good Mother and housewife. She is an excellent painter, like yourself, and like you has been oblig'd by producing Originals to give up Copying . . .

There are many young Edgeworths male and female all of

[1] ME to Mrs. R, n.d. [Sept. 1810].

[2] ME to Mrs. O'Beirne, 2 Aug. 1810.

[3] See below, p. 257.

promise and talent and all living round the same table with this set among whom I have not yet mentioned Miss Edgeworth, because I consider you as already knowing her from her works. In such a Society you may suppose Conversation must be good, but I was not prepared to find it so easy. It is the only set of the kind I ever met with in which you are neither led nor driven, but actually fall, and that imperceptibly, into literary topics, and I attribute it to this that in that house literature is not a treat for Company upon Invitation days, but is actually the daily bread of the family. Miss Edgeworth is for nothing more remarkable than for the total absence of vanity. She seems to have studied her father's foibles for two purposes, to avoid them and never to appear to see them, and what does not always happen, her want of affectation is unaffected. She is as well bred and as well dress'd and as easy and as much like other people as if she was not a celebrated author. No pretensions, not a bit of blue stocking to be discover'd. In the Conversation she neither advances or keeps back, but mixes naturally and cheerfully in it, and tho in the number of words she says less than any one yet the excellence of her remarks and the unpremeditated point which she gives them makes you recollect her to have talk'd more than others. I was struck by a little felicity of hers the night I was there. Shakespear was talk'd of as he always is, and I mentioned what you have lately heard me speak of as a literary discovery and curiosity, that he has borrow'd the Character of Cardinal Wolsey from Campion, the old Chronicler of Ireland. This was new to them and Edgeworth began one of his rattles—

'Well Sir, and has the minute, and the laborious, and the indefatigable and the prying and the investigating Malone found this out?'

Miss Edgeworth said, almost under her breath, 'It was too large for him to see!' Is not that good Epigram? I think it is . . .

I think her very good looking and can suppose that she *was* once pretty. Imagine Miss Wilmot at about 43 years old for such I suppose Miss E. to be, with all the Intelligence of her Countenance perhaps encreas'd and the Sensibility preserv'd but somewhat reduc'd, the figure very smart and neat as it must be if like Miss W's but some of its beautiful redundancies retir'd upon a peace Establishment.

Such is Miss Edgeworth but take her all in all, there is nothing like her to be seen, or rather to be known, for it is impossible to be an hour in her company without recognizing her Talent, benevolence and worth. . . .[1]

[1] Letter of 16 Aug. 1810; E. Œ. Somerville and Martin Ross, *Irish Memories*, new edn. 1925, pp. 49–52.

Bushe refers, perceptively, to Maria's loyalty and discretion in relation to her father. It is perfectly clear that the family had noticed well before 1810 that Edgeworth often made a bad impression on outsiders.[1] Even within the family he had a reputation for tactlessness, and for talking too excitably, that accords with Bushe's word 'rattling'. Those who did not know him attributed his volubility to a desire to shine: it was said of him in Edinburgh in 1803, for example, that he deliberately talked Maria down—'she could not get leave to speak to any-body'.[2] There were others besides Bushe who now summed up the various qualities of his temperament and mind—his vitality, his exuberance, his pride in himself and in his family—into one over-riding characteristic, his 'predominant Egotism'.

From some of Edgeworth's children, too, there came an undercurrent of resistance, although Maria of course remained intensely loyal. While Sneyd was away in England a trivial dispute arose between him and his father, about which Maria had some revealing comments to make:

> Pray my dear Sneyd keep this in mind whenever he gives you any proofs of his sollicitude [*sic*] which vex or plague you at the moment, for men, even *fathers* & authors of practical and professional education are not *perfect*, & in my opinion the exuberances of warm enthusiastic affection are of all faults of human nature the most easily *endured* . . . I know that things sometimes appear to the best judges (and you are not a judge yet) different in absence—& my father very differently by letter & by word of mouth—much depends on manner & look & voice & nameless expressions of countenance.[3]

In general, though, the family circle remained under his spell as the outside world did not. Long after his death Thackeray's daughter met a niece of Mrs. Edgeworth's, and spoke dis-paragingly of Richard Lovell and his hold on Maria, only to find that among the Edgeworths and Beauforts a very different view of him lingered on. 'You do not in the least understand what my uncle Edgeworth was. I never knew anything like

[1] See, e.g., ME's comments on his reception at Clifton in 1791–3 (*Memoirs of RLE*, ii. 143–5, cited above, p. 105).

[2] Joanna Baillie to Walter Scott, 1 July 1813; *Scott's Familiar Letters*, ed. D. Douglas, 1894, i. 300.

[3] ME to CSE, 21 Mar. 1810. For further observations by ME on her father's written style, cf. *Memoirs of RLE*, ii. 333–4.

him. Brilliant, full of energy and charm, he was something quite extraordinary and irresistible. If you had known him you would not have wondered at anything.'[1] In his prime new acquaintances had thought of him like this,[2] but the trail of visitors who came to Edgeworthstown to see his daughter were increasingly inclined to sum him up as a meddlesome old man bent on exploiting Maria's success.

Early in 1809 Edgeworth had been planning a visit to England which for various reasons had had to be postponed, but the urge to take Frances and Maria away had not left him. It was late in 1810 when he disengaged himself from his survey of the bog-lands, but travel in Ireland that autumn remained possible. In October they went to the famous theatricals at Kilkenny Castle, where Maria met Miss Grattan, daughter of the statesman, and heard Thomas Moore. 'I thought Moore recited well—but I don't like his books altogether.'[3] She also found the artificiality of Irish Society disagreeable: 'The whole appeared to me quite *French*.'[4] It was her first glimpse of high life in Ireland, as opposed to the ordinary social contacts of the midlands gentry. It was also the furthest from Dublin she had ever been within the country. For a woman who was by now famous as a sketcher of Irish society, her first-hand knowledge was remarkably limited. Even Kilkenny is barely sixty miles south-west of Dublin; and Maria was never to travel any further till her career as an Irish writer was over. She first visited Killarney as a tourist with Sir Walter Scott in 1825; she never saw the Giant's Causeway (but used a guide-book when she needed to describe it for her novel *Ennui*);[5] and her first visit to the primitive and Gaelic West was her tour of Connemara in 1833.

At least Kilkenny supplied her with up-to-date and first-hand impressions of the Irish aristocracy, which 'told', as she

[1] Anne Thackeray Ritchie, *A Book of Sybils*, 1883, p. 95. Lady Ritchie's informant must have been Lady Strangford, Francis Beaufort's daughter by his first marriage. She was not born till 1826, nine years after RLE's death, but she would have reflected the family view of him.

[2] See above, pp. 40–1.

[3] ME to Mrs. R, Nov. 1810.

[4] ME to SR, n.d. [Nov. 1810]. The theatrical entertainments at Kilkenny were from 1802 to 1819; see *The Private Theatre of Kilkenny*, privately printed, 1825.

[5] See below, p. 372.

would have said, in *The Absentee* (1812) and *Ormond* (1817). So did a three-week trip to Dublin in November, which Edgeworth, Frances, and Maria took in order to hear a series of lectures given by Humphry Davy. Maria had spent very little time in the Irish capital except when she was in transit to and from England, and the visit was useful both because it enabled her to meet professional friends of her father and brothers, and because it introduced her to the commercial life of the city. The view Maria formed of Dublin life, an unusually favourable impression for the post-Union period, is given in *The Absentee*.[1]

Outwardly all this was pleasant and rewarding enough, but Maria's emotional state in November 1810 was far from tranquil. A friend and neighbour of the Ruxtons, George Knox, had been travelling in Sweden, and on his return had had a conversation with Sophy which was quickly passed on to Maria. Knox had met Edelcrantz; what was more, had talked to him intimately; and, although apparently Knox did not think so highly of the Chevalier's abilities as Maria did, he was sufficiently impressed to wonder aloud to Sophy why Maria had not married him. Maria's interest was intense, and she obviously responded to every nuance in Sophy's report of what Knox had said:

> I feel exquisite pleasure at hearing that so good a judge as Mr. Knox was so nearly of my opinion—so entirely of my opinion as to manner and character—As to abilities I hope you will not attribute it to love but to my sane and quite cool judgment (the deuce is in it if 8 long years have not cooled my judgment!) if I say that the printed & published proofs of that ability are such as Mr K if they were in his hands must as a critic admit to be adequate—Has *he* ever in science or belle-lettres produced anything equal to what I can produce on the part of my AUTHOR? I beg pardon for this malicious question, but, much enforced, it was really irresistible—
>
> I would give worlds on the top of worlds to know how that Governor of the poor King of Sweden's son [*i.e. Edelcrantz*] has conducted himself in the late disturbances—I am sure I should be unworthy of the name of Edgeworth unworthy to be a relation of the great & good Abbé E[2] if I did not utterly despise & abjure the

[1] See below, p. 377.

[2] See above, p. 196 n. The disturbance in Sweden was the deposition in 1809 of Gustav IV in favour of his uncle, the Duke of Södermanland (Charles XIII). It was perhaps as well that the loyalist ME could discover so little about Edelcrantz's

friend of a king who could desert him in adversity—*This* I cannot believe or suspect—& it would be inexpressible satisfaction to me to have absolute proof of the contrary—for though he can probably never be any thing to me nor I to him yet merely to keep well with my own dear little self I should rejoice to know that he was worthy of my affection—

How I envy Mr Knox that journey with him!—It is incomprehensible to me how two such reserved men could ever get tolerably acquainted with one another and *how* my impenetrable Chevalier could ever be brought to speak of me or our affairs I cannot comprehend—When Madame Pastoret with all her bewitching address had him tête à tête for the express purpose she could hardly get a word out of him, more than general approbation such as he might have given to his grandmother—nor did he ever let her know how things stood—And yet to Mr K an Englishman—a stranger—the most reserved of Englishman [*sic*]!—This is passing strange!—

I hope my dear S—indeed I am confident that when Mr K asked why I did not marry Edle [*sic*] you answered so as to preclude the possibility of his blaming my father for what was my fault—If I had known my own mind—but that's past and there is no use in thinking of it—except to make myself wretched & ill—which for the sake of my friends & myself I never will do more.[1]

Clearly Maria felt that the subject still had power to make her 'wretched and ill'. Perhaps it was above all the passing of time that in retrospect convinced her she should not have refused Edelcrantz: she was now only two months short of forty-three, so that it was surely too late for her to have a child, and her father, whom she had then felt unable to leave, now might not have long to live. She could not discuss the subject with Edgeworth, although she longed to pass Knox's news on to him:

I wish excessively that my father could have the just pleasure of knowing Mr K's opinion exactly in the words he expressed it to you on the only subject on which we ever materially differed—I owe this to him and yet for the life of me I could not tell it to him—Do you—if you can and if you think it prudent.[2]

'The only subject on which we ever materially differed' was perhaps the question of whether Edelcrantz had loved Maria

activities at this time: he clinched his reputation for opportunism by paying court to the new king's favourite, Gustaf Adolf Reuterholm.

[1] ME to SR, Nov. 1810.

[2] ME to SR, n.d. [Nov. 1810] (another letter).

enough to make her happy: Edgeworth seems to have thought at the time that he did, and Knox also concluded that his interest in Maria had been very genuine. Evidence that this was so seems to have revived Maria's longing for marriage, and she devised a romantic ending to her current tale, *Patronage*, which rearranged the Edelcrantz episode in a pattern that she found much more acceptable.

According to the early editions of *Patronage*, the beautiful heroine, Caroline Percy, falls in love with a German, Count Altenberg, and although she is unhappy at the thought of leaving her parents she agrees to marry him. On her wedding day, immediately after the ceremony, Mr. Percy is suddenly arrested for debt. Caroline believes that in this crisis her duty as a daughter comes first, and (together with another daughter and her mother) she voluntarily accompanies her father to prison. Altenberg is called away to Germany, and so the couple separate without ever having consummated their marriage. But after an interval, in which Mr. Percy is delivered from prison and from his financial troubles, a revolution occurs in Germany which exiles Altenberg for ever, thus enabling Caroline to settle in England with her count within easy access of her father; as, of course, Maria might now have been able to live in Ireland with the former secretary of the deposed Swedish king. In later editions of *Patronage* Maria was forced, partly by larger technical considerations, but partly by readers' objections to Caroline's treatment of her husband, to change this part of her original plot.[1] In the revised version, there was no imprisonment, and the bride did go with her husband to Germany, although she was almost prostrate with grief at being obliged to leave. Once again the providential revolution enabled her to come back and set up home within easy reach of her parents.

The painful revival of Maria's interest in the subject of marriage was evident in 1811, but news of Edelcrantz was almost impossible to obtain. In 1812 Edgeworth asked Dumont to make inquiries of Madame de Staël, who was then travelling in Sweden. Dumont wrote back innocently asking them to repeat the name, which Maria did, in gigantic letters. Nothing seems to have come of this request for news; and gradually, between 1811 and 1813, there was a dying away in Maria's

[1] See below, Appendix C.

obsession with her Swedish chevalier. But after Edgeworth's death she came upon a passage in a book which gave her a curious, complex gratification:

James' Travels in Sweden Norway & Russia contain a *delightful* character of one who was once dear to me & of whom though he is now indifferent to me I like to hear the praise—I rejoice that I did not marry him & that I did not leave my father—but I know it would have given that dear father pleasure to read his praises—There is a note containing an account of his inventions in mechanics & it is really curious & gratifying to me to see how like his inventions & pursuits were to my father's.[1]

Edelcrantz eventually died, unmarried, in 1821, and announcing his death to her aunt and uncle Maria reflected that now at least she must have regretted her situation if she had married him.[2]

By 1811 Maria must have received half a dozen feasible invitations from her family and from newer visitors to Edgeworthstown to go to London on her own, but since her return from Paris she had never desired to go anywhere further than Black Castle by herself. She was quite content to read about the outside world in the *Monthly Magazine* and *Nicholson's Journal*, both of which had a practical and scientific bias, and in the more general and literary *Edinburgh Review*. At Edgeworthstown they bought or borrowed an impressive number of new books, in which the high proportion of French memoirs and novels has already been noted. Maria did not read much new poetry—except Scott's and, rather later, Byron's and Crabbe's, most of which gave her great pleasure—but she must have seen virtually every novel of merit within a few months of its first appearance.

With new books regularly entering the house, Maria did not think of herself as cut off from the intellectual life of England and France, although her attitude to literature was conditioned far more than she appreciated by the specialized atmosphere at Edgeworthstown. In 1804 she could describe Mrs. Barbauld to Pictet as 'the highest literary character in England'.[3] She was

1 ME to Honora Edgeworth, Charlotte Sneyd, and Mary Sneyd, 27 Nov. 1817.

2 ME to Mr. and Mrs. R, 4 May 1821.

3 ME to M.-A. Pictet, 23 Sept. 1804; H. W. Häusermann, *The Genevese Background*, p. 69.

not interested in experimental writing, or in what she called 'fine' writing—that is, selfconsciously 'literary' prose.[1] Her favourite reading might be fiction or non-fiction, but it would be informative and very lucid, 'plenty of facts and as few words as possible'.[2]

Letters from the Continent got through only intermittently because of the war, and Maria had few other correspondents outside Ireland except the small group in Edinburgh. Her acquaintance even by letter with fellow writers is very limited.[3] But there was one correspondent who has already been mentioned as mattering to her intellectually, and who by 1811 was beginning to play a personal part in her life: the utilitarian Étienne Dumont.[4]

Although they had met Dumont, and liked him, in Paris, the Edgeworths were not in touch with him after their return to Edgeworthstown. It was not until 1805, after reading a report that he was to accompany Lord Henry Petty to the latter's estates in Ireland, that Edgeworth first wrote inviting Dumont to visit them, an invitation which he and Maria were to issue again and again in the summers which followed. Dumont did not come, but instead wrote a long series of informative letters which by 1811 had become the most important link between Edgeworthstown and intellectual circles in London. In part the Edgeworths valued Dumont for his French connection—he was the friend and later the memorialist of Mirabeau; but it was his current work in England which proved influential as far as the novels were concerned. Between 1807 and 1810 Dumont

[1] See her letter to Mrs. Inchbald of 14 Jan. 1810, quoted below, p. 310.

[2] ME to Mrs. Marcet, 21 Jan. 1818; Häusermann, op. cit., p. 89.

[3] Apart from a single exchange with Scott, the only writers ME corresponded with before 1813 were Elizabeth Hamilton, Mrs. Barbauld, and Mrs. Inchbald. ME's letters to Mrs. Hamilton have not survived; she refused permission for them to appear in Miss Benger's *Memoirs of the late Mrs. Elizabeth Hamilton*, 1818. But many of her letters to the other two are published in Anna Le Breton's *Memoir of Mrs. Barbauld*, 1874, and J. Boaden's *Memoirs of Mrs. Inchbald*, 1833, vol. ii. The correspondence with Mrs. Barbauld (1743–1825) began in 1804, that with Mrs. Inchbald (1753–1821) in 1809.

[4] Pierre Étienne Louis Dumont, 1759–1829, was born in Geneva but had also lived in St. Petersburg and revolutionary Paris. His most important publications were his translations and interpretations of Bentham's works, and his posthumous *Souvenirs sur Mirabeau et sur les deux premières Assemblées Legislatives* (London, 1832). For an English view of him, see *Memoirs of the Life of Sir Samuel Romilly*, 1840, i. 58–9.

often wrote about the book he was writing, an interpretation of Bentham's work on penology, the *Traités des Peines et des Recompenses* (Paris, 1811); he also discussed the Edgeworths' *Professional Education*, and the most important corrections in the second edition seem to have been proposed by him.[1] As the friend of Romilly and Whitbread, Dumont's interest in education was less experimental and academic, more broadly national than theirs had hitherto been, in their books at least; whereas the Edgeworths tended to write about the intellectual and moral education of individuals, Dumont raised questions about the education of societies. It was true that as an Irish M.P. Edgeworth had campaigned for popular education,[2] but this was an aspect of his work in which Maria had played little or no part. The necessity of maintaining the correspondence with Dumont obliged her for the first time to tackle subjects on which, as she had told her aunt Ruxton on more than one occasion, she had previously never had opinions worth repeating.

Dumont had a very high opinion of the usefulness of the work the Edgeworths had already published on education. Although his letters contained perceptive criticism of other imaginative writers, they scarcely referred to Maria's tales and novels until 1809. The keynote to the earlier letters of the series was struck in the phrase with which he looked forward eagerly to *Professional Education*: 'L'éducation est votre domaine.'[3] After reading only Maria's side of the correspondence, the Swiss scholar H. W. Häusermann supposed that Dumont must have tried to make her less didactic and more receptive to the aesthetic ideas of, for example, Mme de Staël.[4] Dumont did no such thing. On the contrary, in 1811 he made two proposals which were quite in keeping with her most narrowly instructional work to date. The first he hoped she would write as a tale. 'J'aurais voulu faire un conte sur chacun des fausses manières de raisonner en morale et en legislature sur les causes

[1] He thought RLE excessively purist, and from a social viewpoint unduly discouraging, in his insistence that a bad early education was irremediable. For the influence of this idea on the novels, see below, pp. 331 ff.

[2] On 25 Feb. 1799 RLE brought in a bill in the Irish House of Commons for 'the improvement of the education of the people of Ireland'; he was one of the Commissioners appointed to inquire into the subject, 1806–11. See *Memoirs of RLE*, ii. 246–9 and 451–72.

[3] ED to ME, 23 Aug. 1807; University College, London, MSS. Bentham 174/6.

[4] *The Genevese Background*, p. 59.

d'antipathie etc. Les gens du monde ont besoin d'être instruits comme des enfants.'[1] Edgeworth replied that Dumont had 'opened a noble and vast field to her, practicable paths she would do her best to make attractive to common passengers'.[1] Maria seems to have been at least partly under the influence of this hint when she wrote *Harrington*, 1817, and again in the 1820s and 1830s with the unfinished tale *Take for Granted*.

Dumont's other proposal was originally meant for the second edition of *Professional Education*; he wanted Maria to show how a young man can overcome a faulty upbringing and re-educate himself for adult life.[2] Maria liked the idea, not for *Professional Education*, but as a separate tale. She wrote *Ormond*, 1817, as a kind of appendix to the main series of *Tales of Fashionable Life*; so that, whereas the later tales in this series exemplified the principles of *Professional Education*, *Ormond* to some extent qualified them. It also handled the moral theme in a subtler way, again at the prompting of Dumont. He warned her that her didactic purpose showed too blatantly in *Vivian*, one of the second series of *Tales of Fashionable Life* (1812), and that it was even more offensive in *Patronage* (1814). But in advising her to tone down her didacticism, he was speaking as a man of the world and a would-be political reformer; he wanted her to change her tactics, not abandon her aims. He had always spoken with approval of 'le but d'utilité de chacun de vos ouvrages'; the subject she had made her own was, he thought, 'morales domestiques'.[3] The best evidence that Dumont continued in his preference for utilitarianism and rationality over more emotional schools of writing occurs in his account to Maria two years later of Mme de Staël's visit to Bowood:

Mme de Staël a été dans tout son lustre, Lord Lansdowne, Romilly, MacIntosh, Mr. Rogers, Mr. Ward et d'autres encore tenoient le feu electrique dans un mouvement continuel, seule contre tous dans ses attaques contre Locke, contre l'utilité, contre les classifications et les definitions Benthamiques, nous accusant de tuer la religiosité, l'imagination, la poesie, l'enthousiasme du

[1] *Dublin Rev.*, cxlv (1909), 244.

[2] ED to ME, 4 July 1811; MSS. Bentham 174/10.

[3] ED to ME, 18 July 1811, and undated letter [? Mar. 1811]; MSS. Bentham 174/11 and 174/12.

grand et du beau, de reduir les hommes à de viles machines arithmetiques, et de les tromper en morale en leur disant que la vertu [virtu?] étoit la même chose que le bonheur, elle nous étonnoit[?] de la faiblesse de ses raisons et de la vivacité de son eloquence . . . Elle a emporté d'ici le Castle of rack-rent. Elle est charmée d'*ennui* et de *manœuvring*—vous etiez digne de l'enthonsiasme, mais nous nous sommes perdus dans cette triste utilité. Eh bien, la triste utilité vivra plus longtemps que le brillant enthousiasme.[1]

Dumont thus encouraged the Edgeworths to regard themselves as committed utilitarians like himself, and to think of Maria's novels as a convenient form for disseminating the movement's ideas at a simple popular level. In response to their friend's promptings and suggestions, Maria produced *Patronage*, which is little more than a series of illustrations of the themes of *Professional Education*. Although he thought that the moralizing could have been more delicately done, Dumont praised the content, and sympathized perfectly with the intention. Edgeworth was gratified by his approval.

One would think by the complete view which you have taken of *Patronage* that you had seen the sketches of the story—It is intended as

Mental Domestic-Medicine.

Maria has endeavoured to sweeten the dose, but she could not have accomplished her design if she had left out any of the ingredients.[2]

The over-all influence of Dumont on Maria had thus worked powerfully in the direction of ambitious public themes, as he encouraged her to harness her talent for anecdote in order to provide *exempla* for utilitarian ideas, actually in a more wholehearted and consistent spirit than she had previously shown as a didactic writer.

Ironically enough, Dumont also gave Maria a great deal of sophisticated and purely literary advice, of which his warning

[1] ED to ME, 1 Nov. 1813; MSS. Bentham 174/24. Mme de Staël's remark about 'triste utilité' evidently referred to Dumont and his friends at Bowood and not, presumably, to ME at all. But ME misunderstood it and repeated it in 1820 to the Duchesse de Broglie as a criticism her mother had made of herself; the Duchesse denied it, quite soundly as it turns out: 'Elle était incapable!' (*Mem.*, ii. 124).

[2] RLE to ED, 4 Feb. 1814; B.P.U., Geneva, MS. Dumont 33/11.

on didacticism is only one example. He recommended her to read the anonymous *Pride and Prejudice*;[1] and he tried to persuade her that her fashionable portraits would be improved by a little first-hand observation. 'Venez voir nos *fashionables*, ils vous fornissent[?] des volumes de contes . . . Un coup d'œil vaut quelquefois un an de lectures.'[2] At about the same time Maria received four other invitations to go to London: her old school friend Mrs. Hoare asked her in 1810, and in 1811 she was urged to go by her sister Anna Beddoes, by Mrs. Clifford of Herefordshire, and by Mrs. Apreece, the future Lady Davy. Of the latter's invitation Maria observed:

> I would no more go to her than fly. Mrs. Clifford's entreaties go much nearer my heart for I like her & know she likes me—yet I cannot leave my father—I think at his time of life I ought not to do it—and I could not be at ease or happy in another country with the sea between us—except as before excepted. . . .[3]

But when Dumont asked her to go it was a little different. That last sentence, 'except as before excepted', points to Maria's hope that even yet she might marry, if not Edelcrantz then perhaps Dumont himself. This was a thought that she must have discussed not only with Sophy, but with the Sneyd aunts too.[4] His invitation was therefore inevitably more interesting than the others; at the same time, by urging her to come without her father, he had innocently unleashed the same emotional conflict that Edelcrantz had created in her nine years earlier. Maria knew perfectly well what her father's reaction would be. Either not seeing the romantic possibilities, or bluntly welcoming them, he would try to make her go to London on her own. But at the time Dumont's letter came, Edgeworth happened to be out of the house. Maria therefore hurriedly composed a long, confidential reply to Dumont, which placed their correspondence on a more emotional footing while at the same time explaining that she did not wish to come, either alone or in company. The alternative plan, that Dumont should settle for some months of work and companionship at Edgeworthstown, was more congenial to Maria in every way:

> I have tried Paris, and Edinburgh, and Dublin, and know pretty

[1] ED to ME, 14 Apr. 1813; MSS. Bentham 174/18.
[2] ED to ME, 4 July 1811; MSS. Bentham, 174/9.
[3] ME to SR, 30 Aug. 1811.
[4] See below, p. 228.

well what the pleasure of seeing and hearing and beeing seen and heard amount to, and I enjoy amusement, and compliment, and flattery all in their just proportion. But they are as O in my scale compared with domestic life . . . As to the good it might do me as a writer to see the *fashionables* of London, I do not think from my own experience of character that I should expect nearly the advantages from it that you do. I don't think I was much if at all improved as a writer by a winter in Paris or by a visit to Edinburgh or Dublin. The views of character in society are too confined and transitory. There is not time to see justly, the objects are too near. *Travellers* seldom from such cursory observation represent *manners* much less *motives* faithfully. I have I think gained more as a writer by hearing and comparing the representations of persons of sense and of *fools* who have furnished me with facts and observations according to their various ways of seeing and feeling. I have a Father and brother and friends who continually supply me with variety from that world in which I don't live or wish to live.

In a passage in which she was obviously struggling to make herself better known to Dumont, who so far knew her in her intellectual and authorial role, she explained that she was, after all, a very feminine and domestic creature:

If I were only a writer I might perhaps see better and see only as a writer in society, but a number of different feelings—many of them most trifling and foolish perhaps— . . . disturb my spirit of observation and unfit me for a *philosophical spectatress* in the world. For instance I might at a dinner with the grandest and wittiest people in London, be totally absorbed in considering whether the bones in the fish my Father was eating would choke him or not, or (more foolish still) whether my Mother's cap became her or whether the persons who might be complimenting me, thought me idiot or authoress enough to believe them *au pied de la lettre*.[1]

So girlish a note in an intelligent woman of forty-three would not have been to everyone's taste, but Dumont declared himself charmed by it. He thanked Maria for her confidence, and congratulated her on the happy life she led in retirement:

Mais que vous êtes heureuse! vous avez pris toute la jouissance que donne la culture de l'esprit, et vous avez échappé à tous ses dangers, vous n'avez point ce moi des auteurs, ce moi inquiet, qui ne dort jamais . . . Je pense exactement sur ce point de la même

[1] ME to ED, 11 July 1811; B.P.U., Geneva, MS. Dumont 33/11; *Dublin Rev.*, clxv (1909), 248–9.

manière que vous. Je suis persuadé que ces beaux esprits fêtés sont toujours très mécontents d'eux et des autres . . . vous avez la meilleure [satisfaction] de toutes dans le but d'utilité de chacun de vos ouvrages. Ainsi, restez dans votre retraite. . . .[1]

Despite his enthusiasm, retreat was not the life for Dumont, who was used to glittering house-parties at Bowood, or, when in London, went out nightly from his lodgings in the Haymarket; in 1813 Maria was told he had not had to dine at home for four years.[2] He wrote in the summers of 1811 and 1812 of coming to Edgeworthstown, but probably never quite meant it; he was content with long, varied, and by now frequent letters, until early in 1813 Maria could tell him that she, her father, and stepmother would be visiting him in London in the spring.

Mr. and Mrs. Edgeworth, Maria, and Honora crossed the Irish Sea on 30 March by their usual route, Howth–Holyhead. They made for the Bangor Ferry, and thence for the slate quarries at Capel Curig. After this Edgeworth decided on a sudden impulse to go to Liverpool, where the banker and historian of the Renaissance, William Roscoe (1753–1831) entertained them on 5 April. Roscoe showed them the Botanical Gardens he had presented to the public, and his private art collection, and talked to Maria interestingly and impressively;[3] but she did not like the noise and bustle of the manufacturing town, and, in her private heart of hearts, did not feel quite at home among the *nouveaux riches*. In a letter she afterwards regretted, she conveyed to Mrs. Ruxton her sense of the Roscoe family's want of elegance; all of them, especially Mrs. Roscoe, had retained broad Lancashire accents. 'In short though it is in the power of a father's genius to drag a whole family up in the world, yet unless the mother be a woman of education and good manners it seems impossible to give an air of gentility to the family.'[4] To do Maria's good nature justice, this was a comment, and even a subject, that probably would not have occurred to her had she not been writing to Mrs. Ruxton.

[1] ED to ME, 18 July 1811; MSS. Bentham, 174/11.

[2] ME to Fanny Edgeworth, 31 May 1813; *Letters from England*, p. 69.

[3] See, for example, below, p. 268. All ME's letters on this and other English tours are published in *Letters from England*, ed. Mrs. C. E. Colvin, 1971.

[4] ME to Mrs. R, Liverpool, 6 Apr. 1813. But cf. ME to CSE, London, 8 May 1813; *Letters from England*, pp. 10 ff. and p. 48.

Liverpool, where Maria caught cold, and Manchester, where she spent an uncomfortable night in a hotel, struck her as the least agreeable stops of the tour. She much preferred Knutsford, the home of the family of their friend Dr. Henry Holland,[1] and Shrewsbury, where they were entertained by another doctor, Erasmus Darwin's son Robert. Lichfield, their next stop, was still haunted for Edgeworth by the ghost of his wife Honora. Afterwards they stayed for a week with her brother, Edward Sneyd of Byrkley Lodge, Staffordshire, and a further six days at Derby with Edgeworth's friend William Strutt. In the company of a manufacturer and inventor Edgeworth was in his element, and the Strutts enjoyed his company, as the poet Samuel Rogers afterwards learnt to his surprise. 'Moore has been paying a visit to some of the Strutts at Derby, where the Edgeworths passed some time in the summer, and where he found old E. the favourite!'[2] They left Derby on Tuesday 27 April and travelled to Cambridge, which they reached on the evening of the next day. Thursday 29 April was given to paying some visits, and walking round the colleges, Friday the 30th to travelling on as far as Epping. They arrived in London on the morning of Saturday, 1 May, and went straight to Collins's Hotel in Conduit Street, where accommodation had been reserved for them. But they considered the rooms 'small & dear & dark' at £1. 17*s.* a week. Edgeworth went out that afternoon to look for better, and found them at 10 Holles Street, where they settled early in the following week.

Almost the first person Maria met in London was Étienne Dumont, who called to pay his respects in the evening of Sunday, 2 May. Dumont had not chosen a good moment.

I had a dreadful *customary* headache & had gone to lie down—Mrs E. came to summon me downstairs—'Do come if you possibly *can* for M. D— has come a long way on purpose to pay his respects to you'—I was so sick & in such pain I could hardly bear to move—However I crawled down & a most wretched figure I must have made, for I could scarcely speak & I would have given five guineas well counted that he had not called this unlucky evening—but so it

[1] See above p. 211. The future Sir Henry Holland (1788–1873) became a familiar figure in London Society. He was physician both to Caroline, Princess of Wales, and to Queen Victoria.

[2] Rogers to Sarah Rogers, 1 Dec. 1813; P. W. Clayden, *Rogers and his Contemporaries*, 1889, i. 37.

was & there he was!—A fattish, Swiss-looking man in black, with monstrous eyebrows & a red large face like what the little robbins described the gardeners face when it looked down upon them in their nest—I felt at once que l'amour n'avoit jamais passé, et ne passeroit jamais par là—Au reste, he is and will be always to us an excellent friend, a man of first-rate abilities, superior in conversation to anyone I have met with except Sir James McIntosh. Dumont lives the life of a French savant in society—wants nothing more & seems to have sold himself to Bentham as Dr. Faustus sold himself to the devil—This point settled, *completely*, I will now my dear Sophy go on with our public history. . . .[1]

Maria quelled hopeful speculation at Edgeworthstown with the same firmness. 'Tell my aunt Mary that M. Dumont is very plain, very fat, and as far from sentimental as any human being can be.'[2]

There was hardly time to brood over this disappointment, since through Sir Humphry and Lady Davy the Edgeworths' social life began at once. The former Mrs. Apreece was an ambitious hostess, and in her house they could meet precisely the mixed gathering of scientists and 'fashionables' that they had wrongly assumed to be unique to Paris. Other invitations soon followed. On 17 May they were asked to dinner by the scientific Mrs. Marcet,[3] together with Dumont, Malthus, and the popular diner-out John Whishaw.[4] By this time they had also been entertained by other acquaintances who had called on them in Ireland, such as Mrs. Clifford and Lydia White. At the latter's the dinner-party included Sir James and Lady Mackintosh, Miss Berry—'the famous Berry (she is all that is said of her!)'[5]—'and a man who is said to converse better than

[1] ME to SR, [16 May 1813]; *Letters from England*, p. 50. Passage marked 'Private'. For Mrs. Trimmer's *History of the Robins*, see above, pp. 156–7.

[2] ME to Fanny Edgeworth, 31 May 1813; *Letters from England*, p. 69. Dumont several times disappointed by his aloofness when he met ME face to face, although after their meeting in 1813 his letters are more cordial than ever. (See *Letters from England*, p. 116.) For all her unimpeachable respectability, ME was, as we have seen, given to over-enthusiasm, and it would not be surprising if Dumont took fright.

[3] The Swiss-born Jane Marcet (1769–1858) wrote popular books on science, and *Conversations on Political Economy* (1816).

[4] Whishaw, 1764–1840, lawyer, the friend of Romilly, Brougham, and Sydney Smith, held a similar position at Holland House—i.e. that of semi-residential intellectual companion—to Dumont's at Lansdowne House. See also below, p. 405 n.

[5] Mary Berry (1763–1852), the friend of Horace Walpole, and subsequently editor and authoress in her own right.

any man in England—*Mr. Sharpe*; he is called *conversation-Sharpe*—I sat beside him, & thought all the world was right for once.'[1] After dinner the party enlarged and the rooms became so crowded that Maria could list only those with whom she had had a real conversation. Among these were Byron's future mother-in-law and wife, 'Lady Millbank [*sic*] & daughter—daughter is a prodigious heiress—£12,000 per Ann—William look sharp!—I shd. like her much for my sister-in-law (as far as I could see in morning visit & evening rout)—very handsome—18—quite unaffected—sensible conversation—*and* she holds up her head!'[2]

Edgeworth meanwhile was achieving modest things on his own. On 8 May he spoke at a meeting of educationalists, which was organized in order to attempt a *rapprochement* between the warring followers of Lancaster and Bell. Furthermore, the Duke of Bedford called on him to hear about wheel-carriage experiments, and invited him to go to Woburn. At the Archbishop of Armagh's he met Robert Owen, with whom he had a friendly conversation; the two had plenty of interests in common.[3] But, needless to say, it was Maria whom the fashionable hostesses cared about. Mrs. Hope, wife of the wealthy Thomas Hope ('furniture Hope', as Maria succinctly called him),[4] asked them to a grand but intolerably crowded evening; while Lady Elizabeth Whitbread, wife of Samuel Whitbread, the radical Whig M.P., and daughter of Earl Grey, arranged a pleasant dinner-party at which Maria met Sheridan.

As in her series of letters home from Paris, Maria tended to give most space to the women she admired—Lady Lansdowne, Lady Elizabeth Whitbread, and of course Kitty Pakenham,

[1] Richard Sharpe, more correctly Sharp (1759–1835), was intermittently a Whig M.P. and also dabbled in literature. ME met him frequently in London in later years.

[2] ME to Fanny Edgeworth, 18 May 1813; *Letters from England*, p. 66.

[3] *Life of Robert Owen by Himself*, ed. M. Beer, 1920, pp. 152 and 292. ME did not however care for Owen. When she visited his school at Lanark in 1823, she remarked 'luckily for us the tiresome old Owen was not at home' (ME to Honora Edgeworth, 4 June 1823).

[4] Hope was a great collector of furniture and other *objets d'art* at his houses, 10 Duchess St. and Deepdene in Surrey; see Hope's book, *Household Furniture* (1809), and D. Watkin, *Thomas Hope (1769–1831) and the Neo-Classical Idea* (1968). Hope's feeling for the Egyptian and other styles of his day was too advanced for ME's conservative tastes. His wife was of the Irish family of Beresford, a daughter of the Archbishop of Tuam.

Lady Wellington, whom Maria seldom mentioned without an outburst of sentimental enthusiasm.

There could in fact be no doubt about her reception in London. She was having an even more scintillating success than in Paris in 1802–3; she was truly, as many correspondents of the period agreed, one of the 'lions' of the season. Mrs. Edgeworth too was regarded as acceptable company. As for Richard Lovell, Maria as usual approved of him and hoped that others did the same. 'My dear Sophy you & my aunt would be delighted if you saw how *good* my father is in all companies—you would not believe as he desired me to tell my aunt how pretty behaved he is.'[1] But many people thought poorly of Edgeworth's pretty behaviour, as Byron afterwards recalled:

> I thought Edgeworth a fine old fellow, of a clarety, elderly, red complexion, but active, brisk and endless . . . Edgeworth bounced about, and talked loud and long; but he seemed neither weakly nor decrepit, and hardly old . . . He was not much admired in London, and I remember a 'ryghte merrie' and conceited jest which was rife among the gallants of the day,—viz. a paper had been presented for the *recall of Mrs. Siddons to the stage* . . . to which all men had been called to subscribe. Whereupon, Thomas Moore, of profane and poetical memory, did propose that a similar paper should be *sub*scribed and *circum*scribed 'for the recall of Mr. Edgeworth to Ireland'.[2]

Moore did not remember his part in this joke, but there was plenty of other evidence to support Byron's statement that Edgeworth was unpopular in London. John Wilson Croker said as much publicly in his cruel review of Edgeworth's posthumous *Memoirs*. 'In society . . . he was as disagreeable as loquacity, egotism, and a little tinge now and then of indelicacy could make him.'[3]

[1] ME to SR, [16 May 1813]; *Letters from England*, p. 59.

[2] Byron's Journal at Ravenna, 19 Jan. 1821; *Letters and Journals of Lord Byron: with Notices of his Life by Thomas Moore*, iii. 109–10 (3rd edn., 1833).

[3] *QR*, xxiii, 1820, 549. See below, pp. 411–12. Perhaps the nearest to a defence of RLE from a literary pen came from that of Joanna Baillie, the Scottish dramatist. She found ME 'a frank, animated, sensible and amusing woman', and declared that for her sake 'I have taken a goodwill to him in spite of fashion, and maintain that if he would just speak one half of what he speaks he would be a very agreeable man'. (Letter to Walter Scott, 1 July 1813; *Scott's Familiar Letters*, ed. D. Douglas, 1894, i. 299–300.)

In the privacy of various correspondences cutting accounts were exchanged:

Much as I should like to have become acquainted with her [*ME*] the thing was impossible without taking her Papa into the bargain. Now of all the brood of philosophers I have yet seen, there is hardly one down to Thelwall and Dr. Busby whom it seems more impossible to tolerate. There is a degree of Irish impudence superadded to philosophical and literary conceit, and a loquacity that prevents anyone being heard but itself which I never met in any creature to the same degree. He fairly talked down and vanquished all but the stoutest Lion-fanciers of the Bluestocking.[1]

The criticisms came from strictly literary men, who thought Edgeworth unimportant except as his daughter's father. This view of him was so remote from Maria's picture that in 1813 she probably had little idea of what was being said. But within a year slighting references began to find their way into print,[2] and Maria was forced to face up to one of the most painful facts of her later life—that the father whom she idolized was barely known or actively disliked in literary London.

The crowded visit to London lasted a mere six weeks. Maria had hoped to meet Madame de Staël (whom she intended to ask about Edelcrantz), but the French authoress had not arrived by the time the Edgeworths left town. They arrived at Bath on 17 June, and the following day went off to Clifton to spend four days with Emmeline; to Maria's relief, Edgeworth enjoyed Emmeline's company and even went so far as to call her an 'amiable animal'.[3] They had two days with Anna Beddoes and her children, after which Anna went on with them to Mrs. Clifford in Herefordshire. They were now gradually making for home again, and Maria was eager to assure the family circle that she had not the least regret at leaving London:

Of the Dukes & the Duchesses & the Marquisses & the Marchionesses & the Earls & the Countesses innumerable with whose sight cards, and compliments & dinners we have been blessed we shall have leisure to talk in the stillness of Edgeworthstown—but in the

[1] J. B. S. Morritt to Sir Walter Scott, 29 June 1813; *Sir Walter's Postbag*, ed. W. Partington, 1932, pp. 100–1.

[2] See below, p. 273.

[3] ME to Mrs. R, Malvern Links, n.d. [June 1813].

mean time it will give you pleasure to *hear*—especially if you *believe* that my taste is only confirmed by all I have seen felt and understood, in favor of the domestic life I have always led & the dear friends I have always loved.[1]

Maria was no doubt sincere when she wrote this, but she was not objective. The letter was to her friends at Edgeworthstown, and it was meant to reassure them that she had no regrets at coming home. To a Londoner like Dumont she was able to give a more rounded description of how she now felt about Society. Dumont wrote first, shrewdly anticipating what she would say: 'Vous aurez trouvé . . . moins d'esprit, moins de lumières que vous n'aviez peutêtre attendu, et plus d'honnêteté morale, plus de vertu que ne pretendent ceux qui jugent de la Société sans l'avoir connu par eux-même.'[2]

Maria had the candour to admit that he was right:

> You seem to have looked into my mind and to have anticipated all that I should have said to you of the effect which our visit to London has produced on me. I saw more domestic value and less talent than I expected . . . Besides there is a security and sense of reality in studying from life which the most inventive imagination can never attain.[3]

Even though Maria could sincerely say that she felt the same about her home and family, to have recognized 'domestic value' in high society implied a revolution in her thinking. She had made not acquaintances but friends, as the list of her new regular correspondents shows: they included Lord and Lady Lansdowne (who visited Edgeworthstown in August 1813), Sir Samuel and Lady Romilly, and Mrs. Marcet. Through their letters Maria was to hear the latest news of scandals like the Byron affair; even at Edgeworthstown she now knew what was talked of in London, and what was read; she was part of Society. The visit to England laid the first foundations of the gradual change in Maria Edgeworth's personality which occurred in later life. She was more sure of herself and she knew a great deal more about the world, even though she did not want to make outward changes in her life at Edgeworthstown.

She gave that autumn up to earlier commitments—last

[1] ME to CSE, Bath, 18 June 1813.

[2] ED to ME, 24 July 1813; MSS. Bentham 174/19.

[3] ME to ED, 7 Aug. 1813, B.P.U., Geneva; *Dublin Rev.*, clxv (1909), 253.

touches to *Patronage*, a further series of *Early Lessons* from Edgeworth's notes,[1] and a review of Dumont's *Théorie des Peines et des Recompenses*.[2] *Patronage* came out in December, so late in the year that the publisher preferred to date it 1814. In this novel Maria had drawn a harsh picture of London Society, of politics, and some other professions, before she had any first-hand knowledge of what the capital was like. Although she had been innocent of any intention to give offence, some of her detail was taken as considered criticism, and the result was a mild furore in London. As soon as the Reviews arrived at Edgeworthstown, and Dumont reported what people were saying privately, she began a series of changes to the novel which occupied her until the following spring.[3]

A more important domestic event of the spring of 1814 was the home-coming of Lovell on 10 May; Napoleon's fall had freed him at last from internment in France. Although Maria used her customary loyalty in describing a member of the family, Lovell was a stranger to them all, and eleven years of card-playing, drinking, and self-pity had had a visible effect. There was an uneasy period of readjustment until Lovell found an occupation in planning a non-sectarian school for poor children at Edgeworthstown. For a while this common interest helped to break down the family's doubts, and from 1815 Edgeworth was writing of his eldest son with all his natural enthusiasm.

Meanwhile, in April 1814, Edgeworth had fallen ill with his old kidney and intestinal disorders. He was thought to be in serious danger for about three weeks, but was beginning to recover when Lovell came, and later that summer appeared to be well. Although there were evidently doubts about his condition, he took his wife and some of his older children, including Maria, to Dublin for two months in the spring of 1815. Afterwards Maria wrote a sad description to Mrs. O'Beirne of the hopelessness of trying to enjoy themselves while Edgeworth was enduring bouts of violent pain.[4] Later that summer Maria wrote to Dumont—after a long pause, for with

[1] See above, p. 166.

[2] ME had difficulty in finding a publisher for this long article. Parts appeared anonymously in *The Philanthropist*, vii, 1819, and *The Enquirer*, i, 1822. There are MS. sheets in the B.P.U., Geneva.

[3] See below, Appendix C.

[4] Letter of 31 May 1815.

the return of peace he had uprooted himself from London Society and gone home to his native Geneva. Maria summed up the single important development at Edgeworthstown in the intervening months:

> I am ashamed to tell you that I have written nothing these last eighteen months—Indeed, till very lately my mind has scarcely been sufficiently at ease to *think* on any subject but one—my father with his recovering health resumes a strong desire that I should break from my state of idleness—and he cannot wish long in vain for anything in my power to do—I am in perfect health and have no excuse for idleness.[1]

At times pain made Edgeworth irritable with Maria: once for example he upset her by suggesting she cared only for Mrs. Ruxton.[2] Apparently the only writing Maria did throughout 1815 was in Dublin, when she helped her father go over a *Memoir* of the Abbé Edgeworth by her brother Sneyd. Although never formally attributed to Maria, the published book evidently owes a great deal to her; she admitted to Sophy that when it was handed to her 'to be corrected', she had found it in such confusion that it had to be 'completely new written'.[3]

It was not until 1816 that Maria was persuaded by Edgeworth to return to her own literary work, *Comic Dramas* and the two new tales, *Harrington* and *Ormond*.[4] She was too preoccupied with her father's health when she wrote them to make full use either of the new novels she had read, or of the literary ideas she had gleaned from her friends in London.[5] All the same, *Ormond*, especially, shows a greater sophistication, both aesthetic and moral, than any of her earlier tales. It suggests that if her exposure to London had occurred a few years earlier, or if her father's health had not begun to break down in 1814, Maria might have written finer novels than any she is remembered for. But her father died in June 1817, the month that *Harrington* and *Ormond* were published; and this set of tales proved

[1] ME to ED, 12 Aug. 1815; B.P.U., Geneva.

[2] ME to Mrs. R, n.d. [Aug. 1815].

[3] ME to SR, Dublin, n.d. [1815]. Cf. ME and Honora Edgeworth to CSE, Dublin, n.d. [1815].

[4] For the circumstances in which *Ormond* was written, see below, pp. 278–80. Its literary qualities are discussed in Ch. X.

[5] See below, p. 440.

to be the last she wrote for adults for sixteen years. This is how it happened that her exposure to outside influences came too late to matter much in her literary career. Her productive years, like her apprenticeship, belong substantially to Edgeworthstown.

## V

## SOURCES AND SKETCHES

BEFORE she began to write a novel, perhaps at the same time as she drew up a sketch of the plot, Maria Edgeworth was in the habit of recording the 'Object of the Story'. The sketch for *Tomorrow* (one of *Popular Tales*, 1804) is followed by a typical note, headed 'Things to be done'—'to show that those who have the habit of procrastinating may lose fortune, fame, friends and happiness'—and the sketch for an unpublished and presumably unwritten play called *Celebrity* is preceded by a similar declaration: 'The reformation of Lady Helen—the struggle between her affection & her love of celebrity—and the exposing the affection, folly & vanity of the *witlings* form the / *moral* / object of this piece.'

*Ormond*, for which three complete sketches remain, was intended to illustrate a formidable number of didactic propositions. They are listed in some notes headed *Ormond Objects of this story*, which precede the final sketch of the novel:

*Prime object.*

> To shew how a person may re-educate themselves—& cure the faults of natural temper & counteract bad education & unfortunate circumstances.

---

1. *Secondary Objects*—To exhibit the character of an Irish *jobber*—and speculator—to shew how a character of this sort beginning by being *honorable* & generous in private life—but profligate & dishonest in public transactions ends by being *dishonest* in his private as well as his public character & at last quite selfish—mean—treacherous—

2. To shew the consequences in Ireland of the profligacy of such a jobbing gentleman upon his inferiors—both where he favors & where he persecutes.

3. To shew how, one of the lower class in Ireland with the best feelings may from want of education & from the oppression of a persecuting jobber & party spirited gentleman be driven to break the laws—

There are no fewer than nine further Objects for *Ormond*, including observations about the good that can be done in Ireland by a tolerant Anglican, the harm that can be done by a zealous Evangelical, and the superiority of rational attachments to rash engagements made in youth. Yet the Preface to *Ormond* boasts that this is intended to seem less didactic than previous tales: so, somehow, it does, despite the presence of at least half the objects scheduled for inclusion. *Ennui* was another of Maria's best and liveliest stories, but she never lost sight of its original theme, which was the ill-effect on a man's character of a life of fashion. When Sophy Ruxton wanted the amusing coaching scene made the subject of a frontispiece, Maria rebuked her for singling out an episode which in terms of the didactic intention was quite incidental.[1] In a letter to her aunt she showed that for her the nominal subject was the real one:

> I am finishing *Ennui* . . . Luke Whyte breakfasted here again the day before yesterday & I wish to heaven he had told me his history for I am sure it would make a fine companion to *Ennui*—Economy in opposition to extravagance & industry to indolence—But you know my dear aunt I could not well ask the man to tell me that he began life with a pack on his back could I? could you?[2]

Evidence of this kind shows that at the very earliest stage of composition Maria Edgeworth was thinking in terms of a readily definable 'moral'. The didactic element was not imposed at a later stage—neither by Maria nor by her father. On the contrary: the precept really was the starting-point, and far more often than not it was Maria herself who thought of it.

There are a few examples of didactic themes suggested by others. In particular, members of the family circle put forward useful ideas for the children's stories.[3] Some, but not many, of

[1] ME to SR, [? May 1805]. See below, pp. 366–7.

[2] ME to Mrs. R., 4 Apr. 1805. Luke White, who died in 1824 and was about fifty when Maria Edgeworth met him, was a figure of some celebrity. Having begun as the servant of an auctioneer of books, he had become a bookseller on his own account and made an immense fortune. (In 1803 he was able to offer to lend the Irish Government half a million pounds.) He bought estates in Co. Longford, and two of his sons later became M.P.s for the county.

[3] e.g. Mrs. FE's sisters, Harriet and Louisa Beaufort, gave ME the story of *The Orphans*, first published in *The Parent's Assistant* in 1800 (ME to Harriet Beaufort, ? Dec. 1799). *Tomorrow* was developed from an idea by their father, Daniel Augustus Beaufort (ME to Charlotte Sneyd, 2 Apr. 1799; *Mem.*, i. 96). Charlotte Sneyd suggested *Forgive and Forget* (*The Parent's Assistant*, 1800) (ibid.).

the adult tales originated in the same way. *The Modern Griselda* was developed from the *Essay on Self-Justification* at Mary Sneyd's suggestion.[1] Dumont volunteered several subjects.[2] *Harrington*, 1817, evolved partly from one of his hints, partly from a complaint by a total stranger to the family circle. In *The Absentee* (1812) Maria had drawn an avaricious Jewish coach-builder named Mordicai, and an American, Miss Rachel Mordecai, wrote to Edgeworthstown regretting that so moral a novelist should have repeated stale clichés against the Jews. Maria completely took the point, and by way of recompense she produced *Harrington*, a tale intended to expose all irrational prejudice, and anti-Semitism in particular.

In all these cases, as in the stories that originated with Maria, the core of the tale is its instructive theme. But there is not a single known example of a didactic idea for a story that was originally put forward by Edgeworth, whose mind did not work to nearly the same extent as Maria's did in precepts. His contribution came at a later stage, with his characteristic facts.

After choosing a theme, Maria Edgeworth's next step was to assemble material to illustrate it (although, needless to say, the process was not often as calculated as this way of putting it suggests). Here the methods in which her father had trained her began to be strongly in evidence. Just as she and her Sneyd stepmothers collected data for *Practical Education*, so she assembled facts, anecdotes, and eccentric characters who might be put to use in her fiction. She entered some information of this kind in notebooks, although probably much more was carried in her head.[3] Six literary notebooks survive, one very early, one from 1805 to 1807, the rest from the 1820s.[4] There are others, notably one from the Paris visit of 1802–3, which may incidentally have made a repository for material for the novels, but were probably meant first and foremost for use in conversation and in letter-writing. A summary of the contents of the fullest of these notebooks is enough to show what kind of material interested Maria, and where she usually found it.

The literary notebook of 1805–7 is of more interest than the others because it dates from Maria Edgeworth's productive period as a novelist. It includes a closely written 24-page

[1] ME to SR, Nov. 1803.
[2] See above, pp. 221–2.
[3] See below, pp. 262–3.
[4] See Bibliography, below, p. 501.

sequence entitled 'Notes of an account Mr. J. L. Foster gave us of his voyage to Constantinople. Jan 10th 1806'.[1] Apart from this, the majority of the entries are notes from books read especially in preparation for *Professional Education*. Towards the back of the thick, hand-sewn notebook are jottings for other projects —several pages for *Ennui* (including ideas for the sequence about Ellinor's cottage, and one or two Irish phrases evidently heard in real life), a single page entitled 'Notes for Essay on the genius and style of Burke',[2] and a page of observations made by children which is similar to the 'register' kept for *Practical Education*.

The most significant feature of this notebook, as of those that survive from the 1820s, is that it does not record ideas, or sensations, but facts. It shows a mind alert to all kind of miscellaneous information encountered in everyday experience, in conversation, and in books.

When facts like these appear in the novels, it seems that they are relatively unmodified. Maria Edgeworth's stories contain a very high proportion of real-life material, very little that is pure invention. The question arises, then, how Maria Edgeworth made her choice of the documentary material which is so essential an element in her fiction; and the answer seems to have been that she made at least a mental note of any fact that struck her as surprising or unusual.[3] Sometimes an example from ordinary daily life of heroism or generosity has particularly impressed her. Less often her attention has been caught by greed or some other unspectacular form of wrongdoing. In people of her own class, or near it, she is likely to notice personal eccentricity. In peasants she notes oddities of speech, which she takes to be typical of the class rather than the individual. An objective interest in human nature and the way it manifests itself in social custom no doubt lies behind Maria Edgeworth's

[1] See above, p. 180 n.

[2] ME found this task too difficult, and abandoned it. RLE commented: 'I did not think it would be easy to write on Burke's style. Indeed his style is not peculiar like Johnson's or Gibbon's' (RLE to ME, n.d. [1805]).

[3] One such note in Maria Edgeworth's hand on a single sheet records the outburst of an old Irishwoman on hearing of the defeat of an Irish boxer in England: from internal evidence this dates from 1823 to 1824. (Edited by Christina Colvin, *Review of English Literature*, viii, 1967.) ME's glossary to Mrs. Leadbeater's *Cottage Dialogues among the Irish Peasantry* (1811) sets out many more anecdotes evidently collected from life.

liking for facts. But she never makes a general declaration of this kind. The facts in the notebooks do not coalesce with one another or provoke trains of thought. They are merely evidence of a jackdaw-like attitude towards examples of human behaviour.

The same liking for anecdotes, character-sketching, and mannerisms of speech reveals itself in Maria Edgeworth's letters. Although in writing to Dumont she ventured on to theoretical subjects, as a whole her letters contain little original thinking or analysis. The content and manner of the letters is quite as significant as that of the formal notes, since the letters were in a sense an extended notebook kept continuously throughout Maria Edgeworth's working career.[1]

A habit of construction which surrounded a single didactic point with a large number of details, episodes, and characters from life required rich sources of material. At the beginning of her career as a novelist, Maria Edgeworth's life had been very secluded, and she did not have enough first-hand material for her richly miscellaneous books. Her first two tales, *Castle Rackrent* and *Belinda*, the only major tales for adults before she saw society for herself in Paris and Edinburgh, are more indebted than any she wrote later to the nearest sources, that is her father and family history. In *Castle Rackrent* much of the material used can be traced. This time the core round which the detail was arranged was the character sketch of Thady rather than a didactic theme, but the method of assembling real-life data was to prove very much in character. The real-life origin of Thady M'Quirk—Edgeworth's steward John Langan—is well known, since Maria for once made no secret of it:

The only character drawn from the life in 'Castle Rackrent' is Thady himself, the teller of the story. He was an old steward (not very old, though, at that time; I added to his age, to allow him time for generations of the family[)]—I heard him when first I came to Ireland, and his dialect struck me, and his character, and I became so acquainted with it, that I could think and speak in it without effort: so that when, for mere amusement, without any ideas of publishing, I began to write a family history as Thady would tell

[1] ME continued to have access to most of her best letters, at least during her father's lifetime, before her aquaintance outside the family became extensive. Both the Edgeworths and the Ruxtons kept letters, and re-read them at intervals. For examples of what appear to be preparatory character sketches for novels in letters to members of the family, see below, pp. 253–4.

it, he seemed to stand beside me and dictate and I wrote as fast as my pen could go, the characters all imaginary.[1]

Her statement that Thady is the only character drawn from life in *Castle Rackrent* is misleading. She meant by this phrase a conscious, systematic attempt to sketch an individual—and odd references to Langan in her letters certainly confirm that down to incidental gestures Thady was a faithful copy. On the first occasion when she imitated him in a letter, Edgeworth's brother-in-law Francis Fox had been at Edgeworthstown trying to raise men for a force of militia. 'Mr. Fox I believe got but one Recruit out of John Langan & to all our enquiries for my Uncle[,] John shakes his head, puts up his shoulder, or changes from leg to leg which are all in him sad tokens of distress.'[2] Anyone who has read *Castle Rackrent* will recognize Thady's characteristic manner of washing his hands of a difficulty.

But as for her claim that no one else in the novel was taken from life, what about the other most substantial characters, the Rackrents themselves? The first, Sir Patrick, could be any convivial, hunting Irish squire, such as Maria had heard her father describe, or herself read about in the Black Book. His successor, the mean and litigious Sir Murtagh, more specifically resembles her grandfather's uncles, Robert, Henry, and Ambrose, and much of the legal detail in this part of the story is recognizably borrowed from Richard Edgeworth's family history. The third of the line, Sir Kit, is a cheerful insouciant character who might be either of the seventeenth-century John Edgeworths. He also resembles them in going off to England to steal a rich wife. The details of the marriage, however, are taken from an authentic incident in another Irish family. In the novel Sir Kit brings home a wealthy Jewish bride whose intended function is to get him out of his financial troubles, but she refuses to hand over her jewels; he shuts her up in her room, and she is not released until his death in a duel seven years later. This episode appears so incredible that Maria is obliged to add a footnote giving her source, the imprisonment of Lady Cathcart by her husband, Col. Hugh Macguire. Elizabeth

[1] ME to Mrs. Stark, 6 Sept. 1834; *Mem.*, iii. 152. ME borrowed twice from the Langan family: John's granddaughter Kitty was the original of Simple Susan. ME to CSE, 4 Apr. 1808, and *Mem.*, i. 284.

[2] ME to SR, 22 Jan. 1794.

Malyn, Lady Cathcart, married Col. Macguire in 1745; but, when she refused to hand over to him her property and jewels, he abducted her to his home in Co. Fermanagh, where he kept her imprisoned until his death in 1764.[1]

It was therefore by making a strict distinction between the *characters* of the people involved (which were drawn from Edgeworth history), and their *actions* (which came from Col. Macguire and Lady Cathcart), that Maria was able to deny that Sir Kit and his bride were drawn from life:

> There is a fact mentioned in a note, of Lady Cathcart having been shut up by her husband, Mr. McGuire, in a house in this neighbourhood [*i.e. near Edgeworthstown*]. So much I knew, but the characters are totally different from what I had heard. Indeed, the real people had been so long dead, that little was known of them. Mr. McGuire had no resemblance, at all events, to my Sir Kit; and I knew nothing of Lady Cathcart but that she was fond of money, and would not give up her diamonds.[2]

The remaining Rackrent, Sir Condy, the fullest-drawn of the four, is again not a deliberate representation of an individual in the sense Maria meant. But he owed a great deal to the Edgeworth cousin her father had told her about, the young man who frittered away his fortune and died penniless.[3] While Maria preferred to deny that the Rackrents had a source, her father seems to have connected them with this branch of the family. 'In reality the family from whom this picture was chiefly taken has ceased to exist these forty years.'[4] Condy is a complex figure, however, and he may have traits of Paul Elers, Maria's maternal grandfather, whose strange indolence had also taken possession of Richard Lovell Edgeworth's imagination.

The novel has a glossary, a further compendium of facts, for which it is needless to trace each source. Two notes, however, have an unusual history. One, on wakes, was written by Edgeworth. Another, added by Maria to the fifth edition of 1810, illustrates the stratagems employed by the Irish in their endless lawsuits; it describes how a piece of turf was secretly

[1] The full story is told in *The Gentleman's Magazine*, lix (1789), 766–7, and by Edward Ford in *Tewin-Water: or the story of Lady Cathcart*, Enfield, 1876.

[2] ME to Mrs. Stark, 6 Sept. 1834; *Mem.*, iii. 152–3. Co. Fermanagh is not, however, in the neighbourhood of Edgeworthstown.

[3] See above, p. 16 n.

[4] RLE to DAB, 26 Apr. 1800.

buried by night in a neighbour's property, so that a witness could swear that the ground he stood on belonged to his own master. This incident actually occurred during a lawsuit fought between Maria Edgeworth's grandfather and the great-grandfather of a neighbour, a Mr. McConchy.[1] Thus there are a large number of old family sources for the material in *Castle Rackrent*, although these are rare for the later Irish tales. By then, Edgeworth's first-hand experiences, which were very nearly witnessed by Maria, were probably the most important single real-life ingredient. But in both cases, although she had an unusually good vantage-point as her father's assistant, most of her real-life material was not gathered at first hand: it was had from him.

When she came to write *Belinda*, a novel set in English high life (about which she knew much less) she was obliged to rely more heavily still on a single source, her father's youth. It has been obvious to most critics that the half-relevant sub-plot, in which the hero tries to train a wife according to the theories of Rousseau, is based on Thomas Day's experiment with Sabrina Sidney.[2] What has not been noticed is that the most interesting character and much of the main plot comes from Edgeworth's experience in the same period, and that Sir Francis Delaval, the rake who died repentant, must have suggested the character and career of Lady Delacour: Delaval's speech to Edgeworth about his illness and his wasted life is certainly the basis of Lady Delacour's on the same subjects to Belinda.[3]

Sir Francis's political career also supplied some of the odder exploits in *Belinda*. These incidents were at least forty years old when the novel came out, and some of them were objected to as totally improbable. Although anachronistic, they accorded well enough with Delaval's career, and Edgeworth assured Dumont that he could give 'chapter and verse for the female duel and the pigs and the turkeys'.[4] Edgeworth's visit to France in 1772

[1] RLE to Mr. Frederick, 25 June 1812, and note in ME's hand on back fly-leaf of a Butler copy of the 1st edn. of *Castle Rackrent* (see George Watson's edition, Oxford English Novels series, 1964, Appendix A). Similar incidents occur elsewhere in eighteenth-century memoirs, and also in folk stories, but the Edgeworth version seems reasonably reliable, in that it emanates from Richard Edgeworth. Another family lawsuit provided the climax of *Patronage*. See *Patronage*, xii. 398–404 and *Memoirs of RLE*, i. 17–18.

[2] See above, p. 39 n., and *Memoirs of RLE*, i. 214–27 and 337–40.

[3] See above, pp. 28–9, *Memoirs of RLE*, i. 155–6, and *Belinda*, ii. 32.

[4] Undated letter; 'ME and Étienne Dumont', *Dublin Rev.* cxlv (1909), 244.

is utilized forty-five years after it happened for the background of two chapters of *Ormond*, but by that time Maria knew something about Paris at first hand. She guarded against any charge of anachronism by dating the action in the reign of Louis XV, where the material for it properly belonged.

After her visit to Paris, where she met a much wider circle, Maria had far better opportunities of her own to acquire anecdotes for the tales. *Mme de Fleury* is elaborately based on an episode which had happened to Mme de Pastoret; the Château de Fleury is even the name of Mme de Pastoret's country house.[1] A much more amusing character, the French countess in *Émilie de Coulanges*, must have owed a lot to first-hand observation on the Paris trip, although the particular individual Maria may have had in mind has not been identified. The other excellent sketch in that tale, Mrs. Somers, is based on the Sneyd family friend Mrs. Powys. Mrs. Somers, who means to be generous, has a strange, almost neurotic suspicion of other people's attitude towards herself, especially once she has put them in her debt. Maria had got this trait from observing 'our old friend Mrs. P— whom I never in my life saw in possession of a letter five minutes without finding out that "there was something rather odd"—"something unaccountable"—"something really very wrong in it". '[2]

Maria's tendency to build up her tales from character sketches like these, especially in the first half of her career, arose from her knowledge that the Ruxtons loved amusing, odd people. Including the portraits meant that her tales were certain to please the circle at Black Castle, which was of course one of the things Maria most wanted to do. Mrs. Beaumont, the intriguer in *Manœuvring*, was a particular favourite of Mrs. Ruxton's. So of course was Thady, for it was on hearing Maria's imitation of Langan that Mrs. Ruxton had urged her to go on with *Castle Rackrent*.[3]

Moreover, including a mass of material, both character sketches and incidents, meant that Maria could draw her friends into the whole process of composition. This she could do most obviously for the non-fiction, especially when the book was some kind of anthology needing plenty of examples. *Irish*

[1] *Mem.*, i. 156 n. See above, p. 190. [2] ME to SR, Mar. 1804.
[3] See above, p. 174.

*Bulls* was just such a collection of comical blunders. In October 1797, Maria told Sophy that she need not yet begin making her 'pound'; but when four years later Maria was at work on her own account scanning recent satires for 'bulls', she wrote to Harriet Beaufort in England to ask her to do some informal research: 'One English is worth ten Irish Bulls for my purpose.'[1]

The Ruxtons were also asked to look out for material for *Professional Education*,[2] which was thought of from the first as a convenient ragbag of a book. 'I think that our *Professional Education* will be an admirable vehicle for anything we can say on any subject—I therefore wish you my Dr Partner to turn your thoughts to any detached facts that offer themselves to your mind.'[3] For the chapter on the education of a statesman she read several political biographies, such as North's *Life of Lord Keeper Guilford* (1744) and Coxe's *Life of Walpole* (1798). Once acquired, detailed information from sources like these would tend to reappear in the novels she wrote afterwards. Walpole's life, particularly, contributed to the picture of supposedly near-contemporary politics in *Patronage*.

However important books might be as suppliers of incidental material, friends and friends' ideas always mattered more. As late as the 1830s, when Maria was at work on a novel called *Take for Granted*, she was short of ideas to illustrate her theme. The American scholar George Ticknor recounted a conversation he had with her during his visit to Edgeworthstown in 1835: 'She was curious to know what instances I had ever witnessed of persons suffering from "taking for granted" what proved false, and desired me quite earnestly, and many times, to write to her about it; "for", she added, "you would be surprised if you knew how much I pick up in this way".'[4]

The tales were not anthologies in a formal sense, but in practice the word is not inapt. At any rate they often needed a very similar kind of advance preparation. The Ruxtons were

[1] ME to Harriet Beaufort, n.d. [1801]. English bulls were worth more because the book was intended to prove that the Irish were not unique in blundering. See below, pp. 360 ff.

[2] ME thanked Mrs. R for a list of suggestions on 11 Mar. 1808.

[3] RLE to ME, n.d. [1805].

[4] *Life, Letters and Journals of George Ticknor*, 1876, i. 429.

asked to provide some typical real-life information needed for the children's tales:

I am going directly to *The Parents' Assistant*—any stories or anecdotes from the age of 5 to 15 (good latitude & longitude) will suit me—and if you can tell me any pleasing misfortunes of Emigrants, so much the better, for I want to represent the effects of good & bad education in the conduct of two different families of Emigrants—I also have a great desire to draw the picture of an anti-Mademoiselle Panache—A well informed well bred French Governess—an Emigrant lady settled at Bath to introduce young ladies into company—my aunt mentioned some such thing—if I knew the particulars it would be useful to me—Qn. What rank of life are the parents who trust their daughters to this lady? Does she keep a school?[1]

Some years afterwards Maria asked Sophy for material for *Almeria*. Later again she wrote to thank her for supplying a 'hint on selfishness' which had been incorporated in *Leonora*.[2]

One great difficulty facing a woman novelist living on her father's estate in the country was her remoteness from the urban, masculine, professional world. At the beginning of her career Maria Edgeworth, like Jane Austen, scarcely encroached upon these male preserves, but later in her career she did try to get out of the drawing-room. This had a by-product she welcomed, that she was able to call on more members of the family for help. By now her brother Henry was training as a doctor, and her brother Sneyd as a lawyer. Each was asked to supply material about his profession for the novel which dealt with professional life, *Patronage*.[3] Sneyd, who practised in Dublin, was later told to look out for illustrations which may have been wanted for an early version of *Ormond*: 'Inquire for anecdotes of second brothers brought up in luxury improving themselves & working their own way—I have thoughts of such a character for a hero—But don't say *that*—.'[4]

For all the relative superiority of her knowledge of rural

[1] ME to SR, [? Oct.] 1797; *Mem.*, i. 76–7. Mlle Panache, leading character in the tale of that name, is a frivolous, superficial governess: ME characteristically now sought to redress the balance, which she did with *The Good French Governess* (*Moral Tales*, 1801).

[2] ME to SR, 18 June 1802 and Mar. 1804.

[3] ME to CSE, n.d. [June 1810]: 'I am now writing *Patronage*—If you hear of any anecdotes of meritorious people suffering & kept down by want of patronage—or shamefully pushed up by patrons send them to me post.'

[4] Ibid., n.d. [? Jan. 1816].

Ireland, in her Irish tales she still required information about aspects of life, and parts of the country, which she was ignorant of personally. Apart from Edgeworth, with his invaluable knowledge of middlemen and local politics, her chief informant about Ireland was Daniel Augustus Beaufort, who played a particularly important part in supplying material for *The Absentee*.[1]

Lastly there were the informants who supplied material without necessarily being aware of it. Maria Edgeworth would not normally ask anyone outside the family to help with the composition of her novels, but she was alert to the use that could be made of their conversation. During a Christmas visit in 1804 Lord Longford told her 'a great many ex. anecdotes of gaming—eating & drinking—which will all *tell* in *Ennui*'.[2] The most successful single incident in the same tale, that coaching scene which Sophy wanted made the subject of a frontispiece, was supplied or supplemented by material from another friend, Humphry Davy, when he visited Edgeworthstown in July 1806. (After being told this, Byron commented 'So much the better—being *life*'.)[3] Later Maria noted further potential sources in two accomplished gossips on high society, Mrs. Stuart, wife of the Primate of Ireland, and a Mrs. Austin who visited Edgeworthstown for a week in 1811.[4]

Occasionally distinguished men and women appeared in the novels as themselves, because Maria wished to pay them a compliment. A second group of real-life characters were members of her own family circle. For example, a figure identifiable as Edgeworth frequently appears in the children's stories as the wise parent who at the climax bestows appropriate rewards and punishments. In some of the shorter *Popular Tales* and *Comic Dramas* he is shadowy but recognizable in the part of the paternalistic magistrate who is, again, the moral arbiter at the climax. Elsewhere he plays a less god-like role. He is Mr. Percival in *Belinda*, Councillor Molyneux in *Rosanna*, and Mr. Percy in *Patronage*.[5] All these characters are independent gentlemen, happy husbands and fathers, and detached critics of contemporary life.

[1] See below, p. 380.

[2] ME to SR, Christmas 1804.

[3] *Letters and Journals of Byron*, ed. R. E. Prothero, 1896–1904, v. 440. See below, pp. 366–7.

[4] ME to CSE, n.d., [1805 or 1806], and ME to Mrs. R, July 1811.

[5] Lady Davenant in *Helen* also in part resembles him. See below, p. 477.

*Patronage* has several more members of the Edgeworth family. Godfrey, Mr. Percy's eldest son, who suffers from an excess of party spirit, ultimately derived from Maria's eldest brother, Richard, the impetuous Rosamond from Maria herself, and Caroline, the heroine, from her stepsister Honora, who died in 1790.[1] The remaining brothers, the lawyer Alfred and the doctor Erasmus, are not distinctly characterized, but Sneyd and Henry had fulfilled Maria's request to supply some of their adventures. Richard, Maria, and Honora were probably identified with characters in the story in the days when it was the adventurous family saga known as *The Freeman Family*.[2] Maria told Sophy before she began work on *Patronage* proper that she would now eliminate the connection with her own family, but in practice she failed to do this; yet it would be rash to assume from the example of *Patronage*, where family detail is intrusive, that Maria never obtained first-class material from the experience of her younger brothers and sisters. It was Henry's childhood terrors that supplied the opening chapters to *Harrington*, much the best sequence in the book.

The public personalities who occasionally appeared in the novels were usually great men who had earned the gratitude of the Edgeworth family. They were not characterized so much as idealized, but just enough distinctive features were left to enable the original to be recognized. As a rule these figures did not play an important part in the plot. The most suitable role proved to be that of mentor to the hero (or occasionally heroine); the great man either gave him good advice about life, or discovered his hidden merit. The real men and women who made appearances of this kind included the novelist Dr. John Moore (Dr. X) in *Belinda*,[3] the Scottish moral philosopher Dugald Stewart (Dr. Campbell) in *Forester*,[4] the leader of the Irish Volunteers, Lord Charlemont (Lord Y—) in *Ennui*, and the lawyer Charles Kendal Bushe (Lord Chief Justice) in

[1] The evidence for identifying Maria with Rosamond and Honora with Caroline is a pencilled note in a family copy of *Patronage*, and the family tradition handed down by Mrs. H. J. Butler, daughter of Maria's youngest stepbrother. Both are quoted by Slade, p. 150.

[2] See above, pp. 155–6.

[3] Dr. X is identified in the draft to *Belinda* published as an Appendix to the *Memoir*.

[4] RLE to Henry Edgeworth, 11 May 1801.

*Patronage.*[1] Charlemont had been friendly with Edgeworth, Stewart had been host to Henry, and Bushe had encouraged Sneyd. The group of distinguished Frenchmen whom Edgeworth had contacted when he visited France in 1772—Marmontel, d'Alembert, and the Abbé Morellet—are brought into *Ormond.* In *Helen* great men and women do not actually appear, but in the course of the dialogue compliments are paid to Scott, Dumont, and Mme de Staël.

The literary value of the tales depends, or partly depends, on an entirely different kind of real-life sketch, Maria's character studies of people she had seen and been struck by, or heard of through her father. Among the most important examples, several of the peasant characters in *Ennui* and *The Absentee* originated in real life. Edgeworth had an Irish nurse, for example, who gave some traits to old Ellinor. Even if peasant characters as such were not taken from life, many of the speeches they made certainly were.[2] The two Irish plays in *Comic Dramas* were owned to have real-life portraits. 'Christy Gallagher is a genuine Irish character; so is Kathy Roony; but Biddy Doyle is an original.'[3]

The most interesting opportunity to study Maria Edgeworth's extended character-drawing from life is offered by *Ormond.* This tale is built upon a contrast between two types of Irish gentlemen, the Protestant Anglicized jobber, Sir Ulick, and his traditionalist Catholic cousin, 'King' Corny. Both these elaborate portraits are taken from life. The early sketches to *Ormond* describe Sir Ulick as resembling two men, Sir John de Blaquiere and 'T. P.'. De Blaquiere (1776–1812) was a well-known Irish politician and jobber, who acquired a peerage in the bartering of titles that accompanied the Union in 1800. 'T. P.' must have been Admiral Thomas Pakenham, brother and uncle of successive Lord Longfords, and a neighbour of the Edgeworth family.[4] Admiral Pakenham (1757–1836) emerges from Maria's correspondence as a quick-witted, jovial, untrustworthy man, who had already been unflatteringly portrayed in one of her stories. He originally appeared in

[1] Bushe (1767–1843) was Irish Solicitor-General from 1805, and actually became Chief Justice of the Irish King's Bench in 1822.

[2] See below, pp. 361 ff.

[3] RLE to Mrs. Inchbald, 21 May 1817; J. Boaden, *Memoirs of Mrs. Inchbald*, ii. 210.

[4] See above, p. 183.

*Manœuvring* as 'a spirited profligate', but Edgeworth insisted that the character must be wholly changed before publication in case Pakenham was recognized.[1]

Ulick, perhaps because he is an amalgam of two men, has taken on fresh individuality. He reads in the novel like a 'created' character, not like one still tied to his ghostly double in the real world. King Corny is not quite so free. An eccentric, warm-hearted, tyrannical old man, who prefers to live according to the old Irish ways, Corny was based on a close family connection of the Ruxtons, a man named James Corry:[2]

> The first idea of him was taken from the facts I heard of an oddity of a man, like no other I believe, who lived in a remote part of Ireland: an ingenious despot in his own family: one who blasted out of the rock on which his house was built half a kitchen, while he and family and guests were living in the house, who was so passionate, that children, grown up sons, servants and all, ran out of the house when he fell into a passion with his own tangled hair: a man who used, in his impatience in rages, to call at the head of the kitchen stairs to his servants, 'Drop whatever you have in your hand & come here and be d—d![']  He was generous and kindhearted, but despotic, and conceited to the most ludicrous degree, for instance, he thought he could work gobelin tapestry and play on the harp or mandolin better than anyone living.[3]

A single sheet of paper in Maria's handwriting, entitled 'Notes for hist^y of K of B. Islands', indicates how very closely Maria worked to the original character:

> Gout—medecines brewing—quack—Moriarty recovers & King Corny will of gout/insert visit of Sir Ulick/—his passionate temper —whoring of—despotic—injustice—summary justice—number of little children unknown to the law—their mothers plagues of their quarrels—servants pensioned—after King Corny had been mad with them—woman with half her head shaved—Suzy Dunshaughlin —Czar Peter in furies of passion—Sancho Panza in humor & shrewdness—expects prodigious sympathy—Heir presumptive . . . Domestic economy—palace—ingenuity—not a log ever crossed the bar of Dublin but I cd. make as good—cuckoo—savage using

[1] ME to SR, Dec. 1808.

[2] James Corry, of Shantonagh, Co. Monaghan, was married to Mary Ruxton, sister of Mrs. Ruxton's husband John. ME had visited Corry: she describes 'the humours' of his household in a letter of 3 July 1808; F. V. Barry, *Maria Edgeworth: Chosen Letters*, 1931, pp. 153–5.

[3] ME to Mrs. Stark, 6 Sept. 1834; *Mem.*, iii. 151.

civilised arts—conjuror in dark ages—tricks of science—magic lantern—electrical apparatus printing press every thing himself—pair of pumps—fiddle—a chaise & a house to teach the bricklayer to roof it wonderful energy & ingenuity—vanity when a child [*ruled line*] Making a shift—& I'll engage I'll find a substitute—Bobbins to make lace brussels—cow horns—Projects opposed to Sir Ulick—steam engine—ploughing with a bull, a mule & two horses eating each others traces—grand establishment—harness more than their heads worth—Ploughing the half acre—blade of Damascus and the Tomahawk—Stoic & Epicurean . . . Sprained ankle—roaring as he said of himself like a Devil now in hell—better than chewing a bullet—do you think a pig has not satisfaction in squeeling [*sic*]—Reading—heart out of a book—independence of authority—thinks he makes discoveries—Sir I. N.—Locke—I picked that Locke, long ago. . . .[1]

Such a man was too extraordinary not to be recognized instantly, however, by anyone who had met or even heard of Corry. Maria anxiously inquired of her aunt how far she might go in reproducing his peculiarities:

If you recollect when we used to talk over Mr. Corry & when you used to make me laugh by the hour, we agreed that I might introduce such a character provided I did not make it too like the original —Now I am attempting this—My father . . . knows nothing of my plan—therefore I am particularly anxious to know from you how far I may go—and these are my questions—Do you think I may venture to use the handfuls of Hemlock for the gout—The propping up the roof of the house while he builds up to it—the making an [*illegible word*] of dishes with his own hands—the making the post-chaise & violin & building a house with his own hands—I shall not put in the blasting—tempting almost irresistably tempting as it is nor working the goblin tapestry tho' I'd give half a finger for it—the bleeding & watering plants does not tempt me because it is disgusting—The character upon the whole I think would rather flatter him if he read it for my man is represented as a man of extraordinary genius though but half civilised, & though violently passionate & tyrannical, extremely good natured & generous, with the power of attaching in an extraordinary degree—the only offensive paragraph I have yet written is that there appeared in this

[1] ME did not use the chaise, or the relations with women, but the reader of *Ormond* will recognize the gout, the quackery, the bullying of servants, the passion, humour, and shrewdness; Corny's making Ormond heir presumptive; his ingenious devices; the expressions used in his quarrel with Ulick ('blade of Damascus and the Tomahawk'); and the roaring aloud with pain.

character 'a mixture of the savage virtues & vices of the Czar Peter & the shrewd humour of Sancho Panza'[1] . . . the chances are that Mr. Corry himself would never read [the] thing unless he were put on the scent, but my uncle Ruxton & Letty R. certainly would—so my dear Aunt hold a bed of justice directly with Sophy, & before I fall in love any further with my new man, write me word post haste how far I may go—Pray give me your consent, for I am already so far gone that I cannot live without him. . . .[2]

In the event, it seems, she thought she had changed more than she had preserved in changing Mr. Corry into King Corny:

One after another, in working out King Corny, from the first wrong hint I was obliged to give up every fact: except that he propped up the roof of his house and built downwards,—and to generalise all[,] to make him a man of expedients, of ingenious substitutes, such as any clever Irishman in middle life is used to. I was obliged to retain but soften the despotism and exalt the generosity to make it a character that could interest. Not one word I ever heard said by the living man, or had ever heard repeated of his saying [except 'Drop what you have', &c] went into my King Corny's mouth:—would not have suited him. I was obliged to make him according to the general standard of wit and acuteness, shrewd humor and sarcasm of that class of *unread* natural geniuses, an overmatch for Sir Ulick who is of a more cultivated class of acute and roguish Irish gentlemen.[3]

The differences of detail must have been substantial. So, clearly, was the emphasis. Maria found the despotism and conceit of Mr. Corry less endearing in real life than she makes the remnants of these traits in King Corny. She could not have approved of whoring, either, and this is left entirely out in the novel. All the same, there is an inconsequential element about the rich detail of Corny's sayings and doings that derives unmistakably from the anecdotes which circulated about Corry. Corny has a role to play as a major character, one of the two pivots for the novel, the 'overmatch for Sir Ulick'. He remains

[1] This paragraph does not appear in the published novel; it is, of course, in the sheet of notes for Corny quoted immediately above. It is worth noting how close are the details of ME's letter to Mrs. Ruxton with the details on that sheet. These, and the working plan, must all date from the same stage of the novel's development. See below, pp. 278 ff.

[2] ME to Mrs. R, 5 Feb. 1817 (dictated to Fanny Edgeworth).

[3] ME to Mrs. Stark, 6 Sept. 1834; *Mem.*, iii. 151–2. Bracketed words added by editors of *Memoir*.

too much a 'character', an eccentric whose extraordinary actions had obviously caused much hilarity at Black Castle and Edgeworthstown. He still half suggests a lively party-piece; he is not altogether absorbed into the world of *Ormond*.

Certain types of real people affected Maria Edgeworth very strongly. Occasionally her letters give an extended description of a new acquaintance which in itself reads like a preparatory sketch for a character in a novel. Often the strong reaction is one of horror. Maria Edgeworth was for example half amused, half shocked at her first meeting with the well-known London hostess Lydia White or, as Maria had it, Whyte. Miss White arrived unexpected and uninvited at Edgeworthstown, but Edgeworth had met her or knew of her through the gossip that preceded her progress round Ireland:

> I began to think that for once my father had exaggerated when he had described her as an old coquet as well as a wit [but] . . . she really appeared like an old overrouged weather-beaten cast-actress whom one pitied for being obliged to have her neck and arms so very *very* bare . . . she had a sort of drapery loose over her shoulders . . . Corresponding with the dress were the lady's gestures attitudes & voice—all theatrical & affected—not so much eloquence & declamation as Mrs. Apreece but infinitely more wit, repartee & literature—We were all fatigued between admiration & disgust—I never saw so strong a lesson against affectation as she exhibited—It was really melancholy to see what such talents could come to . . . I think Miss Whyte is not a happy woman, at least I should be wretched in her situation—She seems to have a multitude of acquaintance, but no friends—to be at variance with all her relations, or to be indifferent to them, or to despise them—in short to have no family friendships & no *home*, but to lead a wandering desolate kind of life looking to public admiration for what it cannot give—happiness—She will be a miserable old woman—if she has any feeling—but I rather think she has not much—delicacy I am sure she has none; for Dr. B[eaufort] & my father both declared they never heard any unmarried woman say such things as she uttered—I wished myself under the table or underground many & many a time—& here I leave her & cannot say I wish to see or hear her again notwithstanding all her wit & sense & literature—& I think you & even my most tolerant aunt Mary would scarcely have tolerated her.[1]

[1] ME to Charlotte Sneyd, 3 Dec. 1809. Lydia White, who died in 1827, is described more detachedly by Scott as 'what Oxonians call a lioness of the first

Lydia White suggested several details for the hostile vignette in *Patronage* of a fashionable patroness of the arts: Lady Angelica Headingham, in that novel, is another 'aging coquet', with literary pretensions, theatrical manners, and a cloud of diaphanous drapery. But Lady Angelica may also have had connections with another visitor who was already associated in Maria's mind with Lydia White, the wealthy widow Mrs. Apreece.[1] Maria and the Ruxtons were much diverted by her campaign for a second husband, in which she laid siege to several male acquaintances—their neighbour George Knox, the chemist Richard Chenevix, and, most celebrated of all, Sir Humphry Davy, whom she did eventually marry in 1812. (Maria was later to describe him as 'the martyr of matrimony'.)[2] In this case Maria Edgeworth allowed her initial dislike of the two real-life hostesses to prejudice her when she came to write the novel. The sketch that results is monotonously one-sided; Lady Angelica is not nearly so interesting or so complex a figure as the Lydia White of her private description to her aunt.

Another London celebrity whose travels in Ireland nearly took him into *Patronage* was the buck Lord Cranley:

> Lord Cranly [*sic*] (Tommy Onslow that was) who I understand has been long the King's Jester, entertained me much—So frightful mean strange a looking mortal—a thing so unlike nobleman, gentleman or man I think I never beheld! He looked like the lowest species of baboon if you can imagine a baboon that had been both a jockey and a chimney sweeper & had drank [*sic*] hard to boot—yet this creature poured forth anecdote, witticisms & jests & songs without ceasing for hours & kept me in a see-saw of admiration & disgust all night—I hear he *goes* for 3 days—& then he is run down & he can only go the same round again & again—his officers looked so tired of his stories, that I am sure they have heard them 999 times at the least—what a pitiable object is a king's jester out of place—Lord C—gave me a new hint for *Patronage*—[3]

order, with stockings nineteen times nine dyed blue, very lively, very good-humoured, and extremely absurd'. Walter Scott to Lady Louisa Stuart, 19 Jan. 1808; J. G. Lockhart, *Memoirs of the Life of Sir Walter Scott*, 1837–8, ii. 137. Later Maria often met her in London, and came to think more tolerantly of her.

[1] Mrs. Apreece (1780–1855), widow of Shuckburgh Apreece, the heir to a baronetcy, was born Jane Kerr, and was a kinswoman of Walter Scott. For more evidence of Maria's reservations about her, see above, p. 224, and, by implication, below, p. 466.

[2] ME to Mrs. FE, 4 Apr. 1822; *Mem.*, ii. 189.

[3] ME to SR, 12 Oct. 1811.

Lord Cranley does not figure in *Patronage*, or not at least in a recognizable form, but there is a character that aroused speculation and controversy when the novel appeared in 1814. The powerful statesman, Lord Oldborough, was taken to be a portrait of a real political figure, and there was much critical discussion of the propriety of including such a portrait in a novel. For if the statesman was, say, Chatham, then it followed that the king who appears in the novel was George III, who, although insane, was still on the throne.

The Edgeworths always insisted that Oldborough was not drawn from life,[1] and it is true that no recent politician was meant. Oldborough, like Ulick, is an amalgam of two real men. Some of the episodes in his political career—the machinations against him, the details of his fall from power, and his retirement—are based, as already suggested, on detail from Coxe's *Life of Walpole*.[2] But Oldborough's personal attributes—his superficial coldness, his capacity for indignation, and his forbidding presence—belong to a man Maria knew personally, William Stuart, Archbishop of Armagh, the Irish Primate.[3]

*Patronage*, like *Castle Rackrent* and *Ormond*, proves the large part played in Maria's novels by observation from life. It is more than a matter of individual portraits. Oldborough's relations with the heads of two contrasted families provide the whole pivot of the novel's action. On the one hand he has to deal with the obsequious Commissioner Falconer, whose political services he at first finds it expedient to reward; on the other he is friendly with the independent country gentleman Mr. Percy. The contrast between these two relationships is established in an important scene between the three men, in which an unusual number of physical details are given. Oldborough frowns and gestures or moves with a peculiarly impressive deliberation. Commissioner Falconer's bent back is also clearly visualized. Now it seems that Maria did not have much sense of visual detail unless, as for example in the case of Thady M'Quirk, she was drawing from life. It therefore comes as no surprise to discover that within a month of starting

[1] RLE wrote a preface to the 2nd edn. of Feb. 1814 which specifically denied that the novel contained portraits from life.

[2] See above, p. 245.

[3] Wm. Stuart (1755–1822), who became Archbishop of Armagh in 1800, was a son of the politician John Stuart, 3rd Earl of Bute.

work on *Patronage*, she really witnessed a scene at Edgeworthstown which was very similar to the scene in the novel:

I was much entertained whilst the Primate & Bishop [of Meath] were here by their conversation but much more by observing the contrast of their characters—the contrast of a very strong & a very weak character—of inflexible stern integrity & pliant polite address—The *truth* of the Primate gives such value to everything he says—even to his humorous stories! . . . He has two things in his character, which I think seldom meet, a strong taste for humour, and strong feelings of indignation—Where vice appears ridiculous to the observer it often ceases to excite indignation . . . He is a man of the warmest feelings with the coldest exterior I ever saw—A master-mind—It would have diverted you to have seen how he played the bishop at the end of his line—how completely he understood him & how little the bishop cd comprehend or manage such a character as the Primate's—he actually looked, at times, frightened & bewildered, & like a child, who had lost his way in the dark & wanted somebody to help him out—He seemed often to pity my father for his want of address & to be astonished the next minute that the very things which he fancied wd. ruin him with the Primate suceeded better than all his own courtierism . . . You may be sure I *could not but be* charmed with the Primate because I *clearly saw*, that he *clearly saw* & appretiated [*sic*] my father's character—I thank nobody for appretiating his abilities.[1]

The bishop in this encounter, who played the part which was taken in the novel by Commissioner Falconer, was none other than Thomas Lewis O'Beirne, formerly Bishop of Ossory and now of Meath, the devious 'courtier-bishop-secretary' in Edgeworth's dealings fourteen years earlier with the Lord-Lieutenant.[2] Although O'Beirne's promotion in 1797 to the senior Irish bishopric made him a neighbour of the Ruxtons, and hence ultimately a friend of the whole family, Maria's letters continue to accuse him of 'manœuvring', and she never respected him as she did his rather stern, upright wife.[3]

The Primate was a more recent acquaintance. He was a fellow member with Edgeworth of the Irish Board of Education which met between 1806 and 1811. The two men apparently shared many ideas on education, and regarded one another with

[1] ME to SR, ? 28 Apr. 1809. Cf. *Mem.*, i. 224–5, for an illustration of how the editors of ME's letters tampered with them, in this case in order to spare the feelings of the O'Beirnes. The *Memoir*, omits the Bishop from the scene altogether.

[2] See above, p. 121.

[3] See below, p. 477.

mutual respect. Edgeworth's relations with the two churchmen were those of a private, independent gentleman—one, moreover, who despised sycophancy. The bishop was the Primate's subordinate, and his naturally deferential manner underlined this. In *Patronage* the manner of the three men towards one another, and the attitudes which determine what they do and say, come straight from reality, except that they are transferred from the ecclesiastical sphere to the political.

The public's eagerness to see *Patronage* as a *roman à clef* was typical of novel-readers in the period. It is as well to remember that Maria Edgeworth was not alone in being literal-minded. Her contemporary, the Irish novelist Lady Morgan, was exasperated by the unprofitable and often embarrassing speculation that followed the publication of a successful novel containing what purported to be public characters: 'Combine qualities as you may, to the very verge of extravagance, the world will furnish models, trace likenesses, and assign originals.'[1]

As a novel about fashion, politics, and the professions, *Patronage* was uniquely vulnerable, and the reviewers played the game of guessing who was meant by the various minor figures. The Lord Chief Justice was correctly identified by Sydney Smith in the *Edinburgh Review* as Charles Kendal Bushe. Furthermore, it was widely understood that Sydney Smith himself appeared in *Patronage* as Buckhurst Falconer, the reluctant and unsuitable clergyman. The Edgeworths were warned that this rumour must have reached Smith: 'M. Dumont mentions that as Buckhurst Falconer has been generally concluded to be meant for Sydney Smith, we should not be surprised at the asperity of the Edinburgh Review—as he concludes that it is his [*i.e.* Smith's] writing.'[2] Sure enough, there is a clear indication in Sydney Smith's letters that he had taken offence at *Patronage*: 'Everything else I have read of hers I thought very indifferent, even her tale called [Ennui]. If she has put into her Novels people who fed her and her odious father, she is not Trustworthy.'[3]

[1] *Florence Macarthy*, 1818, iv. 144–5 (later edns., ch. 18).

[2] 'The Edgeworthstown Weekly Journal', 1 May 1814 (mock journal in the hand of Mrs. Edgeworth). For Smith's review, see below, p. 273.

[3] Letter to Lady Holland, 20 Jan. 1814; *Letters of Sydney Smith*, ed. C. Nowell Smith, i. 244.

In reality Buckhurst Falconer could not have been directly based on Smith, or any character in *Patronage* on people the Edgeworths met in London in 1813, since the novel was completed, apart from last-minute corrections, before they left home in the spring. But in any case the public was so keen to make identifications that they often chose wrongly. The gauche social rebel Forester, from one of the *Moral Tales*, was generally understood to be a study of the youthful peer Lord Ashburton, whom Maria had not met when she wrote the tale,[1] instead of the individual it was really meant for, Thomas Day. *Leonora* sold well in Dublin when it first came out because the seductress Olivia was mistakenly taken for a portrait of an Irish society woman, Lady Asgill.[2] Vivian was thought to be the rich and wildly extravagant Lord Moira, while in the same novel, and with some plausibility, the author-governess was assumed to be a caricature of Lady Morgan herself, the former Sydney Owenson. Maria's letters do not deny this last charge outright, and it is probably not unreasonable to assume that she had been influenced by stories circulating about Lady Morgan. Still, she was pleased when Sneyd tried to put a stop to the rumours: 'Thank you my dear brother for saying that I never saw Miss Owenson.'[3]

She went to what now seem surprising lengths to prevent the public from linking all but her complimentary characters with real people. She would change a name which suddenly became associated with a family she knew well, even if there was no possible resemblance between the character and the real-life namesake:

Is it not odd that the name of *Beauchamp* should stare me out of countenance again from quite another quarter—Just when I had settled that it was not absolutely necessary to change the name in my little play of my reprobate young slasher *Beauchamp Courtington* on account of your Captain Beauchamp here comes another Beauchamp in Lord Longford's father in law—So there is an imperative necessity to erase 529 Beauchamps—Heaven help my poor aunt Mary who must fall to *scratching* in the midst of the general rejoicing for Lord L[ongford]'s marriage—Now there is a melancholy drawback a *novel* distress he never could have foreseen![4]

[1] Charles Edgeworth to CSE, 2 Apr. 1803. Ashburton was a pupil of Dugald Stewart.

[2] ME to Mrs. R, 8 June 1806.

[3] ME (on back of letter from Mrs. Ruxton) to CSE, 9 May 1812.

[4] ME to Mrs. R, Aug. 1816. Lord Longford, 1774–1835, married Georgiana, daughter of the 1st Earl Beauchamp, in Jan. 1817.

To the contemporary sensitivity about drawing from life should be attributed some of the misleading statements that Maria Edgeworth made about her practices as a novelist. She claimed that she seldom drew from life because she had found that she could not do it successfully. She cited the wife-training episode in *Belinda* as an instance of a real-life episode that did not fit the invented character to whom she had given it.[1] In almost all the cases already quoted in this chapter—except, again, those intended as deliberate compliments—she denied that the character in question was drawn from life. As we have seen, she or her father specifically said that there were not real-life originals for Oldborough, Corny, and everyone in *Castle Rackrent* except Thady.

There is no need to conclude that she and Edgeworth were liars. She meant by 'drawing from life' deliberately painting the portrait of a real-life person, a practice she deprecated because it gave offence, and was in effect a satire. With the latter—hostile caricature, a 'low' form—she did not want to have anything to do. The point of showing how frequently her best characters were on the other hand first suggested by real-life originals, and how closely they continued to resemble them, is merely to reveal the quality of her imagination. It was just as well she went to Paris when she did, and that between 1803 and 1813 there was an increasing flow of visitors to Edgeworthstown, because without these opportunities to meet real-life oddities the stream of her invention might have dried up. She continued to depict English upper-class life because she was able to talk to people who were in it, and in many cases to observe them with the deliberate intention of using some of their traits. The purpose of *Tales of Fashionable Life* was after all to criticize the current vices of high Society. Without first-hand knowledge, or something that passed for it, Maria would have been afraid that her picture was not accurate, and in her eyes this would have been a fatal objection.[2]

It is thus entirely untrue to suggest (as Maria did) that these characters drawn from life were never successful. The reverse is

[1] *Memoirs of RLE*, ii. 349.

[2] This very criticism of ME's treatment of English fashion (i.e. that her picture was as a whole biased and unrepresentative, through lack of first-hand knowledge) was made of *Patronage* in the *QR* in 1814. See below, pp. 346–7. For ME's own confidence at this period that she *did* have enough reliable sources, see above, p. 225.

more nearly the case. Most of her best-known Irish characters, at all levels of the social scale, were based on life, and so were many of her most amusing vignettes of the fashionable English. Yet there was a danger in her method, that the real-life original would bring in some discordant element. Sometimes, as with King Corny, there was too much detail. Sometimes it was the author's attitude to the real-life character, her disapproval (Lady Angelica Headingham) or her admiration (Oldborough, the Lord Chief Justice, the Percy family) that intruded as an unassimilated element into the story.

At the end of her career, Maria was drawn into a discussion of the literary effect of drawing from life. Dugald Stewart's son, Col. Matthew Stewart, was struck by the disadvantages of the practice after reading Maria Edgeworth's last novel, *Helen*. He wrote his letter to his cousin, Mrs. Stark, who was a friend of Maria's, and it was Mrs. Stark who sent the letter on to Edgeworthstown. Col. Stewart had noted from the novel the habit of mind that reacted to external reality by building a 'magazine of facts':

> It is perfectly evident that she paints in general with colours from the life. I have no manner of doubt that she has a vast magazine of a commonplace book in which she has noted down all the traits of character suggested to her by her intercourse with society & if she has not it is beyond dispute that her mind spontaneously performs for her that office. It is in the power which has enabled her to form this magazine of facts that her forte seems to lie.

Stewart put his finger on one difficulty—that Maria was instinctively attracted to eccentrics, who in fact were too odd for the purposes of art:

> It is not enough that a character is true to nature, were it an actual facsimile in all its details, of some living individual known to the author—This will not give it the effect of reality to the reader unless it is consistent with its own probabilities . . . A character which is outré or singular supposing it to be . . . an actual portrait is sure to produce a bad effect on the same principle that conical hills and objects naturally symmetrical however pleasing they may be when we actually see them in a real landscape are among the worst subjects that an artist can choose & for this plain reason that they are not consistent with the usual tenor of beautiful nature—Le vrai peut quelquefois n'être pas vraisemblable . . .

Some of Miss Edgeworth's characters are in my humble estimate too strongly marked with peculiarities. . . .

He summarizes what is to be said aesthetically for and against the practice of drawing from life. He grants that much of the interest of Maria Edgeworth's novels lies in the author's talent as an exact observer of manners and motives, but he also notes that their principal weakness derives from her concentration on the detail, the fact:

These criticisms go intirely to the formation of her characters, & if they are in any respect well founded have probably been occasioned by her own habits of studying human nature in the living examples with which she has been conversant. Her peculiar perfection of observation & discrimination lead to this manner of acquiring her materials & the materials themselves seem to me strongly indicative that they have been so collected [—] I mean very much in detail & as insulated facts & observations. Striking traits of character, remarkable instances of address which have attracted her attention in society instances in which she has detected the true the concealed motives of words & actions & so forth—have been committed to paper or treasured up in her memory . . . This power of observation however admirable may be the degree in which she possesses it & avails herself of it in her writings is not the way in which a power can be acquired of giving a sustained & decided impression of unity to fictitious characters. . . .[1]

The date of the Colonel's letter is one of the most important things about it. As we shall see, by the later 1820s and 1830s the younger inhabitants of Edgeworthstown were also emphasizing the necessity of 'giving a sustained and decided impression of unity' both to characters and to the novels as a whole.[2] But it is fair to say that at the date Maria's novels were written, neither the reviewers nor the great majority of readers thought as much about the broader effect as about liveliness and verisimilitude in the detail; which is of course why her lifelike tales were so much admired and imitated. Maria, as a product of an older period, did not fully understand Col. Stewart's letter; she seldom talked of broad artistic effects, and never seems to have spoken (except in later life, at the prompting of her young relatives) of the desirability of unity. Her first reaction was to deny that she drew from life to the extent the Colonel supposed.

[1] Col. Stewart to Mrs. Stark, 15 July 1834.

[2] See below, p. 459.

The detail of her denial, as it affected Kit and Corny, has already been quoted.[1] Here is the general statement:

I *know* I feel how much *more is to be done, ought to be done* by suggestion than by delineation, by creative fancy than by facsimile copying: how much more by skilful selection & fresh & consistent combination of character than can be effected by the most acute observation of individuals, or diligent accumulation of particulars. But where I have erred or fallen short of what it is thought I might have done it has not been from drawing from the life or from individuals, or from putting together actions or sayings noted in commonplace books from observations or hearsay in society—I have seldom or ever [*sic*] drawn any one character, certainly not any ridiculous or faulty character from any individual—Wherever in writing, a real character rose to my view from memory or resemblance, it has always been hurtful to me, because to avoid that resemblance I was tempted by cowardice, or compelled by conscience, to throw in differences which often ended in making my character inconsistent, unreal. . . .

Again there is the tendency to equate drawings from life with deliberate satire on individuals. 'Certainly not any ridiculous or faulty character' is a tell-tale phrase. Maria goes on to outline her working method as it appears to her. When she compares it with her father's habit of mind as a scientist she is struck by her own casualness, which she has actually had to defend to Edgeworth:

I have no 'vast magazine of a commonplace book'—In my whole life, since I began to write, which is now, I am concerned to state upwards of forty years, I have had only about a half a dozen little notebooks strangely & irregularly kept, sometimes with only words of reference to some book or fact which I could not bring accurately to mind—*At first I was much urged by my father to note down remarkable traits of character or incidents which he thought might be introduced in stories & he often blamed that idleness or laziness as he thought it in me which resisted his urgency, but I was averse to noting down because I was conscious that it did better for me to keep the things in my head if they suited my purpose, & if they did not that they would only encumber me.*[2] I knew that when I wrote down I put the thing out of my care, out of my head, & that although it might be put by very safe I should not know where to look for it: that the labor of looking over a notebook would never do when I was in the warmth & pleasure of

[1] See above, p. 242 and p. 252.

[2] My italics.

inventing—that I should never recollect the facts or ideas at the right time if I did not put them up my own way in my own head: that is if I felt with *hope* or *pleasure* 'that thought or that fact will be useful to me in such a character or story of which I have now a first idea[']: the same fact or thought would recur I knew when I wanted it in right order for invention—In short as Col. Stewart guessed the process of combination, generalization, invention was carried on in my head always best.[1]

Although framed as a denial, this passage is really an admission that Stewart's analysis of her working method was correct. He had not, after all, insisted that the commonplace book was a physical reality. 'If she has not it is beyond dispute that her mind spontaneously performs for her that office.' Her literalness on the subject is a further confirmation of the Colonel's description of her habits of mind. A few years later she tried to recall the terms of her original letter to the Colonel, and again her phraseology did more to support his case than her arguments did to oppose it:

I do recollect also that I answered his supposition that I kept an elaborate commonplace book by telling him the fact—that it was with difficulty that my father had brought me to the sense & to the use & to the habit of noting down facts or ideas gained in conversation—and this I have always done in a very slight irregular manner—that is—not under any commonplace book plan—But just marked with a letter or some sign which I could easily recognize as referring to some subject I intended to write upon—or some story I had in hand or in view—I cannot recollect anything else—[2]

There is a further body of evidence as to how the tales were put together, and again it fits in with Stewart's ideas. When Maria had her theme and a certain number of characters and incidents which illustrated it, she was ready for the first stage of actual composition. Before beginning to write, she made a sketch which she submitted to her father for his approval:

Whenever I thought of writing any thing, I always told him my first rough plans; and always, with the instinct of a good critic, he used to fix immediately upon that, which would best answer the purpose.—'*Sketch that, and shew it to me*'—These words, from the experience of his sagacity, never failed to inspire me with hope of

[1] ME to Mrs. Stark, 6 Sept. 1834; *Mem.*, iii. 148–50.
[2] ME to Miss Bannatyne, 17 Sept. 1838.

success. It was then sketched. Sometimes, when I was fond of a particular part, I used to dilate on it in the sketch; but to this he always objected—'I don't want any of your painting—none of your drapery! I can imagine all that—let me see the bare skeleton.'[1]

The only novel that was definitely not sketched in this way was *Castle Rackrent*.[2] But although there may originally have been a sketch for all the others, most were afterwards mislaid or destroyed. Apart from sketches to three short tales or children's stories, and to various other works which were not written, we now have only a *printed*, not manuscript, version of the sketch to *Belinda*, and three sketches of *Ormond*.[3]

Although they are relatively few, these remaining sketches throw light on Maria Edgeworth's practice as a novelist. It is interesting to see, for example, what she and her father meant by 'the bare skeleton' of a proposed novel. It is also interesting to consider how much of what is best about a particular novel was there at the beginning and how much was added in the course of writing.

There is much more informative material about *Ormond* than any other of the stories for adults. Of the three sketches, it seems that two, headed 'Vesey' and 'Vesay', pre-date the third, 'Ormond', by nearly a year. When the novel was written and dispatched to the publisher, Maria told Harriet Beaufort something of its history:

I think that the amazing & indefatigable pains that Honora in particular & every one of my brothers and sisters have taken in correcting *Ormond* for me will make up for the dangerous celerity with which it was written—Besides I had formed the whole plan & had written two sketches of it above a year ago—So I had long been turning it over & over in my mind. That made it more easy to write the working plan & to go to work upon it quickly—and there is a great deal of difference between writing rapidly & writing in a hurry—whenever I have well considered a subject I think the more *rapidly* I write the more likely I am to preserve a unity of design & spirit through the whole—On the contrary beginning to write before I have well viewed the plan & clearly familiarised my mind's eye with the characters is certain to lead to ultimate failure

[1] *Memoirs of RLE*, ii. 344–5.
[2] ME to Mrs. Stark, 6 Sept. 1834; *Mem.*, iii. 152.
[3] See Bibliography below, p. 501.

or much re-writing & painful alterations—This is what I call *writing in a hurry.*[1]

The two drafts written in 1816 are substantially the same, and almost everything in them also appears in the sketch called 'Ormond'. This, evidently, was what Maria described to Harriet as 'the working plan'. The principal addition in it is the character of Corny, in the third chapter (for, unlike 'Vesey' and 'Vesay', it is already divided into chapters). As far as this point the sketch to *Ormond* is packed with detail, and extremely close to the final novel. The character of Ulick is already present in most of its complexity (as indeed it was in 'Vesey' and 'Vesay').[2] This fullness at the beginning is, to judge by the other examples, characteristic of the sketches, and so is the single fully developed character who dominates the opening scenes; the beginning of the sketch to *Belinda*, with its full portrayal of Lady Delacour, provides an exact parallel. It is evidently no accident that Maria Edgeworth's novels are almost invariably more fully realized at the beginning than at the end.

The later chapters of the sketch headed 'Ormond' have no interesting new characters, and they do not conform so closely to the novel. Just as the last sketch diverged from the earlier ones some way into the plot, so the novel developed at this later point even compared with the last sketch. At a half-way point in the action, Maria now (in the novel itself) decided to send the hero to Paris, and to engage him in a dangerous flirtation with Corny's daughter Dora. Because of Dora's connection with Corny this gives the finished novel an effect of symmetry which is not there in the sketch. The later chapters as sketched promise nothing, in fact, of equivalent interest. Detail follows detail in a largely random, discontinuous sequence.

The most important feature of the sketches as literary documents is this concentration at a superficial level on the plot. There is no generalizing, no simplification, no glossing of the action in order to suggest what the literary effect of a scene is intended to be. Nor is there any attempt to see the detail in terms of the whole. The sketches were not apparently meant to do more than to set out a lively story which incorporated all the heterogeneous mass of didactic aims and illustrative material.

[1] ME to Harriet Beaufort, 8 May 1817.

[2] See the opening page, reproduced facing p. 428.

Their function was certainly not to impose structural unity. The whole manner of narration indicates how the author's concern was more with the contents of individual episodes than with any interrelation between the parts and the whole.[1] It is interesting at this point to reconsider the significance of Edgeworth's exhortation: 'I don't want any of your painting—none of your drapery! I can imagine all that!—let me see the bare skeleton.' This cannot have meant that Edgeworth wanted Maria to simplify and discipline her schemes (which would have been excellent advice). The sketches which survive suggest that he preferred her to limit herself to a strict sequence of facts.

And this is quite in accordance with what Maria says of her father's advice to her in her letter to Stewart. Edgeworth was interested in the detail of her novels, in the liveliness and truth of individual episodes. One has only to recall his volume of the *Memoirs* to understand what his approach to narrative must have been like. It is a very different kind of mind that sees 'the bare skeleton' as a simplification of the finished product, perhaps a mere outline. To Edgeworth the word skeleton no doubt suggested what in fact a skeleton is—a complex of individual bones, each more minutely distinguishable from all the rest than when the flesh is there to cover them.

In her attitude to the observation of character, as in so many of her attitudes, Maria goes back to the decade in which her father reached intellectual maturity, the 1770s: in particular she shares with many English graphic artists of that era a lucid, scientific attitude to objective reality, and thus differs even from the major novelist who most resembles her, the more subjective and emotional Walter Scott. Although only two and a half years older than Scott, she was in tone and temper the natural contemporary of Robert Bage (born 1728) and John Moore (born 1729). This was because she learnt her outlook on human behaviour from her father—who made her curious, but also detached. Even Mrs. Ruxton, on a lighter level, had always encouraged her to look out for entertaining, quirky anecdotes about real people. With such a training it was small wonder that she never admitted the claims of a literary 'truth' which

[1] The manner of the sketches is well illustrated by the page of notes for Corny's character, quoted above, p. 250.

might be distinct from the objective truth of science. Or, rather, she did recognize that claims were made for a 'truth' in fiction that would not stand up to objective analysis—and she thought that such a purely literary approach ought to be resisted.

In spite of her concession by 1820 that real facts in a novel often struck the reader as improbable, she went on believing all her life that this was a risk the serious writer must take. She defended the introduction of facts in an amiable family argument with her brother-in-law, the Revd. Richard Butler, when Butler took much the same line as Matthew Stewart. Maria was prepared to concede the difficulty, but not to abandon her facts: 'I do think that a fact can be very well referred to—a real fact in a fiction as confirming a fictitious fact or character.'[1]

The best illustration of the criteria she used when determining whether to include a character or episode comes in a late letter she wrote to Walter Scott:

> Now I want a bit of advice from you about a character & an episode in my story—When I say episode I mean a part that I can put in or leave out without injury to the rest . . . I once heard a gentleman giving very badly an account of a Scotch chieftain—highlander—I think[,] who had been smitten on a visit to London with a wish to figure in high company—& who had been led on to extravagance of all sorts—to get or keep in the circles of fashionables & in short ended by cutting down his woods & I believe *selling* his Scotch property—perhaps all the time entails make the last impossible.
>
> I want to know from you whether the character be out of drawing—out of Scotch nature—& probability—next whether it would be a national offence to Scotch friends of whom I have many that I would not for a world of novels lose, to draw such a character . . . And by the way I should also ask your opinion whether it would be useful & moral—that I suppose includes the consideration of whether there would be a sufficient *class* of people liable to be influenced by such motives as I should represent—not merely whether the individual character be possible or probable— . . .[2]

Certainly this passage finds Maria considering probability,

[1] Harriet Butler, *née* Edgeworth, to M. Pakenham Edgeworth, 27 Jan. 1837 (letter giving notes of conversations at Harriet's home at Trim, or at Edgeworthstown, which Harriet described as 'Horae Marianae').

[2] ME to Sir Walter Scott, 15 July 1830. National Library of Scotland, MS. 3919.

but it is probability entirely in life, not in relation to her fictional composition. There is no record of an answer from Scott on the point, but apparently Maria Edgeworth's scruples about making her character a Scotsman were not satisfied. The spendthrift absentee landlord who appears incidentally in *Helen* is a run-of-the-mill wealthy young Englishman.

Two incidents in 1813, when she was at the height of her fame, further illustrate her exact and literal notions of truth. While *Patronage* was being printed she went to Longford races, where her observant eye noted two striking details. The trees were black and thick with spectators, as though with huge crows' nests; and as they raced the jockeys' loose many-coloured satin jackets swelled out behind them in the wind. After describing them vividly in her letter, she wondered whether her description of a race in the first volume of *Patronage* (which is scarcely visualized at all) would have benefited if she had been able to include these details. She decided that it 'might not be safe' to have used them. 'In fine races in England it might be out of drawing to represent spectators perched in trees'; and loose jackets, she understood, were probably not current English racing fashion. She obviously knew that what she had seen was more vivid than what she had described, but if it would not make an *accurate* description of an English race meeting she did not want it.[1]

It was also in keeping with her scientific training in making precise definitions that on the whole she avoided the literary device of metaphor. At Liverpool, on her way to London in 1813, Maria and William Roscoe discussed the poetry of their mutual friend Erasmus Darwin. Here was another literary figure who, like Maria, had tried to use a huge body of accurately observed natural fact as the raw material of imaginative literature. Maria and Roscoe agreed that Darwin had not altogether succeeded. His failure, they thought, was not because he had stuck to his facts, but because he had not been content with them:

Mr Roscoe made what appeared to me at the moment to be a new and just observation, that writers of secondary powers, when they are to describe or represent either objects of nature or feelings

[1] ME to Mrs. R, 21 Oct. 1813.

of the human mind always begin by simile: they tell you not what the thing *is*, but what it is *like*.[1]

Maria had almost finished her career before she began to formulate this kind of aesthetic conclusion that conformed to her own practice as a writer. She never expressed general ideas on this subject very distinctly, and on the novel as a form her reviewers are more interesting than she is. But towards the end she does imply something about realism, by producing a book based on the idea that there may be two intellectual approaches to reality: the scientific or exact, and the literary or intuitive. *Harry and Lucy Concluded*, 1825, with its two protagonists based on the scientific R. L. Edgeworth and the literary Maria, does in fact give her thought-out answer to the question of whose truth should stand.

Harry, the young scientist, might be taken by the average educated person as perversely literal, and sometimes he is intended to seem so. Lucy has a cast of mind that most novel-readers might prefer, because she is obviously the more literate. But over-all Harry is certainly meant by the author to seem more admirable than Lucy. He is given all Edgeworth's energy, and in his way he is the more creative and original of the two children. Lucy exhibits the literary mentality almost to the point of satire: instead of examining a thing for what it is, she tries to find analogies for it.[2] In implying that *she* was Lucy, Maria was caricaturing herself. As her admiration for Harry proved, her own intellectual training, even if it never made her feel sufficiently informed about science, still inclined her decisively to the scientific side of the question. One of the Objects she noted for this story was 'that literary and scientific invention should be on the same principles'.[3] By this she seems to have meant, first that science was creative, second that literary 'creation' was secondary if it could not stand up to the same kind of objective test—that is, 'tell you . . . what the thing *is*', not 'what it is *like*'.

There is no doubt that with her respect for miscellaneous fact

[1] ME to Mrs. R, 6 Apr. 1813; *Mem.*, i. 267.

[2] As, for example, during their visit to the foundry, part of which is quoted above, p. 144.

[3] MS. 'Plan and Notes for a new volume of *Harry and Lucy*, begun 16 July 1822'. See Bibliography, p. 501.

Maria Edgeworth appealed to a strong tendency of the times. It is as well not to forget Byron's comment about the fine coaching scene in *Ennui*: 'So much the better—being life.' The poetry of Crabbe and Wordsworth shows the same reverence for the multitudinous unassimilated detail of real life. While Maria had little or no aesthetic instinct to guide her, she had the tremendous historical advantage of having been trained in facts. As a novelist she also had the room to use them. The presence of a mass of accurately observed detail in Maria's Irish novels is undoubtedly one of the factors, probably the most important factor, in making them influential. Thanks to her father's links with the vanguard of scientific empiricism, she herself became a pioneer. Although she has predecessors among the graphic artists, there is nothing quite like her objective precision in the eighteenth-century novel; for the realism even of Defoe and Smollett, though stemming from a similar empirical attitude to external reality, leaves a far less thoroughgoing impression of exactness.

All the same, there is a great difference, as anyone who has read Maria Edgeworth's novels will appreciate, between her realism and that of a truly first-rate artist. Wordsworth talked and wrote about making literature, while Maria began and ended with the facts. Her failure even to attempt to render imaginatively the physical landscape of the industrial Midlands, or of an Irish peasant community, is significant. Although she dealt in reality, it is difficult to think of her as a realist, which implies a conscious literary objective. It is not for nothing that her representative of the literary mentality, Lucy, has such tremendous imaginative limitations. Maria did not think of literature as having the energy and creativeness of science, perhaps because she did not have these characteristics in such abundance as her scientist father, or perhaps because for her novel-writing was a means to a personal end, not quite a fully justified occupation on its own. Whatever the origins of her diffidence on behalf of literature, it had considerable implications for the coherence of the most intellectually ambitious of her tales.

# VI

## A QUESTION OF AUTHORSHIP

As soon as Maria Edgeworth and her father became personally known in London, the first signs of suspicion about the authorship of the novels began to appear. Maria Edgeworth was good humoured and amusing, whereas her father was pompous and a bore. The novels were usually entertaining, like her, but sometimes they were heavy, like him. Surely, then, she had written the lively parts, and he had inserted the rest?

John Ward, the future Earl of Dudley, was one of the most intelligent critics of the novels. Unlike some of Maria's more sentimental admirers, he did not take seriousness to be synonymous with dullness.[1] At first he praised her stories precisely because they were well informed and sociologically accurate. Later, when Jane Austen's novels became available for comparison, he changed his mind. He now thought that the purely factual information in Maria's tales was misplaced, and he hoped that it was Richard Lovell Edgeworth who was responsible for its presence there. If only Maria Edgeworth could have kept her father's influence out, she would have achieved an effect nearer to Jane Austen's:

> Have you read *Mansfield Park*? . . . She has not so much fine humour as your friend Miss Edgeworth, but she is more skilful in contriving a story, she has a great deal more feeling, and she never plagues you with any chemistry, mechanics, or political economy, which are all excellent things in their way, but vile, cold-hearted trash in a novel, and, I piously hope, all of old Edgeworth's putting in. . . .[2]

[1] For an account of his published criticisms of ME, see below, pp. 346–7.

[2] Letter of 11 Aug. 1814; *Letters to 'Ivy'* [*Mrs. Dugald Stewart*] *from the first Earl of Dudley*, ed. S. H. Romilly, 1905. Ward's letter continued: 'By the bye, I heard some time ago that the wretch was ill. Heaven grant that he may soon pop off.' Before meeting the Edgeworths in 1813, Ward did not think the tales over-weighted with political economy. Cf. letters of 28 Sept. 1809, and 3 Sept. 1812, ibid., pp. 76 and 170.

Ward was exaggerating in writing about chemistry and mechanics in the tales, except of course in the educational *Harry and Lucy* series, but the political economy certainly was there on occasion. It was also true that the tales were remarkably detached from personal experience, at least as far as conscious intention went. With *Ennui* and *The Absentee*, especially, Maria was aiming at an effect as near as possible to objectivity. Her whole accumulative, collaborative mode of composition underlines this point. She went about as far as a writer could go towards denying the special role of the author in creative literature.

The method of composition sketched in the last chapter was one which invited a great deal of co-operation from others. Invaluable material was provided by Edgeworth in particular, but also by other members of the Edgeworthstown household, by the Ruxtons, and by the Beauforts. But what about the *writing* of the novels, which was what Ward and everyone else since has meant when they talked of 'interference'? There are extremely important distinctions between some kinds of assistance and others. After asking her relatives for help, did Maria feel morally free to reject their suggestions? If not, did the quantity of their material, and of their sub-editorial criticism later, ever amount to such proportions that the family were virtually Maria's co-authors? Yet another possibility is that Maria was nothing more than a mouthpiece for her father: that he was the original source of everything from Edgeworthstown, and she was his amanuensis. This was her own favourite interpretation. 'In the lighter works . . . I have only repeated the same opinions [i.e. RLE's] in other forms . . . A certain quantity of bullion was given to me and I coined it into as many pieces as I thought would be convenient for popular use.'[1]

Although, as the previous chapter showed in detail, many members of the family made contributions to the novels, it is only Edgeworth's part that has been thought of as 'interference'. At first the speculation sometimes rather favoured him; after he died, for example, some people were sure that Maria would never succeed in writing a novel without him.[2] A solitary modern writer, Desmond Clarke, has taken this view:

. . . two authors extremely disparate in outlook and temperament;

[1] ME to Francis Jeffrey, 18 Dec. 1806 (draft). [2] See below, p. 412.

one blessed with a lively imagination and a sure critical faculty, but with little time, and much too impatient and restive to spend many hours with pen and paper; the other happy with her retentive memory, facile pen, and the nature and temperament to clothe bare ideas with words, and patiently colour the picture roughly and quickly sketched by her father.[1]

But the assumption that he was a bad literary influence has always been commoner. The first charges were the same as John Ward's—simply that Edgeworth wrote the worst passages in the novels himself. Sydney Smith did not scruple to say as much in print when he reviewed *Patronage*.[2] By the later nineteenth century all biographers of Maria, to a woman, disliked Edgeworth, and began to extend the same line of argument to other novels. Specific mistakes and weak passages were ascribed to him, and he became known as the censor of the liveliest strain in Maria. This, roughly, is where his reputation still stands. The most common tendency has been to divide the novels into their naturalistic and didactic elements, allocating the former to Maria and the latter to her father.[3]

The letters show that almost all guesses about Edgeworth's role have been wide of the mark. Mr. Desmond Clarke is wrong if he means that the original ideas for the novels, as opposed to original ideas on education, were Edgeworth's and not Maria's.[4] Certainly Edgeworth was an important source of material, but far from intruding his suggestions, he appears to have produced them so carelessly that Maria was perfectly free not to use them:

He left me always at full liberty to use or reject his hints, throwing new materials before me continually, with the profusion of genius and of affection. There was no danger of offending, or of disappointing him by not using what he offered. There was no vanity, no selfishness, to be managed with delicacy and deference; he had too much resource ever to adhere tenaciously to any one idea or invention. So far from it, he forgot his gifts almost as soon as he had made them—thought the ideas were mine, if they appeared before him in any form in which he liked them; and if never used, he never missed, never thought of inquiring for them. Continually

[1] Desmond Clarke, *The Ingenious Mr. Edgeworth*, 1965, p. 102.

[2] *Edinburgh Review*, xxii, 1814, 433–4. But see above, p. 257.

[3] See Preface, above, and, e.g., Donald Davie, *Heyday of Sir Walter Scott*, 1961, pp. 67 ff., and W. L. Renwick, *Oxford History of English Literature, 1789–1815*, 1963, p. 70.

[4] See above, p. 238.

he supplied new observations on every passing occurrence, and wakened the attention with anecdotes of the living or the dead. His knowledge of the world, and all that he had had opportunities of seeing behind the scenes in the drama of life, proved of inestimable service to me; all that I could not otherwise have known, was thus supplied in the best possible manner. Few female authors, perhaps none, have ever enjoyed such advantages, in a critic, friend, and father, united. Few have ever been blessed in their own family with such able assistance, such powerful motive, such constant sympathy.[1]

Edgeworth was even indifferent to the rare passages he wrote himself, although his fond daughter was not: 'My dear Sneyd I am delighted with Mr. Plunkets having quoted *that* passage from *The Absentee*. The *whole* of it, every word, was written by my father, who dear man, had forgot that he wrote and would scarce believe me. . . .'[2]

Much the commonest accusation against Edgeworth is that his interference, or (more cautiously) his general influence made the novels more didactic. It is all the more striking that none of his surviving criticisms of a book before publication refers to the possible didactic import. Nor was he concerned with over-all shape or structure. As one would expect from Edgeworth's technical approach to his own scientific work, he was much more actively interested in the mechanics of a novel's plot than in its abstract moral quality. His concentration on plot became a byword in his literary discussions with Maria. When in 1813 Maria Edgeworth wrote to Scott in praise of *Rokeby*, she excepted the last canto, which, she thought, squeezed too much story into too little space. On such a point her father, she explained, could never agree with her: 'My father always says "Story! Story! give me story! it is for *all tastes*—All works of fiction that last *must* have good story—Curiosity is a universal passion of all ages."'[3]

If, as was probably often the case, Maria's sketch did not work out all the details of the story to the end, then her father would be ready with a host of ingenious suggestions. That she did not exaggerate his 'ready invention and infinite resource' is amply borne out by a letter about *Leonora*. Although Maria had

[1] *Memoirs of RLE*, ii. 351–2.

[2] ME to CSE, 27 Nov. 1812. See below, p. 281 n.

[3] ME to Walter Scott, 23 Feb. 1813; Nat. Library of Scotland, MS. 3884, f. 78.

been working on this novel for a year, she had not solved the mechanical problem of how to bring about a happy ending. How could Leonora's husband, Mr. L—, honourably extricate himself from his commitments to his mistress, Olivia? Somehow, before he set off with her on an embassy to Moscow, he must discover her true nature, which might best be done by letting him see her correspondence with her confidante, Madame de P—. But it was difficult to think of a natural and creditable means of having him read her letters to someone else. This was just the technical sort of problem that Edgeworth enjoyed:

> I think that the *dirty work* must be done by the waiting maid Josephine from mixed motives of dread of Russian bears and resentment against L— who had never treated her with sufficient gallantry or sufficient generosity—Genl. B— on the contrary may have praised her taste, and her fine eyes, and may also besides trinkets have now and then begged to have her purse mended in which a twenty pound note might have remained by accident—and a lottery ticket (worth £14 or £15) might be given in a very genteel manner —and her watch might be out of order and might not be worth *mending*—he may mount his douceurs to £50—With her assistance Madame de P—'s favourite woman might be induced to *return* Olivia's letters—This however is not quite the thing for the honorable General—Suppose—another way—that Olivia should demand and obtain from Madme. de P— a restoration of her letters—and suppose the packet should be intercepted by the spies set on Mme de P— who is known to be une intrigante—Let the letters be handed about Paris as a specimen of English fidelity and discretion—copies might be sent to the Genl. by some friend at Paris who had been desired to inquire about Olivia and Mme de P—Or suppose—that Olivia regains the letters and that Josephine should send them to Mr. L— to stop his Russian expedition which might be pressed forward—this would entangle the denouement beautifully.[1]

Here was the profusion of advice that Maria described, with no hint in Edgeworth's tone that he cared whether she followed it up (and in fact in this case she did not).

What becomes then of the tenacious legend of the father who dominated and directed his daughter's career? There was one area of decision-making about the novels which in theory was left to Edgeworth: he was in general the arbiter on all matters connected with publication. Or, as Maria put it, 'he is so good to

[1] RLE to ME, 20 Jan. 1805.

[*sic*] manage all authorship business for me and I have found this so much for my interest and my pleasure that I never interfere'.[1]

Some novels were hastened, others delayed, by Edgeworth's good or bad opinion of them. It was Edgeworth who decided that *The Modern Griselda* should be prepared for immediate publication alone, rather than wait to form part of *Tales of Fashionable Life*.[2] Conversely, his dislike of *Leonora* delayed its publication for up to a year. During this period Maria undoubtedly considered publication without his approval to be out of the question; no work of hers was published in his lifetime without his endorsement.[3]

Edgeworth's close supervision of the practical side of Maria's career is illustrated by a letter she wrote in 1813, when she was forty-five and at the height of her reputation:

> My father has been very urgent with me to finish 4 volumes of *Frank and Rosamond*—These by hard labor . . . I have finished . . . After *Frank and Rosamond* were done came *Patronage* to be corrected which I completed but the day before my father went to Town—Then I had a preface of his to *Early Lessons* of 27 pages to *revise*—Sixteen pages rewritten one morning . . . Then about 18 pages of scientific matter was left to me by my father to make into a new volume of *Harry and Lucy* and this I have to do at this moment.[4]

It was Edgeworth, in his role of literary manager, who proposed one of Maria's most successful tales, *The Absentee*. While she was struggling to finish the over-elaborate *Patronage*, in the summer of 1811, Anna Beddoes and her children arrived at Edgeworthstown, and Maria was relieved at the excuse to break off to write a play for them. On 29 August 1811 the new play was enthusiastically received by the family audience, which included the eight-year-old Thomas Lovell Beddoes. 'The Absentee' was a little drama, 'part comic, part pathetic', about an Irish landlord who returns to his estate in disguise and uncovers the dishonesty that has gone on there in his absence.[5]

[1] ME to Lady Romilly, 23 Dec. 1816; Slade, p. 155.

[2] ME to SR, Nov. 1803, to Mrs. R, 3 May 1804, and to SR, Oct. 1804.

[3] ME to Francis Jeffrey, 18 Dec. 1806. There is ample evidence in the correspondence for each novel written after this date.

[4] ME to SR, 16 Oct. 1813. The notes by RLE she refers to are preserved: see Bibliography, manuscript sources, no. 3 (*b*).

[5] ME to SR, 30 Aug. 1811; *Mem.*, i. 242. ME to ED, 7 Sept. 1811; B.P.U., Geneva.

Maria reported that the play received much more praise from the family than it deserved, especially from Edgeworth. He persuaded Maria to send it to Sheridan at Drury Lane, but Sheridan decided, as Maria guessed in advance he would, that the Irish subject-matter made it unsuitable for the London stage.[1] Meanwhile, late in 1811, Maria's publisher began to urge her to complete the second series of *Tales of Fashionable Life* in time for publication in the spring of 1812. It was Edgeworth who once again extolled the merits of 'The Absentee'. He pointed out that an answer to Maria's difficulties lay in combining the play with a sub-plot of *Patronage* which concerned a family of Irish absentees in London. At the end of December Maria had drafted a scheme which included the Tipperarys from *Patronage* and scenes from the play; by 19 February she had written two-thirds, and in April (despite three weeks of violent toothache) she sent the packet off to the publishers.[2] The tale was, her stepmother said, 'less studied, less criticised, less corrected and more rapidly written than any other that Maria had produced'.[3]

Ironically, the Tipperary episode which made the opening chapters of *The Absentee* was available in 1812 only because Maria had resisted her father's earlier ideas about the best place for it. The Edgeworths had long been uneasy about the out-of-date and very unfavourable picture of the Irish given in *Castle Rackrent*. When a fifth edition of *Castle Rackrent* was proposed in 1810, Edgeworth wanted Maria to bring it up to date with a section to be called 'Anecdotes of Jason McQuirk's family since 1782':

> I am sorry I can't give Miles the permit he desires to go on with reprinting Rackrent—But my father wishes to have some *additions* made to it—and I fear in this instance *additions* will not according to the Irish usage of the word be synonymous with improvements —I am inclined to think that I could say better all my father wishes to have said about the modern manners of the Irish McQuirks in the story I am now writing of *Patronage* and I think the prints

[1] *Mem.*, i. 247–8. Sheridan's explanation was that he did not have enough actors to play Irish parts. He also thought that the London audience might not sympathize with the Irish characters.

[2] ME to SR, 29 Dec. 1811; ME to SR, 19 Feb. 1812; and ME to Mrs. R, 2 Apr. 1812.

[3] Mrs. FE to SR, 22 June 1812.

might be there introduced and that this plan would give more time for engraving them properly—All this I have stated and shall restate and re-urge—but in the last event of things you know I must do what my acting and most kind literary partner decides and in the mean time can say nothing to poor Mr. Miles but *Stay a bit.*[1]

This was one of two important occasions, at least, when Maria in the last event of things did not 'do what my acting and most kind literary partner decides'. A more upsetting literary disagreement between the two led to the writing of *Ormond*. The early history of this novel followed the usual pattern, with Edgeworth taking the initiative by suggesting that Maria should turn from one plan to another. In 1816, while she was getting on slowly with *Harrington*, he asked her to pause in order to sketch the other tale or tales which were to be published at the same time:

I have not yet written a word more of the *jewish* because my father has wished me to write some sketches for the other stories wh[ich] are to be written and I have been this week sketching—I have made one wh[ich] he approves but it would take he says two volumes to fill it up and therefore it will not do for this occasion—I have not yet pleased myself in sketches for the present purpose—The sketch he approves is on the bankruptcy plan—You see my dear aunt I obey you and give you enough of my authorship self.[2]

So, because Edgeworth advised her that her new sketches meant too long a tale to fit their plans for a two-volume publication, she returned for the time being to *Harrington*. But she took 'shamefully long about it', and by this time, the autumn of 1816, her father, who was now 72, was obviously failing. He badly wanted to see another of Maria's novels in print before he died; and *Harrington* unfortunately filled only one volume, which was usually considered too short for separate publication. A possibility remained which would have enabled Maria to gratify her father's wishes immediately. She had just finished *Comic Dramas*, the first work for the stage she had

[1] ME to CSE, n.d. [Mar. 1810]. Cf. also Mrs. FE to CSE, 21 Mar. 1810; Nat. Lib. of Ireland, MS. 13176 (21). The prints referred to were drawings by Charlotte Edgeworth of two Irishmen, called Rawley and Tuite. They were eventually published with *Memoirs of RLE*, ii. as an Appendix. The originals are still in the Butler family's possession.

[2] ME to Mrs. R, n.d. [1816]. The sketch 'on the bankruptcy plan' is presumably 'Vesay' as opposed to 'Vesey'; see above, p. 265.

contemplated publishing. *Comic Dramas* were the right length to take the place of 'Vesey', or *Ormond*, in completing the set with *Harrington*.

Maria still thought of her plays as experiments, and she neither wanted them performed nor raised to the status of her established tales by publishing them together in a mixed collection.[1] Edgeworth was just as uncertain about the plays' merits, but, with his characteristic boldness and indifference to public success, he preferred to see something published to nothing at all. In November 1816, he told Miles, the retired partner of their firm of publishers, that in spite of Maria's reluctance he would like *Harrington* published immediately in a set made up by *Comic Dramas*.[2]

In these emotional circumstances it is surprising that Maria went on refusing to let her father persuade her. The disagreement between them must have been sharp, for in the course of it Edgeworth wrote Maria a letter which very much upset her. After he was dead she recalled to her stepsister '. . . the night you brought me *that* letter from my father which threw me into utter and helpless despair—if you had not, like my good angel, inspired me with hope I never, *never* could have recovered courage to go through with that which had I *not* accomplished what should I feel now!—and for all the rest of my life!'[3]

The course of action Maria went through with was embarking on a new tale long enough to publish with *Harrington*. She had her subject ready to hand in the sketches of 'Vesey' and 'Vesay' which she had only recently drawn up for her father's inspection. Nevertheless, with Edgeworth visibly weakening, she was terrified that the book would not be ready in time. Shortly after beginning *Ormond*, she tried to reveal something to Mrs. Ruxton about what was happening:

> In the first place I cannot explain to you exactly why I am so earnest to finish what I am now writing but you must take it on my word that it is essential to my happiness and to my going on *well with my father*, it is a new story and that is all I can tell you, I have not yet decided on the title, indeed I have not said as much as this to anybody out of this house but I cannot leave you groping in the

[1] ME to Mrs. R, Aug. 1816.
[2] RLE to Miles (family copy), 26 Nov. 1816.
[3] ME to Honora Edgeworth, June 1817.

dark as to what I am about. In answer to Sophy's question whether things are going on well with me—they are going on well *now*— . . . My father is not to see any of this while I am writing it and I am not sure that he will see it till it is printed—He knows nothing of my plan.[1]

Edgeworth did learn of the existence of *Ormond* while she was writing it. By 16 February his wife was reading it to him, chapter by chapter, and with characteristic lack of rancour he threw himself into helping Maria get it done quickly. He ordered her to write no letters until the main task, the writing, was completed. Meanwhile he made tremendous efforts to give his own kind of assistance, which had to be done at the same pace as her rapid writing if it was to be of any use.

My father is quite satisfied about *Ormond* and I am as you may guess overpaid a thousand times for the labor it cost and the confinement to which it necessarily subjected me. I never saw nor could I have conceived anything equal to the energy and exertions of my father in correcting and re-correcting this story over and over again sometimes hearing it read and dictating corrections for 4 or 5 hours together—between the fits of dreadful sickness and often to the point of actual exhaustion—It was a proof of persevering and energetic affection such as only he cd. give—It was at the time often very painful to receive, but now it is well over delightful to reflect upon.[2]

In this case his collaboration actually included some writing, as well as the more usual cutting and correcting. After only three months, the novel was got off early in May to the publisher, Rowland Hunter—who, having failed to understand the need for urgency, nearly let them down by his leisureliness. Francis Beaufort went to see him in London and insisted that he should farm the novel out to two printers. By these exceptional means an advance copy was handed to Edgeworth on his birthday, 31 May, but after all he did not live to see *Ormond* published. On the morning of the day he died, 13 June 1817, news came that the two tales would be out in London on the 21st, but Edgeworth had already lost consciousness, and never heard it.

[1] ME to Mrs. R, 5 Feb. 1817 (dictated to Fanny Edgeworth).
[2] ME to Harriet Beaufort, 8 May 1817.

*Ormond* is an extreme case in the literary relationship between Edgeworth and Maria, and what we know of its history tells us a great deal about Edgeworth's role in the evolution of the novels. Maria can never have had more motive for falling in with his advice than in these months when he was dying. Even so, she was capable of refusing to take it. Later Edgeworth took an extraordinary interest in *Ormond*, and spent many painful hours working on it. He did not contribute nearly so much to the great majority of the tales—*Ormond* is certainly exceptional in this respect. Again, it is the slightness of his material contribution which is impressive.

It is true that Edgeworth wrote three passages in the novel himself. (Only two others definitely by him can be identified in the whole of Maria Edgeworth's fiction, although there may in reality have been a few more.)[1] One of Edgeworth's passages in *Ormond* was a key scene, King Corny's death; it is not certain where his writing begins, since afterwards Maria found it too distressing to look in the book for the reference. He also wrote several pages of chapter 30, from Moriarty's meeting with Ormond in Paris, to almost the end of the chapter. This sequence includes the real-life story of Michael Dunne, a Navan shop-keeper, who had confided to Edgeworth the story of his exploits in escaping from prison. The third passage written by Edgeworth was the reunion of Moriarty Carroll with his wife in chapter 31, from 'Lie back, Moriarty . . .' to '. . . we proceed to Castle Hermitage'.[2]

The Michael Dunne episode, like the note in *Castle Rackrent* and Sir Terence O'Fay's anecdote in *The Absentee*, contains real-life material which had come within Edgeworth's experience. Like similar sequences written by Maria, they are lively, but rather too clumsily documented; it is very obvious that they were taken from life. Edgeworth's two shorter passages from *Ormond* are strongly emotional and pathetic; they illustrate that responsiveness of his which his critics have hardly noticed, yet which is one of the outstanding qualities of his volume of

[1] He contributed a note to the Glossary of *Castle Rackrent* (see above, p. 242). In *The Absentee* he wrote the sequence in which Sir Terence O'Fay uses racing cant, from 'Well, and did not I make up for that . . .' to '. . . was not that famous?' (ch. 5; x. 86–7). The passage is based on a real-life anecdote (ME to CSE, 27 Nov. 1812).

[2] ME to CSE, 27 Mar. 1818; *Mem.*, ii. 7–8.

*Memoirs.*[1] None of the passages written by him, it goes without saying, contains any trace of didacticism.

Beyond the writing of three passages, what other specific contributions did Edgeworth make to *Ormond*? When the two earlier drafts were drawn up, he preferred one version to another, but afterwards Maria began work from her third draft, or 'working plan', which at the time he did not see. Also at the earlier stage, he had advised her against starting work on the tale; afterwards of course she started without his knowledge. At this time she meant to write it entirely without him, as she certainly wrote *Modern Griselda* and presumably *Castle Rackrent.* She did not ask his advice (but the Ruxtons' instead) about adding the controversial character of King Corny. Even in the case of *Ormond,* when she was specifically writing a story to give her father pleasure, there are no specific artistic decisions which can be shown to be his and not hers.

By far the most persistent story about Edgeworth's interference with the novels concerns his supposed meddling with the sketch to *Belinda.* Unlike the other sketches,[2] this has been available for inspection for over a century, since it was printed as an Appendix to the *Memoir of Maria Edgeworth.* In the sketch, Lady Delacour dies of cancer, which certainly means that before the novel was finished Maria changed her mind about the end. In the fully written version Lady Delacour's illness turns out to have been a delusion, she reforms, and the reader leaves her enjoying domestic bliss with her boorish husband. If the original tragic conception was Maria's, and the feeble and inconsistent climax to the novel was her father's, *Belinda* seems—at a superficial glance—to go a long way to justify Edgeworth's critics.[3]

[1] See above, p. 18. Apart from its lively treatment of Thomas Day, his volume is memorable for its haunting, often emotional descriptions of, e.g., Mrs. Hungerford (i. 88–9), the crippled lady in the French château (i. 292–5), the poor Scotch girl lost in London (i. 354–6), the well-born beggar woman (i. 356–8), and, above all, the bereaved clergyman (i. 385–91).

[2] The MS. sketches are unhelpful in establishing the extent of RLE's 'interference'. On the early ones (e.g. to *The White Pigeon*) he pencilled in comments, but the three sketches to *Ormond* were written when he was almost blind, and most of the others date from after his death.

[3] The critics who have made much of the change have not noticed that in other respects Lady Delacour is treated with more depth and sympathy in the novel than in the sketch, and that her most unpleasant characteristics are transferred to a new character, Mrs. Freke, who suffers an odd, ritualistic version of the punishment that was to have been meted out to Lady Delacour—she is caught in a mantrap.

The statement that it was Edgeworth who changed the ending to *Belinda* first appeared in Helen Zimmern's *Maria Edgeworth* (1883). Miss Zimmern utilized the *Memoir* very freely, and she was obviously much struck by the Appendix on *Belinda*. When she compared this sketch with the finished novel, she arrived at some confident conclusions which she assumed could be applied to Maria Edgeworth's work as a whole:

> We have Mrs. Barbauld's testimony that Miss Edgeworth wrote *Castle Rackrent* unassisted by her father, and judging how infinitely superior in spontaneity, flexibility, and nervousness of style, force, pith, and boldness, it is to those of her writings with which he meddled, it is forcibly impressed upon us that Mr. Edgeworth's literary tinkering of [*sic*] his daughter's works was far from being to their advantage . . . Had Lady Delacour died heroically, as Miss Edgeworth had planned, and as the whole course of the story leads the reader to expect, the book would have been a success . . . Again, it is on Miss Edgeworth's spoken testimony to Mrs. Barbauld that we learn that she meant to make Lady Delacour die, but that it was her father who suggested the alteration; and since it was a part of the Edgeworthian creed to believe in such simple and sudden reformations, she accepted his counsel, to the artistic injury of her tale. It was Mr. Edgeworth, too, who wrote and interpolated the worthless, and highflown Virginia episode in which Calrence Hervey takes to the freak of wife-training after the pattern of Mr. Day. The incident is quite out of keeping with the character of Clarence, who is depicted a wooden dandy, but not a romantic fool. These changes, willingly submitted to by Miss Edgeworth, who had the most unbounded belief in her father's superior wisdom on all points whatsoever, also mark his idiosyncracy, for Mr. Edgeworth was a most rare and curious compound of utilitarianism and wild romance.
>
> It is almost possible, in Miss Edgeworth's works, to venture to point out the passages that have been tampered with, and those where she has been allowed free play. . . .[1]

This passage is worth studying because it has been so influential. Augustus Hare follows Miss Zimmern confidently with the assertion that '*Belinda* was much marred by the alterations made by Mr. Edgeworth, in whose wisdom and skill his far cleverer daughter had unlimited and touching confidence'.[2] Two years later the same facts—this time attributed to Miss Zimmern, not Mrs. Barbauld—reappeared in

[1] Helen Zimmern, *Maria Edgeworth*, 1883, pp. 52–4.

[2] Augustus Hare, *The Life and Letters of Maria Edgeworth*, 1894, i. 70 n.

the preface to a new edition of *Belinda* by Anne Ritchie, Thackeray's daughter. They seemed to her so significant that she added a distinctly hostile sketch of Edgeworth as man, father, and literary collaborator. Similarly, Emily Lawless, in 1904, made her two chapters on *Castle Rackrent* and *Belinda* turn on the fact that Edgeworth was away when *Rackrent* was being written, while 'upon none of Miss Edgeworth's books did her father's editorial hand fall so heavily, or with such destructive effect as upon this unfortunate *Belinda*'.[1] Of the later critics who have discussed *Belinda*, Elton, Baker, and Professor Renwick do not mention Edgeworth's alleged part in changing the plot, but Mr. P. H. Newby repeats Miss Zimmern's charges in full,[2] using the story of the evolution of *Belinda* as the most damaging known example of Edgeworth's literary interference; and so it would be, if it were true.

Miss Zimmern's influential assertion rests, however, on no authority except her own. She named Mrs. Barbauld as her source, but it was another revision which brought in Mrs. Barbauld: after she chose *Belinda* for her selection of British Novelists in 1810, Maria, with her father's help, made substantial alterations to the text.[3] Miss Zimmern may have confused these corrections, which were made nine years after publication, and did not affect Lady Delacour, with the changes made between the first inception and the novel as written.

As for her other accusation, that Edgeworth wrote the Virginia episode, here she is simply mistaken; Maria refers to this sequence in the *Memoirs* in terms which leave no doubt that she and not he was the author.[4] (In any case it is unwise, again, to make too much of this change; the sequence it replaces, in which Clarence Hervey was to have acquired a seat in the House of Commons, is unlikely to be much of a loss to literature.) Without these two celebrated examples, we are left with no evidence that Edgeworth decisively changed the course of the novels when he saw the sketches. His concern at this stage

[1] Emily Lawless, *Maria Edgeworth*, 1904, pp. 99–100.

[2] P. H. Newby, *Maria Edgeworth*, 1950, pp. 53–4.

[3] See Appendix C, where RLE's annotated copy of the second edition is described. Evidence that RLE helped to make these changes was also available to Miss Zimmern in the letter from ME to Mrs. Barbauld of 18 Jan. 1810; A. Le Breton, *Memoir of Mrs. Barbauld*, 1874, pp. 136–7.

[4] *Memoirs of RLE*, ii. 349.

was almost certainly to supply detail to fill out the plot. His interest in the more mechanical side of novel-writing no doubt had the disadvantage that it encouraged his daughter's own tendency to think in terms of incident and episode rather than of the novel as a whole. But in the specific instances where we really do know what Edgeworth advised, we are unlikely to quarrel with him. When Maria was undecided how to end *The Absentee*, Edgeworth encouraged her to finish with a letter from Larry the postilion.[1] They both wrote one, and Edgeworth decided that Maria's was better. This instance of his 'interference' is much more characteristic of him than the influential *Belinda* story. It illustrates his interest in technical problems, his ready invention, and his genuine absence of egotism 'when writing is in question'.

Once the legend about *Belinda* is cleared out of the way, there is very little to support the traditional view of Edgeworth's part in the novels. The whole conception that he either inserted passages conveying his views, or sought in general to influence the novels so that they did convey his opinions, is based on the hostile nineteenth-century reading of his character and of his relationship with Maria. Of course he threw himself into the task of 'correcting' her stories with his usual energy. Sometimes, as in the case of *Leonora* which we are about to come to, his 'corrections' included radical criticisms. But it was much more common for him to take the subordinate position of supplier of detail, or the still less exalted role of proof-reader. 'It is not only a laborious but a very humble office to correct the writings of another.'[2] The point in short is that Edgeworth was a very busy man with plenty of interests of his own who also believed in encouraging his children with whatever they chose to do—Lovell with chemistry, Sneyd with poeticizing, William with engineering, Maria with novels. He was naturally very proud of her because of all the praise she received. But nothing he said about the novels suggests that he thought himself more involved with them than with any other work his children produced.

[1] The *Mem.*, i. 251, attributes this idea to RLE. Harriet Butler, in a letter to F. Y. Edgeworth of 4 May, 1886, claims that it originated with Maria, but she also denies that RLE wrote any of *The Absentee*, and this we know to be untrue. See above, p. 281 n.

[2] See above, pp. 147–8.

It is of course true that in a letter already quoted he addressed her as his 'Dr. Partner'.[1] That letter refers not to a novel but to a book he undoubtedly initiated and supervised—*Professional Education*, a case in which he could legitimately think of himself as part-author. There are plenty of other examples of his special interest and sense of involvement in the educational books.[2] He did regard Maria as his spokesman when he had something he wanted to say. 'We—or rather Maria, who is always meant by "we" when writing is in question.'[3]

But he did not claim the same property rights in the novels: on the contrary, he liked to speak of them as Maria's. Critics have accused him of writing prefaces to her tales which exaggerated the connection with his own work, and therefore seemed to insinuate that much of the credit originated with him. The *locus classicus* is his preface to *Tales of Fashionable Life*, where he tried to place the fiction precisely within their joint educational programme:

> It has . . . been my daughter's aim to promote, by all her writings, the progress of education, from the cradle to the grave. Miss Edgeworth's former works consist of tales for children—of stories for young men and women—and of tales suited to that great mass which does not move in the circles of fashion. The present volumes are intended to point out some of those errors to which the higher classes of society are disposed.
>
> All the parts of this series of moral fictions . . . have . . . arisen from that view of society which we have laid before the public in more didactic works on education. In *The Parent's Assistant*, in *Moral* and in *Popular Tales*, it was my daughter's aim to exemplify the principles contained in *Practical Education*. In these volumes, and in others which are to follow, she endeavours to disseminate, in a familiar form, some of the ideas that are unfolded in *Essays on Professional Education*.[4]

It is difficult to make Edgeworth's scheme work precisely as he described it, or not to suspect him of some rationalization after the event. He was still less convincing when he made the same claim for *Castle Rackrent*: 'What we have already published

[1] See above, p. 245.

[2] e.g. his letter to her quoted above on p. 158.

[3] See above, pp. 139–40. The reference here is to the account he meant to publish of his political dealings in Co. Longford.

[4] Preface to *Tales of Fashionable Life*, 1st series, 1809.

has always tended to improve the education of our country: even *Castle Rackrent* has that object remotely in view.'[1]

The question is not, however, whether Edgeworth expressed the relationship between the fiction and the educational principles in quite the right terms; it is whether he invented the relationship, or whether Maria intended it to be there: and the latter is, unquestionably, the case. The later group of tales and novels which includes *Vivian* and *Patronage* has the derivation from *Professional Education* which Edgeworth attributes to it.[2] Earlier, although Edgeworth himself was taking relatively little interest in the fiction, Maria was sufficiently influenced by her series for children to have a broad didactic plan in mind. Just as the children's literature was adjusted to the age of its readers, so the stories for adults written between 1803 and 1813 were carefully calculated to suit their different audiences. *Popular Tales*, 1804, was meant for those of the lower orders who could read, and the stories in it were accordingly about tradespeople and the characteristic problems of their lives. It was written in a plainer variant of Maria Edgeworth's normal prose style. *Tales of Fashionable Life* (two series, 1809 and 1812) aimed to regulate the manners of the upper classes; and both *Modern Griselda* (1805) and *Patronage* (1814) although eventually published separately, were originally intended to form part of *Tales of Fashionable Life*. *Harrington* and *Ormond* (1817) were supplementary stories which in effect extended the series. In other words, almost all Maria's fiction between *Belinda* (1801) and *Helen* (1834) was conceived within a single plan which linked it with Edgeworth's formal work, and this was meant by her 'to disseminate, in a familiar form, some of the ideas that are unfolded' in the 'more didactic works on education'.

Yet Edgeworth's conversation with Maria in 1805 about their doing another academic book together has him referring to her 'pretty stories and novellettes' as, by implication, not 'useful', and hence 'unworthy of his partner, pupil and daughter'.[3] Decidedly therefore it was not he but Maria who really did try to insist from first to last that the fiction and the educational

[1] RLE to Lady Spencer, 11 May, 1803.

[2] See below, pp. 329 ff.

[3] ME to SR, 26 Feb. 1805. The passage is quoted above, p. 209.

books were indivisible. As the story of her entire development shows, it was she who felt most anxious to maintain the idea of a partnership. The idea that the fiction must be seen as part of his work, so that it would contribute to his greater glory (an ironic hope if ever there was one) emanated from her. No doubt it is a very twentieth-century interpretation to guess that her motive in writing was to stimulate a continuous response from the father who had begun, in her childhood, by not responding to her enough. But it is nevertheless fair to notice how thoroughly she used the tales in her relationship with him. Sometimes, as in the case of *The Modern Griselda*, she wrote them in secret in order to make a present of them later:

> I shall work hard with the hopes of having something to read to my father—This has always been one of my greatest delights and strongest motives for writing—*Lazy Lawrence*—*The Bracelets* and *The Limerick Gloves* and *The Prussian Vase* were all written whilst my father was out somewhere or other, on purpose to be read to him on his return.[1]

Afterwards a printed copy of *The Modern Griselda* was thrust into his hands without a title-page, to see if he could guess who had written it. (It is surprising that she was prepared to use this ploy; it had not worked when she tried it with *Belinda* on Mrs. Ruxton three years earlier.)[2] At other times she maintained his interest with a tactic which she described as 'a female spirit of opposition'—that is, she argued back. She was willing to assert herself on minor issues in the case both of *Ormond* and *Leonora*. (In both cases she sought and got support from other members of the family first.) But perhaps the greatest gratification she had from success as an author was that at times it made her father dependent on her. Once, after his death, she recalled the time that he had had to do an article for the *Edinburgh Review*, when he 'urged me to assist him—to assist my father!'[3] Edge-

[1] ME to SR, Nov. 1803. Afterwards *Manœuvring* was written for RLE's birthday in 1808 (ME to Mrs. R, 26 May 1808).

[2] ME wrote *Belinda* while the Ruxtons were living in England. She deliberately kept knowledge of it from them in order to put a copy into her aunt's hands as 'Mrs. Robinson's posthumous work' (Mrs. FE to Harriet Beaufort, 28 May 1801). Cf. also *Mem.*, i. 105–6. The joke misfired, because Mrs. R interpreted Maria's curious refusal to praise the book as jealousy of another author. Neither Maria nor Mrs. R ever cared for *Belinda* after this.

[3] ME to Harriet Beaufort, 15 Dec. 1817. The article in question was a review of John Carr's *Stranger in Ireland* (1806). See below, pp. 371–2.

worth had on occasion hinted that she might tone down her praises of him, but he was in fact touched by her devotion and grateful for the literary help. On his deathbed he told her that 'no daughter since the creation of the world had ever given a father more pleasure'.[1] The knowledge that her writing pleased him was her chief motive all along in doing it; the stories, like the letters, were not written for the public but for particular individuals in the family:

> Notwithstanding my being an authoress and a philosopheress by profession and reputation, nevertheless I have only the smallest conceivable portion of public spirit or general philanthropy. It would have been a sad thing for the world if I had been appointed l'orateur du genre humain, for unless affection for some individual had prompted or inspired the exertion I should not have said one word, certainly never have got through a sentence. Seriously it was to please my father I first exerted myself to write, to please him I continued. He has abundance of public spirit. He by degrees enlarged my views, one circle succeeded to another larger and larger, but the first stone was thrown the first motion given by him, and when there is no similar moving power the beauteous circles vanish and the water stagnates.[2]

'Partnership' was more real to her than it was to Edgeworth. Since she was convinced that her writing was inspired by him, and meant for him, she could not believe at first when he died that she would ever return to novels, even to reading them. 'As to literature you judge rightly that the *charm* is gone. The *partnership* the most delightful literary *partnership* of thought and affection that ever existed is ended.'[1]

Her father was her most important partner, but not by any means the only one. The tales for adults, as opposed to the children's stories and educational books, really seem to have begun in order to give pleasure to her aunt, and the Ruxtons were just as influential as Edgeworth in the first half of her career; they apparently knew of and participated in everything she wrote between the early children's stories and *Ormond* in 1817, with the single exception of *Belinda*. The Beauforts were

[1] ME to ED, Sept. 1817; *Dublin Rev.*, cxlv (1909), 260.
[2] ME to ED, 18 Sept. 1813; *Dublin Rev.*, cxlv (1909), 256.

also often asked to read something through before publication, though not so much as a matter of course.[1] And all along, a subject neglected so far, there was the part played by the household at Edgeworthstown.

Maria as we saw did not get along well with the siblings nearest her in age, who were jealous of her career as an author. But she found a role with her younger brothers and sisters, both as a teacher and, more importantly, as an inventor of stories. Her most fruitful period in the latter role was the seventeen-nineties, when nearly all her best stories for children were written.[2] During Edgeworth's marriage to Frances, when on the whole Maria was writing for adults, she found other means to involve the entire household and thus strengthen her position in it.

It was at this time that she evolved her characteristic method of composition. She did the writing herself, and thought her best work was written quickly. With *Castle Rackrent*, for example, 'there was literally not a correction, not an alteration made in the first writing, no copy and as I recollect no interlineation—It went to the press just as it was written—Other stories I have corrected with the greatest care and remodelled and rewritten'.[3] Two of the other three Irish tales were also written exceptionally fast. The 105,000 words of *The Absentee* were produced in three and a half months, and *Ormond*, which is 15,000 words longer, in two weeks less.[4] But these works were carefully planned in advance—or parts of them were. Maria acknowledged that this was important. 'Whenever I have well considered a subject I think the more *rapidly* I write the more likely I am to preserve a unity of design and spirit through the whole.'[5] Certainly the novel she took four years to write—*Patronage*—was one of her least successful.

This rapid careless way of writing on was possible only (she claimed) because a loyal band of helpers was waiting to receive the text. It was, Edgeworth would tell her, ' "my business to *cut* and correct—yours to write on" '.[6] Probably she regularly overwrote, and afterwards left the job of cutting to the family. At any

[1] See above, p. 174 and below, p. 298.

[2] See above, pp. 157 ff.

[3] ME to Mrs. Stark, 6 Sept. 1834; *Mem.* iii. 153.

[4] See above, pp. 277 and 280.

[5] ME to Harriet Beaufort, 8 May 1817.

[6] *Memoirs of RLE*, ii. 346.

rate she deliberately used this method with her last novel, *Helen*.[1] 'Correcting' the novels was from first to last a family responsibility, and it was taken very seriously. Edgeworth stressed the importance of this revision prior to publication:

If my daughter has obtained any literary reputation, it has not been won, by sudden fits of exertion, but by patient changes and corrections which have cancelled more than three-fourths of what she had written—*Ennui*, one of her best performances, was totally rewritten, so was *Vivian*; and *The Absentee* had been written first in a theatrical form, before it appeared as one of the Fashionable Tales.[2]

For him the advantage of this method was that the text was carefully checked, since he did not have a high opinion of Maria's accuracy:

The confusion of names which is the constant fault of all you write is to be met with in these fair pages—Burdon for Barker and Oh fie! Angelina for *Lady Frances*.

One sheet was turned wrong side out—fie fie fie—will you never mend. . . .[3]

But an incidental advantage was that it saved Maria herself a great deal of time. As she neared the end of a novel, her critics would begin work on the early chapters, so that writing and revision was going on simultaneously. All along Edgeworth had impressed on Maria the value of neat, industrious habits. Her days were accordingly divided into compartments, so that she could write, correct, and still maintain the other activities of a busy life, letter-writing, walking in the garden, riding out, doing business, and talking with family and friends. The best description of her working day comes from a period after her father's death, but its orderliness is typical of her whole life:

Before breakfast walk 2 miles (never miss except rain). After breakfast set [*sic*] awhile and read letters (of yours when so happy).

From half after ten to half after eleven correct what may have been read night before of *Helen*.

From half after eleven till two—or always till half after one—read *Helen* to Aunt Mary in my room—I read to her what Harriet afterwards reads to all in the evg.

[1] See below, p. 460.

[2] RLE to Mrs. Hofland, 28 Dec. 1815.

[3] RLE to ME (fragment), n.d. [early 1800].

2 or ½ Luncheon—After Luncheon rest awhile—Honora insists half an hour—So then it is past 3 —and I must go out again till four.

From four till 5 I write *Helen*—I have some of the last chapters to rewrite before we come up to them and at an hour and half a day that will be as much as I can do.

From 5 till ¼ after six letter writing—and much of that and more than I can do and be ready which I assure you always am (almost) for dinner.

After dinner sleep till tea never fail snugly like a dormouse . . . After tea till eleven Harriet reads *Helen*. . . .[1]

The point for Maria was not speed so much as getting everyone involved together. Charlotte and Mary Sneyd faithfully performed humble secretarial tasks like altering a name throughout a manuscript.[2] The heyday of Maria's stepbrothers and stepsisters as critics on the whole came in the 1820s and 1830s, when once again Maria used her writing to cement her ties with the family. But all along she enjoyed hearing her stories read out in the evening, listening to everyone's reactions, and incorporating their suggestions in the text. Sending off the play 'The Absentee' in 1811 led to the kind of family involvement she loved. 'It was copied in a single night: we all sat round the library table, and each taking a portion, it was completed by twelve o'clock in eight different handwritings.'[3] Guessing who the eight must have been gives an idea of the composition of 'The Committee of Education and Criticism', as Maria called the older part of the family circle. Presumably they were Maria herself, her father, Mrs. Edgeworth, the two Sneyd aunts, Honora (born 1791), William (born 1794), and Anna Beddoes, who was only a brief visitor to Edgeworthstown.[4]

Usually she did not show her novels to anyone outside the family circle before publication. *Professional Education* was a different matter: the various chapters went to a number of outsiders, including Étienne Dumont, Lord Selkirk, James

[1] ME to Fanny Wilson, 12 Jan. 1833.

[2] See above, p. 258.

[3] *Mem.*, i. 247.

[4] ME's other literary confidant in the domestic circle was her stepbrother Sneyd (CSE), born 1786. He had some literary aspirations of his own; e.g. he wrote a long poem called 'Indur', and the *Memoirs of the Abbé Edgeworth* (1815), which ME was obliged drastically to rewrite (see above, p. 234). As a lawyer Sneyd was often away on circuit. For ME's principal literary advisers in later years, see below, pp. 459–64.

Keir, and Judge Fox. Independent vetting was not thought necessary in the case of the novels, with the single exception of *Leonora*. Since Maria was not publishing this tale as part of a series, but in a single volume by itself, Edgeworth felt it had to aim at a particularly high standard of correctness.[1] Besides, its theme embroiled Maria in problems of verisimilitude and propriety, for which women of the world were the best judges. So Edgeworth for once allowed or encouraged Maria to send this novel out, to her old friend Lady Moira, and to Mme Gautier in Paris and Lady Spencer in London. From Maria's replies to those of their letters which have not survived, it is clear that almost all their comments referred to style, verisimilitude, or morality. So indeed did those of the Ruxtons:

> Thanks for your most kind and judicious criticisms on Leonora's letters—that I think them judicious may be best proved to you by my having already written entirely over again 40 pages of Mr. L's letters—You shall see him quite a new man— . . . my father may hurry it off to Johnson—but I shall prevent that if I can because I wish to profit *more* by your corrections—not yours and my aunts only Madam—but my uncle's. Thank him for his great kindness in sending me so full a list . . . —Singularly happy the woman who has such friends—*Extraordinarily* happy the authoress![2]

> Yesterday I had a most agreeable letter from Madame Gautier (dated 15th Sepr). A packet containing Popular tales and a copy by my aunt Mary of the two first of Olivia's letters and the Dutchess's long moral letters which I sent the 19th March had just reached Paris . . . as I said that Madame Gautiers was a *most agreeable* letter you may guess that she praises popular tales—But she praises much more the Dutchess's letters, which she wants me to let Pictet translate and publish in the Bibliotheque Britannique.[3]

Lady Spencer's comments were, obviously, entirely typical:

> *Leonora* is delightful; I have twice read it through and hope to read once more when it [is] given to the world—I would have every young married woman profit by the wholesome advice so admirably given in it—on no rock do they founder so often as on unguarded female friendship—it is my horror and you may therefore conceive my satisfaction when I perceived that your incomparable pen had drawn so accurate a picture of the dangers so dreaded, and so often

[1] ME to SR, 22 July 1804, and RLE to ME, 4 Aug. 1804.

[2] ME to SR, 18 July 1804.

[3] ME to SR, Oct. 1804.

witnessed by me in this dissipated and fearless period . . . [*Leonora*] so exactly accomplishes the object I have long wished to see executed, that I could not resist expressing my satisfaction at finding all my ideas so delightfully realized by you—Go on dear Madam amuse edify and instruct as you are so well able to do—and every mother will gratefully confess her obligation to you.[1]

Only Edgeworth refrained from joining the chorus of feminine praise about *Leonora*. In a letter written at the time when the novel first seemed nearly finished, he expressed his doubts about its appeal:

Your critic partner father friend has finished your [*Leonora*].[2] He has cut out a few pages one or two letters are nearly untouched; the rest are cut and scrawled and interlined without mercy—I make no doubt of the success of the book *amongst a certain class of readers provided* it be reduced to one small volume and provided it be polished ad unguem—so that neither flaw nor seam can be perceived by the utmost critical acumen—

As it has no story, to interest the curiosity, no comic to make the reader laugh nor tragick to make him cry it must depend upon the development of sentiment—the verisimilitude of character and elegance of style which the higher classes of the literary world expect in such a performance in lieu of fable and of excitement for their feelings—These you well know how to give; and your honest gratitude towards a favoring public will induce your accustom'd industry to put the highest finish to the work—In this purpose I advise you to revise it frequently when you are *drunk* and *sober*—and to look upon it as a promising infant committed to your care, which you are bound by many ties to educate and bring out when it is fit to be presented—The design is worthy of that encouragement which you have already received; it rests on nature, truth, sound morality and religion and if you polish it it will sparkle in the regions of moral fashion—You will perhaps be surprised to hear that I have corrected more faults of style than in anything I have ever corrected for you.—Mr. Ruxtons criticisms have except one been adopted by me—and I hope when you have corrected it again, that he will have the goodness to revise it a second time—[3]

[1] Lady Spencer to ME, n.d. [1805]. As the sister-in-law of the celebrated Duchess of Devonshire and of Lady Bessborough, Lady Spencer had an admirable view of 'this dissipated and fearless period'.

[2] The MS. originally read 'your anonymous love story'. ME probably made the emendation prior to publishing the letter in the *Memoirs*.

[3] RLE to ME, 4 Aug. 1804; *Memoirs of RLE*, ii. 353-4.

Only a month later, Maria summarized his views for her aunt in terms less flattering to *Leonora*. His objections would surprise those who have thought that he wrote the didactic parts of the novels himself: 'My father continues to think Olivia and Leonora flat and spiritless and stuffed with morality —but he says it will be recommended by Governesses and read by Misses . . . I shall correct it with all possible care—partly I suppose from the female spirit of opposition.'[1] By October, despite Madame Gautier's praise, his hostility had hardened still further, and Maria was forced to lay the book temporarily aside:

> . . . they [the letters] are gone up to the garret by particular desire for some months—Perhaps they will appear better when they come down again after this prudent retreat—My father is still their determined foe—He says Olivia is a chambermaid and writes not like a *demi*rep but like a whole *rep* and in this particular he brings my uncles opinion in support of his own—But he adds that after a great deal of correcting the volume may be made good for something—[2]

Edgeworth's judgement in this case was better than that of any other of Maria's literary advisers. This is not surprising, for the virtuous ladies she deliberately consulted were all carried away by enthusiasm for the theme; a man was better placed to criticize the lack of action and the unusual poverty of characterization. Olivia—to whom both Edgeworth and Ruxton objected—is indeed a cardboard Other Woman, just the figure that a respectable and sheltered spinster might be expected to draw.

However, Edgeworth had the power of postponement, not of veto; by June 1805 *Leonora* was at the printer's, and in October Johnson sent proof-sheets to Edgeworthstown for the family's last thoughts. At last Edgeworth did begin to come round, not because he thought much of the novel as a whole, but because Maria had at last succeeded in giving one scene the pathos that to him was the next best ingredient to comedy and incident:

> As we journeyed to Pakenham Hall he [RLE] read the sheet of *Leonora* which was the letter written immediately after her husband's leaving home with Olivia—you may remember that he formerly

[1] ME to Mrs. R, Sept. 1804. [2] ME to SR, Oct. 1804.

called this the letter of a kitchen maid—But I assure you he could scarcely read it without crying and he repeatedly said it is truly pathetic—it is excellent &c—I am in hopes he will like the whole bit by bit—and my aunt protests she will refrain from extolling it —But does not keep her word—[1]

In the end pathos, and the chorus of feminine praise, won the day, and *Leonora* (which had been ready, as Maria once thought, in the summer of 1804) was finally published in February 1806.

This is another interesting case because it shows how criticism from within the family compared with the comments Maria had from outsiders. The traditional view has always been that Edgeworthstown, and especially Edgeworth himself, was out of line in being exceptionally didactic and doctrinaire. *Leonora*, the only case of a novel shown to outsiders, proves that the reality was very different. It was the women of the world who praised the didactic theme, and Edgeworth who complained of the lack of life. He thought *Leonora* failed for the very reason that most of its critics since have thought it failed—because it was 'flat and spiritless and stuffed with morality', and because it had 'no story, to interest the curiosity, no comic to make the reader laugh nor tragick to make him cry'.

The revisions that Maria made to the novels for subsequent editions reinforce the same point, that the Edgeworth family did not have unusually prudish or pedantic notions. Once the novels were published, corrections could be supplied by outsiders, and in fact frequently were. Maria did not change the text of her novels in response to their broad aesthetic criticisms, even if she agreed with them; not many novelists do. But she did feel obliged to make other kinds of alteration, which sometimes merely affected a single word, but in two cases completely changed the second half of the novel.

By modern standards she went to great trouble with her fiction after publication. Apart from faults of grammar and other purely verbal errors, which she invariably corrected, there were two kinds of mistakes which she felt bound to take seriously. One was a breach of good taste, an action or expression which did not meet the best standards. She thought

[1] ME to Mrs. FE, Thursday [latter part of 1805].

herself as much a lady when she appeared before the public in writing as she was when she went out into the world in person, and deplored the social vulgarity and impropriety in, for example, the novels of her Irish rival Lady Morgan.[1] Equally important was accuracy about facts. Accidental impropriety and inaccuracy were therefore powerful arguments against a particular passage. Conversely, discovery of a new fact which appeared to support what was already written in a novel might induce her to make an addition to the text.

The Irish novels, which went into several editions, have a typical post-publication history. All had at least one cut or insertion. Although Maria Edgeworth resisted her father's plan for a major supplement to the fifth edition of *Castle Rackrent* in 1810, she added the long footnote giving the history of a family lawsuit.[2] In 1813 *Ennui* gained a similar new footnote, added to Davy's sequence about different travellers' experiences in Ireland.[3] On the other hand, a reference to Lady Geraldine's loud voice was dropped as indecorous from the second collected edition of 1833; Maria marvelled that it had survived so long.[4] Grace Nugent, heroine of *The Absentee*, in the third edition of 1812 lost a speech in which she had referred to a kept mistress.[5] But in 1818, another paragraph, containing a further comic incident from real life, was added to the humorous set piece, Mrs. Raffarty's dinner-party.[6]

The changes made to *Belinda* and *Patronage* are too complicated to set out here in full.[7] Again, they are mostly connected with errors of fact or impropriety. If any further reminder is needed that in this period the public had some very literal and proper ideas, there is the objection made by Mrs. Inchbald to a word in *Patronage*. In that novel a vain politician, the Duke of Greenwich, feels insulted because Lord Oldborough fastens a letter to him with a plebian wafer instead of a seal. ('I wonder how any man can have the impertinence to send me his spittle!'[8]) Mrs. Inchbald objected that this was a word she thought Maria 'could not have written and ought not to have known how to spell'. But Maria had picked up the

[1] See below, p. 448.
[2] See above, pp. 277–8 and pp. 242–3.
[3] See above, p. 247.
[4] ME to Harriet Butler, 22 Dec. 1831.
[5] ME to Miss Waller, 16 Aug. 1812.
[6] See below, p. 377.
[7] See Appendix C.
[8] *Patronage*, ch. 8; xi. 132.

expression in real life, it did illustrate the character of a vain man, and after consideration she decided to keep it. 'I have now changed the word *severe* into *coarse* . . . but I cannot alter, without spoiling, the *fact*. I tried if *saliva* would do, but it would not: so you must bear it as well as you can, and hate his Grace of Greenwich as much as you will—but don't hate me.'[1]

Since she was writing to please her family circle, anything idiosyncratic about their literary tastes is relevant to her career. The Beauforts, who had received a scientific education, were certainly exact, and Mrs. Edgeworth's sister Harriet, especially, seems over-literal. She objected to one of the best scenes in *Belinda*, the one in which Lady Delacour is so torn by suspicion and jealousy that she loses control over herself. 'The tears rolled fast down her painted cheeks; she wiped them hastily away, and so roughly, that her face became a strange and ghastly spectacle.'[2] Harriet thought that bringing in a mundane article like rouge at this stage, and allowing Belinda to refer to it, was unnatural and ill-judged.[3] Otherwise she seems to have concentrated on points of grammar, although it is unfair to make too much of this, since the 'corrections' that everyone was always asked for implied small verbal emendations rather than fundamental criticism.

There were only three family critics whose intimacy with Maria was such that they could conceivably have had any consistent influence over her—Sophy, Mrs. Ruxton, and Edgeworth. The Ruxtons' letters as a whole have not survived, and from Maria's in reply it is difficult to get a clear picture of Sophy's tastes. At Black Castle, as at Edgeworthstown, they did not read the *Lyrical Ballads*; but they did read Scott's poems as they were published, and later Byron's. Sophy had read all the poetry and novels that a young woman in Jane Austen's social circle might have read; she had also worked her way through *The Wealth of Nations*, annotating it, which

[1] ME to Mrs. Inchbald, 14 Feb. 1814; J. Boaden, *Memoirs of Mrs. Inchbald*, 1833, ii. 195–6.

[2] *Belinda*, ch. 15; ii. 263–4.

[3] ME to Harriet Beaufort, n.d. [1802]. Instead of defending the rouge because it is thematically connected with the *mask* that Lady Delacour hides behind (see below, p. 312), ME wrote back very prosaically about why it was natural for Belinda to bring the subject up. But she kept the rouge.

means of course that she was no Catherine Morland. But nor was she an advocate of serious topics in novels as opposed to frivolity. She particularly liked the coaching scene in *Ennui*, and thought the attack on press-ganging in *Patronage* out of place.[1] She had her own contacts with the Irish, and knew, or thought she knew, how small farmers talked; she said that Farmer Gray in *Rosanna* reasoned too closely.[2] Sophy was used as a confidante by both Maria and Lovell when they fell in love, and perhaps the topic she most often took up after reading through a tale was the handling of the romantic interest. She did not see *Belinda* before publication, but the claim afterwards that Belinda was a jilt and 'cold-hearted' may well have come from Black Castle. Sophy certainly persuaded Maria to rewrite passages in *Leonora*, *Vivian*, and *Patronage* because she did not like what characters did or said when they were supposed to be in love.[3]

A clearer picture of Mrs. Ruxton's tastes can be pieced together, which is useful, since Mrs. Ruxton mattered a great deal more than Sophy to Maria. Mrs. Ruxton was a lady, and cared about being one, as her refusal of Thomas Day suggested. 'Her grace and charm of manner were such that a gentleman once said of her "If I were to see Mrs. Ruxton sitting in rags as a beggar on the doorstep, I should say 'Madam' to her!"'[4] She strongly objected to improper passages in the books they all discussed, and in this limited sense would have been an effective censor of Maria's novels. There was, for example, an expression in *Irish Bulls* which she thought disgusting, and Maria hastily promised to take it out in the next edition, adding that she had no ambition 'to emulate the dirty part of Swift's fame'. She explained how the unfortunate phrase had got into the book: 'My father was so charmed with the original expression as it came fresh from the lips of John Langan that he would have it inserted.'[5] Presumably because of its theme, Mrs. Ruxton approved of *Leonora*. But in her wit and vivacity she was said after all to resemble her brother, and prudery was not the most important feature of her criticism. She loved

[1] See Appendix C.

[2] ME to SR, 22 July 1804. Again, ME did not agree and she made no change.

[3] ME to SR, 22 July 1804, 30 July 1804, Dec. 1808, and June 1811.

[4] *Mem.*, i. 19.

[5] ME to SR, 1 Aug. 1802.

lively character sketches, and it was she who encouraged Maria to go on with *Castle Rackrent* because Thady was so good a character. She always appears to have singled out the individual characters and not to have thought of the novels as wholes. The Irish tales, which were full of vignettes and entertaining detail, were favourites. 'I think *Ormond* superior to anything you have yet written . . . superior to *The Absentee*, *Ennui*, all of them.'[1] She must have sanctioned the sketch of King Corny in *Ormond*, although since the original was her husband's brother-in-law the character could potentially have been a great embarrassment. Mrs. Beaumont, the adroit lady in *Manœuvring*, was her favourite single sketch. Conversely, she hated lifelessness in any of the tales. Belinda was too cold to be a girl after her heart, and she detested Alfred Percy, the virtuous lawyer in *Patronage*.[2] Maria once reported how her aunt had roundly denounced a play as 'the tamest, weakest thing she ever saw of mine'.[3] Maria's letters to Black Castle show what kind of an influence her aunt was—and of course Maria's letters to her aunt are part of her evolution as a writer. The most important qualities that Mrs. Ruxton drew out of Maria were her talent for lively detail and well-observed comic touches. The polished high comedy of Maria's best early vein—*Belinda*, *The Modern Griselda*, *Manœuvring*, and so on —were particularly suited to her aunt, who was noted (like some of Maria's best characters) for witty and polished conversation.[4] Mrs. Ruxton was one reason the novels came into being at all, and, although she did not consciously try to influence the way they were written, she was in a sense the presiding genius of the first half of Maria's career as a writer of fiction.

Ample evidence has already been provided for determining Edgeworth's tastes. Like his sister, he loved lively detail—humour and pathos, racy speech and striking characters, and above all 'story, story, story'. It is typical of him that he thought *Ennui*, which is structurally weak but excellent in detail, the best of the *Tales of Fashionable Life*.[5] His literary preferences

[1] Mrs. R to ME, 27 July 1817. [2] ME to Mrs. R, 28 Jan. 1814.

[3] ME to Charlotte Sneyd, 19 Nov. 1808. [4] See below, pp. 320–9.

[5] ME and RLE to Walter Scott, 4 Feb. 1815; Nat. Lib. of Scotland, MS. 3886, f. 65.

were certainly not out of the ordinary in the first half of the nineteenth century—the enormous middlebrow success of Dickens was to prove that. In fact Edgeworth was regarded not only by the family but by their publisher as a good judge of what the ordinary public would like. Before publication he went on record as believing that *Leonora* was uninteresting, *Patronage* too didactic to succeed, and *Comic Dramas* merely 'slight productions'.[1] Sure enough, these were the books the critics liked least, although perhaps only *Patronage* actually lost money.[2]

As a scientist and educationalist Edgeworth thought originally, but in literary matters he did not. He therefore had no sense of the literary significance of Maria's use of Irish material. He assumed that the Irish tales were too local in interest to last, and wondered rather obscurely if the success of *The Absentee* was 'too much owing to the provincialism and patois of some of the characters'. He had no worries about the more run-of-the-mill *Modern Griselda*—'a peculiar favourite of mine—I think its chief merit is elegance'.[3] He valued more than a modern reader would the verbal correctness which came from careful checking of Maria's work, and therefore implicitly encouraged her own tendency to undervalue the more creative and imaginative aspect of writing; just as his interest in detail and real-life facts made her concentrate on these, and neglect the whole design.

His literary ideas were those common to the age of sentiment. He read fiction in order to sympathize with characters, not to judge them. If he thought at all of the purpose of art, it was in outworn neoclassical terms, as 'an imitation of life'—without perceiving that the subjectivity of his age called for radically new forms. Yet the significant thing about him is that as a scientist he did have a fresh approach to one aspect of life, the external. Working empirically, he had acquired a sophisticated sense of how society worked. Maria's early novels were entirely traditional in their 'realism', and Edgeworth did not take them intellectually seriously. He called them 'mere

[1] ME to CSE, 21 Oct. 1817, and Preface to *Comic Dramas*, 1817.

[2] See below, pp. 346–7, and Appendix B.

[3] RLE to Galignani and Maradan, French publishers of *The Modern Griselda* and *The Absentee*, 15 July 1815.

pretty stories and novellettes' and instead got Maria to settle down to *Professional Education*, which forced her for the first time in public to consider questions right outside the drawing room. Coupled with his earlier influence on her education, Edgeworth's request to Maria to write this book for him is the really significant instance of his affecting her career. What it did was to turn Maria away from the feminine type of novel that came most easily to her, and set her off on the sequence that included *Ennui* and *The Absentee*, the two most influential tales she wrote.

The fact that for several years before this she was publishing tales which did not specially interest or impress him shows that he was a long way from the Svengali of vulgar imaginings. It was only after she caught a glimpse, through Paris and afterwards through Dumont, of an intellectual high society, that she summoned courage to tackle her father's serious interests in the terms of her own genre. Once she did this, she inevitably began to draw on the understanding of an Irish estate that he had given her, and the deductions about the entire Irish economy that could be drawn from Edgeworthstown's example. The habits of accurate observation in which her father had trained her were not used after this merely to characterize individuals, but also to give a balanced picture of the real-life manners and speech of the Irish peasantry. The tales she wrote that contemporary critics liked best were unusually objective and well informed. *Ennui* and *The Absentee* were admired for their intellectual qualities and their grasp of reality—because, in fact, they reflected Edgeworth's wider and more intellectual masculine interests rather than Mrs. Ruxton's necessarily more restricted feminine ones. After her father's death, Maria recalled a characteristic suggestion he had made to her:

> I am more and more convinced of the wisdom of my fathers advice to me to read the papers constantly—to keep up the knowledge of all the *real* interests of the world and to exercise the judgment daily upon the great subjects on which the minds of the first people in the country are exercised—This is particularly necessary to a dealer in fiction.[1]

Although she claimed to have been persuaded that fiction

[1] ME to Mrs. FE, 28 Jan. 1819; *Letters from England*, p. 166.

ought to deal in 'the *real* interests of the world', her last novel, *Helen*, was to prove something of a hybrid, with the private and domestic theme better handled than the documentary social material. Again this suggests that Maria herself was naturally most at home in the narrower feminine compass. But her reputation was made with *Ennui* and *The Absentee*, and it is this part of her career that ensured her literary importance. Most people have supposed that in the Irish novels she was most herself, and it seems to follow that in the English novels she would have owed more to Edgeworth. But in reality the reverse was the case. Of course she used his experiences to fill out her English novels, like *Belinda*, but she used it in the Irish tales too. What is more to the point is that the English 'drawing-room' tales of her first phase focus on individual character sketches, are light and pleasing in tone, and are not quite serious—even if they are often incidentally didactic.[1] The tales of her next phase, especially the Irish ones, tackle bigger questions. It is only in them that Maria draws on her father's intellectual concerns, and employs his scientific methods, which is the point at which Edgeworth's presence is seriously felt in her tales.

Where then does her didacticism come from? A purely literary answer would be 'from the moral tale', and it is certainly more reasonable to put it down to Maria's up-bringing on Voltaire and Marmontel than to blame any of her relatives. On the other hand, purely literary explanations are not in keeping with the atmosphere at Edgeworthstown. There is no evidence that the advantages of the moral tale over the novel, or vice versa, ever came under discussion at the time when Maria was a practising writer. She wrote very spontaneously—influenced of course unconsciously by literary precedent, but also moved by private considerations nearer home. The didactic passages are peculiarly Maria's, in a sense that nothing else in the tales is. They are the one element that no one ever asked her to put in. They reflect her obsessive desire to promote her father's opinions, such as the advantages of domestic over public life, or the importance of financial and moral independence. Alternatively they show how

[1] e.g. the first chapter of *Belinda*, 'Characters', where each introductory sketch of the principals in the action is followed by a short homily.

anxious she was not to write mere novels, but instructive tales that fitted in with his work and were not unworthy of his serious reputation as a scientist.

It will be objected that this is no way to become a novelist. Novels, like any works of art, are written for their own sakes, or at least not as an incidental part of an emotional dialogue with other people. The fragmentariness of her stories, the way in which real life is allowed to intrude, the frequent animus against metropolitan life and society, are all among Maria's most obvious defects as a novelist, and they can be linked with her attitude towards composition. Meanwhile, Edgeworth himself appears to have been unaware that Maria meant her novels to bring his name to the world's attention. Since he thought it a sign of a manly character to scorn 'popular or any kind of applause', he was the last man to employ a publicist. Nor would he have cared if he could have seen how much his fancied connection with her novels would have caused him to be abused. 'Posthumous fame is in reality nonsense.'[1] But Maria herself badly wanted to have established what indeed seems to be the sober truth, that she owed her literary importance to the training and attitudes she received from her father.

[1] RLE to John Foster (dictated to ME), 10 June 1817 (three days before his death); letter in Foster collection, Public Record Office of Northern Ireland, MS. 36184.

# VII

## TALES OF TWO WORLDS

*Castle Rackrent* (1800), Maria Edgeworth's first successful work of fiction for adults, evolved almost by accident. Her second, *Belinda*, was highly derivative. Maria did not care much for either of them afterwards. She positively disliked *Belinda*,[1] and only grudgingly rated *Castle Rackrent* seriously when its popularity obliged her to. Her next group of tales, which at their best were light and witty sketches centred on one or two well-conceived characters, were really her first assured work for adults. After this, from 1809, she began to publish a quite different style of fiction, which her contemporaries acclaimed because, they said, it marked a new phase in the formal development of the novel.

This summary of Maria Edgeworth's career would not have aroused any surprise or dispute among those first critics, but it differs sharply from accounts given from the latter half of the nineteenth century to the present day. *Castle Rackrent* and *Belinda*, if not much read, are now generally remembered by name, whereas other tales that both she and her contemporaries thought her most important are forgotten. In the late nineteenth century there was a shift in taste to more introverted novels, so that those of Maria's fictions which were character-centred came to be preferred (even when they were palpably immature) to the broader surveys of society which she produced later. The following chapter sets her career in a perspective which aims to be more balanced, as it is certainly more historical. For after exploring her career as it occurred, we may conclude that Maria Edgeworth's contemporaries often wrote more wisely and interestingly about her than many of her critics since.

### 1. *The First Phase: Comedy and Characterization*

*Castle Rackrent* owed its success to the portrait of its narrator, Thady M'Quirk, to which, as we know, the story of the Rackrent dynasty was fitted in two separate pieces.[2] There is

[1] But partly for personal reasons; see above, p. 288 n.

[2] See above, p. 174.

only one other fully drawn character, Sir Condy, and the great bulk of the so-called action is a miscellany of real-life events and information.[1] The presence of such a high proportion of documentary material ought to make *Castle Rackrent* one of the most fragmentary of Maria's tales, but giving the story to Thady to tell has a wonderfully cohesive effect. Although he is not the principal figure in the action, but a mere bystander, he dominates the book, so that the Rackrents' various doings serve the central aesthetic purpose of revealing his character and attitudes. Thus Maria's original tactic of developing her character sketch of John Langan by finding an appropriate story, or, as it turns out, stories, for him to tell turns out to be one of the strengths of the finished version.

In editing *Castle Rackrent* recently, Mr. George Watson praised its originality and technical skill. The device of a narrator who is not an active participant in the story, and, what is more, is not a reliable witness, seems to be both original and technically extremely promising; but the word skill is not the best one to use in the context. It may be that Thady's dominance over the welter of incident gives the story more unity and perhaps more imaginative force than anything else Maria wrote, but it certainly does not allow the story to speak for her. She found it unpalatable that she had made the quaint, archaic narrator more interesting than the Rackrents, who as landlords had in reality a more significant part to play in Irish life. Her motives in taking to fiction were not to act as an amanuensis to John Langan; on the contrary, the viewpoint she wanted to adopt was English and forward-looking. At the most personal level she had a good landlord in mind, and it had been impossible to get either him or his example into Castle Rackrent.[2] This is why she never used the technique of an idiosyncratic narrator again, although it had proved an excellent vehicle for combining her gift of recreating character, with her fund of Irish material.

*Castle Rackrent* was so successful with the critics and public that it was impossible afterwards for Maria to resist the temptation of producing more fiction for adults. The difficulty

[1] See above, pp. 240–3.

[2] The discrepancy between *Castle Rackrent* and ME's ideals in writing fiction about Ireland is dealt with more fully in the next chapter. See below, pp. 355 ff.

was the question of form. Of possible genres the most obvious was the one the public bought in quantity, the three-volume novel. Edgeworth had long ago lifted his ban on novel reading, and Maria had consumed as they came out most novels of any merit produced in England in the 1790s—Moore's, Godwin's, Holcroft's, Bage's, Mrs. Radcliffe's, Mrs. Inchbald's, and so on. But the novel still had a low intellectual reputation, often on the grounds that it depicted silly, sentimental behaviour, a dangerous example to young girls; and even the intellectual novelists of the 1790s had not made the form respectable, since they were associated with radicalism and with sexual promiscuity.[1]

Maria therefore joined the group of rational women writers of this period whose first novels were so to speak anti-novels. In the Advertisement to *Belinda* she declared war on the form. 'The following work is offered to the public as a Moral Tale—the author not wishing to acknowledge a Novel . . . So much folly, errour and vice are disseminated in books classed under this denomination, that it is hoped the wish to assume another title will be attributed to feelings that are laudable, and not fastidious.' Jane Austen was to make gentle fun of the Advertisement. 'I will not adopt that ungenerous and impolitic custom so common with novel writers, of degrading by their contemptuous censure the very performances, to the number of which they are themselves adding.'[2] In spite of this, both *Northanger Abbey* and *Sense and Sensibility* have much in common with *Belinda*, just as the two novelists' juvenilia in the 1790s often reveal similar attitudes. Maria's *Whim for Whim* and *Angelina*, like Jane Austen's *Volume the First* and *Volume the Second*, burlesque some of the commoner clichés of sentimental fiction. Afterwards both novelists move away from these self-conscious literary beginnings in the direction of naturalism, but their early novels retain traces of parody and satire.[3]

[1] Cf. RLE's views on Godwin's sexual attitudes, described above, p. 206 n. ME's *Angelina*, like her friend Mrs. Hamilton's *Memoirs of Modern Philosophers*, 1800, satirizes advanced novels, particularly those that depict daring and free-living women (like Mary Hays's *Memoirs of Emma Courtney*, 1796).

[2] *Northanger Abbey*, ch. 5. For other novelists who refused to employ the word novel, see J. M. S. Tompkins, *The Popular Novel in England, 1770–1800*, 1932, p. 26n.

[3] It is of course significant that according to Cassandra Austen *Sense and Sensibility* was begun in November 1797, and '*Northanger Abbey* was written

*Belinda* is not a burlesque, but it does introduce archetypal situations of the sentimental novel, and handles them in a highly rational manner that has the effect of bringing convention face to face with reality.

Formally the three-volume *Belinda* is very much a novel, and it borrows unashamedly from other novels of the period, especially those of Fanny Burney, Elizabeth Inchbald, and John Moore. Moore's influence is perhaps confined to the didactic spirit in which Lady Delacour was conceived, and it is best left to a consideration of Maria's general debt to the moral tale. Mrs. Inchbald supplied a pleasing manner, and Fanny Burney provided the plot. The action of *Belinda* is fundamentally the same as that of *Evelina* and *Cecilia*, namely the adventures of an *ingénue* making her début in high society. The situation gives scope for social comedy and social criticism, as through Belinda's eyes the reader meets a succession of characters at morning visits and masquerades. The vignettes introduced in this way are also often very much in the Fanny Burney tradition. There is for example the foolish baronet Sir Philip Baddely, who proposes to Belinda and to his astonishment is rejected. He is directly in the line of social comedy that passes from Fanny Burney to Jane Austen, and his description of the Queen's breakfast at Frogmore is as good as anything of its kind to be found in either:

'It was the finest sight and best conducted I ever saw, and only wanted Miss Portman to make it complete. We had gipsies, and Mrs Mills the actress for the queen of the gipsies; and she gave us a famous good song, Rochfort, you know—and then there *was* two children upon an *ass*—damme, I don't know how they came there, for they're things one sees every day—and belonged only to two of the soldiers' wives—for we had the whole band of the Staffordshire playing at dinner, and we had some famous glees—and Fawcett gave us his laughing song, and then we had the launching of the ship, and only it was a boat, it would have been well enough—but damme, the song of Polly Oliver was worth the whole—except the Flemish Hercules, Ducrow, you know, dressed in light blue and silver, and—Miss Portman, I wish you had seen this—three great coach-wheels on his chin, and a ladder and two chairs and two children on them—and after that, he sported a musquet

about the years 98 and 99'. Jane Austen, *Minor Works*, ed. R. W. Chapman, 1954, memorandum facing p. 242.

and bayonet with the point of the bayonet on his chin—faith! that was really famous! But I forgot the Pyrrhic dance, Miss Portman, which was damned fine too . . . and there was some bon-mot (but that was in the morning) amongst the gipsies about an orange, and the stadtholder—and then there was a Turkish dance, and a Polonese dance, all very fine, but nothing coming up to the Pyrrhic touch, which was a great deal the most knowing, in boots and spurs—damme, now I can't describe the thing to you, 'tis a cursed pity you weren't there, damme.'

Lady Delacour assured Sir Philip that she had been more entertained by the description than she could have been by the reality.[1]

The relationship between Belinda and her fashionable mentor, Lady Delacour, resembles the similarly chequered friendship between Fanny Burney's Cecilia and Mrs. Delville. *Belinda* also apes *Cecilia* (as well as many other eighteenth-century novels) by introducing a pastoral interlude, the episode where Clarence Hervey finds Virginia in a cottage in the forest. In short, Maria Edgeworth has taken two series of events from her father's youth—Sir Francis Delaval's life and death, and Thomas Day's attempt to train a wife[2]—and fitted them to the format of Fanny Burney's first two novels.

In copying Fanny Burney Maria thought she was aiming at something far superior to the common run of novels.[3] Even so, *Belinda* is not so much a mere imitation as an effort to present the same material more intelligently. In choosing between her various suitors, Evelina is supposed to be looking for true politeness; Belinda's criteria, moral seriousness, strength, and integrity, are a great deal more intellectually impressive. Evelina pretends to be a critic of Society, but really falls in with its assumptions, whereas Belinda is intelligent and independent. Maria Edgeworth's fresh attitude to convention is always being demonstrated; there could scarcely be a more refreshing dismissal of eighteenth-century pastoral idylls than her brisk comment when Virginia prefers a moss rose to a pair of diamond ear-rings:

And yet there was more of ignorance and timidity, perhaps, than of sound sense or philosophy in Virginia's indifference to diamonds; she did not consider them as ornaments that would

[1] *Belinda*, ch. 11; ii. 183–5.

[2] See above, p. 29 and p. 39 n.; and *Belinda*, ch. 26; iii. 180.

[3] Advertisement to *Belinda*.

confer distinction upon their possessor, because she was ignorant of the value affixed to them by society . . . These reflections could not possibly have escaped a man of Clarence Hervey's abilities, had he not been engaged in defence of a favorite system of education or, if his pupil had not been quite so handsome.[1]

Through this kind of narrative tone, and through her choice of a rational heroine, Maria gave her borrowed material the stamp of her own personality and of her education, which was greatly superior to Fanny Burney's. After her exposure to some highly emotional writing in novels of the 1790s, her style was consciously anti-romantic. Of practising novelists, Mrs. Inchbald had what Maria considered to be the most desirable manner:

> You excel, I think, peculiarly in avoiding what is commonly called *fine writing*,—a sort of writing which I detest; which calls the attention away from the *thing* to the *manner*, from the feeling to the language; which sacrifices every thing to the sound, to the mere rounding of a period; which mistakes *stage effect* for *nature*. All who are at all used to writing, know and detect the *trick of the trade* immediately; and, speaking for myself, I *know* that the writing which has least the appearance of literary *manufacture*, almost always pleases me the best. It has more originality; in narration of fictitious events, it most surely succeeds in giving the idea of reality, and in making the biographer, for the time, pass for nothing. But there are few who can, in this manner, bear the *mortification* of staying behind the scenes. They peep out, eager for applause, and destroy an illusion by crying, *I* said it; *I* wrote it; *I* invented it all! Call me on the stage and crown me directly![2]

In love scenes or emotional scenes between 'straight' characters Fanny Burney had employed an inflated rhetoric. '"Oh, Sir", cried I, "will you so soon abandon me?—am I again an orphan?—Oh, my dear, my long-lost father, leave me not, I beseech you! . . ."' Maria avoided the incongruity which this kind of style introduced between serious and comic dialogue. For her, as for Elizabeth Hamilton and Jane Austen, the afflatus that was commonly used in the fiction of the period to communicate deep emotion evoked laughter rather than tears. But, being an Edgeworth, Maria also had

[1] *Belinda*, ch. 26; iii. 179–80.

[2] ME to Mrs. Inchbald, 14 Jan. 1810; J. Boaden, *Memoirs of Mrs. Inchbald*, 1833, ii. 154–5.

serious intellectual objections, which are best summarized by her comments a few years later on Madame de Staël's eloquent but often imprecise style of speaking and writing:

> I do admire eloquence, but I think I should soon be heartily tired of it if it could not be translated into common sense . . . There is no answering metaphor or allusion by reason and argument. In the midst of her antipathy to anatomy she forgets how much painting owes to it, how impossible it is to cover by the finest drapery any defects in the original proportion of the figure. The anatomy of the mind is just as necessary to the orator as the anatomy of the body to the painter.[1]

In maintaining a consistent style Maria Edgeworth succeeds where Fanny Burney fails. The dialogue of Maria's intelligent people is much better than her predecessor's; in fact it is one of Maria's first and least noticed achievements that in dialogue she can make even self-aware characters reveal motives hidden from themselves.

*Belinda* is the first of a series of Edgeworth stories in which attention focuses on an eloquent woman. Lady Delacour, by far the best-remembered character in the novel, is a leader of fashion, and a sense of verbal style is part of her character. She scores effortlessly off her boorish husband at the breakfast-table, prides herself on *l'éloquence du billet*, and, unlike some supposedly polished people in novels, invariably suggests a sophisticated woman of the world:

> 'Am not I the most virtuous of virtuous women', said Lady Delacour, 'to go to court such a day as this? But', whispered she, as she went up stairs, 'like all other amazingly good people, I have amazingly good reasons for being good. The Queen is soon to give a charming breakfast at Frogmore, and I am paying my court with all my might, in hopes of being asked; for Belinda must see one of their galas before we leave town, *that* I'm determined upon.—But where is she?'
>
> 'Not at home', said Clarence, smiling.
>
> 'O, not at home is nonsense, you know. Shine out, appear, be found, my lovely Zara!' cried Lady Delacour, opening the library door. 'Here she is—what doing I know not—studying Hervey's Meditations on the Tombs, I should guess, by the sanctification of her looks. If you be not totally above all sublunary considerations,

[1] ME to ED, 7 Aug. 1813; *Dublin Rev.*, cxlv (1909), 253.

admire my lilies of the valley, and let me give you a lecture, not upon heads, or upon hearts, but on what is of much more consequence, upon hoops. Every body wears hoops, but how few—'tis a melancholy consideration—how very few can manage them! There's my friend Lady C—; in an elegant undress she passes for very genteel, but put her into a hoop and she looks as pitiable a figure—as much a prisoner, and as little able to walk, as a child in a go-cart. She gets on, I grant you, and so does the poor child; but getting on, you know, is not walking. O, Clarence, I wish you had seen the two lady R.'s sticking close to one another, their father pushing them on together, like two decanters in a bottle-coaster, with such magnificent diamond labels round their necks!'[1]

The achievement here is that despite her polish and knowingness Lady Delacour is as transparent in her way as Sir Philip Baddely in his. The rapidity of her speech often seems feverish, and this puts the reader in mind of the very fact she wants to keep secret—that she believes herself to be dying of cancer of the breast. The polish is both real and assumed, a genuine quality and a façade. It is part of the mask Lady Delacour wears to keep up appearances, and often the moments at which she is choosing her words most carefully are those in which her mental suffering reveals itself.

The transparency of Lady Delacour's dialogue is well illustrated in a scene which is potentially one of the most hackneyed in the novel: it can fairly be compared, for example, with the meeting between Evelina and her father.[2] Belinda has been hoping to bring Lady Delacour to a sense of duty towards her daughter, Helena, who is away at school and seldom comes home. After preparing the ground carefully while Lady Delacour is ill, Belinda suddenly confronts her with Helena. Unfortunately Helena has been staying with Lady Anne Percival, of whom Lady Delacour is jealous; therefore she is mistrustful of the present of some goldfish which Helena has sent her, and suspiciously demands to know where they originally came from:

'Lady Anne Percival gave them to me, ma'am.'

[1] *Belinda*, ch. 5; ii. 89–90. Francis Jeffrey later observed that with Lady Delacour ME had shown her superiority over other novelists in the 'faithful but flattering representation of the spoken language of persons of wit and politeness of the present day', *Ed. Rev.*, xx (1812), 103.

[2] See above, p. 310.

'And how came her ladyship to give them to you, ma'am?'

'She gave them to me', said Helena, hesitating.

'You need not blush, nor repeat to me that she gave them to you; that I have heard already—that is the fact—now for the cause: unless it be a secret. If it be a secret which you have been desired to keep, you are quite right to keep it. I make no doubt of its being necessary, according to some systems of education, that children should be taught to keep secrets; and I am convinced (for Lady Anne Percival is, I have heard, a perfect judge of propriety) that it is peculiarly proper that a daughter should know how to keep secrets from her mother: therefore, my dear, you need not trouble yourself to blush or hesitate any more—I shall ask no farther questions: I was not aware that there was any secret in the case.'

'There is no secret in the world in the case, mamma', said Helena, 'I only hesitated because—'

'You hesitated *only* because, I suppose you mean. I presume Lady Anne Percival will have no objection to your speaking good English?'

The flustered child at last manages to say that the goldfish were given to her as a prize:

'And is this all the secret? So, it was real modesty made her hesitate, Belinda? I beg your pardon, my dear, and Lady Anne's: you see how candid I am, Belinda. But one question more, Helena: Who put it into your head to send me your gold fishes?'

'Nobody mamma; no one put it into my head. But I was at the birdfancier's yesterday, when Miss Portman was trying to get some bird for Mrs Marriott, that could not make any noise to disturb you: so I thought my fishes would be the nicest things for you in the world; because they cannot make the least noise, and they are as pretty as any bird in the world—prettier, I think—and I hope Mrs Marriott thinks so too.'

'I don't know what Marriott thinks about the matter but I can tell you what I think', said Lady Delacour, 'that you are one of the sweetest little girls in the world, and that you would make me love you if I had a heart of stone, which I have not, whatever some people may think—Kiss me, my child!' The little girl sprang forwards, and threw her arms round her mother, exclaiming, 'O, mamma! are you in earnest?' and she pressed close to her mother's bosom, clasping her with all her force.

Lady Delacour screamed, and pushed her daughter away.[1]

[1] *Belinda*, ch. 13; ii. 217–19. The passage where Lady Delacour's rouge runs is another example of a dramatic scene handled quietly and naturalistically. See above, p. 298.

This is an excellent scene, subtle in detail and eloquent in conveying the novel's broader themes. But it is no use pretending that *Belinda* is always so successful; in some respects it is a very immature book. Among Maria's considerable borrowings from other novels are a number of literary clichés. Lady Delacour may talk well, but a woman nursing a tragic secret, gloomy at home and dazzling abroad, is far from completely natural, and the knowledge that she was based on Delaval is not enough to make her fully plausible. Maria did not know highly fashionable women at first hand, and after Delaval her characterization of Lady Delacour owed most to her melodramatic notions about the misery of living in Society. There is more than a touch of the theatre about Lady Delacour's double life, and the business with the masks at the ball, when she and Belinda are mistaken for one another.[1] The novel even ends with a formal curtain speech. It is no wonder that after reading it Sheridan suggested that Maria should write for the stage.

A commoner objection to *Belinda* has always been its heavy-handed didacticism. This takes the form both of a moralistic running commentary, and of subordination of character and incident to the manufacture of a perfectly just conclusion. All the changes made to *Belinda*, in the course of writing and in preparation for Mrs. Barbauld's edition of 1810, show how seriously Maria took her responsibility to set a good example. She fell in unfortunately with the almost universal late-eighteenth-century assumption that 'the business of fable was to illustrate moral truth; it was an *exemplum* anchored to a text'.[2] Often the very writers who were most anxious to be

[1] ME's fondness for the old stage trick of the disguised character who eavesdrops on the rest is mentioned in connection with her plays, above p. 152 n. Strangely enough, when ME was writing plays she did not use the idea of the double character at all interestingly. In her novels she has characters divided against themselves, in her plays merely characters whose real identity is not known to the other people on the stage. The contrast is nicely demonstrated by *The Absentee*, where the opening scenes were in narrative form from the beginning, while the Irish sequence began as a play (see above, pp. 276–8). The mixed, complex characterization is all in the opening part, while the Irish sequence depends for its personal interest upon the routine device of the disguised hero who will reward the good people and punish the villains at the final curtain. Marianne Moore has turned part of *The Absentee* into a play—not, significantly, the Irish sequence, but the more fully characterized English scenes which ME developed all along through narrative and dialogue.

[2] J. M. S. Tompkins, *The Popular Novel in England, 1770–1800*, p. 72–3.

sensible and rational—that is, to avoid romance and depict the world as it really was—were also those most committed to concluding with a proper distribution of rewards and punishments. Mrs. Inchbald's *Simple Story*, probably Maria's favourite novel by a contemporary, is a case in point.[1] So too is John Moore's *Zeleuco* (1789), which has as its theme the proposition that people who behave wrongly and selfishly are generally punished in this world for their misdeeds. As we shall see, the philosophical format of *Zeleuco* (which itself obviously owes more to the moral tale than to the three-volume novel) was henceforth to be used more often by Maria than its most obvious alternative, the narrative form based on a central character's quest for a partner in marriage. *Zeleuco* is worth bearing in mind in relation to *Belinda* because it demonstrates again what even comparison with Fanny Burney showed—that it is a mistake to think of Maria Edgeworth as more didactic than her contemporaries or immediate predecessors. On the contrary, from the children's stories onwards she shows a strong impulse away from literary precedent in the direction of naturalism; and it is characteristic of her that the one really fresh element in *Belinda*, the dialogue, is natural.

It has to be admitted that so far Maria had found it by no means easy to reconcile her liking for the natural with her belief in the exemplary, and that her difficulty had become particularly obvious, as so often in this period, in *Belinda*'s long-drawn-out and painfully forced conclusion. It was probably with some relief, therefore, that she turned next to the length she had become accustomed to in writing for children, that of the short or medium-length tale.[2] *Rasselas*, *The Vicar of Wakefield*,

[1] It ends: '[The reader] has beheld the pernicious effects of an *improper education* in the destiny which attended the unthinking Miss Milner—On the opposite side, then, what may not be hoped from that school of prudence—though of adversity —in which Matilda was bred?

'And Mr. Milner. . . had better have given [away] his fortune. . . so he had bestowed upon his daughter *proper education*.'

[2] She never intentionally wrote another three-volume novel. *Patronage* grossly over-extended itself in the course of writing, and had to be published in four volumes; *Helen*, designed for two volumes, came out at the publisher's request in three; but everything else ME wrote for adults was shorter. *The Modern Griselda* and *Leonora* were published as single volumes, *The Absentee* is about the same length, and *Ormond* is a little longer. *Vivian*, *Ennui*, and *Manœuvring* each take up less than a full volume, while the shortest tale, *The Dun*, has about 12,000 words.

the philosophical fables of Voltaire and the more worldly stories of Marmontel had maintained their prestige throughout Maria's apprentice years, and as late as 1815 a critic discussing Jane Taylor's *Display* still took it as a matter of course that the tale was a distinct literary form; he defined it as shorter *and more probable* than the novel, and praised it as much for relating 'the natural occurrences and simple incidents of life' as for its philosophical or moral seriousness. (According to this reviewer, Johnson, Goldsmith, and Maria Edgeworth were the best writers of tales in English.[1]) In 1802 Maria was thus setting off along a well-trodden path, and, sure enough, she approached the moral tale for adults just as she had approached the three-volume novel, by copying the best examples she knew. *Almeria* and *The Dun*, both written that summer before she went to Paris, are literary exercises, half way between story and essay, in which every episode is as closely tied to the philosophic theme as it is in *Rasselas*. *The Dun* sets out the consequences of not paying debts; *Almeria* proves that getting on in the fashionable world is no way to happiness.

Unquestionably the modern reader's expectations about naturalistic fiction, which are very much shaped by the subsequent development of the novel and to a lesser extent of the short story, seriously interfere with appreciation of a didactic tale. Yet it would be fair to say that given the convention not a great deal is actively wrong with *Almeria*. Since the structure of the tale hammers home the point continuously, the cultivated, retired family, the Elmours, have no need to point it out themselves, which makes them the most tolerable of Maria's model households. To be more positive, there are several examples of the nice touches of observed behaviour that are Maria's forte. The heroine's adroit transfer from one patroness to another is amusingly done, and the snubs she receives from the higher-born but less well-off are entirely convincing; there is a nice irony when Almeria in her turn tries to be rude to old Mrs. Wynne, who is too good a woman at first to understand, and when she at last does understand

[1] *Eclectic Review*, N.S. iv, 1815, pp. 157–8: 'The Tales of Maria Edgeworth, distinguished by a character wholly original, form a series of the most ingenious and instructive moral lessons that have ever proceeded from the pen of an individual.'

is too secure to mind. Almeria's humiliations, coupled with the intermittent workings of her conscience, lead naturally to the climax of the story, the moment when she bursts into tears in front of the Elmours.

*Almeria* makes out its case neatly, in fact; what it lacks is an articulate character at the centre of the action who will give Maria scope for dialogue. It is the negative case which proves the positive, for every one of Maria's successful early tales contains a key character who talks revealingly and well: first the Irishman Thady, afterwards the sequence of high-born ladies beginning with Lady Delacour. Maria's powers of characterization depend on allowing her characters to reveal themselves through speech, and in the nature of the heroine, and the format, she is not at her liveliest in *Almeria*.

Then there is the question of the theme itself. Some allowance must be made for the premise of virtually any reader of the period—that didacticism *as such* is not out of place even in the novel, while it is the *raison d'être* of the moral tale. Many fine novels—*Tom Jones*, for example, and *Mansfield Park*—have didactic messages that are perfectly explicit, and in each case central to the novelist's purpose. The difficulty with Maria Edgeworth's early tales is not then that she is trying to make a point, but that the point is, first, naïve, and, second, too bluntly stressed. *Almeria* has the same theme as *Belinda* and *Letters of Julia and Caroline* (the second story in the three-part *Letters for Literary Ladies*):[1] the sharp contrast in each story between happiness at home and misery in the fashionable world. (*Belinda* was even originally to have been called *Abroad and At Home*.) The origins of this theme, in Maria's experience at school, in London in 1792, in Ireland via her father in the 1790s, and lingeringly, persistently, through the influence of Thomas Day, have already been accounted for.[2] Whatever the value of retirement as an ideal in eighteenth-century literature, Maria's obsession with it was a major technical handicap when she set out to write naturalistic social novels of the first decade of the nineteenth century. She was so bent on showing that socialites were bad that she was biased against nearly all her minor characters, and accordingly handled them with an animus that over the length of a

[1] See above, p. 173.

[2] See above, Chs. I and II.

novel or long tale becomes monotonous. Fanny Burney's heroines go out into the world without interesting thoughts in their heads, and little equipment for acquiring any, but at least they are fresh and unprejudiced. Maria's cleverer and more sensible Caroline and Belinda have their minds made up from the start; and it is not much use their being able to tell the value of moss roses and diamond ear-rings if they cannot discriminate finely between one fashionable figure and another.

Reference has already been made to the various, almost contradictory results of the social experience of 1802–3 on Maria's fiction.[1] On the one hand she was encouraged to relax her early didactic grimness in favour of a lighter touch; on the other, the wish to communicate with her French friends, and in particular with Edelcrantz, deterred her from using naturalistic detail of a purely local kind. In the thinnest and most abstracted of the tales, *Leonora*, Maria reacts with her usual sensitivity to the particular reader she has in view, both by providing an unspecified setting and (what is for her more important) by placing less reliance than usual on nuances of speech.

Yet again there are all the signs of literary derivativeness. She borrows from her own *Letters of Julia and Caroline*, which in its turn had owed a great deal to Madame de Genlis's *Adèle et Théodore*.[2] A fresher, negative inspiration is Mme de Staël's *Delphine*, which gave Maria much of her material for the seductress Olivia and Olivia's friend, Mme de P—, and probably decided her to stick to the letter-form. Other features of the structure and plot are freely adapted from Goethe's *Sorrows of Werther*, 1774, which was widely regarded in England as an improper book because it was interpreted as condoning an adulterous passion. Maria's central triangle, Mr. L—, his wife Leonora, and his mistress Olivia, roughly mirrors Goethe's triangle of Lotte, her husband Albert, and Werther. There was nothing unconscious about the fact that *Leonora* is as much an unsympathetic rewriting of *Werther* as it is of *Delphine*, since these were for Maria the key novels of the emotional school. 'I determined to set about *Leonora* and to read *The Sorrows of*

[1] See above, p. 200.

[2] See above, p. 149.

*Werther* in their black binding by way of preparative for the genuine sentimental style.'[1]

*Leonora*, written between 1803 and 1805, thus had Maria doing virtually everything she should not have done. Her talent was as a reporter of the social scene, not as a satirist or parodist. The letter-form, although it could be lively when well handled, was not her *métier* either. Instead of using letters to report dialogue, as Fanny Burney does with Evelina's, she let each character in turn utter a monologue setting out general theories about philosophy and morals. 'It is easy to discover, that it was not so much the story, as the moral, that Miss Edgeworth was anxious about, and that she intended this fable merely as a vehicle for those disquisitions on affected sensibility and conjugal duty with which it is very copiously adorned.'[2] Two of her three principals are supposedly in the grip of physical passion, and here both her lack of personal experience and her sense of propriety are severe handicaps.[3]

Edgeworth's gloomy view, that *Leonora* lacked detail and interest and was too moralistic ('it will be recommended by Governesses and read by Misses') must have had some influence on the manner of the new tales begun about this time. The letters Maria was writing to the Ruxtons, the most polished, assured, and witty as a series that she had written yet, meanwhile proved that potentially Paris had taught her a new ease, as well as greatly increasing her store of anecdote. The trio of tales which are in a sense companion pieces to *Leonora*, in that they are written or planned about the same time in 1803, and have features of plot in common, are much more tailored to the untheoretical audience at home than to Maria's formalistic notions about Parisian literary tastes.

On her return from Paris Maria was still committed to the plan she started with *Almeria* and *The Dun*, a two- or three-volume set of moral tales pointing out the foibles of the fashionable. But after encountering intellectual high society

[1] ME to SR, Nov. 1803. ME's edition was probably the translation by Wm. Render, D.D., 1801, which was bound in black velvet.

[2] F. Jeffrey, *Edinburgh Review*, viii (1806), 207.

[3] Most inappropriately ME sent *Leonora* (which she still thought of as the most French of her tales) in 1818 to Stendhal as a gift. For his remarks the following year on her deficiencies as a novelist of passion, see below, p. 395 n.

she was no longer inclined to condemn the entire metropolitan upper class out of hand; she was free to do what she had long since delighted in doing in her letters to Mrs. Ruxton—avoid generalities, tell anecdotes, and bring individuals to life. Between 1803 and about 1808, in addition to *Leonora* and *Popular Tales*, she worked on a group of stories which are basically extended sketches of one or two contrasted characters.

The first of them, *The Modern Griselda*, was written very quickly, like most of Maria's best tales. Beginning only in November 1803,[1] by mid December she had finished her light comedy about a silly wife who wears out her husband's patience, and ultimately his affection, by insisting on having the last word on every subject.

Griselda's tactics in debate give Maria splendid scope for humour, and once again her story centres on a figure who can be fully characterized by the way she talks. Griselda is another articulate woman, though not this time a clever one. It is surprising to recall that her speeches, the very heart of the tale, were actually the last element to be composed, since the story is expanded from Maria's amusing *Essay on the Noble Art of Self-Justification*. Her fine ear for the mannerisms of her own sex is well demonstrated in the marital conversation over the breakfast-table, after Griselda's husband has noticed from his newspaper that two friends have got married:

'Mr Granby! . . . But why do you call him our friend? I am sure he is no friend of mine, nor ever was; I took an aversion to him, as you may remember, the very first day I saw him: I am sure he is no friend of mine'.

'I am sorry for it, my dear; but I hope you will go and see Mrs. Granby?'

'Not I, indeed, my dear.—Who was she?'

'Miss Cooke'.

'Cooke!—but there are so many Cookes.—Can't you distinguish her in any way? Has she no Christian name?'

'Emma, I think—yes, Emma'.

'Emma Cooke!—No, it cannot be my friend Emma Cooke—for I am sure she was cut out for an old maid'.

'This lady seems to me to be cut out for a good wife'.

'May be so—I am sure I'll never go to see her—Pray my, dear, how came you to see so much of her?'

[1] See above, p. 203.

'I have seen very little of her, my dear: I only saw her two or three times before she was married'.

'Then, my dear, how could you decide that she is cut out for a good wife?—I am sure you could not judge of her by seeing her only two or three times, and before she was married'.

'Indeed, my love, that is a very just observation'.

'I understand that compliment perfectly, and thank you for it, my dear.—I must own I can bear any thing better than irony'.

'Irony! my dear; I was perfectly in earnest'.

'Yes, yes; in earnest—so I perceive—I may naturally be dull of apprehension, but my feelings are quick enough: I comprehend you too well. Yes—it is impossible to judge of a woman before marriage, or to guess what sort of a wife she will make. I presume you speak from experience; you have been disappointed yourself, and repent your choice'.

'My dear, what did I say that was like this! Upon my word, I meant no such thing; I really was not thinking of you in the least'.

'No—you never think of me now: I can easily believe that you were not thinking of me in the least'.

'But I said that only to prove to you that I could not be thinking ill of you, my dear'.

'But I would rather that you thought ill of me than that you did not think of me at all'.

'Well, my dear', said her husband, laughing, 'I will even think ill of you, if that will please you'.

'Do you laugh at me?' cried she, bursting into tears. 'When it comes to this, I am wretched indeed! Never man laughed at the woman he loved! As long as you had the slightest remains of love for me, you could not make me an object of derision; ridicule and love are incompatible, absolutely incompatible. Well, I have done my best, my very best, to make you happy, but in vain. I see I am not *cut out* to be a good wife. Happy, happy Mrs. Granby!'[1]

*The Modern Griselda* has of course a didactic point to make. Griselda is contrasted with Emma Granby, and Emma is clearly introduced into the action solely to show how a sensible wife behaves. But there is no hint that she is fonder of cultivated domesticity than Griselda, or that Griselda would have been less idiotic had she not lived in Society. Emma is simply the more sensible woman and the more desirable wife among two individuals. Byron, indeed, thought he had found a real-life Emma in his future wife. In a letter to Lady Melbourne of

[1] *The Modern Griselda*, ch. 3; i. 278–80.

18 September 1812, he said that Miss Milbanke reminded him of Emma Granby in *The Modern Griselda*—'whomever I *may* marry, that is the woman I would wish to have married'.[1] By any criterion Byron's remark is a little startling, but certainly it says something for the subdued didacticism of *The Modern Griselda*. Not many Edgeworthian 'pattern' women would have been selected for Byron's bed or indeed breakfast-table.

*Émilie de Coulanges* shows the same tendency to focus on individuals, probably because it too was devised as early as 1803.[2] As with *The Modern Griselda* the tone is light and the comedy centres on the speeches of acutely observed leading characters. One of these is the Comtesse de Coulanges, a Parisian émigrée who has fled from revolutionary France to London. This lady is befriended by a wealthy Englishwoman, Mrs. Somers, who insists on sharing her house with the Countess and her daughter, Émilie. Shortly afterwards Mrs. Somers presses upon her friend a large sum of money, with which, unknown to them, she had intended to buy a Guido and a Correggio for her drawing-room. Having made this sacrifice, she begins to feel dissatisfied with her guests, which is reasonable enough where the Countess is concerned. Complacent in her natural Parisian superiority, and insensitive to others, Mme de Coulanges blandly fails to appreciate Mrs. Somers's generosity: 'You see her humour—English humours must not be trifled with—her humour, you see, is to give.' But Mrs. Somers also unfairly blames Émilie, who although baffled by their hostess's complex moods, is sensitive enough to feel them. Once again, the characters are displayed and their relationships developed in a series of dialogues. But at this period of her career Maria Edgeworth's technique becomes increasingly sophisticated. She experiments, for example, with switching between speech and private reflection summarized in narrative, a device which anticipates Jane Austen:

> One day, some of her visitors, who were admiring the taste with which she had newly furnished a room, inquired for what those two compartments were intended, looking at the compartments

[1] J. Murray, *Lord Byron's Correspondence*, 1922, i. 79.

[2] *Mem.*, i. 175. The story was not completed, however, until early 1809. ME to Margaret Ruxton, 13 Mar. 1809.

which had been prepared for the famous pictures. Mrs Somers replied, that she had not yet determined what she should put there: she glanced her eye upon madame de Coulanges and upon Émilie, to observe whether they *felt as they ought to do*. Madame de Coulanges, imagining that an appeal was made to her taste, decidedly answered, that nothing would have so fine an effect as handsome looking-glasses: 'Such', added she, 'as we have at Paris. No house is furnished without them—they are absolute necessaries of life. And, no doubt, these places were originally intended for mirrors'.

'No', said Mrs Somers, dryly, and with a look of great displeasure —'No, madame la comtesse, those places were not originally intended for looking-glasses'.

The countess secretly despised Mrs Somers for her want of taste; but, being too well bred to dispute the point, she confessed that she was no judge—that she knew nothing of the matter; and then immediately turned to her abbé, and asked him if he remembered the superb mirrors in madame de V—'s charming house on the Boulevards.[1] 'It is', said she, 'in my opinion, one of the very best houses in Paris. There you enter the principal apartments by an ante-chamber, such as you ought to see in a great house, with real ottomanes, covered with buff trimmed with black velvet. . . .'

Mme de Coulanges goes on to an extended description of the house, its mirrors, and its pictures, a choice of subject which is disastrous in the circumstances. She also manages to convey that only Parisians have the taste to own such houses and art collections. Émilie changes the subject to a theme which ought to have been more tactful, but to her bewilderment she pleases Mrs. Somers even less:

'I used to love to see madame de V—, in the midst of all her fine things, of which she thought so little. I never saw a woman (did you, mamma?) who seemed better suited to be mistress of a large fortune—no ostentation—no formality; but so easy, and so desirous that every body round her should enjoy all the advantages of her wealth. Her very looks are enough to make one happy—all radiant with good-humoured benevolence. I am sure one might always salute madame de V— with the Chinese compliment, "Felicity is painted in your countenance" '.

This was a compliment which could not be paid to Mrs Somers at the present instant; for her countenance was as little expressive of

[1] Obviously Mme de Vindé's: the Edgeworths visited the house and admired its treasures in 1802 (Mrs. FE to Harriet Beaufort, 6 Dec. 1802).

felicity as could well be imagined. Émilie, who suddenly turned and saw it, was so much struck, that she became immediately silent. There was a dead pause in the conversation. Madame de Coulanges was the only unembarrassed person in company; she was very contentedly arranging her hair upon her forehead opposite to a looking-glass. Mrs Somers broke the silence by observing, that, in her opinion, there was no occasion for more mirrors in this room; and she added, in a voice of suppressed anger, 'I did originally intend to have filled those unfortunate blanks with something more to my taste'.

Madame de Coulanges was too much occupied with her ringlets to hear or heed this speech. Mrs Somers fixed her indignant eyes upon Émilie, who, perceiving that she was offended, yet not knowing by what, looked embarrassed, and simply answered, 'Did you?' This reply, which seemed as neutral as words could make it, and which was uttered not only with a pacific but with an intimidated tone, incensed Mrs Somers beyond measure. It put the finishing stroke to the whole conversation. All that had been said about elegant houses—antechambers—mirrors—pictures—amateurs—throwing away money; and the generous madame de V—, *who was always good-humoured*, Mrs Somers fancied was meant *for her*. She decided that it was absolutely impossible that Émilie could be so stupid as not to have perfectly understood that the compartments had been prepared for the Guido and Correggio, which she had so generously sacrificed; and the total want of feeling—of common civility—evinced by Émilie's reply, was astonishing, was incomprehensible.

The more she reflected upon the words, the more of artifice, of duplicity, of ingratitude, of insult, of meanness, she discovered in them. In her cold fits of ill-humour, this lady was prone to degrade, as monsters below the standard of humanity, those whom, in the warmth of her enthusiasm, she had exalted to the state of angelic perfection. Émilie, though aware that she had unweetingly offended, was not aware how low she had sunk in her friend's opinion: she endeavoured, by playful wit and caresses, to atone for her fault, and to reinstate herself in her favour. But playful wit and caresses were aggravating crimes: they were proofs of obstinacy in deceit, of a callous conscience, and of a heart that was not to be touched by the marked displeasure of a benefactress.[1]

The unhappy Mrs. Somers is perhaps too complex a figure to fit into a short, supposedly comic tale: at any rate, Maria

[1] *Émilie de Coulanges*, ix. 313–17. For Mrs. Somers, see above, p. 244.

never found an appropriate resolution to her neurotic suspicion and dissatisfaction. This tale, like several of the others, is partly spoiled by its sudden ending in a perfunctory and outrageously contrived wedding that fails to resolve the conflicts of character that have been created.

A story first planned a month later,[1] *Manœuvring*, is one of the few Edgeworth tales to have a good comic plot. The complications of the action are brought about by the resourceful manœuvrer herself, and they are in the accelerating, desperately self-entangling vein of formal farce. The protagonist is a capable, disingenuous widow, Mrs. Beaumont, who has resolved to marry her daughter and son to the wealthy, unattractive Sir John Hunter and his silly sister, despite the wish of both her children to marry into the neighbouring Walsingham family. Mrs. Beaumont's attempt to influence her not very clever but honest son against Miss Walsingham and in favour of Miss Hunter is a nicely judged duel between a polished, accomplished, insincere mistress of conversational art and a direct young man who speaks his mind. An opportunity for a crisp Jane Austen-like summary of a scene in narrative comes when Mrs. Beaumont tries to parade Albina Hunter in front of John to best advantage:

> . . . She now, by a multitude of scarcely perceptible inuendoes, and seemingly suppressed looks of pity, contrived to carry on the representation she had made to her son of this damsel's helpless and lovelorn state. Indeed, the young lady appeared as much in love as could have been desired for stage effect, and rather more than was necessary for propriety. All Mrs Beaumont's art, therefore, was exerted to throw a veil of becoming delicacy over what might have been too glaring, by hiding half to improve the whole. Where there was any want of management on the part of her young co-adjutrix, she, with exquisite skill, made advantage even of these errors by looks and sighs, that implied almost as emphatically as words could have said to her son—
>
> 'You see what I told you is too true. The simple creature has not art enough to conceal her passion. She is undone in the eyes of the world, if you do not confirm what report has said'.
>
> This she left to work its natural effect upon the vanity of man.[2]

[1] ME mentioned what seems to have been the first idea for *Manœuvring* to SR in Dec. 1803. She did not actually write it until May–June 1808, 'for my father's birthday' (ME to Mrs. R, 26 May 1808).

[2] *Manœuvring*, ch. 7; viii. 195–6.

The lady's manœuvres are threatened by the sudden appearance of honest old Mr. Palmer, a friend of Mrs. Beaumont's late husband. Mr. Palmer is rich, and inclined to leave his West Indian fortune to the Beaumont children, but he will clearly change his mind if he gets an inkling of Mrs. Beaumont's intrigues. Mrs. Beaumont estimates that by playing on Mr. Palmer's hypochondria she can dispatch him back to the West Indies before his eyes are opened:

Mrs Beaumont left a note to her favourite Dr Wheeler, to be sent very early in the morning. As if by accident, the doctor dropped in at breakfast time, and Mrs Beaumont declared that it was the luckiest chance imaginable, that he should happen to call just when she was wishing to see him. When the question in debate was stated to him, he, with becoming gravity of countenance and suavity of manner, entered into a discussion upon the effect of hot and cold climates upon the solids, and fluids, and nervous system in general; then upon English constitutions in particular; and, lastly, upon *idiosyncrasies*. This last word cost Mr Palmer half his breakfast: on hearing it he turned down his cup with a profound sigh, and pushed his plate from him; indications which did not escape the physician's demure eye. Gaining confidence from the weakness of the patient, Dr Wheeler now boldly pronounced, that, in his opinion any gentleman who, after having habituated himself long to a hot climate, as Jamaica, for instance, should come late in life to reside in a colder climate, as England, for example, must run very great hazard indeed—nay, he could almost venture to predict, would fall a victim to the sudden tension of the lax fibres . . . Mr Beaumont and Amelia, in eager and persuasive tones of remonstrance and expostulation, at once addressed the doctor, to obtain a mitigation or suspension of his sentence. Dr Wheeler, albeit unused to the imperative mood, reiterated his *dictum*. Though little accustomed to hold his opinion against the arguments or the wishes of the rich and fair, he, upon this occasion, stood his ground against Miss and Mr Beaumont wonderfully well for nearly five minutes; till, to his utter perplexity and dismay, he saw Mrs Beaumont appear amongst his assailants.

'Well, I said I would submit, and not say a word, if Dr Wheeler was against me', she began; 'but I cannot sit by silent: I must protest against this cruel, cruel decree, so contrary too to what I hoped and expected would be Dr Wheeler's opinion'.

Poor Dr Wheeler twinkled and seemed as if he would have rubbed his eyes, not sure whether he was awake or in a dream. In his perplexity, he apprehended that he had misunderstood Mrs Beaumont's note, and he now prepared to make his way round again through the solids and the fluids, and the whole nervous system, till, by favour of *idiosyncrasy*, he hoped to get out of his difficulty, and to allow Mr Palmer to remain on British ground. Mrs Beaumont's face, in spite of her powers of simulation, lengthened and lengthened, and darkened and darkened, as he proceeded in his recantation; but when the exception to the general axion was fairly made out, and a clear permit to remain in England granted, by such high medical authority, she forced a smile, and joined loudly in the general congratulations.[1]

In the very nature of things Mrs. Beaumont is bound to overstep the mark in the end; there is never any sense that she is merely the villainess getting her necessary come-uppance. The honest people already half see through her, and in the end she is caught in a marriage plot herself, when Sir John Hunter proves a match for her in more senses than one. The notion that honesty is the best policy is certainly central, and no reader can miss it; but the moral is not more disagreeably enforced in *Manœuvring* than in many comedies where the simple and good are predestined to come off best.

If Maria Edgeworth's career had stopped at this point she would have deserved more recognition than she has had for her contribution to the techniques of comedy. In the first half of *Belinda*, in *The Modern Griselda*, *Émilie de Coulanges*, and *Manœuvring*, she pioneered some of the most successful features of Jane Austen's novels. Maria's concern in this early phase was with character, and the interaction of character, in a limited social context. It was no doubt Mrs. Ruxton's love of style and a polished manner, joined to her delight in vivid characterization, that encouraged Maria to concentrate at first on the kind of character she rendered so well. Lady Delacour, Griselda, Mme de Coulanges, and Mrs. Beaumont are all women of her own class who are highly articulate, conversational, and persuasive. By the interest that she showed in talk as such, Maria did a great deal to refine dialogue and to establish a thoroughly consistent naturalism. She also put a premium on lucidity and rationality. The quality of discrimination

[1] *Manœuvring*, ch. 5; viii. 174–6.

in her main characters created the mental climate of a new, more civilized comedy, in which wit and entertainment did not preclude a serious inquiry into values.

Did not preclude it—but did not fully exploit the opportunity. The relation between Maria Edgeworth's comedies and Jane Austen's is an extremely interesting one, which in spite of the critical attention Jane Austen has received never seems to have attracted any notice. Jane Austen was reading Maria's tales during the long fallow period before she published anything. The Austenian juvenilia and first drafts, written in the seventeen-nineties, were grounded in burlesque and always strongly literary in their inspiration. Yet when Jane Austen published her first novel, *Sense and Sensibility*, in 1811, she had already moved a long way towards her mature vein of naturalism. What part Maria's polished comedies played in that evolution has never been examined, and perhaps cannot be established. But certainly many of the techniques that Jane Austen later used so successfully—the subtly revealing dialogue, the intelligent principal characters, the relation between the intelligence of those characters and a continuously analytical narrative tone—were all to be found first in Maria Edgeworth. It would be surprising if so perceptive a literary intelligence as Jane Austen's did not recognize in someone else's work the techniques that she could use to get below the superficial surface of drawing-room comedy.

Jane Austen could, while Maria apparently could not. The meticulousness of Maria's dialogue has been illustrated, and this, together with the natural elegance of her ordinary narrative prose, gives her tales an atmosphere of intelligence that distinguishes them from almost all naturalistic fiction since Sterne.[1] But how intelligent really are the novels of the first half of her career? *Belinda* and *Almeria* strive over-earnestly to make a doubtful generalization that reveals all Maria's emotional immaturity and lack of experience. The later tales like *Manœuvring*, though pleasing, have nothing much to say. They were planned in the period when she still felt diffident

[1] To say this is not to underrate the intelligence of philosophical novelists like Godwin and Bage. The difference is that ME is primarily interested in recreating the ordinary everyday world, not in a system of ideas; by her day the divorce between one kind of novel and another was almost complete, and it was she who brought back intellect into the representation of common life.

about handling general ideas, apart from very limited points affecting individuals, or the merest platitudes, such as that it is better to be straightforward than devious. It is a point in favour of *The Modern Griselda*, *Émilie de Coulanges*, and *Manœuvring* that they lose the automatic animus against fashionable people, and concentrate on individuals; but a point against them that the three central figures are observed from the outside, as essentially no more than extended character-sketches.

The complaint so commonly raised against Maria Edgeworth, of didacticism, seems legitimate in the case of her first three tales set in the fashionable world, where the point made is intrinsically dubious, clumsily handled, and over-emotional. But a serious novel does have a serious subject. Jane Austen's do: *Mansfield Park* has quite as much to say about education as Maria's most notoriously didactic novel, *Patronage*; and it says more than *Belinda* or Mrs. Inchbald's *Simple Story*, both of which also labour intermittently to prove that the Maria and Julia Bertrams of this world come to a bad end, and the Fannys inherit the earth. One of the most important differences is that in Jane Austen's novels the central characters live in a sustained and continuous world of moral choices, and the issues are understood, or come to be understood, by the heroines themselves. Maria on the other hand does not at first use the intelligence of her characters sufficiently. Although all too moralistic in her own incidental comments, in the first phase of her career she is still fundamentally shy of committing herself wholeheartedly to a serious subject, and examining it through the consciousness of her clever heroines. At this stage she was no more ready to reason independently in her books than she was in her letters. But her intellectual timidity, her fear of giving offence by expressing decided views, gradually receded under the influence of Étienne Dumont and the work she did with her father on *Professional Education*.

## 2. *The Second Phase: Public Life*

Maria began reading in preparation for *Professional Education* in 1805, although most of the writing of the book was not done until 1807–9. It is the tales written in 1805–6 and 1809–12 that are most thoroughly pervaded by its influence.[1] *Patronage*, with its six young men pursuing five different professions, in places reads like a deliberate adaptation of the educational treatise for the popular-novel-reading public. But *Ennui*, *Mme de Fleury*, *Vivian*, and *The Absentee* are also deeply influenced, and all of them illustrate the two main themes of *Professional Education*.

Since he finished the earlier phase of his work on education, Edgeworth had had the problem of placing his three surviving sons by Elizabeth Sneyd in appropriate professions.[2] After the broad, methodological approach of *Practical Education*, he therefore turned to utilitarian questions. What professions should a father encourage his son to follow, and how could he best prepare him? The answers he arrives at are distinctive and revealing. *Professional Education* is an odd, complex book, both a rag-bag of miscellaneous ideas and a statement of two fundamental principles, which are distilled from Edgeworth's personal experience as well as his life's work in education.

Most characteristically, the book proposes that the first consideration in choosing a boy's career is whether it will enable him to maintain his personal independence. In politics, diplomacy, and the church a man relies on others for his advancement; the army, at least in peacetime, is also a doubtful proposition; the best professions are law and medicine, where he can rise by his own unaided efforts. The case of the eldest son is of course rather different. If he is to inherit an estate, Edgeworth argues that he should be educated to administer it. Edgeworth's own experiences convinced him that the landowner's was the key profession, especially in the agricultural economy of Ireland. He also in most cases acts as magistrate, so that not merely the livelihood, but also the security, the freedom, even perhaps the lives of the poor depend on the landlord. It goes without saying that the country gentleman's

[1] *Ennui* was begun in 1804, but substantial work was done on it between Apr. and June 1805. Probably then, possibly in 1809, it was virtually rewritten. See above, p. 291. *Mme de Fleury* was sketched in Paris in 1803, but not written until Jan. 1806 (ME to SR, 5 Jan. 1806). *Vivian* was written in 1809, *Patronage* between May 1809 and Oct. 1813. For *The Absentee*, written 1811–12, see above, pp. 276–7.

[2] As we have seen, Henry trained as a doctor, Sneyd as a lawyer. RLE thought at one time of making William a potter, but Josiah Wedgwood the younger warned him that the difficulties would be insuperable (Eliza Meteyard, *A Group of Englishmen*, 1871, pp. 344–6). William became an engineer instead.

function as the natural leader of his neighbourhood requires him to live on his estate.

The second theme of *Professional Education* is that early education is so powerful a factor in determining character that a boy can be trained for his chosen career virtually from birth. This is an extension, even a *reductio ad absurdum*, of the Locke–Hartley doctrine that environment matters more than heredity. Both Mrs. Edgeworth and Étienne Dumont tried to make Edgeworth qualify his extreme view a little, but their most persuasive efforts seemed only to make him more doctrinaire.[1] Maria characteristically kept out of controversy, but her tales of the period in fact take her father's side of the question.

It is startling to see how faithfully the plots of the five stories most influenced by *Professional Education* repeat its double message. It must have been of this group of tales that Captain Francis Beaufort was thinking when he remarked over dinner to the painter Joseph Farington that 'she and Her Father, Mr. Edgeworth, have adopted certain notions and maxims and they take this method of publishing them to the world, which they could not hope to do with any effect if given only as *Aphorisms*'.[2] Certainly it is only with the stories influenced by *Professional Education* that Edgeworth's 'notions and maxims', as opposed to Maria's partisan emotions about her father, really begin to see the light of day in her fiction.[3]

The hero of *Ennui*, Lord Glenthorn, who is very wealthy, has been vaguely educated with no profession in view. His adult life is spent in a search for any kind of stimulus to ward off boredom, but nothing, not even a lively period in Ireland, satisfies him for long until he loses his title and estate and has to train for the Bar in order to support himself. In *Mme de Fleury*, on the other hand, a group of poor children have been trained by a wealthy Parisian lady in various crafts suitable to

[1] His own volume of autobiography, the *Memoirs*, vol. 1, which was written in 1809, seeks to demonstrate the truth of this favourite proposition in terms of his own life. See above, p. 19 n. The structural similarity between RLE's episodic volume of memoirs and ME's tales of this period is worth pointing out: both present a series of isolated incidents, and relate the hero's handling of each to the success or otherwise of his education.

[2] J. Greig (ed.), *The Farington Diary*, vii (1927), 227.

[3] See RLE's preface to *Tales of Fashionable Life*, 1809 (quoted above, p. 286), the first time he publicly claimed a connection between the educational books and the fiction.

their station in life. When the Revolution comes, the children can support themselves and their benefactress too, which is certainly more than she can have bargained for when she launched them in life. Every one of them proves to be loyal and industrious, whereas the ill-educated children who are introduced as foils are thriftless and treacherous and come to a bad end.

Vivian is another wealthy young man who has not been prepared for any particular profession. He has good intentions, and, we are told, talents, but he has been injudiciously indulged as a child by a widowed mother. The result is that he is totally lacking in self-reliance, or *moral independence*.[1] He gets a seat in the House of Commons, which, as we know from *Professional Education*, is not the wisest course of action. He is seduced physically by the wife of another politician and morally by the pressures of party. Before the end he has married a woman he does not love and has totally lost his reputation for political integrity.

*Patronage* is another novel set in England, and so literal a re-working of the chapters of *Professional Education* on the various professions that a summary of the plot would be tedious. But a last tale which is linked with *Professional Education* is easy to overlook. The first third of *The Absentee*, the part featuring the absentee family in London, as part of *Patronage* was of course brought into being as a further illustration of the same themes. The Clonbronys, the central family in *The Absentee*, came into existence in order to show how corrupting it is when gentry desert their estates and flock to the capital. *The Absentee* has a sub-plot, which involves the hero in a quest to clear away a shadow on the birth of Grace Nugent, the girl he loves. No one who reads *The Absentee* can see any immediate connection between the two plots, but their occurrence in one context becomes explicable once the connection with *Professional Education* is understood. Lord Colambre has determined that he cannot marry Grace if she is illegitimate. His scruples do not arise from his pride of rank, but because he knows that as a small child Grace was brought up by her mother. If it is true that this mother was unchaste, the dominant influence on

[1] In his upbringing by his mother, and in the defects of character that resulted, he must have been meant to represent all that RLE was not.

Grace's early education was a corrupt one. Colambre's refusal to overlook this fact is another attempt by Maria to prove that environment and early education determine character.[1]

The theme that character is formed decisively in early childhood is a difficult one for a novelist to handle. The implication is that adult characters have little or no capacity to learn from experience; their natures were already determined, well before the action of the novel begins. It is interesting to compare *Mansfield Park* again to see how Jane Austen gets over the difficulty. The sense of continuous progress in that novel does not arise from real change or development in the characters, but from gradual enlightenment in those still capable of redemption. Maria, who makes much less effort to see through a problem in literary terms, allows characters to learn to see their mistakes in *Ennui*, *The Absentee*, and *Harrington*, although she does not succeed in having enlightenment come steadily and naturally until *Ormond* (1817).[2] With the other tales of this phase she falls into the obvious trap. Almost all the characters in *Mme de Fleury*, *Vivian*, and *Patronage* are divided into sheep and goats, which is which having been determined long ago by their parents' notions about education.

*Ennui*, *Mme de Fleury*, *Vivian*, *The Absentee*, and *Patronage* resemble one another structurally, again on account of this awkward theme. The plots differ from the reasonably continuous stories Maria Edgeworth had devised for *The Modern Griselda* and *Manœuvring*. Lord Glenthorn in *Ennui* and *Vivian*, for example, are confronted with a series of more or less independent adventures. In every episode the hero fails to meet the challenge he is faced with because of a weakness of character brought about by defects in his education. Naturally a story constructed with this aim in mind is repetitive and discontinuous. An effect similar to this is present in Maria's longer stories from the beginning; it is there in *Castle Rackrent*, *Belinda*, and *Almeria*, for example; and this is not surprising, since from the beginning Maria acknowledged a debt to Moore's

[1] In *The Absentee* Colambre's motives are obscure, and two of CSE's friends described his attitude as 'prudery'. ME was content to reply that 'for explanation of his principles and feelings they must wait for *Patronage*' (ME to CSE, 27 Nov. 1812). Cf. *Patronage*, ch. 4; xi. 67–75.

[2] Jane Austen's example may have helped to bring about the less emphatic treatment of the theme in *Ormond*. See below, pp. 440 ff.

*Zeleuco*, which is constructed on precisely this principle. However, with her characteristic tendency towards naturalness, Maria had hitherto been producing a more relaxed, flexible, and detailed version of the novel-with-a-purpose than was customary in her period. The effect of didacticism often seems more intrusive in the tales of her maturity; not, really, because she had changed her underlying approach, but because with her increasing intellectual self-confidence she was now far more aware of what she wanted to say.

The other theme derived from *Professional Education* is handled much more successfully. The contrast demonstrates, indeed, how dangerous it is to make sweeping generalizations about the literary consequences of trying to handle theoretical 'notions and maxims' in fiction. Without her father's theme of the moral implications of a man's profession Maria would have been a much less interesting and significant novelist than in fact she is.

Hitherto she had excelled as a humorous writer who, on the whole, dealt with relatively superficial personal foibles. When she took up the subject of a man's moral independence she was moving towards different and profounder truths about the human personality, although at first she stated rather than explored them. With *Ormond* (1817) and *Helen* (1834), her last two tales, she was eventually to reveal a depth of interest in the social influences that make people what they are, the distinctive mannerisms of a class, and of a sub-group within a class, that did not come remotely within the range of anything written before the era of *Professional Education*.

The stories of the group under discussion, from *Ennui* to *Patronage*, do not attempt this kind of research into character, but they are more serious than the early tales in other ways. The most refreshing feature of them, after a long period in which most of the abler novelists were women, is that they touch upon masculine concerns. Maria Edgeworth's early tales are as feminine as Jane Austen's, and are set, like them, in the woman's world of drawing-rooms and husband-hunting. Not just the best characters, but *all* the important characters are women—Julia and Caroline, Belinda, Lady Delacour, Almeria, Griselda, Leonora, Olivia, Mrs. Somers, Mme de Coulanges, Émilie, Mrs. Beaumont.

Once she begins to make use of *Professional Education*, Maria Edgeworth is naturally dealing with a different sphere of interest. *Ennui*, *Vivian*, and *The Absentee* have heroes instead of heroines, and in *Patronage*, which is about families rather than individuals, the men have more to do than the women. High Society is only one element in these tales. They also take the characters into politics or the professions, or into the peasant's workaday world, where rent day matters a great deal more than the Queen's breakfast at Frogmore.

What this implies will emerge more clearly from a separate examination of the Irish tales. But even in the English tales influenced by *Professional Education*, Maria establishes a connection never before consciously made in the novel, the economic connection between an individual and his wider social context. She draws in short for the first time on the social ethos her father learnt from his Lunar contacts: she sees society as an organism and relates a man's virtue to the contribution he is willing or able to make to the general welfare. Jane Austen, it is true, draws a moral inference from her male characters' professions. It is a proof of their value that Edmund Bertram becomes a clergyman, Knightley is an energetic landowner, and Wentworth a brave and competent sailor. But the emphasis in Jane Austen's novels is primarily on the character, whereas with Maria Edgeworth it is equally on his economic and social context, that is on society itself.

This innovation is one of the two really interesting features in Maria Edgeworth's later tales. The other is a fundamental change in her technique to meet the demands of her much wider subject-matter. In every tale she wrote for adults until now, with the important exception of *Castle Rackrent*, she concentrated on a relatively small group of characters from her own class. But, especially when she had to handle landlords in action,[1] she now found herself dealing with far wider social spheres, and with characters whose experience and manners divided them *as a class* so profoundly from their superiors that normal techniques of characterization through dialogue became irrelevant. An upper-class character can be

[1] ME presents English landowners—e.g. Vivian, Mr. Percy in *Patronage*—but she tends to avoid English lower-class characters. The remarks made about new techniques in the dialogue therefore apply only to the Irish tales.

given nuances of speech that distinguish him plainly from his peers. An Irish peasant speaks in an idiom so foreign to the cultivated English ear that it is difficult, even impossible, to characterize him fully as an individual; instead he becomes a representative of his class.[1] In dealing with her wider Irish subject-matter, therefore, Maria Edgeworth had to employ a different approach to dialogue. In putting words into a peasant's mouth, she was sometimes capturing a turn of phrase commonly used by the peasantry; at other times she was introducing the reader to facts or customs; at her most inward she threw light on what she considered to be a common trait in Irish peasant character. Thus the tales of this period are not only more concerned with broad issues, and with a world of affairs peopled by men rather than women. At least when they are set in Ireland, they also introduce a parallel innovation in dialogue, which again has the effect of focusing the reader's attention outward, on the real-life social behaviour of a class, rather than inward, on the personality of an individual.

In the first phase of Maria's career much material is borrowed from life, but there is less interest in documentation for its own sake than in the second phase. *Ennui*, *The Absentee*, and *Ormond*, particularly, but also to a lesser extent *Madame de Fleury*, *Vivian*, and *Patronage*, present facts and incidents as real-life evidence which helps to make out a case. The reader is given clearly to understand that the 'background' is more than background. In the Irish tales it is actually more central than any individual character. Because of this, 'truthfulness' takes on a new significance, and in fact takes precedence among the author's claims for the reader's attention.

These innovations interested her contemporaries so positively that they were prepared to overlook, or at least to minimize, a considerable number of faults. And in any case, although the central characters were much less individualized than they had formerly been, there were enough good minor figures in the later tales to prove that Maria Edgeworth's sense of comedy had not deserted her. In *Vivian*, for example, she created the

[1] This seems to be the case, at least, where the peasant is presented together with another character or characters who do *not* speak in dialect. The effect of strong contrasts of idoms of speech is to obliterate the subtler nuances of individual personality. For ME's preference for scenes in which an upper-class English-educated character is present, see below, p. 363.

affable, commonplace peer Lord Glistonbury, who during a stroll in the garden confided his ideas for his son's education:

> 'Now, my idea for Lidhurst is simply this;—that he should know every thing that is in all the best books in the library, but yet that he should be the farthest possible from a book-worm—that he should never, except in a set speech in the house, have the air of having opened a book in his life—mother-wit for me!—in most cases—and that easy style of originality, which shows the true gentleman. As to morals—Lidhurst, walk on, my boy—as to morals, I confess I couldn't bear to see any thing of the Joseph Surface about him. A youth of spirit must, you know, Mr. Vivian—excuse me Lady Mary, this is *an aside*—be something of a latitudinarian to keep in the fashion: not that I mean to say so exactly to Lidhurst—no, no—on the contrary, Mr. Russell, it is our cue, as well as this reverend gentleman's', looking back at the chaplain, who bowed assent before he knew to what, 'it is our cue, as well as this reverend gentleman's, to preach prudence, and temperance, and all the cardinal virtues'.[1]

In all the tales of the group, except *Madame de Fleury*, highly quotable passages like this still helped the reviewers to fill out their copy. Even in *Patronage*, longest and as a whole the least readable of the Edgeworth novels, there are many scenes among the Falconer family that are equal to Maria Edgeworth's most polished vein of comedy. There is besides in these later tales some of the deeper inquiry into personal motives, inhibitions, and failures that was to emerge at its best in Maria's last novel, *Helen*. Glistonbury's daughter, Lady Sarah, is an outwardly frigid, inwardly passionate woman whom a later-nineteenth-century novelist might have made much of. Lord William in *Patronage*, who suffers from Maria's own youthful defect, *mauvaise honte*, is another study in a new, more serious, and more natural style. The opening chapters of *Harrington* describe the obsessive terrors of a boy of six,[2] and again they show an aspect of Maria Edgeworth's talent that was to be given full scope only in *Helen*.

Although the polished light comedies centred on character were behind her, it would not be difficult to prove that Maria's command of amusing dialogue and, especially, her capacity to

[1] *Vivian*, ch. 2; ix. 33–4.

[2] Based on the nervous terrors of Henry Edgeworth as a child: see above, p. 248.

enter into private experience improved as she grew older. All the same, it was for their handling not of character but of society that the tales of this period impressed her contemporaries more deeply than any of the other stories she had written. Encouraged by Dumont's interest in society and in facts about Ireland, primed by the research into masculine worlds that she had done for *Professional Education*, she scored her greatest success with a series of tales that were technically imperfect but fascinating in what they had to say.

### 3. *Contemporary Preferences*

It is impossible to understand Maria Edgeworth's career without recourse to her earliest critics, since she enjoys a unique advantage among English novelists: she is the first of any stature to be regularly and intelligently reviewed. What was said in print about the tales as they came out affected the manner of her own later stories, and, what is more important in general, it also influenced the consensus of opinion over a decade or more about what the novel could and should attempt to do.

*Letters for Literary Ladies*, *Castle Rackrent*, and *Belinda* were not much noticed, or if they were noticed they were not much examined. The *British Critic*'s complete review of *Castle Rackrent*, for example, runs as follows:

> This is a very pleasant, goodhumoured and successful representation of the eccentricities of our Irish neighbours. The style is very happily hit off; and the parallel to his [*sic*] story, we apprehend, has been too frequently exhibited. The character of 'honest Thady' is remarkably comic, and well delineated; and we are not at all surprised that the publication should, in so short a time, have passed through two editions.[1]

With the appearance of the two great Reviews during the first decade of the nineteenth century the situation was transformed. The *Edinburgh Review* from 1802 and the *Quarterly* from 1809 established the principle of selecting for review only books which seemed to merit it. The articles, which might extend to twenty pages or more (assisted, it is true, by extensive

[1] *British Critic*, xvi, 1800, 555. *Castle Rackrent* was anonymous until the third edition of 1801.

quotation) were often general essays as well as examinations of a particular book. The effect of such detailed attention on contemporary poetry—on the Lake poets, Byron, and Keats in particular—has been recognized. But it is at least arguable that a higher standard of reviewing had more influence on the course of the novel, since this was a form which had never commanded good criticism.

The *Edinburgh* reviewers who superseded the publishers' hacks of journals like the *British Critic* were, or soon became, men of some literary standing, but in the novel (if not in poetry) their scope was at first limited by the scarcity of novels worth writing about. Maria Edgeworth was lucky therefore that from about 1804 until 1812 or 1814 she received a respectful attention that in a richer period no single minor artist would have been able to command. For intelligent reviewers, looking for something of significance to write about, the unusual interest of the subject-matter and the manner of treatment in Maria Edgeworth's Irish tales in particular was a godsend. Being rather more concerned with the novel as a form than Maria was, they saw aesthetic implications in what she was doing. While she merely worried about how far her stories reported reality, her early reviewers began to draw certain conclusions about realism. They took up the challenge with enthusiasm. Indeed, for the *Edinburgh* and more particularly for the *Quarterly*, 1809 and 1812, the years in which *Ennui* and the *The Absentee* were published, were landmarks in the history of the novel.

Maria's first serious reviewer was Francis Jeffrey, editor of the *Edinburgh Review*. Jeffrey chose to review most of Maria Edgeworth's tales and novels himself—*Popular Tales*, *Leonora*, the first and second series of *Tales of Fashionable Life*, and *Harrington and Ormond*. One of the most important features of his criticism of Maria Edgeworth is that he thoroughly approves of her didactic intention. *Popular Tales* remains for several years his favourite among her works. He considers it

> an attempt, we think, somewhat superior in genius, as well as utility, to the laudable exertions of Mr Thomas Paine to bring disaffection and infidelity within the comprehension of the common people, or the charitable endeavours of Messrs. Wirdsworth [*sic*] & Co. to accommodate them with an appropriate vein of poetry.

Both these were superfluities which they might have done very tolerably without.[1]

As far as Jeffrey is concerned, the social utility of *Popular Tales* is 'so truly laudable as to make amends for many faults of execution'.

This sentence gives a not unfair idea of Jeffrey's habitual reaction to works of art. But he recognized that even Maria's usefulness, that is her effort to criticize and correct behaviour in the circumstances of ordinary life, depended on her capacity to re-create normal day-to-day existence convincingly. For this reason he modified his belief that *Popular Tales* was her best achievement when the two Irish tales, *Ennui* and *The Absentee*, were published. He accepted that in *Ennui* there was a more exact representation of real life than anything Maria Edgeworth had achieved earlier. The low-life Irish figures were drawn with unique precision, and even the treatment of the Irish aristocrats was 'more original and characteristic than that of *Belinda*—and altogether as lively and natural'.[2] Of these two Irish tales—or 'moral fictions' as he calls them—he uses the word 'perfect'. Nothing compares with them, unless it is 'the best tales of Voltaire'. He is confident in describing *Ennui* as 'more rich in character, incident and reflection, than any English narrative with which we are acquainted'.

Jeffrey's views are worth dwelling on because of their representativeness. He writes as a humane, forward-looking, but essentially philistine bourgeois, and so mirrors the tastes of the average cultivated middle-class reader of the early nineteenth century. His Scottish background places him within the liberal, rational, practical tradition which is broadly characterized as utilitarianism. And in England, despite unrepresentative opposition from many of the best poets, the Anglo-Scottish empirical tradition is beyond question the dominant intellectual movement of the period. Jeffrey is a liberal but not a radical. In aesthetic matters he is a conservative because like the Edgeworths and their friends among French intellectuals he is frightened of the social and moral evils which he associates with the introspection of the great poets. No doubt he particularly admires Maria Edgeworth's

[1] *Ed. Rev.*, iv, 1804, 330. [2] Ibid. 1809, 383.

novels because they direct the reader's attention to the recognizable 'real' world, and, by implication, urge him to make the best of it. This is to be 'progressive' as Jeffrey understands it. He is unsympathetic to experiments with form, and does not in general look out for originality, although he also thinks that Maria is original. Even at his best Jeffrey is not a subtle or daring critic, and at his worst he is inadequate. Yet it is easy to be unfair to him. He is not blinded by partiality.[1] He knows that Maria can fail; but in her work he detects that quality of idealism and faith in progress which was perhaps convincingly expressed only by the pioneering generation of the Industrial Revolution, perhaps was no longer appropriate in a more ruthless Malthusian universe, yet evidently could still appeal to the decent instincts of the liberal middle classes. At any rate, Jeffrey's admiration, and his association of Maria's name with all that was socially healthy and responsible, are among the most important factors in the growth of her reputation.

The great rival to the *Edinburgh Review*, the *Quarterly*, begins only in 1809. Since it sets out to repair the deficiencies of the *Edinburgh Review*, the *Quarterly* tries to improve on Jeffrey's treatment of new writing, and it is disposed to be more sympathetic to experiment. If the interests of Church and State seem threatened, the *Quarterly*'s Tory critics can on occasion be vituperative, and the notorious excesses of John Wilson Croker are too well known to need recalling. But on most literary subjects the *Quarterly*'s reviewers are more sensitive and open-minded than the *Edinburgh*'s. During the first decade of the *Quarterly*'s existence, until *Blackwood's Magazine* and the *London Magazine* appear in often successful rivalry, an able group of critics use its pages as a forum for determining what the novel is and can be.

The *Quarterly*'s treatment of Maria Edgeworth is unexpectedly sympathetic. To begin with the Review inherited a political suspicion of productions from Edgeworthstown,[2] fed by the most notorious symptom of the Edgeworths' radicalism, the absence of reference to religion in *Practical Education*. The

[1] Cf. his respectful but decisive panning of *Leonora*, which begins 'Miss Edgeworth always writes with good sense, and with good intentions: but this is not among her best doings' (*Ed. Rev.*, viii, 1806, 206).

[2] The animus was stronger against RLE than against ME. See below, pp. 411–12.

*Bibliothèque Britannique* and Abraham Rees's *Chambers' Cyclopaedia*, both adopting the educationalists' viewpoint, had already argued the case against this omission at length.[1] But the charge of irreligion was one that supporters of the Church, and other committed critics, were happy to return to over and over again, even in relation to the novels, where religion was never touched on.[2] For about fifteen years the *Quarterly* seems to have had an editorial policy of introducing the subject whenever it dealt with the Edgeworths. William Gifford, the editor, wrote a paragraph deploring Maria Edgeworth's attitude to Christianity and inserted it in a review by Henry Stephen of the first series of *Tales of Fashionable Life*, because, he thought, Stephen had not given the point enough weight.[3]

All the same, having dealt their blow for party principle, reviewers in the *Quarterly* do Maria Edgeworth full justice. Perhaps, like Jeffrey, they sense her innate conservatism; what is certain is that they are more interested than Jeffrey in the quality of the tales as fiction. The characteristic that Henry Stephen, J. W. Croker, John Ward, Walter Scott, and Richard Whately all find in Maria Edgeworth's writing is a new degree and kind of realism.

Before Gifford comes to his assistance, Henry Stephen considers Maria Edgeworth interesting because she ventures to dispense common sense to her readers, to bring them within the precincts of real life and natural feeling. He praises the probability of her stories, and the charm they derive from her undeviating attention to nature, although he fears that without

[1] See above, p. 169 n.

[2] ME, who was a more conventional Christian than RLE (although she does not seem pious by nineteenth-century standards) was understandably nettled by the repeated imputation that her heroines are not Christians. After slurs by Croker in the *Quarterly* and John Foster in the *Eclectic Review* (viii, 1812), she composed a note for private circulation on behalf of the heroine of *The Absentee*: 'Lady Colambre refers the [*Quarterly*] Reviewer to page 148 of the 2nd vol. of *The Absentee*. . . she trusted, that in this Christian land none could have so little Christian charity as to suspect her of being an infidel. Clonbrony Castle, 26 August, 1812.' Her brother Sneyd satirized this kind of criticism with a burlesque review of *Tales of Fashionable Life*, supposedly published in *The Christian Observer*. In some quarters Sneyd's review was taken seriously. See *Letters from England*, pp. 23 and 24n.

[3] *QR*, ii, 1809, 148–9. The evidence for Gifford's authorship of this passage is presented by H. and H. C. Shine, *The Quarterly Review under Gifford*, Chapel Hill, 1949, p. 8.

any element of romance the result must at times seem a little dry to the reader brought up on commoner novel theories and situations.

Croker, writing three years later, fully accepts Maria Edgeworth's decision to reject romance. In fact he takes 'an undeviating attention to nature' to be a *requirement* of the naturalistic novel, and he criticizes Maria Edgeworth only for her failure to live up to her own high standards. In handling the *manners* of characters, and in making her people individual, she is unrivalled among modern novelists; he can think only of names like Cervantes and Fielding for comparison. In devising natural characters to serve her morality, she is even superior to Fielding. So far Croker thinks that she is excellent. Where he finds her less good is in her handling of plot and incident, that aspect of her novels which is not naturalistic. Too often, as in the case of *Ennui* and *Émilie de Coulanges*, she is content with a hack romantic conclusion. Elsewhere she borrows episodes from life without sufficient attention to the difference between the real in life and the 'real' in fiction. 'While the *vrai* is the highest recommendation of the historian of real life, the *vraisemblable* is the only legitimate province of the novelist who aims at improving the understanding or touching the heart.'[1]

It is on the subject of Ireland that Maria writes with her most extreme and characteristic fidelity to real-life fact. Naturally her critics try from the first to define what is original about her handling of Irish material. It could not be said that to write about the Irish was in itself new, for, as the reviewers constantly mention, Irishmen had been familiar, even hackneyed figures in at least one branch of eighteenth-century literature for at least forty years before *Castle Rackrent*.

It is impossible to appreciate the effect Maria Edgeworth created with her peasant characters without comparing them with the literary Irishmen her readers knew. There was not one stereotype but two. The first was prone to the 'bull', or verbal blunder, and according to popular myth he was likely to utter one of these every time he opened his mouth. Bulls were much in evidence in newspapers, biographies, and

[1] *QR*, vii, 1812, 329. This is very similar to the objection later raised by Col. Stewart (see above, pp. 260 ff.), which ME rejected.

travels of the period. The second cliché, the 'stage Irishman' of late-eighteenth-century sentimental comedy, was not an absurd or blundering figure. Nor was he the sentimentalized hot-headed, hard-drinking, warm-hearted Paddy of twentieth-century popular literature. The best-known eighteenth-century stage Irishmen were probably Charles Macklin's Sir Callaghan O'Brallaghan (*Love à la Mode*, first performed 1759); Richard Cumberland's Major O'Flaherty, who was so successful in *The West Indian* (1771) that he was brought back in *The Natural Son* (1784); and Sheridan's Sir Lucius O'Trigger (*The Rivals*, first performed 1775) and Lieutenant O'Conner (*St. Patrick's Day*, 1775). These characters are based on a single type; they are gentlemen, soldiers, and usually lovers as well, brave, belligerent, impetuous, inconsistent, generous, and warm-hearted. They are highly fallible, but their very faults are meant to endear them to the audience.

The 'stage Irishman' was bound to become stereotyped once he regularly became isolated from his natural context. The English characters by whom he was surrounded were not 'stage English', but individuals. Charles Macklin did set *The True-born Irishman* (1762) in Ireland, so that in this play the Irish characters are fully differentiated people. Indeed, the best of them, Mrs. Diggerty, so strongly resembles Lady Clonbrony of *The Absentee* that it seems possible that she influenced Maria Edgeworth's portrait. Mrs. Diggerty is an aspirant to high Society who in describing London life exclaims: 'Veest! imminse! extatic! I never knew life before—everything there is high, tip top, the grande monde, the bun tun—and quite teesty.'[1]

Macklin's success with Mrs. Diggerty is a significant pointer. Maria Edgeworth handles the Irish better than her eighteenth-century predecessors above all because she places them in their natural context in Ireland. An Irish setting for a novel before *Castle Rackrent* was most unusual; although it was not totally unknown, for the example of Smollett in *Humphry Clinker* (1771) had prompted a few obscure novels set at least nominally in Scotland, Wales, or Ireland.[2]

[1] It is on account of her careful pronunciation of 'teebles and cheers' that Lady Clonbrony provides ammunition for her English mimics (*The Absentee*, ch. 1).

[2] Novels set in Ireland include *The Reconciliation: or the History of Miss Mortimer*

Even rarer than the regional setting was sustained, accurate regional dialect. Rustic characters had spoken in a stereotyped Mummerset since the time of Squire Western, but there were only isolated attempts to capture the distinctive ways of speech of other regions. Maria Edgeworth's Irish tales break new ground by reporting the speech and customs of the Irish characters with what the Irishman Croker vouches for as documentary accuracy. It is the idiom of the peasantry which seems to the English reader most distinctive, but the critics recognize that Maria also characterizes the other classes of Irish society by their speech.[1]

The reviewers are deeply impressed by the accuracy with which the real-life Irish are reported in Maria's novels. Croker singles out Larry the postilion, from *The Absentee*:

> His letter to his brother, with which the volume concludes, is, to our judgment, quite perfect in its peculiar stile; cunning and simplicity, sense and folly, burlesque and pathos, are there mingled without incongruity or confusion, and present one of the most faithful descriptions of Irish manners, and one of the best specimens of Irish phraseology which even Miss Edgeworth herself has produced.[2]

Croker is equally interested in her ability to distinguish her Irish characters by class one from another. He is fascinated by this sociological concern in her novels, and it is here, he claims, that her truly valuable contribution lies:

> —in the accurate discrimination of the various classes of Irish society, all marked with the lively traits of their common origin, yet distinguished by the several peculiarities of their respective stations and characters. Other writers have caught nothing but the general feature, and in their description, everything that is Irish is pretty much alike, lords, peasants, ladies and nurses: to Miss Edgeworth's keen observation and vivid pencil, it was reserved to separate the genus into its species and individuals, and to exhibit the most accurate and yet the most diversified views that have ever been drawn of a national character.[3]

It is important to notice that in this, as in all other strictly

*and Miss Fitzgerald* (1783), *Anthony Varnish* (1786), and *The Minor: or, the History of George O'Nial, Esq.* (1787). All are anonymous.

[1] e.g. her description of the speech of Lady Geraldine in *Ennui*, quoted below, p. 371.

[2] *QR*, vii, 1812, 341.

[3] Ibid., 336.

contemporary reviews of Maria Edgeworth, there is no reference to national consciousness, the emotional sense of national identity which is so strong an element in Lady Morgan and, later, in many of the imitators of Scott. Croker is interested in Ireland as a large, stratified society, and his remarks would apply if Maria Edgeworth had set out to write about Yorkshire. It is to the credit of this much criticized reviewer that he was the first to notice that Maria Edgeworth's ability to see her characters in terms of class, and to define class characteristics accurately, opened the way to a new kind of realism. He sees this development as part of a natural historical evolution in the novel, away from the general to the specific. After the exaltation of Raphael, Correggio, and Murillo—Croker's analogy for the classical period which produced *Gil Blas* and *Tom Jones*—the novel is now 'minute and Dutch'. Its characters are not in general terms, '*men*, but Irish, Scotch and French'.[1] Here then is an early claim that in the nineteenth century the novel is entering a new phase, based on documentation of accurately observed fact in the real external world.

Other critics quickly accepted that a new era had dawned, and the standard of realism expected of a so-called naturalistic novel was raised accordingly. When after the publication of *The Absentee* Maria Edgeworth returned in *Patronage* to an English setting, her own Irish tales were used as a stick to beat her with. The intelligent John Ward, the future Earl of Dudley, observes that her characterization of English society is inaccurate *as a whole*. 'What we have to complain of in her representation of society, is not so much the inaccuracy of any particular sketches, as the general effect of the whole group.' Ward notices how she is prejudiced against public life, the old bias that gradually reasserts itself a few years after the Paris visit. 'There are two classes of person whom Miss Edgeworth seems to view with no very charitable feelings—those who are engaged in ambitious pursuits and those who compose what is sometimes called "fashionable company" in the metropolis.' Ward, a former M.P. himself, and a future Foreign Secretary, refuses to accept Oldborough as a plausible English politician. He believes that 'Society' has also been travestied:

[1] *QR*, xi, 1814, 355.

The greater part of her characters that are not absorbed in business or buried in seclusion are represented as foolish, selfish, worthless people . . . We at once admit that there are persons moving in 'the fashionable world' as silly, as coarse, and as void of feeling as any Miss Edgeworth has represented. But the number is comparatively very small . . . She does not willingly admit the idea of virtue and sense except in retirement.

Ward attributes the pervasive inaccuracy of her picture of English life to lack of first-hand knowledge. 'Miss Edgeworth, though enjoying the friendship of many of the most distinguished persons in this country, and the esteem of all, has taken only an occasional and cursory view of English society.' When she writes about Ireland she knows her subject at first hand, and the result, both in individual sketches and in the representation of the whole, is entirely different:

Miss Edgeworth knows the Irish nation thoroughly—not merely in those broader and more general characteristics that distinguish it from this and from all other nations, but in those nicer shades that mark each class of society. All the materials are drawn from her own stores, and she is never obliged to supply the defect of actual observation by hearsay or conjecture . . . Her merit was not that of describing what had never been described before—it was greater, it was that of describing well what had been described ill—of substituting accurate finished resemblances, for clumsy confused daubings by the sign-post artists of modern comedy.[1]

Maria was at the height of her literary reputation when the first novels of Jane Austen and Walter Scott were published, so that her tales were always an available yardstick for critics to measure the stature of her two rivals. Jane Austen's naturalism was received favourably, and with much more understanding than it might have commanded before 1809.[2] Both Scott and Whately give due credit to Jane Austen for being consistently naturalistic, in her plots as well as in characterization, whereas Maria Edgeworth, the pioneer of this kind of writing, tolerates 'absurd and lucky denouements'.[3] It is often claimed that Jane Austen was insensitively reviewed,

[1] *QR*, x, 1814, 309.

[2] Cf. the doubts expressed by Henry Stephen in that year as to whether a novel without romantic colouring could maintain the reader's interest: cited above, pp. 342–3.

[3] R. Whately, review of *Northanger Abbey* and *Persuasion*, *QR*, xiv, 1820, 355.

but her early critics are quick to praise her for taking a step further what they see as the important modern development in the novel, the effort to reproduce 'a correct and striking representation of that which is daily taking place'.[1] They even notice, although they do not make enough of it, that Jane Austen has solved the outstanding technical problem left by Maria Edgeworth, that of devising an *action* which is significant and shapely and yet to all appearances natural.

Critics begin informally to draw up their rules during the period that Maria Edgeworth is writing, often directly stimulated by her tales. They are inclined to expect three things of a would-be naturalistic novelist. The most obvious, and probably the most important, is that he must be able to suggest in detail the quality of ordinary daily life. But it is almost equally important that his characters should not be individual eccentrics, but plausible members of a group, occupation, or class, so that the world of the novel accurately reflects real-life society.[2] Lastly, the representation itself, the novel as a whole, should aim to seem coherent and natural. Before her career was over Maria Edgeworth was widely felt to have failed to meet the last requirement. She was a pioneer, and in some ways still pre-eminent, in her rendering of real life, she had done remarkable things in rendering people of different classes, but she was not the equal of some others as a maker of novels.

A late word by a contemporary critic on Maria Edgeworth's general achievement as a social novelist comes from the *New Monthly Magazine*'s anonymous review of *Tremaine*. Nowadays Robert Plumer Ward's *Tremaine* (1825), although not perhaps much read, is often cited as supposedly the first of the novels of fashionable life of the 1820s, the 'silver fork' school of Lister, Bulwer Lytton, and Disraeli. But this contemporary reviewer takes it for granted that *Tremaine* fits naturally into the movement inaugurated by Maria Edgeworth, the movement towards an accurate analytical social realism:

> *Tremaine* is, notwithstanding the writer's somewhat fastidious deprecations to the contrary, nothing else but a novel. It is a novel, however, sui generis; though resembling, more than any other class,

[1] W. Scott, review of *Emma*, *QR*, xiv, 1816, 193.

[2] For ME's own conscious intention to make her characters representative of their class, see her letter to Scott of 15 July 1830, quoted above, p. 267.

that of which Miss Edgeworth's are the only truly valuable specimens we possess. It resembles those admirable works, inasmuch as it discards all romantic exhibitions of passion and sentiment, and depends, for its power of interesting the heart, and exciting the imagination, on its vraisemblance alone;—it resembles them in its vigorous and at the same time refined and delicate delineation of character, and its absolutely unexaggerated truth of manners; and also in confining those manners to the present day;—it resembles them in the excellent moral lessons, touching the conduct of real everyday life, which it is not only calculated but intended to inculcate, and which, in fact, it cannot be read, by no matter whom, without inculcating;—it resembles those hitherto unrivalled works in all these particulars, and is (we will venture to say it) inferior to them in none of these, as far as it goes. It differs from Miss Edgeworth's Tales, in being absolutely free from that crying defect which the very warmest of her admirers (amongst whom we are proud to reckon ourselves) cannot either overlook or forget, and which, while it takes away from them that specific, homogeneous character, without which they cannot be regarded as perfect works of art, does what is still more important, in robbing them of the power of producing those admirable practical effects which their otherwise astonishing merits might command. We allude, of course, to the singularly complicated and artificial plots of Miss Edgeworth's stories. It cannot be doubted that these greatly injure the general effect of the works of which they form so important a part, by destroying their verisimilitude as wholes . . .

These elaborately artificial plots of Miss Edgeworth's Tales, united with their otherwise perfect truth of delineation, give to them a mixed character, and prevent them from being regarded as either true pictures of what we are, or ideal ones of what we might or ought to be; leaving them hanging, like Mahomet's coffin, between the heaven of the one, and the mere earth of the other, without absolutely belonging to either. Now, in regard to the above particular, the singular work more immediately before us perhaps stands alone. At any rate, with all the separate truth of detail, as far as it goes, which belongs to the capital productions to which we have in part compared it, it has also a general truth of effect which they are without;—in fact, with some very trifling exceptions, the whole of Tremaine may be taken, so far as regards the reader, as neither more nor less than a portion of human life in the nineteenth century.[1]

[1] 'Review of *Tremaine, or the Man of Refinement*', anon., *New Monthly Magazine*, xiii, 1825, 328.

Scott's debt to Maria Edgeworth will be considered later in the fuller context of a discussion of the Irish tales. Naturally the critics are fully aware of the link between the novelist of Ireland and the novelist of Scotland. But Croker, at any rate, is anxious to make the point that *Waverley* resembles some Edgeworth tales more than others:

> We have heard *Waverley* called a Scotch *Castle Rackrent*; . . . the resemblance consists only in this, that the one is a description of the peculiarities of Scottish manners, as the other is of those of Ireland; and [that] we are far from placing on the same level the merits and qualities of the works. *Waverley* is of a much higher strain, and may be safely placed far above the amusing vulgarity of *Castle Rackrent*, and by the side of *Ennui* or *The Absentee*, the best undoubtedly of Miss Edgeworth's compositions.[1]

'The amusing vulgarity of *Castle Rackrent*': Croker means something specific by this, and it is not a philistine point but a defensible one. *Castle Rackrent* focuses within itself on the character of Thady, and therefore takes a limited and eccentric view of the Irish scene. In the two later tales there is a more ambitious task in hand: 'The peculiarities of low manners are made auxiliary to the development of national character.'[2] Again, Croker shows that he thinks the writer of fiction can and even should aim at rendering society as a whole. This is something *Castle Rackrent* does not attempt, and Croker is claiming that it is the worse for not attempting it.

Croker's preference for the later tales on this account seems to have been usual in his day. Maria herself apparently liked *The Absentee* best: 'Look for me in *The Absentee*, she said.'[3] In 1817 various correspondents wrote to her comparing *Comic Dramas* and *Harrington and Ormond* with her earlier tales. The Ruxtons and two new English friends, Lady Romilly and John Whishaw,[4] all showed unanimity in their choice of the best among her works. *Ormond* was, Mrs. Ruxton thought, 'superior to *The Absentee*, *Ennui*, all of them', and Lady Romilly confirmed that in London it was regularly 'class'd with *Ennui* and *The Absentee*, which I think have always been the most

[1] *QR*, xi, 1814, 356.

[2] *QR*, xii, 1815, 508 (Review of *Guy Mannering*).

[3] *Letters of Anne Thackeray Ritchie*, 1924, p. 227.

[4] For Whishaw's reputation as a literary sage, see below, p. 405 n.

popular'.[1] These private friends did not give reasons for the high reputation of *Ennui*, *The Absentee*, and *Ormond*, by comparison with the still well-known *Castle Rackrent*. Croker surely speaks for them, though, when he finds in the three later tales a higher degree of intellectual seriousness, a greater relevance to the real world—in a phrase, a new, nineteenth-century realism which is essentially scientific in spirit. Judged by contemporary standards, Maria Edgeworth's earlier vein of comedy, however entertaining, did not equal either in interest or originality her mature treatment of Irish society.

[1] Mrs. R to ME, 27 July 1817; Lady Romilly to ME, 1 Aug. 1817. Cf. J. Whishaw to ME, 27 May 1817, and SR to ME, 23 July 1817.

# VIII

## THE IRISH TALES

THADY M'QUIRK, narrator of *Castle Rackrent*, is the most celebrated, extended, and probably the best character sketch Maria Edgeworth ever made. She was able to bring the old man to life as he would have looked, and as Langan did look: Thady scratches his head under his wig, puffs at his pipe, and moves slowly, an old man and a perpetually puzzled one. His wig does double service as a duster; his greatcoat is buttoned round his neck like a cloak, so that the sleeves 'are as good as new, though come Holantide next, I've had it these seven years'.

But in the last resort what brings Thady to life is Maria's mastery of his idiom and attitudes. 'He tells the history of Rackrent family in his vernacular idiom, and in the full confidence that sir Patrick, sir Murtagh, sir Kit, and sir Condy Rackrent's affairs will be as interesting to all the world as they were to himself.'[1] One of the most important points in the first section of the book is this unconscious provincialism, which is meant to strike the English reader as highly absurd. Thady assumes that the whole world lives within a jaunting-car ride of Castle Rackrent. When Sir Patrick dies, for example, he has a fine funeral: 'All the gentlemen in the three counties were at it.' This is Thady's most distant horizon, while the real focus of his interest is much more local still: 'As I have lived so will I die, true and loyal to the family.'

The source of comedy is the eccentricity and superficial inconsistency of his comments, which in fact follow logically from his loyalty to the Rackrents. There is for example the fluctuating tone of his remarks about the wife of the third Rackrent he served under, the Jewish bride of Sir Kit. When he first sees her he is startled by her ugliness. She puzzles him by her total ignorance of Ireland, especially the sights and names he has grown up with since boyhood, and he concludes

[1] Preface to *Castle Rackrent*, i. 5.

that she must be a little mad. But as she is now Lady Rackrent he feels obliged to defend her: 'I took care to put the best foot foremost, and passed her for a nabob in the kitchen.'[1] He pities her when her husband shuts her in her room, although loyalty to Sir Kit prevents him from saying anything, and the moment that Sir Kit dies in a duel Thady automatically transfers his allegiance to the 'Jewish' as lady and head of the house. But as soon as he discovers her desire to leave Castle Rackrent with all possible speed, he loses interest in her, and his sympathies revert to Sir Kit. 'Her diamond cross was, they say, at the bottom of it all; and it was a shame for her, being his wife, not to show more duty, and to have given it up when he condescended to ask so often for such a bit of a trifle in his distresses, especially when he all along made it no secret he married for money.'[2]

Thady's commentary does not dominate the second, longer section of the book to the same extent. When Sir Condy is driven by his debts out of Castle Rackrent into the lodge at the gate, Thady goes with him, since it is natural for him to prefer his old master to the new owner, his own son Jason Quirk. Thady's declaration for Condy makes him a participant in the action, but a subordinate one; attention from now on is focused on the last of the Rackrents, and the plight he is in when everyone but Thady has deserted him. The pattern of the earlier section is that a mass of material, often from Edgeworth family sources, is used to illuminate Thady's attitudes. The second section tells a much more coherent and in itself interesting story, but it is not primarily about Thady, and apart from suggesting his puzzlement when he has to choose between loyalty to his own family and to the Rackrents, it does not add to what we already know of his character.

There are not two but three distinct stages in the evolution of *Castle Rackrent*. The first fits Maria's own description of the genesis of the tale.[3] She wanted a dynasty of landlords, each of whom would possess a vice characteristic of his species, in order to provide a suitable vehicle for Thady. The first part must have been written between the autumn of 1793 and 1796, probably early in that period rather than late. Two years after it was completed, she added Sir Condy's story, presumably

[1] *Castle Rackrent*, i. 26. [2] Ibid., 36. [3] See above, pp. 240–1.

because the situation of a dissipated and abandoned figure particularly interested her. Another motive may have been to find a literary vehicle for some of the election scenes she had heard about from her father in January and February 1796.[1] If this was a direct incentive, 1796 would be a plausible date for the second half of the tale.

It is not difficult to imagine why Maria might have wanted to draw a spendthrift landlord more directly than she had treated any of the earlier Rackrents. She had the vivid example of the cousin Edgeworth remembered from his youth, and at times there are also touches of Elers, even Delaval, about Condy. All had fallen from a high or moderately high estate, had squandered their money, been neglected by their friends; and two of them had died bitterly repentant. Edgeworth was fascinated by these three men, whom he must have described vividly to Maria. Even without her father, she could have found a Sir Condy in the last of her dissipated forebears, Protestant Frank, who died deep in debt and a fugitive from his estate.[2]

The last stage in the evolution of the tale is the Glossary. The entire text of *Castle Rackrent*, with its footnotes, was already in print when the family decided that some further explanation for the public was needed.[3] For the printer's convenience the Glossary therefore had to be bound up with the preliminaries of the first edition of 1800, while in later editions it followed in its more natural position at the end of the text. At the end of October 1798 Maria was preparing to send the manuscript to Johnson in London, and the complete book with Glossary was published in January 1800. The date of the Glossary at least can therefore be pinpointed. It was compiled in 1799, probably in the latter half of the year after the family returned from England.

The time of composition is important, because it helps to explain both the existence of the Glossary and the kind of point it tries to make. The Edgeworths had just returned from a tour in which they had renewed intellectual contact

[1] See above, p. 120, and *Castle Rackrent*, i. 51 ff. The painter Joseph Farington records that Capt. Francis Beaufort told him that *Castle Rackrent* was written '8 years before it was published' (entry for Mar. 1819; *Farington Diary*, ed. J. Greig, 1928, viii. 217). Although Beaufort is in general an unexceptionable source, it has to be admitted that ME was out of Ireland in 1792, and that she did not see Mrs. R, which makes the story difficult to accept as it stands.

[2] See above, pp. 15–16.

[3] See introductory note to Glossary.

with Edgeworth's English friends, and had discussed Ireland's Union with England from the English end. 'The commercial and mercantile world with which we have mixed . . . look upon it as madness in the Irish to oppose what they think so advantageous.'[1] Suddenly it must have seemed to the Edgeworths that the onus was on the Irish to prove that the English were getting a bargain; so that the light entertainment Maria was about to produce, which presented the Irish as comic and irresponsible, was anything but timely. Moreover, the book, if published now as it stood, would make an odd companion piece with Edgeworth's economic arguments to the Irish House of Commons and his appeals for a more progressive policy in education. All this helps to explain the self-conscious intellectuality and *Englishness* of the Glossary: the Edgeworths were not merely interpreting Thady to an audience unfamiliar with his type, but were trying to dissociate themselves from his primitive attitudes. Some of the notes, especially the first four, are facetious and patronizing, but most are of serious scholarly and especially antiquarian interest, reflecting Edgeworth's membership of the Royal Irish Academy, and probably Beaufort's too. One of the notes was, as we know, composed by Edgeworth;[2] another, which from a literary viewpoint contains very interesting matter, must originally have been supplied by him. When Maria describes a scene in which two peasants wrangle in front of the 'Editor' in his capacity as Justice of the Peace, it is clearly her father and not herself who is meant.

The most recent editor of *Castle Rackrent*, considering the decision to add the Glossary for the benefit of the English reader, observes that to a modern reader the Edgeworths seem 'over-solicitous'.[3] His assumption here is that their motive in supplying the Glossary was to make sure that the general public would find its Irish idioms intelligible. Now the Edgeworths had certainly spent time worrying about this, as the footnotes to the text and the Preface show. They 'had it once in contemplation to translate the language of Thady into plain English; but Thady's idiom is incapable of translation, and,

[1] Mrs. FE to DAB, Hill Top, nr. Birmingham, 23 Apr. 1799; Nat. Lib. of Ireland, MS. 13176(4).

[2] See above, p. 242.

[3] George Watson, introduction to *Castle Rackrent* in Oxford English Novels series, 1964, p. xx.

besides, the authenticity of his story would have been more exposed to doubt if it were not told in his own characteristic manner'.[1] As Mr. Watson rightly points out, the twentieth-century reader finds this fear exaggerated because he has become accustomed to dialect in fiction, and so has no difficulty in following Thady's turns of phrase; some of which, like 'let alone' as a conjunction, have become common usage, as the Edgeworths foresaw they might. Accurate reporting of dialect was so rare in the eighteenth century that Maria had no reason to take it for granted that Thady's manner of narration would not prove an insuperable block. But in spite of these early doubts the Edgeworths had in fact resolved to go ahead with the book as it stood—Irishisms and all—before they were struck with the further doubts that made them add the Glossary. The most cursory inspection of the Glossary shows that it was not meant as a means of overcoming a linguistic or even a cultural barrier. Its function, which became necessary because of the special political circumstances of 1799, was to update the book and make it a means of introducing more serious sociological information about Ireland.

The date of publication of this pioneering and soon very celebrated Irish novel—in the very year of Ireland's Union with England—has been taken to be enormously significant in terms of the story's meaning. '*Castle Rackrent* was to be the brilliant requiem of the Protestant Nation, for Maria Edgeworth had seen its history as the life of a family which rose from obscurity, fought bravely, lost meanly, and at last perished in squalor and pride.'[2] She had seen nothing of the kind. The Preface is most insistent that the characters in the story are not the same generation as the one on the point of uniting itself with England:

> The Editor hopes his readers will observe, that these are 'tales of other times'; that the manners depicted in the following pages are not those of the present age: the race of the Rackrents has long since been extinct in Ireland, and the drunken Sir Patrick, the litigious Sir Murtagh, the fighting Sir Kit, and the slovenly Sir Condy, are characters which could no more be met with at present in Ireland, than Squire Western or Parson Trulliber in England.[1]

[1] Preface to *Castle Rackrent*, i. 6.

[2] Thomas Flanagan, *The Irish Novelists, 1800–1850*, New York, 1959, p. 23,

At least one of Maria's later tales, as well as a mass of contemporary evidence, proves that the race of the Rackrents was not extinct in 1800, yet in a perfectly literal sense *Castle Rackrent* does tell 'tales of other times'. The material is drawn more consistently than in any other Edgeworth tale from the past, particularly from a family history that goes back as far as a hundred and fifty years—which helps to explain why, deplorable though the Rackrents are, they do not shock Maria. Had rack-renting landlords been common in her own day in Co. Longford, her moral indignation would probably have asserted itself; but since most of the landowners lived elsewhere, and few were ever seen at Edgeworthstown, she had no axe to grind on this occasion. A note of personal complaint is heard only once, when the characterization of Thady is held in abeyance for half a page while he pronounces a diatribe against middlemen, and a long footnote in the Edgeworths' own tones is added for good measure.[1] Apart from this Maria is free to exercise her natural bent for character sketching and anecdote. This is both the strength and weakness of *Castle Rackrent*. It does not give away Maria's personal immaturity, as the other early tales do. But if it exposes little, it also expresses little.

In the very nature of its material *Castle Rackrent* is one kind of historical novel, but at a more serious level it is the least historical of Maria's tales. There is no sense of the impending future in it—no clash between the Rackrents' values and those of the people replacing them. *Castle Rackrent* has been read as a forerunner of *Waverley* in its historical awareness. 'Sir Condy is a historical as well as a national type; like the Baron Bradwardine in Scott's novel, he is the man who lives by the barbaric standard of honour in a commercial society where that standard can no longer apply.'[2] But who in the novel represents the new commercial ethos—is it Jason? Certainly not in the Edgeworths' eyes, because Jason made his fortune as agent to the estate, through the carelessness of the absentee Sir Kit: he was the parasite of the old system, not the herald of a new. It was the very absence in *Castle Rackrent* of a sense of Ireland's economic possibilities that the Edgeworths regretted in 1799;

[1] *Castle Rackrent*, i. 21–2.

[2] D. Davie, *The Heyday of Sir Walter Scott*, 1961, p. 66.

they would not have taken such pains to provide a modern ethos in the Glossary had they felt that it was present in the book.

For reasons which have largely to do with Ireland's later history, the modern reader is likely to sympathize with Thady and to see his attitudes as genuinely rooted in native Irish custom. Because he does so he misses the ironic point that Maria makes very clearly in the first section of the narrative. The Preface states that if it is truth we are concerned with, an illiterate peasant is a more useful narrator than an educated person, because his prejudices and absurdities are too blatant to be mistaken by the reader. With a confidence in objective truth typical of the Enlightenment, the Edgeworths did not allow for a reader who might use historical insight to account for Thady's attitudes. The first half of the book, in which Thady's prejudices, provincialism, and blind partiality for the Rackrents are heavily stressed, only partially gets across to most modern readers. We tend to see all these qualities as typical of a peasant, and therefore as part, a very truthful part, of Maria's impersonation of Thady. She expected us to feel more surprised and more critical, to reject actively his indulgent view of the Rackrents, and supply the correct, the enlightened, moral frame of reference.

This is how Thady's inconsistency and narrowness of vision probably appeared to its first readers. Conceivably it would still have done so if *Castle Rackrent* had been in one part instead of two. The addition of Sir Condy, and Thady's more active part in relation to him, decide the issue against the grain of the first section of the book. It is impossible for a rational person to approve of Sir Murtagh and Sir Kit, so that when Thady insists on doing so he is being absurd; equally it is impossible not to sympathize with Sir Condy, particularly when his opponents are the family of his flighty wife, and Jason Quirk. The effect of the closing episode is therefore to change the reader's attitude towards Thady's loyalty. The book ends with a totally different meaning from the one with which it began. The pathetic circumstances of the generous Sir Condy's death, almost alone and unmourned at his own gate, makes it possible to read *Castle Rackrent* as a not unsympathetic account of the passing of old-fashioned landlordism.

This was just what the Edgeworths were afraid of. They were gratified by the tale's instant success. 'My father asked for "Belinda", "Bulls", &c, found they were in good repute —"Castle Rackrent" in better—the others often borrowed, but "Castle Rackrent" often bought.'[1] It went into five English editions before inclusion in the first Collected Works, and for several years after its appearance the Edgeworths would hear stories of how it was read and enjoyed in high places. 'We hear from good authority that the king was much pleased with Castle Rack Rent—he rubbed his hands & said what what—I know something now of my Irish subjects.'[2] During his visit to London in 1805 Edgeworth also learnt that 'Mr. Pitt is a great admirer of Castle RR—& Lord Carhampton says it is the best book he has read since he learnt to read'.[3]

Just the same they were worried that it would be resented by the Irish themselves, especially if the limited vision and mistaken loyalty of Thady was not taken ironically, while his picture of the Rackrents was accepted as an up-to-date description of the Irish gentry. One acquaintance did object to it as a travesty, but most people in their own circle tactfully assured them that it was 'a representation of past manners that should flatter the present generation'.[2] Mrs. Edgeworth asked her brother William, who had a Church living near Cork, to find out how it was received there. His reply shows that many people were reading it as a 'straight' account of present-day Irish society, and in fact liked it or disliked it with that criterion in mind:

One *lady* told me she did not like it at all because it was so severe and she feared so true a satire on her dear country—Another who is a native in the West Indies & never lived above a couple of years in Ireland said it was 'very entertaining sure'—but as to being a picture of the manners of Ireland, that was nonsense 'for I never saw nothing like it'—a revd. gentleman said the other day that it was not in the least a true picture of Irish manners, '& how should it?—for I hear the author is some low fellow that never was in

[1] The report of the Leicester bookseller who ran a circulating library; see above, p. 188.

[2] RLE to DAB, 26 Apr. 1800.

[3] RLE to ME, London, 17 May 1805. Lord Carhampton had been the Irish Commander-in-Chief in 1796–7. See above, p. 121.

Ireland in his life & evidently does not know how to write'—But except by these, I have heard it exceedingly admired both 'as a picture of Irish squires' 'as a piece of good satirical writing'—'a good imitation of the style of the narrator'—and as 'an entertaining tale'.[1]

This letter justifies the anxiety the Edgeworths had felt. The fact that Thady has as it were captured *Castle Rackrent*, and successfully imposed his personality upon it, is evidence of Maria's great gift for characterization, and her remarkable powers of filling out a portrait through the nuances of speech. On the other hand the tale as a whole is at odds with itself, and at odds with Maria. The ironic message of the first half is cancelled out by the pathos of the second. The result is that *Castle Rackrent* has always been taken to mean the opposite of what the Edgeworths believed: that the passing of thoroughly selfish and irresponsible landlords is to be regretted when they come from a native Irish family and can command a feudal type of loyalty from some of their peasants.

At this stage in her career as a novelist Maria had not formed any plans to write a tale which better represented her or her father's views about Ireland;[2] it will be remembered that she did not yet regard the tales, which were primarily hers, as a vehicle for serious social material. But *Castle Rackrent*, with its apparent nostalgia and its emphasis through Thady on Irish foolishness and backwardness, certainly needed to be atoned for. An apology duly came in the form of *Irish Bulls*,[3] an essay which is not fiction (although it contains three short stories) but is so relevant to Maria's development as an Irish writer that it must be considered together with the tales.

*Irish Bulls* is an essay on the 'bull', or comic verbal blunder, which is supposed to be characteristic of the Irish when speaking English.[4] The authors (named as both R. L. and Maria Edgeworth) have two principal points to make. One is that plenty of people beside the Irish make comic blunders. The

[1] Wm. Beaufort to Mrs. FE, 2 Oct. 1800; Nat. Lib. of Ireland, MS. 13176 (5).

[2] Later on RLE wanted her to correct *Castle Rackrent* itself by adding another generation which brought the picture of the Irish gentry up to date. See above, pp. 277–8.

[3] *Irish Bulls*, Conclusion, i. 246.

[4] See above, p. 243.

other, that many Irish 'blunders' have a natural explanation, and that the speech of the lower-class Irish is in fact exceptionally expressive.

The parts of the book which deal descriptively with Irish speech remain original and alive. The best chapter, 'Irish Wit and Eloquence', sets out examples of Irish lower-class usage with spirit, and as far as possible with accuracy. It is with *Irish Bulls*, in fact, that the Edgeworths first make extensive use of their direct records of Irish phrases and speeches, which from now on are used as freely to document character-sketches in the stories as the observations of children were used in *Practical Education*. No hearsay anecdotes or traditional Irishisms are used in the serious analytical part of *Irish Bulls*. 'The examples we have cited are taken from real life, and given without alteration or embellishment.'[1] Nearly all were spoken to one of the two authors personally, most of the best to Edgeworth while he was acting as a magistrate, or canvassing the county.[2] He had an excellent memory as well as the family talent for mimicry which Maria inherited. As far as possible he tried not to improve on his originals (although no doubt this was not always possible) and the version Maria copied down was believed by both to be of genuine sociological value as an accurate specimen of speech and 'manners'. A dispute between two peasants who appeared before Edgeworth demanding justice is characteristic of the examples of Irish speech they collected:

A thin tall woman wrapped in a long cloak, the hood of which was drawn over her head, and shaded her pale face, came to a gentleman to complain of the cruelty of her landlord.

'He is the most hard-hearted man alive, so he is, sir', said she; 'he has just seized all I have, which, God knows, is little enough! and has driven my cow to pound, the only cow I have, and only dependance I have for a drop of milk to drink . . . Oh! if it had but been my lot to be tenant to a *gentleman born*, like your honour, who is the poor man's friend, and the orphan's, and the widow's—the friend of them that have none other. Long life to you! and long

[1] *Irish Bulls*, ch. 10; i. 196.

[2] *Memoirs of RLE*, ii. 336–8. ME attributes to her father the notes on the Dublin shoeblack (ch. 8), and, from ch. 10, the speech of the poor freeholder and the exchange between the poor widow and her landlord quoted here.

may you live to reign over us!—Would you but speak three words to my landlord, to let my cow out of pound, and give me a fortnight's time, that I might see and fatten her to sell against the fair, I could pay him then all honestly, and not be racked entirely, and he would be ashamed to refuse your honour, and afraid to disoblige the like of you, or get your ill-will. May the blessing of Heaven be upon you, if you'll just send and speak to him three words for the poor woman and widow, that has none other to speak for her in the wide world.'

. . . The landlord appeared; not a gentleman, not a rich man, as the term landlord might denote, but a stout, square, stubbed, thick-limbed, gray-eyed man, who seemed to have come smoking hot from hard labour . . .

'And now have you done?' said he, turning to the woman, who had recommenced her lamentations.

'Look at her standing there, sir. It's easy for her to put on her long cloak, and to tell her long story, and to make her poor mouth to your honour; but if you are willing to hear, I'll tell you what she is, and what I am . . . She is one that is able to afford herself a glass of whiskey when she pleases, and she pleases it often; she is one that never denies herself the bit of *staggering bob*[1] when in season; she is one that has a snug house well thatched to live in all the year round, and nothing to do or nothing that she does, and this is the way of her life, and this is what she is.—And what am I? I am the father of eight children, and I have a wife and myself to provide for. I am a man that is at hard labour of one kind or another from sunrise to sunset. The straw that thatched the house she lives in I brought two mile on my back, the walls of the house she lives in I built with my own hands; I did the same by five other houses, and they are all sound and dry, and good to live in, summer or winter. I set them for rent to put bread into my children's mouth, and after all I cannot get it! And to support my eight children, and my wife, and myself, what have I in this world', cried he, striding suddenly with colossal firmness upon his sturdy legs, and raising to heaven arms which looked like foreshortenings of the limbs of Hercules—'what have *I* in this wide world but these four bones?'[2]

The footnote to this passage says that it was taken down a few minutes after it was spoken, and in the *Memoirs* too Maria claims that it is unembellished fact. Edgeworth 'repeated, and

[1] Author's footnote: 'slink calf', *OED*: the skin or flesh of a premature calf.

[2] *Irish Bulls*, ch. 10; i. 193–5.

I may say acted' the speeches, which 'I instantly wrote word for word, and the whole was described exactly from the life of his representation'.[1] The scene is typical, and interesting, because it is an example of the Edgeworths' dispassionate reporting. They do not invent an artificial climax; they do not guess who is telling the truth, or inquire further into motives than they can see; the sole purpose of the scene is to reproduce 'the thing as it is'.

The groups of speeches in *Irish Bulls*, by which the Edgeworths demonstrate 'the eloquence, wit and talents of the lower classes of people in Ireland', are forerunners of many fine passages of lower-class dialogue in the Irish tales written afterwards—passages that sometimes carry a footnote stating them to be 'Fact' of 'Verbatim'. As a process the Edgeworths' habit of collecting speech-specimens was careful, fairly systematic, and carried out for the purposes of science, not of literature. Because their material was intrinsically so lively, it was to be the richest ingredient in the Irish tales, although never 'made over', as it were, into fiction. Maria's native scenes do not show peasants in the ordinary circumstances of their lives among themselves; like those in the scene from *Irish Bulls* just quoted, the peasants in the novels are always observed by an Anglo-Irish witness, either a landlord or a gentleman travelling about the country.[2] The primary purpose of the Irish tales was always to show as much and no more than the Edgeworths could vouch for in life.

Authentic detail in the style of *Irish Bulls* was later to prove the most influential characteristic of the Irish tales, but, especially after *Castle Rackrent*, Maria was nearly as much bent on improving Ireland's image with the English public as on serving the abstract interests of truth. Since one of her most persistent aims was to predispose the English in her country's favour, she evolved a stereotype of the Irish character, fallible, but loyal and warmhearted. 'Little Dominick', 'The Irish Mendicant', and 'The Irish Incognito', short stories introduced as *exempla* of the argument of *Irish Bulls*, all centre on these

[1] *Memoirs of RLE*, ii. 338.

[2] Typical conversations are for example Lord Colambre's in *The Absentee* with the postilion Larry about evasions of the law (ch. 10; x. 184ff.), and Michael Dunne's confession in *Ormond*: the original of the latter speech was repeated to RLE and written down by him. See above, p. 281 n.

lovable Edgeworthian Irishmen who are in fact the prototypes for Maria's later studies of their race.[1]

*Irish Bulls* therefore shows how on reflection the Edgeworths thought Ireland ought to be presented. As scientists they wanted to document details of speech and custom as they really were; perhaps incompatibly, they also wanted to dispose the English reader in Ireland's favour. Furthermore, there was the whole range of Edgeworth's political opinions about Ireland, which Maria had not yet found a way of conveying to the public; these views were in a sense very English and non-nationalistic, to do with expanding industry, reforming agriculture, and so giving Irishmen a standard of life which equalled that of their English opposite numbers. Although not explicitly political at all, *Irish Bulls* has the detached viewpoint and the forward-looking policies of the later Irish tales, rather than the apparent nostalgia of *Castle Rackrent*. A typical feature is that the authors not only introduce English ideas, but actually speak of themselves as English—'We were neither *born nor bred* in Ireland';[2] furthermore, warned off perhaps by Thady, they speak of Ireland's past with some disrespect. 'We are more interested in the present race of its inhabitants than in the historian of St. Patrick, St. Facharis, St. Cormuc; the renowned Brien Boru . . . or even the great William of Ogham; and by this declaration we have no fear of giving offence to any but rusty antiquaries.'[3]

Irish traditions meant to the Edgeworths the survival of irrational and inefficient habits: they thought that extensive education among all classes was the best remedy for tradition.[4]

[1] The characteristic is most marked in Irishmen who appear incidentally in tales and novels set in England, e.g. O'Brien in *Patronage*, and O'Neill in *The Limerick Gloves* (*Popular Tales*). Standardization in characterizing low-life characters like these is also linked to ME's interest in documenting the speech and manners of their class, which has a way of limiting individuality (see above, pp. 335–6). Middlemen are regularly as grasping as peasants are careless and lovable. But ME's high-life Irish characters, though still warm-hearted, are more varied—e.g. Lady Geraldine in *Ennui* (see below, p. 371) and Ulick and Corny in *Ormond* (see below, pp. 382 ff.).

[2] Conclusion, *Irish Bulls*, i. 247.

[3] Ibid., i. 248. Cf. also ch. 11; i. 200.

[4] ME has come under heavy fire for this opinion from Irish nationalists (see below, p. 389). The problem of maintaining ancient cultural traditions while trying to modernize a country is an extremely difficult one, and no doubt the Edgeworths' solution was a brutal simplification. Whether any alternative is more likely to succeed is still open to question.

*Castle Rackrent* had contained antiquarian material in its Glossary; the Edgeworths had been mildly interested in it in the past (as when Edgeworth constructed his moose's skeleton for Edmund Burke), and Dr. Beaufort was more actively so. Within a few years Lady Morgan was to draw extensively on remote Gaelic memories for her first successful novel, *The Wild Irish Girl* (1806), and Scott of course had profounder ideas about the past as a determining influence on the present. But with *Irish Bulls* the Edgeworths turned their back on this vein. Historical novels, as Edgeworth afterwards declared, gave 'to truth all the disadvantages of fiction'.[1]

The faults of *Ennui*, Maria's next Irish tale, are so glaring that few modern critics have bothered to give it a second glance. It has a most improbable plot, in which the hero turns out not to be the man he thinks he is, the wealthy Earl of Glenthorn, but a peasant's son who was changed at nurse. Even worse, he regains the very same estate that he has just lost, by meeting, wooing, and winning the girl who happens to be heir-at-law. The earlier part of the tale, while not quite so implausible, is didactic and tiresomely repetitive. A sequence of episodes is designed not to forward the action but merely to repeat the same point, that Lord Glenthorn is too shallow and ill informed to be capable of escaping ennui for long.[2]

In spite of these faults, *Ennui* is perhaps the best of Maria's Irish tales except *Ormond*. Its historical importance is greater than *Ormond*'s, and for that matter *Castle Rackrent*'s too. It helped to inaugurate a new style of sociological realism, not just by chance but because it made subtle and valid points about society and social relationships. The reason that its quality has escaped attention is that the merits of the book are virtually confined to the central chapters, in which the hero goes to live in Ireland.

Lord Glenthorn is Irish-born, but he has spent most of his childhood, youth, and early manhood in England; he returns to his Irish estate only in his mid twenties, and as a stranger. At this time he is a sick man. He is recovering from a serious head injury, and he is apparently subject to periodic bouts of

[1] RLE to Étienne Dumont, n.d., *Dublin Rev.* cxlv, 1909, 244.

[2] See above, p. 331.

neurotic depression, which Maria merely describes as 'ennui'. In many of these details Glenthorn resembles Maria herself on her return at the age of fourteen to Ireland, when she was convalescing after her serious eye trouble, and still under the shadow of her disturbed childhood and adolescence.[1] In describing Glenthorn's responses she draws on her own memories of 1782, and gives by far her most sensitive account of the impression Ireland makes upon a stranger.

Glenthorn's first journey across Ireland introduces him to the expedients of a few more backward people than he has ever known;

> From the inn yard came a hackney chaise, in a most deplorable crazy state; the body mounted up to a prodigious height, on unbending springs, nodding forwards, one door swinging open, three blinds up, because they could not be let down, the perch tied in two places, the iron of the wheels half off, half loose, wooden pegs for linchpins, and ropes for harness. The horses were worthy of the harness; wretched little dog-tired creatures, that looked as if they had been driven to the last gasp, and as if they had never been rubbed down in their lives; their bones starting through their skin; one lame, the other blind; one with a raw back, the other with a galled breast; one with his neck poking down over his collar, and the other with his head dragged forward by a bit of broken bridle, held at arms length by a man dressed like a mad beggar, in half a hat and half a wig, both awry in opposite directions; a long tattered great-coat, tied round his waist by a hay-rope: the jagged rents in the skirts of his coat showing his bare legs marbled of many colours; while something like stockings hung loose about his ankles. The noises he made, by way of threatening or encouraging his steeds, I pretend not to describe . . . Then seizing his whip and reins in one hand, he clawed up his stockings with the other: so with one easy step he got into his place, and seated himself, coachman-like, upon a well-worn bar of wood, that served as a coachbox . . .
>
> In vain the Englishman in monotonous anger, and the Frenchman in every note of the gamut, abused Paddy: necessity and wit were on Paddy's side; he parried all that was said against his chaise, his horses, himself, and his country, with invincible comic dexterity, till at last, both his adversaries, dumbfounded, clambered into the vehicle, where they were instantly shut up in straw and darkness. Paddy, in a triumphant tone, called to *my* postilions, bidding them 'get on, and not be stopping the way any longer'.

[1] See above, pp. 81 ff.

Without uttering a syllable, they drove on: but they could not, nor could I, refrain from looking back to see how those fellows would manage. We saw the forehorses make towards the right, then to the left, and every way but straight forwards; whilst Paddy bawled to Hosey—'Keep the middle of the road, can't ye? I don't want ye to draw a pound at-all-at-all'.

At last, by dint of whipping, the four horses were compelled to set off in a lame gallop; but they stopped short at a hill near the end of the town, whilst a shouting troop of ragged boys followed, and pushed them fairly to the top. Half an hour afterwards, as we were putting on our drag-chain to go down another steep hill,—to my utter astonishment, Paddy, with his horses in full gallop, came rattling and *chehupping* past us. My people called to warn him that he had no *drag*: but still he cried 'Never fear!' and shaking the long reins, and stamping with his foot, on he went thundering down the hill. My Englishmen were aghast.

'The turn yonder below, at the bottom of the hill, is as sharp and ugly as ever I see,' said my postilion, after a moment's stupified silence. 'He will break their necks, as sure as my name is John.'

Quite the contrary: when we had dragged and undragged, and came up with Paddy, we found him safe on his legs, mending some of his tackle very quietly.

'If that breeching had broke as you were going down the steep hill,' said I, 'it would have been all over with you, Paddy.'

'That's true, plase you honour: but it never happened me going down hill—nor never will, by the blessing of God, if I've any luck.'[1]

This *tour de force* clearly comes straight from life; part of it, as we know, from Humphry Davy in 1806, although part seems already to have been in existence before Maria heard his reminiscences on that occasion.[2] Glenthorn's arrival at his ancestral home is in another style, one which looks forward to the atmosphere of Scott's novels rather than to any other piece of writing by Maria. As he penetrates deeper into a more primitive part of Ireland, Glenthorn has been unable to find a good inn, or even a change of horses, and he decides to travel on into the night towards his castle. The road stretches ahead in the moonlight along the edge of the sea. Glenthorn's weariness, and the forlornness of the countryside, and the silence of

[1] *Ennui*, ch. 6; vii. 50–4.

[2] See above, p. 247. There is enough room for doubt about the date of SR's letter praising this passage (referred to above, p. 237) to leave a possibility that Davy did supply the entire matter for this episode, as Byron obviously believed.

the carriage wheels on the sand, are all details which contribute to an exotic effect of foreignness in the place, like Scott at his best. The travellers come upon the castle quite suddenly. After the silence of the sand, the coach wheels are rumbling over a wooden drawbridge, and in the courtyard beyond they are met by a confusion of lights and noises, 'the strange and eager voices of the people'. Nothing could convey more forcefully than this night and the following days that Glenthorn is a total stranger in Ireland.

His bemused meetings with the peasantry have been quoted in connection with Maria Edgeworth's own early reactions to her father's estate.[1] Glenthorn's whole experience as a landlord is in fact based on Edgeworthstown in the 1780s and 1790s. Not that he knows enough to be a model progressive landlord, as Edgeworth tried to be. But he has an instructor, his agent M'Leod, who is a student of Adam Smith. M'Leod does his best to instil progressive ideas into Glenthorn, for example urging him not to give indiscriminate charity to the unfortunate, but to encourage the industrious and thrifty. M'Leod believes in short leases, which enable the landlord to retain control over his estate, financial incentives to encourage efficiency, and the abolition of feudal rights and duties. Without any visible sign of success, he tries to explain to his employer the wider concepts of the free market and the division of labour. He also shows him round the non-denominational village school which he and Mrs. M'Leod have established in the belief that an ignorant peasantry cannot prosper in competition with more modern communities. M'Leod's advice to Glenthorn provides the fullest statement given in the Irish tales of how the Edgeworths thought a good landlord should behave.

Almost all the detail about the estate is drawn with peculiar immediacy from Maria Edgeworth's own observation.[2] The story is set in 1798, the year of the Rebellion, and some of Glenthorn's experiences are a thinly disguised rendering of Edgeworth's own difficulties at the hands of the Protestant bigots in County Longford.[3] For example, Glenthorn becomes estranged from his Protestant fellow magistrates when he re-

[1] See above, pp. 88–9.

[2] i.e. unlike most of the detail in *Castle Rackrent*. See above, pp. 240–3.

[3] See above, pp. 136 ff.

fuses to condone Orange brutality and illegal repression. Afterwards he is pelted by an Orange mob in a near-by town, as Edgeworth was, and appears at the time to be in danger of his life.

At this point Maria leaves her documentary evidence and takes off in a wild flight of romance, one of those leaps from observed fact to literary cliché for which her contemporaries have been quoted taking her to task.[1] The rebels plan to kidnap Glenthorn in order to force him to join them, but he learns about the plot and succeeds in capturing the entire rebel gang. Glenthorn's public proof of his loyalty is so much more glorious than Edgeworth's efforts to clear his name in 1798 that this climax may have been irresistible for Maria; a less devoted daughter, or more dedicated artist, might have considered that what really did happen in County Longford—Edgeworth's bitter demands for an inquiry, his failure to get a clear verdict in court, and his final decision to meet his neighbours half-way—is probably as near as real life usually gets to a happy ending.

Elsewhere, free from filial piety, *Ennui* gives a beautifully observed study of the difficulties of an Irish landowner. The subtlest of the topics dealt with is Glenthorn's relationship with his tenants, or rather his failure to establish a satisfactory relationship, even with the nurse, Ellinor. Before he discovers that she is in reality his mother, Glenthorn is grateful to Ellinor for her devotion to him, and he decides to give her a splendid present. His choice, as misguided as all his benevolent attempts, is a pretty cottage in the English style. At last, after many delays and frustrations, the little house is built and painted and papered to his satisfaction, a charming contrast to the squalid hovel in which Ellinor has lived all her life. The result is foreseeable:

> Her ornamented farm-house became, in a wonderfully short time, a scene of dirt, rubbish, and confusion. There was a partition between two rooms, which had been built with turf or peat, instead of bricks, by the wise economy I had employed. Of course, this was pulled down to get at the turf. The stairs also were pulled down and burned, though there was no scarcity of firing. As the walls were plastered and papered before they were quite dry, the paper

[1] See above, pp. 347–9.

grew mouldy, and the plaster fell off . . . Some of the slates were blown off one windy night: the slater lived at ten miles distance, and before the slates were replaced, the rain came in, and Ellinor was forced to make a bedchamber of the parlour, and then of the kitchen, retreating from corner to corner as the rain pursued, till, at last, when 'it *would* come *every way* upon her bed', she petitioned me to let her take the slates off and thatch the house; for a slated house, she said, was never so warm as a *tatched cabin*; and as there was no smoke, she was *kilt* with the *cowld.*

In my life I never felt so angry . . . In a paroxysm of passion, I reproached Ellinor with being a savage, an Irishwoman, and an ungrateful fool. 'Savage I am, for anything I know; and *fool* I am, that's certain; but ungrateful I am not', said she, bursting into tears. She went home and took herself to her bed; and the next thing I heard from her son was, 'that she was *lying in the rheumatism*, which had kept her awake many a long night, before she would come to complain to my honour of the house, in dread that I should blame myself for *sending of* her into it *afore* it was dry'. The rheumatism reconciled me immediately to Ellinor; I let her take her own way, and thatch the house, and have as much smoke as she pleased, and she recovered. But I did not entirely recover my desire to do good to my poor tenants.[1]

Ellinor's original effort to do good to Glenthorn turns out even worse. She never meant him to know he was not her foster son but her real son, whom she exchanged as a baby with the sickly little heir. She is surprised into telling him the truth when she thinks that Ody, another of her sons, is among the rebels whom Glenthorn is about to commit to prison. When she learns that Ody is after all not involved, she assumes that Glenthorn will simply keep the secret as she has always done. She cannot understand the English moral code which forces him to give up the whole inheritance to his foster-brother, who is now a blacksmith. Ellinor's own morality is not so impersonal; she recognizes obligations only to the nearest of those around her. Her disapproval of her son's determination to make the truth known is so intense that when she finds she cannot alter it she wills herself to die. The stubborn interviews between the two reveal the impassable barriers between an upper-class Englishman and a peasant Irishwoman, whatever their blood relationship. Ellinor is something rare and perhaps new as yet

[1] *Ennui*, ch. 8; vii. 91–3.

in literature, a peasant character who is treated with respect. Instead of laughing at her or patronizing her, Maria accepts that hers are the attitudes of a woman of her race and class. There is no attempt at a sentimental deathbed reconciliation. In *Ennui*, for perhaps the first time in any novel, personal relationships are shown entirely mastered by social circumstances. The mother and son are able to love one another, on Ellinor's side with an extraordinary self-effacing devotion; but her sacrifice of her child as a baby means that he is brought up in a different class and culture, so that, whether he knows he is her son or not, they can never speak to one another with real understanding.

At home on his estate Glenthorn faces one by one the problems of an Anglo-Irish landlord among a native Irish peasantry. The other side of his existence as an Anglo-Irishman is his social life among his equals. At the neighbouring great house of Sir Harry Ormsby he meets and falls in love with the lively, distinctively Irish Lady Geraldine:

> She looked, spoke, and acted, like a person privileged to think, say, and do, what she pleased. Her raillery, like the raillery of princes, was without fear of retort. She was not ill-natured, yet careless to whom she gave offence, provided she produced amusement; and in this she seldom failed; for, in her conversation, there was much of the raciness of Irish wit, and the oddity of Irish humour.[1]

Maria uses Lady Geraldine's wit and knowledge of Ireland as a tool to give the reader an outspoken commentary on a succession of upper-class Irish types. The lacklustre hero is not in the nature of things lively enough to pass judgements on the people he meets at Ormsby Villa, but Lady Geraldine can do it for him. She employs her frank tongue at the expense of the corrupt Dublin politician, Lord O'Toole, the 'fast' English tourists, Mrs. Norton and Lady Hauton (who are figures of more consequences in provincial Ireland than they are at home), and the would-be author of a book on Ireland, Lord Craiglethorpe.

This last portrait is sailing nearer the wind of personal caricature than Maria usually allowed herself to go. She and her father had recently reviewed John Carr's *Stranger in Ireland*

[1] Ibid., ch. 9; vii. 100.

(1806).[1] They had found it 'a book of stale jests', trivial and anecdotal, and useless by comparison with the only fit model for such a 'Tour', which was Arthur Young's serious analysis of the Irish economy. The fatuous Lord Craiglethorpe, going from one country house to another with his notebook at the ready, is just such an author as John Carr. Lady Geraldine mocks him to the company by supplying him 'with the most absurd anecdotes, incredible *facts*, stale jests, and blunders, such as were never made by true-born Irish-man'.[2]

Afterwards Glenthorn travels round Ireland, and, although he does not have the impudence to write a book, he is a superficial tourist of the Craiglethorpe stamp. Needless to say, Maria is not interested in the picturesque qualities of the places he visits, having never been to them herself.[3] Lady Morgan, in *O'Donnel* (1814), sends a similar fashionable party to the Giant's Causeway, in order to introduce her native Irish hero against a suitable setting of barbaric grandeur. When Maria sets Glenthorn there she does not even write her own description of the scenery, but instead borrows (with acknowledgement) the account given by Dr. William Hamilton in his scholarly *Letters Concerning the Northern Coast of the County of Antrim* (1786).[4]

The point of making Glenthorn travel about is to show how inadequately he understands his own country. Glenthorn sees his deficiency clearly in retrospect:

As to the mode of living of the Irish, their domestic comforts or grievances, their habits and opinions, their increasing or decreasing ambition to better their condition, the proportion between the population and the quantity of land cultivated or capable of cultivation, the difference between the profits of the husbandman and the artificer, the relation between the nominal wages of labour and the actual command over the necessaries of life:—these were questions wholly foreign to my thoughts, and, at this period of my life, absolutely beyond the range of my understanding. I had travelled through my own country without making even a single

[1] *Ed. Rev.*, x, 1807.

[2] *Ennui*, ch. 9; vii. 109–10.

[3] See above, p. 215.

[4] *Ennui*, ch. 13; vii. 165. In the same chapter she uses a guide-book account (quoted as a footnote) of a stag-hunt on Lake Killarney, rather than make her hero describe it in the text. For ME's distaste at this period for writing about scenery, see above, p. 143.

remark upon the various degrees of industry and civilization visible in different parts of the kingdom. In fact, it never occurred to me . . . that political economy was a study requisite or suitable to my rank in life or situation in society. Satisfied with having seen all that is worth seeing in Ireland, the Giants' Causeway, and the Lake of Killarney, I was now impatient to return to England.[1]

It has been Lady Geraldine's function to show Glenthorn what an Irish gentleman should be, just as it is M'Leod's to try to teach him to be a landlord. Lady Geraldine's mother manœuvres to get him to propose and eventually he summons up enough energy; but Geraldine refuses him. As the arbiter of gentlemanliness, she is not satisfied that his rank makes Glenthorn a somebody: 'For, do you know, I think somebody is nobody.'

Her view, and M'Leod's, is that a landowner has a specific social and economic role which it takes education to play. During the greater part of the action, Glenthorn is too ignorant to be effective in Irish society, even with benevolent intentions. This is why he can make no lasting progress while he remains an earl. The sudden loss of his title, or rather the impoverishment which accompanies it, forces him to get a professional training as a lawyer. Once he has acquired the necessary education, and demonstrated his ability to advance by his own efforts, he becomes for the first time fit to play his part as a gentleman. The end, which is apt to read like conventional romance, is intended to show how a man's personal salvation is bound up in his actions as a member of society.

Granted that Glenthorn's moral progress from selfish private man to social man is not handled successfully throughout, its presence in *Ennui* is a reason for claiming this tale as one of Maria's most interesting. The life of the landlord is realized in fiction for the first time, and his working relationships with tenants, employees, and neighbours are handled with freshness and truth. At its most convincing Glenthorn's experience is based on Edgeworth's; not merely the detail of administering the estate at Edgeworthstown, but the whole ideal of social utility which Edgeworth had learnt from the Lunar generation. The scheme of *Ennui* is to show Glenthorn how his society works from top to bottom, so that he can earn by enterprise the place

[1] *Ennui*, ch. 14; vii. 170–1.

he once merely inherited, as in a true sense a leader of the community. Glenthorn's road to salvation was laid down in the naïve and heroic era of eighteenth-century economic expansion; whether or not his moral insights were to provide an acceptable code for the later nineteenth and twentieth centuries, it is fair to say that in the Irish context of 1805 technical knowledge and a sense of responsibility were relevant enough themes to preach to the gentry.

*The Absentee* is nowadays probably better known and more admired than any other tale by Maria Edgeworth except *Castle Rackrent*. It has twice been reprinted this century, presumably for its witty, caustic opening chapters featuring the Clonbrony family in London. The demoralized Lord Clonbrony, the social climber, Lady Clonbrony, and the ladies of the *ton* who secretly laugh at her, form a memorable, indeed an excellent, group. This sequence, in Maria's most brilliant comic manner, is consistently well written, and technically sophisticated. Lady Clonbrony's crowded party is established with all the freedom and flexibility of the cinema; the reader joins first one group and then another, or follows Lady Clonbrony about the room, or eavesdrops on the interior monologue of her son, Lord Colambre, who is an indignant observer of the scene. Lady Clonbrony's protestations about her English birth—or, later, the summary of her opinions about love and marriage—are worthy of Maria's successor in the art of feminine character study, Jane Austen.

As a comedy of manners, the opening sequence of *The Absentee* is as good as anything Maria Edgeworth wrote. It is amusing, perceptive, and sophisticated, the manner she had perfected earlier at its best. Essentially, though, it is directed at a few individual characters rather than at their wider social context, which is, or in the author's view ought to be, Ireland.

The literary merits of *The Absentee* are mostly confined to these first scenes in England. It is *Ennui* in reverse, in that once the hero sets foot in his native country most of Maria Edgeworth's vitality seems to leave her. The two worst sequences in the Irish parts of *The Absentee* were adapted (hastily, as we know) from the play for children of the same name. Parts of Colambre's arrival in Ireland must have been specially written in 1812 to fuse the two blocks of material together, and some of the minor characters and speeches which were added later are lively enough.[1] But Colambre's visits to the two parts of his father's estate, which obviously come from the drama, are among the few insipid pages which Maria Edgeworth wrote about Ireland. Like *Rosanna* (one of the *Popular Tales*) and *The Rose, the Thistle and the Shamrock* (*Comic Dramas*), they are sentimental idylls out of key with Maria Edgeworth's best manner when describing the peasantry, which is based on observation from life.

The concluding section of *The Absentee* is almost exclusively taken up with disentangling a sub-plot about the good name of the heroine's mother. It is not relevant to the theme of absenteeism, and indeed can scarcely be made intelligible without reference to *Patronage*.[2] As a whole, therefore, *The Absentee* is very uneven, and in its treatment of Ireland is by far the least successful of Maria Edgeworth's four Irish tales. Yet it was probably the most influential of them all, and Maria Edgeworth herself preferred it to the others. Why?

The answer is that with *The Absentee* she produced the first 'national' novel that was fully recognizable as such; she stumbled apparently by chance on a number of techniques that moved the centre of interest decisively from the hero to his environment. It has been objected that Colambre's character does not develop, since he is virtuous to start with. But this is clearly a willing sacrifice of interest on the part of the author; she wants to make sure that Colambre is acceptable to the reader as a reliable witness of Irish life. In *The Absentee* the personal drama and action of *Ennui* are exchanged for devices which enable the author to present her own view of Ireland with authority. She makes Colambre detached enough to appreciate the degradation of his parents in London, and well enough informed to assign it to its proper cause, their neglect of their function as Irish landowners.

As a visitor to Ireland, Colambre has what Glenthorn lacks, an educated eye. On arrival in Dublin he makes friends with

[1] The full story of the writing of *The Absentee* is given above, pp. 276–7. For Larry the postilion's letter, which was added at the last moment to end the tale, see above, p. 285.

[2] See above, p. 332.

a soldier, Sir James Brooke, who supplies him with an enlightened reading-list about contemporary Ireland. At the top of the list is the book Craiglethorpe should have been trying to imitate, Arthur Young's *Tour in Ireland.* Young was not of course a tourist at all, but a celebrated agricultural economist, whose 'tour' gathers facts on such subjects as the soil, the face of the country, climate, rental, products, tenantry, the labouring poor, food, clothing, habitation, livestock, emigration, religion, the price of provisions, roads, tithes, absentees, population, manners and customs, the corn trade, manufactures, revenue—and so on, in what amounts to a general survey of the topography and economy of Ireland. Brooke also recommends the survey of Ireland by Edgeworth's father-in-law, D. A. Beaufort, whose *Memoir to a Map of Ireland* sets out a comparable mass of information which the author collected while studying the country region by region for the purposes of making his map.[1]

A reading-list for a study of Irish sociology and economy is no way to establish the country imaginatively—'vile cold-hearted trash in a novel' was what John Ward called it.[2] The intellectual justification is given by Brooke, who says that a visitor must have an authoritative context into which he can fit his own observations, or he will be unable to discriminate between the typical and the unique. Colambre's picture of Ireland is bound to be rich in first-hand evidence, and after he has taken Brooke's advice he will also be able to judge how far his observations represent the country as a whole.

To translate Arthur Young's survey into fiction is an unusual enterprise for a novelist. Most readers will find that Maria falls between two stools, producing a work that is too impressionistic by comparison with its models, and far too literal for a novel. Certainly the principles of relevance in the Irish scenes of *The Absentee* have little to do with the plot, but refer back to the remarks Maria gave Brooke in the sixth chapter. Each

[1] ME might have made Brooke add a third work, Edward Wakefield's *An Account of Ireland, Statistical and Political*, 2 vols., 1812, on which Edgeworth co-operated. Maria actually helped to correct Wakefield's book in Feb. 1812, as she was writing *The Absentee*. But she did not think much of Wakefield—'Such a scrawl!—such style—and so little in the 100 pages of description I have read that I am quite in despair' (ME to CSE, Feb. 1812).

[2] See above, p. 271.

episode in Ireland contains a degree of documentation that links it very closely with real life. Within the limits of fiction they create when taken together a serious (if optimistic) study of Irish society as a whole.

Beginning in Dublin, Colambre sees something for himself of the buildings and architecture, and Brooke sketches in for him an account of polite social life since the Union.[1] The most important class to meet in the city are the trades-people. Colambre studies their financial practices, and gets a more entertaining view of their social moves when the 'grocer's lady', Mrs. Raffarty, invites him to dine at her villa:

> At length one course was fairly got through, and after a torturing half hour, the second course appeared, and James Kenny was intent upon one thing, and Lanty upon another, so that the wine-sauce for the hare was spilt by their collision; but, what was worse, there seemed little chance that the whole of this second course should ever be placed altogether rightly upon the table. Mrs Raffarty cleared her throat, and nodded, and pointed, and sighed, and set Lanty after Kenny, and Kenny after Lanty; for what one did, the other undid; and at last the lady's anger kindled, and she spoke: 'Kenny! James Kenny! set the seacale at this corner, and put down the grass cross-corners; and match your macaroni yonder with *them* puddens, set—Ogh! James! the pyramid in the middle, can't ye?'
>
> The pyramid, in changing places, was overturned. Then it was that the mistress of the feast, falling back in her seat, and lifting up her hands and eyes in despair, ejaculated, 'Oh, James! James!'
>
> The pyramid was raised by the assistance of the military engineers, and stood trembling again on its base; but the lady's temper could not be so easily restored to its equilibrium. She vented her ill-humour on her unfortunate husband, who happening not to hear her order to help my lord to some hare, she exclaimed loud, that all the world might hear, 'Corny Dempsy! Corny Dempsy! you're no more *gud* at the *fut* of my table than a stick of celery!'[2]

Poor Mrs. Raffarty, with her classical villa half demolished and restored in the picturesque style, is as near to a comic *tour de force* as anything in the Irish scenes of *The Absentee*; but she is good only in a particular way. Like the irrepressible

[1] Recently seen by ME at first hand; see above, p. 216.

[2] *The Absentee*, ch. 6; x. 120–1. The last sentence of this quotation does not appear in the first edition. It was added to the fifth edition of 1818.

coach-driver in *Ennui*, she has the vitality which must have belonged to an original in real life; in common with so many of Maria's incidental character sketches, she is never made to realize her potential as a character in a novel.[1]

Having learnt something of Dublin, Colambre now ventures out of the capital into the countryside. At first, he has the worst possible guide for a man who wishes to form an unprejudiced picture of Irish life. He has fallen in with an English tourist in Ireland, a fashionable woman called Lady Dashfort, who is highborn, arrogant, and daring. This lady has an ulterior motive for wishing Colambre to take home an unfavourable impression of Ireland—she wants him to marry her daughter, and settle in England. So she introduces him to Killpatrickstown, a Castle Rackrent which has in spite of everything survived into the nineteenth century. There Colambre sees the Gaelic tradition of unlimited hospitality carried to lengths which are ruining a titled family. The tenants on the estate owe their places not to industry but to old possession and personal ties with the family. Far from commending them as so many Thadys for their loyalty, Maria briskly describes their attitude to 'the family' as servility and flattery.

It is necessary for Colambre to see Killpatrickstown, since such estates still exist. But to claim, as Lady Dashfort does, that all Ireland is like this would be repeating the imputation that *Castle Rackrent* is a fair picture of the country in the first decade of the nineteenth century. From two other members of the local aristocracy Colambre learns a more favourable and, Maria claims, balanced impression of the Irish landed gentry. He meets the Catholic soldier and antiquarian, Count O'Halloran[2] (the only example in Maria Edgeworth's fiction of an Irish Catholic whom Englishmen think of as a gentleman), and

[1] Mrs. Raffarty's character is not entirely without structural significance: she is a counterpart for Lady Clonbrony in middle life, while Lady Dashfort, as an upper-class Englishwoman in Ireland, is Lady Clonbrony's mirror image. But little or nothing is done to develop these resemblances after the characters are first introduced.

[2] O'Halloran probably derives at least in part from Lord Trimleston, a Roman Catholic who kept a similarly exotic household. This peer gave medical treatment to RLE's mother, after she was partially paralysed, about the year 1754. There were few other aristocratic Catholic families within the Edgeworths' circle of acquaintance.

Lady Oranmore, an idealized representative of the Anglo-Irish aristocracy.

With his household full of strange pets, curios, books, and antiquities, O'Halloran promises well enough, but he has little to do except be a credit to his class and religion. He is there for the same reason as Lady Oranmore—because Maria's scheme dictates it. She goes on over-organizing Colambre's tour for the same reason. He comes to his father's property, which, conveniently, is divided into two parts: one is a model estate, very like Edgeworthstown, the other an example of the deplorable difference an unscrupulous agent could make to the rentroll of a property and the living standards of its tenants.

The heart of what Maria has to say about Ireland is, as always, the relationship between landlords and the peasantry. Because of Lord Clonbrony's absenteeism, there is no landlord in this case, but an agent. First Colambre is given a chance to study a good agent in Mr. Burke, who is in charge of the Colambre estate. Like M'Leod in *Ennui*, Burke runs a school and does his best to train the tenantry in the proper skills of their trades. The Garraghty brothers, extortioners who are rack-renting the Clonbrony estate, are on the other hand typical of the middlemen the Edgeworths were more familiar with in Co. Longford. Colambre disguises himself as a mining engineer and so is able to observe at his leisure the way the entire estate is administered in his father's absence.

The intellectual virtue of *The Absentee* thus consists in its ability to place the individual in his class context. The London scenes establish the individuals, the Clonbronys, who have misguidedly removed themselves from their proper place. The Irish scenes sketch their society, Ireland, in such a way that the functions and duties of the landlord are made clear. Among all Maria Edgeworth's tales, *The Absentee* was in its day probably the most influential. The very obtrusiveness of the scheme by which it is organized probably drew attention to its interest as sociology, as the new 'national' novel. The subtler and more complex *Ennui* might at first be read as the personal drama of a redeemed rake, and so not given full credit for its sociological insight; although after *The Absentee* appeared the similarity of the themes was obvious to Maria's reviewers.

The fault of *The Absentee*, at least while the hero is in Ireland, lies in the obvious subordination of the characters and the action to the over-all aim of making a representative picture of the country. Even worse, Maria seems to have been determined this time to present Ireland favourably. There are too many 'good' characters—O'Halloran, Lady Oranmore, Burke, the widow O'Neil—whose function seems to be to make up for every Rackrent, Jason Quirk, and idle tenant in the Edgeworthian canon to date.[1] The sense of responsibility that emanates from the Irish part of *The Absentee* is overwhelming. It is clearly significant that in the Irish parts of her book Maria Edgeworth drew heavily on the help of one of her principal authorities, D. A. Beaufort himself:

> The tide of gratitude has just rushed over my mind, and while it flows full and strong let me pour it out to you in thanks for the kind sympathy, for the valuable counsel you gave me when I was meditating the character of the good and bad agents in *The Absentee*. If you approve them thank yourself for it—I hope Count O'Halloran and the animals show you that they are all much the better for your reforming sympathy backwards and forwards with magical activity and alacrity from broadwheeled waggons to Count O'Halloran Major Benson Captain Williamson *&c*. . . .[2]

Prompted more than anything else perhaps by Dumont's sociological interest in Ireland, she has virtually abandoned characters for ideas. *The Absentee* belongs to the short phase in her career when she is overinvolved with abstractions, which is why it is less good as a novel about Ireland than either *Ennui* or *Ormond*, the last of the Irish tales.

*Ormond* has the virtues of its two predecessors, but it is a better novel than either. The tales written between about 1809 and 1813 showed Maria trying, seldom very successfully, to make fiction out of one of the main ideas of *Professional Education*, that character was formed decisively by early education; *Ormond* (1817) benefits from having been written as a concession to the opposite view, that a man could change for the better.[3]

[1] Burke in particular seems to have been meant to atone for the hostile portraits of middlemen in *Castle Rackrent* and *Ennui*. ME sent a message to a friend of her aunt's who had once blamed her for criticizing the Irish that she had now 'endeavoured to draw in *The Absentee* a good Irish agent' (ME to Mrs. R, 13 July 1812).

[2] ME to DAB, 29 June, 1812.

[3] See above, p. 222.

Harry Ormond succeeds in learning from his own experience in early adult life. The process by which his character is formed therefore becomes central to the action of the novel; and it is his character which is under scrutiny, not a single aspect of it. Writing her last tale but one, Maria at last knowingly makes a personal history rather than a vice the centre of interest. The title of *Ormond* was presumably chosen, as the title of *Helen* (1834) certainly was,[1] to emphasize that we are about to read the story of an individual, whereas *Ennui* and *The Absentee* belonged to a stricter and more didactic category. Harry Ormond is an orphan whose father has died, apparently penniless, in India. He has been brought up by an Irish friend of his father's, Sir Ulick O'Shane, and when the story begins he is an uneducated and naïve boy of about nineteen. In spite of many errors, he endears himself from the first to the other characters because he is good-natured and generous, and gradually he learns prudence and stability to fit him for his adult role in life. The character and development of Ormond is deliberately copied from Fielding's Tom Jones, although Maria's reading of Fielding is conditioned by early-nineteenth-century moral ideas, and feminine ones at that. She regards some of Tom's characteristics as unsuitable for imitation, particularly his weakness for women;[2] but she has borrowed the idea of a warm and lovable central character, who corrects his own shortcomings, and acts as a moral touchstone for the more calculating characters around him. Despite her good intentions over didacticism, Maria has included some priggish passages, and two priggish characters, one of whom happens to be the heroine. Nevertheless, *Ormond* has, for once, a consistent theme, which divides the interest between the hero and his environment, and can be sustained with reasonable continuity throughout the book.

The interest of the opening chapters lies in the contrast

[1] See below, pp. 458–9. The gradual change in ME's attitude to didacticism is dealt with more fully below, pp. 440 ff. The process began with the hostile reception of *Patronage* in 1814, and ME's greater willingness by this time to listen to advice from London. The Preface to *Harrington and Ormond* states categorically that in the case of Ormond 'the moral . . . does not immediately appear, for the author has taken peculiar care that it should not obtrude itself upon the reader'.

[2] On moral grounds ME excluded *Tom Jones* from a book-list she drew up for Irish secondary schools in 1815.

between the two men who successively act as guardians to Ormond, Ulick and Corny. They represent two types of Irishmen: Corny is a Catholic, who retains a virtually feudal hold over his native Irish peasantry, whereas Ulick, an Anglican for reasons of policy, is a sophisticated, worldly Anglo-Irish politician, more at home in Dublin than in the countryside.

Corny and Ulick are closely observed in terms of the roles they have chosen to play. Corny has the positive virtues of sincerity, self-reliance, and independence. But it is significant that his kingdom is an island. He is cut off socially from the rest of Ireland, and therefore from his equals. He is ignorant, in spite of his quaint learning from Gaelic tradition and from the classics. Certain forms of self-sufficiency—painstakingly making things himself when it would be cheaper to buy them, farming obstinately by the old methods—are not virtues to Maria, although Corny thinks they are, but manifestations of his ignorance. When Harry lives with Corny in the Black Islands, he scarcely has to call on his intellect. Hunting by day, carousing by night, flattered by the admiration of the common people, 'prince' Harry stagnates intellectually and morally.

Ulick, on the other hand, is eminently sociable. He lives in the company of his equals and superiors, as host to a succession of important or fashionable people. His aim in life is to manipulate everyone else to his own advantage. He makes his way by pleasing, and thus has no more personal integrity than he has a real stake in the countryside.

While Ormond lives in the Black Islands he has his first serious romantic adventure. Corny has a pretty daughter, Dora, with whom Ormond is soon boyishly in love. Dora is, however, tied to an engagement which illustrates the primitive code of honour of her father and his people. Before she was born Corny promised her in marriage to the eldest son of a *stalko*, a dispossessed gentleman of the old Irish stock. Her fiancé is 'White' Connal, a boorish, money-making farmer, or, as Corny puts it, 'the purse-proud grazier and mean man—not a remnant of a gentleman!' Luckily for Dora, 'White' Connal is killed in a hunting accident, whereupon she is automatically offered to his brother, 'Black' Connal. The new suitor, who like so many Irish Catholics has served in the French army, is as different as possible from the old; in

Ormond's eyes at least, he is a Frenchified fop. But Dora is encouraged by her aunt, Mlle O'Faley, who has also lived in France, to let the thought of life in Paris sweep her off her feet. In her three suitors (for Ormond as Corny's favourite would have made an obvious husband), Dora is confronted not only by three men but by three ways of life. Corny feels that he cannot break his word to old Connal, much as he would like to; but as it happens Dora, after flirting with Ormond, does not ask her father to break the contract. In marrying Black Connal, rather than Ormond, she makes a moral mistake, which amounts to rating lightness, or *légèreté*, as Connal complacently puts it, above Ormond's more genuine quality as a human being. The importance of Dora's quandary in the structure of the book is that it established the outlines of the moral landscape which also surrounds Ormond.

Corny dies in a hunting accident, and Ormond returns to the mainland to stay with a benevolent Anglican clergyman, Dr. Cambray,[1] under whose guidance his serious formal education now begins. But it is not long before Sir Ulick reappears to claim Ormond as his ward again, and we soon learn why—Ormond has come into a fortune after the death of his Indian stepmother. Ulick, as usual, is activated partly by real affection for his ward, partly by his politician's instinct to gain control over a rich young man and his money.

With Ulick to stage-manage him, Ormond now meets his own class, the wealthy Anglo-Irish. Unlike Glenthorn he is fresh, vigorous, and capable of discrimination. He dislikes both the malice and the languor that he finds in most of Ulick's guests; while in politics he learns to hate the arrogance and oppression of Orange bigots like Sir Ulick's son, Marcus, and the Evangelical Mrs. M'Crule. (For the sake of balancing the account, Maria gives Corny a drunken and bigoted priest for a confessor, Father Jos, who proves that partisan feeling in Irish life does not all come from the Protestant side; but, as usual in an Edgeworth novel, the worst villains on the Irish scene are to be found in the Protestant middle class.)

It is in coming to know the English-educated brother and sister Herbert and Florence Annaly that Ormond arrives at what is for Maria the heart of the matter, for they are the first

[1] For Dr. Cambray's connection with DAB, see above, pp. 140–1 and n.

Anglo-Irish to set him a standard he can admire. Corny, who loved his tenants, was nevertheless a tyrant who treated them like children. Ulick buys goodwill (and high rents) by favouring his people in the courts or turning a blind eye on their lawbreaking. In Maria's view the two land systems they stand for, the Gaelic of pre-Conquest days and the Anglo-Irish of the seventeenth and eighteenth centuries, are equally discredited, and it is only the rational, modern-minded Annaly who has either the will or the ability to improve the lot of the Irish as a whole. Whereas modern critics have called Maria's view of estate administration patronizing, she charged the primitive Corny with this offence; she believed that it was the landlord of the new type who treated the peasantry like rational beings. This therefore is Ormond's conclusion; he comes to appreciate Annaly's aims and to feel the limitations of both Corny and Ulick as landlords and gentlemen. At the same time he admires his English friend's family life, for in the Annaly household the domestic relationships are stable, formal, and mutually respectful,[1] a strong contrast with the warm-hearted confusion of the Black Islands. Not that the Annalys are meant to lack heart—but heart is an Irish characteristic, and Maria, associating it both with muddle and with partisanship, necessarily feels that justice should come first. In the cause of justice the Annalys intervene on behalf of a Catholic boy, Tommy Dunshaughlin, when Protestant bigots try to deny him a scholarship; as usual in the Irish context it is the Catholics who stand to gain most from the introduction of true judicial impartiality. Seeing all this, Ormond comes like Dora to regard the choice of a partner in marriage as a decision about a way of life; and thus he makes up his mind to marry Florence Annaly.

But there is another test in store for him first. So far the alternatives he has been faced with have been either the Irish way or the English. Then, as the result of a misunderstanding, Ormond comes to believe that Florence means to refuse him. He hurries impetuously abroad, and his destination is Paris, where Dora and her husband, Black Connal, are happy to receive him.

[1] This of course coincides with ME's perception of Edgeworthstown; the marked formality with which the family there treated one another was referred to above, p. 136.

The Paris Maria describes here is the dazzling society of just before the Revolution. It is Maria Edgeworth's most effective account yet of a crowded social panorama: the *mores* of the French fashionable world are shown to be hopelessly corrupt by English standards—far worse in sexual matters than the *mores* of Lady Delacour's circle—but this time she sketches in the corruption with sophistication and actually humour. When Ormond demands to know if there are any chaste women at Dora's crowded assembly, Mademoiselle O'Faley is at first confident that she can find him twenty:

'To begin with, there, do you see that woman standing up, who has the air as if she think of nothing at all, and nobody thinking of her, with only her husband near her, *cet grand homme blême*?—There is madame de la Rousse—*d'une réputation intacte*!—frightfully dressed, as she is always. But, hold, you see that pretty little comtesse de la Brie, all in white?—Charmante! I give her to you as a reputation against which slander cannot breathe—Nouvelle mariée—bride—in what you call de honeymoon; but we don't know that in French—no matter! Again, since you are curious in these things, there is another reputation without spot, madame de St. Ange, I warrant her to you—bien froide celle-là, cold as any English—married a full year, and still her choice to make;—allons, there is three I give you already, without counting my niece; and, wait, I will find you yet another', said mademoiselle, looking carefully through the crowd.

She was relieved from her difficulty by the entrance of the little abbé. . . .[1]

Ormond is greatly struck by Dora's beauty, which has bloomed with the addition of French elegance. He is also visited by an insidious form of temptation, that of finding himself accepted within the charmed circle of fashion. The French assume that he is, or will become, Dora's lover, and Ormond's heart is certainly touched by Dora; but still at the back of his mind and hers there are Anglo-Saxon inhibitions. Although both of them are influenced by the brilliance of Paris, as a principle they prefer English domestic stability to French volatility.

Ormond is not called upon to test his moral strength for too long. On learning that Ulick's bank is collapsing, he leaves

[1] *Ormond*, ch. 27; xiv. 266–7.

Paris at once for Ireland, and is in time to save most of his own fortune, although the bank fails. When he gets to Castle Hermitage he finds that Ulick is dead, whether naturally or by his own hand his servants will not reveal. Ulick's hurried secret burial is very different from Corny's splendid funeral earlier in the book, and Maria Edgeworth allows the common people to draw a last moral from the lives and deaths of the two men:

They compared him with King Corny, and 'see the difference!' said they: 'the one was the *true thing*, and never *changed*—and after all, where is the great friends now?—the quality that used to be entertaining at the castle above? . . . What is it come to? See, with all his wit, and the schemes upon schemes, broke and gone, and forsook and forgot, and buried without a funeral, or a tear, but from Master Harry.'[1]

Ormond too accepts the valuation of the ordinary Irish. He marries Florence and prepares to settle in Ireland, to be a very different kind of landlord from either Ulick or Corny. Either of their estates is available for him to buy; Ulick's is the better bargain, but Ormond remembers the bond of affection he had with the peasantry in Corny's Black Islands. In allowing the issue to be decided by the latter consideration, Ormond blends Irish warmth of heart, the common characteristic even of Ulick and Corny, with the cooler qualities he has adopted from the Annalys.

*Ormond* has the most interesting plot yet devised by Maria Edgeworth. Admittedly she does not handle the hero's progress to maturity with as much art as Jane Austen handled Emma's the year before; but Ormond's moral development has an original feature, in that it is not merely self-discovery, but a growth in his understanding of Ireland. The device of introducing Ormond as a natural, unthinking Irish boy, and turning him during the course of the action into an educated Englishman enables her to show Ireland with an intimacy she could not achieve in *Ennui* and *The Absentee*, where the narrators are both outsiders. At the same time it does not prevent her from introducing the high standard of moral discrimination which she associates with an English education. Corny's native Irish

[1] *Ormond*, ch. 31; xiv. 323.

world, in which the *stalko* maintains his threadbare pride by means of an outmoded code of honour, could have been penetrated only by a native Irish hero. Ulick's Anglo-Irish circle, reaching upwards to the Lord-Lieutenant and outwards into the middle classes, demands intelligent criticism by an Englishman. In making Ormond belong in both worlds, Maria has had to sacrifice the fresh response to Ireland that only an outsider like Glenthorn can experience; Ormond is almost unnaturally at home everywhere, so that he does not suffer from the frustrating failures in communication which are among the most lifelike sensations of *Ennui*. But for a view of Ireland that is both broad and intimate, the situation of the homeless, fatherless, Irish–English Ormond is much the most convenient vantage-point.

The heroes of *Ennui* and *The Absentee* were sent off to get to know Ireland with an embarrassing lack of literary tact. Ormond's search for a role takes him about more naturally, and enables him to see deeper. He gets nearer to the Irish peasantry than the two protagonists who have come over from England, and sees the two great sources of strife in Ireland, land and religion, from the viewpoint of both camps, since he is not so wholly committed to the landed Protestants as his predecessors.

What it is to be Irish is further clarified by contrast with the neighbouring alternatives. Ireland is provincial and often boorish. The point is established when the two half-French characters are introduced into the Black Islands. With her exact ear for the minutiae of speech, Maria Edgeworth is able to play with the dialogue of Mlle O'Faley and Black Connal. Both prefer to speak in polished French, which in the novel is carefully rendered in unexaggerated but sufficiently stilted English; but when Miss O'Faley has to speak English she utters a vulgar and often incorrect brogue that is comically at variance with her elegant French *persiflage*. The difference between her two idioms underlines the difference in the state of culture in France and Ireland, but it also suggests that when grafted on to Irish characters French civilization does not necessarily take root.

In fact, we get in *Ormond* an early and extended use of the 'international theme', which is employed effectively by many nineteenth-century artists,[1] and consummately by Henry James. Dora's wry story could easily have been used by James—indeed was, in *Portrait of a Lady*. Dora did not want the Irish Irishman, White Connal, or the English Irishman, Ormond, but preferred the Frenchified Black Connal, just as Isabel Archer preferred the Italianate American Gilbert Osmond. Both heroines are over-influenced by superficialities, taking the style to be the way of life, and both discover too late that their husbands' style hides a code of moral values which their own upbringing teaches them is corrupt. Dora ends like Isabel a prisoner, who is unwilling to leave her husband but cannot love him. Dora is not as subtly done as Isabel, and Ormond quite lacks the fine consciousness of a Ralph Touchett or Lambert Strether; but his sense of Paris as a moral and aesthetic entity, an alternative culture by which he might live, if he chose to do so, is an apprehension which foreshadows theirs.

The perception of places, or rather societies, as having a moral character which the hero must accept or reject is apparently an innovation of Maria Edgeworth's generation. Jane Austen had indeed already published *Emma*, and Maria Edgeworth had read it—or, rather, had begun it.[2] In *Emma* the characters inhabit at one and the same moment a natural landscape, and a clarified landscape of the moral consciousness. The Ireland which is shown in *Ormond* in this respect resembles Jane Austen's Highbury. Corny's 'kingdom', insular in every sense, and Ulick's far more elaborate Anglo-Irish world, with foundations as shallow as those of the Ascendancy itself, are simultaneously real and symbolic societies. They are contrasted with an aristocratic Paris that is seen as fatally artificial and isolated from the life of ordinary French people. Ormond has a better chance of happiness in Ireland because he has had experience of both sides of a community that is divided along lines of race and religion. Besides, Maria will not admit that the Irish situation is as hopeless as the French one shortly before the Revolution. Economic progress can do much; and she believes that the English, or Anglo-Irish, can bring it, through their respect for stability and their sense of social responsibility.

[1] Historical novelists use it in the first half of the nineteenth century: Scott, of course, and Bulwer Lytton in *The Last Days of Pompeii* (1834). But the extended contrast of national character and values is certainly rare so early.

[2] See below, p. 445.

*Ormond* is thus both more intellectually satisfying and less aesthetically flawed than the earlier Irish tales. It resembles them in ranging over Irish society as a whole, but for the first time successfully links the ambitious survey of a whole community with the moral development of an individual. For this reason—and despite the challenge offered by the individual and endearing *Castle Rackrent*—*Ormond* stands the test of re-reading better than any other of Maria Edgeworth's tales.

In spite of the sophistication of Maria Edgeworth's best studies of Ireland in fiction, she has had very little honour in her own country; most modern Irish critics have tended to approach her from a more or less dogmatic nationalist position, and have therefore found her defective. Stephen Gwynn, for example, condemns her because she is not 'in full national sympathy with Ireland or even with Ireland's rights to be considered a nation'. He deplores her lack of respect for the native Irishman, whether gentleman or peasant. 'The limitations of Maria Edgeworth as an Irish novelist are the limitations of her power to apprehend what Thady Quirk [*sic*] really stood for and signified.'[1] Padraic Colum compares her very unfavourably with Turgenev:

> To Maria Edgeworth the Clonbroneys [*sic*] are absentees from their property and their province; to Turgenev such people are absentees from their station and their country. Their country! How intensely Ivan Turgenev thinks of Russia, its language, and its culture. Maria Edgeworth is lukewarm about such ideas. She belongs to the settlers in Ireland, and she has no notion what Irish culture could mean. It has never occurred to her that people might be more dignified if, instead of speaking with an Irish brogue, they spoke in the Irish language. And yet when she was writing the English language was foreign to the bulk of the Irish people. She is not prepared to lash the people in *The Absentee* because they are out of relation with the culture of their race. In *Ormond*, however, she shows a benevolent interest in 'the King of the Black Islands', that fine old man who prefers to live in accordance with the customs and traditions of an Irish noble of another day.[2]

It is ironic that Turgenev apparently took a different view

[1] *Irish Literature and Drama*, 1936, p. 54.

[2] Padraic Colum, 'Maria Edgeworth and Ivan Turgenev', *British Review*, xi, July 1915, 112–13.

of Maria Edgeworth's manner of handling the Irish peasant. According to an anonymous obituarist of Ivan Turgenev, it was the novelist's elder brother who, after visiting Abbotsford and meeting Maria Edgeworth, introduced him to her tales and to the idea of treating peasants sympathetically in fiction. The elder Turgenev concluded, claims the article, that

> Maria Edgeworth had struck on a vein which most of the great novelists of the future would exclusively work. She took the world as she found it and selected from it the materials that she thought would be interesting to write about, in a clear and natural style. It was Ivan Turguéneff himself who told me this, and he modestly said that he was an unconscious disciple of Miss Edgeworth in setting out on his literary career. He had not the advantage of knowing English. But as a youth he used to hear his brother translate to visitors at his country house in the Uralian hills passages from 'Irish Tales and Sketches', which he thought superior to her three-volume novels. Turguéneff also said to me, 'It is possible, nay probable, that if Maria Edgeworth had not written about the poor Irish of the co. Longford and the squires and squirees, that it would not have occurred to me to give a literary form to my impressions about the classes parallel to him [them] in Russia. My brother used, in pointing out the beauties of her unambitious works, to call attention to their extreme simplicity and to the distinction with which she treated the simple ones of the earth.'[1]

Doubts have been expressed about this story: the details it gives, especially the English visit, hardly fit Turgenev's brother. Yet the obituarist may have been guilty only of a simplification. Two other Russians, of literary tastes and liberal views, actually did visit Scott and meet Maria Edgeworth. Either of these men—Alexander Turgenev (not related to the novelist) or Vladimir Davidov[2]—might have passed his knowledge on to Turgenev or to his brother. Although the link is conjectural, it is plausible enough on internal literary grounds. In Turgenev's tales as in

[1] 'Turguéneff: by one who knew him', *Daily News*, 7 Sept. 1883. It is interesting that the obituarist thinks of ME as impressing Turgenev with her semi-scientific reporting of the manners of the Irish peasantry. Stendhal, on the other hand, read her as a novelist of character rather than as a novelist of society. See Introduction above, p. 2, and Stendhal's *Molière, Shakespeare, La Comédie et La Rire*, Paris, 1930, p. 268.

[2] See Gleb Struve, 'A Russian Traveller in Scotland in 1828', *Blackwood's Mag.*, cclviii, 1945, and 'Russian Friends and Correspondents of Scott', *Comparative Lit.*, ii, 1950; and *Letters from England*, pp. 450–1, 480, and 492.

Maria's, the peasant is studied by an alien upper-class observer; viewed with apparent objectivity, he becomes an explicable human being instead of a bundle of inhabited rags.

In the light of this similarity, why have nationalists been so critical of Maria Edgeworth? The answer must be that there are some more modern ways of apprehending Ireland which are alien to her rational approach. Colum is right to remark that she does not think of Ireland as a mystical entity nor of the Irish as racially distinct from the English. Nor does she place her peasants in their characteristic physical context: unlike Scott and Carleton, unlike even Galt, she makes almost no use of landscape.

Her failure even to attempt to realize Ireland physically can reasonably be accepted as in absolute terms a shortcoming; it means that her novels, though full of real-life detail, seldom re-create a complete world. But the absence of nationalism which in Ireland seems to have damaged her reputation more is not a shortcoming in the same sense. Her Irish critics have failed to perceive how thoroughly Maria belongs, intellectually as well as aesthetically, with the generation which matured before the French Revolution. The political ideals she expresses in her father's lifetime are based on the battle-cries of 1782; if she has any revolutionary inspiration it comes not from France but from America. Her goal is to gain for her Irish characters, regardless of their religion, the rights enjoyed by their English counterparts. And so her strategy is not to prove that the Irish are unique, and therefore worthy of nationhood, but to show them in essence the same, and therefore worthy of equality.

To charge her with lack of patriotism shows a lack of historical awareness. The fervent 'patriots' of Edgeworth's political generation before the Union were the Protestants, not the Catholics. In rejecting the emotional Protestant cry of 'nationhood' the Edgeworths thought they were preferring the claims of the whole nation against the privileged part of it.[1] By emphasizing that Ireland is socially and economically indivisible, Maria Edgeworth reminds her English readers of the presence of the deprived nine-tenths of the population, the Catholic peasantry. She might not be interested at this stage

[1] See above, pp. 115–19 and 136–41.

of her life in political principle; she was very aware of good practice, at the level of the individual estate, and by focusing her criticisms of the gentry and the Protestants here she gave her mature Irish tales a distinct political meaning.

Most criticism of Maria Edgeworth from within Ireland has been based on confused and unhistorical thinking. There has been a tendency for example to think of *Castle Rackrent* as the most 'pro-Irish' of the tales, because it is dominated by a portrait of a peasant; but, as we have seen, Thady's irrationality was in reality held up for criticism, even ridicule, and the indulgence shown to a bad landlord in Condy made the Edgeworths themselves believe that they had done Ireland a disservice. *Ennui*, *The Absentee*, and *Ormond*, all of which urge the Anglo-Irish to take their duties seriously, are more specifically political, and more liberal in their underlying tendency, than ever *Castle Rackrent* was.

Another objection to the three mature tales has been the harmoniousness of their conclusions, with each Anglo-Irish hero settling down to run a model estate, like Edgeworthstown; and, by implication, succeeding. Again, Maria's optimism deserves defending, as in part a matter of history: she shared it with the Lunar circle, Arthur Young, and Adam Smith. It should not be forgotten either that the Napoleonic Wars (during which *Ennui* and *The Absentee* were both written) kept agricultural prices artificially high, so that in the countryside it seemed not unreasonable to hope for a sunny future; a collapse came after 1814, and, sure enough, both financial instability and increased sectarian bitterness are faithfully reflected in *Ormond*.[1]

It is true that in her works Maria speaks to the Anglo-Irish, not to the native population; and also that what she asks for—greater toleration, a greater sense of commitment to the country—requires a change of heart in individuals rather than a change of national status for Ireland. Nationalists have not liked the underlying assumption, that the way ahead lay in the

[1] The best single instance of the historical accuracy and explicit liberalism of *Ormond* is the treatment of White Connal, who has made a fortune in generally hard times by turning over from arable farming to grazing. This was a common strategy after 1814, since meat and dairy products did not slump so badly as corn. Naturally it was unpopular with the peasantry, many of whom were dispossessed to make way for the sheep; and in making White Connal a contemptible purse-proud figure ME shows where her own sympathies lie.

integration of the community within itself, and with England; it seems that they prefer Lady Morgan's heroines, harp-playing Gaelic princesses, to Maria's prosaic Anglo-Irish heroes. Yet even after the Union it was still—to be realistic—the Anglo-Irish landlords who had more influence over the country's future than any other class of men (while Gaelic princesses were, needless to say, a negligible force). If then it is the underlying historical realities which count, Maria's sober efforts to reveal Protestant abuses of power, and to urge England to govern better, showed more political insight than anything else written in fiction in her generation except the novels of Scott.

Of course it is true that politically Maria Edgeworth did not succeed—her fellow landlords were not converted to the policy she advocated for them. As optimists on principle, she and her father probably overestimated the chances of success. Inheriting the religious indifference of the Enlightenment, they did not foresee the intensity with which sectarian quarrels were to be conducted in the nineteenth century. They also badly underestimated the rising tide of native Irish nationalism. Whatever the position had been when Edgeworth formed his views in the eighteenth century, by the time *Ormond* was written it was too late for an English Protestant landowner (which Ormond elects to be) to lead the mass of the population anywhere, even to prosperity. It took a Catholic of native Irish descent—like Corny in the novel, or O'Connell in real life—to win a following among the people.

Even so, comparison of the facts of Edgeworth's political experience with the novels shows that the extent of Maria's naïvety has been greatly exaggerated. At least she was able to avoid some of the simplicities into which the nationalist critics like Colum and Gwynn fell in their turn. She favoured the Irish peasantry, and occasionally sentimentalized them, but she was too honest intellectually to try to whitewash them altogether. In her novels, native ignorance has to bear nearly as much responsibility for Ireland's backwardness as the maladministration of the Anglo-Irish. The intellectual limitations of, say, Ellinor and Corny are among the most important facts we know about them. Corny as she actually draws him is more intelligently conceived than the idealized version of him outlined by her nationalist critic—'that fine old man who prefers to live in accordance with the customs and traditions of an Irish noble of another day'.

Although Maria Edgeworth as a 'national' novelist has not satisfied nationalist tastes, she achieved something better than they were looking for. When her English contemporaries describe her as the founder of the 'national' novel, they mean an aspect of her writing that is equally relevant in portraying any large community—her discovery how to draw a modern society with all its parts functioning in their real-life relation to one another. In *Ormond* she makes an additional point about Ireland when for the purposes of comparison she introduces the cultures of two other societies. But isolating what is peculiarly Irish is never the main intention; in *Ennui*, *The Absentee*, and *Ormond* the aim is to explore how a modern community works, and through the experience of the hero to show that civilized man is, morally speaking, a social animal rather than an isolated individual.

The national novel that Maria initiated was, as we have seen, intelligently received by her earliest critics, but, more important for her literary significance, it was also understood by Walter Scott. When *Waverley* appeared in 1814, it was followed by 'a postscript, which should have been a preface'. In this, Scott states that he has tried to describe the types created by Scottish circumstances,

> not by a caricatured and exaggerated use of the national dialect, but by their habits, manners and feelings; so as in some distant degree to emulate the admirable Irish portraits drawn by Miss Edgeworth, so different from the Teagues and 'dear joys' who so long, with the most perfect family resemblance to each other, occupied the drama and the novel.

Contrary to the general modern opinion,[1] it was not *Castle Rackrent* that prompted *Waverley*, but *The Absentee*. This important fact emerges quite clearly from Scott's subsequent descriptions of how his novel came to be written. In 1805 he wrote a third of the first volume, that is to say the chapters set in England, but was discouraged by a friend from continuing. He laid the novel aside, and when he moved to Abbotsford in

[1] See for example Mr. George Watson, in his preface to *Castle Rackrent*, Oxford English Novels series, 1964, especially pp. vii–viii.

1811 he put it away and forgot it.[1] Next year, in the summer of 1812, he read *The Absentee*, which he liked so much that he sent a letter of congratulation to Maria. (He had written before to ask Maria to expand on a reference in *Ennui* to a tale about an Irish hero called Blackbeard,[2] but he did not know the Edgeworths personally.) According to the account he wrote in 1829, 'the extended and well-merited fame of Miss Edgeworth' was one of the circumstances which recalled the manuscript of *Waverley* to his memory. He must have been thinking of the reception of *Tales of Fashionable Life*, particularly the second series in 1812, because it was not until the autumn of 1813 that he took out the manuscript and added to the opening in England the Scottish scenes which are what really matter.

*Waverley* has of course much more in common with *The Absentee* (and with *Ennui*) than it has with the eccentric *Castle Rackrent*. Maria Edgeworth's maturer Irish tales provide the models for Scott's attempt to sketch a whole society. Individual characters and their private relationships are subordinated in Scott, as in Maria Edgeworth: Scott's Captain Waverley, like Maria's Glenthorn and Colambre, is remarkable as a hero for the attention he does not command. He is a colourless alien, an idealized representative of the English reading public, sent to explore their neighbour's world. In Scott's novel, as in Maria's, the hero's affairs of the heart take second place to his involvement in the affairs of the nation. Maria is more interested in economics, Scott in politics, but both agree that it is society rather than private life that rightly commands attention.[3] In short, Scott follows Maria Edgeworth in making the community his real central character. In his novels, as in hers, there is an almost pedantic interest in documentation from real life. A profusion of detail—facts about customs, dress, above all

[1] General Preface to Collected Edition of Scott's novels, 1829.

[2] ME sent a long reply on 29 Dec. 1811 (Nat. Lib. of Scotland, MS. 3881, ff. 142–3), in which she explained apologetically that she had forgotten any further details, and lost her original reference.

[3] Cf. ME to ED, 29 Apr. 1823; *Dublin Rev.*, cxlv, 1909, 265. Stendhal sighed over their deliberate avoidance of love as a subject. 'C'est la mode; cette pauvre passion est en disgrâce auprès de nos romanciers modernes, Mme de Genlis, Miss Edgeworth, W. Scott. Savez-vous pourquoi? C'est qu'ils ont assez d'esprit pour savoir que pour le peindre, il faut l'avoir senti.' Letter to Adolphe Mareste, Florence, 18 July 1819; *Correspondence*, ed. by H. Martineau and V. del Litto, Paris, 1962, i. 980.

idioms of speech—gives an entirely new richness to the portrait of society. Furthermore, Scott makes an impressionistic attempt to render the community as a whole, aristocracy, bourgeoisie, peasantry, Lowlanders and Highlanders, the new men and the men in decline. His characters are no more isolated individuals than hers are; they are representatives of their respective classes.[1] These features of Scott's near-contemporary Scottish novels are precisely the features of the 'national' novel as Maria Edgeworth developed it. They are not merely incidental to Scott's work, but are the sources of its strength.

If it is a weakness to write principally for a foreign audience, then clearly Maria Edgeworth and Scott have faults in common as well. Scott liked to think that his novels would be of service to his country, by teaching the English to overcome the remnants of their eighteenth-century antipathy to everything Scottish:

> Without being so presumptuous as to hope to emulate the rich humour, pathetic tenderness, and admirable tact, which pervade the works of my accomplished friend, I felt that something might be attempted for my own country, of the same kind with that which Miss Edgeworth so fortunately achieved for Ireland—something which might introduce her natives to those of the sister kingdom, in a more favourable light than they had been placed hitherto, and tend to procure sympathy for their virtues, and indulgence for their foibles. . . .[2]

This ambition, which may not have much to do with the making of art, reminds us that the general aesthetic approach of Scott and Maria Edgeworth was in some respects very similar. Just as Maria Edgeworth moved in non-literary circles, so Scott had more respect for men of action, statesmen, and soldiers than for men of letters. Lockhart quotes at length a revealing conversation he had with the two novelists at Edgeworthstown in 1825, in which they agreed that they put the claims and affections of everyday life before the demands of art. They also cared more for the experience and language of

[1] For evidence that both meant their characters to be responsible and representative, cf. ME's letter to Scott of 15 July 1830, quoted above, p. 267.

[2] Preface to Collected Edition of his novels, 1829. In a letter of May 1818, Scott praised ME for her 'transcendent' merit 'of raising your national character in the scale of public estimation' (H. J. C. Grierson, *Letters of Sir Walter Scott*, v. 42).

ordinary people than for the elaborate sentiments to be found among sophisticated classes and in literature.[1] Their interest in the day-to-day life of common people and distaste for aestheticism no doubt encouraged them to use the prosaic, 'unliterary' novel at a time when so much more artistic energy and talent was being devoted to poetry.

Scott was, of course, a greater writer than Maria Edgeworth, and some of the reasons for this can be glimpsed from the preface to *Waverley* of 1829. As a man, living in a society which was not culturally, religiously, and racially divided in two, Scott knew his subject as a whole more naturally than Maria Edgeworth knew hers. He could claim to have enjoyed 'free and unrestrained communication with all ranks of my countrymen, from the Scottish peer to the Scottish ploughman'. He is richer, more diverse, and never so sketchy and theoretical as Maria Edgeworth in the Irish scenes of *The Absentee*.

On some subjects Scott consciously differed from Maria.[2] He was much more instinctive and romantic in temper, and his view of history, unlike hers, was conditioned by the French Revolution; change, in his novels, is a dynamic, irresistible pressure destroying much that is valuable and often proving tragic to the individual caught in its path. Scott's view of history fits in brilliantly with the panoramic sweep across a modern (or near-modern) society which he adopted from Maria's tales; his version, with the historical dimension added, shows society changing, while she presents it static. Therefore, although he shares so many virtues with Maria Edgeworth, the effect of Scott's novels is different, and the picture he presents of society has proved more acceptable to subsequent generations. Again, Maria is a transitional figure. She has the serenity of the Enlightenment, and the hopefulness of the pioneers of the Industrial Revolution; but she is important in literary history because she also, within these limits, looks forward to the nineteenth century.

For, just as Jane Austen's naturalistic treatment of drawing-room life is preceded by Maria Edgeworth's, so is Scott's realism in depicting a modern community in its entirety. It is

[1] J. G. Lockhart, *Memoirs of the Life of Sir Walter Scott*, 1837–8, vi. 59–61.

[2] e.g. his private strictures on *Harry and Lucy Concluded*, 1825: Walter Scott to Joanna Baillie, 12 Oct. 1825; *Memoirs of the Life of Sir Walter Scott*, vi. 82–3.

with *Ennui* and *The Absentee* that the English novel first comes to grips with its great preoccupation in the first half of the nineteenth century, organic society as reshaped by the Industrial Revolution. Identifying herself intellectually with her father, Maria Edgeworth writes from the viewpoint of the most highly self-conscious section of the new manufacturing classes; she speaks in fiction with the voice of the Lunar Society and Adam Smith. This is no mere curiosity of literature, nor a dead end like that other product of their circle, the scientific poetry of Erasmus Darwin. Maria's novels belong to the main stream of her form's development. Instead of becoming associated, like Darwin's poems, with outmoded techniques, they introduce the objective, pseudo-journalistic approach to the social scene which successive nineteenth-century novelists could build on. Before Maria, heroes and heroines are relatively free of their environment: they are individuals. After her, characters in fiction are increasingly dominated by their social and economic circumstances, and it is a short step to that mid-nineteenth-century fictional universe in which the heroes and heroines are commonly seen as society's prisoners. In the gradual transition from the world of Tom Jones to the world of Dorrit and Dr. Lydgate, there is no doubt where Glenthorn, Colambre, and Ormond belong; for all of them end as cogs in the social machine. It is true that Maria is a transitional figure, and that she does not share those insights into the evils of the new industrial order that early nineteenth-century historical experience was to give its artists. With a hopefulness shared by few of her successors, Maria Edgeworth's heroes voluntarily choose what she believed to be the enlightened path. Yet from the viewpoint of the novel's evolution, Maria's approval of her heroes' optimism is not so significant as the educated consciousness she gives them in relation to the social and economic realities of their world. Well-meaning and forward-looking, they are vehicles for the first discriminating studies of an entire society in fiction.

# PART III

# INDEPENDENCE: 1817–1849

## IX

## LIVING WITHOUT HER FATHER

RICHARD LOVELL EDGEWORTH died at seven o'clock in the evening on 13 June 1817. Although he had spent many months enduring pain, often for hours at a time, he had remained in command of himself and everything around him—'the Soul' of the household, as one old friend put it.[1] He spent the first half of 1817 ordering the affairs of his estate, supervising the completion of his last experiments on clocks and carriages, helping Maria with *Ormond*,[2] and dictating parts of his autobiography, which he meant her to complete after his death. His family thought his energy phenomenal, a view confirmed by the record they kept of letters dictated by him on all kinds of subjects in the last two years of his life. He had a deliberate policy, based on the example of the Scottish empiricist Thomas Reid, of keeping himself and the household busy as his death drew near.[3] While Maria was engaged on *Ormond*, and forbidden to write letters, another daughter, Fanny, was kept unusually busy as her amanuensis. Honora wrote most of Edgeworth's own correspondence. It was a typical example of Edgeworth's manner in handling the family, as was his well-executed leave-taking. He followed the common custom of the period in finding appropriate words of advice, encouragement, and thanks for his wife and daughters, and for William, the only son at home. 'I did not know how *much* I loved Maria till I came to the parting with her.'[4]

Maria had been steeling herself to face the loss of her father for months, even years. In 1813, she had spoken to the writer Joanna Baillie of what his eventual death would mean to her. Miss Baillie now wrote sympathetically, recalling her words:

[1] Mrs. M. Powys to ME, 25 June 1817.

[2] See above, p. 280.

[3] *Memoirs of RLE*, ii. 296–7. RLE read Dugald Stewart's *Life of Reid* (1802) on his way home from Edinburgh in 1803.

[4] ME to Mrs. R, ?14 June 1817. See also above, p. 289, and *Black Book*, pp. 209–10.

'I remember that when I had the pleasure of seeing you here, you spoke to me as if in the event of your father's death, every happiness and pursuit for you in this world would be closed, and at present you will think so.'[1]

Maria was indeed desolated. Immediately after Edgeworth's death she was so ill that she had to go to Black Castle for nursing by Mrs. Ruxton, who was 'more like him [her father] than anyone now living'.[2] All that summer she was incapable of exerting herself, except in what she referred to as 'the sacred cause' of her father's memory. She corresponded with Sir Richard Phillips about the obituary he was proposing to publish in his *Monthly Magazine*, and she scanned the other journals for notices, observing, for example, with surprise and pain that Francis Jeffrey did not take the opportunity of a review of *Harrington and Ormond* to pay tribute to Edgeworth in the *Edinburgh Review*. She was also very sensitive to the tone of letters from friends. Some of them addressed their condolences to her, rather than to Mrs. Edgeworth; not only was Maria better known, but the special nature of her relationship with her father was generally recognized. 'Father, friend, husband—he was all to *you*—Addison says "the most interesting of all human affections is that which subsists between a father and daughter" and this holy, happy union has been perhaps preserved and enjoyed by you more than any woman in existence.'[3] Mrs. Inchbald, on the other hand, alienated her by writing a routine letter criticizing *Ormond*, which not only failed to express sympathy but unfortunately characterized Corny's death—a scene written by Edgeworth himself—as 'ludicrous'.[4]

Between October 1817 and January 1818 Maria was back at Black Castle for more nursing by her aunt. All that year she could find no pleasure in novels because she associated them so strongly with her father: she noted the publication of Godwin's *Mandeville*, but felt no desire to read it. Her own *Ormond*, 'that poor Orphan Book', remained hateful for many years because it brought back the last months of her father's life. In 1824 she

[1] Joanna Baillie to ME, 1 July 1817.

[2] ME to Honora Edgeworth, 4 July 1817.

[3] Mrs. Barbara Hofland to ME, 1 July 1817.

[4] Maria was much struck by 'the harshness, the total want of human, not to say feminine feeling in writing in such a way to a daughter in such circumstances' (ME to Mrs. CSE, Aug. 1817.)

was obliged to read it before it was republished as part of the first collected edition of her novels, and even then the task was painful.

Although in time she resumed her old activities, nothing was ever to diminish her immense respect for Edgeworth's memory. 'The love-powders which her father certainly gave her have not lost their effect after his death', as Joanna Baillie reported to Scott four years later.[1] Scott soon had opportunities of his own to observe their continuing potency, for the many letters Maria wrote to Abbotsford in the 1820s often referred to Edgeworth, whom Scott had never met, and always with the same vivid sense of loss. Even in the eighteen-thirties Maria could not speak of her father without gratitude, or, of course, emotion: '"Nobody can know what I owe to my father; he advised me and directed me in everything; I never could have done anything without him. These are things I cannot be mistaken about, though other people can,—I *know* them." As she said this, the tears stood in her eyes and her whole person was moved.'[2]

She cared much more for his reputation with the public than she had ever cared for her own. In 1834, for example, she asked the sister of the author of an article on the telegraph to have her father named as the unacknowledged pioneer in the field: 'Nothing you could do for myself could give me so much pleasure.'[3]

On the day before Edgeworth died he dictated to Maria a letter to his publisher in which he stated that he had written 480 pages of autobiography, and that Maria was to add 200 more. He added that he required her to perform this task within a month of his death, but in the margin of the letter we see the addition which Maria must have added silently: 'I never promised.' The idea that someone other than herself should be given the *Memoirs* was unthinkable, yet immediately after his death she was scarcely in a condition to begin work on any book. She begged her father's friend and executor, Francis Beaufort, to give her his moral support in her decision to delay publication:

[1] Letter of 2 Feb. 1822; *Private Letter-books of Sir Walter Scott*, ed. W. Partington, 1930, p. 263.

[2] *Life, Letters and Journals of George Ticknor*, 1876, i. 428.

[3] ME to Miss Martha Cowper; C. Hill, 'Some Unpublished Letters of Maria Edgeworth', *Hampstead Annual*, 1897, p. 129.

If you *cannot*—be silent on the subject—for I feel that no argument, no motive or influence but that which can never more be exerted over my mind—that *allpowerful* motive which brought out powers of which I was unconscious—could enable me to write at this time for the public.[1]

Beaufort suggested that Christmas 1818 would be a sufficiently early date to aim at. By August 1817 Maria had already begun work, but only at correcting her father's section of the manuscript. He had written part of the narrative of his early years in 1809, part in the early months of 1817, and shortly before his death he had also dictated memoranda and notes to help Maria with the more difficult subjects she would have to take up, notably Irish politics. She began by reading through his narrative, making only such minimal alterations as were absolutely necessary:

I should not think myself justified in *changing* a single sentiment expressed by him—But if I found any passage which I thought might be injurious to his credit I would suppress it in the publication—drawing [a] pencil lines across it in his own manuscript . . . and in his ms will be visible every alteration or suppression I make —Hitherto in reading it, which I do (an hour a day) to my aunts and Honora we have found only two passages that I wished not to publish—and they & Mrs. E were quite of my opinion—all the other corrections were merely verbal or transpositions of passages of narrative to preserve order.[2]

Even though she was determined to make as few changes as possible, the task of editing imposed a strain on her. Late in 1817 she had a severe attack of her old eye trouble, which made work on the *Memoirs*, together with the necessary research for it among old letters and papers, a severe physical as well as emotional burden throughout the first half of 1818.

But by the summer of 1818 she had completed a draft of her own part of the narrative, 1782–1817, which was to make up the second volume of the book. Her friend Lady Lansdowne had been pressing her since 1813 to visit her country home, Bowood, one of the celebrated gathering-places of Whig high Society in the decades before the Reform Bill. Maria now

[1] ME to F. Beaufort, 19 July 1817.

[2] ME to CSE, 17 Aug. 1817. RLE's MS., with ME's pencil corrections (as trivial as she suggests) is now in the National Library of Ireland, Dublin, together with her list of emendations to it (MS 7360).

accepted the invitation on behalf of herself and her stepsister Honora, although her motives on her own account were anything but social:

> I have told Lady L— that I cannot stir till I have completely finished what I am writing & till I have given time to my friends in Ireland to read & form & impart their opinions to me—My mother must read it—You must read it at Black Castle—and I believe it should be read at Collon—This cannot all be accomplished before the end of July—I have therefore begged Lady L— would name any time after the beginning of August . . . *My* chief object in going to England is to hear Francis Beaufort's Mr Dumont's & perhaps Mr Wishaw's opinions of *the life* before it is published.[1]

Maria and Honora arrived at Bowood in September 1818,[2] and duly circulated the manuscript to some of the most trusted of their English friends. Among those who read it at Bowood were Dumont, Lady Lansdowne, and Dugald Stewart, who, although old and ill, was still an appropriate commentator on much of Edgeworth's life. From Bowood she went to Epping, home of Capt. Francis Beaufort's father-in-law, Capt. Wilson, partly to see friends, but partly too so that more people could see the manuscript. She made a special journey to show it to Mrs. Sabrina Bicknell, formerly Sabrina Sidney, Thomas Day's one-time ward and intended wife, who might well feel embarrassed at having her early history published in full.[3] After a further fortnight at Bowood Maria went to Byrkley Lodge to get the Sneyds' approval for two other highly delicate episodes, Edgeworth's courtship of Honora and, more especially, Elizabeth Sneyd.[4]

The advice both of people who were personally concerned, and outsiders who moved in the world, was very necessary on

[1] ME to Mrs. R, Spring Farm, New Town, Mt. Kennedy (CSE's home), 20 May 1818. ME's reference to John Whishaw in this context is explained by his tremendous reputation for critical sagacity; for which, however, Sydney Smith had a characteristic explanation. 'Whishaw's plan is the best; he gives no opinion for the first week, but confines himself to chuckling and elevating his chin; in the mean time he drives diligently about the first critical stations, breakfasts in Mark Lane (with Ricardo), hears from Hertford College (Malthus), and by Saturday night is as bold as a lion and as decisive as a court of justice' (quoted by Lady Seymour, *The Pope of Holland House*, 1906, p. 33). ME however did not in the end consult Whishaw.

[2] ME's letters written during this visit are published in *Letters from England*, pp. 75 ff.

[3] See above, p. 39 n.

[4] See above, p. 70.

this occasion. By now even Maria recognized that her father had made enemies, and she had an inkling of what a hostile reviewer of the *Memoirs* might say from 'that abominable passage about him in the Ed[inburgh] Review of Patronage'.[1] Therefore in her text she went out of her way to emphasize that her father's latinate written style and his manner in public did not agree with the warm personality that he showed to his family.[2] As for the controversial marriage to Elizabeth Sneyd, no tact in presentation could be too great; one of the few cuts Maria made in her father's text in fact came in this part of the narrative. The discrepancies between her description of his role in politics, and the views he had actually expressed at the time, have already been noted. She took great care to represent his political activities as orthodox and constitutional, and while omitting any description of his true opinions on such tendentious subjects as the French Revolution, stressed his later disapproval of Bonaparte.

On the question of just how far she should try to convey her own attachment to her father she was anything but a good judge. Francis Beaufort, who shared his family's gifts of tact and personal insight, saw that in spite of her literary gifts she was not an ideal choice as Edgeworth's biographer:

> That clear succinct style of narrative—The epigrammatic anecdote—The terse moral induction, neatly introduced—And that touching pathos which is produced not by copious and exuberant climax but by Simplicity—all these abound in your writing and are the life of Biography. But, there is another quality still wanting and which in you particularly will require an effort of more than common fortitude—I mean *judgment* of selection.[3]

Something went wrong between Maria and Dumont that September at Bowood, which may have been connected with Dumont's embarrassment at finding that Maria's 'judgment of selection' had left much to be desired. He told her afterwards that he felt too close to the subject to be a good judge of it. At the time his manner was unforthcoming—Maria wrote later of his 'stickishness', and at the time she complained in a letter to Frances that he conversed agreeably only 'towards the

[1] ME to Harriet Beaufort, 15 Dec. 1817. See above, p. 273.
[2] *Memoirs of RLE*, ii. 333–4.
[3] Francis Beaufort to ME, 28 July 1817.

dessert'.[1] In the early stages of work on the *Memoirs*, Maria had read Mme de Staël's biography of her father, the financier Jacques Necker, and had complained that it was not sufficiently intimate and domestic. Her own narrative emphasized how important Edgeworth's family had been to him, and, at least in the first draft, it dwelt on the intense love that she had felt for her father since childhood. These intimate passages were too much for Dumont, who must have felt that Maria was delivering herself up to the far from tender mercy of the Reviews. He advised her to take out some of the most emotional passages.[2] On questions of propriety Maria had decided to accept her friend's opinions. After a series of largely social visits in London in the spring of 1819, she left her father's manuscript with the publisher, but in May brought her own volume back to Edgeworthstown in order to make the necessary changes and cuts.

A revised text was ready by the end of that year, and Hunter wrote that he would publish the book in the early summer of 1820. All along Maria had looked forward to publication with 'almost a superstitious terror . . . how shall I ever be able to endure to see all that I hold most dear & sacred approached by the unhallowed hands of unfeeling persons?'[3] As the time grew near she decided not to endure it. She had been tempted for some years by invitations from friends on the Continent, both the survivors of her old circle in Paris, and Dumont in Geneva. Her stepsisters by her father's last marriage were now arriving at marriageable age, and without Edgeworth Maria took upon herself the responsibility for widening their opportunities. But again, as in 1819, her private motives for travelling were not so much bound up with the stepsisters as with her father's *Memoirs*. Her plan was to stay out of the country until it was no longer talked about.

Maria crossed the Channel with the twenty-one-year-old Fanny and nineteen-year-old Harriet on 22 April 1820, and within a few days was introducing them to the old friends of 1802 who still survived. M. and Mme de Pastoret and Mme Gautier were as charming, and as welcoming, as ever; but the

[1] ME to Mrs. FE, Pregny, Switzerland, 10 Aug. 1820, and Bowood, [Sept. 1818]; *Letters from England*, p. 93.

[2] See above, p. 57.

[3] ME to Mrs. Marcet, 10 Oct. 1817; H. W. Häusermann, *The Genevese Background*, 1952, p. 85.

Abbé Morellet and Mme Delessert were dead, Mme Suard had turned into 'a wild old Frenchwoman'[1] who embarrassed them in company, and Mme Récamier, although still elegant in manner, had grown fat and was living in poverty in a convent. Quite apart from the changes made by time, Maria did not find Parisian life as attractive now as in 1802. 'Maria was nearly brought to own that she had thought less well of the French the more she had seen of them.'[2]

The conversation has lost much by what the French have gained in liberty—during Napoleon's time none dared to whisper of politics—now, none can speak of anything else—the ultras are the most furious because the weakest—the Liberals the most noisy, because they have much appearance and little reality of object or of sense—the Buonapartists are the most silent because the most afraid, and the Royalists quietly hold their tongues and the reins of power.[3]

An acid summary of the successes and disappointments of the tour was given by a decidedly homesick Harriet, in these and other letters to the Edgeworths and Beauforts. Harriet Edgeworth had inherited the wry detachment of her mother's family, and there is all the difference in the world between the tone of her reports in 1820 and Maria's in 1802; especially when Maria was writing to the gentle Mary Sneyd, who disliked hearing ill of anyone. Harriet was even capable of passing on her observation that Maria, who was impervious to flattery of herself, swallowed it whole when it was directed at a sister. 'Maria is delighted when the English say lovely and the French say charmante to her face about Fanny.'[4] Harriet's summing up a month later of the real success that Maria had enjoyed is all the more convincing:

Indeed Maria is treated by foreigners of all nations in the most distinguished and at the same time most gratifying manner, not as an odious author but as a delightful gentlewoman—not as one who must be received because she has written but as one whom everybody is glad to know because they have when unknown given them pleasure, and whom everybody is glad to be intimate with

[1] ME to Charlotte and Mary Sneyd, 7 July 1820; *Mem.*, ii. 71.
[2] Harriet Edgeworth to Honora Edgeworth, Paris, 29 June 1820.
[3] Harriet Edgeworth to Harriet Beaufort, La Celle, 4 June 1820.
[4] Harriet Edgeworth to Harriet Beaufort, Paris, 7 May 1820.

because when known she is seen to be all that is most agreeable in her most agreeable books—Indeed she well deserves all the attention she receives for well as I knew her I did not know the extent of all her talents—the extent of her modesty I was well acquainted with —but the best idea I can give you of her is to say that after displaying all that is most brilliant to Princesses and Peers, or after the deepest arguments with the most celebrated and the most scientific she goes to order our gowns, or to continue a new habit shirt—or to talk nonsense or sense with us—how astonished would some of her solemn admirers be if they were to see her rolling with laughter at some egregious folly and still more would some of the brilliant wits be at the quantity of fancy and talent she wastes on us.[1]

August to mid October was spent in touring Switzerland. Their principal hosts were the Moilliets. Mrs. Moilliet was Amelia, the daughter of James Keir, now married to a man of Swiss descent who had a house at Pregny with a glorious view of Mont Blanc. There Maria saw Pictet again, and the Marcets, and of course Dumont, who revelled in the beauty of his native country: 'He loves Mont Blanc next to Bentham, above all created things.'[2] Dumont accompanied them on a six days' tour round the shores of Lake Geneva, in the course of which they visited Mme de Montolieu, Gibbon's friend; he also went with them to Coppet, Mme de Staël's former home, where her son received them cordially. Much of their time in Switzerland was given over to simple sight-seeing with the Moilliets. They went together on a three weeks' tour of the cantons, throughout which Maria maintained her unfailing cheerfulness despite great heat, fleas, and some terrifying roads. Again Harriet was deeply impressed.

She is indeed a wonderful creature and though I talk of peace at Geneva I never saw her so surrounded or so adoringly attended to—Rows of four deep encircled her chair and Fanny and I are scolded from her orbit—which is very fair but very hard because the best conversation and cleverest people are always talking to her without considering what she says herself.[3]

On the way back they stopped at Lyons, a depressing experience because no one they saw there remembered Edgeworth

[1] Harriet Edgeworth to Harriet Beaufort, La Celle, 4 June 1820.
[2] ME to Mrs. FE, Pregny, 10 Aug. 1820; *Mem.*, ii. 95.
[3] Harriet Edgeworth to Mrs. FE, Berne, 1 Sept. 1820.

or the work he had been so proud of in 1772.[1] In the last week of October they reached Paris again, and there the first news—not of the *Memoirs*, for they had discussed them with Dumont—but of the *Memoirs*' reception by the English Reviews got through to Maria. The *Quarterly* had been so offensive that the family at Edgeworthstown had decided against writing to her about it, but Dumont sent an indignant letter of sympathy after her from Geneva,[2] and Mrs. Marcet a similar one from London.

It must have surprised those who knew her best, and knew how tense the writing of the *Memoirs* had made her, that she now behaved very calmly. In a letter to her aunt she brushed the review aside. 'Never lose another night's sleep or another moment's thought on the *Quarterly Review*—I have never read and never will read it.'[3] She knew that the family would suppose her distressed, and she took pains to reassure them:

> You would scarcely believe my dear friends the calm of mind and the sort of satisfied resignation I feel . . . I suppose I had during the two years of doubt and extreme anxiety I endured exhausted all my power of doubting—I *know* that I have done my very best—that I have done my duty without shrinking from any personal consideration and I firmly believe that if my dear father could see the whole he would be satisfied with me.[4]

Maria did not read the *Quarterly*'s review until 1835, nor did she make any effort to discover who had written it. The author was in fact John Wilson Croker. As a considered judgement on the literary merits of the *Memoirs*, Croker's article was actually in a minority, for the equally influential *Edinburgh Review* and *London Magazine* both expressed qualified approval.[5] Yet even here a note was sounded which must have jarred on nerves as sensitive as Maria's. The *London Magazine*'s critic hinted that Edgeworth's influence on the novels was probably less benign than she supposed; it also dissented gently from her estimate of his abilities as a scientist, and allowed a note of comedy to creep in where she certainly saw nothing amusing: 'Mr Edgeworth began to marry at twenty, and continued the

[1] See above, pp. 43–4.
[2] ED to ME, Geneva, 7 Nov. 1820; *Mem.*, ii. 126.
[3] ME to Mrs. R, Paris, Nov. 1820; *Mem.*, ii. 126.
[4] ME to Mrs. FE, 15 Nov. 1820; *Mem.*, ii. 128.
[5] *Ed. Rev.*, xxxix, 1820, 121–48, and *London Magazine*, i. 1820, 555–65.

practice till late in life. In fact, matrimony and mechanics seem to have monopolised his fidelity.' A columnist in the same magazine had still less regard for a daughter's tender feelings:

> We persist in thinking Mr Edgeworth's life a tiresome, vain, inglorious book... and his own account of his own jokes, and his own account of himself, who can bear it?—His daughter may be pardoned her affectionate praise of him:—but the public is not his daughter. He eulogises himself deplorably; and really, if we may judge from his own account, upon very slender grounds.[1]

Byron came to similar conclusions in the privacy of his journal;[2] it was clear that the impression of pomposity Edgeworth had left in London in 1813 was not forgotten by the literary coterie.

John Wilson Croker was particularly anxious to review the *Memoirs* for the *Quarterly*: he had, he told the editor, William Gifford, 'some *personal object*'. John Murray, the publisher, readily agreed: 'You will do a service by taking it out of the hand of Southey who is decided for praising them.'[3] Croker did not know Edgeworth, and it is difficult to see what his 'personal object' can have been. It is possible that his hostility is entirely accounted for by political animus, since as a practising Tory politician Croker was in the habit of attacking the works of Whigs; the review certainly speaks slightingly of the part Edgeworth played in Irish politics in 1782, 1798, and 1800. But, characteristically, Croker attacks Edgeworth the man on many other grounds at the same time. He accuses him of lying repeatedly about the importance of his own role in different projects, and is vindictive about the four (or, as he will have it, five) marriages; and in the course of accusing Edgeworth of bad taste he crudely insults him for his description of the death of Maria's mother, Anna Maria. 'If the family cat had died in kittening, the circumstances could not be noticed with less ceremony.'[4] His respectful reviews of Maria's novels had proved that he had no personal quarrel with her,

[1] *London Mag.*, ii. 1820, 269; cf. also ii. 123, 156, and 242.

[2] See below, p. 413.

[3] See letters of Murray to Croker and Gifford to Murray, quoted Shine, H. and H. C., *The Quarterly Review under Gifford, 1809–1824*, p. 71.

[4] Croker could not know, of course, that ME had also felt unhappy about her father's narration at this point, and had made emendations. See above, p. 404.

but he could not find much to say for her performance on this occasion. 'She is too rhetorically panegyrical—too pompous about trifles—somewhat too querulous—and as little amusing as the nature of memoir writing would permit her to be.'[1]

Where Croker led the way with such energy, others soon followed: more and more writers now gratuitously introduced Edgeworth's name into articles about Maria's books, very seldom to his advantage. The *North American Review*, for example, declared itself confident that her ability to write had not been buried with her father, and urged her to publish something in order to justify its faith. Maria's reaction to this suggestion was bitter—'a truly American proposal to a daughter to come out and dance a fandango on her father's grave to show how much better she could do without him than with him'.[2] In the same year she was hurt by more spiteful jibes at her father, in the *New Monthly Magazine* and *Blackwood's*, which had the effect of making her resolve never to be publicly associated with either journal in future. When she gave John Gibson Lockhart her *Essay on Bores* to publish as he saw fit, she stipulated that the piece must be anonymous if it appeared in *Blackwood's*.[3]

The Reviews' campaign against her father made Maria shy of publishing for adults. In the early 1820s she seemed to have arrived at a situation where a reference to her was likely to be accompanied by abuse of Edgeworth. In any context other than *Blackwood's* it scarcely mattered whether *Essay on Bores* was anonymous or not, since it was too short to attract the attention of reviewers; and children's books were in a similar position. But any more substantial piece of work acknowledged to be hers seemed doomed to drag her father's name before the public once again:

> I have a motive yet untold for wishing to publish anonymously. —I have a fear that reviewers or other newspaper writers might follow up a line of criticism which they commenced—the *only one* which could really hurt my happiness—the setting my father's fame & name in competition—whether in praise or blame to me this would be odious—I should reproach myself for having brought

[1] J. W. Croker, *QR*, xxiii, 1820, 530.

[2] ME to Sir Walter Scott, 18 Feb. 1824; Nat. Lib. of Scotland, MS. 3898, f. 74. Cf. *North American Review*, xvii, 1823, 383–6.

[3] ME to J. G. Lockhart, 23 Aug. 1825; Nat. Lib. of Scotland, MS. 923, ff. 49–50. Cf. ME to Thomas Campbell (copy), 22 Sept. 1824.

it on by publishing again—I should say to myself—Why could I not have avoided it by ceasing to write—or by writing only as I have done ever since 1817 children's books which no reviewer can ever think worth mentioning. . . .[1]

Maria was writing busily between 1818 and 1825, and not paralysed by grief, as most biographies of her have stated. Just the same, she did not publish a substantial work of fiction for adults between *Ormond* in 1817 and *Helen* in 1834. From 1820 until about 1828, the reviewers' campaign against her father was the most important single cause of the break in her career as a novelist.

In spite of the grief that she felt at her father's death, and the pain the *Memoirs* caused her before and after publication, as a private woman Maria realized herself more fully after 1817 than ever before. In middle age she at last began to strike outsiders as a very positive personality. As late as 1813 this had usually not been so. Byron, for example, remembered her from that year as 'a nice little unassuming "Jeanie Deans-looking bodie" . . . Her conversation was as quiet as herself. One would never have guessed she could write *her name*; whereas her father talked, *not* as if he could write nothing else, but as if nothing else was worth writing.'[2] The painter Joseph Farington noticed that she was much more fully accepted in Society in 1819 than she had been on the first visit.

She is now in great request, and passes her time at present in visiting families of distinction[.] When she was in England with her father 3 or four years ago, she was much sought for, but it was ascribed to curiosity to see a person much celebrated for her works. She is now invited by those who wish to have the pleasure of her conversation.[3]

Isaac D'Israeli put the difference down to a marked change in Maria's own manner:

The literary comet in our *conversaziones* this season was Maria Edgeworth, who took up an odd whim of introducing and being

[1] ME to Sir Walter Scott, 17 Nov. 1824; Nat. Lib. of Scotland, MS. 868, f. 108.
[2] Byron's Journal at Ravenna, 19 Jan. 1821; *Letters and Journals of Lord Byron* (3rd edn., 1833), ed. Thomas Moore, iii. 110.
[3] *Farington Diary*, Mar. 1819, ed. J. Greig, viii (1928), 217.

introduced. It was all Souls' day with her. She is monstrously ugly, and I saw her in a Shepherdesses hat. She says nothing, but a great deal. In her father's lifetime, when she came up to London, she was like a sealed fountain; but now, being on her own bottom, she pours down like the falls of Niagara.[1]

There is probably something in D'Israeli's explanation for the change in Maria. Now that her father was dead she had to go into company alone, or as the chaperone of her step-sisters. In 1820 she had managed the whole elaborate journey across England, France, and Switzerland, and, if only to avoid political disputes, she had not merely taken part in conversation but often done her best to lead it.[2] Back in England that December, 1820, she had stayed a few days at Bowood again, and spent Christmas at Easton Grey, near Malmesbury, Wiltshire, with the family of the sociable Thomas Smith.[3] She no longer thought of herself as in mourning; the fad of house-parties at the time was charades, and Maria's letters are full of boisterous impromptu theatricals in which she and dignitaries like Lord Lansdowne and the historian Henry Hallam participated with gusto.

After less than a year, in October 1821, she was off from Edgeworthstown again with Fanny and Harriet for a full winter season in London.[4] Their entertainment began with a series of visits to country houses. At the first, Wycombe Abbey, the home of Lord Carrington, William Wilberforce was a fellow guest. They went on to David Ricardo's home, Gatcombe Park, where Maria was pleased with their host's 'very composed manner' and 'continual life of mind'.[5] There followed in rapid succession Bowood, Cirencester (Lord and Lady Bathurst), and Deepdene, the exotic Surrey home of Mr. and Mrs. Thomas Hope. The three Edgeworths began the New Year in a more homely atmosphere at Hampstead, first with the Carr family,[6]

[1] Isaac D'Israeli to Byron, 10 Dec. 1822; *Letters and Journals of Lord Byron*, ed. R. E. Prothero, 1898–1904, vi. 86n.

[2] e.g. an undated fragment of Harriet's describes a quarrelsome dinner-party at Mme Suard's (May or June 1820).

[3] Smith, d. 1822, was the friend and correspondent of John Whishaw, and neighbour of the Ricardos and Lansdownes. See Lady (Elizabeth) Seymour, *The Pope of Holland House*, 1906, pp. 6 ff.

[4] For the letters of this visit, see *Letters from England*, pp. 238 ff.

[5] ME to Mrs. FE, Gatcombe Park, 9 Nov. 1821; *Mem.*, ii. 151.

[6] See below, p. 430.

and afterwards with the Carrs' neighbours Joanna and Agnes Baillie; but by mid January 1822 they were again enjoying a scientific house-party at the home of the Whig M.P. and agriculturalist Sir John Sebright, together with a distinguished trio of fellow guests, Dr. Wollaston, Mrs. Marcet, and Mrs. Somerville. A few days later they were at Mardoaks with Sir James Mackintosh. Maria was gratified that Fanny and Harriet should have the opportunity of seeing people reputed to be among the cleverest and liveliest in English high Society, and, moreover, naturally, as they appeared in their own homes. At the most celebrated houses, Bowood, Deepdene, and elsewhere, there had sometimes been ten or more other guests, but the Ricardos and Mackintoshes had entertained them simply, almost as members of the family. In any case the effect was relatively intimate, but the smaller parties, with their opportunities for establishing real friendships, were what Maria preferred. 'The two new literary persons Fanny most wished to see in coming to England were Ricardo and Mackintosh. She has seen them in the best manner in their own families and at leisure to be not only wise and good but agreeable. Harriet and she have *heard* more of their conversation . . . than they could . . . during a whole season in London.'[1] Maria learnt from it too; country houses were to provide the setting, country-house conversation one of the themes, of her remaining novel, *Helen*.

At the end of January they went to stay with Lady Elizabeth Whitbread at Grove House, Kensington, and were settled in a house of their own, 8 Holles Street, by early March. The three months of London society which followed were unquestionably Maria's most brilliant at any time in the capital. They were received 'in six different and totally independent sets, of scientific, literary, political, travelled, artist, and the fine fashionable of various shades'.[2] Maria's name got them admitted to Almack's and into conversation with the prison reformer, Mrs. Fry, in Newgate; as Whishaw put it, 'their [the Edgeworths'] friendship was expended like gold leaf over a prodigious surface'.[3] Maria had two kinds of weapon in her

[1] ME to Mrs. FE, Hertford College, 23 Jan. 1822; *Letters from England*, p. 334.

[2] ME to Mrs. R, 10 Apr. 1822; *Mem.*, ii. 193.

[3] Whishaw to Sydney Smith, 17 Apr. 1822; Lady Seymour, *The Pope of Holland House*, p. 247. Cf. Joanna Baillie to W. Scott, 2 Feb. 1822; W. Partington, *Private Letter-books of Sir Walter Scott*, 1930, p. 263.

armoury, her talent for anecdote and mimicry and her vast, unusually solid reading. Since her books had led people to expect a very well-informed woman, it was generally her humour and unpretentiousness that attracted favourable comment. Sydney Smith summed it up later when he observed: 'She does not say witty things, but there is such a perfume of wit runs through all her conversation as makes it very brilliant.'[1] Others who met her also tried to refine on exactly where her ability really lay. 'In her conversation she is brilliant, and full of imagery to a degree which would in writing be a fault.'[2] The perceptive Harriet made a not dissimilar observation, which confirmed that Maria's style in conversation must have been very different from the rational tone in which the novels were written. 'Maria seldom argues well—she is generally in a passion with the dispute or the disputer before she has gone far, and if not in a passion often prefers wit to logic.'[3] An American visitor, George Ticknor, who met her later at Edgeworthstown, said that she *did* talk like the novels, but in the manner of the liveliest dialogue, not the narration:

> What has struck me most today in Miss Edgeworth herself, is her uncommon quickness of perception, her fertility of allusion, and the great resources of fact which I can call nothing else but extraordinary vivacity. She certainly talks quite as well as Lady Delacour or Lady Davenant, and much in the style of both of them, though more in that of Lady Davenant.[4]

No doubt a great deal of her success in society in 1822 was due, when all is said, to her still current reputation as a writer. But, though this gave her the original entry, she established her place because people came to like her for being 'warm-hearted and kind, a charming companion, with all the liveliness and originality of an Irishwoman'.[5]

Even in this disparaging period, relatively few adverse comments were made about her. Isaac D'Israeli's has already been quoted. Mrs. Josiah Wedgwood reported that her neice

[1] Lady Holland, *Memoirs of Sydney Smith* (3rd edn., 1855), p. 446.

[2] R. P. Graves, *Life of Sir W. R. Hamilton*, Dublin, 1882–9, i. 162 (from his description of a visit to Edgeworthstown, 27 Aug. 1824).

[3] Letter to Harriet Beaufort, 7 Feb. 1822.

[4] *Life, Letters and Journals of George Ticknor*, 1876, i. 427. For Lady Delacour's conversation, see above, pp. 311–13; for Lady Davenant's, below, pp. 468–9.

[5] Martha Somerville, *Personal Recollections of Mary Somerville*, 1873, pp. 155–6.

Eliza Wedgwood had met Maria, and found her affected, certainly an uncommon accusation.[1] More plausible was the view of Mrs. Eliza Fletcher, who met her the following year in Edinburgh: Mrs. Fletcher thought Maria over-effusive.[2] Now that the barrier of reserve was broken down, she could also give offence simply by talking too much. Thomas Moore, who originally liked her for her unpretentiousness, became exasperated with her on her next visit to London, at a breakfast of Samuel Rogers's, because, he asserted, she did not know when to stop:

> Miss Edgeworth, with all her cleverness, anything but agreeable. The moment any one begins to speak, off she starts too, seldom more than a sentence behind them, and in general contrives to distance every speaker. Neither does what she say[s], though of course very sensible, at all make up for this over-activity of tongue.[3]

Her family were aware that she occasionally became over-excited. Harriet was relieved when Maria returned to Edgeworthstown at the end of this particular visit to find her 'so perfectly free from feverishness or over-talking or laughing or anything & so delightfully and unceasingly entertaining—It really is a new existence to be with her again.'[4] At times, obviously, the strain of performing in company over-stimulated her, as it had done her father. But, unlike Edgeworth, she was never accused of 'rattling'. Nor was she silly, or pretentious, or malicious, as the great majority of fine talkers could be at some time or other. Because of her great gifts of good humour and sense, Society did not tire of her during the period that it was gradually ceasing to read her. And Maria in her turn was pleased with her new friends. After her season in 1822 she completely reversed the judgement her father had made in 1805, when he stated that London Society never could be as

[1] Mrs. J. Wedgwood to Mme Sismondi, 8 Apr. 1822; Emma Darwin, *A Century of Family Letters*, 1915, i. 143.

[2] *Autobiography*, 1875, pp. 156–7. Mrs. Fletcher's dislike was reciprocated by the Edgeworths. 'I am sure Mrs Fletcher is enough to drive anyone of weak nerves distracted without anything more' (Harriet Butler to Honora Edgeworth, 22 Feb. 1828). But ME could certainly gush on occasion: see those of her letters published by H. W. and I. Law in *The Book of the Beresford Hopes*, 1925, which the editors describe, with justice, as reminiscent of Mr. Collins.

[3] Thomas Moore's diary, entry for 29 Apr. 1831; *Memoirs, Journal and Correspondence of Thomas Moore*, ed. Lord John Russell, 8 vols., 1853–6, vi. 187.

[4] Harriet Butler to Fanny Wilson, 15 July 1831.

good as Paris. 'The great variety of society in London, and the solidity of the sense and information to be gathered from conversation, strike me as far superior to Parisian society.'[1]

There was one more expedition from home in this unusually eventful half-decade of Maria's life: in May 1823 she set off with her stepsisters Harriet and Sophy for Scotland. Among her first hosts were the aged Dugald Stewart and his wife at their country home, Kinneil House. Afterwards Maria renewed her acquaintance with Robert Owen, and toured his school at Lanark,[2] before arriving in Edinburgh in the first week in June. Apart from making contact with old friends of 1803, like the Alisons, Maria's great object was at last to meet Scott.[3] Although it was nearly ten in the evening when they reached their lodgings in Edinburgh, she could not resist the note he had left urging them to call then and there at his town house. She found him occupied more to his taste than hers, listening to a performance of Gaelic songs by the boatman of the Laird of Staffa. On one of the following days she met another old correspondent, Francis Jeffrey. Then she went off with her stepsisters for a five-weeks' tour of the Highlands, before the highlight of the tour in early August, a fortnight's visit to Scott's home at Abbotsford.

Maria's stay with Scott and his family was unquestionably one of the most delightful experiences of her life. She wrote enthusiastic letters home which praised Scott for his generous nature and easy manner, his affection for his family, and of course his genius.[4] To her, as to many of her contemporaries, he was the unchallenged literary giant of their day; she probably admired him more than any other great man she ever met.

[1] ME to Mrs. R, London, 10 Apr. 1822; *Mem.*, ii. 193. Cf. RLE to ME, quoted pp. 206–7 above.

[2] A full description of this visit is given in ME to Honora Edgeworth, 4 June 1823. ME did not like the school, largely because she thought the pupils did not understand their lessons.

[3] She had been corresponding with him regularly since reading his generous tribute to her in the 'Postscript, which should have been a Preface' to *Waverley*. See *Mem.*, i. 303–9. Other letters between them are published in Lockhart's *Life of Scott*, 1837, W. Partington, *The Letterbooks of Sir Walter Scott* (1930), and *Sir Walter's Postbag* (1932), and H. J. C. Grierson, *Letters of Sir Walter Scott*, 12 vols., 1932–7.

[4] Published by R. F. Butler, 'ME and Sir Walter Scott', *RES*, new ser. 9, 1958.

Scott liked her too, as Lockhart bears witness: that month was, he says, one of the happiest in Scott's life.

> Never did I see a brighter day at Abbotsford than that on which Miss Edgeworth first arrived there—never can I forget her look and accent when she was received by him at his archway, and exclaimed, 'Everything about you is exactly what one ought to have had wit enough to dream!' The weather was beautiful, and the edifice, and its appurtenances, were all but complete; and day after day, so long as she could remain, her host had always some new plan of gaiety. One day there was fishing on the Cauldshields Loch, and a dinner on the heathy bank. Another, the whole party feasted by Thomas the Rhymer's waterfall in the glen—and the stone on which Maria that day sat was ever afterwards called 'Edgeworth's stone'. A third day we had to go further afield. He must needs show her, not Newark only, but all the upper scenery of the Yarrow, where 'fair hangs the apple frae the rock',—and the baskets were unpacked about sunset, beside the ruined chapel overlooking St. Mary's Loch—and he had scrambled to gather bluebells and heathflowers, with which all the young ladies must twine their hair,—and they sang, and he recited until it was time to go home beneath the softest of harvest moons.[1]

Lockhart, who could be difficult, liked Maria almost as much as his father-in-law did.[2] Between the younger members of the two families rather more coolness was felt. The Edgeworths did not take to Scott's daughters at first (although they thought they improved on acquaintance), and Anne Scott's comments when the guests left also suggest a certain detachment. 'I like Miss Edgeworth very much, though she talks a great deal, and does not care to hear others talk. There was a dreadful scene at parting. The great Maria nearly went into fits, she had taken such a fancy to us all.'[3] Nor did every social occasion go quite so smoothly as the picnics lyrically described by Lockhart. In the privacy of her letters home Harriet wrote of a dinner after which Sir Walter wanted to go to sleep, but a lady called Miss

[1] J. G. Lockhart, *Memoirs of the Life of Sir Walter Scott*, 1837–8, v. 292.

[2] See Introduction above, p. 3. Lockhart was acting as a good friend to ME at the time of writing his *Life of Scott* (see below, pp. 464–5), which may account for the rather formal complimentary strain of his references to her. His letters written at the time, although also favourable, sound more detached.

[3] Anne Scott to Miss Millar, 8 Sept. 1823; *Letters to a Governess*, ed. P. A. Wright-Henderson, 1905, p. 86.

Setchky 'who had a face like a squashed centipede[']s [&] sitting down at the pianoforte, after a tremendous prelude began such a yelling as precluded all repose'. Next morning in the landau Sir Walter declared to his wife, Anne Scott, and Harriet, that 'Miss Setchky ought to be assassinated, to which we all cordially agreed'.[1] Harriet's description in many ways accounts better than Lockhart's for the success of the visit: Scott and Maria resembled one another not only in many of their opinions and literary practices,[2] but in their pleasant unpretentious good humour and warm manner. Both of them liked to like and be liked. After this they wrote to one another frequently, and Scott returned Maria's visit in August 1825; then he and Lockhart carried her off on a tour of the Lakes of Killarney. But by this time financial trouble was in the offing, not just for Scott but for the Edgeworths as well. There was to be no more travelling for Maria for the time being, and, when she said goodbye to Scott in Dublin on 15 August 1825, it was for the last time.

There were already signs at Edgeworthstown in the early 1820s that the estate was in difficulties, but at that time Maria herself was not in a position to know the full facts. In spite of her experience as his assistant for thirty-five years, Edgeworth had not left her with any further role in running the estate after his death. This was because there were traits in her character which he mistrusted, especially her anxiety to please; he thought she would be too liable to grant favours, and to give away her capital to anyone in the family who asked for it. On his deathbed he warned her against the dangerous softness of her nature, while praising Lovell, his principal heir under the marriage settlement with his second wife Honora, as 'wise and economic'.[3]

Edgeworth had taken great care in drawing up his will. Lovell was the immediate legatee of about a third of the estate, and after ten years he was to have it all. In the meantime the larger portion was set aside and its rents went into a Trust, which was to pay legacies and annuities to Mrs. Edgeworth, Maria, and the younger children. Edgeworth named two trustees

[1] Letters to Lucy and Honora Edgeworth, 30 July and 7 Aug. 1823; *REL*, v, 1964, 64–5.

[2] For which see above, pp. 394 ff.

[3] Memorandum by ME, quoted *Black Book*, pp. 209–10.

outside the immediate family, but most unfortunately one of them, Lord Longford, felt unable to act, and the family (presumably led by Mrs. Edgeworth and Maria) decided to have Lovell made trustee. In 1817 they were full of gratitude to him, because he had behaved generously in asking them all to stay on as before at Edgeworthstown. In return they wanted to show their confidence in him as head of the family; with the result that for several years not merely a third but the whole of the estate was Lovell's sole responsibility.

Even a sterner and more methodical man than Lovell would have had difficulty in fulfilling his father's instructions to the letter. In making his will (which was signed as early as 8 December 1814), Edgeworth had calculated the income of the Trust estate at £2,500 (Irish)[1] a year, and from the sale of two properties, which he directed, he expected a further large lump sum. But by now the war had ended, and land values had declined sharply. The legacies which (in accordance with marriage settlements) he left to his children, and the annuities of £400 a year for his widow, and £500 a year for Maria, could not in fact be met from the income which the Trust lands yielded after 1817. Indeed, before many years were up, Lovell could scarcely find money for the annual payments, let alone hope to raise the principal in 1827. He believed (wrongly, as it turned out) that the Trust was in debt to him rather than the other way round, and at last, at the end of 1822, he asked Mrs. Edgeworth to take over the business of receiving the Trust's rents and administering its business. Mrs. Edgeworth found that Lovell's accounts were in confusion, that rents were in arrear, and that there was no hope of getting tenants on the Trust lands, the poorer parts of the estate, to pay up in the near future. She took on an agent, George Hinds, who collected the rents and henceforth kept the Trust accounts in good order.

But Lovell had still not confessed his private debts, nor the debts of the admirably conceived school which he was running at Edgeworthstown. Afterwards Maria declared that he was not a villain, but a coward; he could not face the family with disagreeable truths. At last, late in 1825, he made a clean breast of it. He was deep in debt, to the extent, as it turned out, of £26,000. Lovell now put his affairs into Maria's hands and

[1] The Irish £ was worth 18*s*. 6*d*. English.

'empowered me to act as his agent and to call in his debts and devise, if I could, with the aid of the rest of the family, some means of extrication'.[1]

Money was tight everywhere in 1826, and raising a loan was no easy matter. Maria faced the problem with a toughness that reflected ironically upon her father's deathbed pronouncements. A lawyer told her there was nothing to be done but sell or mortgage immediately. But Maria was as firmly persuaded as her father and grandfather that land must never be allowed to go out of the family; she therefore followed a policy of selling at a fair valuation to Sneyd and William, and raising loans within the family, especially from herself and Honora.[2] The immediate need was to meet the bills and interest payments that were already due, and this could not be done without the help of the tenants:

> All his [Lovell's] tenants joined in giving me assistance either by advancing the rents due somewhat before the time of payment, or by refraining to claim debts due to them till it should be convenient to pay, or by lending whatever sums they could spare even for a few months trusting that I would repay them punctually on the day I promised & requiring nothing from me but my word—refusing to take any interest for these most useful and timely loans. I cannot recollect without strong emotions of gratitude these proofs of our tenants affection & the more touching they were to me that they thought they owed whatever they could do for his children to my father's memory who was the best of landlords and friends to them—With this assistance at our utmost need we were able to pay all the bills which became due at that date. Not one was dishonoured.[3]

At the same time Maria attacked the creditors, tempting them with the prospect of ready money if they moderated their demands, or threatening them with exposure if their claims were exorbitant. In two or three years she had halved Lovell's debt, that is brought it down to between £12,000 and £13,000. From now on they could raise no more large sums, and the debt had to be paid off in small amounts year by year.

[1] ME's Memorandum, 'Appendix . . . to my grandfather's Black Book', 2 Apr. 1839 (Irish State Paper Office).

[2] ME lent £4,000 or £5,000, Honora £2,000. ME's money was from her books and from gifts by RLE (see above, p. 102); Honora had inherited Sneyd money, like the other children of the Sneyd wives.

[3] Ibid. Most of Lovell's tenants were gentlemen farmers.

Meanwhile the problem of the Trust estate had to be faced. Lovell generously insisted on extending the original ten-year term until all the legacies of his brothers and sisters could be paid off. The family calculated that for the Trust to meet its liabilities would take a further seventeen years from 1826, so that Lovell was voluntarily giving up the greater part of his inheritance for sixteen years beyond the date set in his father's will. In this way, by a co-operative family effort, which Maria worked out and supervised, they weathered the crisis of 1826–7, and kept almost all the estate together.

Maria's success in handling Lovell's debts gave her a role in the family which she had never enjoyed before. Together with her stepmother Frances she was now the dominant figure, in fact if not in law. There was no strength of character in the sons of Edgeworth's Sneyd marriages,[1] and the women made a better job of holding the estate together than Lovell, Sneyd, and William could have done. Maria in fact emerged as a woman of unexpected strength. After spending two-thirds of her life emphasizing her dependence on her elders, she had learnt to share with Frances the leadership of the family.

Not all her activities within the family circle were as well judged as her handling of the estate. In 1819, for example, she intervened in the life of her favourite stepsister, Fanny, in a way that does more credit to her affection than her good sense. The brother of Capt. Francis Beaufort's wife Alicia—Lestock Wilson, a young City business-man—had fallen in love with Fanny and asked her to marry him. Fanny was at first well disposed; but Maria, thinking that Fanny had an *entrée* to a far more distinguished world than Lestock's, persuaded her to look higher. Like Lady Russell's interference in Anne Elliott's life in *Persuasion*, Maria's advice was well meant, and it was never resented; but the result was much the same. Ten years later, on 1 January 1829 (Maria's sixty-first birthday), Fanny married

[1] RLE summed up the common characteristics of his Sneyd children, and indeed the Sneyd sisters (excluding Honora), when he coined the word 'Sneydism'. 'The Sneyd part of all my children is the best in every circumstance but two—strength of lungs and self-confidence—I do not mean courage but that ready belief in the power of our own abilities and the independence of our own exertions—Upon these I have always endeavoured to rely' (RLE to Charlotte Sneyd, Paris, 29 Nov. 1802).

Lestock after all. In 1829 there was no opposition from Maria, for as Fanny was nearly thirty, and in poor health, it was no longer realistic to suppose that she could do better than marry a man who loved her devotedly and had the means to support her. The respect that Maria had come on mature reflection to feel for the sterling qualities of Lestock can be gauged from *Helen*, which was written in the first years of Fanny's marriage: one of the central figures in that book, General Clarendon, resembles Lestock in having every attribute that could be desired in a husband, except brilliance.

Part of Maria's moral progress in the 1820s was to learn one of the hardest parts of the parent's responsibility, when to abdicate. She felt a sense of loss with each depletion in the family circle over the years. Mrs. Edgeworth's sons were the first to go: Francis went to Charterhouse School in 1819, and Cambridge in 1827, while Michael Pakenham was away from 1823, first at Charterhouse, afterwards at the East India College—Hertford College, later Haileybury; he left for India in the spring of 1831. Sophy, the third daughter, had a pretty face and a sweet singing voice; she was the first girl to leave on her marriage in March 1824 to her second cousin and neighbour, Capt. Barry Fox. The marriage of Harriet in August 1826 deprived Edgeworthstown of a more forceful and amusing personality; she too married an Irishman, the clergyman Richard Butler, who was Rector of Trim, Co. Meath, when Harriet married him, and later became Dean of Clonmacnoise. Fanny's departure for London with Lestock in 1829 was the worst blow of all for Maria, both because Fanny would be further away and because since infancy she had been the child nearest Maria's heart. Why this was so is not clear from Fanny's intelligent but rather reserved letters; the entertaining Harriet has a much more universal appeal.

Maria never said, and perhaps never thought, that her horizons became more confined after the mid 1820s. But after that brilliant half-decade, when she had introduced her three stepsisters into high Society in England, the Continent, and Scotland, she saw all three make less than brilliant marriages with neighbours or within the family. Once her stepsisters had gone, there was less incentive for Maria herself to go into Society. Meanwhile the circle at home diminished, not merely because the young people went away, but because of the loss one by one of the much-loved older generation. Daniel Augustus Beaufort died, aged eighty-four, in 1821; Charlotte Sneyd in 1822; John Ruxton in 1825. An even more shocking death, in May 1829, was that of one of the three remaining sons of Edgeworth's Sneyd wives, William, aged thirty-five, from pneumonia. In the same year Mrs. Ruxton had a serious illness which recurred in 1830; and it may have been partly in order to avoid being a spectator at her aunt's deathbed that Maria set out that October to stay with Fanny at 1 North Audley Street in London.

There was no question of getting away from personal sorrow in the capital. Maria was followed by the news that her aunt Ruxton had died not long after her departure, on 1 November 1830. As usual Maria's letters did not dwell on mournful subjects, but her aunt had been a strong influence in her life for nearly fifty years, and this was her severest loss since her father. In any case the London world she knew, Whig social and intellectual high life, was a product of the Regency era, and it was breaking up under the changed conditions of the years preceding Reform. Many old friends were dead or dying. The preceding year, while at home, she had heard of the death of Dumont, which had called to mind 'so many thoughts of mine, so many feelings connected with literature[,] with my father, with my happiest days!'[1] In London she learnt from the Lockharts and others of Sir Walter Scott's failing health; he had already had more than one paralytic seizure, although he did not die till 1832. She found both the Duchess of Wellington and Thomas Hope very ill, and both died during her stay in London, within a few days of her last call on them. Again and again she was reminded of a conversation she had had at Hope's house in 1819, in the presence of the Duke of Wellington, when she had quoted Mme de Staël's 'On dépose fleur à fleur la couronne de la vie', and Lord Harrowby had replied with Johnson's

> Year follows year, decay pursues decay
> Still drops from life some withering joy away.[2]

[1] ME to Mrs. Marcet, 25 Oct. 1829; H. W. Hausermann, *The Genevese Background*, p. 153.

[2] ME to SR, 2 Apr. 1819; *Mem.*, ii. 37. As usual ME (or Lord Harrowby) was

After returning to Edgeworthstown in July 1831, Maria made only two more visits to London, from December 1840 to May 1841, and from November 1843 to April 1844. It would be wrong to suggest that she struck the people she met on these visits as any less cheerful, or even on occasions brilliant, than before. But now that she had a domestic centre in London in North Audley Street her visits to the capital had the flavour of a family visit rather than a season in town. Fanny's health meant that much of Maria's time had to be spent at home; and even when Fanny was well, the Wilson–Beaufort influence militated against a highly fashionable existence. Maria saw her old friends, including the Lansdownes, Sydney Smith, and Samuel Rogers. But few of her new acquaintances were politicians and literary men; more were scientists, geographers, and travellers. By the 1840s other and greater novelists had come to the fore, and Maria's was no longer a current literary name. She retained her popularity among people who knew her, but she was no longer the 'lion' of 1813 to 1822.

Maria's visits to Fanny in London after her marriage were also less frequent than they might have been, because fresh financial troubles kept her at home. In 1833 Lovell reluctantly confessed to more secret borrowing, to the sum of £3,000. What the family openly complained of was that he had lied, and broken his promise not to borrow again; in private they probably also felt that his heavy drinking made him intolerable to live with. They now gathered together and agreed to take concerted action to protect themselves and the estate. The next brother, Sneyd, agreed to buy the whole of Lovell's remaining property, and also to take upon himself the payment of his debts, while Lovell was allowed an annuity of £250. Lovell went off to live in Liverpool, and Sneyd returned to his home in Kent, leaving Mrs. Edgeworth as tenant of the house, and Maria to continue as agent.

She performed this function for Sneyd until 1839, when she was 71. In this year her stepbrother Francis came back to act as agent to the Trust estate in place of George Hinds, and

not quite accurate. Johnson wrote: 'Year chases year, decay pursues decay, / Still drops some joy from with'ring life away': a significantly better version (*Vanity of Human Wishes*, ll. 305–6).

gradually Maria relinquished the running of Sneyd's lands to him as well. By this time she had seen the estate through fifteen arduous years, a fact which is essential to an understanding of the woman she became in old age. The family's financial trouble was in a sense the making of her. The weakness and dependence which those who knew Maria best had always associated with her was ground out of her on this seemingly unending treadmill. She was faced after 1826, and even more after 1833, with a situation in which neither she nor the family could afford for her to be a Rosamond, perpetually extricated from her difficulties by a parent. The continued existence of Edgeworthstown as the family home depended on her prudence, and her own description of how difficult it was to act as an agent throughout this period certainly underestimates the reality. She had to go against the grain of her nature in order to keep the estate together. When, for example, Sneyd wanted to take a short cut by finding someone who would lend money below the usual rate of five per cent, it was Maria, most un-Rosamond-like, who recommended caution. She did not think they would find any quick way of clearing off the arrears of debt:

> All that can be done as far as I see at present in these affairs must be by endurance and forbearance, by the strictest economy & punctuality in the payment of interests—One half year's unpunctuality would throw the next into such embarrassment that it would be absolutely impossible to pay these accumulated interests & any fresh loan could not be made without selling land to pay for it.
>
> The alarm would instantly spread and a forced sale must ensue. That is the evil which I deprecate and which only the continual vigilance of an agent who is a friend and one of the family can prevent . . . Nor could anyone else have motive sufficiently powerful and constant to sustain him (or her) under the continual petty difficulties and temptations to deviate from the strict line of penurious duty into the path of danger and destruction . . . It would be sufficiently irksome even to any one of the family, if a man, to be a mere *locum tenens* machine receiving with one hand and paying with the other & appearing to have neither power or [*sic*] will to do any good or kindness to any one of the tenants who pay their rents so well and are so friendly and obliging *to the family* and so grateful to the liberal landlord of better days—As a woman I have been better able to bear this situation and these awkward and to a generous mind painful trials than any man of the family could have

been . . . I flatter myself that I am by this means useful to my family . . . from the confidence which the persons both receiving interests and the tenants needing repairs and consideration of various sort have for one whom they have known and had dealings with for above half a century and whom their beloved landlord, my father, first introduced to them.[1]

Thanks therefore to persistence and hard-headedness, she brought the family out of their worst financial straits, although the Edgeworths were never again as comfortably off as they had been in the palmy days of Irish landlordism before 1814.

The remnants of her father's family which Maria did so much to hold together were by now scattered in Ireland and England; Edgeworthstown House was merely a symbolic centre. The Sneyd element was still represented there by the pleasant, intelligent, and self-effacing Honora (born 1791), and by the aged Mary Sneyd. But Honora left home in March 1838, on her marriage to Francis Beaufort, who had been left a widower in the previous year.[2] Aunt Mary died, aged 90, in 1841; she had lived under the same roof with Maria for almost half a century, and had been one of the most devoted and useful of the 'committee of education and criticism'. After Honora's departure, Lucy was the only stepsister left at home; and Lucy too was eventually married, in 1843, to the Irish astronomer Dr. T. Romney Robinson. Meanwhile in her old age Maria lost three of her youngest stepbrothers and sisters by death—Sophy in 1837, Francis in 1846, and, most distressing of all, Fanny in 1848.

Yet, in spite of so much change, and private reason for sorrow, she went evenly on. The daily pattern of her life—an early morning walk, an afternoon drive—maintained the formality she approved of in domestic affairs, and allows no prying into her states of mind. In appearance she remained neat, active, and agreeable, and she kept herself busy according to the pattern of life her father had laid down in what she called 'my happiest times'. Edgeworthstown House remained the centre not only of the scattered family, but of a further 'family' of old tenants and servants who occasionally wrote to her from as far afield as

[1] ME to Mrs. FE, 29 Nov. 1833. Cf. Memorandum, 'Appendix . . . to my grandfather's Black Book', 2 Apr. 1839.

[2] For Beaufort's career, see above, p. 130 n.

Chapter                    30 pages—

Sir Ulick O'Shane comes into his drawing
room after a late sitting — remarks on
a formal circle — character of Sir U O'Shane
& Lady O'Shane — history of his 3 marriages
— his connexion with Lady A & her daughter
character of Lady A — how she & Sir
U had been at variance why he wishes
his son Marcus to marry Miss A—
A ball this night was to have been opened
by Marcus & Miss A — but Marcus had
dined out with his friend young Ormond
— at Mr C— O'Shane's — K of the B— Islands — Lady

FROM MARIA EDGEWORTH'S SKETCH FOR ORMOND

PLATE VI

THE FAMILY CIRCLE AT EDGEWORTHSTOWN, 1837

Sketch of Harriet Butler reading Lover's *Rory O'More*. (From left) Mary Sneyd, Harriet, Maria, and Mrs. Edgeworth

America and India. It was her natural home, both because of all these ties and because of the presence there of her great friend and stepmother, Frances; while nearby in County Meath was Harriet's cheerful house at Trim, as congenial an alternative in Maria's last years as Black Castle had been during her father's lifetime. Maria visited Trim and was in her usual spirits in April 1849. Back home at Edgeworthstown with Frances she was taken ill: according to the *Memoir*, she returned from a drive on 22 May complaining of a pain around her heart, and died a few hours later. A family letter says that after a mild illness lasting a few days, she suddenly worsened and died in Frances's arms. In either case her unobtrusive exit matched the spirit of her life, as her stepmother noted. 'She had always wished to die at home, and that I should be with her—all her wishes were fulfilled.'[1]

In her later years Maria had looked back on her long life and reflected on its consistency. 'The same in my friendships and in my views of what did then and has always made me happy—the love of those I love and domestic life.'[2] And this was essentially true, despite the changes she had seen since Edgeworth's death. Even in her most fashionable period, she had preferred English country houses to London high life, the naturalness of Scott's conversation to the brilliance of Mackintosh's,[3] even vulgarity, such as she detected in Ricardo's family, to lifeless elegance like that of Lord Carrington's daughters (although, she could not help adding in the last case, 'I would rather be without both these defects').[4] The fact that she became famous made little difference either to her taste or her manner, since it was in keeping both with her sincerity, and her sense of decorum, that she never enjoyed being lionized;[5] she liked to be a woman and a lady, not 'Mrs. authoress'.

The last point is borne out by the friends she made in old age. In the 1830s and 1840s she made few fresh men friends, but

[1] *Mem.*, iii. 265.

[2] ME to Fanny Wilson, Christmas 1841.

[3] ME to Mrs. R, 8 June 1823; R. F. Butler, 'Maria Edgeworth and Sir Walter Scott', *RES*, ix, 1958; and Mrs. S. C. Hall, *Art Journal*, xi, 1849, 227.

[4] ME to Mrs. FE, 9 Nov. 1821.

[5] ME's reflections on this process are published in *Thoughts on Bores*, eventually published anonymously in the annual *Janus* of 1826.

increasingly came to appreciate unpretentious motherly older women, not unlike herself. One was Mrs. Martin of Ballinahinch;[1] another Joanna Baillie, who was five years older than Maria; a third Miss Baillie's neighbour, Mrs. Carr. Maria drew a typical distinction between Mrs. Carr and her more elegant daughter Isabella (Lady Culling Smith):

> I am very glad that Mrs. Carr's daughter was so well received & cherished—I am sure Mrs. Carr would have felt it a great deal more warmly for her than she did for herself—But that is because the mother's nature is warmer at heart than the daughter's—People can only feel as much as they can . . . All the time I don't mean to say that she has not feeling enough—Only I like more—Give me Mrs. Martin for the matter of that.[2]

In the past her father had taught her to admire men and women of integrity, the kind of figure based on Honora and Thomas Day and represented in the novels by the forbidding statesman Lord Oldborough. Now that Edgeworth was dead Maria chose for herself warmer, more expressive people, and she had the confidence in her judgement to stand by it in print.[3]

Maria's later life is most striking for this, that at last she found her natural personality and the scale of values that went with it. In the past she had become self-conscious if required to describe anything beautiful, whether paintings in the Louvre or a natural landscape. While she did not develop any remarkable talents as a descriptive writer, she did learn in later life to take pleasure in the beautiful (if not in the sublime), and she was no longer timid about saying so:

> The lanes about this place are delightful—full of dogroses & singing birds & every figure we meet—old man old woman, boy or girl with pitcher—ass with faggots or ploughman plodding home—picturesque—& even the *pigs*—*Morlands*—Yesterday evening returning home by sunset we heard a boy playing a flute or flageolet in a wood on the other side of the water so agreeably all the while we were coming up the hill and seeing the light of the sunset on the trees—I have much more pleasure infinitely more in my old age in

[1] ME met Mrs. Martin while touring Connemara in Oct. 1833. The fine letter to M. Pakenham Edgeworth of Mar. 1834 which describes the tour has been published by H. E. Butler, *Tour in Connemara and the Martins of Ballinahinch*, 1950.

[2] ME to Mrs. FE, 29 Nov. 1833.

[3] See below, pp. 475–8.

the sight of the beauties of nature than I ever had in youth—It seems as if I had come into the possession of the fortune of my senses late in life—and like all people not used early to riches I suppose I am inclined to make a sort of *parvenu* boasting of them.[1]

Maria's earlier novels contain few descriptive passages and often suffer from the lack of a physical setting, while *Helen*, which in so many respects reflects Maria's new-found areas of awareness, is 'placed' in a pleasant Southern English countryside.

At the same time, Maria knew where to draw the line. Her family and friends mattered far, far more than inanimate nature to her. When her erratic stepbrother Francis gave as a reason for settling in Italy the fact that he liked the climate and the landscape, Maria was half diverted, half appalled at his sense of priorities:

It is most difficult to judge for one whose feelings are so different absolutely different from one's own.—I am so little influenced by climate—it makes so small a portion of my happiness compared with *persons*—*Things* he says are so much more permanent—meaning sky & trees & statues etc![2]

During her father's lifetime she had greatly exaggerated her need for him, and to a lesser extent for Aunt Ruxton. The warmth of her expressions, and her fondness for 'petting', had been mistaken by her friends, and by herself as well, for weakness. What Maria evidently did need was the security of her home, and while the home was governed by an older generation she played the appropriate role of the daughter who was happy to be guided by wiser heads than her own. Having taken her docility at face value, the family were afterwards astonished at her underlying toughness of mind. She revealed this partly in her shrewdness with money, partly in her ability to endure the loss of one much-loved friend after another. Long before, in 1806 when Charlotte was dying, Maria had thought that she would be most useful if she was cheerful, and so she remained in later life in the face of every successive shock. Like her manner of running the estate, her good humour showed a

[1] ME to Fanny Wilson, Hamstead Hall, nr. Birmingham (the home of the Moilliets), 2 July 1831.

[2] ME to Fanny Wilson, 12 Aug. 1831.

remarkable ability to discipline personal feelings and tastes in the interests of the family circle. That was why, in delivering her formal *éloge* on Maria's life, Mrs. Edgeworth put the emphasis on her powers of control rather than of expression, and on her head rather than her heart:

> . . . Her genius, her vast capacity for every species of knowledge, her infinite cheerfulness: and with all her bright fancy, and all her never-failing wit, the wonderfully practical nature of her mind. The most remarkable trait in her character was the prudence with which she acted; the command which she had acquired over her naturally impetuous nature and boundless generosity of spirit.[1]

[1] *Mem.*, iii. 265.

# X

# WRITING WITHOUT HER FATHER

THE story of Maria's life in her last three decades leaves unanswered an outstanding question: why in a period of growing self-knowledge and self-fulfilment, in private life the most effective years of all, she succeeded in publishing so little of importance.

After meeting her at parties, the fashionable 'Conversation' Sharp had a graceful explanation for her failure to publish a novel which delighted Maria—'she is too busy being happy'.[1] But Sharp was not quite accurate, and in approving of what he said Maria was, as so often, over-influenced by sentiment; the implication was that she had ceased to have literary ambitions, and this was not true at all.

From 1818 to 1825 writing seems to have kept her as busy as ever. In spite of her despair about literature as an occupation at the end of 1817, she went to work promptly on her father's *Memoirs* in 1818 and 1819. Later in 1819 she nearly completed a new two-volume book in the *Early Lessons* series, *Rosamond* (1821), together with *The Most Unfortunate Day of My Life* (unpublished until 1931). Nor was she idle during her foreign tour of 1820. Two new chapters were needed for *Rosamond*, and Maria, hearing of this while staying at Pregny in Switzerland, sat down immediately to compose the episodes of 'The Bracelet of Memory' and 'Blind Kate'.[2] On her return she wrote another instalment of *Early Lessons*, the three-volume *Frank*. Her visit to England in 1818 and 1819 finds many echoes in *Frank*, and it comes as no surprise to find that the family were reading over the letters of the tour while Maria was engaged in writing it.[3] In 1821–2 came the nine-months' visit to England, during which she wrote nothing. After she returned to Edgeworthstown,

[1] ME to Mrs. Lazarus, n.d. [1831]. Richard Sharp (1759–1835), *littérateur*, Whig M.P., and diner-out, met ME on successive visits to England.

[2] ME to Honora Edgeworth, Pregny, 1 Oct. 1820.

[3] Honora Edgeworth to SR, in copy of letter from CSE to Harriet Edgeworth, 10 Feb. 1821, postmark 2 Apr. 1821.

she went to work on *Harry and Lucy Concluded*, which fills four volumes, and is both a scientific textbook and one of the most impressive and interesting of Maria's books for children.

These years were in fact so busy that the usual question asked by her biographers, why did she not write?, is a false one. What her family and friends did want to know at the time was why she wrote only for children. The reason she gave Scott—that children's books did not get reviewed—goes a long way to explain her failure to publish anything more substantial in the 1820s.[1] Within the family, she also suggested that she had a positive duty to finish the series which had been so central an element of the literary partnership. 'I could never be easy writing anything else for my own amusement till I have done this, which I know my father wished to have finished.'[2]

But *Harry and Lucy Concluded* did finish the series in 1825, and after this Maria told her friends that she had every intention of resuming her career as a writer of fiction for adults. For two or three years more, when she was trying to disentangle the affairs of the estate, she had less time for writing than at any previous period of living at home, and to the vexation of some of her relatives she produced nothing. 'It is indeed a most deplorable thing that a mind like hers should be chain'd down to accounts—though it was so noble a thing the undertaking them—I should like to see her writing something really great—coming forth once more & vindicating her throne to herself.'[3] It was time she was short of, and not inclination. In fact she was anxious to take up her pen if only as a means of making money; the profits of *Harry and Lucy Concluded* had been set aside in advance to pay college fees for her brothers Francis and Pakenham.[4] The urgent need (for the first time in her career) to write for money finally decided the question of novels versus children's books and articles, since the latter paid both author and publisher less—except when successful enough to have several editions, as *Harry and Lucy Concluded* was not.[5] On the

[1] See above, pp. 412–13.

[2] ME to Mrs. R, 7 Aug. 1822; *Mem.*, ii. 206.

[3] Francis Beaufort Edgeworth to Fanny, Cambridge, n.d. [Jan. 1826]. ME received letters on this theme from Mrs. R and CSE, especially in 1827–8.

[4] ME to Walter Scott, 17 Nov. 1824; Nat. Lib. of Scotland, MS. 868, f. 108.

[5] See Appendix B.

other hand a novel that was known to be hers should still get a good price; Lockhart estimated it surprisingly high, in view of the uncertainty in the publishing trade. Advising her to let Scott handle the business side, he told her that for a full-length novel she might expect between £1,000 and £1,500.[1] So large a sum at this time must have been a decisive argument, and Maria was convinced.

It was at this point, when she had to begin a full-length tale from the beginning, that Maria felt the full psychological effect on her writing of the absence of her 'literary partner'. Edgeworth might have contributed little to the text of the novels, but at certain stages in their composition his ability to reassure Maria had been invaluable. It is true, as her critics have never tired of pointing out, that she wrote two good stories, *Castle Rackrent* and *The Modern Griselda*, without assistance from him in the early stages, but then the germ of these two tales was unusually substantial; *Castle Rackrent* evolved from a fairly elaborate verbal imitation of a real man, *The Modern Griselda* from an essay which contained much of the necessary material for the novel.[2] It was while her literary ideas were in a more germinal state than this that she seems to have lacked confidence in them. Before 1817 she had been able to take her tentative suggestions to her father, who seldom remained in a state of doubt—'Sketch that, and show it to me'. Now that he was dead, her diffidence about embarking on a fresh plan was very real. She had plenty of ideas, but she did not know which were the good ones.

Throughout the 1820s she tried to get Scott to take Edgeworth's place as her literary mentor:

> I want you to tell me whether you think a subject promising which I am turning in my head for another popular or fashionable tale if I can make it into either—*Travellers*—of various classes—with their faults follies, humors . . . If you should be so kind as not to forget my case do pray lend me a helping hand—Throw me a few

[1] J. G. Lockhart to ME, n.d. [1828], Nat. Lib. of Scotland, MS. 936, f. 6. It was about this time that the publisher Cadell wrote to Scott urging him to keep his name before the public, and citing ME as an example of a novelist who had unwisely let her reputation grow cold (R. Cadell to WS, 21 Mar. 1828; W. Partington, *Letter-books of Sir Walter Scott*, 1930, pp. 361–2). Apparently Scott and Lockhart were more optimistic about her chance of success.

[2] See above, pp. 174 and 238.

hints out of your abundance—above all things hinder me from setting off on a wrong road if you think it would lead to nothing—I have lost him who used to judge for me & give richly.[1]

Scott urged her to go on with *Travellers*, and supplied her with an anecdote she might use; but he begged her not to publish anything anonymously, and eventually she accepted his advice: 'You have settled for me that I am not to write anonymously.'[2]

*Travellers* remained in her mind for several years, and she made several pages of notes for it. One of the characters was to have been a bigoted Orangeman, who would have provided an opportunity for Irish dialogue, and for making the sort of points about the Irish political scene that were made in *Ormond*. But *Travellers* never progressed beyond the notebooks. While Maria was still engaged on volumes for children, Washington Irving brought out his *Tales of a Traveller* (1824), which she was so convinced had forestalled her that even Scott could not persuade her otherwise.[3]

Another plan considered at this time got further, but eventually came to nothing. *Take for Granted*, worked up from the hint Dumont gave as long ago as 1812, existed in some form in manuscript in the spring of 1821,[4] and Maria did more work on it late in 1828 and early in 1829. There was even 'an announcement in the *Lit. Gazette* that Miss E. is *far advanced* in a novel in 3 vols to be called *Take for Granted*'[5] but, although the title was right, the rest of the *Gazette*'s story was wrong. Maria had not advanced far, because Scott and Lockhart had persuaded her that she must produce a *novel*, and the scheme of *Take for Granted* had proved unsuitable:

I have cried *halt* in *take for granted* but only *halt*—I found that it could afford only a short story from the radical vice of its having a *tethered* subject—tethered to one point—and I thought that having been so long lying by I had better not produce a *mouse* only—

[1] ME to Walter Scott, 11 Oct. 1824; Nat. Lib. of Scotland, MS. 3899, f. 157. Cf. also ME to Scott, 15 July 1830, quoted above, p. 267.

[2] Scott to ME, 15 Oct. 1824; *Letters*, viii. 395–402, and ME to WS, 15 July 1830; Nat. Lib. of Scotland, MS. 3919, f. 227.

[3] ME to CSE, 20 Mar. 1827.

[4] Honora Edgeworth to SR, in copy of letter from CSE to Harriet Edgeworth of 10 Feb. 1821, postmark 2 Apr. 1821.

[5] ME to Mrs. R, 18 Mar. 1828.

Therefore I have turned my hand to a *longer*—I did not say a better thing—That's to be proved—a novel in *only* two volumes I hope. . . .[1]

She resumed *Take for Granted* in 1834–6, and again in 1838, when she ended by burning 100 pages of manuscript.

But to return to 1828, the year when she began her serious efforts to produce a novel without her father. Even before she put *Take for Granted* aside, she was forced to apologize to Mrs. Ruxton, who was especially eager to see the promised novel. Maria had to admit that once again she had been beguiled into producing a long tale for children: *Garry-Owen*, which she had felt obliged to write for a young friend of Lockhart's, Crofton Croker, who was editing an annual called *The Christmas Box*. After this, at last, she did begin work in earnest. For six months early in 1829 she toiled at the new 'novel in *only* two volumes', about which there is little information except that the setting was London and one character was to be a Scottish absentee.[2] She applied to her stepsisters Fanny and Harriet for the kind of advice she might once have received from her father, and at one stage at least Fanny responded with radical criticisms, which Maria eagerly welcomed:

I have been impatient to finish up the rewriting of the ms to the place where it ended when you read it. I have now accomplished it and I send two chapters and will send the other two next post. I think my most urgent and most agreeable motive has been to prove to you my dear that you have not done me harm or discouraged me but that on the contrary you have excited and inspirited me . . . The Irishman whom you approved is kept for his proper place—so is the sarcastic man whom you liked and the two fine ladies—nothing is wasted that was worth the —— part of a farthing—But all the rubbish has been burnt for I could not bear the sight of it and besides should have been very sorry that thereafter anybody should have conned over those pages and *fancied* that something might have been better as it was at first.[3]

Although the last sentence seems to imply lingering doubts about Fanny's judgement, it was in line with Maria's general policy to destroy any passage which she did not like. This practice was much invoked in 1829: she wrote to Lockhart in June that she had 'torn to pieces day after day I am sure 300

[1] ME to J. G. Lockhart, 8 Feb. 1829; Nat. Lib. of Scotland, MS. 934, f. 72.

[2] See above, p. 267.

[3] ME to Fanny Wilson, 14 Feb. 1829.

pages within this six months from being dissatisfied with them—Especially during these last 6 weeks what I forced myself to write, I could not after all bear to read.'[1] The abortive novel of 1829 has therefore disappeared with unusual completeness from her well-documented life—neither theme nor title survives—but some of the material was made over into *Helen*. In the latter novel Helen voluntarily gives up a fortune which her uncle had put in trust for her, in order to pay off his debts. A more substantial episode like this was to have appeared in the novel of 1829:

> Mr. Strickland is to be here again with Mr. Boddenham—this evening . . . When this man's father's bank was in peril—old Boddenham from anxiety was in danger of a paralytic stroke—his son had a large property entailed which the creditors of the bank could not touch—To save his father he immediately gave up the whole—except a few hundreds for himself & his wife to live upon—sunk down from his high estate at once & rose in the opinion of all the good how much above the great—he prolonged his father's life two years by the sacrifice—The bank broke afterwards . . . Now my dear you have read my sketch of the story I am writing—I hope you recollect that it was my written intention that my hero should lose his fortune by his father of aristocratic famy. having given his name as a sleeping partner in a bank—& that his generous conduct should &c.—The only new circumstances of which I shall certainly avail myself are the palsy & the *settled property* which will increase the generosity & pay a due tribute to Boddenham that will be known only to self and friends—I hope you will remember that I had actually *written* my intentions. . . .[2]

This scheme of 1829 was at least promising enough to yield three hundred pages, while many other plans that Maria sketched after her father's death seem to have produced nothing at all. On the back of some rejected sheets of *Harrington*, for example, are those sketches which never turned into tales—'The Modern Lucretia', 'Celebrity', and 'The Life and Death of a Divorcée'. *Take for Granted* and *Travellers* were also meant for tales, and there were obviously periods after 1817 when Maria

[1] ME to J. G. Lockhart, 8 June 1829; Nat. Lib. of Scotland, MS. 923, f. 59.

[2] ME to Fanny Wilson, 3 Mar. 1829. The hero of ME's anecdote is presumably Charles Thomas Bodenham, of the Catholic family long resident at Rotherwas, Herefordshire. ME later confessed that transplanting his story into *Helen* was a mistake, because it was irrelevant to the theme (*Life, Letters and Journals of George Ticknor*, 1876, i. 428).

Edgeworth preferred the idea of another series of popular or fashionable tales to the more arduous task of writing a full-length novel. The later eighteen-thirties were years when some such plan was in her mind. As late as 1841, when she was already seventy-three, she was making detailed sketches for a story she called 'Nora' or 'The Fair Parvenue', which turned on the problems created by educating a girl out of her station: the germ of this idea had been in her head since 1834.

In the fifteen years following *Helen* in 1833, she managed to complete only one story, and that was for the juvenile audience which she found least demanding. *Orlandino* (1848) illustrated the advantages of temperance, and the profits went to raise money for the victims of the Irish famine. Maria's benevolence provided the motive for a last, unambitious effort, long after her natural will to write had gone.

Looking back on Maria's repeated failures after 1828 to write a novel, Mrs. Edgeworth came to a simple conclusion:

> She had long hesitated as to writing any work of fiction without that support and sanction to which she had been accustomed from her father in all her previous works . . . to write a tale which was to bear comparison with *Belinda* or *Patronage* seemed to her for many years to be, without her father's encouragement, an impossibility.[1]

When at last *Helen* was completed, after unusual worry and uncertainty, Maria's own account of her five-year struggle to produce a novel is very similar to her stepmother's: 'You cannot conceive (even knowing me as you do) how much I was afraid myself to venture what had not his correction & his sanction—for many many years that feeling deterred me from any attempt in this line.'[2]

Yet there had been relatively little difficulty in finishing the children's stories or the *Memoirs*. Perhaps Maria would have explained this by pointing out that these were continuations of schemes that she and her father had started together. Rightly or wrongly, her view, and the family view, was that she needed Edgeworth's general support behind her at some stage in the process of authorship. Lacking the commoner incentives to write, such as the desire for fame or the need for some kind of

[1] *Mem.*, iii. 77.

[2] ME to Mr. Bannatyne (PS. to letter to Mrs. Stark), 14 May 1834.

private self-expression, she found the task of seeing a book through to completion much more difficult than in the days when his more confident and assertive personal style over-rode her domesticated one.

But perhaps the most interesting difficulty that Maria had to face when she tried to write novels in 1830 and thereafter is that she was obliged to take the novel itself more seriously than before. The shift in her aesthetic ideas which began about 1813 obliged her to make changes in the narrative approach she had been using immediately before that date. While still isolated at Edgeworthstown the Edgeworths had been able to subordinate the fiction Maria wrote to the educational programme that she worked on with her father. Exemplary fiction, whether it set out to demonstrate general moral truths or to convey facts, might have seemed a relatively simple matter. Novel-writing was not—or not, at least, now that so many revolutionary aesthetic ideas had gained ground. From 1813, Maria was exposed to two fresh sources of influence, new people and new books. Within a few years, she could look back on *Patronage* (1814), and see why so many people disliked it, and how inferior it was to *Waverley*:

> The sad & irremediable fault of *Patronage* is that the moral *saute aux yeux* at every turn in every corner, in every page, in every line beginning middle & end the poor reader meets it & curses the useless light—Useless because too glaring—especially for tender eyes—I will do better next time & take for my motto
>
> 'Our story has a moral—and no doubt
> You all have wit enough to find it out.'[1]

The first source of new opinions, her greatly enlarged circle of friends in England, undoubtedly had some influence over her. For example she became more sensitive to her metropolitan audience and therefore more aware of what might please a sophisticated class of reader. Both *Ormond* and *Helen* revealed a disposition to amuse fashionable people, where *Patronage* merely hectored them.

At the same time it remains clear that Maria's new friends

[1] ME to [? Dr. Holland], n.d. [1817]; National Library of Ireland, MS. 8145 (ix). Cf. ME to Mrs. Inchbald, 14 Feb. 1814; *Memoir of Mrs. Inchbald*, ii. 195: 'To the good of our moral we were obliged to sacrifice; perhaps we have sacrificed in vain. Wherever we are tiresome, we may be pretty sure of this.'

did not change her ideas as much as they might have; in aesthetic matters most of them were conservative. The Whig aristocracy that mingled at Holland House and Bowood prided itself on being intellectual, but it was no more 'advanced' in the arts than it was radical in politics. 'Literature' in these circles did not mean creative literature, fiction, and poetry, as Fanny underlined when she declared that the literary men she most wanted to meet were Ricardo and Mackintosh.[1] Similarly Maria recommended the Smith family of Easton Grey by remarking that 'they have had for their intimate friends most of the literary people of London etc. Sydney Smith—Horners—Tennant—Wollaston—Whishaw—Romilly etc'.[2] In another letter, it is true, she adds the more radical Burdett and Hobhouse to the list, but they too were politicians rather than writers, and in any case never friends of hers.

The social structure of English society in fact ensured that she did not meet many creative writers. Byron (whom Maria did meet briefly in 1813) and Shelley were in Italy in 1821–2; but Coleridge, Southey, Lamb, Hazlitt, Godwin, Cobbett, and Peacock would all have been available in London had she or her stepsisters shown any interest in meeting them. Whig high society, which in its reverence for utility was prepared to idolize scientists and political economists, tended to act more exclusively towards creative writers. Harriet Martineau speaks of 'the spirit of clique, and the prejudices of party, and the atmosphere of complacency and mutual flattery, and bookish gossip, and somewhat insolent worldliness in which the Whig literary society . . . revelled'.[3] This was a very hostile view, and certainly not Maria Edgeworth's own; yet one can see even from her favourable account of the circle in her letters how an opinion like Harriet Martineau's came to be held. There were worlds elsewhere.

Maria's social success therefore took her into very different circles from those in which the family had moved during her youth. Her father had positively avoided London in favour of provincial intellectuals, who were radical in politics and had

[1] See above, p. 415.

[2] ME to Mrs. FE, Easton Grey, 22 Nov. 1821.

[3] Harriet Martineau, *Biographical Sketches*, 1869, 'Mrs. Marcet'. Jane Marcet, political economist, scientist, and writer for children, was a friend of ME's, and their circles overlapped.

no social pretensions in the capital. Maria had not seen enough of most of the Lunar circle to think of them as her own friends; nevertheless, the intellectual influence of the Midlands, felt at second hand through her father, emerges in the most important tales of her heyday.

When it came to her own generation of intellectuals, Maria obviously chose not to make use of some of the openings she was offered. The literary circle which Anna Beddoes had entertained in Bristol in the 1790s inter-connected with the Lunar group through the younger Wedgwoods and through Dr. Beddoes himself. Maria was too discreet to say much during her visit to Bristol in 1799, but in fact she did not much care for Anna's friends—'self-opinionated provincials of the Bristol school'.[1] As for the factory-owners in the Midlands, Maria had less real interest in technology than her father, and she was rather more of a snob. On her visits to the survivors of Edgeworth's circle after Edgeworth's own death, she was very ready to pay tribute to good sense in the men, or good nature in the women. She recognized the intellectual stature of James Watt, and kept up social contacts with Keir's family, the Moilliets; but Keir had been one of the most gentlemanly of the Lunar circle. She visited Erasmus Darwin's son Robert, and Josiah Wedgwood the younger, but between her and some of the other younger Wedgwoods there was a mutual reserve.[2] It is difficult to sum up her attitude towards 'provincials' and industrialists without exaggerating the element of social superiority on Maria's side, yet it cannot be denied that the gulf between herself and the Roscoes or Strutts was more important to her than it had ever been to her father.[3]

Social considerations as well as intellectual ones determined what new friends she made after 1813. She never met the two literary celebrities whom Anna knew at Bristol, Coleridge and Southey. If Wordsworth had not called at Edgeworthstown on

[1] See above, p. 142. [2] See above, p. 417.

[3] Cf. what also appears to have been a gradual change in her attitude to Thomas Day. In 1781 she seems to have sympathized with his hostility to Society (see above, pp. 74–5); by 1799, when *Forester* was written, she had found intellectual objections, no doubt prompted by family experience at that time (see above, p. 164); and in 1818, when Lady Lansdowne praised Day's character as depicted in RLE's *Memoirs*, ME reflected decisively: 'Had she seen him, she would not have endured his manners however 24 hours' (ME to Mrs. FE, Sept. 1818; *Letters from England*, p. 99).

his tour of Ireland in 1829 she would never have met him either. Her reaction to Wordsworth on this occasion is not unrelievedly hostile, nor is it perhaps unbalanced; but it does show a naturally kindly observer at her most detached. Although she later came to admire at least one of his poems, she had little general sympathy with him as a writer, and here she seems to show less respect for his occupation of poet than she would have shown for almost any other intellectual profession:

I enjoyed the snatches of Mr. Wordsworth's conversation & I think I had quite as much as was good for me or for *him* in my opinion—He is sensible—but has an abundance, a superfluity of words—and he talks too much like a book & like one of his own books—neither prose nor poetry—He seems as if he had been too much accustomed to be listened to and that he had learned to listen to himself—You know the French expression—'Il s'écoute'—Not that he is absolutely presuming or conceited or *vain* in manner—It is rather a soft slow proud-humility tone—very prosing—as if he were always speaking *ex cathedra* for the instruction of the rising generation and never forgetting that he is MR. WORDSWORTH—the author and one of the poets of the lake—But under all this slow, slimy, circumspect tiresome *lengthiness* there is a vein of real humour and whenever this breaks through and that he lets himself laugh & describe naturally without picking his words or thinking of his character he is very amusing and agreeable—At all times he is I am persuaded a really good man—He has a good philosophical bust too though very plain—a long thin gaunt looking face—much wrinkled and weather-beaten—of the Curwen style figure & head and face & tone & manner—but with a more cheerful and benevolent expression—He has contrived very comfortably to travel all over Europe with different rich travellers[.] I hope they were none of them so impatient as I am of longwinded speakers as I am [sic] & then all was well—Mr. Marshall & his son with whom he came here seem to doat.[1]

She was not much in sympathy with other innovating poets of the period. She teased a young man in Paris, for example, for affecting the fashionable Byronic mode. 'She laughed at his

[1] ME to Mrs. R, 27 Sept. 1829; partially published, *Mem.*, iii. 35, and E. Inglis-Jones, *The Great Maria*, 1959, pp. 219–20. Wordsworth travelled with John Marshall of Leeds and Hallsteads, and his son James. He reminded ME of his own neighbour, the agriculturalist John Christian Curwen of Workington, Cumberland. For the latter's account of his visit to Edgeworthstown in Oct. 1813, see his *Observations on the State of Ireland*, 1818, ii. 212–20.

anti-French nature efforts to be "triste", and ridiculed his fondness for "le vague" in poetry.'[1] She warned her stepbrother Francis not to ape the example of Thomas Lovell Beddoes, who at nineteen, while still an Oxford undergraduate, had recently made a name for himself with *The Bride's Tragedy*:

> I cannot agree with you in admiring Tom Beddoes' play—But I am glad you have picked out the two best thoughts in it—and even these are only conceits—bordering upon nonsense. I do not think that an idea or expression's being *quite new* is always a proof of its being quite good—Many young writers are run away with & misled by this idea of originality—Unless a thing be good it is not valuable & therefore not admirable for being *original*—tho original it may be absurd & fantastical—Do not give up your own good sense & taste form*ed* or form*ing* on the best classical models—I should be very sorry that you were 'caught by this jingling of a name'—very sorry that you were to catch the vile contagion of imitating Tom.[2]

It became increasingly clear that she preferred scientists to poets. When she and Francis played the game of who in the world they would most like to see arrive at Edgeworthstown, Francis chose Coleridge, Maria the astronomer Herschel. '"What of all people in all countries in the whole world" said Francis, who wondered I did not prefer one of his poets. ["]Yes in the whole world["] persisted I.'[3] Herschel arrived unexpectedly the next day, whereas Coleridge was never seen at Edgeworthstown.

The circles she moved into in the 1820s were therefore scarcely likely to revolutionize her literary ideas overnight; yet fashions were changing, and Maria was exposed to them. The novel proper was experiencing a tremendous revival in prestige, largely because of Scott, but also through Jane Austen and a few lesser figures. Except in 1817, Maria had been reading new novels continuously, and her comments show that she was both ready to learn from her contemporaries, and ready to resist their example.

Her first reaction to Jane Austen was only qualified approval. She thought that most of *Mansfield Park* was very like life, and

[1] *Mem.*, ii. 79.

[2] ME to Francis Edgeworth, Apr. 1823; *Studia Neophilologica*, xxxiii, no. 2, 1961, p. 227.

[3] ME to SR, 27 Sept. 1827.

very enjoyable,[1] and later she was greatly impressed by the naturalness of *Persuasion*: 'Don't you see Captain Wentworth, or rather don't you in her place feel him taking the boisterous child off her back as she kneels by the sick boy on the sofa? And is not the first meeting after their long separation admirably well done? And the overheard conversation about the nut?'[2]

On the other hand she found the behaviour of General Tilney in *Northanger Abbey*, 'packing off the young lady without a servant', 'quite outrageously out of drawing and out of nature'. For her Jane Austen's novels aimed at verisimilitude above anything else, and although she generally admired the manner in which they captured the surface of daily life, her early reaction was to wonder whether such a goal made for interesting novels. She was content to repeat Mrs. Marcet's observation about *Northanger Abbey* and *Persuasion*: 'One grows tired at last of milk and water even tho the water be pure and the milk sweet.'[3]

Her reaction to *Emma* showed that she still failed to grasp the lesson that Jane Austen had to teach her, how to introduce natural detail within an equally natural yet significant story. Jane Austen, who admired Maria Edgeworth, sent her a copy of *Emma*, but after reaching the end of the first volume Maria passed the remaining two volumes on to a friend, observing:

> . . . there was no story in it, except that Miss Emma found that the man whom she designed for Harriets lover was an admirer of her own—& he was affronted at being refused by Emma & Harriet wore the willow—*and smooth, thin water-gruel* is according to Emma's father's opinion a very good thing & it is very difficult to make a cook understand what you mean by smooth thin water gruel![4]

And the family went on to Frances Jackson's *Rhoda*, which Maria liked 'much—50%—better than *Emma*'.

But this turned out to be an interim judgement after all. Ten years later Maria Edgeworth had learnt enough from Jane Austen, or from other writers who had learnt from Jane Austen, to make recognizable efforts to imitate her natural way with a

1 ME to SR, 26 Dec. 1815.

2 ME to Mrs. R, 21 Feb. 1818; *Mem.*, ii. 6.

3 ME to Mrs. Marcet, 24 Feb. 1818; H. W. Häusermann, *The Genevese Background*, p. 90.

4 ME to Sneyd and Harriet Edgeworth, n.d. [1816].

plot. By 1833 she could even write of an admiration for Jane Austen as a 'sign of good taste'.[1]

Her first reaction to Scott's novels was that they were much more interesting. She thought *Waverley* 'a work of first-rate genius'; she did not like *Guy Mannering* quite so much, although Meg Merrilies was 'a character worthy of Shakespeare'; and both she and her father were delighted with *The Antiquary*.[2] For Maria the outstanding characteristics of Scott's novels were, from the first, warmth and generosity. In private and public she frequently paid tribute to Scott's wholesome, better-than-life view of human nature:

> To work his ends, there is never aid from any one of the bad passions of our nature. In his writings there is no private scandal—no personal satire—no bribe to human frailty—no libel upon human nature . . . His morality is not in purple patches, ostentatiously obtrusive, but woven in through the very texture of the stuff. He paints man as he is, with all his faults, but with his redeeming virtues—the world as it goes, with all its compensating good and evil yet making each man better contented with his lot. Without our well knowing how, the whole tone of our minds is raised—for, thinking nobly of our kind, he makes us think more nobly of ourselves![3]

When she praises Scott for 'making each man better contented with his lot', presumably she is thinking of the spirit of acceptance with which each of his novels ends. His great historical turmoils are resolved or promise to be resolved in a *modus vivendi* whereby all classes and sects can live in harmony together. But, unlike Maria, Scott had not used overt didacticism in order to make the point. When she referred to this at Edgeworthstown in August 1825, he observed: 'The rats won't go into the trap if they smell the hand of the ratcatcher.'[4] Although Dumont had tried to make the same point more than a decade earlier, it was probably from reading Scott that Maria effectively learnt how to suppress her over-cerebral commentaries, and instead to convey her optimistic vision of life by giving moral stature to her characters. She called Scott's ability

[1] ME to M. Pakenham Edgeworth, 10 Sept. 1833.

[2] ME to Mrs. R, 13 Oct. 1814; *Mem.*, i. 303; ME to Mrs. O'Beirne, n.d.; ME to Mrs. CSE, n.d. [1816]; and RLE to ME, n.d. [1816].

[3] *Helen*, i. 267.

[4] ME to Mrs. R, 19 Dec. 1825; *Mem.*, ii. 265.

to do this his 'moral enthusiasm', and it was perhaps the tendency in all his writing, poetry as well as prose, that she liked best. She praised it for example in his *Life of Napoleon*: 'I like the moral enthusiasm of Scott far better than the mocking wit of Voltaire—To interest his fellow-creatures a writer must be interested for them—Always laughing will not do—Man has a serious regard for himself—and woman too.'[1]

However, her strong personal and moral admiration of Scott did not blind her to some of his faults as a writer. In discussing the *Life of Napoleon* she had also referred to the slovenly style, and she saw perfectly clearly that his later novels were not so good as his early ones. She thought the first volume of *Redgauntlet* 'excruciatingly tedious', and told Scott himself that for the conclusion of *St. Ronan's Well* 'he ought to be carbonadoed'.[2] Although she might have felt reluctant to admit it, during the decade that her admiration for Jane Austen increased, not much occurred to maintain her respect for Scott as an artist.

Scott and Jane Austen were not of course the only novelists available to influence Maria Edgeworth in the 1820s, when the standard reached by lesser practitioners was probably higher than in any decade of Maria's life so far. Most of these minor figures fell under the influence of one or other of the great novelists, Scott or Jane Austen, or of Maria herself. There were two dominant genres in the 1820s, with as yet little cross-fertilization between them—novels of English high life, and 'regional' novels, which were usually set in Scotland or Ireland. Maria seldom 'tomahawked' (as Harriet put it); she was almost too ready to praise any reasonably literate beginner. Yet as time went on, for reasons that became important in her own career, she was more at home with the novels that dealt primarily with her own class than with the ones that were set in Ireland.

It is probably misleading to define Thomas Love Peacock's satires as novels; but they were immediate favourites at Edgeworthstown, from *Nightmare Abbey* onwards. More orthodox novels that Maria also praised included R. P. Ward's *Tremaine* (1825),[3] T. H. Lister's *Granby* (1826), Disraeli's *Vivian Grey*

[1] ME to Fanny Edgeworth, 31 Aug. 1827. Cf. ME to Mrs. Stark, 6 Sept. 1834; *Mem.*, iii. 157–8.

[2] ME to SR, 7 Aug. 1824, and to Honora Edgeworth, 28 Jan. 1824.

[3] See above, pp. 348–9.

(1826), and Thomas Hamilton's *Cyril Thornton* (1827), all of which had a more or less natural English setting. Her patience was tried only by really silly productions in this genre, for example by Lady Caroline Lamb's *roman à clef*, *Glenarvon* (1816), or by Mrs. Purvis's novel of high life, *Almack's* (1827).

Her reaction to the lesser Scottish and Irish novelists was more mixed. Lady Morgan was perhaps something of a special case, since from her higher social position Maria had always found her rival intolerably vulgar. It was further ground for offence that some critics had thought it appropriate to lump Miss Edgeworth and Lady Morgan into one category, for the sake of comparison:

> What a shameful mixture in this book [*Florence Macarthy*] of the highest talent & the lowest malevolence and the most despicable disgusting affectation & *impropriety*—& disregard of the consequences of what she writes—I love O'Leary—& wish *that* admirable original character could be taken out of this heap of trash—I do not think the Crawleys *well* done—except perhaps some part of old Crawley —Vulgar as he is & incredible as I perceive it is to the English that such a man could be admitted in company there are such in Ireland.
>
> My general feelings in closing this book are shame & disgust— & the wish never more to be classed with *novel* writers when the highest talents in that line have been so disgraced.
>
> Oh that I could prevent people from ever naming me along with her—either for praise or blame—Comparisons are indeed odious —God forbid as my dear father said I should ever be such a thing as that—
>
> It was for want of such a father she has come to this.[1]

In the early 1820s a school of Scottish regional novelists became established in the shadow of Scott. Maria does not appear to have read the extremely natural and detailed John Galt (whose *Annals of the Parish* must surely owe something to her *Castle Rackrent*); but she did approve unreservedly of Susan Ferrier's *Marriage* and *Inheritance*, and on the whole she liked the Scottish novels of Lockhart. Yet, strangely enough, Maria scarcely ever expressed a special interest in Irish or Scottish novelists by virtue of their subject-matter. She never praised them as attempts, like her own *Ennui* and *The Absentee*, to

[1] ME to Mrs. FE, 28 Jan. 1819; *Letters from England*, pp. 166–7.

sketch in the life of a whole society. She was much more interested in the characters, and in their feelings. This was really in keeping with the sentimentalist tradition in which she had been brought up. With advancing age, Maria was discovering her own deepest convictions; and she found that all along she had liked fiction which appealed to her heart. In 1812, the very year of her great success with *The Absentee*, she was capable of deprecating her own study of manners in favour of the highly wrought passion and drama of the Richardsonian tradition:

We have been reading *Cecilia* again . . . Upon the whole the plan is excellent—the great passions—avarice—family pride—extravagance—love—are strongly seized & these general history pictures of human nature will last longer than any portrait-painting however exquisite or any of the mere sketches of flying follies & manners of the day—such as your Lady Clonbrony &c—The history of Albany I had not sufficiently observed before in *Cecilia*—It is one of the finest pieces of writing I ever read—The character of Delville is charming—the scene with Mrs Delville in which she breaks a bloodvessel—very fine—her whole character *superior*—Lady Honoria Pemberton exquisitely entertaining.[1]

Maria's natural liking for stories that focused on passionate private relationships had been kept in check later in her father's lifetime because her highest aim then had been to portray everyday life in a highly literal way, for the purpose of conveying information or influencing behaviour. In the 1820s, when overt didacticism became unfashionable, social realism too seemed to lose ground in her estimation; certainly her critical concern was for the emotions of the central figures in a story, rather than for the factual detail in the background. Her first response to Scott had been admiration for his sympathetic characterization, and for the fundamental optimism of his social philosophy. But she seemed to become increasingly aware of the extent to which Scott concentrated on background and a multitude of minor characters at the expense of his heroes, and although in her Irish tales she had done precisely the same she was critical of the effect achieved:

The hero of the book [*Redgauntlet*] is more paltry and pusillanimous than any of his usual paltry heroes—Swathed in a long riding

[1] ME to SR, 13 Dec. 1812.

skirt: and with a lady's mask!—Did ever any body but Scott venture to conceive a hero in such a plight—His heroes are mere sticks round which he twines his flowers—& the less the stick is seen the better.[1]

This was not a sympathetic way of referring to a technique which Scott had actually borrowed from her own *Ennui* and *The Absentee*.[2] The criticism makes one all the more curious to know exactly what she thought Scott's 'flowers' were. It would be an odd term for that aspect of his realism he had modelled on hers, the accuracy and scale with which he had drawn his portrait of an entire society. Sure enough, sociological realism was the kind of virtue he praised in her writing, not she in his. What she liked was the vigour of his peasants, like Meg Merrilies; the warmth of his understanding of other individual characters; and above all the optimism. From this it is fair to deduce that the specific social and political connotation of Scott's novels was less attractive to her than the romantic element that had been present in his writing since the era of *Lady of the Lake* and *Marmion*. In other words, Maria did not understand the most important historical contribution she herself had made to the novel. If anything, her exposure in the 1820s to new writers and fresh literary ideas turned her against the broader, analytical type of novel which her own Irish tales had helped to pioneer.

For when she encountered a school of novelists who imitated Scott's social panorama, but not his optimism, her general reaction was to disapprove. On different occasions she used the word 'genius' of three at least of the new Irish novelists who began to publish between 1825 and 1830. She praised the Banim brothers, Griffin, and Carleton for their accuracy and their power, but never considered these qualities enough; fundamentally she could not admire any of them because of their often bitter tone in handling explosive Irish issues.

Maria Edgeworth's failure to write about Ireland after 1817 has been explained in a number of ways. It would have been entirely consistent with the Maria of earlier years, for example, if she had felt a 'national novel' too ambitious an enterprise when Edgeworth was no longer there to advise her. Actually Maria was far more confident about publishing her own views

[1] ME to Honora Edgeworth, 13 Aug. 1824. [2] See above, pp. 394 ff.

on national politics—or, at least, on circulating them among virtual strangers—than she had ever been before. Her new friendships with Whig political families, the Lansdownes, Romillys, and Whitbreads, must have forced her to talk rationally about Ireland's affairs. She sent letters to all these which often bore on politics; more strikingly, she came later to embark on at least three correspondences on specifically political themes—in the 1820s with Ricardo and in the 1830s with Richard Jones, each time on the dependence of the Irish economy on the potato; and in the later 1820s with Thomas Spring Rice, later Lord Monteagle, on Catholic Emancipation.[1]

In the 1820s Maria was an eager supporter of the movement to extend full rights to Catholics, and, although depressed by delays at Westminster, she was so sure that Emancipation would prove effective when it came that in general she remained optimistic. By now she had quite abandoned the feminine shrinking from political debate which had so strongly characterized her in the 1790s. An observation which she was to put into the mouth of a leading character in *Helen* expressed her later view:

> Let me observe to you, that the position of women in society, is somewhat different from what it was a hundred years ago, or as it was sixty, or I will say thirty years since. Women are now so highly cultivated, and political subjects are at present of so much importance, of such high interest, to all human creatures who live together in society, you can hardly expect, Helen, that you, as a rational being, can go through the world as it now is, without forming any opinion on points of public importance. You cannot, I conceive, satisfy yourself with the common namby-pamby little missy phrase, 'ladies have nothing to do with politics'.[2]

Throughout this decade, therefore, Maria had no reason to give up the idea of another novel about Ireland, and indeed she had every intention of writing one. Scott urged her that it was her duty to pour oil on troubled waters,[3] and she seems to have accepted the obligation. The notebooks of the 1820s

[1] For the correspondence with Ricardo, see F. Y. Edgeworth (ed.), *Economic Journal*, xvii, 1907. Some letters to Spring Rice are published in M. Hurst, *Maria Edgeworth and the Public Scene*, 1969; for the MSS. see Bibliography, pt. 1, sect. 4.

[2] *Helen*, ii. 233.

[3] Letter to ME, 15 May 1827; *Letters*, x. 211.

contain a great deal of Irish material, some of it excellent,[1] and as late as 1834 Maria could declare that 'the scene of the next story I write, if ever I do write again shall be in Ireland'.[2] Ironically enough, that forecast was true: *Orlandino*, 1848, does have an Irish setting. So for that matter had *Garry-Owen*, 1829, another tale intended for adolescents.

The existence of these two unimportant stories only underlines the fact that she never did write the Irish novel she might have done. As virtual mistress of Edgeworthstown during this period of intense political activity, she had an unrivalled view of Irish political affairs, and her letters prove that she had become an interested observer both of the local and national scene. The trouble was that her observations were now unsuitable—or so she thought—as raw material for fiction.

The full history of Maria Edgeworth's political experience in the 1830s is told elsewhere, and there is no need to repeat it here in detail.[3] Irish politics helped to interrupt her career as a novelist because, as O'Connell's campaigns led the Catholic peasantry into opposing their Protestant landlords, she wavered in the sympathy for the lower orders which had previously been one of her motives for writing about Ireland. The election of 1832, when even some of the Edgeworthstown tenants voted against the Edgeworths' known wishes, was a deeply disillusioning experience for her.[4] She concluded that a novel which described events like these would set a poor example, and was better left unwritten:

> It is impossible to draw Ireland as she now is in a book of fiction —realities are too strong, party passions too violent to bear to see, or care to look at their faces in the looking-glass. The people would only break the glass, and curse the fool who held the mirror up to nature—distorted nature, in a fever. We are in too perilous a case to laugh, humour would be out of season, worse than bad taste. Whenever the danger is past, as the man in the sonnet says, 'We may look back on the hardest part and laugh'. Then I shall be ready to join in the laugh. Sir Walter Scott once said to me, 'Do explain why Pat, who gets forward so well in other countries, is so

[1] Two such notes have been published by Mrs. C. E. Colvin, 'Unpublished MSS. by Maria Edgeworth', *REL*, viii, 1967.

[2] ME to Mrs. Lazarus, 10 Nov. 1834.

[3] In M. Hurst, *Maria Edgeworth and the Public Scene*, 1969.

[4] ME to Fanny Wilson, 22 Dec. 1832.

miserable in his own'. A very difficult question; I fear above my power. But I shall think of it continually, and listen, and look, and read.[1]

Since the danger did not pass, she could not plead Ireland's cause with sincerity before the English public, or argue that an individual's duty lay in identifying his interests with his country: two of her principal themes when she established herself as an Irish writer. 'Really though I wrote a story called *The Absentee* I begin to think that it is but reasonable that a country should be rendered fit to live in before we complain more of Absentees.'[2]

In the 1830s she was caught in the classic position of a moderate liberal in times of revolution. The violence of the extremists calling for change alienated her; and as far as they were concerned she was not much better than any other upholder of the Anglo-Irish Establishment. The personal tragedy for Maria was that the nation-wide sectarian struggle was carried into Edgeworthstown itself. In the worst crisis of her father's lifetime, 1798, he, although a landlord, had been on the same side as his Catholic tenants, but in the early 1830s that tradition was broken. Worse even than 1832 was the election of 1835, when the Edgeworthstown tenants had to choose again between 'the family's' known wishes on the one hand, and their priest's instructions on the other. Maria's own view was plain. She thought it was part of the understanding between landlord and tenant, part as it were of the contract, that a tenant should support what was known as his landlord's interest; which in this case meant voting for the Conservatives. Among the tenants of longest standing, three of the Catholics—Woods, Langan, and Dermod—voted for the White brothers, who were Liberals and Repealers.

Sophy's husband Barry Fox was active in Longford politics on the Conservative side. Fox was greatly annoyed by the defection of some of the Edgeworthstown tenants, and in the absence of the legal landlord, Sneyd, he decided on his own initiative to punish the three defectors. He summoned them to bring in the hanging-gale, an instalment of rent due from the tenant to the landlord which by custom was left in arrear;

[1] ME to Michael Pakenham Edgeworth, letter begun 14 Feb. 1834; *Mem.*, iii. 87–8. Cf. *Life, Letters and Journals of George Ticknor*, i. 429.

[2] ME to Fanny Wilson, 4 Jan. 1839.

and it was to Maria, as agent, that old Dermod and his son came to pay their money. At this moment, when a tenant had refused the landlord his customary rights, and she was retaliating in the name of the family, she must have thought that the spirit of co-operation which the Edgeworths had stood for in Ireland, the political theme of her Irish tales, belonged to a hopeful time that was over and done with:

> Accordingly . . . enter Dermod, hobbling and bent . . . and followed by his young son, who presently fell to crying. I endeavoured to keep automatically to my receiver of rents and I fell to counting the money. . . . Dermod went on paying his rent and saying that when once paid one comfort was it could not be asked for again. But he and his father before him had been paying rent to Miss Edgeworth and her father and grandfather etc., and the son went on sobbing and I counting and miscounting.
>
> Barry very mildly, and in a most gentlemanlike manner, said it had given him great concern etc. But what he had begun he would go through with and he told Dermod that he considered he was doing him a service in protecting him against his priests, who, as he knew, had forced him to vote against his landlord. To this fact of being forced by priests to vote against his landlord against his will Dermod acceded. 'Why, there it is then and it was as much as my life was worth and my son's too to do the contrary. Count it again *dear* (to me), for I don't know is it right or wrong.' His hands trembled so between anger and pity for himself and various contending emotions that I am sure he knew no more than a fish what he was doing, and he looked to his son to *count*, who was in *no condition* either with his head upon his knees. Barry repeated that they would now be safe against the priests' oppression for that they would have it to say that their landlord had forced them to pay their rent and against another time. Dermod, throwing his old head back with a vigorous resolution, interrupted and declared that never more would he be in such a scrape, for that the very minute he got home he would burn the scrap of paper or parchment that brought all the trouble upon him (meaning the registration of his vote). I think Barry said this would do him no good and exit. The thoughts of the number of years I had received rent from that old good tenant in my father's time all worked upon me. I am ashamed to tell you my finale—that tears began flow, and though I twinkled and rubbed them out and off they did come—and Honora came in and Mr Hinds was by and it was all shameful.[1]

[1] ME to CSE, 12 Feb. 1835; M. Hurst, *Maria Edgeworth and the Public Scene*, pp. 78–9.

If she had been able to capture the full significance of this scene in a novel, what a novel it might have been. But to do so she would have had to write about the bitterness of the 1830s with the full freedom of the best novelists of that decade, a change in her notions of social responsibility which she was never able to make. She might praise Griffin's 'warm strong Michael Angelo drawing',[1] but at heart she did not agree with his readiness to explore the harsh realities of Irish life. Her criticism of the new school shows even more clearly than her scattered remarks about Scott that she did not in the least understand the nature of her own achievement as a novelist. Her importance to her own generation and indirectly to their successors was as a realist, but as a product of the Enlightenment she had never thought and never did think that realism was an adequate end by itself.[2] The two Irish novelists she really seems to have liked best in the early 1830s are almost forgotten now, but her approval of them is significant. One was George Brittaine, author of *The Recollections of Hyacinth O'Gara* (1829), *The Confessions of Honor Delany* (1830), and *Irish Priests and English Landlords* (1830). The technique of the first two novels seems to owe something to *Castle Rackrent*, and the third to *The Absentee*, but that would not be why Maria liked them. They are even more didactic than her own tales, and are directed strongly against priestly interference in politics. Maria's approval of them is an indication of how far she had travelled politically since the strongly anti-Orange tales she wrote in her father's lifetime. Her approval of three rather feeble performances also shows how far she was still out of tune with Romantic ideas about the integrity of art, how little she had learnt to take her own craft seriously.

The other Irish stories which Maria most enjoyed reading

[1] ME to Fanny Wilson, 26 Sept. 1829.

[2] ME was never in sympathy with the increasingly powerful realistic fiction written during her old age, but continued to judge novels by their moral themes. She seems to have detested many of the works of Dickens. See also her censure of 'M. de Balzac's most beautifully written immoralities' (ME to Mrs. S. C. Hall, 23 Apr. 1838; *Art Journal*, xi, 1849), and her remarks on Mrs. Gaskell's *Mary Barton*, on which she wrote a lengthy criticism six months before her death: 'The book is ably done so far as graphic description; but is not calculated to produce any good result . . .' (ME to Lady Beaufort (Honora), n.d. [Dec. 1848 or Jan. 1849]; R. D. Waller, 'Letters Addressed to Mrs. Gaskell by Celebrated Contemporaries', *Bulletin of the John Rylands Library*, xix, 1935).

were Mrs. Anna Maria Hall's sentimental, idealized *Sketches of Irish Character*. 'I sat up till near one o'clock last night in spite of your brother's bally-ragging to finish it for it had a nook in my heart but leave it I could not—I think it touching —simple—beautiful & true Irish.'[1]

None of Maria's critical views need occasion surprise if taken in conjunction with her own novels. Her attitude to literature was not in essentials dissimilar from Dr. Johnson's: she regarded it as a serious matter, but serious in relation to life, not to art. Her perspectives were thus very much of her own time, or rather of her father's time, and all that is odd in her comments on novels of the Reform era is that they show so little elasticity of mind. The story of her later life can be seen as in so many ways a triumph: strength emerging from apparent weakness. But Maria in old age has her less attractive aspect too: an upper-class Whig with her circle of ageing contacts, a political progressive outpaced by the speed of change, a literary innovator who did not appreciate the best writing of the period. For intellectually the self-discovery of her later years (in all subjects perhaps except science) was largely a matter of discovering that in her time, unlike her father in his, she was naturally conservative. The central belief of her life, both in relation to her family and to Ireland, was the importance of maintaining a cheerful, harmonious exterior. When she found irreconcilable conflicts in life, her reaction was first to write in order to propose remedies, second to fall silent; rather than depict the country in turmoil, she allowed her career as an Irish novelist to come to an end.

Maria's attitudes to public themes in the novel are a reminder that Edgeworth had always supplied the intellectual impetus in their partnership, and that the political stance in *Ennui*, *The Absentee*, and *Ormond* reflects his mind rather than hers. When she was intellectually assertive in her fiction, she was repeating his ideas. She had of course very considerable literary virtues which were independent of him, such as the easy elegance of her style. But the grace and humour of her dialogue, especially, is displayed at its most characteristic in her

[1] ME to Fanny Wilson, 23 July 1829. Mrs. Hall (Mrs. Samuel Carter Hall) became a personal friend of ME's. Her manner as an author appears to have been influenced by ME's, particularly by *Moral* and *Popular Tales*.

English scenes, not her Irish ones. Accurate peasant dialogue, like informed representation of society, reflects the side of her which was most closely associated with him. The woman she became without her father was therefore not a natural pioneer, in society, in politics, in literature, or anywhere else. The new 'masculine' novel with which she had made her name did not express her preferences or personality.

But if at past sixty Maria was now to sit down to compose a novel that *did* express herself—that was, for example, intimate and emotional—she would still have to learn techniques that she had not been using in her father's lifetime. It was a real achievement that she was able to do this in her mid-sixties, and an indication of the deepening of her character in those later years. She might turn her back on one area for painful analysis, the controversially social; she did not shirk questions which arose from her personal life. 'Look for me in *The Absentee*', she had once said, altogether wrongly. When Maria Edgeworth wrote the tale which expressed herself, she wrote *Helen*.

# XI

## *HELEN*

*Helen* is more richly based on first-hand knowledge than the rest of Maria Edgeworth's work. Both the central characters reflect herself, and there is much that is autobiographical in their experiences. The settings and many lesser figures also come from direct observation. In spite of this, or because of it, the novel was one which proved exceptionally difficult to write. Although the first unambiguous reference to it came on 3 May 1830 ('I am thinking three hours a day of *Helen*'), the book was not published until February 1834.

The first departure from earlier practice was to base the novel not on a didactic theme but on a strong situation involving three characters. Maria found the main plot of *Helen* in Crabbe's verse tale *The Confidant* (*Tales*, 1812). In the original story, Anna, the wife of a yeoman called Stafford, is blackmailed by her friend Eliza, who knows that at the age of fifteen Anna had an illegitimate child. Crabbe's version ends easily and happily, for although Stafford discovers his wife's secret, he willingly forgives her. Maria transposes the story into high life and makes considerable changes in the characters and motives of the three principals. Crabbe's villain, Eliza, becomes Maria's heroine, the would-be honourable Helen, while the wife in Maria's version is the more guilty of the two women; her Lady Cecilia, though well-meaning and affectionate, is weak, and it is she who ensnares Helen rather than the other way around.

All along Maria was aware that in writing about three people rather than to a didactic theme she was attempting a new departure. She wanted the public to be aware of it too, and therefore she firmly rejected her publisher's advice to go back to her old style of title.

> The nature of the story depending more on the development of various characters and on the *interest* excited by Helen herself than on any particular point or moral would not admit of such a sort of

title as *Ennui* or *Manœuvring* or *The Absentee*—I have been reproached for making *my moral* in some stories too prominent—I am sensible of the inconvenience of this both to reader and writer & have taken much pains to avoid it in *Helen*—I will not therefore give a title that shall promise what I have tried *not* to perform.[1]

For Maria to ask anyone for literary advice was always a sign that she was emotionally involved with that person to a special degree, and she now used the writing of *Helen* to foster her relationships with her father's youngest children, especially Fanny and Harriet.[2] When, on her return from London in the autumn of 1831, Maria began to work on the novel in earnest, she sent the manuscript to Fanny, instructing her to return it, cut and corrected, at the rate of forty pages a week. Maria begged Fanny to interpret the commission boldly:

> I entreat you my dear to cut away with unsparing hand all superfluous descriptions and begin by shortening as much as ever you can of the character of Irdale [Churchill] which I know is lengthy & out of proportion—I will put him in some action with Beauclerc if I can hereafter . . . I beg you will correct with pen & ink not your cowardly pencil which gives me double double toil & trouble—& doubly felt needless mortification & provocation—to see that you cannot trust your own taste when I do implicitly.[3]

Fanny, who had the literary interests of most younger members of the family, set great store on getting the principal characters properly engaged in a good plot, but there was no longer any need to persuade Maria of this: 'I quite feel all you say about the advantage of putting characters in action & making them shew themselves instead of describing them.'[3] The weakness of the novel in this respect was destined to be the nominal hero, Helen's fiancé Granville Beauclerc, who had no part to play in the plot derived from Crabbe. Fanny seems to have been troubled by this from the beginning, and to have advised strengthening and filling out Beauclerc's role in various ways. She suggested that Maria should bring him in earlier,

[1] ME to J. G. Lockhart, 12 May 1833; Nat. Lib. of Scotland, MS. 923, ff. 55–6.

[2] The Ruxton sisters, Sophy and Margaret, were still alive, almost alone among her old literary advisers, but she delayed showing them *Helen* until it was nearly finished, and then declared: 'I won't tear it to pieces for them—that's poz' (ME to Fanny Wilson, 4 Jan. 1833).

[3] ME to Fanny Wilson, 1 Nov. 1831.

and Maria did so.[1] A little later Fanny supplied material for Beauclerc's new scenes, in the form of 'observations upon the slender and uncertain grounds on which even the cleverest men build their systems'.[2] Fanny's suggestions did not really meet the point that the hero had nothing to do; but it was not easy to solve this problem without cutting him out altogether, and, despite the evidence of Fanny's ruthlessness in 1829, in general the stepsisters liked to propose amendments rather than wholesale changes. Maria adopted Fanny's ideas with energy, and after much rewriting in the winter and spring of 1832, she gave the manuscript in April to Harriet Butler.

Harriet's principal role, like Fanny's, was probably simply to cut. Maria had resolved to keep *Helen* down to two volumes,[3] but her method was to let her invention carry her freely on, leaving it to the sisters to cut back the narrative to the requisite length. At the same time she encouraged Harriet, as she had encouraged Fanny, to make more general criticisms:

> I quite agree with you that the Irish should be left out of this story for *more reasons than you* or Mr. B. give . . . I was going to remodel a chapter in which there was an Irish lady whom Fanny had thought too long—I have now made short work of it and cut her out—she will be a good character elsewhere but took too much room here & had not room enough to shew herself well after all & was lugged in by head & shoulders & I am heartily glad she is out . . . In these additions I daresay I have repeated some ideas & perhaps the same words in other parts & you will cut out—please . . . But I need not teach my grandchild to suck eggs—I should be very glad if you could squeeze out more whey out of the curds to leave me still more room in this volume but if you can't you can't. . . .[4]

In the uneasy days of 1832, the Butlers' objection to the presence of Irish characters may well have been political.[5] At other points in the novel they were asked to adjudicate on aesthetic and moral issues:

> Pray consider whether the moral of *Helen* was in any part too

[1] ME to Fanny Wilson, 16 Apr. 1832.

[2] ME to Fanny Wilson, 5 June 1832.

[3] ME's preference for the shorter length was noted above, p. 315 n. In 1824 she remarked of Lady Morgan's *Salvator Rosa*: 'It is in two volumes and would have been twice as good if it had been compressed into one—Good books & precious stones are made by compression' (ME to Mrs. R, 4 Nov. 1824).

[4] ME to Harriet Butler, 1 May 1832.

[5] See above, pp. 452 ff.

prosy or prominent—May be all the time Mr. Butler has not the least idea what the moral is—If so I shall say tant mieux—If several morals—so much the better still—If the Genl be not *upright* you must *plumb* him between you. . . .[1]

A third sister, Lucy, also made her contribution. As the novel was being published, Maria wrote regretting that she had allowed Lucy, who was in poor health, to exert herself so greatly:

At any rate now it is done, I take all the good thankfully, and assure you that the part you wrote for me would not I think have pleased the family-public so well as it has done if you had not so helped me by your mind still more than by your hand. For your good taste stopped me always when I was going wrong—and encouraged by your approving sympathy when I was going right, I spoke on with a warmth and fancy which I could not have any other wise commanded—Every body observes that Lady D's histy. and Lady Cecilia's have more the force of *reality* of real natural speaking than any other of the narrative parts . . . that you had so much pleasure in writing that history of Lady Davenant & Cecilia's confession for me is delightful to me to believe.[2]

At first glance these letters, particularly the second, seem to imply that Lucy 'wrote', in the sense of devised, two scenes of *Helen*, one of which (Lady Cecilia's confession) is particularly fine. This was not the case. Maria told Ticknor that she dictated the passages to Lucy, a person of sure taste, in order to achieve a natural effect of spoken narrative; when Lucy's pen hesitated, Maria changed the words.[3]

By early in 1833, Maria was ready to have an incomplete second version read out to the family circle of critics at Edgeworthstown.[4] The purpose of reading the text aloud was to detect minor errors of grammar, or factual inaccuracies. All the family then resident appear to have been involved, and letters discussing points of detail then passed between Harriet and Honora, and Harriet and Mrs. Edgeworth.

1 ME to Harriet Butler, 12 Aug. 1832.

2 ME to Lucy Edgeworth, 30 Jan. 1834 and 3 Mar. 1834.

3 *Life, Letters and Journals of George Ticknor*, i. 428–9. The MS. of Cecilia's confession survives: see Bibliography, pt. 1, section 3 (*e*). It has comparatively few emendations except some substantial cuts, as one might expect of a passage composed in this way.

4 For ME's account of her working day while this was done, see above, pp. 291–2.

By April there was a complete draft, and in early May Fanny and Lestock arrived at Edgeworthstown for a family council, to which the Butlers were also summoned. *Helen* then received its final preparation for publication, a process which occupied the household until the end of August or beginning of September 1833.

At the proof-reading stage Maria had perforce to rely on the family, for she was stranded in Connemara that autumn while the first proofs were arriving at Edgeworthstown.[1] She wrote to ask Honora to look over the opening chapters and return them to the publisher, declaring that 'whatsoever *yees* do I am sure I shall approve'.[2] She was even more emphatic in exhorting Fanny in London to act freely on her behalf: 'Remember that you are to exercise your judgment & to decide without appeal in the last resort both as to corrections that have been made and as to any that you see occasion to make.'[3]

When later in 1834 the novel was corrected for a second edition, Maria brought in her stepbrother Francis, and rebuked him and Fanny in the now familiar terms for their timidity:

> You might both have altered to your taste and might have been sure I should have been pleased. However to prove to you that I don't say do as you please from mere laziness I have considered & reconsidered and rewritten Francis's & my own mixing them together so *as to make it my own*—as Honora & aunt Mary say it now does. I hope you & F. will approve—if you do not pray alter it till you do—I particularly like the speech Francis has put into Beauclerc's mouth & wish he had written more for him—It is much more according to my own idea of his character & way of talking than what I put into his mouth.[4]

As ever, it is easy to be misled by the manner in which she begged co-operation from her family, or described the contributions her relatives had made. She exaggerated when she wrote to Fanny, Harriet, Lucy, and the others, because she was very fond of them and wanted them to believe they shared her writing with her. She gave a typical reason for refusing to alter a detail that Francis disliked: 'It is Emmeline's not my own—& if I made it my own it would not answer my purpose

[1] See above, p. 430 n.

[2] ME to Honora, 2 Nov. 1833.

[3] ME to Fanny Wilson, 18 Nov. 1833.

[4] ME to Fanny Wilson, 2 Sept. 1834.

in putting it in for she would not feel it to be hers.'[1] But, significantly, Emmeline's contribution seems to have been restricted to a single metaphor of little interest to anyone but Maria or Emmeline themselves. As for her requests to her stepsisters to be bold, these almost certainly arose from her awareness that they were usually quite the reverse. Although she did not stand on her dignity, her new advisers could hardly speak to her with the same freedom as her father, her aunt, Daniel Augustus Beaufort, and even Sophy had once done. Harriet, although she deplored 'bringing in a real man like Dumont', diffidently told her mother that 'unless you advised & thought it very worth while I would not think of hinting it to M. as I know she will not like to take it out'.[2]

Thus it was that essentially Maria had to judge for herself, and most modern readers would probably feel that, especially in the largely domestic genre in which *Helen* is written, she gained much more than she lost from being forced to stand on her own feet. Maria still could not bring herself to believe this. When in the end she had to concede that she and Fanny had failed with the hero, she added that she would not have made this mistake if her father had been there to apply his more decided standards: 'In the sketch of *Helen* I had not the judgment I formerly had to help me to see if the anatomy was correct.'[3] As she wrote the book, she worried about her own ability to maintain the reputation which she still thought she owed to her father. She told her old friends in Scotland that she was 'more anxious far (and for good reasons) about this book than any I ever sent into the world':

> I thank you with all my heart for the *nervousness* you felt about my venturing again before the public—and it is a *heart*felt as well as a *head*-felt satisfaction to me that you do not think I have lowered what my father took such pains to raise for me . . . You may conceive what consequence it is to my happiness to be assured by friends on whose sincerity & judgment I can depend that I have not done what they think I ought to repent or be ashamed of.[4]

[1] Ibid. ME's sister Emmeline King evidently supplied the comparison between fashionable conversation and gaslight, 'which lights at a touch, and at a touch can be extinguished' (*Helen*, ii. 31).

[2] Harriet Butler to Mrs. FE, 20 Mar. 1833. Cf. *Helen*, ii. 45–6.

[3] ME to Mrs. Stark, 6 Sept. 1834; *Mem.*, iii. 155. See also above, p. 311.

[4] ME to Mrs. Stark and Mr. Bannatyne, 14 May 1834.

A great deal of manuscript evidence remains, which confirms that *Helen* was written with painstaking care and with much secretarial help, especially from the younger members of the family. There are four manuscript fragments of the novel, including the one in Lucy's hand, and the British Museum possesses a complete copy, which is the only complete manuscript of an Edgeworth novel to survive. This presumably is the fair copy prepared by the family council and sent to the publisher in August or September 1833. It bears all the signs of that Edgeworthian characteristic, careful re-reading and proof-correcting by others; and comparison between the manuscript and the printed version of the novel shows that afterwards something of the same process was gone through again. The substantial changes visible in the manuscript are almost invariably simple cuts, while the lesser changes are adjustments of style—a redundant word is left out, a clarifying word inserted, or a sentence rearranged. These changes of detail confirm the impression left by earlier literary manuscripts. They show how correct, accurate, and responsible the Edgeworths tried to be, and how much interest as a family they took in Maria's books. But if, as appears to be the case, the family committees never exercised more authority than in the case of *Helen*, their labours had little effect on the literary quality of the novels, one way or another.[1]

The business aspect of publication, the masculine area which Edgeworth had once managed for Maria, was entrusted to that shrewd professional, John Gibson Lockhart. The publisher whom Lockhart chose was Richard Bentley. 'He did not sell the whole copyright to Bentley only this edition of a thousand copies—for which he is to give me what Lockhart tells me is the largest copyright that ever was given for a novel viz £600—and if he prints 200 more he is to give me £200 more.'[2]

Lockhart had done well by her, and in all Maria made £1,100 from *Helen*.[3] A further £200 of it came in when Bentley decided that the novel he had accepted for publication in two volumes would be better after all in three. Maria,

[1] See also Appendix C.

[2] ME to M. Pakenham Edgeworth, 10 Sept. 1833.

[3] Memorandum by ME, Sept. 1842, given in Appendix B below.

although she had set her heart on an impression of brevity, submitted in the end to Bentley and Lockhart as meekly as she had usually fallen in with her father's judgement on points like these:

You find that I did not swear or kick but behaved like a reasonable woman & a lady moreover & pockets my £200 with a very good grace. In short I do not understand the publishing & bookselling trade—and Bentley & Lockhart do—I have satisfied my own conscience which is *my point*—I know that far from having stretched a single page or a single sentence to *make out* a third volume—I have cut away as much as ever I could—cut it to the quick—and now it matters not whether it be printed in 2 or 3 volumes—If tiresome in 3 to the ear it would be equally so in 2 & would look worse to the eye the bookfanciers tell us.[1]

In the event, despite her lack of assurance and her many calls for assistance, *Helen* is peculiarly Maria Edgeworth's own book. With the exception of some detail in the hawking scene, which was supplied by Lord Berners and his family,[2] she was drawing on first-hand experience throughout. As John Ward had observed in connection with *Patronage*, Maria's earlier novels set in England had lacked the social authenticity of those set in Ireland, but this is not true of *Helen*. Only a reader of Maria's letters from London and from great houses like Bowood can know how closely her last novel compares with her real-life perceptions of Whig high Society. Many individual scenes and characters are drawn from life—the scandal-mongering dentist, St. Leger Swift, was Honora's dentist, Waite,[3] and the wit Horace Churchill was based on the poet Samuel Rogers. A single instance from one of the letters, a description of a dinner-party of Lady Davy's which Maria attended in 1831, shows that she moved in London that season with the deliberate expectation of finding material for *Helen*:

Well sounding party—number right for table—and Davy's fine plate & good dinner & champagne & all sorts of wines—And yet

[1] ME to Honora Edgeworth, 2 Nov. 1833.

[2] ME wrote to Lord Berners, whom she knew kept hawks, for information about the sport. Her letter drew a reply from an old lady called Wilson, of Kirby-Cane, Norfolk, who gave her 'all the particulars in a most simple interesting exact manner'. Letter in ME's hand, no addressee or date [? May 1833].

[3] ME to CSE, 14 Mar. 1834.

it did not do well—Rogers was cross & Lady Davy marked it and was cross to him when he would not eat flesh & would not like her Virgin her Madonna del Sisto—Then Lord Mahon who was pert after his fashion vexed Rogers more & more—& then his Lordship blundered about something and Rogers had him down & coolly & spitefully trampled on him—and though they talked over all the beauties of art and nature all over the world afterwards yet still there was a leaven of malice that spotted all—The *bad butter* you know— . . .

Of all the back-biters *ever I seen* dead or alive Rogers is beyond compare the most venemous [*sic*] audacious & universal—and at last it can hardly be called backbiting—for he bites before the backs are turned—He was *at it* to me against Lady D—when she was within a foot of us—and his answer to me when I warned him that he must be heard—

'And if I am!—When I mention no names . . . I might be talking of the Queen of Sheba—There! there! did you see that?—her look & his (Lord Ashburners [*sic*—?Ashburnham]) it will not be her fault if it does not come to something . . .'

Then she came quite close & instantly Rogers's look and tone changed and he was all oily flattery—with a *taste* of persiflage for the saving of his credit *for satire & taste* with the bystanders—At the last dinner where I met Rogers he & Mr. Hay were more than flirting disgustingly with Lady Lyndhurst—This night he said to me We have never met since we were in company with that *terrible* woman—Very terrible you seemed to think her when you were sitting beside her—There I protest I told Hay as we were coming in that he must be victim that night (. . .) Oh what can a man do—a gentleman—he can't go away when the woman begins—he can't leave her to herself you know—Besides she can *hate* as well as love—Oh she is an underbred creature—who is pushing herself forward & it wont do The ladies can't bear this[.] I think I shall learn some good lessons for my next novel—But reality is beyond fiction—too strong—would not be believed.

The insincerity of this London life strikes me more now than when I was younger—perhaps I am more a stander by & am more *let behind the curtain* and have no objects of my own—for sisters & self—Besides it all appears to me now so little worth while!—[1]

Samuel Rogers had qualities to recommend him. Although comfortably off rather than rich, he had the good taste to

[1] ME to Harriet Butler, 29 Mar. 1831; *Letters from England*, pp. 509–10. The scene in the novel where Horace Churchill backbites the departing guests, almost before they are safely out of earshot, is in vol. i, pp. 283–300.

surround himself in his house in St. James's Place with exquisite objects of art; yet he also had a reputation for helping other writers in need. In 1844 Maria was able to refer to him (having apparently forgotten Lady Davy's party) as 'dear, goodnatured old man'.[1] But the sketch given in this letter and in *Helen*, of a man who alternately flattered and slandered, was also confirmed independently by Abraham Hayward and Harriet Martineau:

> He was, plainly speaking, at once a flatterer and a cynic . . . He would begin with a series of outrageous compliments, in a measured style which forbade interruption; and, if he was allowed to finish, would go away and boast how much he had made a victim swallow. He would accept a constant seat at a great man's table, flatter his host to the top of his bent, and then, as is upon record, go away and say that the company there was got up by conscription—that there were two parties before whom everybody must appear, his host and the police . . . The relation which this propensity of his bore to his position was direct. It placed him at great men's tables and kept him there, more than any other of his qualifications. His poetry alone would not have done it. His love and knowledge of Art would not have done it; and much less his wealth. His causticity was his pass-key everywhere. Except the worship paid to the Railway King for his wealth, we know of nothing in modern society so extraordinary and humiliating as the deference paid to Rogers for his ill-nature.[2]

Although dinner-parties of the kind where Horace Churchill was a guest occur in *Helen*, they are a subordinate part of the main characters' experience. Maria disclaimed any intention of writing another of the fashionable, implicitly adulatory novels of London Society that had become popular in the later 1820s; she had some contempt for 'the exclusive or *Almack* nonsense' which aimed to give the reader tantalizing glimpses of a gilded life from which he—or perhaps more often she—was excluded. Crowded fashionable scenes were not to play a central part in *Helen*, which was set rather in the everyday life of the Whig aristocracy:

> I have had opportunities of living in intimacy with several

[1] ME to Mrs. FE, 8 Apr. 1844; *Mem.*, iii. 237.

[2] Harriet Martineau, 'Memoir' of Rogers first published in the *Daily News* of Dec. 1855; reprinted in *Biographical Sketches*, 1869, pp. 372–3. Cf. also the essay by Hayward in *Ed. Rev.*, 1856, reprinted in his *Selected Essays*, 1878.

families of the highest rank in England, & therefore felt that I might securely venture on drawing their domestic manners and habits of life—more difficult and dangerous to a writer to attempt than any of the pictures of London life, which deal in generalities and admit of exaggeration for effect. I own I was ambitious to draw what I thought I knew, and I have been gratified by the assurance of many who live in that sphere that I have not over or under drawn.[1]

The accuracy which comes from first-hand observation is apparent in the first two volumes, where Maria attempts to do for English country-house life what she had formerly done for Irish society as a whole. The result is a leisurely panorama of the English upper-class scene which is far truer to life than anything she attempted before her father's death.

The greater part of *Helen* is set in the country mansion Clarendon Park. To this house comes the nineteen-year-old Helen Stanley, who has recently been left alone in the world after the death of her uncle and guardian. She has been invited to live with her childhood friend, formerly Lady Cecilia Davenant, and Cecilia's husband General Clarendon, so far a stranger to Helen. The more important of the two actions involving the heroine concerns her relations with this couple, and with Cecilia's mother, Lady Davenant; the admittedly inferior sub-plot introduces a romance between Helen and the General's ward, Granville Beauclerc.

The main action is, however, slow in developing; virtually the whole of the first two volumes instead find it more interesting to explore Helen's new world, Society as it appears to a newcomer at Clarendon Park. The key to this first half of the book is to be found in a remark made by Lady Davenant, when she encourages Helen to compare the merits of two men, Beauclerc and Horace Churchill, by the style and meaning of their conversation:

'It has been said', continued Lady Davenant, 'that it is safer to judge of men by their actions than by their words, but there are few actions and many words in life; and if women would avail themselves of their daily, hourly, opportunities of judging people by their words, they would get at the natural characters, or, what

[1] ME to Miss Martha Cowper, 1834; Constance Hill, 'Some Unpublished Letters of Maria Edgeworth', *Hampstead Annual*, 1897, pp. 127–8.

is of just as much consequence, they would penetrate through the acquired habits; and here, Helen, you have two good studies before you.'[1]

For two volumes the reader is given, through Helen's consciousness, the opportunity of judging people daily by their words. The subject of this part of the novel is the upper class in conversation, not so much in the privacy of their intimate relationships, as in more public settings, in the drawing-room, dining-room, and grounds of a large country house.

The grand style in conversation is provided by Lady Davenant herself, a powerful political and intellectual woman who is as much at home in foreign capitals as in London. In private, as in her conversations with Helen, her tone is that of a highly intelligent, reasoning and feeling woman. Her longest speeches, even her narrative of her life, maintain the imprint of a forceful personality through their distinctive style, which is emphatic, sarcastic, and generalizing. Her manner is that of a woman who has become accustomed to authority. The style Lady Davenant employs in public, which it is odd to find a visitor to Edgeworthstown comparing with Maria's,[2] compels admiration rather than amusement or liking; she does not so much shine in a drawing-room, as subdue it. The great weapon in her armoury is the 'sentence', a memorable statement memorably uttered, which renders further discussion otiose: 'How much we owe to such men as Mr. Churchill, who make us feel detraction virtue!'[3]

If Lady Davenant is the great utterer of sentences in the novel, Horace Churchill is the master of anecdote. Maria gives a favourable account of him when he sets out to amuse the company with a variety of curious facts and stories, although in other scenes she censures him strongly for personal malice and for plagiarism. She gives far more of Horace Churchill's conversation than his role warrants, which suggests that the old interest in social documentation was not dead, only relegated to a less central part. Churchill the anecdotalist clearly resembles half a dozen wits whom Maria heard, not Samuel

[1] *Helen*, i. 312.

[2] *Life, Letters and Journals of George Ticknor*, 1876, i. 427. See above, p. 416.

[3] *Helen*, i. 292.

Rogers only but Sydney Smith, Sir James Mackintosh, 'Conversation' Sharp, and Robert Plumer Ward.

Lady Davenant's weightier style, with its concern to establish truth, contrasts very favourably with Churchill's superficiality and heartlessness. The hero was meant to make the same point: Helen, at least, admires Beauclerc's generous praise of great men, and despises Churchill's mean habit of detraction. Beauclerc's character owes much to Maria's stepbrother Francis Edgeworth, who was talented but impulsive and wayward.[1] Unfortunately Maria was torn between the two opposing goals of comparing her hero favourably with Churchill, and indulgently exposing Francis's foibles. Not surprisingly, the character that emerges in the novel is out of focus. Maria uses the word 'brilliant' to describe Beauclerc, but in fact he seems immature, and considerably less charming than the erratic but humorous personality suggested by Francis's letters.

Helen's friend Lady Cecilia, on the other hand, is realized with great success, and perfectly fits the author's description of her. She has none of her mother's intellect, but she has much more sympathy with the people around her. It is Cecilia's moral weakness to try to give pleasure at all costs. Maria adroitly gives her dialogue from the beginning a habit of inaccuracy that seems trivial, even charming, and yet is indicative of the ominous pliancy in her character. Later, when she is thoroughly entangled in lies, Cecilia's imprecision takes on a more serious moral colouring. Knowing Helen to be innocent, she deliberately takes her part in such a way that those listening will be doubly convinced of her guilt: 'It is indeed to me a painful subject, for Helen has been my friend from childhood, and I have so much reason for loving her!'[2] Cecilia's subtle indirections are contrasted in turn with the crueller innuendos of some of the minor characters, and with the frank manner of her mother, her husband, and the General's sister, Esther.

Of all these, it is the General and Miss Clarendon who offer

[1] Thomas Carlyle characterized Francis Edgeworth in his *Life of Sterling*, 1851 (Centenary edn. of Carlyle's works, 1897, xi. 130–2) as 'the good little Frank . . . a composed, dogmatic, speculative, exact and not melodious man. He was learned in Plato and likewise in Kant; well-read in philosophies and literatures; entertained not creeds but the Platonic or Kantean *ghosts* of creeds. . . .'

[2] *Helen*, iii. 172.

the most striking contrast in style. Esther's rudeness is made to seem so out of keeping in the context of the polite world that it often shocks, as Maria means it to. While the General is less gauche, he is unusually deliberate in his own choice of words, and when he listens to others he attends to the literal meaning rather than the suppressed implication. By doing so he seems to lack sophistication, and inevitably, as a man of action rather than an intellectual, he cannot compete in brilliance with the social and political stars that marriage with Cecilia Davenant has brought into his house.[1] Yet in the last volume his literalness becomes increasingly impressive. He sounds the note of truth, and it is his evasive wife who is out of harmony.

The earlier parts of the novel, especially, thus set out to combine that interest in personal style which Maria had always shown in rendering the speech of her own class, with the more general intellectual ambitions of the Irish tales. Two house parties in this section of the novel have, typically, almost no narrative function, but they are essential if a representative picture is to be given of the whole range of English upper-class life. The first organized occasion brings in the fashionables—Churchill, and two sisters, the malicious spinster Lady Katrine Hawksby and the unfaithful wife Lady Castlefort. Later, at a political gathering, a much broader range of social types are brought together, and aristocrats rub shoulders with 'cits', to the embarrassment, Maria suggests, of all.

While Maria's record of conversational styles has a special fascination for the historically minded reader, it must be confessed that the more familiar English setting robs it of the imaginative dimension of her rendering of Irish life. Even in the Irish tales, the author's insistence that an example of speech or behaviour is a 'fact' is likely to disturb the novel-reader's sense of illusion; and in an English country house the presence of so much unassimilated documentation seems altogether harder to justify. The effect is often lifeless: even 'brilliant' conversations are less than brilliant when they are not made to seem relevant. The compliments to Scott, Dumont, and Madame de Staël are even more out of place, as Harriet feared they would be. In short, Maria's one attempt at a panoramic

[1] It is this feature of the General's character that derives most directly from Fanny's husband Lestock Wilson. See above, p. 424.

survey of English society is not executed with any newly acquired skill, and, unlike the similar Irish material, it has neither the unfamiliarity nor the depth of social analysis to sustain the reader's attention.

Then, at last, after nearly two volumes of sociological material, the personal drama begins to develop. Cecilia has misled her husband about an unimportant affair she had with another man before she met him. Knowing that it was what the General wanted to hear, she has assured him that he was her first love. Suddenly an anonymous correspondent sends him a packet of Cecilia's youthful letters to the other man, a Colonel D'Aubigny; and although there is nothing immoral or even improper about the letters, they leave no doubt that the woman who wrote them was in love with the man she was addressing.

At this time, Lady Davenant, who is in precarious health, is about to set off for St. Petersburgh. Cecilia persuades Helen that it would be dangerously upsetting if Lady Davenant discovered that her daughter had been telling lies, however trivial. Reluctantly Helen consents to let the General and Lady Davenant think that it was she, Helen, who wrote the love-letters to D'Aubigny. She believes it will be only a matter of a few days, until after Lady Davenant's departure, before Cecilia confesses the whole story to the General. But Cecilia cannot find the courage to tell her husband. Day by day she has more lies to recant; meanwhile rumours begin to tarnish Helen's reputation, and threaten her engagement to Beauclerc. Hints of scandal appear in the newspapers, and Cecilia and the General discover independently that a much-exaggerated version of the correspondence is about to be published. The General is able to stop the book from appearing, but by this time he has lost all confidence in Helen's integrity. In her own eyes, too, she is guilty of falsehood and a serious betrayal of trust. Lady Davenant had begged her to protect Cecilia from the consequences of her weakness of character, and Helen sees that by supporting Cecilia in her deception of her husband she has helped instead to corrupt her.

Helen leaves the General's house, releases her fiancé from their engagement, and takes refuge in the home of the uncompromising Esther Clarendon. Under the management of this uncomfortable nurse, she recovers painfully from what was in effect a nervous collapse. Months pass, a baby is born to Cecilia, and still she does not confess. Guilt and anxiety poison her feeling for her husband, and lead to further difficulties, until she is half estranged from him. At this point Lady Davenant comes home, seriously ill, and on seeing her mother Cecilia at last finds the courage to tell the whole story. Helen's reputation is restored, but Cecilia has to undergo a further period of uncertainty before her mother intercedes successfully with Clarendon and saves the marriage.

As a sustained drama of personal relationships, the last volume of *Helen* is superior to anything else in Maria's tales. The plot moves forward rapidly from the moment that Lady Cecilia comes to Helen with her first request for help (although that, almost incredibly, is not until volume ii, page 279). From this point the novel's key relationships—Helen and Cecilia, Helen and the General, the General and Cecilia—are subjected to increasing pressure. The change in Cecilia is admirably conceived; her affection for Helen, even her love for her husband, cool involuntarily as she uses one and dupes the other. For Helen the conspiracy means a greater and greater strain, until her life is as confused as a nightmare. At a ball in London, the evening before the fatal letters are to be published, Helen, who knows nothing, half hears whispered rumours about herself. The rhythm of the prose suggests her abnormal nervous state as she is carried home in the coach. 'All the time [she] felt as in a feverish dream, watching the lights of the carriage[s] flit by like fiery eyes, while she thought only of the strange words she had heard, and why they should have made Beauclerc angry with her.'[1]

Next day Cecilia goes in secret to her cousin Lady Castlefort to find out what she knows about the scandal, and what revelations are still to come. Louisa Castlefort is brought with difficulty to reveal that there is a copy of the unpublished book in the house, and that it is to be read aloud this very morning to a breakfast-party which her sister has assembled. As usual with Maria's writing, the surface tone of the dialogue is poised and witty, but this time there is another element which is rarer

[1] *Helen*, iii. 73.

in her work—tension; we are at the climax of an action which has been building up with quickening pace for half a volume. The scene between the two contrasted fine ladies therefore has an urgency and complexity which make it unusually interesting. More than once Cecilia is on the point of failure, for the frivolous Lady Castlefort is far more interested in her own troubles than in Helen's:

'. . . I understand it all perfectly, and I pity you from the bottom of my heart: so now, my dear Louisa—'

'I tell you, my dear Cecilia', pursued Lady Castlefort, continuing her own thoughts, 'I tell you, Katrine is envious of me. Envy has been her fault from a child. Envy of poor me! Envy, in the first place, of whatever good looks it pleased Providence to give me.'—A glance at the glass.—'And now Katrine envies me for being Lady Castlefort. Heaven knows! now, Cecilia, and you know, she need not envy me so when she looks at Lord Castlefort; that is, what she sometimes says herself, which you know is very wrong of her to say to me—unnecessary too, when she knows I had no more hand in my marriage—'

'Than heart!' Cecilia could not forbear saying.

'Than heart!' readily responded Lady Castlefort; 'never was a truer word said. Never was there a more complete sacrifice than my mother made of me; you know, Cecilia, a poor, young, innocent, helpless sacrifice, if ever there was one upon earth.'

'To a coronet', said Lady Cecilia.

'Absolutely dragged to the altar', continued Lady Castlefort.

'In Mechlin lace, that was some comfort,' said Cecilia laughing, and she laughed on in hope of cutting short this sad chapter of sacrifices. But Lady Castlefort did not understand raillery upon this too tender point. 'I don't know what you mean by Mechlin lace,' cried she pettishly. 'Is this your friendship for me, Cecilia?'

Cecilia, justly in fear of losing the reward of all her large lay-out of flattery, fell to protesting the tenderest sympathy.[1]

Publication is stopped, but it is a Pyrrhic victory: Helen collapses into the depression which keeps her many weeks in retirement in Wales, while Cecilia's suffering barely ends with the book. The last volume deals with a prolonged emotional crisis, the only situation of its kind in a novel by Maria Edgeworth.

At first sight the moral of *Helen* conforms with that of the

[1] *Helen*, iii. 103–4.

earlier tales of fashionable life, which is to say that it is critical of the life led by the upper classes in society. Many of the individuals who represent the fashionable world in the novel are more or less unpleasant—Horace Churchill, for example, and the sisters Lady Katrine and Lady Louisa. Among the major characters, the obvious moral defaulters are Cecilia and Helen. They tell trivial lies, as people in Society do, out of an anxiety not to cause an equally trivial degree of pain. There is a danger that the very virtues of a highly civilized world, good manners, elegance, and grace, place too high a value on pleasing others. The most straightforward deduction from the story is that it is wrong to put this generally admirable consideration before integrity.

But this is only a small facet of the moral theme of *Helen*, which in reality differs so radically from Maria Edgeworth's earlier tales about fashion that it almost seems to reverse the point they made. The heroines of the earlier stories, such as Belinda and Caroline, stood apart from the social scene because they disapproved of it. 'Social life' in *Helen* means something very different from the social climbing and husband-getting which go a long way to make up Maria's first representations of Society. The theme of contrasting styles of talk is expanded until the novel is dealing with the whole area of communication between people, intimate as well as formal. Instead of approaching the subject of high life with automatic hostility, Maria gives a generous allowance of humanity and goodwill to all her major characters, so that their problems become the general human problems of sensitive people who have to live in close proximity with one another. *Helen* is sociologically much more specific than the earlier tales of fashionable life, but at the same time its theme is more universal.

It is true that at first sight Cecilia is the obvious sinner, because she has proved a liar and a coward. But there is another inference to be drawn from the plot of *Helen*, and this is the one that Maria Edgeworth herself preferred:

> I must tell you that she [Mrs. Moore] discovered a moral in *Helen* which I certainly wished to impress but which few people except herself & my own particular family have ever noticed. Most people[,] said she[,] tell me that the moral of *Helen* is that wish to abide by truth—Very well—But we all knew that before—That's

too common a moral—But the moral I draw from *Helen* is from that fine Lady Davenant's character that mothers talented mothers should take care not to make their children afraid of them so as to prevent them from telling the truth & trusting them with their faults & secrets at the time when youth most want anothers counsel & assistance. In short the moral of Lady Davenant's character is that talents should make themselves objects of Love not fear.

My dear Lucy after this it would be superfluous to add that I think her an amazingly clever woman.[1]

If Cecilia lied to her mother, it was because she longed to please her, and found herself unable from childhood to do so. It is an indication of Maria's insight into feminine dependence that she makes Cecilia choose a husband who in his awe-inspiring reserve strongly resembles Lady Davenant. Cecilia's relations with her husband repeat the pattern of her relations with her mother. She longs to please them both, but they stand aloof, watching her; the more frightened she is, the more she resorts to evasions and downright lies. Yet in the last resort there is a generosity about Cecilia which reflects critically upon the formal virtue of the two people who presume to judge her; profound human relationships depend on something more—on something more expressive—than merely telling the literal truth.

Esther suffers from the same rigidity as her brother and Lady Davenant. She wants Helen to recover her health, but she has none of the sympathy an invalid needs in a nurse. The plot poses the question, who has the greater capacity to give happiness to others?—Cecilia, or Esther Clarendon? Maria's own opinion disposes of the theory that she meant the unbending Miss Clarendon to stand for an admirable purity—'odious creature!'[2] Yet in her boorish manners and her preference for retirement, Esther is a female Thomas Day; her principled love of justice (not to speak of her aloofness) recalls the first Honora; time was when Maria might have felt obliged to venerate Esther, as indeed some of her Scottish friends did. Mrs. Stark wrote to say that she knew (and evidently approved of) a real-life Miss Clarendon. Maria replied: 'I must confess that I do not think I could much love my own Miss Clarendon for I am full as much influenced I am ashamed to say by

[1] ME to Lucy Edgeworth, 6 Jan. 1836.
[2] ME to Lucy Edgeworth, 3 Mar. 1834.

*manner* especially in living with any body in every day life as ever poor dear Lady Cecilia was.[1]

There is even more personal significance in relation to Maria in Lady Davenant's part in the novel. As a person of impressive presence and unbending integrity, she is one of those Edgeworthian characters who stand for the personal ideal that Richard Lovell Edgeworth and Mrs. Ruxton taught Maria, the ideal of classical nobility and virtue. Maria actually declared that Lady Davenant reminded her of her father (and also of their friend Mrs. O'Beirne, whom she had once described as 'true steel to the backbone').[2] One of Lady Davenant's speeches to Helen is based on actual advice Maria was given by Edgeworth, especially the emphatic warning against weakness he uttered on his deathbed:

> It must not be what I please, my dear child, nor what I think best; but what you judge for yourself to be best; else what will become of you when I am in Russia? It must be some higher and more stable principle of action that must govern you. It must not be the mere wish to please this or that friend;—the defect of your character, Helen, remember I tell you, is this inordinate desire to be loved, this impatience of not being loved. . . .[3]

It is no wonder that Maria had such insight into the experience of Helen and Cecilia, since a craving for the affection of an impressive, rather awe-inspiring older person had been the mainspring of her own emotional existence through the greater part of her life. That is why the implications of *Helen* are so surprising, and why they signify a new maturity in Maria. Her earlier rendering of herself in fiction, in the characters of Rosamond in *Early Lessons*, and Rosamond Percy in *Patronage*, had been studies in humility, almost in self-abasement; the two Rosamonds were saved from the disastrous consequences of their imprudence only by the watchful despotism of a parent. This time praise and blame are more fairly distributed among the characters, who are all, as it were, adult and morally equal. Lady Davenant is the first of Maria's

[1] ME to Mrs. Stark, 14 May 1834; *Mem.*, iii. 138–9.

[2] ME to CSE, 14 Mar. 1834.

[3] *Helen*, i. 67. Cf. above, p. 420, and ME to Mrs. O'Beirne, n.d. [1811]: 'Even my father who says the defect of my character is an inordinate desire to be beloved allows me to exult in the hope of possessing a little portion of Mrs. O'Beirne's love.'

magisterial parent-figures to be subjected in her turn to impartial criticism. If Cecilia is at fault, her mother is partly to blame. Talents should be objects of Love, not Fear. In short, Maria rejects her father's heroic, unyielding idea of virtue and replaces it with a softer, more feminine and domestic scale of values.

Some of the technical improvements in *Helen*, the strong plot and the subdued didacticism, are no doubt due to the example of other novelists, or to Maria's exposure to somewhat more sophisticated literary influences. But perhaps the most impressive of her achievements in the novel arises from an extra-literary source, the strengthening in confidence that came in her sixties from years of self-reliance. She had always believed, and been encouraged to believe, that failure in 'civil courage' was her weakness, so that in *Helen* she took a subject which was emotionally as well as socially part of her own experience; but, refreshingly, she now accepted the fault without exaggerating it, and even modestly proposed that there were circumstances in which her fault was worth more than her father's virtue. The heroines of the earlier tales, who turned their back on social life in favour of strenuous independence, had something in common with Esther Clarendon. In *Helen* Maria replaces this most tenacious of her old themes with the idea that the happiness of people we love may justly be put before, or at least alongside, personal integrity. Of all her tales, it is the only one with a theme she could be said to have lived.

To a modern reader *Helen*, or rather the latter half of it, is likely to seem the best of Maria's tales set in England, but in her own day it could not command the space that *Tales of Fashionable Life* had received in the Reviews. The friendly Lockhart wrote what proved to be the only substantial piece of criticism in an English journal.[1] *Helen* was received with more overt enthusiasm in America, where literary fashions were slower to change. The Revd. W. B. O. Peabody, writing in the *North American Review*, believed that on moral grounds

[1] *QR*, li, 1834, 481 ff. Coleridge recorded, however, 'how much noise this work was making and the great interest it had excited' (letter to Eliza Nixon, 9 July 1834; *Letters*, ed. E. H. Coleridge, 1895, ii. 774). Translated into Swedish in 1836–7, it suggested the plot for Frederika Bremer's *A Diary* and afterwards for an important part of Mrs. Gaskell's *Wives and Daughters*.

Scott and Maria Edgeworth were the best of all novelists, and that (by the same criteria) Miss Edgeworth had this time outdistanced even Scott.[1] With the help of such friends and sympathizers Maria ended her career as a novelist creditably, although not gloriously. It is clear that her reputation was now entering the slough from which it has never emerged, except for the brief period of interest shown in her as a woman rather than a writer at the close of the nineteenth century. As early as 1867 Abraham Hayward (in the course of reviewing the *Memoir of Maria Edgeworth*) could assume that he was writing for a generation that had scarcely read her except as a writer for children.[2]

For *Helen*, although once republished (in 1838), did not quite fit into the current genre of 'silver-fork' novels, and Maria's name must have seemed quaintly old-fashioned beside those of Bulwer Lytton, the Countess of Blessington, Lady Charlotte Bury, and Mrs. Gore. The difference between Maria and most of her comparable rivals was that the rest were fashionable in every sense; they depicted high life from the inside, with the intention of charming, amusing, and perhaps provoking in the reader a tinge of envy. It was certainly no part of their scheme to apply a common scale of human values to their elegant scenes.

A minor novel of the day with which *Helen* can be conveniently compared is Emily Eden's *The Semi-Attached Couple*. Although not published until 1860, it was written some thirty years earlier. Like *Helen*, it is set in a great house immediately after the marriage of the owner; and, again, the marriage is subjected to strain because of a difference in temperament and values between a dour husband and an outgoing wife. Their domestic life is seen against a prolonged house-party, which includes a political week-end. Indeed, if Emily Eden had not specifically claimed that she wrote her novel before the passing of the Reform Bill of 1832, one would suppose that she had deliberately set out to give the Tory equivalent of the Whig Maria Edgeworth's *Helen*.

*The Semi-Attached Couple* is scarcely a classic, yet on occasion it has been highly praised. One of its editors, for example,

[1] *North American Review*, xxxix, 1834, 167ff.
[2] *Ed. Rev.*, cxxvi, 1867, 458ff.

rashly claims that it is 'better than *Sense and Sensibility*'.[1] It has amusing dialogue, good minor characters, and over-all it is more entertaining than *Helen*. Yet in the end comparison with this gay but superficial near-pastiche reflects credit on Maria. Aesthetically, it is true, she belongs to a more primitive stage of the novel's development, so that *Helen* is no more equal than the Irish tales to accommodating all the real-life material put into it. Furthermore, the energy, vision, and hope of her father's lifetime is somewhat diminished now. Yet the outlook on life is a serious one, the moral feeling is true, and the quality of intellect shown in incidental ways is still rare for the novel in the period. The first two volumes of *Helen* differ sharply from the comedy of *The Semi-Attached Couple* in that they are trying to make a serious examination of the life of the English upper classes; and when the two writers are compared handling the relations between husband and wife, the contrast is even more decisively to Maria's advantage. Partly because in *Helen* so much has already been conveyed about the nuances of personal style, we can take Cecilia's trivial lies both as telling us something crucial about life in civilized society, and as revealing a way of being that is unique to her; there is nothing like the depth of that in Emily Eden. If a novel cannot be called great, or even successful, unless it is technically more controlled than any of Maria's, nevertheless it can command a special kind of respect. It was within the capacity of Maria Edgeworth, and not of most of her contemporaries or immediate successors, to write a novel of high life that was at various levels a novel of social life, and thereby to justify writing one at all.

[1] John Gore. Introduction to his edition of *The Semi-Attached Couple*, 1927, p. v.

# EPILOGUE

## A LITERARY PERSPECTIVE

'WHEREAS Jane Austen was so much the better novelist Maria Edgeworth may be the more important.'[1] The critics who agree that this must be so have tended to focus their discussion on the merits and demerits of *Castle Rackrent*, parts of *The Absentee*, and even *Belinda*. If only Maria had asserted her independence of her father, she could have written about Lady Delacour without giving her a happy ending, or, better still, have continued in the native Irish idiom of *Castle Rackrent*. The chapters which precede have shown how dubious these traditional lamentations are, and how illogical. For if Maria had gone on in her earliest vein, or written according to her natural disposition, she would have been unlikely to have had any real significant influence on the course of literary history.

Posterity's guess that Maria depended too much on other people is fair enough, although the story is more complex than nineteenth-century biographers supposed. It was her family and not merely her father which was the central influence in her work throughout her life. Paris in 1802 and London in 1813 made some impression on her, and the effect of general social experience shows itself towards the end of her life in *Helen*. But from first to last the family audience was at the forefront of her consciousness. The early works which have been praised because they have been regarded as free, or in part free, of Edgeworth, do not escape the imprint of the family. Far from it. The most direct influence on the entire first half of Maria's career was her literary, lady-like, and humour-loving aunt Mrs. Ruxton, who liked fiction that was polished and entertaining.

But it is the middle stage of her career, when Maria consciously tried to express her father's ideas, which matters

[1] P. H. Newby, *Maria Edgeworth*, 1950, pp. 93–4. Quoted and enlarged on by Walter Allen, *The English Novel*, 1954, Pelican edn., pp. 103 ff.

historically. By getting her to do the spade-work on *Professional Education*, Edgeworth obliged her to make up her mind on general masculine subjects which she had previously refused to have opinions on. The interest Dumont expressed in these ideas, coupled with the questions in his letters about Ireland, were more factors which encouraged her to aim her tales at men of more intellectual weight than the received idea of the novel-reader. Not everyone has thought the change an improvement. The desire to inform someone like Dumont rather than amuse someone like Mrs. Ruxton accounts for the heavier texture of tales of this group, which at their worst (for example in parts of *Patronage*) can be positively leaden. All the same, it was on account of these intellectually ambitious tales, not for her sketchier entertainments, that Maria was praised by her contemporaries for raising the status and enlarging the scope of the novel. The modern reader who cares about her historical importance had therefore better read *Ennui*, from the well-received and influential *Tales of Fashionable Life*, rather than the earlier, less responsible *Castle Rackrent*, which the *Edinburgh* and *Quarterly* reviewers were happy to think she had left behind her.

Just how important an innovation was Maria's? Describing someone as historically more important than Jane Austen may have sounded impressive when the phrase was coined, but since Jane Austen lacked disciples it is really not saying much. A comparison with a novelist of another period who did wield influence may be more illuminating. With Defoe the novel first began to emerge as an independent genre, a fictional narrative in prose for a middle-class readership which dealt recognizably with daily life. Defoe's adventurers and adventuresses are expressive symbols of the tradesman and entrepreneur on his way up in the world. Their religious protestations, and their unconscious egotism, express the ethos of the Dissenter trading classes, and Defoe's matter-of-fact style perfectly conveys the businessman's untheoretical, anti-aesthetic temper. Defoe identified himself too completely with the middle classes to make an effective judge of them; instead he was their spokesman, and he reproduced them with a historical accuracy that would seem astounding as a piece of analysis, if only we could feel that it was fully understood by Defoe himself.[1] Richardson and Fielding, each in their way greater artists, had more to say about the middle classes; but because they *were* artists, who selected and moulded, they did not give so literal a report of what the middle classes in life were really like. Nor perhaps would the achievements of the great novelists of the seventeen-forties have been possible but for Defoe's feat of mirroring the manners and morals of 'the middle station' in the near-documentary form which proved appropriate for that subject and that readership.

Some writers on the novel treat its history as one of evolution; others believe that it has no history at all. If it has an intelligible development between the eighteenth and the nineteenth century, for sociological and historical as well as literary reasons this was interrupted towards the end of the eighteenth century. The great eighteenth-century novelists were all men, and their concerns were not just love and marriage but also money and land. Clarissa's relations with her family are as important as her relations with Lovelace, and morally Tom Jones's reconciliation with Squire Allworthy counts for more than his reunion with Sophia. Both these novels focus on the central character's moral nature in terms of his dealings with society; although society in the eighteenth-century novel is depicted impressionistically, through a number of typical individuals like James Harlowe, Mrs. Sinclair, Allworthy, and Lady Bellaston, rather than painstakingly established as it is in the nineteenth century.

An elaborate combination of factors, felt not only in the novel but also in poetry and drama, drastically reduced the scope of fiction in the last decades of the century. Brilliant though it is, Sterne's *Tristram Shandy* has many of the early signs of a period of decadence: its strong theoretical preoccupation, and its interest in states of feeling, combine to

[1] The extent to which Defoe was a conscious artist has of course been hotly debated of recent years by critics such as Ian Watt (*The Rise of the Novel*, 1957), J. R. Moore (*Defoe: Citizen of the Modern World*, 1958), M. E. Novak (*Economics and the Fiction of Daniel Defoe*, 1962, *Defoe and the Nature of Man*, 1963, etc.), and G. A. Starr (*Defoe and Spiritual Autobiography*, 1965). This is not the place to engage in a full-scale debate with Defoe's partisans; it will be evident from the nature of my comparison with ME that I have adopted the less flattering view of his artistry, although not of his historical importance.

weaken the all-important interaction between the characters and their social environment. It is true that Sterne is often precise about time and place. But his attitude to external reality is equivocal: as a sentimentalist, he implicitly exalts states of feeling, and denies real importance to external factors (except, significantly, chance) in the lives of his characters. Lesser talents in this period were more wholehearted about the social world. But in the hands of Fanny Burney and Elizabeth Inchbald, who as women had the disadvantages of limited education and experience of life, the novel is intellectually far more trivial than under their great male predecessors. The cult of sensibility was even less concerned with the circumstances of social life in the real world; and the tale of terror, though interesting at its best in its handling of the psychology of individual characters, was remotest of all from daily reality. The philosophical novelists of the 1790s had the considerable virtue of taking up public themes again, but they did so in a theoretical spirit, and the sheer intellectual interest of their subject-matter does not outweigh the thinness of their rendering of real life. Without its original foundation in the world of affairs, the three-volume novel had become insubstantial.

Encouraged by her two domestic circles, Maria began her career as a novelist in typical feminine style, in the not despicable but minor tradition of Fanny Burney. She sketched a number of people amusingly, observed upper-class conversation very well, and conveyed impeccable sentiments. Apart from the aberration *Castle Rackrent*, she wrote in this way during the period to about 1808, as long as she was thinking of her audience as primarily made up of women. When after this she began to direct her fiction towards a more serious general public, she began for the first time to tap her own and her father's intellectual milieu. Her really important innovation was to report Ireland as accurately as she could, in the same literal spirit and with the same disregard for aesthetic considerations as Defoe had shown in reporting his world. The result was a fresh lease of life for the novel, and a new fashion for social documentation, although by now, in the early nineteenth century, the science of political economy had taught the educated novelist a great deal about society. Maria wrote about the lives of the peasants and about the relations between the classes in Ireland. She also took up general topics like a man's obligations to society and his need on his own moral account to find a role in the social structure. She 'invented nothing', but reported the facts, which was in keeping with the intellectual training her father had got within the Lunar group.

By taking up worldly topics and dealing with them in a prosaic, documentary fashion, Maria came near to repeating Defoe's prescription for the novel. Like him, she was a faithful spokesman for the middle classes at a time when they were strongly in the ascendant. The historical importance of Defoe and Maria Edgeworth does not rest on their artistry; on the contrary, it has a great deal to do with their evident lack of interest in art as such. They achieved success and were widely imitated because they dealt in impersonal and hence in apparently objective terms with real life as their readers knew it. It was not only in contrast with romance writers that they struck their public as admirably serious. It was also in contrast with greater artists, who perhaps preferred the ideal to the actual, or the pattern to the fact.

The reason for Maria Edgeworth's literary importance lies in her development of the techniques of documentation, and in her intelligent understanding of the social scene. The social novel became the dominant form of the first half of the nineteenth century, both in England and Europe, not because of individual writers but because it studied middle-class life and reflected middle-class attitudes. Its explicit reference to real life and fascination with detail was the literary counterpart of the empiricism of the industrial innovators, and so it naturally appealed to the educated but not aesthetic prosperous classes, and to the rapidly expanding proletarian readership. Not only for Maria Edgeworth and Scott, but for Dickens, Thackeray, Mrs. Gaskell, and George Eliot, society itself often becomes the central character: the sub-title 'a novel without a hero' could be applied far more widely than to *Vanity Fair*, and Hardy's description of one of his works as a novel 'of character and environment' excellently defines the most distinctive quality of the best English fiction of the nineteenth century. For Maria Edgeworth's genre, so often nowadays called in a derogatory way 'the provincial novel', does not exist as a separate entity, as the study of its first critics has shown. Her successors may have had a different (and often much more critical) attitude to society, but their concern was, like hers, a detailed and accurate re-creation of the organism as a whole, and not of individuals extrapolated from it. There is the same unbroken line of development as between Defoe and the great novelists of the 1740s.

How much is an innovator worth? In the late 1820s, the 1830s, and 1840s sociological insights would have made their way into the English novel from France, or, more probably, would have been felt spontaneously by the English themselves. How much did it matter to Dickens, Thackeray, and the rest that a flourishing social novel came into being in England two decades earlier than in France, in the form of the provincial or national novel?

There has never been a thorough-going analysis of Scott's influence on the English novelists of the next generation.[1] We know, of course, that they read him. What is equally apparent is that they did not share his attitude to society; the images that came to Thackeray and Dickens when they depicted the contemporary world were Vanity Fair and the Marshalsea Prison, comparisons which conveyed their sense of a corrupt, self-perpetuating structure that dominated and destroyed individual lives. It would never have occurred to Scott or to Maria Edgeworth to use such images. They shared with Ferguson and Burke a sincere respect for society as the natural product of an evolutionary growth; the process to which they regularly subject the heroes of their most typical novels, of learning to know their own nation, is an enriching, not a disillusioning, experience. An individual grows from irresponsibility to a sense of himself as Civil Man, just as a community has advanced from barbarous disunity to its modern ordered complexity.

In order to express their conception of the relation of the

[1] In *The Novelists of the Eighteen-Forties*, 1954, Mrs. Tillotson, for example, effectively denies a connection, by treating social realism as an innovation of her decade. The Marxist Georg Lukacs (*The Historical Novel*, trans. 1962) deals with the question of Scott's influence on the European novel as a whole, but in too general a style to throw much light on the specific issue of the debt to him of later English novelists.

individual to the social framework, it was appropriate for Maria Edgeworth and Scott to employ a colourless hero who underwent a series of adventures and met a succession of carefully differentiated people. The purpose of this technique was to bring 'the background' into the foreground, which was where they wanted it. Dickens and Thackeray also have a habit of using uninteresting, often immature central figures, who pale in interest compared with the rich panorama for which the consciousness of the hero merely provides a medium. Granted that these later writers belonged to far bitterer times, and tended to see the individual as the passive victim of the social machine, they might usefully have invested their central figures with rather more human potential (if only to have it destroyed); alternatively, in so far as social satire was their object, they might have been expected to employ more critical or reflective observers. But they do not do either of these things.

The English novelists of the first half of the nineteenth century constitute a school with very distinct characteristics, for which they have not in recent years received enough credit. In breadth of scope, attention to detail, and sociological accuracy the mid-nineteenth-century figures far exceed anything attempted in the eighteenth century. *Tom Jones* and *Vanity Fair* may resemble one another in some of their narrative devices, but they are a world apart in their grasp of the social framework and especially the implications of class. It may be, therefore, that criticizing Dickens or Thackeray or Scott for failing to pay more attention to their heroes and heroines is like so much neo-classical criticism of tragedy; it is the malpractice of deriving from observations of one type of novel the retroactive rules for all novels. The fact is that most English novels between Maria Edgeworth and Thomas Hardy are not primarily about the central characters but about environment, or, at the most, about characters seen specifically within an environment. French and Russian novelists do more to isolate the innerness of their heroes and heroines than any English novelist of the period, even George Eliot. On the other hand, the English novel, relatively weak at this kind of analysis, is scarcely excelled in its powers of recreating the external world, whether it is Dickens's London, George Eliot's Midlands, or Hardy's Wessex. And this is an achievement which would certainly have met with the approval of its pioneers, who had no higher ambition than as artists to realize, as moralists to preach acceptance of, the thing as it is.

Maria Edgeworth's is an ironic career. From first to last her personal preference was for a domestic setting and the company of a few intimates. The one novel which really expresses her tastes, *Helen*, succeeds when in the latter half it becomes intensely feminine. She was thus the last person in the world who would have wished on her own to pioneer the 'loose baggy monsters' of nineteenth-century fiction. This was a tradition which in many ways would have been distasteful to her. In its liveliness, vulgarity, and intermittent radicalism it not only describes but expresses the ethos of a commercial world in which, in her lady-like heart of hearts, Maria did not feel at home. But then she did love her father, and he supplied many of the qualities that were needed; he was intellectually more detached than she from the gentry, and he was spontaneous, energetic, and empirical. Through her devotion to Edgeworth, and despite herself, Maria brought Lunar practicality and the Lunar social ethos into the novel, and in doing so helped to set it on a course which it held for over half a century.

## APPENDIX A

# THE CHILDREN OF RICHARD LOVELL EDGEWORTH (1744–1817)

| (1) | (2) | (3) | (4) |
|---|---|---|---|
| Anna Maria Elers (1743–73) | Honora Sneyd (1751–80) | Elizabeth Sneyd (1753–97) | Frances Anne Beaufort (1769–1865) |
| Richard (1764–96) m. Elizabeth Knight, 1788 | Honora (1774–90) | Elizabeth (1781–1800) | Frances Maria (1799–1848) m. Lestock Wilson, 1829 |
| Lovell (b. and d. 1766) | Lovell (1775–1842) | Henry (1782–1813) | Harriet (1801–89) m. Richard Butler, 1826 |
| Maria (1768–1849) | | Charlotte (1783–1807) | Sophia (1803–37) m. Barry Fox, 1824 |
| Emmeline (1770–1847) m. John King, 1802 | | Sophia (b. and d. 1784) | Lucy Jane (1805–97) m. T. Romney Robinson, 1843 |
| Anna Maria (1773–1824) m. Thomas Beddoes, 1794 | | Charles Sneyd (1786–1864) m. Henrica Broadhurst, 1813 | Francis Beaufort (1809–46) m. Rosa Florentina Eroles, 1831 |
| | | William (1788–90) | Michael Pakenham (1812–81) m. Christina Macpherson, 1846 |
| | | Thomas Day (1789–92) | |
| | | Honora (1791–1858) m. Francis Beaufort, 1838 | |
| | | William (1794–1829) | |

Among the children of the first marriage, Richard, Emmeline, and Anna had issue. Of the fourth, Sophy, Francis, and Michael Pakenham had children. Descendants of Richard, Anna, Sophy, and Michael Pakenham are still living. There was no second generation from either of the Sneyd marriages.

APPENDIX B

# MARIA EDGEWORTH AND HER PUBLISHERS

THE history of the Edgeworths' relations with their publishers, Joseph Johnson and his successors, provides valuable evidence of Maria Edgeworth's commercial success as a writer. Johnson, the radical and friend of the Godwin circle, was regarded by Edgeworth as a personal friend, although his dilatoriness in replying to letters was often an irritation; one of the few actions that ever caused serious annoyance was his commissioning Thomas Holcroft to write mottoes at the head of each of the *Popular Tales*, 1804.[1] Johnson made more than he expected out of *Tales of Fashionable Life* (1809), and on his deathbed later that year he asked his heir to make sure that a proportion of the profits went to the author (*Memoirs of RLE*, ii. 356).

The business was taken over by Johnson's two nephews, and on Maria's behalf Edgeworth dealt with one of them, John Miles, until about a year before the latter's retirement at the beginning of 1815. This association covered the years of Maria's most consistent success, so that not unnaturally relations between Edgeworth and Miles were very amicable: the sum of £1,050 for the second series of *Tales of Fashionable Life* contrasts with the £300 Johnson had given for *Belinda*. It also compares favourably with the sums received by other successful novelists: Lady Morgan received £550 for *O'Donnel*, 1814, and in the same year Constable offered £700 for *Waverley*, which Lockhart thought a high sum. 'When we recollect what the state of novel literature in those days was, and that the only exceptions to its mediocrity, the Irish Tales of Miss Edgeworth, however appreciated in refined circles, had a circulation so limited that she had never realized a tithe of £700 by the best of them—it must be allowed that Constable's offer was a liberal one.'[2]

In the same year as *O'Donnel* and *Waverley*, no doubt encouraged by the great success of *Tales of Fashionable Life*, Johnson's other nephew Rowland Hunter seriously over-reached himself. He offered £2,100 for *Patronage*—considerably too much, as he found when he could not sell the second edition.[3] In order to recoup his

[1] But for ME's reservations about his politics, see above, p. 124.

[2] *Memoirs of the Life of Scott*, iii. 124. Scott refused the £700 and took a half-share in the profits: a better bargain.

[3] It is not clear why the second edition failed (see below, p. 499 n.), unless it was damaged by the unfavourable reviews *Patronage* received. With ME at the height

losses, Hunter resorted to paying less than usual for the *Continuation of Early Lessons*. The Edgeworths reluctantly accepted this arrangement, but they felt they had even more to put up with in 1817, when Hunter failed to understand the need for speed in publishing *Harrington and Ormond*; Edgeworth became so irritated with him that in his last weeks he advised Maria to take the *Memoirs* to John Murray.[1] However, she decided against this additional complication; Hunter got both the *Memoirs* and all the sets of children's books which she completed in the 1820s. But they did not do so well as Hunter expected, probably because of the generally depressed state of the market, and he wrote more than once asking her to accept less than he had contracted for.[2] She agreed in every case, but at last, after the appearance of *Little Plays for Children* in 1827, she asked him to make proposals he would abide by. In the course of Hunter's reply (which again proposed a cut in payments) he claimed that on the whole he had lost by publishing her books. That being so, Maria wrote, it was better for them both to put an end to their connection.[3]

Maria was inclined to blame Hunter severely for what she thought of as his personal mismanagement of her affairs. But it is fair to say that in the 1820s there were economic factors which spelled trouble even for the ablest publishers. As for Maria's saleability, the tide of literary taste was clearly turning against her. This fact was slower to affect the educational writing than the fiction: her children's books went into far more editions than the novels in the second quarter of the nineteenth century.[4] But, in spite of Collected Editions of her Works in 1825, 1832–3, and 1848, reprints of individual novels now became rare—and it was the novels which had made the real profits. Thus the high price adroitly extracted by Lockhart from Bentley for *Helen* in 1833 obscures the fact that Maria probably reached her peak as a selling author in

of her fashionable reputation, the first edition began by selling remarkably well. '8000 copies of the first edition of *Patronage* were disposed of on the day when it was published—1500 of a second edition were bespoke and fifteen hundred more have been printed' (ME to ED, 19 Feb. 1814; B.P.U., Geneva). The size of the first printing compares with 3,000 for the first edition of *Comic Dramas*, 1817, the only other figure I have been able to trace.

[1] RLE to R. Hunter, 11 June 1817. See above, p. 280.

[2] ME to Fanny Wilson, 7 Feb. 1834. ME was particularly annoyed when Hunter claimed that on the last collection of children's stories he lost hundreds of pounds because she changed the title from 'Late Lessons' to *Harry and Lucy Concluded*.

[3] ME to Rowland Hunter (copy 18 Nov. 1827). Supplementary information about ME's later relations with Hunter is given by the Revd. William B. Sprague in his *European Celebrities*, 1855, quoted by Grace A. Oliver, *A Study of Maria Edgeworth*, 1882, p. 484. Sprague visited Edgeworthstown in 1836.

[4] e.g. there were seventeen editions of *Early Lessons* up to 1848.

1812–14, before her reputation began to suffer from comparison with Scott and Jane Austen.

List written by Maria Edgeworth and dated September 1842:

| | | £ s. d. |
|---|---|---|
| *Parent's Assistant* | | 120— 0— 0. |
| *Practical Education* | | 300— 0— 0. |
| *Letters for Literary Ladies* | | 40— 0— 0. |
| *Castle Rackrent* | | 100— 0— 0. |
| *Moral Tales* | | 200— 0— 0. |
| *Early Lessons* | | 50— 0— 0. |
| *Belinda* | | 300— 0 —0. |
| *Bulls* | | 100— 0— 0. |
| *Explanations of Poetry* | published under RLE's name | 40— 0— 0. |
| *Letter to Lord Charlemont* | | 3—12— 0. |
| *Griselda* | | 100— 0— 0. |
| *Popular Tales* | | 300— 0— 0. |
| *Leonora* | | 200— 0— 0. |
| *Fashionable Tales*, 1st part | | 900— 0— 0. |
| *Professional Education* | | 300— 0— 0. |
| *Fashionable Tales*, 2nd part | | 1,050— 0— 0. |
| Johnson's acct. pd. | | 78—16—10. |
| *Patronage* | | 2,100— 0— 0. |
| *Early Lessons*, cont. | | 210— 0— 0. |
| *Comic Dramas* | | 300— 0— 0. |
| *Harrington and Ormond* | | 1,150— 0— 0. |
| *Memoirs* | | 750— 0— 0. |
| *Rosamond*—Sequel— | | 420— 0— 0. |
| *Frank* | | 400— 0— 0. |
| *Little Plays* | | 100— 0— 0. |
| *Harry and Lucy Concluded* | | 400— 0— 0. |
| *Helen* | | 1,100— 0— 0. |
| | | £11,062— 8—10. |

As usual with the Edgeworths, the money Maria made from her books was carefully accounted for. She made a mark in red ink beside those works written and published after her father's death, and counted these sums earned in difficult times peculiarly her own to spend on her dearest object, the family circle. 'I spent of this sum in delightful travelling to France Switzerland and Scotland and England including nine or ten months residence in France and two winters in England about Two thousand pounds—& I had the pleasure of giving to my brother & sister & near relatives from copyright of *Helen* about £600—and the remaining £500 I used in purchasing principal . . . With Comic Dramas £300 I had the pleasure of paying a debt of my father's to Catherine Billamore [the housekeeper]. He left to me the privilege of paying his personal debts of which this was the only one I ever heard of.'

## APPENDIX C

# THE POST-PUBLICATION HISTORY OF *BELINDA* AND *PATRONAGE*

REFERENCE has already been made in the text to Maria Edgeworth's practice of correcting her novels for subsequent editions.[1] Although most of the novels which were reprinted received minor alterations, only two, *Belinda* and *Patronage*, were substantially changed after their first publication.

The criticism to which Maria responded in the case of *Belinda* was a substantial one, and difficult to cure: Belinda's becoming engaged to another man, Mr. Vincent, after previously feeling attracted to the hero, Clarence Hervey, was considered to be the action of a jilt.[2] Maria tried to tackle this difficulty, and one of the improbabilities in the Virginia episode, by making some very minor additions to the second edition of 1802:

> We have explained that the picture with which Virginia fell in love was some *time* in her possession—We have detailed Lady D's recovery, and we have added a few sentences to explain that Belinda would have loved Clarence better than any other person *always* if he had declared any attachment to her, but that she had turned her thoughts *from* him when he made no declaration of love to her—In the last scene he is *now* made distinctly to avow his passion for her—There are many other faults but we did not think it would be wise to botch . . .[3]

This, however, was not nearly radical enough, and later on, when Mrs. Barbauld chose the novel for her 'British Novelists' series, Maria had a more leisurely opportunity to consider its 'many other faults'. She found it a daunting prospect: 'I really was so provoked with the cold tameness of that stick or stone Belinda that I could have torn the pages to pieces—and really have not the heart or patience to *correct* her—as the hackney coachman said "Mend *you*! better make a new one".'[4]

[1] See above, pp. 296–8.

[2] Probably the view of the Ruxtons, who disliked the novel (see above, p. 288 n.). In print it was put most forcibly by *The Monthly Review*, xxxvii. 1801, 368–74, which observed that the heroine's first love should have been 'an almost sacred bond'.

[3] ME to Harriet Beaufort, n.d. [1802]. It was *The British Critic*, xviii. 85, which had objected so strongly to the climax of the Virginia episode.

[4] ME to Mrs. R, 26 Dec. 1809; *Mem.*, i. 229–30.

But the problem had to be tackled, and Edgeworth began the work by reading through the text and marking off all the speeches in which Belinda appeared to encourage her second suitor too decisively.[1] (He also found some small errors of grammar, and unnecessary circumlocutions or addresses to the reader.) Maria worked through the text making the changes (most of which were cuts), and afterwards outlined them to Mrs. Barbauld. 'By taking out her consent to marry [Mr. Vincent], I hope I shall in some degree, satisfy all parties. Belinda is but an uninteresting personage after all, but I cannot *mend* her in this respect, without making her over again—and indeed without making the whole book over again.'[2]

The revisions to *Belinda* are an interesting instance of the importance placed in this period on improper *actions*, which, since they were considered to invite imitation, were invariably shunned by right-thinking novelists. Quite apart from allowing Belinda to set so dubious an example, in the first edition Maria had innocently married Mr. Vincent's black servant, Juba, to a white country girl, Lucy. By 1810 she had the gravest doubts about the implications of such a marriage: 'My father says that gentlemen have horrors upon this subject, and would draw conclusions very unfavourable to a female writer who appeared to recommend such unions; as I do not understand the subject, I trust to his better judgment.'[3]

In order to get rid of the mixed marriage Maria had to conjure up an entirely new character, a hard-favoured white man called Jackson, who provided a bridegroom for Lucy. It would have been simpler to cut out Lucy's marriage altogether, since in terms of the plot it was quite incidental, but Maria valued the moral point that true love need not begin with physical attraction. As the reader can well imagine, both these substantial changes made for reasons of propriety to the 1810 edition of *Belinda* had the effect of weakening the second half of the novel still further, although they left the best scenes with Lady Delacour unimpaired.

The changes made after publication to *Patronage* were even more

[1] RLE's own copy, inscribed in ME's hand 'from his literary partner', carries his pencil markings in the margin beside passages he thought should be changed. He rarely suggests an alternative word or phrase, and then only in the case of a grammatical correction.

[2] ME to Mrs. Barbauld, 18 Jan. 1810; A. Le Breton, *Memoir of Mrs. Barbauld*, 1874, pp. 136–7. Cf. ME to Mrs. R, 25 Dec. 1809; *Mem.*, i. 229–30, and 9 Jan. 1810.

[3] ME to Mrs. Barbauld, 18 Jan. 1810. Cf. ME to Mrs. R, 9 Jan. 1810: 'My father has great delicacies and scruples of conscience about encouraging such marriages.'

extensive, in response to the heaviest and most explicit criticisms any novel by Maria Edgeworth ever encountered. Étienne Dumont summarized for her the views of 'le beau monde' in London, including the general point which everyone who has read the novel must have felt, that *Patronage* is too long and too didactic. In addition, and with more practical effect, Dumont drew Maria's attention to the 'parti nombreux' of physicians, surgeons, churchmen, lawyers, and politicians who were objecting to the manner in which she had treated their various professions. It was a particular misfortune, Dumont added, that the inclusion of one or two details enabled the readers to date the action in or near the present day, which encouraged critics to try to identify characters and incidents.[1]

Almost all the substantial alterations to *Patronage* set out to correct the professional objections pin-pointed by Dumont. Most were made at speed: *Patronage* went into a second edition in February 1814, and a third in April of the same year. Edgeworthstown was snowed up in January, and the fourth volume of the first edition was late in arriving, so that in spite of Maria's desire to make quick amends all but one minor cut missed the second and had to wait for the third edition.[2] The interest of this edition of April 1814, which presents the novel in what was to prove an intermediate state, is that it shows clearly the kind of correction to which Maria gave priority.

Of the professions whose methods of preferment *Patronage* described, the one most reasonably aggrieved was the medical. In the first edition there was a corrupt election to St. George's Hospital, a surgeon of which (described in the text as a 'farrier') was shown brutally and incompetently treating a broken leg. Dumont's remonstrances were reinforced by Sir Samuel Romilly; Maria wrote reassuringly in reply, and in another letter to one of her brothers outlined how she proposed to put the matter right :

> We have re-written the whole of the odious Frumpton scene about the broken leg—have broken the leg in the street & had the man carried into a shop instead of a hospital & have made Erasmus quarrel with Frumpton in favor of the hospitals—Pray make this known to your friends if any of

[1] ED to ME and RLE, 26 Jan. 1814; see also above, p. 257. Elsewhere ED was able to tell ME that *Patronage* had an admirer in that dedicated critic of existing institutions, Jeremy Bentham. 'Notre Philosophe Bentham qui est tres bon juge est enchanté, enchanté c'est le mot, il ne voudrait pas souffrir qu'on retranchât le moindre chose' (ED to ME, 14 Feb. 1814).

[2] The solitary cut of substance in the 2nd edn. is difficult to account for: this is Godfrey Percy's embarkation letter, ch. 9; i. 277–82, which was inessential but also inoffensive.

them care about the matter—We hear that the supposed attack upon the London hospitals has made a great *combustion* in London.[1]

This change had consequences in other scenes, and involved Maria in more rewriting than any other alteration to the third edition.

Eradicating the legal errors, the task Maria faced next, was potentially even more troublesome. Two mistakes in law could be, and were, put right relatively easily. Maria altered Alfred Percy's first triumph in court, because it turned on the *statute of limitations*, the application of which she had misunderstood; and she emended the legal phrase *mesne rates* to *mesne rents*.[2] Unfortunately the whole climax of the plot rested on her third legal mistake. She had committed Mr. Percy to prison for an alleged debt, which still had to be proved in a court of law; the entire effect of the court scene in the final volume depended on the dramatic reversal which restored Mr. Percy to his old estate from the depths of a debtor's prison. Mr. Percy's imprisonment was a legal impossibility; yet this time even the scrupulous Edgeworths baulked at the trouble involved in taking it out. Maria consulted her father's old ally, Judge Fox, and was relieved to hear his opinion: 'After ¾ of an hours sitting and careful investigation it was determined to leave things exactly as they are—because as he says none but lawyers will see the errors & men of sense will allow in a work of fiction all that . . . in short cannot be altered without diminishing interest or *truth* of character.'[3]

For the time being, then, the legal blunder was left; but there were still public men to be placated. In one scene Maria had shown the inhumanity of press-ganging; despite the objections of the Ruxtons and at least one reviewer, Maria on her father's advice left it in, but she dropped a particularly offensive half-sentence.[4] She could do little about the attempts to identify Oldborough, except through her father to deny that portraits were intended.[5] She accepted the criticisms of a scene in which Lord Oldborough confers with the King, and here the rewriting (obviously done in haste, since inconsistencies remain) seems designed to remove implied criticisms of the King's attitude, as well as any personal characteristics which might suggest George III.[6]

One more change had to be made to prevent readers from dating

[1] ME to CSE, 26 Feb. 1814. Cf. letter to Lady Romilly of same date, quoted Slade, pp. 146–7.

[2] *Patronage*, ch. 40; xii. 381 ff.

[3] ME to Mrs. R, Mar. 1814.

[4] ME dropped the imputation that a bribe might obtain a man's release, which was the aspect of the episode that offended Capt. Francis Beaufort (ME to CSE, 11 Feb. 1814). For discussion of whether the episode as a whole should have been included, see ME to SR, 25 Jan. 1814; *Mem.*, i. 297, Honora Edgeworth to CSE, Jan. 1814, and John Ward, *QR*, x, 1814, 312.

[5] See above, p. 255 n.

[6] *Patronage*, ch. 37; xii. 315–18.

the action, and again it was the court scene which suffered. Maria had borrowed her denouement from an incident in family history: on the critical document which disinherited Mr. Percy was a seal, and under the seal a sixpence; but when it was uncovered the sixpence proved to have a date later than that of the document, which of course proved that the document was a forgery. In the original version, it was the King's head—George III's, when it should have been George II's—which decided the issue, meaning, of course, that the King in the novel seemed to be George III; in rewriting Maria was obliged merely to state flatly that the date on the coin was later than the unspecified date on the document.[1]

Mrs. Inchbald's criticisms of 'spittle' have already been mentioned.[2] Two other scenes offended the delicacies of readers. In one, Buckhurst Falconer saved a gluttonous bishop from choking by blowing down his ear. In another a miser, to avoid waste, forced a footman to drink up the remains of every bottle of medicine in the house. Maria defended all three scenes stoutly on the grounds that they had really happened, but she modified each one in detail in order to make them as decorous as the facts would permit.[3]

These then were the changes Maria made at her first opportunity—the third edition of April 1814—in response to the criticism *Patronage* encountered when it came out. The broad aesthetic objection, that the novel was too didactic and too long, took a second place: two insignificant cuts were made, but there was no attempt as yet to cut back systematically in the duller parts of the novel.[4]

The decision Maria arrived at with Judge Fox, to leave alone the legal blunder by which Mr. Percy went to prison, did not satisfy the censorious and literal-minded readers of the period. In May 1815 she received a long and detailed letter from a lawyer, signing himself 'Lycurgus', who listed all her legal mistakes (including those she had emended in April 1814). Perhaps at his instigation, Maria did eventually undertake the elaborate alteration of the end—eliminating the debtor's prison, and dispatching the heroine to Germany—which she had hoped would never be necessary. Maria's stepmother recollected that the new version appeared in 'the third edition of 1815', and Mrs. B. C. Slade follows her account; but in fact the rewritten conclusion was not

[1] *Patronage*, ch. 42; xii. 404. Cf. *Memoirs of RLE*, i. 17–18.

[2] See above, pp. 297–8.

[3] ME to Mrs. Inchbald, 14 Feb. 1814; J. Boaden, *Memoirs of Mrs. Inchbald*, 1833, ii. 195–6, and Preface to the 3rd edition of *Patronage*.

[4] Alfred Percy lost a superfluous passage of praise, and the lively play scene was also shortened.

published until the first Collected Edition of Maria's novels in 1825.[1] The literary effects of the change as usual tended to be unfavourable, but this time there were compensations: while dramatically a great deal was lost by saving Mr. Percy from prison, something was also gained by preventing Caroline from accompanying him there on her wedding day.[2]

In one other respect the 1825 version of *Patronage* was superior to any previous one, for it had been subjected to a series of substantial cuts which reduced the original 285,000 words to about 250,000. The Falconer family and Lord Oldborough are left virtually untouched, but the Percy family lost most of the passages of authorial commendation which had made their section of the novel tedious. Most of the cuts were not made by Maria herself, for where no rewriting was required she was always ready to leave changes to the family circle. It is clear from the family correspondence that the bulk of the work on the Collected Edition of 1825 was done by the stepsisters Honora and Harriet; ironically, therefore, the only changes undertaken with the intention of improving *Patronage* as a novel were left to others.

Taken as a whole, the changes Maria made after publication have a mildly deleterious effect on the merits of the novels concerned. The simple cuts in the last version of *Patronage* succeeded in removing some of the Percy family's prosiest moments, but most other alterations, in *Belinda*, *Patronage*, and elsewhere, were designed to remove a cause of offence, so that the new version tended to be more neutral and discreet and thus from a literary viewpoint less interesting than the old. It may well be that Maria Edgeworth was particularly ready to work on *Belinda* and *Patronage* because she recognized that both novels had serious artistic failings; nevertheless, in correcting them she limited herself to certain clearly defined categories of mistake which were not primarily aesthetic.

[1] See *Mem.*, i. 314, and Slade, p. 153. Mrs. Slade also gives the date of the third edition as 1815, but this is a simplification. I have seen two copies with 'Third Edition, 1814' on the title-page, and two copies entitled 'Third Edition, 1815'; the contents of both versions are identical, and the ending is as in the first edition. Mrs. FE is probably correct in associating RLE with the changes: it seems likely that the end was rewritten in time for a new edition in 1815, but because Hunter had printed too many copies of the second edition (RLE to Lovell Edgeworth, 25 May 1817) the old sheets of April 1814 were still available to be used up.

[2] See above, p. 218.

# BIBLIOGRAPHY

## 1. PRINCIPAL MANUSCRIPT SOURCES

1. National Library of Ireland, Dublin.

Two related collections of Edgeworth family letters:

(*a*) Edgeworth–Butler letters, *c.* 1770–1817. MSS. 10166–7.

This, the first part of the most important collection of Edgeworth letters, contains several hundred letters from ME, together with hundreds more from other members of her family. It is arranged in four boxes in chronological order, but it is not yet catalogued.

(*b*) Beaufort–Edgeworth letters, to 1817. MS. 13176.

A smaller, complementary collection of the Beaufort and Edgeworth families, including letters from ME, RLE, and Mrs. FE.

2. Private possession (Edgeworth) Butler family: Edgeworth–Butler letters and Beaufort–Edgeworth letters, 1818–*c.* 1849.

The second and considerably larger parts of the collections described in 1. Although still in the hands of the descendants of Michael Pakenham Edgeworth (ME's youngest stepbrother), these too are destined for the National Library of Ireland. All letters cited in the text above come from 1 (*a*) and 2, unless otherwise stated, and are treated collectively as a single entity.

3. (Edgeworth) Butler family: literary MSS.

(*a*) Educational register. Two notebooks in the hand of Mrs. H. Edgeworth, 1778–9; one by Mrs. EE from the 1790s.

(*b*) Further educational material:

RLE's draft letter to Mrs. Barbauld, with longer essay, also in form of letter.
Notes for *Harry and Lucy*, 2 in a Sneyd handwriting.
*Harry and Lucy Cont.*: RLE material.
*Harry and Lucy Concluded*: ME's sketch and pieces of MS., etc., with comments by Davies Gilbert (Davies Giddy).

(*c*) 6 literary notebooks in ME's hand (see text above, pp. 238–40).

(*d*) Literary sketches for: *Tomorrow*; *Simple Susan*; *The White Pigeon*; *Ormond* ("*Vesey*")—three versions; *Harrington*; 'Life and death of a divorcée' (unwritten story); 'Celebrity' (unwritten); 'The Modern Lucretia' (unwritten).

(*e*) Fragments of literary manuscript:

'The Education of the Poor': incomplete MS. by ME.
*The Mental Thermometer*, MS. in Harriet's hand.
*Patronage*, page of MS. in ME's hand, with corrections by RLE; and extract of Fénélon for use in *Patronage*.

Pieces of MSS. for *Comic Dramas*.

Pieces of MSS. for *Harrington*, cancelled early version (with three unwritten sketches on back; see above).
*Garry-owen*: incomplete MS.
Pieces of MSS. for *Helen*, and notes.
Piece of MS. for 'Nora' (unwritten tale of *c.* 1840).

(*f*) Erratum slips: *Ormond* (2) and *Frank* (*A Sequel*).

(*g*) Miscellaneous notes:
'Langan! Langan!': note of Irish speech.
Notes on travels of J. L. Foster.

(*h*) Verses:
2 by ME to Mrs. R, 1 to Sir Philip Crampton.
Miscellaneous family verses in volume given to Alison family.

(*i*) Publishing accounts and note of sales of copyright: 6 items.

(*j*) MSS. by other members of family:
Fragments of RLE MSS. for *Readings on Poetry* or *Explanations of Poetry*.
'The Palace in the Forest': MS. in hand of Harriet Edgeworth and ? by her.

4. Private possession, Hubert Butler, Esq.: *The Most Unfortunate Day of My Life*, literary MS.

5. National Library of Ireland: other manuscripts.

In addition to scientific and other papers relating primarily to RLE, these include:

(*a*) MS. of RLE's *Memoirs*, vol. i, in RLE's hand, with ME's corrections and cancellations. MS. 7360.

(*b*) Cancelled pages of RLE's *Memoirs*, vol. ii, in ME's hand. MS. 11132, 1st folder.

(*c*) Memoirs of the family of Edgeworth since the Revolution in 1688, 3 vols., and Memoirs . . . of the Edgeworth family, 1 vol.: 'The Black Book of Edgeworthstown'. MSS. 7361–4.

(*d*) ME's correspondence with Mrs. Mary Leadbeater, author of *Cottage Dialogues*, 1810–13. Ballitore Papers, Bundle E, 1–40.

(*e*) ME's letters to Sir W. R. Hamilton, *c.* 1830. MS. 11132, 3rd folder.

(*f*) ME's correspondence with Thomas Spring-Rice, 1st Baron Monteagle, 1824–50. Monteagle Papers, MS. 13346. Further letter, same series, MS. 13371.

(*g*) ME to Mrs. Moore (copies), 1835–49. MS. 495.

(*h*) Letters of ME (in French) to Mme de Vindé.

6. Trinity College, Dublin.

(*a*) Journal of Revd. D. A. Beaufort (incomplete). MS. 4024 (K. 6. 57).

(*b*) Letters of ME to Sir Philip Crampton, surgeon. Crampton's *Correspondence and Estate Papers*, MSS. 4018–19 and 4176–85.

7. The British Museum, London.

(*a*) 9 letters from ME and RLE to Mrs. Inchbald (printed in J. Boaden, *Memoirs of Mrs. Inchbald*, ii, 1833). Egerton MS. 2158.

(*b*) MS. of *Helen*, in different hands, most ME's. Add. MSS. 28524–5.

8. The Bodleian Library, Oxford.

(*a*) 2 letters from ME, 1802 and 1814. MS. Montagu d. 7 (25433). 1 letter from ME, 1823. MS. Montagu d. 19 (25437).

(*b*) Literary MSS.: *The Bracelets*, MS. Eng. misc. d. 647; 'The Double Disguise' (unpublished play), Dep. c. 134; 'Whim for Whim' (unpublished play), MS. Eng. misc. d. 684.

(*c*) Letters and papers of the Beddoes family: Letters of Anna Beddoes to Mrs. Leonard Horner, 1811–14 and 1819–20, MS. Eng. lett. d. 222, ff. 55–93; and Beddoes papers, MS. Dep. c. 135.

9. Bibliothèque Publique et Universitaire, Geneva.

(*a*) 53 letters from ME and RLE to Étienne Dumont, 3 Oct. 1805–6 July 1822. MS. Dumont 33/11.

(*b*) 10 letters from ME to Étienne Dumont, 14 Nov. 1820–27 July 1828. MS. Dumont 75, ff. 1–53.

(*c*) Further letters to M.-A. Pictet and others.

(*d*) MS. of review by ME and RLE of Dumont's *Théorie des Peines et des Récompenses par Monsieur J. Bentham* (published 1811–22; see Bibliography, section 2, below).

(For list of Edgeworth letters in private hands in Switzerland, to Pictet, Mrs. Marcet, and others, see H. W. Häusermann, *The Genevese Background*, 1952, pp. 215–17.)

10. University College, London.

(*a*) 43 letters from Étienne Dumont to ME and RLE, MSS. Bentham 174/2–53 (in French).

(*b*) ED's 'Renvois', 6 pages of notes and definitions summarizing Benthamite theory for the Edgeworths. MS. Bentham 174/1.

11. National Library of Scotland, Edinburgh.

More than 50 letters from ME (some with RLE) to Scottish correspondents.

(*a*) Abbotsford Collection: the correspondence and documents of Sir Walter Scott and J. G. Lockhart. MSS. 851–938. (The material in this collection was published in H. J. C. Grierson, *The Letters of Scott*, 12 vols. 1932–7.) Letters to Scott, which are arranged chronologically (MSS. 865–9), include 2 from ME, 1 from RLE, and ME's notes of Scott's tour in Ireland, 1825. Letters to and from Lockhart, MSS. 923–35. ME's correspondence with Lockhart and his wife, 1826–47, arranged together, MS. 936.

(*b*) Walpole Collection: letters to Sir Walter Scott, 1796–1831), acquired by Sir Hugh Walpole in 1921. (Partially published in W. Partington's *Private Letter-books of Scott*, 1930, and *Sir Walter's Postbag*, 1932.) Arranged chronologically, with some misplacing, MSS. 3874–92. Approximately 40 letters of ME (some with RLE) to Scott, i.e. the great majority, are in this collection.

(*c*) Constable Collection, MSS. 668–84, and Letter-books of Archibald Constable, MSS. 789–92, include letters to and from ME.

(*d*) Miscellaneous letters from ME, e.g. to Basil Hall, 1818 (MS. 3220, f. 117); to Miss Chandler, n.d. [early 1790s] (MS. 2255, f. 42); to Joanna Baillie, 14 Nov. 1817 (MS. 3888—Walpole Collection); and in Watson Collection (MSS. 577–600), 2 letters.

(*e*) Lockhart's letters to Bentley about ME's publishing affairs, MS. 3649, ff. 171, 183, 197–207.

(*f*) Diary in Harriet Edgeworth's hand of tour in Ireland with Scott in 1825. MS. 911, f. 50.

(*g*) Spurious portrait of ME, printed in *La Belle Assemblée*, *c.* 1810. MS. 2256, f. 13.

12. Royal College of Surgeons.

Letters to Joanna Baillie. Hunter–Baillie Collection, vol. v, ff. 83–99.

13. Huntington Library, California.

Letters and papers, including letters of ME to Fanny Robinson, 1782–6. (19th-century copies in Butler family possession.)

14. Birmingham University Library. 31 letters to J. M. Moilliet (son-in-law of James Keir).

## 2. PUBLISHED WORKS OF MARIA EDGEWORTH

### A. COLLECTIONS

[*Works*]. 13 vols., Boston, etc., 1822–5; 20 vols., New York, 1835–6.

*Tales and Miscellaneous Pieces*, 14 vols., 1825.

*Tales and Novels*. 18 vols., 1832–3, 1848, 1857; 10 vols., 1893; 12 vols., 1893.

*Classic Tales* (a selection), with a biographical sketch by G. A. Oliver. Boston, etc., 1883.

*Tales*. Ed. A. Dobson, 1903. [Children's stories.]

*Tales that Never Die*. Ed. C. Welsh, introd. by C. E. Norton, New York, 1908.

*Selections from the Works*. Ed. G. Griffin, introd. by M. C. Seton, [1918].

### B. INDIVIDUAL WORKS

[The children's tales especially have an elaborate bibliographical history. Here the date of the first edition only is given, except in the case of those novels which were changed substantially in subsequent editions. For details of later editions in all other cases see *Cambridge Bibliography of English Literature*, vol. iii, 1969.]

*Adelaide and Theodore*, 1783. Tr. from Mme de Genlis, *Adèle et Théodore*. Only 1 vol. printed, recalled before publication; probably anon. No known copy.

*Letters for Literary Ladies, to which is added An Essay on the Noble Science of Self-justification*, 1795 (anon.). 1st signed 1799 [2nd edn.].

*The Parent's Assistant: or stories for children.* 3 vols., 1796, 6 vols. (signed), 1800. (The contents of volumes appearing under this title are not necessarily identical: for example, the edition of 1800 adds 8 new stories, and omits 3 transferred to *Early Lessons*, below.)

[*A Letter to Lord Charlemont on the Tellograph and the Defence of Ireland*, 1797. By RLE, with ME's assistance.]

*Practical Education*, 2 vols., 1798. With RLE. 3 vols., 1801 (as *Essays on Practical Education*).

*Castle Rackrent, an Hibernian tale*: taken from the facts, and from the manners of the Irish squires, before the year 1782, 1800 (anon.). 1st signed 1801 [3rd edn.].

[*Early Lessons*]. *Harry and Lucy*, pts. i–ii, 1801; *Rosamond*, pts. i–iii, 1801; *Frank*, pts. i–iv, 1801; tenth volume, other stories, 1801–2.

*Moral Tales for Young People*, 5 vols., 1801.

*Belinda*, 3 vols., 1801. Appeared in Mrs. Barbauld's British Novelists series, 1810, with major alterations in latter part of story.

*The Mental Thermometer*, 1801 (Juvenile Library, vol. ii).

*Essay on Irish Bulls*, 1802. With RLE.

*Popular Tales*, 3 vols., 1804.

*The Modern Griselda: a tale*, 1805.

*Leonora*, 2 vols., 1806.

'John Carr's *Stranger in Ireland*', *Ed. Rev.*, x, 1807 (anon.; with RLE).

*Essays on Professional Education*, by R. L. [and Maria] Edgeworth, 1809.

*Tales of Fashionable Life*, vols. i–iii (*Ennui*, *Almeria*, *Madame de Fleury*, *The Dun*, *Manœuvring*), 1809; vols. iv–vi (*Vivian*, *Emilie de Coulanges*, *The Absentee*), 1812.

*Cottage Dialogues among the Irish Peasantry*, by Mary Leadbeater, with notes and a preface by Maria Edgeworth, 1811. Irish and later edns. omit ME's preface and notes.

*Patronage*, 4 vols., 1814. In the 1825 Collected Edition there are substantial changes, including rewriting of the last volume. (See Appendix C.)

*Continuation of Early Lessons*, 2 vols., 1814. Continuation of *Harry and Lucy* (substantially RLE), *Frank*, *Rosamond*, above.

'On French Oaths', *Irish Farmers Jnl.*, iii, 1815 (anon.).

[*Memoirs of the Abbé Edgeworth*, 1815, by C. Sneyd Edgeworth, revised by Maria Edgeworth.]

*Readings on Poetry*, 1816. With RLE; preface and last chapter by ME.

'Memoir of Mrs. Elizabeth Hamilton', *Monthly Magazine*, xlii, pt. ii, 1816. ('Sd. E'.).

*Comic Dramas, in three acts*, 1817 (*Love and Law*, *The Two Guardians*, *The Rose, the Thistle and the Shamrock*).

*Harrington, a tale*; *and Ormond, a tale*, 3 vols., 1817.

'A review and analysis of the *Théorie des Peines et des Récompenses par Monsieur*

*J. Bentham*, redigée en Français d'après des manuscrits par Monsieur E. Dumont', *The Philanthropist*, vii, 1819, and *The Enquirer*, i, 1822. (Anon.; with RLE. Both versions incomplete.)

*Memoirs of Richard Lovell Edgeworth, Esq.*, 2 vols., 1820. Vol. i by RLE, vol. ii by ME.

*Rosamond: a Sequel to Early Lessons*, 2 vols., 1821.

*Frank: a Sequel to Frank in Early Lessons*, 3 vols., 1822.

*Harry and Lucy Concluded: being the last part of Early Lessons*, 4 vols., 1825.

*Thoughts on Bores*, *Janus*, Edinburgh, 1826. Anon.; first acknowledged in Collected Edition, 1832–3.

*Little Plays for Children*, 1827 (*The Grinding Organ; Dumb Andy; The Dame School Holiday*).

*Garry-Owen: or the Snow-woman*, in *Christmas Box*, 1829; with *Poor Bob the Chimney-sweeper*, 1832.

*Helen, a tale*, 3 vols., 1834.

*Orlandino*, Edinburgh, 1848 (Chambers' Library for Young People).

*The Most Unfortunate Day of my Life*: being a hitherto unpublished story, together with *The Purple Jar* and other stories, 1931.

## C. PUBLISHED LETTERS

Boaden, J. (ed.). *Memoirs of Mrs. Inchbald*, including her familiar correspondence, 2 vols., 1833.

Davy, J. *Fragmentary Remains of Sir Humphry Davy*, 1858.

*A Memoir of Maria Edgeworth*, with a selection from her letters by the late Mrs. [Frances] Edgeworth, 3 vols., 1867 (privately printed).

Constable, T. *Archibald Constable and his Literary Correspondents*, 3 vols., Edinburgh, 1873.

Le Breton, Anna L. *A Memoir of Mrs. Barbauld*, including letters and notices of her family and friends, 1874.

Graves, R. P. *Life of Sir W. R. Hamilton, including selections from his poems, correspondence and miscellaneous writings*, 3 vols., Dublin, 1882–3.

Hare, A. J. C. *The Life and Letters of Maria Edgeworth*, 2 vols., 1894.

Hill, Constance. 'Some Unpublished Letters of Maria Edgeworth', *Hampstead Annual*, 1897.

'The Correspondence of Ricardo with Maria Edgeworth', *Economic Jnl.* xvii, 1907.

Grey, R. 'Maria Edgeworth and Étienne Dumont', *Dublin Rev.*, cxlv, 1909.

Law, H. W. and I. *The Book of the Beresford Hopes*, privately printed, 1925.

Butler, H. J. and H. E. *The Black Book of Edgeworthstown and other Edgeworth Memories, 1585–1817*, 1927.

—— 'Some Unpublished Letters: Sir Walter Scott and Maria Edgeworth', *MLR*, xxiii, 1928.

Partington, W. (ed.). *The Private Letter-books of Sir Walter Scott*, 1930.

—— *Sir Walter's Postbag*, 1932.

Barry, F. V. (ed.). *Chosen Letters*, 1931. Includes 8 unpublished letters.

Waller, R. D. 'Letters addressed to Mrs. Gaskell by celebrated contemporaries', *Bull. John Rylands Lib.*, xix, 1935.
Romilly, S. H. (ed.). *Romilly–Edgeworth Letters, 1813–1818*, 1936.
—— 'The Lost Letters of Maria Edgeworth', *QR*, cclxviii, 1937.
Hone, J. *The Moores of Moore Hall*, 1939. Includes some of her letters to the Moore family.
Butler, H. E. (ed.). *Tour in Connemara, and The Martins of Ballinahinch*, 1950.
Häusermann, H. W. *The Genevese Background*, 1952. First publication of a number of her letters preserved in or near Geneva.
Butler, R. F. 'Maria Edgeworth and Sir Walter Scott: unpublished letters, 1823', *RES*, N.S., ix, 1958.
Donner, H. W. 'Echoes of Beddoesian Rambles', *Studia Neophilologica*, xxxiii, no. 2, 1961. Includes some of her letters about Thomas Lovell Beddoes.
Colvin, Christina. 'Two unpublished MSS. by Maria Edgeworth', REL, viii, 1967.
—— *Maria Edgeworth: Letters from England*, 1971.
Hurst, Michael. *Maria Edgeworth and the Public Scene*, 1969.

## 3. SECONDARY WORKS

[Two categories of book are included in this list: (i) Substantial reviews, all literary or biographical studies, and general literary works giving separate attention to the novels of ME. (ii) Works devoted wholly or partly to the Edgeworths' achievements in a non-literary sphere (e.g. education). No attempt is made to give every title cited incidentally in the text above.]

[Pictet, C.], review of *Practical Education, Bibliothèque Britannique*, xii, 1799.
Review of *Castle Rackrent, Monthly Rev.*, May 1800; *British Critic*, Nov. 1800.
Review of *Belinda, Monthly Rev.*, April 1802.
Pictet, M.-A. *Voyage de trois mois en Angleterre, en Écosse et en Irlande*, Geneva, An. 11 [1802].
Seward, A. *Memoirs of the Life of Dr. Darwin*, 1804.
[Jeffrey, F.], review of *Popular Tales, Ed. Rev.*, iv, 1804.
—— review of *Leonora, Ed. Rev.*, viii, 1806.
—— review of *Tales of Fashionable Life*, vols. i–iii, *Ed. Rev.*, xiv, 1809.
—— review of *Tales of Fashionable Life*, vols. iv–vi, *Ed. Rev.*, xx, 1812.
—— review of *Harrington and Ormond, Ed. Rev.*, xxviii, 1817.
—— review of *Memoirs of Richard Lovell Edgeworth, Ed. Rev.*, xxxiv, 1820.
[Stephen, H. J., and Gifford, W.], review of *Tales of Fashionable Life*, vols. i–iii, *QR*, ii, 1809.
[Croker, J. W.], review of *Tales of Fashionable Life*, vols. iv–vi, *QR*, vii, 1812.
—— review of *Memoirs of Richard Lovell Edgeworth*, *QR*, xxiii, 1820.
Foster, J., review of *Tales of Fashionable Life*, vols. iv–vi, *Eclectic Rev.*, viii, 1812.
Wakefield, E. *An Account of Ireland, Statistical and Political*, 2 vols., 1812.
[Smith, S.], review of *Patronage, Ed. Rev.*, xxii, 1814.
[Ward, J., later 1st Earl of Dudley], review of *Patronage, QR*, x, 1814.
Review of *Harrington and Ormond, Blackwood's Mag.*, Aug.–Sept. 1817.

Review of *Memoirs of Richard Lovell Edgeworth*, *London Mag.*, May 1820.

'Miss Edgeworth's Tales and Novels', *Fraser's Mag.*, Nov. 1832. [Review of 1832 Collected Edition.]

[Lockhart, J. G.], review of *Helen*, *QR*, li, 1834.

—— *Memoirs of the Life of Sir Walter Scott*, 7 vols., Edinburgh, 1837–8.

[Peabody, the Revd. W. B. O.], review of *Helen*, *North Amer. Rev.*, xxxix, 1834.

Hall, Mrs. S. C., 'Edgeworthstown: Memories of Maria Edgeworth', *Art Jnl.*, xi, 1849; xxviii, 1866.

Hayward, A. 'Miss Edgeworth', *Ed. Rev.*, cxxvi, 1867.

Hillard, G. S. (ed.). *Life, Letters and Journals of George Ticknor*, 1876.

Oliver, Grace A. *A Study of Maria Edgeworth, with Notices of her Father and Friends*, Boston, 1882.

Ritchie, Anne Thackeray. *A Book of Sybils*, 1883.

Zimmern, Helen. *Maria Edgeworth*, 1883.

Krans, H. S. *Irish Life in Irish Fiction*, New York, 1903.

Lawless, Emily. *Maria Edgeworth*, 1904. English Men of Letters Series.

Grey, R. 'Heavy Fathers', *Fortnightly Rev.*, July, 1909.

Ward, W. 'Moral Fiction a Hundred Years Ago', *Dublin Rev.*, cxliv, 1909.

Hill, Constance. *Maria Edgeworth and her Circle in the days of Buonaparte and Bourbon*, 1910.

Paterson, Alice. *The Edgeworths: A Study of later Eighteenth Century Education*, 1914.

Colum, P. 'Maria Edgeworth and Ivan Turgenev', *British Rev.*, xi, 1915.

Michael, E. F. *Die irischen Romane von Maria Edgeworth*, Dresden, 1918.

Woolf, V. 'The Lives of the Obscure: the Taylors and the Edgeworths', *The Common Reader*, 1st series, 1925.

Darton, F. J. H. *Children's Books in England*, 1932.

Tompkins, J. M. S. *The Popular Novel in England, 1770–1800*, 1932.

Scott, W. *Letters*. Ed. H. J. C. Grierson, 12 vols., 1932–7.

Baker, E. A. *History of the English Novel*, vi, 1935.

Gwynn, S. *Irish Literature and Drama*, 1936.

Slade, B. C. *Maria Edgeworth 1767–1849: a Bibliographical Tribute*, 1937.

McHugh, R. J. 'Maria Edgeworth's Irish Novels', *Studies*, xxvii, 1938.

Millhauser, M. 'Maria Edgeworth as a Social Novelist', *N & Q*, 17 Sept. 1938.

Palfrey, T. R. 'Maria Edgeworth and Louise Swanton Belloc', *N & Q*, 25 March 1939.

Longford, Christine. 'Maria Edgeworth and her Circle,' *Irish Writing*, vi, 1948.

Armytage, W. H. G. 'Little Woman', *Queen's Quart.*, lvi, 1949.

'Humours and Moralities', *TLS*, 20 May 1949.

Clarke, Isabel C. *Maria Edgeworth: her Family and Friends*, 1950.

Newby, P. H. *Maria Edgeworth*, 1950.

Leclaire, L. *Le Roman régionaliste dans les Îles britanniques, 1800–1900*, Clermont Ferrand, 1954.

Flanagan, T. *Irish Novelists 1800–1850*, New York, 1959.

Inglis-Jones, Elisabeth. *The Great Maria*, 1959.

Inglis-Jones, Elisabeth. *The Lord of Burleigh*, 1964.

Simon, B. *Studies in the History of Education, 1780–1870*, 1960.

Davie, D. *The Heyday of Sir Walter Scott*, 1961.

Renwick, W. L. *English Literature, 1789–1815*, 1963 (Oxford History of English Literature, vol. ix).

Schofield, R. E. *The Lunar Society of Birmingham*, 1963.

Colvin, Christina. 'A Visit to Abbotsford', *REL*, v, 1964.

—— 'Maria Edgeworth's Literary Manuscripts in the Bodleian Library', *Bodleian Library Record*, viii, no. 4, 1970.

—— (with Marilyn Butler). 'A Revised Date of Birth for Maria Edgeworth', *N & Q*, Sept. 1971.

Houston, Janetta M. M. 'A Critical Study of the Works of Maria Edgeworth', 1964. Unpublished thesis for the University of Oxford, MS. B.Litt. d. 1038.

Watson, G. Preface to his edition of *Castle Rackrent*, Oxford English Novels series, 1964.

Clarke, D. *The Ingenious Mr. Edgeworth*, 1965.

Swinnerton, F. *A Galaxy of Fathers*, 1965.

Hawthorne, Mark D. *Doubt and Dogma in Maria Edgeworth*, Gainesville, Florida, 1967.

Newcomer, J. *Maria Edgeworth the Novelist: a bicentenary study*, Fort Worth, 1967.

*Cambridge Bibliography of English Literature*, iii, 1969.

Sister Eileen Kennedy, S.C. 'Genesis of a Fiction: the Edgeworth–Turgenev relationship', *ELN*, vi, 1969.

# INDEX

Titles of books are listed under the name of the author, except published works of Maria Edgeworth, which are given individually. For the complete list of her works in order of publication, see Bibliography.